Inside OS/2® 2, Special Edition

Mark Minasi
Bill Camarda
John Little
Marlene Semple

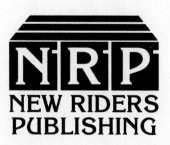

NRP
NEW RIDERS
PUBLISHING

New Riders Publishing, Carmel, Indiana

Inside OS/2 2, Special Edition

By Mark Minasi

Published by:
New Riders Publishing
11711 N. College Ave., Suite 140
Carmel, IN 46032 USA

Printed in the United States of America   2 3 4 5 6 7 8 9 0

Library of Congress Cataloging-in-Publication Data available upon request.

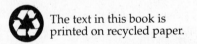 The text in this book is printed on recycled paper.

Publisher
David P. Ewing

Associate Publisher
Tim Huddleston

Acquisitions Editor
John Pont

Managing Editor
Cheri Robinson

Product Director
Michael Groh

Production Editor
Nancy Sixsmith

Editors
Rob Tidrow, Rob Lawson, Tim Huddleston, Peter Kuhns,
Geneil Breeze, Cheri Robinson, Lisa Wagner

Technical Editor
Bret Curran

Editorial Secretary
Karen Opal

Book Design and Production
Christine Cook, Scott Cook, Lisa Daugherty, Dennis Clay Hager,
Roger Morgan, Juli Pavey, Amy Peppler-Adams, Angela M. Pozdol,
Michelle Self, Susan M. Shepard, Greg Simsic, Alyssa Yesh

Proofreaders
Carla Hall-Batton, John Kane, Sean Medlock,
Linda Quigley, Suzanne Tully

Indexed by
Suzanne Snyder, Tina Trettin, Loren Malloy

Dedication

To the Next Generation: Donna Cook, Scott Tucker, Kris Ashton, David Stewart, and Jim Booth. "Make it so ..."

About the Authors

Bill Camarda specializes in writing about computer and telecommunications topics for large corporate clients. Formerly an editor at *Family Computing Magazine*, he is author of *Bringing the Computer Home*.

John W. Little is the Manager of Network Services for Future Now, Inc. He has been a technology consultant to many large companies, has specialized in OS/2 since its release, and continues to focus on communications. Little holds many industry certificates and is a teacher. He is a technical editor and author, contributing regularly to national magazines. Little has been involved with computers since 1981 and is involved with several projects for IBM, Lotus, Microsoft, and others.

Mark Minasi, owner of Mark Minasi and Company, is a respected consultant and educator in the fields of advanced PC operating platforms and PC technology. He is a contributing editor for *Compute*, *BYTE*, and *AI Expert*, and coauthor of Que's *Using OS/2*. Minasi has written several books on PC troubleshooting and maintenance. He routinely speaks to large and small groups as a consultant and as a seminar instructor and has served as Vice President of the Washington, D.C. Capital PC User's Group.

Marlene C. Semple is a consultant and the head of Marlene C. Semple Communications Services in Orlando, Florida. She studied journalism at the University of Miami and George Washington University and received a Master of Education degree from Loyola University. Semple is a writer and editor for magazines, book publishers, and educational publishers in the East and Midwest and also was president of Chicago Women in Publishing in 1976. In the past, she planned and developed information for personal computer users, became a software usability specialist, and was an OS/2 usability team leader during the development of OS/2 2.0.

Acknowledgments

Thanks to the many people who made writing this book possible. First and foremost, thanks to Kris Ashton who collected OS/2 applications and wrote Chapter 8; thanks much, Kris. In addition, thanks to my trusty staff, Donna Cook and Scott Tucker, who express mailed, photocopied, laplinked, and generally supported me in all ways possible. Thanks a million to the folks who sent me applications for analysis; good luck to you brave pioneers—may 32-bit applications make you all 32 million dollars. Thanks to IBM for the betas and other support. And hats off to the New Riders crew—nice work!

Thank you to the editorial staff at New Riders Publishing, including Tim Huddleston, Rob Tidrow, Brad Koch, Peter Kuhns, Rob Lawson, Cheri Robinson, Nancy Sixsmith, Lisa Wagner, and Geneil Breeze.

Thank you, Bret Curran, for doing an excellent job as technical editor. Your work was thorough, on time, and is greatly appreciated.

Thank you, Jverg Bonkaenel at IBM, for allowing New Riders to use PM Camera.

Thanks to Mike Groh for his help in tracking and completing the more difficult parts of the book, and for writing the introduction.

Trademark Acknowledgments

New Riders Publishing has made every attempt to supply trademark information about company names, products, and services mentioned in this book. Trademarks indicated below were derived from various sources. New Riders Publishing cannot attest to the accuracy of this information.

3COM and 3+ Open are registered trademarks of 3Com Corporation.

Post-it is a trademark of 3M Company.

PostScript logo is a registered trademark and Adobe Type Manager is a trademark of Adobe Systems Incorporated.

PageMaker is a registered trademark of Aldus Corporation.

Warning and Disclaimer

Foreword

Leland R. Reiswig, Jr.
Assistant General Manager, Programming
Personal Systems
IBM Corporation

When IBM announced in 1984 that we were working on an advanced operating system that could "multitask DOS programs and provide access to more memory than current versions of DOS," (as we said at the introduction of the AT), no one—ourselves included—could have guessed that we'd end up with a system as powerful and feature-rich as the one we ended up with. OS/2 2.0, the result of hundreds of programmer-years of effort, represents an operating system for your desktop that is more powerful than those IBM shipped with its mainframes in the late 1960s.

Users of OS/2 will gradually discover that it is a treasure trove of features, but what I think you'll find most useful is OS/2's breadth as an application platform. Not only is OS/2 2.0 a complete foundation for a new generation of powerful 32-bit applications, it also provides a home for older DOS applications, a finer home in fact than the one that they have under DOS itself. In one phrase, that is OS/2's greatest strength: it's not only got more of the future built in, it's got more of the past built in.

"More of the past," indeed. You know that I promised that OS/2 would be a "better DOS than DOS," and I think that we succeeded. If you've just gotten a copy of OS/2, try out a few trusty old DOS programs in this new environment. See how much easier it is to use your favorite word processor in a DOS box with over 720K of free RAM, a DOS box where extra memory can be gotten with a mouse click or two. You'll be amazed by the number and variety of options that you can adjust for DOS sessions.

Amazed ... and perhaps scared, a bit. There is a lot more in OS/2. And that's where a book like this one will prove to be a good investment, a perfect companion to the PC world's newest operating system, a system revolutionary in many ways. The authors and New Riders Publishing are to be commended for a thorough and complete look at the new world of 2.0. Read this book next to your computer—you'll find yourself saying, "Hey! let me try that out" with nearly every page.

Table of Contents

Introduction

In the spring of 1992, IBM introduced Version 2.0 of OS/2, the most advanced operating system available for personal computers. With Version 2.0, OS/2 provided enhanced features that changed the way people used computers. OS/2 emerged as a platform on which tightly integrated applications could dynamically exchange data in a seamless fashion. The new OS/2 environment also provided a more colorful interface with proportionally spaced fonts, a wider range of video and printer drivers, and updated screen graphics. Through these enhancements, OS/2 made powerful personal computers more accessible than ever to unskilled users.

OS/2 promises to make a substantial impact on personal computing for years to come. Every OS/2 user will benefit from truly powerful memory-management features, the potential for integrated multimedia capabilities, and advanced object-oriented data management. These advanced capabilities enable you to become productive with *all* the applications you run under OS/2—whether they are OS/2-specific applications, older DOS programs, or even Microsoft Windows applications.

Inside OS/2 2, Special Edition prepares the PC-literate individual to take full advantage of OS/2's powerful environment. Whether you are an advanced user of MS-DOS or a first-time OS/2 user, *Inside OS/2 2, Special Edition* can help you shorten the learning curve and quickly realize the benefits of this powerful operating system.

OS/2 represents a shift from the command line to a graphical computing environment. To a DOS command-line expert, OS/2 requires a new way of thinking. Under OS/2 2.0, you interact with the computer in a much more fluid and visual manner than is possible with the command-line interface. You can activate most OS/2 commands by clicking the mouse on menu options or by using the mouse pointer to press on-screen buttons. You no longer have to remember arcane command-line syntax, with its potential for spelling errors and missed options.

If you are a beginning computer user, you will find that OS/2 offers a natural way to interact with your PC. In any OS/2 application, you can initiate most functions by simply selecting the desired data (usually through simple mouse movements) and then choosing the desired operation (again, usually by using the mouse).

How This Book is Different from Most OS/2 Books

Inside OS/2 2, Special Edition is designed and written to accommodate the way you work. The authors and editors at New Riders Publishing know that you probably do not have a great deal of time to learn OS/2, and that you are anxious to begin using OS/2 to help you become more productive in your daily work.

This book, therefore, does not lead you through endless exercises for every OS/2 function and does not waste your time by repeating clearly obvious information. Each chapter introduces you to an important group of related OS/2 concepts and functions, and quickly shows you how these aspects of OS/2 relate to your computer system. The chapters also lead you through the basic steps you must follow to incorporate each new concept and function into your own computing work. This book's tutorials, however, are fast-paced; they help you become productive in the shortest time possible once you understand the concepts and functions involved.

Later in this introduction, you will find descriptions of each of this book's chapters and appendixes.

Who Should Read This Book?

Inside OS/2 2, Special Edition is written for two types of reader: experienced PC users who are new to the OS/2 environment, and experienced OS/2 or Microsoft Windows users who want to upgrade to OS/2 2.0.

Experienced PC Users Who are New to OS/2

If you are in the first group of readers, you are comfortable with personal computers, and particularly with MS-DOS versions 3.3 and higher. This book assumes that you have experience using DOS command-line applications and text-based user interfaces. This book also assumes that you are anxious to become productive with OS/2 2.0. As an experienced user of personal computers, this book makes the following assumptions about you:

- You are an experienced PC user who understands basic computing concepts and is familiar with basic computer components, such as hard disks, printers, and so on.

- You know that a file is the computer's basic information container and that files are hierarchically arranged in directories.

- You know that computers use different kinds of files: text, data (which may be text), executable, and so on. (Executable files normally have an EXE file name extension and text files usually have TXT or DOC extensions.)

- You can type and know the location of the keys on the keyboard.

- You do not have time to read long passages about computer and software basics; rather, you want to start working with OS/2 2.0 as soon as possible.

If you are an experienced MS-DOS user who has not yet made the transition to OS/2, read the following section.

The Benefits of OS/2 2.0 to New OS/2 Users

OS/2 dramatically shortens the time required to learn a new application. Several years ago, IBM established the Common User Access (CUA) conventions for all well-behaved OS/2 applications. These conventions specify the screen's overall appearance, the placement of menus and menu options, the mouse actions, and other aspects of the user interface that are important for rapid access to the software's functions.

All OS/2 applications provide a common method of interacting with the computer. You find a consistency in the actions you must take to interact with most OS/2 applications. For instance, the steps required to save a file are the same in every CUA-compliant application. Similarly, you cannot accidentally erase or write over an existing file without first receiving a warning. In OS/2 applications, help is always available by clicking on the Help option in the menu bar at the top of the screen.

You will find OS/2's *visual* approach to computing a very pleasant experience. Most of your interaction with OS/2 is through mouse actions (pointing and clicking), and a keyboard equivalent exists for every mouse action.

OS/2 2.0 enables you to transfer your existing DOS applications to the OS/2 environment—even those applications that require expanded memory, exclusive use of serial ports, or very high-resolution graphics. The good news is that you do not have to abandon your favorite character-based DOS application when you move to OS/2.

The Benefits of This Book to New OS/2 Users

Many OS/2 books are available, ranging from very basic books to advanced, specialized books for experienced users. Only a few OS/2 books make a genuine effort to present information with comprehensive explanations, practical examples, and a minimum of hand holding.

Because of the depth of the topic discussions and the breadth of coverage in *Inside OS/2 2, Special Edition*, you can use it as a reference long after you have mastered the OS/2 interface.

If you have never used OS/2, you should start with Chapter 1 and work through Chapter 4. These chapters introduce you to OS/2's graphical nature and to the impact OS/2 has had on users in the last few years. Skip over any sections that appear obvious or do not interest you. You can always return to these sections later.

The later chapters of this book deal with more advanced topics that you will encounter as you gain experience with OS/2. Whenever possible, practical examples and illustrations are drawn from popular OS/2 applications.

In these later chapters, you will discover the benefits of OS/2 2.0's preemptive multitasking, capability to run multithreaded applications, 32-bit architecture, and advanced memory management. These features combine to provide the user with seamless integration across many kinds of applications. The productivity gains possible from OS/2's integration capabilities are substantial.

This book's sections on running DOS and Microsoft Windows applications under OS/2 are a valuable resource if you want to move existing DOS or Windows applications to the OS/2 environment. OS/2 2.0 provides a sound platform for any DOS or Windows application—even those that require exclusive use of the computer's resources, such as memory, serial ports, and graphics. In fact, your DOS and Windows applications may even run faster and more reliably under OS/2.

OS/2 Users Who Want To Upgrade to OS/2 2.0

If you fall into the second group of readers for whom *Inside OS/2 2, Special Edition* is written, you are an experienced user of an earlier version of OS/2 or Microsoft Windows. You either have upgraded to OS/2 2.0, or you are considering making the upgrade. This book introduces you to the capabilities that are new to OS/2 2.0. You can learn how to apply OS/2's latest enhancements to your own computing work without relearning the OS/2 concepts and functions you already know through your own experience. Specifically, this book makes the following assumptions about you:

- You are familiar with the mouse and mouse actions.
- You know how to use dialog boxes and selection lists.
- You understand the concept of windowed applications and you know how to use OS/2's maximize and minimize buttons.
- You are familiar with the OS/2 desktop, program groups, and icons.
- You know how to start and run applications under OS/2.

If you already are an OS/2 user who is upgrading to OS/2 2.0, read the following section.

The Benefits of OS/2 2.0 to Experienced OS/2 Users

If you are upgrading from an earlier version of OS/2, you will find that version 2.0 offers even more power and value than the earlier versions.

The advanced memory-management and preemptive multitasking capabilities of OS/2 2.0 provide a more stable environment than anything available before. Task-switching is faster and more fluid than in other operating environments; you can exchange data between applications more easily than ever before.

OS/2 effectively isolates multitasked applications from one another and from the operating system itself. This feature provides an extremely stable environment for running multiple applications simultaneously.

The OS/2 2.0 user interface is faster, more colorful, and more flexible than that of previous versions. Many OS/2 desktop applications have been updated to incorporate new features.

The OS/2 Lan Server provides the networked office environment with stable, reliable, and secure network services including shared printer and file access, remote communications capabilities, and advanced network management facilities.

The Benefits of This Book to Experienced OS/2 Users

In contrast to many books on OS/2 2.0, *Inside OS/2 2, Special Edition* does not overstate the obvious. For example, this book does not show you how to install OS/2 or OS/2 applications (although an appendix provides step-by-step instructions and information on installation options). The book emphasizes practical examples that demonstrate the subject material without belaboring the point. You should work through as many examples as you like, and feel free to experiment. As you already know, OS/2 keeps you from damaging anything in the process.

If you already are an experienced OS/2 user, you may want to skip the first two chapters. Starting with Chapter 3, you will find information on customizing the Presentation Manager Desktop. The following chapters explain file management under OS/2 and the built-in OS/2 "applets," and touch on the advanced features of version 2.0.

The later chapters look at making the most of your applications under OS/2. A large part of this book is devoted to advanced topics such as networking and connectivity issues, optimization, and batch programming with the REXX batch language.

The appendixes provide detailed descriptions of the installation options available with OS/2 and a survey of currently available OS/2 applications.

How This Book Is Organized

Inside OS/2 2, Special Edition is designed both as a tutorial to help new users learn to master OS/2 2.0, and as a reference guide that you can use over and over, long after you have mastered the basics of OS/2. The book is divided into parts, each of which covers a specific group of OS/2 concepts and functions. The parts progress from simple to complex.

Part One: Getting Started

Part One introduces the new OS/2 user to the OS/2 environment. In this part of *Inside OS/2 2, Special Edition*, you learn the history of this exciting operating system and adopt a new approach to computing as you move from the DOS command line to the OS/2 graphical interface. By mastering the elements of the OS/2 interface, you prepare to begin working with applications in the OS/2 environment.

Chapter 1, "OS/2 Background," discusses the leadership position OS/2 has achieved in the realm of personal computing. The chapter surveys the history of OS/2, from its inception in 1984 as an advanced operating system for the IBM AT through its latest incarnation as version 2.0. This chapter also touches on the future of OS/2 and discusses in clear, precise terms the significant advantages of this powerful operating system.

Chapter 2, "Getting Started with the OS/2 Workplace Shell," studies the basic elements of the OS/2 environment and OS/2 applications. You master the various parts of the OS/2 interface, including scroll bars, drop-down menus, selection lists, icons, and buttons. This chapter also describes basic mouse actions that you can use to interact with OS/2.

Chapter 3, "Organizing and Customizing the Workplace Shell Desktop," offers a basic look at the OS/2 environment, including OS/2 objects, their behavior, and your interaction with them. You learn to construct the desktop by adding program groups and items, and by moving and resizing groups. The chapter also shows you several ways to start applications from the desktop.

In Chapter 4, "Managing Files with OS/2 2.0," you are introduced to the different file systems that are built into OS/2. Although you may choose a traditional DOS-like file system, you may choose instead to take advantage of OS/2's High Performance File System

(HPFS) to reap the benefits possible with this advanced architecture. The chapter introduces the principles of both of these systems and explains how to manage files in the OS/2 environment.

Part Two: Doing Business with OS/2

In Part Two, you become comfortable with the OS/2 desktop by manipulating OS/2 and OS/2 applications. You start with basic OS/2 facilities and progress through more complex OS/2 operations by using the operating system's built-in applets and advanced commercial applications. Through copious examples, you learn how to optimize your OS/2, DOS, and Windows applications in the OS/2 environment.

Chapter 5, "OS/2 Mini-Applications," shows you that your knowledge of OS/2 applies to virtually all OS/2 applications. You can move from one OS/2 application to another without learning a whole new set of commands and without mastering a different interface.

Chapter 6, "OS/2 and DOS Programs," shows you how to use your existing DOS applications in the OS/2 environment. OS/2 2.0 makes it easier than ever to integrate DOS applications into the OS/2 environment. This chapter surveys the advanced management of DOS processes running under OS/2 and memory optimization techniques. Finally, this chapter discusses specific versions of DOS, including DR DOS 6.0.

Chapter 7, "Running Windows Programs under OS/2," clarifies the tasks and considerations when running new or existing Windows applications in the OS/2 environment. The material in this chapter explains why the performance of these programs may actually be better when run under OS/2 than their native environment.

Chapter 8, "A Sampling of OS/2 Applications," surveys a representative sample of commercial OS/2 applications, and emphasizes the consistency of the OS/2 interface across these applications. Available OS/2 programs range from sophisticated database, graphics, and word processing applications to simple utilities that complement the built-in OS/2 applets.

Chapter 9, "Working Smarter with OS/2," shows you how to truly maximize OS/2 applications with OS/2 multitasking capabilities. This chapter describes the enhanced Dynamic Data Exchange (DDE) and Object Linking and Embedding (OLE) facilities of OS/2 2.0. Through practical examples, this chapter shows you how easily you can move data among applications.

Chapter 10, "OS/2 Connectivity," is a comprehensive guide to the networking capabilities of OS/2. Through in-depth discussions of the various networking and connectivity facilities available in OS/2 2.0, the process of enterprise-wide computing is simplified and made more accessible. This chapter is surely to remain a reference to OS/2 networking long after you have mastered the OS/2 interface.

Part Three: Using OS/2's Power

It is easy to overlook some of the most powerful features of a so-phisticated operating system such as OS/2. With so many features that are new and exciting, even the most significant benefits of OS/2 may not be explored by the new user. This section of *Inside OS/2 2, Special Edition* deals exclusively with information that will enable you to fully utilize all the major features of OS/2.

Chapter 11, "Understanding the Power of the Command-Line Interface," shows you how to bypass Presentation Manager and directly access the command-line interface for low-level operations. Input and output redirection, pipes, and boot options are discussed in detail.

Chapter 12, "Optimizing OS/2," teaches you techniques to fine-tune OS/2 for optimum performance and to reduce the chance of problems in the future. The chapter covers memory management, video optimization, operating-system parameters, disk access, and printing.

Chapter 13, "Writing Batch Programs Using REXX," introduces you to REXX, the powerful scripting language that is built into OS/2. REXX enables you to automate many routine system-management tasks that are a part of any operating system.

Part Four: Appendixes

Inside OS/2 2, Special Edition includes two appendixes. These appendixes offer in-depth discussions of topics not covered earlier in the book.

Appendix A, "Installation," shows you how to set up OS/2 on your system and describes the various installation options. This appendix also lists some of the most commonly asked OS/2 questions and their answers. You also learn how to use third-party device drivers.

Appendix B, "Current OS/2 Applications," is a survey of most of the commercially available applications for OS/2. This appendix should serve as a reliable source for the tools required in your work.

Part Five: Command Reference

Inside OS/2 2, Special Edition contains an extensive command reference.

Conventions Used in This Book

Throughout this book, certain conventions are used to help you distinguish the various elements of OS/2, DOS, their system files, and sample data. Before you look ahead, you should spend a moment examining these conventions:

- Shortcut keys are normally found in the text where appropriate. In most applications, for example, Shift-Ins is the shortcut key for the Paste command.

- Key combinations appear in the following formats:

  Key1-Key2: When you see a hyphen (-) between key names, you should hold down the first key while pressing the second key. Then release both keys.

  Key1,Key2: When a comma (,) appears between key names, you should press and release the first key and then press and release the second key.

- On-screen, OS/2 underlines the letters of some menu names, file names, and option names. For example, the File menu is displayed on-screen as <u>F</u>ile. The underlined letter is the letter you can press to choose that command or option. (In this book, however, such letters are displayed in bold, underlined type: **<u>F</u>**ile.)

- Information you type is in **boldface**. This convention applies to individual letters and numbers, as well as text strings. This convention, however, does not apply to special keys, such as Enter, Esc, or Ctrl.

- New terms appear in *italic*.

- Text that is displayed on-screen, but which is not part of OS/2 or a OS/2 application—such as DOS prompts and messages— appears in a `special typeface`.

Special Text Used in This Book

Throughout this book you will find examples of special text. These passages have been given special treatment so that you can instantly recognize their significance and so that you can easily find them for future reference.

Notes, Tips, and Warnings

Inside OS/2 2, Special Edition features many special sidebars, which are set apart from the normal text by icons. The book includes three distinct types of sidebars: "Notes," "Tips," and "Warnings."

A *note* includes "extra" information that you should find useful, but which complements the discussion at hand instead of being a direct part of it. A note may describe special situations that can arise when you use OS/2 under certain circumstances, and tell you what steps to take when such situations

arise. Notes also may tell you how to avoid problems with your
software and hardware.

 A *tip* provides you with quick instructions for getting the
most from your OS/2 system as you follow the steps
outlined in the general discussion. A tip might show you
how to conserve memory in some setups, how to speed up a procedure, or how to perform one of many time-saving and system-
enhancing techniques.

 A *warning* tells you when a procedure may be dangerous—that is, when you run the risk of losing data,
locking your system, or even damaging your hardware.
Warnings generally tell you how to avoid such losses, or describe
the steps you can take to remedy them.

New Riders Publishing

The staff of New Riders Publishing is committed to bringing you the
very best in computer reference material. Each New Riders book is
the result of months of work by authors and staff, who research and
refine the information contained within its covers.

As part of this commitment to you, the NRP reader, New Riders
invites your input. Please let us know if you enjoy this book, if you
have trouble with the information and examples presented, or if you
have a suggestion for the next edition.

Please note, however, that the New Riders staff cannot serve as a
technical resource for OS/2 or OS/2 application-related questions,
including hardware- or software-related problems. Refer to the
documentation that accompanies your OS/2 application package
for help with specific problems.

If you have a question or comment about any New Riders book, please write to NRP at the following address. We will respond to as many readers as we can. Your name, address, or phone number will never become part of a mailing list or be used for any other purpose than to help us continue to bring you the best books possible.

New Riders Publishing
Prentice Hall Computer Publishing
Attn: Managing Editor
11711 N. College Avenue
Carmel, IN 46032

If you prefer, you can reach New Riders Publishing at the following FAX number:

(317) 571-3484

Thank you for selecting *Inside OS/2 2, Special Edition*!

I

Getting Started

OS/2 Background

Getting Started with the OS/2 Workplace Shell

*Organizing and Customizing
the Workplace Shell Desktop*

Managing Files Using OS/2 2.0

OS/2 Background

If you are an experienced DOS user, changing to OS/2 requires major changes in your expectations of an operating system and in how you get your work done. OS/2 offers many new features, including the Workplace Shell, the High Performance File System, and 50-line CONFIG.SYS files.

This chapter looks at the history of OS/2, from its preannouncement in 1984 to the release of OS/2 in March of 1992. You learn the strengths and weaknesses of OS/2 compared to other operating systems and explore whether OS/2 is the right operating system for you.

Looking at OS/2's History

For many users, using OS/2 2.0 is their first experience with large amounts of memory and multitasking. OS/2 is a complex program that did not spring from a programmer's head in one day. Like an ancient city built on the ruins of earlier cities, OS/2 is built on the foundation of yesterday's hardware. The story begins in 1984.

Looking Back to 1984:
A New Operating System for the AT

On August 1, 1984, IBM unveiled a new member of its PC line. The AT, which stands for *Advanced Technology*, was billed as the world's first multiuser personal computer. Publicity photos showed the AT attached to two "dumb" terminals (that is, terminals without any computing power of their own).

This new computer was supposed to handle *multitasking*, which is the capability to run more than one program at a time on the same computer. You could connect terminals to it, and the AT theoretically could use up to 16 megabytes of memory and run five times faster than an XT. A new operating system that exploited the special features of the AT also was promised.

After the introduction of the AT, the new operating system did not live up to its promises. The new operating system, DOS version 3.0, was developed mainly to recast DOS from assembly language into C language, which was popular with system developers. DOS 3.0's most significant and only new feature of the promised new operating system was its support for the 1.2M high-density floppy disk drives that accompanied the AT.

The industry wanted to know what had happened to the multitasking capability. IBM responded that they were working on a new version of DOS that would handle multitasking and memory larger than 640K.

The 8088 and the 80286: Power versus Compatibility

The AT was built on what was then the most powerful CPU available from Intel. Intel designed the 8088 CPU, the processor used in the PC and XT. Because backward compatibility was of paramount importance, IBM turned to Intel for the next generation of desktop machines.

Like all technology companies, Intel was hindered and helped by its *installed base*—existing customers who used Intel products. Intel's large installed base was a tribute to the Intel engineers who designed general-purpose CPUs that offered good performance at a reasonable price. The disadvantage of Intel's installed base was that Intel did not have the freedom to develop a new CPU at the risk of incompatibility with its existing line of products.

Understanding Real and Protected Modes

The PC's 8088 CPU can address no more than 1024K of memory.
The 80286 can address 16,284K of *RAM* (Random-Access Memory),
but to support the installed base, a 286 CPU must boot in 8088-
emulation mode. In other words, the 80286 runs as an 8088 until the
CPU is told to do otherwise. In 8088-emulation mode, the 286 can
address only 1024K of memory. When the 80286 CPU emulates an
8088, the 80286 is said to be in *real mode*. The 80286, therefore, is
actually two CPUs in one: a fast implementation of the old 8088
CPU, and a new processor that can address 16 megabytes of
memory.

Because DOS was designed for the 8088, the 80286 must remain in
real mode when running DOS and DOS programs. The full power
of the 286 cannot be realized by DOS programs. A new operating
system was needed to support the 286 when the AT was introduced.

The new capabilities of the 286 appear in protected mode. *Protected
mode* makes it possible for programs to use more memory and
protects memory for applications. Multitasking occurs when multiple programs coexist in the PC's RAM. In a four-megabyte system
running a spreadsheet and a word processor, for example, the
operating system takes up two megabytes of RAM, the spreadsheet
takes up one megabyte, and the word processor takes up one megabyte. For the three programs to coexist, each must remain within its
boundaries. Protected mode creates and protects these boundaries
and prevents one program from using the memory of another.

In a protected-memory system, the operating system loads the
application. The application then makes an allocation request for
RAM from the operating system. If the operating system has
enough RAM, the application is assigned the memory. The newly
allocated spaces are then registered by the operating system in an
area in the 80286's memory called the *Global Descriptor Table (GDT)*.
From that point on, all memory accessed by the application is
scrutinized by a part of the 80286 CPU called the *Memory Management Unit (MMU)*. If an application tries to access areas of memory
that are out of the allocated space, the MMU immediately senses the

violation and triggers an alert called a *GP Fault*. Each operating system handles GP faults differently. Microsoft Windows, another protected-mode environment, responds with the message `Unrecoverable Application Error` when it detects a GP fault. OS/2 shuts down any programs that violate memory boundaries. This memory protection is built into the 286 CPU, and is the basis of all advanced PC operating systems.

Using DOS in Protected Mode

Theoretically, DOS can be adapted easily to protected mode. DOS applications, however, are *single-tasking*—they can perform only one function at a time. When programmers create a DOS application, they usually write the program so that it detects and uses exclusively the system's available resources. These programs are not designed to ask for access to memory or hardware devices. To rewrite DOS programs so that they use the 80286's protected mode involves massive rewriting of program code.

This protected- versus real-mode dichotomy answers the question often posed by DOS users of why an 80286-based computer (or an 80386 or 80486) does not use all of its memory. DOS programs are tied to real mode because they do not work in protected mode without massive rewriting, and the CPU must be in protected mode to address memory beyond one megabyte.

Looking Back to 1985: the 80386

In April 1985, Intel introduced a powerful new processor, the 80386. The 386 has the two processor modes of its 80286 predecessor—real mode and protected mode—and two more of its own.

Working with Segments: the "Nuisance Barrier"

As you have seen, the 286 allocates specific portions of memory, called *segments*, to protected mode applications that request memory. Segments are used in the 8088 architecture, but the 8088 does not offer protected memory. The capability to segment memory is in general a positive CPU feature, but the 80286 has a major design problem associated with segments. For purposes of compatibility with the 8080, a CPU even older than the 8088, segments on an 8088 can be no larger than 64K. Backward compatibility concerns prompted Intel to keep the 64K limitation on segments in the 286 CPU.

This design decision was probably the most unfortunate one made by Intel on the 80286. Each data or code object must fit within 64K because no segment can exceed this amount. A designer of a spreadsheet program that uses megabytes of memory must chop up those megabytes into dozens of 64K segments and then must manage those segments. This "nuisance barrier" has discouraged many programmers from examining 286 programming more closely. On a mainframe or mini running a UNIX or MVS operating system, such barriers do not exist.

Using Big Segments on the 386

The 80386 not only raises maximum memory to 4096M, but also removes the 64K segment size barrier. This feature is important to today's software developers. In graphics programs, for example, a typical full-screen image of VGA resolution can require 256K of memory; a higher resolution image may need 1024K of memory. The most convenient way to handle a single piece of data such as an image is to create an area in memory called an *array* that you can manipulate. On an 80286, a 1024K array must be implemented as 16 separate 64K segments because of the CPU's 64K segment size maximum. A 386, on the other hand, can allocate a single 1024K segment, which is called *linear addressing*.

As you might expect, a potential compatibility problem exists with larger segments. For this reason, the 80386 supports another mode besides real and 286-protected mode—*386-protected mode*.

Understanding V86 Mode

You can convert programs easily from 286-protected mode to 386-protected mode. 386-protected mode basically does everything 286-protected mode does. To convert from real mode to protected mode is more complicated. Many DOS real-mode programs probably will never be converted to 386-protected mode because of the extensive rewriting that is required. Intel did not realize this in 1981 when it introduced the 286. The debut of the 386 in 1985 included a fourth processor mode—*virtual 8086* or *V86* mode. V86 mode is best described as the DOS multitasking mode. V86 mode enables OS/2 to support DOS programs without posing major problems for the operating system's designers.

Some DOS programs direct all screen operations through DOS. DOS passes on the request to change a screen image to the video hardware using software called the *BIOS*, the *Basic Input Output System*. Most DOS programs, however, do not go through DOS. Instead, the programs directly control the hardware, and the new screen characters are placed right into the video board's screen buffer.

This practice causes problems for an operating system trying to multitask two DOS programs. Suppose, for example, that you command Lotus 1-2-3 to calculate a large spreadsheet and then you run dBASE while 1-2-3 is calculating. The 1-2-3 blinking Wait message appears in the upper right corner of the screen while dBASE is running because 1-2-3 does not direct its screen operations through DOS. The two programs write data simultaneously to the same screen. If 1-2-3 directed all of its screen operations through DOS, the multitasker program could work with DOS to intercept the appearance of the 1-2-3 "Wait" box. The screen would clear and the dBASE dot prompt would appear. Ordinary software, such as a simple DOS multitasker, cannot solve this problem.

To solve the problem, V86 mode divides a 386 computer into multiple PCs. Instead of making 1-2-3 and dBASE share the same PC, V86 mode creates a *virtual* PC for each program. In 486 mode the program can manipulate only a section of memory that is mimicking the video hardware rather than the actual video hardware.

The combination of 386-protected mode and virtual 8086 mode makes the 80386 a powerful CPU. 386-protected mode represents the future—V86 mode supports the past. Nevertheless, few people in the business thought that the 386 would appear on desktops anytime soon. The 286 CPU introduced by Intel in 1981 did not appear in a commercial product for three years.

A Note on the Term "386"

If you have an 80386SX or 80486-based computer, you may wonder how your machine applies to the terms used in this chapter for the 80386 CPU. For the purposes of this book, 386 refers to any computer based on the 80386DX, 80386SX, 80386SL, 80486DX, or 80486SX computer. Although these CPUs vary in speed, essentially they are the same in terms of the software they can run.

Looking Back to 1986: Early Disappointments

Although most of the world was unaware of OS/2 in 1986—OS/2 had not yet been named—the new operating system was problematic. Microsoft had been working on a multitasking version of DOS since 1983. A major problem with the 80286 CPU—the target processor of the first version of OS/2—nearly ended the project. The problem is that once the 286 is shifted to protected mode, it cannot shift back to real mode. Running DOS programs requires real mode, meaning that OS/2 would not be able to support DOS programs. If the problem had not been solved, OS/2 would have been totally incapable of running DOS programs. At one point in the OS/2 development project, Microsoft insiders confided to *PC Week* that early developer's kits would be available in the summer of 1986. Although Microsoft created a solution to the protected-to-real mode problem, it delayed the project. Its kits did not appear until the fall of 1987. These factors and others led to many changes to OS/2, as indicated by its different names. OS/2 was first named DOS 3.0, then DOS 4.0. A product named DOS 4.0 was actually shipped (not the one made generally available in 1988). It could multitask DOS programs if the programs were written to use DOS 4.0's multi-tasking capabilities. The 286 operating system was renamed DOS 5.0 (again, not the product shipped in 1991), then CP/DOS, DOS286, and ADOS (Advanced DOS).

For developers, the emergence of the 80386 made matters worse. Despite the expectation that 386s would not appear in the mass market until around 1988, hardware designers already were building the 386 CPU into mass-market products. Compaq started the influx of 386s on desktops with a top-quality Deskpro model that appeared only one year after the introduction of the 386 CPU by Intel. Many developers felt that an operating system for the 386 was needed more than a 286 operating system. The new product did not arrive, however, mostly because of the sheer complexity of the operating system. Microsoft had never built anything on this scale.

Looking Back to 1987: OS/2 1.0

In April of 1987, IBM announced its anxiously awaited next generation of microcomputers, the PS/2. At the same time, the new 286-based protected mode operating system was named OS/2. IBM had used OS/360 as the front-end of its popular line of early mainframes, and offered the OS/400 for the AS/400 minicomputer products ("midrange," as IBM calls them). The name OS/2 hinted at the operating system's true mission: to link the desktop to the computer center. This goal has been OS/2's area of greatest success. OS/2's largest customers are companies that want to develop mainframe programs inexpensively, not PC DOS users looking for big memory or multitasking.

In July 1987, the first versions of OS/2 were released to developers willing to risk $3,000 to be part of the Software Development Program. Despite the uncertain nature of the test-version ("beta") code, the developer world was excited about OS/2 1.0. Most major software companies had at least a small OS/2 development group. During this time, a single political event occurred that limited the prospects for OS/2.

Reacting to a perceived Japanese attack on the American semiconductor business, the Reagan administration convinced Japanese semiconductor manufacturers to raise the price of memory chips to allow U.S. semiconductor companies to compete. Unfortunately, by that time, few U.S. makers of memory chips remained. The result was a shortage of memory chips. The price of RAM chips skyrocketed to four times their previous cost. This scared many buyers away from memory purchases at the very time PC vendors were advising people that they would need four megabytes of RAM to run the upcoming OS/2.

On December 8, 1987, IBM and Microsoft released OS/2 1.0. This version did not have a graphical interface, would not work with a mouse, and could not support hard disks larger than 32M; but it was a beginning. Almost a year later, graphics appeared in OS/2, and support for large hard drives came in another year.

You may wonder why IBM and Microsoft shipped an incomplete product so early. The Macintosh's increase in popularity may have been a factor. Macintosh computers appeared in 1984, but until 1987 only attracted a small yet loyal following. By 1987, however, a Macintosh was not such an odd computer to buy. The appearance of PostScript and PageMaker (a high-quality printer standard and a desktop publishing program) made the Macintosh a good choice for some uses. IBM may have wanted to strike back at the Macintosh's graphical user interface (GUI). Shipping OS/2 1.0 early enabled IBM to promise this feature in the near future.

Looking Back to 1988: OS/2 1.1

In 1988, many vendors were developing for OS/2, but most did not want to release anything until IBM and Microsoft released the version of OS/2 with the Macintosh-like GUI called Presentation Manager (see fig. 1.1). *Presentation Manager*, or PM, enabled developers to build graphical applications, but required massive programmer retraining.

Figure 1.1:
A typical
Presentation
Manager screen.

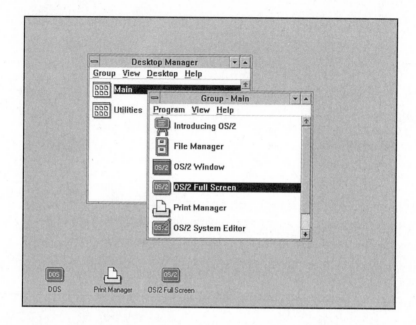

At the same time, the advent of the 386 caused many people to doubt the usefulness of OS/2. By 1988, about one quarter of business computer sales were 386-based. Experts continued to worry that an operating system for the 286 was a waste of time. An operating system for the more powerful 386 seemed inevitable. As a result, OS/2 sales decreased.

Sales of IBM's new PS/2 computer, based on the Micro Channel bus, also dropped. To boost sales, IBM embarked on a dual mission of software and hardware promotion, spreading the word about the PS/2 and OS/2. Their efforts were designed to instill in the minds of PC buyers that OS/2 was the operating system of the future, and that the Micro Channel bus, found only in the PS/2, was the best hardware to support the new multitasking operating system. Even the names—OS/2 and PS/2—reinforced the point that IBM's new operating system and new hardware were made to go together. This approach, however, scared away many potential OS/2 buyers who thought that they had to buy IBM hardware to use OS/2. This misunderstanding, combined with OS/2 compatibility problems on about 20 percent of PC clones, hurt sales considerably.

On Halloween of 1988, OS/2 1.1 shipped. The new version included the Presentation Manager graphical user interface and optional support for drives larger than 32M. IBM and Microsoft managed to include these features by making the same changes to disk structure that PC and MS-DOS 4.0 had done a few months before. Version 1.1 had some compatibility problems, however, and was notoriously buggy. In an attempt to bolster OS/2 sales, Microsoft renamed Windows 2.0 the "Windows Presentation Manager 2.0." OS/2 1.1 did not have database, communications, or LAN support. These features would come later in OS/2 1.1's Extended Edition.

Looking Back to 1989: The High Performance File System (HPFS)

While the public waited for the release of OS/2's Extended Edition, IBM and Microsoft representatives vigorously promoted OS/2. By then, programs were available that demonstrated OS/2's true power. Hamilton C Shell offered the kind of advanced user interface that Peter Norton is famous for in the DOS arena. The shareware communications program Logicomm was in its second version, and Microsoft was shipping its popular Word program with both the DOS and OS/2 versions in the same box. Most major database products—Informix, Oracle, R:BASE, FOCUS, SQLBase, and SQL Server—were by then running under OS/2. MicroFocus COBOL also had arrived on the market, attracting dozens of companies with its compatibility with mainframe COBOL.

Soon after Comdex 1989, IBM and Microsoft released OS/2 1.2. The new version offered an improved Presentation Manager and a new file system, the *High Performance File System (HPFS)*. HPFS, which is discussed in detail later in this chapter, completely revamped OS/2's file-management capability. Previously, OS/2 used the same file system as DOS—the File Allocation Table, or FAT, system. FAT-based systems handled large files poorly, however, and a new system was needed because OS/2 had become home to many database products. HPFS was added to OS/2's long list of major differences from DOS.

Another important addition to OS/2 1.2 was the REXX batch language. REXX is an SAA language used to write simple programs without the use of a compiler and other programming tools. REXX is not appropriate for large programs, but it is a powerful alternative to the limited batch language of DOS that OS/2 had supported since 1981. IBM originally thought that REXX would only be used for mainframe communications. As a result, it made REXX available only to users who purchased OS/2 1.2's Extended Edition.

By late 1989, work had begun on three new operating environments. The most well-known of these was Microsoft Windows version 3.0. OS/2's delays and poor sales prompted Microsoft to begin showing quietly a new version of Windows that not only ran Windows programs but also multitasked DOS programs—something that OS/2 could not do. Windows programs rewritten to use Windows 3.0 could access megabytes of memory, as opposed to the 640K-barrier of Windows 1 and 2. The opinion that the 386-based computer was the future was correct. The 286 was the best-selling computer for one year only. In 1989 consumers bought 386 computers (more than any other). The time for a 386-based version of OS/2 had arrived. Microsoft in Redmond and IBM in Armonk began telling the world that they were working on a complete rewrite of OS/2 called version 2.0, as well as OS/2 3.0. Version 2.0 would exploit the larger memory-addressing capabilities of the 386 CPU and would multitask existing DOS programs. OS/2 2.0's release was unofficially scheduled for mid-1990. Version 3.0 would not only incorporate the features of 2.0, but would also be machine-independent—it could be implemented easily on non-PC architectures such as the Macintosh, or RISC machines such as IBM's RS/6000, the Sun, or HP workstations.

IBM reacted nervously to Microsoft's development of Windows, and began displaying a version of OS/2 that did not demand as much memory as version 1.2. This slimmed-down version was the work of IBM without any Microsoft assistance. Nevertheless, as the decade ended, the question of what operating system to use was harder to answer than it had been at any other time in the 1980s.

Looking Back to 1990: Windows 3.0

At Microsoft's Systems Seminar in January 1990, Microsoft representatives described the course that Microsoft intended to follow with its operating systems products. OS/2 versions 2 and 3 were on track and looking good. Early beta copies of OS/2 2.0 already had been sent to beta testers. OS/2 2.0's designers basically left the body of OS/2 unchanged and added support for larger memory and DOS multitasking. The beta version that appeared in the summer of 1990 seemed to be a solid enough product to market. If IBM had done that, OS/2's place in the market today would no doubt be different.

Microsoft Windows 3.0 was released on May 21, 1990. To run well, Windows needed a 386-based computer with at least four megabytes of memory (the memory shortage was over by then), VGA graphics, a mouse, and a 60M or larger hard drive. OS/2 required the same configuration in 1988, which was considered a disadvantage of the operating system. With Windows, however, users welcomed a product that could use the 386's power. Windows took the world by storm, selling more copies in the first month than OS/2 had sold in three years. Developers noticed that Microsoft had a winner on its hands.

The success of Windows put developers in a difficult situation. They spent three years and many dollars on OS/2 development and did not see a market for their product. Windows development was irresistible by comparison. Consequently, the OS/2 development teams became primarily Windows development teams, and only a few programmers were left to work on OS/2 development.

No releases of OS/2 occurred in 1990; IBM delayed 2.0's release until early 1991. IBM received some good news in 1990, however, when Hewlett-Packard supplied its printer drivers for the popular LaserJet line of printers. For years, the lack of HP support had hindered both IBM and Microsoft. Nevertheless, the release of these printer drivers came too late to help OS/2 version 1.*x*.

Looking Back to 1991:
IBM and Microsoft Go Their Separate Ways

Nobody knew when OS/2 2.0 would be released. IBM did not admit that such a product was under development, but the PC community knew that something was going on in the operating system arena. A front-page article in the *Wall Street Journal* proclaimed OS/2 dead. The article also announced that Microsoft would end its part in OS/2 development and turn it over to IBM. All future Microsoft operating system development would grow out of Windows and DOS. OS/2 version 3.0, the future architecture-independent version of OS/2, would eventually become Windows NT. NT, which stands for *New Technology*, was Microsoft's name for its new core software that would run on many different types of computers. NT also would run UNIX and OS/2 programs and would be the most comprehensive desktop operating system. Microsoft promised NT by the end of 1992, an ambitious goal in light of the delays encountered by previous large operating system products. Before 1991 ended, however, Microsoft retracted the promise of OS/2 and UNIX support by late 1992.

Early in 1991, IBM shipped OS/2 version 1.3. This new version, with a faster user interface, was a slimmed-down version of 1.2. Version 1.3 also included a powerful font engine designed by Adobe Systems, the makers of the PostScript language. The font engine, called *Adobe Type Manager*, could accommodate fonts built in the Adobe Type 1 format, the most widely used format in electronic fonts.

Late in 1991, IBM announced that OS/2 2.0 would not ship until March of 1992. The reason for the final delay was IBM's former ally, Microsoft.

Hostility between IBM and Microsoft increased throughout 1991. After Microsoft's public denouncement of IBM in the *Wall Street Journal*, IBM announced changes in its view of LANs. The LAN world has been dominated for years by Novell, Inc. of Provo, Utah. Since 1986, Microsoft and IBM had been trying to cut into Novell's large market share. The most recent attempts had been the OS/2-based LAN Manager and LAN Server mainly developed by Microsoft. In February 1991, IBM announced hardware and software that would connect a PC LAN to a mainframe at high speed—as long as the LAN was Novell. Microsoft retaliated with the announcement of major revisions to LAN Manager version 2.1 that would not support IBM's existing LAN Server, although previous versions of LAN Manager were interchangeable with LAN Server.

Later in 1991, IBM announced that OS/2 2.0 would be a "better Windows than Windows," and "a better DOS than DOS," by running Windows programs faster and by multitasking DOS applications. This announcement seemed to justify another delay of three months.

Introducing OS/2 2.0 in 1992

OS/2 2.0's long-awaited arrival in March 1992 seemed more like the beginning for new operating system development, rather than the end of a process.

With more than one million copies sold, OS/2 has now joined the ranks of the most popular PC operating systems.

Understanding OS/2 and Systems Applications Architecture (SAA)

In 1988, IBM admitted a shortcoming in its line of computers: incompatibility. Despite IBM's success in selling microcomputers, mainframes, and minicomputers, these three markets were separate.

To illustrate this incompatibility, suppose that you open a video rental store and need a computer to keep your accounts. Your local IBM salesperson sells you a PS/2 Model 90 and Lotus 1-2-3. You use 1-2-3 to build the accounting system you need. When you expand to several stores, a single PC is not enough. Your IBM salesperson then sells you an AS/400 minicomputer, or a midrange. You soon discover that the midrange does not offer 1-2-3 on its menu of startup options, does not use a mouse, and is very different from your PS/2. The IBM salesperson assures you that what you need is a language called RPG.

After some struggling, you learn RPG and rework your 1-2-3 files in the new language. Eventually, you own a national chain of video stores. Although the AS/400 is a capable machine, it cannot handle the workload of many stores. The IBM representative configures a full-featured IBM 390 mainframe for you. Recalling your last venture into a new architecture, you ask if 1-2-3 or RPG is the preferred development tool on this computer. The answer is no, and you are directed to yet another development tool built around a language called COBOL. Again, you must retool and reimplement your software in COBOL.

Many companies experience these problems when they move between levels of IBM computers. In contrast, programs that run on the smallest Digital Equipment Corporation (DEC) MicroVAX run basically without modification on the largest DEC processors. Cross-platform incompatibilities hurt IBM's market share, and IBM wanted to do something about it. This was not a simple matter, however. Unlike mainframes and minicomputer programs, which are limited interactively, PCs run interactive programs. They have graphical screens, mice, and other devices rarely found on larger systems. The communications link between the main processor and the user terminal is something of a bottleneck, especially when compared to the PC's quick text display capabilities. Mainframe applications usually are built by professional programmers using complex tools. Although the same kinds of programs also are used on the PC, many accounting systems are built on Lotus 1-2-3 and macros written by nonprofessional programmers.

IBM developed *Systems Applications Architecture (SAA)* to solve incompatibility problems. SAA consists of three parts:

- **Common Communications Access.** Ensures that all IBM computers, both large and small, can communicate with each other.

- **Common Programming Interface.** Ensures that a program written on the mainframe can be recompiled and run correctly on the PC or midrange.

- **Common User Access (CUA).** Determines how the computer looks to the user. A person accustomed to the microcomputer version of a program can learn quickly to use the mainframe version without the need for excessive retraining.

Understanding Common Communications Access (CCA)

Micro-to-mainframe data transfer has never been an easy task. Initially, IBM did not think that thePC would ever communicate with the mainframe. For this reason, they did not build any PC-to-mainframe links. Today, more PCs are connected to IBM mainframes by non-IBM communications hardware than by IBM-made communications hardware. DCA's IRMA boards, for example, consistently outsell IBM's 3270 emulation boards.

The many ways that PCs and mainframes communicate compound the problem. It is almost impossible for a company to develop a single software package that enables any PC to communicate with any mainframe by using any communications standard. The alternative was to narrow the field of communications standards. CCA supports a type of communication called Logical Unit type 6.2, or LU 6.2. LU 6.2 is a peer-to-peer communication method rather than a master-slave communication method. In *master-slave communications*, one side controls the communication. Master-slave is easy to define and to write software for, but it is limited in many ways. Master-slave, for example, does not work on some PC LANs with workstations that need to communicate with other workstations. Peer-to-peer communication is more work for the designer, but is more flexible in the long run. When LU 6.2 is paired with another standard—Physical Unit type 2.1, or PU 2.1—it is called Advanced Program-to-Program Connection, or APPC. Part of SAA compliance is support of APPC. You learn more about communications in Chapter 10.

Common Programming Interface (CPI)

If you are a mainframe programmer using a third-generation programming language, you probably do much of your work in COBOL, the COmmon Business Oriented Language. COBOL still is popular because of its versatility and age. Scientific and engineering mainframe programmers commonly use FORTRAN, the FORmula TRANslator. Many programming tools that are better than either FORTRAN or COBOL exist, but these two languages remain popular.

If you are a developer in the PC world, you probably use C language. C's popularity also can be attributed to timing and tradition. Neither C nor COBOL can claim to be *the* programming language because C has not transferred to the mainframe world and COBOL has not taken over the desktop. Regardless of the advantages of each language, SAA supports C, COBOL, FORTRAN, RPG (for midranges), and REXX, a powerful batch language discussed in Chapter 13.

If all these languages are SAA and the PC is supposed to be SAA-compliant, why are these languages unavailable for PCs? SAA is intended for PC hardware that runs OS/2. IBM makes no promises about SAA in the DOS environment. REXX, APPC, FORTRAN, and others can be found in a DOS implementation from a vendor. IBM, however, is implementing these languages for OS/2 and making them an important part of its overall computing strategy.

Common User Access (CUA)

Although communications and programming compatibility are of interest to systems administrators and programmers, most computer users are not highly trained computer professionals. When an application is shifted from the mainframe to the desktop, massive retraining is required. CUA was designed to help programmers write applications that look basically the same on the PC and on a terminal attached to a minicomputer, midrange, or mainframe.

SAA also offers a standard set of key assignments. For example, F1 is the help key for most applications; F3 is generally the exit key, although many OS/2 utilities do not respond to F3; and F10 gains access to the command menu on a screen.

Previous IBM standards, such as the networking standard SNA—Systems Network Architecture—were developed to promote sales of hardware or software. SAA was designed to make it easier for computers to communicate, to make more software available across platforms, and to enable users to move between platforms without retraining. For many programmers, SAA is a welcome addition to OS/2.

Pink—The Next Generation of Macintosh Software

IBM took the idea of cross-platform paths one step further—beyond the IBM line of computers. In 1991, IBM began working with Apple to create a new operating system, code-named Pink.

The Pink operating system appears to be more of a collaboration between Apple engineers than between Apple and IBM. The design team of the current Macintosh operating system, System 7, sat down with two piles of paper cards—blue ones and pink ones. Ideas that the developers thought they could implement in time for System 7's release were written on blue cards. Ideas that were desirable, but would have to wait for the next development cycle—System 8—were written on the pink cards. System 7 is the Blue operating system. Pink is the next generation of Macintosh operating software. IBM's main concern is getting it to run on the 386- and 486-based PS/2s, as well as on the Power PC.

The Power PC is a new line of desktop micros that IBM is developing, based on its popular UNIX desktop, the RS/6000. The 6000 is designed around a Reduced Instruction Set Chip (RISC) main processor developed by IBM in the late 1980s. The RS/6000 is popular because it offers a good price-to-performance ratio. The RS/6000 can be a desktop computer, but does not run DOS or DOS applications without extra hardware. The Power PC will be a scaled-down version of the 6000. Before the Power PC finds a place on America's desktops, however, it needs software. Pink is the intended software for this computer.

> **NOTE** Pink, if completed, will be a remarkable operating system. It is intended to run on three completely alien systems—the Intel 386/486 CPU, the Motorola 680X0 series used by the Macintosh, and the RISC chip of the 6000 for the Power PC.

Pink may worry OS/2 users, who say "What about us? Where does OS/2 fit in?" IBM has said only that "There will be a migration path to Pink." Before you worry, remember that the intended release date for PINK is 1995. This goal is optimistic, considering the delays of OS/2.

Exploring OS/2's Advantages

If you are thinking of switching to OS/2, you need to know its advantages over DOS. The three main advantages of OS/2 are as follows:

- **Multitasking.** OS/2 enables you to run multiple processes simultaneously.

- **Larger Memory.** OS/2 removes the 640K barrier that DOS users are so familiar with and eliminates the memory manager that wastes time under both DOS and Windows.

- **Graphical User Interface (GUI).** OS/2 offers a GUI that is easy to learn and use with OS/2 applications, including SAA compliance.

Other important features of OS/2 are as follows:

- Excellent backward compatibility for DOS and Windows applications

- Well-integrated networking support

- Built-in Adobe Type Manager

- A redesigned file system (HPFS) that enables better naming conventions, offers faster disk access, and decentralizes allocation information

- Unified device support through driver programs that simplify application installation and support

- Application protection—no `Unrecoverable Application Error` messages

- The incorporated REXX language, which is far more powerful than the DOS batch language

Any of these features would make an operating system worth a second look. The following sections discuss each of these items.

Using OS/2's Multitasking Capabilities

As mentioned earlier, *multitasking* is the capability to run multiple programs at the same time on the same computer. *Context switching* or *task-switching* enables you to load multiple programs into a computer at the same time but run only one program at a time. Both applications do not run simultaneously. To shift from one application to another, you click the mouse button or use a few keystrokes—you do not have to exit one program and wait while another one loads.

Context-switching capabilities are helpful in many cases, but you might want programs to continue to run after you have switched away from them. If you switch from dBASE while sorting a file, for example, the file is not sorted when you return to dBASE; the process is suspended until you reactivate dBASE.

Newcomers to OS/2 often question the benefits of multitasking if they can do only one thing at a time. Every user has to wait for the computer at some point. If you have ever sat and waited while your computer prints, downloads or uploads data, compresses data, sorts files, or runs any other operation that takes time but does not require user intervention, you can appreciate multitasking. On a multitasking system, a few mouse clicks can start another program simultaneously while one of these processes is running.

A well-written OS/2 word processing program, for example, enables you to save your file in the background, instead of making you wait while the hourglass appears on-screen and the drive light flashes. An OS/2 E-mail program automatically dials your E-mail service, checks your mailbox every hour or so, and notifies you only when you have mail.

In multitasking, the program that you currently are working with—the program that accepts your keystrokes—is the *foreground task* (in the foreground). The other tasks—the ones that disappear into their folders when minimized—are the *background tasks* (in the background). In the Workplace Shell, the window that you currently work with has the *focus*. Focus and foreground are almost the same thing.

The differences between foreground tasks and the focus are explored in the multitasking discussion in **NOTE** Chapter 12. This chapter also shows you how to tune your OS/2 system.

Although multitasking is beneficial, it does have some disadvantages. Under DOS, you start one program at a time; you cannot start a second task until the first task is completed. DOS is like a desktop that has room for only one piece of paper; you are never given the opportunity to mess up your workspace. In the OS/2 environment, the capability to open dozens of programs at the same time can create a messy-looking screen and more opportunities to lose work, much like a desk piled high with half-finished projects. In addition, a multitasking computer closely resembles a mainframe. Mainframes generally are served by a full staff of people who specialize in multitasking and system tuning. With OS/2, the user must play the role of the system administrator. This responsibility scares some users away from a complex environment like OS/2 or Windows.

Using OS/2's Big Memory Capabilities

The primary limitation of DOS is memory. OS/2 extends its programs well beyond DOS's memory confines by giving more memory to programmers and to programs.

More Memory for Programmers

Programmers can write many more applications for OS/2 than for DOS because OS/2's memory is easier to utilize, and the CPU offers much more assistance in the debugging process.

The original PC CPU, the 8088, can address only 1024K. (The CPU is only partially responsible for the DOS 640K barrier.) Even more annoying, however, is a less-publicized limitation: the 64K segment.

Every piece of program and data must reside inside a *segment*, which is an area in memory. References to specific locations inside segments are called *offsets*. Most PC programs have at least three segments: a *code segment* for the program, a *data segment* for the data, and a *stack segment*. A *stack* is a temporary storage area used by the PC to mark its place in a current process after an interruption. In figure 1.2, you see a computer program with code, data, and stack segments.

The program instructions (in the code segment) tell the CPU to retrieve a data value at the 14th location within the data segment. This is a two-step process. The program tells the CPU in which segment to look and what offset to use within that segment. If necessary, multiple segments can be used in a program. Segmentation is a common architectural feature in CPUs, and it is beneficial in many ways. The problem with 8088 segments is that they cannot be larger than 64K. This is why the BASIC language that Microsoft shipped with DOS could only accommodate programs no larger than 64K, or one segment. The early VisiCalc spreadsheet for the PC also was limited to spreadsheets no larger than 64K. In addition, the 64K-segment limit forces the DOS COPY command to go back and forth between a disk drive and memory when copying files. DOS can read only 64K worth of data before it runs out of memory; it then must write the data and go back for more.

Figure 1.2:

Using segments and offsets to point to data in a program.

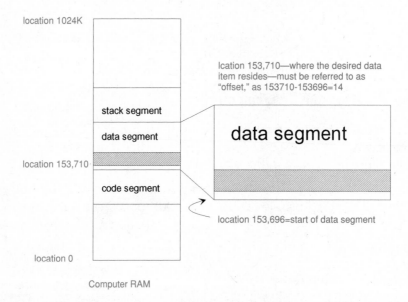

location 1024K

lcation 153,710—where the desired data item resides—must be referred to as "offset," as 153710-153696=14

stack segment

data segment

data segment

location 153,710

code segment

location 153,696=start of data segment

location 0

Computer RAM

If those examples do not convince you of the disadvantages of 64K segments, consider the system resources used by Microsoft Windows, which you can see in the **H**elp **A**bout window in the Program Manager. This critical memory area needed by Windows is a segment that can be no larger than 64K. When the critical area fills up, Windows cannot start another application, although you may have megabytes of free memory.

The problem of the 64K boundary is worse in the 80286 CPU. The 80286 can address up to 16M of RAM. This memory addressing is still segmented, however, and the segments cannot exceed 64K.

Lotus 1-2-3 versions 3.0 and 3.1 can access all 16M of a 286 computer's RAM, but it must allocate that 16M of RAM in separate 64K segments. For this reason, a number of software vendors refused to support the 286's extended memory. Because OS/2 version 1.*x* used 286-processor mode, good mainframe programs should have been available under OS/2 1.*x* or Windows 3.*x*. These programs never appeared because the 64K segment problem does not exist in the mainframe world. This oversight on the part of the 286's designers prompted Microsoft's Bill Gates to label the 286 "a brain-damaged chip."

The developers of the 80386 CPU finally fixed the problem. The 386 processor mode addresses 4096M of memory, and no size limitation is imposed on the segments. The segments can be as large as 4096M. The 386 CPU also supports the old 8088 and 286 processor modes.

More Memory for Programs

DOS was built for the 8088 CPU, which was designed over 14 years ago. The DOS memory limitation is a hassle for more than 60 million DOS users. DOS forces even a 50 MHz, 80486-based computer to act as a 50 MHz 8088. Even worse, extended memory is available in the 80286 through the 80486 CPUs, as you see in Table 1.1, but the memory is wasted unless you have an operating system that can use it.

Table 1.1
Maximum Addressable Memory for
CPU and Machine Types

CPU	Maximum Addressable Memory
80386SX	16M
80386SL	16M
80386DX or any kind of 80486 w/ISA bus	16M
80386DX or any kind of 80486 w/MCA or EISA	4096M

It seems that the memory size limits of the 80386DX or 80486 can end your memory problems forever. (The 80286 CPU is not included in Table 1.1 because OS/2 version 2.0 does not run on it.) The memory sizes shown in Table 1.1 refer to Random-Access Memory (RAM). Typically, an OS/2 workstation has 6M of RAM and 100M or more of hard disk space. You can exploit fully the 4096M addressing capability of the 80386DX and 80486s in OS/2 version 2.0. (Four *gigabytes* equal just over four billion bytes.) This capability frees developers from having to shoehorn powerful programs into a mere 640K. Furthermore, if you have struggled with a DOS memory manager program, such as Quarterdeck QEMM or DOS 5.0's EMM386.EXE, you know that they take time and effort to use effectively. The extra effort usually results in no more than an extra 128K to 192K of free space. OS/2 has made memory managers obsolete; they are unnecessary except for some features that are used for DOS compatibility.

OS/2 enables you to use *virtual memory*, which is hard or floppy disk space that is used as RAM. If your computer only has one megabyte of free memory, but you want to run a two-megabyte program, OS/2 can run the program. OS/2's virtual memory uses disk space as if it were RAM space. Although virtual memory is considerably slower and should be used only if necessary, you can use it to run a large application easily.

You probably do not realize how much time you spend working around limited memory space. After you use OS/2 for one month, however, you may surprise yourself at the increase in productivity.

Using OS/2's Graphical User Interface (GUI)

The graphical user interface (GUI) was explored first at Xerox Corporation's Palo Alto Research Center (PARC) in the early 1970s. OS/2's original GUI was the Presentation Manager. For nearly two years, OS/2 version 2.0 betas were built around the Presentation Manager.

Windows users notice the resemblance of Presentation Manager to Windows. A beta version of OS/2 that shipped in late 1991 introduced something totally new to OS/2's graphical environment—the Workplace Shell. An opening screen for the Workspace Shell is shown in figure 1.3.

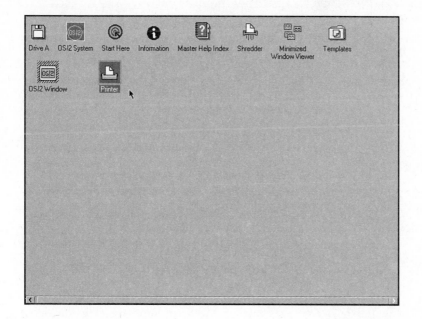

Figure 1.3:

A typical Workplace Shell screen.

The Workplace Shell resembles the Presentation Manager, but uses some new and interesting concepts. Although many developers have been slow to adjust to the Workplace Shell, it is worth the effort to learn to use it. Chapters 2 and 3 cover this new addition to the OS/2 GUI.

Graphical User Interfaces (GUIs) are very popular. Every platform wants to add graphics, even older operating systems like UNIX. GUIs use graphics, symbols, and easily accessible menus to simplify the task of learning to use—or remembering how to use—an application. GUIs are sometimes called *WIMP interfaces*. WIMP is an abbreviation for the parts of the GUI: Windows, Icons, Mice, and

Pull-down menus. *Windows* are the graphical windows on-screen that can be resized and rearranged by the user. *Icons* are small pictures that represent objects, such as data, programs, and peripherals. An icon sometimes takes the place of a file or application name. *Mice* are pointing devices that you use to select an on-screen control. *Pull-down menus* show the user currently available options or future options. Pull-down menus usually display unavailable options in another color, such as gray.

Previous versions of the OS/2 GUI, the Presentation Manager, looked like Microsoft Windows and functioned similarly. The new Workplace Shell is much different. Unlike other GUIs, the Workplace Shell uses the right mouse button. The right mouse button is rarely used in most GUIs, but is essential in OS/2 2.0. At first glance, the Workplace Shell looks a lot like the Macintosh shell, but a closer look reveals many differences.

Employers favor GUIs because they make a machine more accessible. A program that hides its commands behind a bad interface presents a learning challenge to a beginner. dBASE III, for example, is a good program, but its forbidding dot prompt does not invite you to experiment. The OS/2 GUI, on the other hand, is very friendly. A menu appears, even if you click on the empty Workplace Shell background. In addition, after you learn one GUI application, you probably can understand all GUI applications. The same interface for other programs uses the same key for help and other capabilities that you use under the GUI.

GUIs also are the best working environment for occasional program use. Tax software, for example, is helpful, but users must relearn it each year because it is used once or twice. An occasional user can learn to use a GUI-based package much more quickly.

Using DOS and Windows Programs on OS/2

Concurrent CP/M86, TopView, the original DOS 4 (the limited-distribution multitasking version), OS/2 1.*x*, and Windows 1 and 2 were brilliant efforts to create a powerful new platform for multitasking and running memory-intensive graphical programs. Their failure in the marketplace can be attributed largely to one reason: they did not support existing applications. MultiMate or WordStar could run under IBM's TopView product with hours of work, but not very well. Lotus 1-2-3 2.2 ran under OS/2 1.3's DOS compatibility box, but only with restricted memory capabilities and no access to expanded memory. IBM and Microsoft—two large, capable companies—did not build anything to draw people away from DOS until Windows 3.0 was released.

Windows 3.0 does not do much more than Windows 1 and 2. More memory is available for applications in Windows 3.0, but expanded memory has always been available, as anyone who uses Micrografx Designer or Excel knows. Windows 3.0 not only runs existing DOS programs, but also runs more than one existing DOS program at the same time. Users made it clear that they wanted an operating environment that ran existing DOS applications.

Clearly, backward compatibility was an important design goal for OS/2. As early as 1989, the OS/2 2.0 beta offered better support for multitasking DOS applications than the latest version of Windows. Some of the features that the 2.0 beta offered include:

- OS/2 DOS boxes which have from 624K to 724K of free memory. Windows and DOS 5.0 DOS boxes have a maximum of only 596K of free space.

- Programs running in EGA, VGA, and XGA graphics modes (except for seamless Windows 3 applications) can run in a window under OS/2 2.0. In addition, graphics programs can be made to fit in a one-fourth sized window under OS/2 2.0.

- Sound can be disabled in a DOS box under OS/2 2.0, a convenient feature if you work at home or in a crowded office. This is not a Windows option.

OS/2 2.0 might have been released in late 1990—the beta was certainly good enough—had it not been for Windows. OS/2 sold about 200,000 copies in the first four years of its life. Windows, on the other hand, sold 8,000,000 in the first year and a half. IBM decided that OS/2 had to emulate Windows. IBM first announced that it would build a Windows-to-OS/2 translator. The intrinsic set of commands that controls Windows are called the *GDI*—the *Graphical Device Interface*. Similar commands under OS/2's graphical Presentation Manager and Workplace Shell are called *GPI*—the *Graphical Program Interface*. These two interfaces perform the same functions, but they do them differently. The command to draw a line, for example, may be `lineto` on one system, and `moveto` on the other. Such an interface between a program and an operating system is called an *API—Application Program Interface*. The GDI is Windows' Application Program Interface; GPI is OS/2's graphical API. Figure 1.4 shows the Windows and OS/2 APIs.

Figure 1.4:
OS/2's and Windows' APIs.

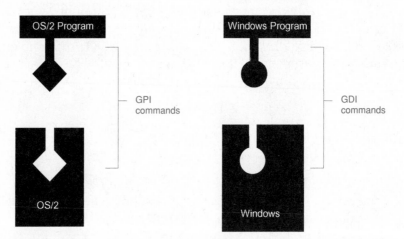

Because the Windows and OS/2 APIs do things differently, Windows programs are difficult to run under OS/2. To solve the problem, IBM developed a system of translation, as depicted in figure 1.5.

Translators are slow, however, and speed was a priority for OS/2. For this reason, IBM announced that it would augment the OS/2 APIs with the Windows APIs, instead of translating the Windows API, as shown in figure 1.6.

Windows Program

Windows OS/2
API translation
layer

OS/2

Windows Program

OS/2

Figure 1.5:
One approach to
Windows under
OS/2: an API
translator.

Figure 1.6:
The final OS/2 and
Windows API
approach.

This design goal was a bold move for IBM because the Windows API is as varied as the OS/2 API. IBM's decision to supplement the OS/2 API with Windows' API resulted in a delay of OS/2 2.0's release for another 15 months. Nevertheless, the effort has been worth it. Nearly every Windows program runs as fast under OS/2 as under Windows. This capability, however, may work against OS/2's long-term future as an operating system platform. OS/2's support of Windows programs is so good that some developers may see no need to develop OS/2 products. Shortly after the introduction of OS/2 2.0, Microsoft released Windows 3.1, which incorporates a few new features not found in Windows 3.0. Programs written for 3.1 did not run under the initial release of OS/2 2.0. The December 1992 release of OS/2 includes a faster graphics "engine" and Windows 3.1 support.

Using OS/2's LAN Connectivity Capabilities

In DOS, Local Area Networks (LANs) are something of an afterthought. Any LAN administrator can tell you many stories of incompatible network shells and insufficient memory. DOS was designed to live by itself without interference from the outside world. LANs literally intrude upon the structure of DOS.

Communications by nature require multitasking. If you are interrupted by the telephone while working on a project, you must make a mental note of where you are in the project before you answer the telephone. While you are talking, the information about the interrupted task remains in the back of your mind until you return to your work.

Building communications systems without multitasking is risky. Many LAN crashes under DOS can be attributed to the lack of multitasking. Most LAN products try to alleviate this problem by including simple multitasking capabilities. To work properly, however, multitasking must be built into the operating system, not merely tacked on as an afterthought.

OS/2 is an ideal platform for networking. LANs generally have a *server* that serves as a central repository for data and peripherals such as printers. The PCs that use this data are called *workstations*. The term "workstations" also describes a class of desktop microcomputers that run UNIX. Servers usually do not run DOS; instead, they run multitasking operating systems such as Novell NetWare, UNIX (used by Banyan VINES), and OS/2 (used by Microsoft's

LAN Manager, IBM's LAN Server, and the former 3Com's 3+ Open software). Currently, OS/2 is used mostly as the operating system for network servers.

You can run one operating system on the server and a different one on the workstation. The workstations run a translator program that converts the requests from DOS to the format used by the server. The translator program is called the *network shell* or *network redirector*.

OS/2's APIs—commands that programs can issue to the operating system—can transport data over a network, share peripherals over a network, enable one computer to use another's printer, and re-motely execute programs. To execute programs *remotely* means to start a program on one computer (computer A) that runs on another computer (computer B). Computer B does all the CPU work, and transports the screen output to A. Computer B also accepts key-strokes from A, making computer A work like a terminal for B. Computer B shows nothing of the program on its own screen; it does all the work in the background. This is valuable for companies that mainly work with programs that are not demanding for CPU power, such as small spreadsheets and medium documents. The company can keep costs down by placing many inexpensive com-puters and a single fast computer on the network. Users can then move work to the fast computer when necessary.

 Chapter 10 discusses networking OS/2 in detail.

Using OS/2's High Performance File System (HPFS)

Since 1981, DOS has kept track of the location of a file on a disk by using the *File Allocation Table*, or FAT. TheFAT was useful when a 360K floppy disk was considered spacious. As disk sizes grew, however, the FAT became a disadvantage. When DOS 3.3 arrived in 1987, the FAT's problems became obvious. DOS 3.3 supported hard disks up to 32M in size, but by then, some computers had disks larger than 32M.

DOS 3.3 included a fix for this problem by enabling you to partition a disk into multiple logical drives. *Logical drives* enable you to make an 80M drive appear as three drives: a 32M C drive, a 32M D drive, and a 16M E drive. Although this fix is beneficial, it is limited by the number of letters in the alphabet. A 660M drive, for example, cannot be divided into logical drives—if you tried to divide this size, you would run out of letters. Later versions of DOS offered a patch that solves this problem, but caused compatibility problems with existing programs. These programs took a year or two to fix. Even with these patches, the FAT-based file system suffers from other shortcomings:

- File names can be no longer than eight characters followed by a period, then three characters. This "8.3" naming convention leads to some odd file names.

  HPFS file names, on the other hand, can be 254 characters or more. You also can use lower- and uppercase letters in making file names.

- The FAT maintains all file location information in a single location out on the edge of the disk. Suppose, for example, a file is located toward the center of the disk. To read that file, the disk's head, a structure somewhat like an audio turntable's tonearm, must move out to the disk's edge to retrieve location information about that file. Then, once the disk knows where to look for the data, the disk head travels back in toward the center to retrieve some of the file's data, then travels out to the edge to get some more file location information, and so on.

  HPFS physically places the file information data near the file, minimizing disk head movement.

- The FAT offers no space for descriptive file information. If you want to attach a note about a file, such as author and date of creation, FAT has no place to store it. The only descriptive information FAT accepts are the DOS attributes—hidden, read-only, archive, and system.

HPFS allows up to 64K of extended attributes for each file. *Extended attributes* can be any kind of information that you want to attach to a file. OS/2 even offers extended attributes for disks, based on the FAT file system, that have not been formatted with HPFS.

- The FAT file system has no provision for finding files easily because it places file names into a directory in the order that they are created. A program that must access a directory containing 1,000 entries does so slowly because the program must read and interpret each file name. (Imagine trying to find a number in a telephone book that is not arranged alphabetically.)

HPFS automatically sorts file names to enable you to find a particular file quickly. In addition, many PC applications use databases, and database operations do not always read a file sequentially. Instead, they jump around the file by performing a *random-access read*. Random reads are significantly slower under the FAT than under HPFS.

HPFS does have a few drawbacks. You cannot use most backup software to back up files with long names; special software is required. If you run real DOS—not the DOS emulation that comes with OS/2—the part of the disk formatted under HPFS is invisible when you run DOS. You learn more about HPFS and file management in Chapter 4.

Taking Advantage of OS/2's Single Driver

When the Hewlett-Packard LaserJet III printer arrived on the market, people purchased them enthusiastically. The series III had scaleable fonts, faster graphics, more memory, and a lower price tag than the series II. Buyers soon realized, however, that DOS programs were not compatible with the series III, but OS/2 applications were.

DOS requires a separate small program for each application to support your printer, screen, mouse, and keyboard. These small programs are called *drivers* and are shipped with the application. They are kept separate from the main program to enable software designers to add support for new printers. Under OS/2's Workplace Shell and Presentation Manager, however, all programs share a single driver program. With OS/2's single driver system, upgrades are easy and programmers are freed from the tedious task of writing many different drivers. The single driver system also creates a new market for more powerful drivers.

Drivers are essential to system speed. Hewlett-Packard, for example, released Windows drivers for the series III line of printers in April 1991. The new drivers replaced the drivers shipped originally with Windows 3.0. The installation of the new drivers increased Windows' print speed by 30 percent. The driver-based architecture of OS/2 creates a market for high-performance driver software. If IBM releases low-quality drivers for the LaserJet under OS/2, another company may seize the opportunity and write its own faster drivers.

If Lotus develops a high-quality printer driver for 1-2-3 in an operating environment other than OS/2, the new driver benefits only 1-2-3; other programs continue to print with their less-efficient drivers. In OS/2, however, improved drivers benefit programs such as 1-2-3 and WordPerfect equally. Shared drivers also forced the market to build better drivers in the Windows world. The initial Hewlett-Packard drivers for Windows did not produce the kind of quality that Aldus, the makers of PageMaker, wanted. They wrote their own drivers, and their changes were incorporated in the shrink-wrap HP drivers. Similarly, Micrografx assisted in building some of the graphics code for OS/2, so that OS/2 can serve as a high-quality platform for its drawing and charting packages. This not only helps Micrografx, but also any competitors that build similar packages. You learn more about installing and using drivers in Chapter 12.

Using Adobe Type Manager in OS/2

In 1986, laser printers and page layout software were introduced that created a new use for the personal computer: desktop publishing. *Desktop publishing* software enabled users to create typeset-quality publications using a number of typefaces, fonts, and designs.

Adobe Systems created *PostScript* for the Macintosh, which is a printer control language that includes fonts that can be resized instantly. PostScript eliminates the need to decide beforehand what sizes you want; you simply pick any size, and the printer handles the rest. The one drawback to PostScript is that you need a PostScript printer.

Adobe came up with a solution to this printer problem—the Adobe Type Manager (ATM). ATM is a program that attaches itself to your printer's driver. Windows users must buy a copy of ATM, but OS/2 users find it built into the system. As a result, you now can buy just one copy of a typeface and plug it directly into dozens of applications. You can even use it under Windows.

Using OS/2's Application Protection

In a multitasking operating system, applications must cooperate. In the earlier discussion of real and protected modes, you learned that protected mode enables multiple programs to coexist in memory without being overwritten by the memory needs of another application. If an application tries to go outside of its allotted memory area, the CPU's memory-management hardware senses this and generates a GP (Global Protection) fault. The GP fault is a high-priority error that generally causes the operating system to terminate the application.

In Windows, a global protection fault results in an *unrecoverable application error* (UAE). Windows is incapable of determining which application created the UAE because it does not spend all its time in protected mode. If an application violates another application's space while the processor is in real mode, the violation is not recognized until the processor switches back to protected mode.

Windows' response is to terminate the current foreground application, even if the foreground application is not at fault. OS/2, on the other hand, can determine which application violated memory space. This is an important feature because you want to know which appli-cation is causing the problem. Windows does not give you this opportunity.

Using OS/2's REXX Batch Language and SAA Support

DOS has had a number of problems that have been fixed slowly by Microsoft, IBM, or another party. DOS's inadequate batch language is one problem that remains unsolved. Third-party products such as 4DOS, BAT, and the Norton Batch Enhancer solve the DOS batch language inadequacies.

A batch language enables you to take a number of tasks and assign a name to the tasks. If you want to put data on a floppy disk onto your hard disk, you probably would transfer the data using the following steps:

1. Create a subdirectory on the C drive. For this example, name it \TARGET.

2. Make \TARGET the default subdirectory.

3. Insert the floppy disk into drive A.

4. Type **COPY A:*.* C:**.

A common mistake for users who perform the preceding task is to omit step two. If step two is skipped, all the files are copied to the root directory of drive C. You can create a batch file named FLOPCOPY (or whatever you want to call it) to hold all the commands needed to perform the task. Instead of performing steps 1–4, you simply enter **FLOPCOPY TARGET**. If you write the batch file well, it can be used to put data from a floppy disk onto any subdirectory by using such commands as **FLOPCOPY JUNK** or **FLOPCOPY GR8TSTUF**.

You can use a DOS batch file to perform the preceding steps. DOS batch files cannot query the user about preferences, keep data structures, do math, or perform other basic things that any programming language can do. The addition of REXX language is a major advantage for OS/2 users. Batch files can make your life easier. After you read about REXX in Chapter 13, you will be able to make batch files quickly.

REXX is part of the overall SAA support mentioned earlier in this chapter. The rest is CUA compliance, LAN Manager support of communications protocols, and the IBM-issued language compilers that are matched by SAA-compliant cousins on the minicomputer and mainframe platforms.

Exploring OS/2's Disadvantages

The disadvantages to using OS/2 may be too great for some users. To run OS/2, for example, a computer must have at least the following elements:

- An 80386SX processor
- 4M of RAM
- 60M hard disk drive
- Microsoft, IBM, Mouse Systems, or others
- VGA display

These requirements are for the basic system. With this system, little hard disk space remains for applications after loading OS/2, and the system runs slowly. The realistic minimum platform for OS/2 is the following configuration:

- An 80386DX processor running at 25 MHz or faster
- 8M of RAM with expansion capabilities
- 120M hard disk drive
- Microsoft, IBM, Mouse Systems, or VisiOn mouse
- VGA display

Be prepared to buy some hardware if you commit to OS/2 or any GUI (the hardware requirements for Windows are less extensive). Cost of new equipment is not a concern for most companies. The biggest concern is what to do with all the old XTs, ATs, and slow 386s. You learn more about OS/2 hardware requirements in Appendix A.

OS/2 software also can be expensive, costing as much as $500 per copy, depending on its features. In addition, upgrades can be expensive, especially for a large organization. Fortunately, organizations can upgrade applications at their leisure because OS/2 2.0 is backward compatible with DOS and Windows. This is an improvement over OS/2 1.0, which required new versions of applications.

In addition to the hardware and software costs, switching to OS/2 requires retraining expenses because it represents major changes for users. Your company needs to justify the long-term benefits of switching to OS/2 to supplement the short-term inconvenience of changing to a new system.

Incompatibility with Some DOS Programs

All VPMI and DPMI DOS multitaskers face the same challenge: they must make distinctly separate programs run simultaneously. In some cases this is impossible—some programs, such as games, communications programs, and disk defragmenters, will never work under anything but DOS. For most users, such incompatibilities are seldom more than an annoyance. Others, however, may find that their mission-critical software does not run under OS/2. These users must decide whether to change to OS/2, to use OS/2's "dual boot" feature to run DOS and OS/2, or to rebuild their software so that it works under OS/2.

Windows programs generally run well under OS/2. A few Windows programs, however, are written with the little-used 32-bit "back door" that enables Windows programmers to write true

32-bit 386 programs under Windows 3.0. Although no major Windows applications use this 32-bit back door, some development tools are written in this manner. The most notable example is Smalltalk for Windows, which also is available for OS/2.

Working with a Scarcity of OS/2 Programs

Early OS/2 users will find that the variety of applications available for DOS does not exist for OS/2. Chapter 8 discusses currently available OS/2 applications,. As you have seen, the excellent backward compatibility of OS/2 for most DOS and Windows programs alleviates the lack of software until more OS/2 applications appear.

As time passes, more and more OS/2 applications will be developed. For example, Lotus, WordPerfect, and Computer Associates are currently working on OS/2 applications.

Working with Unusual Hardware

The wide base of users for DOS and DOS-compatible machines has made possible the nearly limitless supply of hardware for any need: numerical controllers for process automation; data-acquisition devices for manufacturing control; devices to aid the sight-impaired and those without use of their limbs; and mundane devices such as high-resolution monitors, touch screens, optical storage media, and tape drives.

Generally, DOS supports these devices either through software installed in a CPU (a Read-Only Memory or ROM), a program called a device driver, or both. In either case, these programs are real mode programs not suited to OS/2's protected-mode environment. New drivers must be written before OS/2 can recognize and support these devices.

Owners of old devices may wonder what they can do if the company that made their devices goes out of business. OS/2 is capable of making virtual device drivers of old DOS device drivers, enabling the drivers to run in the DOS sessions. Although OS/2 and Windows programs cannot access the devices, DOS programs can use these drivers.

Summary

Microsoft and IBM bit off considerably more than they could chew when they announced in 1984 that a more powerful, 286-oriented operating system would appear "soon." Quirks of the 286 architecture delayed OS/2's opening, and uncontrollable political events (the RAM shortage) and bad marketing hurt OS/2 1.0. As the next few years passed, OS/2 continued to improve, albeit within the constraints of the 286 platform: it received a graphical user interface, a better file system than the FAT-based system that DOS uses to this day, and incorporated the powerful Adobe font engine. 2.0 rounded out the growth of the operating system with the power of the 386: more memory and solid DOS multitasking.

Add to all of that OS/2's lesser-known advantages. It was built from the ground up with networking in mind, making LAN integration easier. The REXX language makes it possible to write some fairly sophisticated programs with tools as easy to use as the System Editor. The Workplace Shell brings a new object-oriented environment to the computer screen, one that may improve greatly the productivity of most users.

OS/2 has come a long way from the naive, hopeful announcements made in 1984. OS/2 draws its power from the 80386's protected mode, and the CPU's capability to address literally billions of bytes of memory. OS/2 also enables you to multitask existing DOS programs by using its virtual 8086 mode.

Even though OS/2 2.0 has advantages and disadvantages, its benefits greatly outweigh the negative aspects of this powerful operating system. OS/2 can multitask OS/2, DOS, and Windows programs. It ties all of its capabilities together with a graphical user interface that is more than just another Macintosh clone. (You might see the innovative features of the OS/2 GUI incorporated into future Macintosh system releases.) Add these advantages to the extra functionality of the driver-based I/O system and a central repository for fonts, and you have all the elements for a software success.

The Workplace Shell is different in many ways from competing computer operating environments. It is the key to unlocking much of the power of OS/2; that is why you start your tour of OS/2 in the next chapter, "Getting Started with the Workplace Shell."

Getting Started with the OS/2 Workplace Shell

The object-oriented Workplace Shell is new to OS/2 2.0. It looks different, is organized differently, and behaves somewhat differently from Presentation Manager (PM), the user interface utilized in previous versions of OS/2. This chapter introduces the Workplace Shell, discusses the advantages of graphical user interfaces, explains IBM's Common User Access strategy, and helps to get you started using the mouse, the keyboard, and the objects in the Workplace Shell.

In the PM interface, most functions were grouped under the Desktop (or Program) Manager, the File Manager, and the Print Manager. You opened the Desktop Manager window to run programs in windows, you opened the File Manager to work with your files, and you opened the Print Manager window when you needed to change some print settings or take other actions to get your jobs printed. But in the Workplace Shell, these previous managers have disappeared, and you do all your work from one screen, the desktop.

The File Manager and Desktop Manager are now program, folder, and data-file objects. The Print Manager has been subdivided into an object for each printer and queue. The Control Panel consists now of objects such as Mouse, Keyboard, and Color Palette. The Task List is now the Window List. Program groups are program folders on the desktop. In figure 2.1, the OS/2 System folder has been opened. You can see the following objects in the open windows: Productivity, Games, Command Prompts, System Setup, Startup, and Drives. All these objects contain other objects.

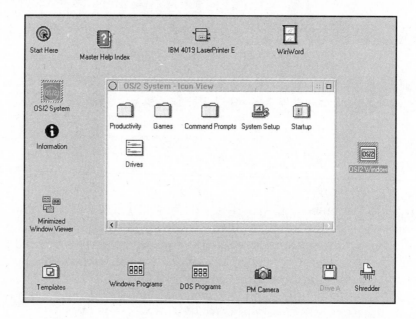

The desktop presents an object-oriented graphical user interface. The desktop covers your entire computer screen. On the desktop you see pictures (icons) that represent objects you work with. To interact with this graphical interface, you use a mouse, a keyboard, or both to manipulate the objects on the screen.

You start a program, for example, by double-clicking your mouse on a program object. You create a letter object by peeling off a blank form from a stack of forms. You print a letter by moving the letter object to a printer object (this action is sometimes referred to as *drag-and-drop*).

Understanding GUI Features

Graphical user interfaces contain visible elements with which you interact by using pointing devices. In simple graphical user interfaces, you point to an element, such as Print on a menu, and select it by clicking on the element with a mouse. The program responds with an action such as presenting a box with fields that you select or fill in. More complex GUIs produce rectangles (windows) that you can move and size with a pointing device. State-of-the-art GUIs, such as the OS/2 Workplace Shell, are object-oriented. You manipulate icons that represent objects to produce, for example, documents and charts, to print them, and to store or discard them.

Graphical user interfaces make using a computer easier because user interactions are consistent, applications communicate effectively, and the GUI hides the complexity of the operating system.

User Interface Consistency

The consistency of the graphical interface contributes to its ease of use. Once you have learned how to do something, you should be able to utilize that same action anywhere in the interface and get the same results. The procedure for inserting text in a document, for example, should be the same no matter where in the GUI you do it.

Software products that are developed under the same user interface guidelines exhibit a look-and-feel consistency. The similarities in their appearance cause you, even as a first-time user, to recognize the interface as one you are familiar with. You start using the products with confidence, expecting that they all will respond similarly. Consistency not only makes you comfortable, but it shortens the time you need to begin doing real work with a new software product.

The Workplace Shell focuses on objects, which behave in a similar manner. If you point to an object and press the right mouse button, for example, the pop-up menu of the object is displayed. This menu contains only the functions that are currently available for that object. These functions typically include the following:

- Open
- Help
- Create another
- Copy
- Move
- Create shadow
- Delete

Functions that are specific for an object (Print, for example) are added to this basic menu.

Because the behavior of all objects is consistent, you soon learn how to interact with them to accomplish your work.

Graphical Information

Pictures can convey information more quickly than words can. The graphical user interface displays pictures (called *icons*) of objects and actions so that you can quickly understand what you can do with a software product. Many icons also have labels. Studies have shown that computer users learn faster when icons are labeled than when just the icons are shown. Simple concepts, such as an arrow indicating that more information is available on the next page, do not require labels, but the more complex the concept, the greater the need for a label.

Icons are pictures that represent objects such as files, documents, printers, and programs.

As software developers know, icons that represent actions rather than objects can be quite difficult to design so that users understand them. For this reason, you will probably not see as many action icons as object icons in graphical user interfaces.

On-Screen Object Orientation

The object-oriented interface presents icons that you manipulate directly by using a pointing device. The higher the degree of object orientation, the greater the degree of direct manipulation. For example, to print a document, you simply move the picture of the document object to a picture of a printer object on the screen. You drag the object with your pointing device, most often a mouse. Once you learn this technique, you can apply it any time you want to print a document. If your workstation is connected to several printers, you can print your document on any of those printers by going through the same motions: dragging the object and dropping it on a printer.

Interface Flexibility: Mouse or Keyboard

Graphical user interfaces are designed to be used with a pointing device. Most GUIs, however, accept keyboard input as well. Some users prefer to use a keyboard for certain functions, such as moving blocks of text. You often see users interact with a GUI by switching between mouse and keyboard, depending on which is handier at the moment.

Most actions performed with the pointing device have keyboard equivalents.

IBM states that a mouse or other two-button pointing device is required for the graphical interface of OS/2, 2.0. You can, however, use a keyboard with the command-line interface and even with the

Workplace Shell. Nevertheless, most users (even those who have never worked with a mouse before) find the mouse a more natural way to interact with graphics.

On-Line Help

Help that is available at the touch of a mouse or a key is another advantage of GUIs. In some products, you select the word "Help" somewhere on the screen. In other products, you click on a Help icon.

 The on-line help sometimes contains information that is not available in the printed documentation.

Most of the information about OS/2 2.0 for end users is on-line. Not all of this on-line help is repeated in the printed manuals. The manuals give information about installation, getting started, and migrating from Microsoft Windows and previous OS/2 versions. But for step-by-step help while you are using the Workplace Shell, you need to look on-line.

 The extensive OS/2 2.0 on-line help system includes more than 5,000 entries.

In the Workplace Shell you can find help for doing tasks and for working with objects. Once you become familiar with the basics of the object-oriented interface, you will probably use the Master Help Index more than any other source of help. The Master Help Index includes a powerful search capability. You can request a search of only the help titles in the index itself or a full text search. You specify how wide you want the search to be. It can go beyond the help text to include on-line manuals.

Figure 2.2 shows the Master Help Index opened to the beginning of the C section. You click on a letter tab at the right to go to that section. Notice the vertical and horizontal scroll bars. You click on a row in the scroll bar to see more information in the direction that the arrow points. To display other letter tabs, click the upward-pointing or downward-pointing double arrows, which are positioned above and below the letter tabs.

Figure 2.2:

The Master
Help Index.

Other sources of information in the Workplace Shell include the Start Here tutorial, which is a subset of the Master Help Index organized by high-level basic tasks; a glossary of Workplace Shell terms; and an on-line manual, the Command Reference. The home of these information objects is the Information folder, an icon on the desktop. You can open the Information folder to view the contents of any information object. If you want to keep an information object handy for frequent use, you can move it out of the folder to the desktop.

If you find that you do not use the Master Help Index frequently, you can keep it in the Information folder. Then the Workplace Shell start-up time is reduced.

Defining CUA in OS/2

The object-oriented Workplace Shell was the first product to be developed according to new user interface design guidelines published by IBM in October 1991. What CUA means to computer users is that operating systems and other applications have a more consistent look and feel than in the past.

CUA's Role in IBM's Strategy

The IBM Common User Access (CUA) user interface, implemented as the OS/2 Workplace Shell, plays an important role in the corporation's plan to develop consistent products that can communicate despite operating in different computing environments. The vision is that software and hardware will be so consistent and connectable that workstation users do not have to know when they are accessing a mainframe or network computer. Data will be stored in the most appropriate place so that users can retrieve it and share it as necessary.

IBM's long-range plan for consistency and connectivity is known as Systems Application Architecture (SAA). In addition to the CUA user interface, SAA includes:

- Common Programming Interface (CPI)—the languages and services programmers use to develop software that can run in all SAA environments

- Common Communications Support (CCS)—the architecture and protocols that interconnect the SAA systems

- Common Applications that conform to the CUA interface

Software developers who are writing new applications to run under OS/2 2.0 use the *CUA Guide to Interface Design* so that their applications are consistent with the Workplace Shell. CUA applies both to IBM and non-IBM products. IBM assists software developers in designing products that comply with the CUA guidelines.

 Developers can obtain the CUA design guide from IBM representatives or branch offices.

The CUA user interface has been evolving since the mid-1980s. The first version, published in 1987, was developed for personal computers. In 1989, two versions evolved: one for programmable workstations, the other for nonprogrammable terminals. The two versions were consistent insofar as it was possible, but the nonprogrammable interface was limited in graphical features. The 1991 version, CUA 3 or CUA '91, exploits the graphical capabilities of personal workstations, as is evident in the OS/2 Workplace Shell.

Advantages of CUA

The major advantage of Common User Access is the consistency that compliant applications exhibit. Once a user has learned how to save a file, get help, and resize a window in any OS/2 application, this learning is transferrable to all OS/2 applications. Training time is greatly reduced, improving efficiency.

CUA includes the following key components:

- **Common Presentation.** The appearance of components (title bar, scroll bars, mouse cursor, and so on) is consistent across all OS/2 applications. In fact, often the location of components is consistent. The vertical scroll bar (if there is one), for instance, is always located at the right edge of the active window.

- **Common Interaction.** The interface components (buttons, scroll bars, and so on) all work the same way. For instance, you always press a screen button by pressing a mouse button.

- **Common Process Sequence.** CUA specifies an object-action sequence of operation. The object is selected before the action to perform is specified. For example, when printing a document, you specify the document (object) by clicking on it and dragging it to the printer icon to be printed (action).

- **Common Actions.** Objects with a similar appearance always behave in a similar manner. A Cancel button, for instance, always cancels (stops) the pending operation. An OK button always means the user accepts the pending action.

According to the CUA guidelines, when the software you use complies with the CUA specifications and has been tested for usability, you should find the products satisfying to use, efficient, and appropriate for the work you want to do.

Usability testing is a requirement because, even though software developers follow CUA's direction, the guidelines are general enough to allow some freedom in interpretation. Usability testing is a check to be sure that the new software product is easy to learn, easy to use, and useful. The testing procedures range from evaluation of early prototypes by usability specialists to formal laboratory studies. Test subjects are representative of the product's intended users. In early phases of product development, employees of the software development company may act as test subjects. As the product nears completion, test subjects with appropriate experience are recruited from outside the company to participate in product usability testing. Sometimes test subjects are customers who have used previous versions of the products or plan to use the new product in their work.

Usability specialists feed back results of testing, along with recommendations for improvements, to the product developers and, if CUA guidelines are involved, to CUA. After changes are implemented, the product is tested again. This cycle of testing and retesting is repeated until the product is judged to be ready for shipment.

When software developers follow the usability-oriented guidelines of CUA, the software product should exemplify three important design principles:

- The user, not the computer, is in control of the interaction. For example, error messages give helpful information so that the user can take appropriate action.

- The user does not have to remember all the operational details of the software product. The program, for example, may display a menu of functions from which the user can choose instead of requiring the user to memorize commands.

- The user will find the product easy to learn and use because the interface is consistent in appearance and function. Each Workplace Shell object, for example, has the same basic pop-up menu, whether it is a printer or a letter.

Using Workplace Shell Objects and Implements

To interact with the graphical interface of the Workplace Shell, you use either the mouse or the keyboard to manipulate the objects on the screen. Select the objects you need, and then take action by selecting from menus or by moving objects. Focusing on the objects you work with rather than on your tools (software applications) may require a shift in your approach, but ultimately you benefit because you can concentrate on the products of your work. Even if you have been a command-line user, you probably will find the graphical, object-oriented interface easier to work with because you do not have to memorize commands, syntax, and parameters. In addition, you can more easily take advantage of the rich function of OS/2 2.0 through the graphical interface.

The Mouse

The mouse is the pointing device most commonly used with GUIs. The Workplace Shell is designed for the mouse, and using one is strongly recommended. OS/2 2.0 also supports other pointing devices, such as trackballs and touch screens.

Even if you have never used a mouse before, you need not be concerned about learning mouse techniques. With a little practice, you can easily learn the three basic mouse techniques: pointing, clicking, and dragging. Then you will be ready to realize all the benefits of OS/2 2.0.

Pointing

The first time you use a mouse, take a few minutes to experiment with moving it around on your working surface. Find a comfortable position to hold the mouse in your hand. Move the mouse around, noticing how the movement you make is translated to the movement of the mouse pointer on the screen.

 The position of the mouse pointer is indicated by an arrow or some other symbol on the screen.

The mouse pointer shows up on the screen as an arrow or some other symbol that moves as you move the mouse. The tip of the arrow communicates with the system. For the system to register that you are pointing at a particular place on the screen, you must be sure to place the tip of the pointer on the object or text.

Point at an object now. Next, pick up the mouse so it is not touching the mouse pad or working area, hold it in the air, and move it around. The position of the pointer on the screen does not change. Place the mouse down on the surface again and move it around. Now you see the pointer moving on the screen. Whenever the mouse is in an awkward position on your working surface—too close to the edge or too close to the computer or other objects— simply pick it up and put it down again in a more comfortable position or where there is more room to maneuver. This procedure does not change the position of the pointer on the screen.

Clicking

Clicking the mouse selects or opens an object or menu item. A single click causes a highlight to appear on the object. Click again, and you open the object. A window appears so that you can see the object's contents.

You can accomplish both these steps in one step by double-clicking. Move your mouse pointer to the object you want to select. Then press the left mouse button twice to open the object. You can start programs in the same way.

You may need a little practice with the timing of the clicks in a double-click. You need to press quickly enough to tell the computer that the two clicks are one action but slowly enough for them to register. Try not to jerk the mouse while double-clicking because you may accidentally move the pointer off the object. OS/2 2.0 is implemented for a two-button mouse. You need a mouse that has at least two buttons. The on-line and printed instructions for OS/2 2.0 always refer to the left button as button 1 and the right button as button 2. The instructions are written this way because you can change the mouse button settings so that the right button is button 1 and the left button is button 2.

Being able to change button assignments is useful for people who hold the mouse in their left hand.

Dragging

In OS/2 2.0, you click the left button to select or open an object, and you click the right button to move an object. Moving objects on the screen by using only the mouse (not by selecting Move from a menu) is called *dragging*. Always use the right button for dragging actions.

The use of both mouse buttons is a change from previous versions of OS/2, in which the left button was used for all mouse operations.

To drag an object:

1. Move the mouse pointer to an object.

2. Press the right button and hold it down.

3. Move the mouse pointer to the place you want to drop the object. You can see that you are dragging the object with the pointer.

4. Release the right button.

You can move a window on the screen by using the same technique:

1. Point to the horizontal bar in which the title of the window is displayed.

2. Press the right button and hold it down.

3. Drag the window to the place where you want it.

4. Release the right button.

Being able to drag a window out of the way is often useful. You can, for instance, keep a help window open and refer to it while performing an action if you move the help window to one side.

Using Pop-Up Menus

You also can use the right button to display the pop-up menu for an object. A *pop-up* menu contains the actions that you can perform with that particular object. The basic pop-up menu choices are Open, Help, Create another, Copy, Move, Create shadow, Delete, Print, and Find.

To display an object's pop-up menu:

1. Point to the object.

2. Press the right button.

The OS/2 2.0 desktop is an object that covers your screen. Other objects are on the desktop. The desktop object is always open; you never see an icon for the desktop.

To display the desktop's pop-up menu:

1. Point to an empty space on the desktop.
2. Press the right button, or press Shift-F10.

To select a choice from a pop-up menu, click on it with the left button. To shut down OS/2 2.0, you should always use the Shut Down choice on the desktop pop-up menu.

Using the Mouse with Ctrl

You can perform many actions on an object by manipulating it with a mouse instead of using the pop-up menu. Some of these actions require you to use a key in combination with the mouse.

Copy an Object

To make a copy of an object:

1. Point to the object.
2. Press and hold down the right button.
3. Press and hold down the Ctrl key.
4. Drag the object to the place where you want a copy.
5. Release the right button and the Ctrl key to drop the copied object.

The preceding technique is especially useful when working with data file objects. You can, for example, make a copy of a letter this way.

Select Multiple Objects

To select more than one object:

1. Press and hold down the Ctrl key.
2. Point to the first object with the mouse.
3. Click on the first object using the left button.

4. Click on the other objects, one at a time.

5. Release the Ctrl key.

Now you can perform other actions on the objects you selected, such as moving, copying, and deleting. You might want to copy several data-file objects to disk drive A, for example. Or you might want to move them to a different folder.

The Keyboard

You also can interact with the Workplace Shell through the keyboard. Because the Workplace Shell is designed to be used with a mouse, almost all instructions in on-line help and the manuals are written for the mouse. Common User Access guidelines, however, require that a keyboard equivalent must be available for each mouse action, and, in general, OS/2 2.0 follows this guideline.

Using Keyboard Fast Paths

You may find that it is sometimes easier to use the keyboard than the mouse. It might be quicker, for example, to open an OS/2 2.0 command prompt window and type **FORMAT** instead of opening the Drives folder, pressing the right mouse button to display the pop-up menu for Drives, and clicking on Format disk in the menu.

 Underlined letters in menus indicate keyboard fast paths.

To assist keyboard users, each menu option has one letter underlined. Press the key for that letter to select the option.

When you need to look through a long, alphabetized list (the Master Help Index, for example), you can press a letter key to jump directly to that section. Say you want to find information on installing a new printer. Open the Master Help Index, press the I key to go right to the I section. Then you can move down through the I entries by using a mouse or the Page Down key until you find the installation information you are looking for.

Table 2.1 shows the single-key assignments that are available in the Workplace Shell.

Table 2.1

Single-Key Assignments

Key	Action
Arrow keys	Move among objects
Spacebar	Select an object
Enter	Open an object; select a menu choice
Del	Delete an object
Home	Select first choice in object pop-up menu
End	Select last choice
Letter key	Select menu choice with underlined letter
Esc	Remove window, cancel mouse action
F1	Display help
F2	In Help, display General Help
F5	Refresh
F6	Switch window pane
F9	In Help, display Keys Help
F10	Switch to menu bar
F11	In Help, display Help Index
Page Down	Move to next page
Page Up	Move to previous page
Print Screen	Prints contents of object
Tab	Move to next position in entry field

Users sometimes have difficulty remembering key combinations that require Alt, Ctrl, or Shift. This memory task is somewhat simplified in OS/2 2.0 because, as Table 2.2 shows, almost all key combinations for windowing actions begin with Alt.

Table 2.2
Alt-Key Combinations

Keys	Action
Alt-Tab	Switch to next window
Alt-Esc	Switch to next window or full-screen session
Alt-Home	Switch DOS program between window and full screen
Alt-down arrow	Display drop-down list or box
Alt-up arrow	Display drop-down list or box
Shift-F10	Display pop-up menu for desktop
Alt-Insert	Copy an object and place it on clipboard
Alt-Backspace	Undo
Alt-F4	Close a window
Alt-F6	Switch between a window and a Help window
Alt-F7, arrow keys	Move a window
Alt-F8, arrow keys	Size a window
Alt-F9	Hide a window
Alt-F10	Maximize a window

Ctrl-key combinations are used for a variety of actions, as shown in Table 2.3. Ctrl-Esc, which displays the Window List, is an important key combination to remember.

Only a few key combinations utilize Shift. These key combinations are shown in Table 2.4. One very useful combination is Shift-Esc, which displays the pop-up menu of an open window.

Table 2.3
Ctrl-Key Combinations

Keys	Action
Ctrl-Alt-Del	Restart or reboot the computer
Ctrl-Esc	Display Window List (list of started programs or objects
Ctrl-Insert	Copy an object or group of objects and place it on clipboard
Ctrl-/	Select all objects
Ctrl-\	Deselect all objects
Ctrl-Spacebar	Select one object and deselect all others
Ctrl-right arrow	Move cursor to end of next word
Ctrl-left arrow	Move cursor to beginning of previous word

Table 2.4
Shift-Key Combinations

Keys	Action
Shift-Esc	Display pop-up menu of window
Shift-Insert	Paste contents of clipboard onto object
Shift-F8	Switch between single and multiple selection
Shift-F10	Display pop-up menu for selected object
Shift-Alt-Backspace	Redo (undo last undo)
Arrow keys-Spacebar	Select one or more objects and add to those previously selected
Spacebar-Shift-arrow keys	Select multiple objects and deselect all others.

Screen Objects

As you see later in this chapter, objects typically have several views. For example, folder objects can have an icon view, a tree view, and a detail view. There is also a settings notebook, which controls aspects of the object. The following sections discuss objects in a little more detail, in order to make them more easy to conceptualize and understand.

- **Program Objects.** *Program objects* are easy for users to understand because they are like icons on the Windows desktop. Program objects are "pointers" to a program, whether the program is a machine language file (having an EXE or COM extension) or a REXX or batch command file (having a CMD or BAT extension).

- **Data Objects.** *Data objects* stand in for data files. These objects are the "hooks" that the operating system uses to enable you to manipulate a data file. By dragging a data file object from one disk drive object to another disk drive object, you cause the operating system to move a file from one drive to another.

  By dragging the object corresponding to a text file to the system editor object (a program object), you instruct the operating system to start the system editor and load the text file into the system editor. By dragging a data file object to the Shredder object, you instruct the operating system to delete a file. When you drag a data file over to your printer object, the file gets printed (assuming that the printer object knows how to print the file; it does not know how to print a file using an obscure format). The process of dragging instructs the operating system to do something.

- **Folder Objects.** Every filing system needs an organization paradigm. The analogy of file folders in a filing cabinet is an good one: because users have worked with paper filing cabinets, the notion that a drive is a file cabinet (and that the file cabinet contains folders with data) is a simple one to understand. OS/2's Workplace Shell takes it a step further, and gives you access to folders inside folders inside folders, ad infinitum (more like ad nauseum). If you are experienced with DOS, you are familiar with the notion of subdirectories. A subdirectory is represented in WP5 as a folder. A subdirectory inside a sub-directory, therefore, is just a folder inside a folder.

TIP If you are fairly DOS-literate, and you have been poking around your disk trying to figure out what files corre-spond to the Desktop, the Information folder, and the like, here's a tip: all folders—even the Desktop—are just normal subdirectories on your hard disk.

To find out a folder, (or other object's) "true name," follow these steps:

1. Open the object's pop-up menu by either right-clicking on it or by pressing Shift-F10.

2. Left-click on **O**pen, and then on Settings. You see the object's *settings notebook* (discussed later in the chapter), as well as objects that look like notebook tabs to the right of the window.

3. Click on the tab labeled **F**ile. You see an area titled Physical name: containing two fields: Path and Name. Together, they tell you where the item that is the actual folder is.

NOTE For example, if you open the settings for the Desktop itself (right-click on any exposed part of the background) you see a path of C:\ (assuming that the boot drive is C) and a name of OS!2_2.0_D (assuming that the operating system is on a FAT partition). This means that the desktop is the subdirectory C:\OS!2_2.0D. If you check on the OS/2 System Folder, it reports a path of C:\OS!2_2.0D, which is the Desktop itself, and a name of OS!2_SYS. A quick look at the directory structure of the disk reveals that there is, indeed, a subdirectory called C:\OS!2_2.0D\OS!2_SYS.

- **Device Objects.** *Device objects* seem the most "magical" of the Workplace Shell objects—dragging an object over to a printer has no analog in DOS; there never was a central clearinghouse for printing because printer control was the concern of each application. Similarly, the Shredder is a fairly new notion, although many computer users have heard of the Macintosh "trashcan."

  In general, device objects are device drivers, programs that control a piece of hardware, or a built-in facility in the operating system. There is no separate subdirectory or program for many of these items; you find no File setting in their settings notebook.

If you are still confused about objects, do not try to understand what they are—just practice using them.

The Desktop

The OS/2 2.0 Desktop is actually a folder object, although you never see it presented as a folder icon. It takes up the entire screen and contains all other OS/2 2.0 objects.

When you open an object on the desktop, you see that object's contents. The Shredder, however, does not hold objects. When you drop an object on it, it asks you to confirm that you want to delete the object. If you answer yes, the Shredder immediately deletes the object.

The Start Here object contains a list of basic tasks and related help objects to get you started using OS/2 2.0.

OS/2 System is a folder object that contains the following objects:

- **Startup.** At first this object is empty, but you can put programs here that you want to have started each time OS/2 is started.

- **Productivity.** This object contains tools, such as Sticky Pad, To-Do List, Seek and Scan Files, PM Chart, Calculator, OS/2 System Editor, Enhanced Editor, and Data Update, depending on which ones you have installed.

- **Games**. This object contains games such as OS/2 Chess, Jig-saw, Cat and Mouse, Scramble, Reversi, and Klondike Solitaire, depending on which ones you have installed.

- **Command Prompts**. This object contains command lines for OS/2, DOS, and WIN-OS/2 (Microsoft Windows running under OS/2) presented in full-screen format, plus OS/2 and DOS command lines in windows.

- **Drives**. This object contains objects for the disk drives in your computer (A, C, and so on).

- **System Setup**. This object contains Color Palette, Font Palette, Country, System, Sound, Migrate Applications, Device Driver Install, Mouse, Selective Install, Keyboard, System Clock, Spooler, and Scheme Palette. Figure 2.3 shows the System Setup object opened in icon view.

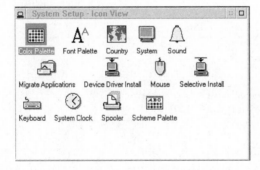

Figure 2.3:
Contents of
System Setup.

The Templates folder contains samples of various types of objects, such as printer, icon, folder, data file, bit map, and program.

You can use a sample from the Templates folder to create a new object of that type by simply pointing to the sample and then dragging a copy of it to another place on the Desktop.

Drive A on the desktop is a shadow of drive A in the Drives folder. It is placed here to give you easy access to it. When you open the drive A object, you see the contents of any disk you have in this disk drive.

The printer object represents the printer you have installed. You can drag objects to the printer object to print them. If you open the printer object, you see information about print jobs. You can have several printers on your desktop.

The Information folder contains the OS/2 tutorial, glossary, and, if you installed them, Command Reference and REXX Information. In figure 2.4, the Common Reference, Tutorial, and Glossary are shown.

Figure 2.4:

Contents of Information folder.

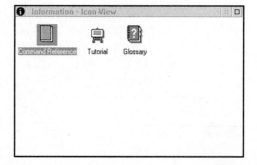

The first time OS/2 2.0 starts up after installation, the Tutorial is opened on the desktop. This is the developers' way of saying, "You should go through this tutorial now." The tutorial is a valuable introduction to the new world of OS/2 2.0.

The Glossary is helpful because it explains many of the terms used in the Workplace Shell. As you use on-line help, you might notice terms highlighted with a gray box. This highlight indicates that there is a glossary definition for the term. Double-click on the highlighted item to see the definition.

TIP You can add or delete information objects to save storage space. To add an information object, use Selective Install in the System Setup folder. To delete, drag the object to the Shredder.

Workplace Shell Windows

When you open a Workplace Shell object, the contents are displayed ina window. Windows present themselves in the following three ways: tree view, icon view, and details view.

- **Tree view.** In tree view, OS/2 shows you the contents of a folder hierarchically. Although a hierarchical method does not always make the most sense, tree view works well for the drive C folder, for example, because drive C: has many folders (and folders inside folders). You see a tree view of drive C in figure 2.5.

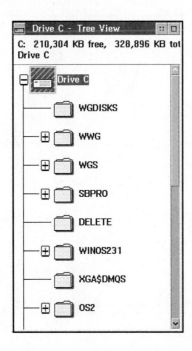

Figure 2.5:

Tree view of drive C.

- **Icon view.** In Icon view, OS/2 shows the objects inside a folder represented by their icons. Although it can appear cluttered, it works well for the OS/2 System Folder.The System Folder's icon view is shown in figure 2.6.

Figure 2.6:

Icon view of the
System folder.

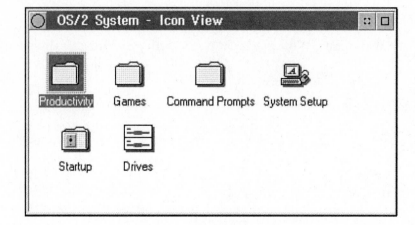

- **Details view.** In Details view, you see a list of every object (and other information about that object). It is similar to a DIR directory listing that you see from a DOS or OS/2 command line. A Details view of a drive folder is shown in figure 2.7.

Figure 2.7

Details view of a
drive folder.

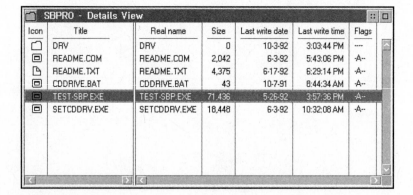

Program Windows

Application program windows generally follow CUA guidelines, adding more elements as necessary for their specific functions. Most have a menu bar just under the window title bar.

In the Workplace Shell, folder objects, including the desktop, do not have menu bars. The action choices for objects are in the objects' pop-up menus.

Figure 2.8 shows a window from the Enhanced Editor (EPM), which comes with OS/2 2.0 in the Productivity folder. The menu bar contains the choices <u>F</u>ile, <u>E</u>dit, <u>S</u>earch, <u>O</u>ptions, <u>C</u>ommand, and <u>H</u>elp.

At the far left of the window title bar is the *title bar icon*, a miniature icon that represents the object from which this window is derived. When you select the title bar icon, a pull-down menu appears with choices that you use to control the window itself: <u>R</u>estore (to previous size), <u>M</u>ove, <u>S</u>ize, Mi<u>n</u>imize, Ma<u>x</u>imize, <u>H</u>ide, <u>C</u>lose, and <u>W</u>indow list. Formerly, this menu was called the system menu or control menu, but window menu would have been a more descriptive title because its choices are only for manipulating the window.

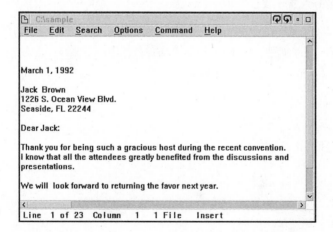

Figure 2.8:
Enhanced Editor primary window.

Sometimes a title bar icon menu includes both the window controls and the pop-up menu for the object. This lengthy combined menu typically includes the following choices: Open, Refresh, Sort by, Help, Create another, Copy, Move, Create shadow, Delete, Window, Find, Select, Arrange, and Close.

When you select a choice on the horizontal menu bar, a pull-down menu is displayed. In the Enhanced Editor, The Search pull-down menu contains the choices Search, Find next, Change next, and Bookmarks. An arrow to the right of a choice in a pull-down menu means that there is another menu, called a *cascaded menu*, relating to the choice. The cascaded menu for Bookmarks contains the choices Set, List, Next, and Previous. An ellipsis (three dots) follows both Set and List.

An ellipsis to the right of a menu choice means that when you select that choice, a secondary window (dialog box) is displayed in which you enter more information about your choice. The EPM window in figure 2.9 shows a secondary window for the Search choice.

You type the necessary information in the Search and Replace fields and then select the check boxes for the options you want. Check boxes are typically used when you can make several choices; they are not mutually exclusive. When you select a check box choice, an X or a check mark is placed in the box.

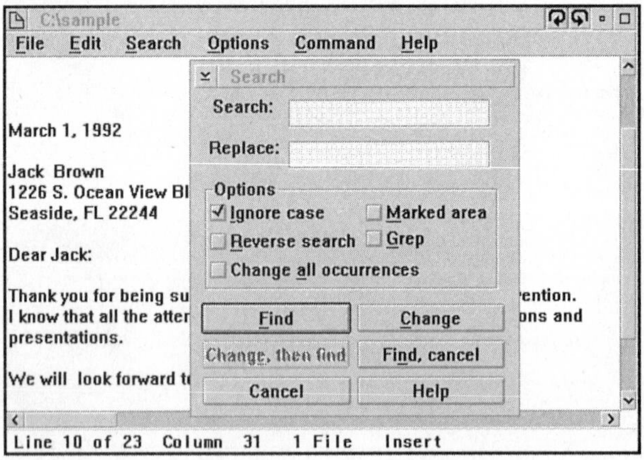

Figure 2.9:

Secondary window (dialog box).

At the bottom of this secondary window are push buttons for Find; Change; Change, then find; Find, cancel; Cancel; and Help. You must select one of these push buttons to dismiss this window before you can go on to another action. Select Cancel to remove the window without making any changes.

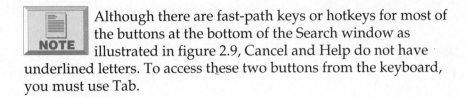 Although there are fast-path keys or hotkeys for most of the buttons at the bottom of the Search window as illustrated in figure 2.9, Cancel and Help do not have underlined letters. To access these two buttons from the keyboard, you must use Tab.

Figure 2.10 illustrates other window controls. This is the secondary window for the File Print choice. You select one of the printers shown in the list box. Then you select a radio button for **D**raft mode or **W**YSIWYG mode. The WYSIWYG—What You See Is What You Get—choice enables you to preview the format of the document before you print it. You can then make any adjustments you want before you print it. Radio buttons are given that name because, as on some radios, you can push only one button among several to indicate your choice.

Figure 2.10:

Secondary window for File Print.

Another secondary window control (not shown here) is the drop-down list. When the secondary window is displayed, only one choice is visible, with a down arrow beside it. When you highlight it, other choices are displayed. They drop down from the default. Use the scroll arrows to find the choice you want, and then select it.

Because the drop-down combination box is a variation of the drop-down list, its appearance is similar to the drop-down list. In this control, however, you can type in your own entry in a list of objects or settings.

Some applications use a control called a tool palette, or toolbar. In a drawing application, the tools include drawing implements, shapes, and so on. An editor or word processor can include a toolbar with choices for type face, type size, type styles, and formatting. CUA recommends that the application be designed so that when you select one of the tools, the mouse pointer changes to indicate the operation you can perform with the tool. The graphical design of windows and their controls makes them easier to use and offers flexibility to the application developer.

Summary

This chapter has introduced the new OS/2 2.0 user interface, the object-oriented Workplace Shell; discussed the advantages of graphical user interfaces; explained IBM's Common User Interface strategy; and shown you how to get started using the mouse, the keyboard, and the objects in the Workplace Shell.

The next chapter will show how you can organize and customize your desktop so you can work efficiently and comfortably. Chapter 3 covers the use of Workplace Shell pop-up menus and settings notebooks. It discusses using the mouse to start a program on the desktop, moving from program to program, and using the Window List. The chapter further explains sizing windows, customizing window actions, arranging icons, and securing the desktop. Chapter 3 also includes a section about customizing with System Setup objects.

Organizing and Customizing the Workplace Shell Desktop

The Workplace Shell is highly customizable. You are in control, and the desktop is yours to personalize as you wish. This chapter shows how you can organize and display the objects on the OS/2 2.0 desktop according to your preferences.

Of course, you can change the colors on the screen. You can even create colors of your own. You can change the typeface of the text you display and print. You can even change the size and style of the text in the labels of the icons on the screen. Do you like a tidy desk? You can hide windows you are not using or minimize them and have them put inside the Minimized Window Viewer. Then your desktop does not have a cluttered appearance. Do you prefer to have the windows you minimize shown on the desktop so that you can see and get to them easily? Then change your window settings so that minimized windows can be placed on the desktop. Inside a window or on the desktop, you can have the icons neatly arranged in rows with just a click of the mouse button. You also can move individual icons around on the desktop or in and out of folders— wherever they are convenient for you.

In the Workplace Shell, you usually can choose from several ways of accomplishing the same result. You can try them all, and then use the one you prefer or the one that is most convenient at the time. To create a new data-file object, for instance, you can select Create another on the pop-up menu of an existing data-file object; or peel off the top layer of a data-file template; or make a copy using a notebook. This is only one example of the customizing and organizing information available in this chapter.

Working with Workplace Shell Menus

In the Workplace Shell, two new mechanisms give users greater capabilities in interacting with the operating system: pop-up menus and Settings notebooks. Neither of these tools was in earlier versions of OS/2.

Using Pop-Up Menus

Every object on the desktop has a pop-up menu of the basic actions you can perform with that object. To display the pop-up menu for an object that has not been opened, move your mouse to the object and right-click.

Each pop-up menu is specific for an object. The following choices are common to many pop-up menus:

- Open
- Help
- Create another
- Copy
- Move

- Create shadow
- Delete

An arrow to the right of a choice means that a submenu provides more choices. Click on the arrow to see the other choices.

Open, for instance, may have these choices: Settings, Icon view, Tree view, and Details view. You can select any of these choices according to the way you want to look at the object. The Settings choice is discussed in the next section. The other views are discussed later in this chapter.

After you open an object, you can display its pop-up menu in two ways:

- Right-click once on a space inside the window but away from any objects.
- Left-click on the title bar icon in the top left corner of the window.

To display the pop-up menu for the desktop, right-click on an empty space on the desktop. The desktop pop-up menu includes Shut down, which you should use to power off your computer.

 How to use pop-up menu choices in specific situations is explained in the remainder of this chapter.

Using Settings Notebooks

The Settings notebook is an important mechanism for customizing the appearance and behavior of objects. To display a Settings notebook, select Open Settings on the pop-up menu of an object. A Settings notebook looks like a paper notebook with tabs, as shown in figure 3.1.

Figure 3.1:

Settings notebook for program object.

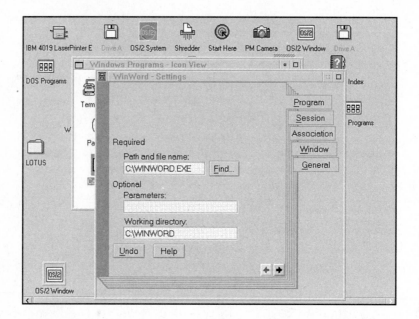

Each Settings notebook is specific for an object. The Settings notebook in figure 3.1 is for a program object. It has sections for **P**rogram, **S**ession, Association, **W**indow, and **G**eneral as indicated by the tabs on the right side of the notebook. Each section can have several pages.

In figure 3.1, the Settings page for **P**rogram currently is displayed. The fields on this page are for the path and file name of the program, any start-up parameters you might want to add, and the working directory. You can click on the Help button for an explanation of each of these fields. You might have to fill in or change the information displayed if this program does not start correctly.

Click on the arrows at the bottom right of the page to go to the next page or go back a page. You also can click on a tab to go to one of the following sections:

- **S**ession, which shows what kind of session the program runs in (OS/2, DOS, or WIN-OS/2 for Microsoft Windows programs)

- Association, which shows the file types associated with this program object

- Window, which shows how minimized windows behave in this program and what happens when you select this program object when the program is already open (displays the existing window or opens another one)

- General, which shows the icon title and the icon, and tells whether a template is available for creating duplicate objects

You can change any of the settings, and the changes are made automatically. You do not have to take any action to save the changes you make. Click on the Undo button to reverse the changes you just made or click on the Default button to return to the system's original settings.

Starting and Ending Programs

To start a program on the desktop, you can use the mouse; open an associated data file; or use the command-line interface. To close a program object, once again you have a choice: double-click on an icon or use a menu.

Double-Clicking To Start a Program

When you start a program in the Workplace Shell, you are really opening a program object. The easiest and quickest way to open an object is to move your mouse pointer to it and double-click the left button. The object opens, and its contents are displayed in a window.

The first time you start OS/2 2.0, you might not have any application programs installed except the ones that come with OS/2. You might have, for instance, the games or productivity tools you selected to install. You can practice starting those by simply following these steps:

1. Open the OS/2 System folder by double-clicking on it.

2. Open either the Games or Productivity folder in the OS/2 System window.

3. Double-click on one of the program objects in the window.

Using the Pop-Up Menu To Open a Program Object

You also can open a program object by selecting Open on the pop-up menu of the object. To display the pop-up menu of an object that has not been opened, right-click on the object.

With the Productivity folder object open, display the menu of a program object, such as To-Do List. The first choice on the menu is Open. To start the program To-Do List, left-click on Open.

Opening a Data Object Associated with a Program

Another way to open a program is to open a data object associated with the program. For instance, you can associate a letter with a word processing program. Then you can simply double-click on the letter (data object) to open the letter and simultaneously start the word processing program.

You can associate a single data object with a program, or you can associate all data objects of that type with a program. For example, you can associate one spreadsheet with one spreadsheet program and a second spreadsheet with a second spreadsheet program. You also can associate all spreadsheets that have the extension WK1 at the end of their names with the same spreadsheet program.

To associate a data-file object with a program by file name:

1. Display the pop-up menu for the program by left-clicking on the icon.

2. Hold down the left mouse button, move the mouse across the **O**pen choice to **S**ettings, and release the button. The Settings notebook displays.

3. Click on the Association tab.

4. Type the file name of the data-file object you want to associate with this program.

You also can associate all data-file objects with a certain file name using this same method. For example, to associate all data-file objects with names that end in DOC with the same word processing program, type ***.DOC** in the file name field.

To associate data-file objects with a program by type:

1. Display the pop-up menu for the program by left-clicking on the icon.

2. Holding down the left button, move the mouse across the **O**pen choice to **S**ettings, and release the button. The Settings notebook displays.

3. Click on the Association tab.

4. Select one or more file types from those displayed.

5. Click on **A**dd.

Starting a Program from a Command Line

If you know the command for starting a program, you can start it from a command line, as follows:

1. Open the OS/2 System folder.

2. Open the Command Prompts folder.

3. Open a DOS or OS/2 window or full-screen session.

4. At the command prompt, enter the start-up command for the application program.

Starting a Program from a Drive Folder

Yet another way to start a program is to open the drive object where the program object is and start it from there. If, for instance, you want to start a Windows program that is on drive C, do the following:

1. Open the OS/2 System folder.

2. Open the Drives object.

3. Open the Drive C object. (Default view is Tree view.)

4. Open the Windows object if you have Windows applications installed.

5. Display the pop-up menu of the program you want to start.

6. Select **O**pen **P**rogram.

You might want to move programs that you use frequently onto the desktop so that they are easily accessible.

Closing a Program Object

The easiest way to close a program object, or any other object, is to double-click on the title bar icon in the upper left corner of the object's window.

You also can use a menu: with the title bar icon menu displayed, click on Close.

Moving from Program to Program

As you work with the Workplace Shell, you might have several windows open at the same time. You might keep the Master Help

Index open so that you can refer to it from time to time. You might, for instance, want to integrate information from two other windows into a third window. It is a simple matter to move among open windows using either the mouse or the keyboard.

Selecting a Window Using the Mouse

If a portion of a window is visible, click on it to bring that window to the foreground. It then becomes the active window. You can tell which is the active window because its title bar and border are highlighted.

Selecting a Window Using the Keyboard

You can switch from window to window using the keyboard by pressing Alt-Tab. To switch to the next window or full-screen session, press Alt-Esc. To switch between a window and a Help window, press Alt-F6. (For other key assignments, see Chapter 2.)

Activating and Using the Window List

The Window List displays the titles of all open windows. You can use it to find which windows are open, to switch to another window, and to do other actions with the open windows. To display the Window List, press both mouse buttons once over an empty space on the desktop, or, from the keyboard, press Ctrl-Esc.

An especially useful action of the Window List is to close several or all windows to tidy up your desktop. You can use the technique called *swiping* for this. To close all windows, make sure you are in the Window List and follow these steps:

1. Press and hold down the left mouse button and drag the mouse pointer down the list to highlight all window titles shown in the Window List.

2. Right-click on one of the titles to display the object's pop-up menu.

3. Click on Close.

 To close selected windows, hold down Ctrl and click on only the window titles you want to close.

You may notice that desktop is always displayed on the Window List. Because you must have the desktop open to use the Workplace Shell, you cannot close it. Even though you select desktop when getting ready to close all windows, you cannot close it accidentally. If you right-click on the desktop title in the Window List to display the desktop pop-up menu, the only choices available here are _S_how and _H_elp. If, however, you display the desktop pop-up menu on the desktop itself, more choices are available, including the important choice Shut _d_own.

As you become accustomed to working with the Window List, you will probably find that some of its functions are quite useful to you. You can quickly show or hide several open windows, as described later in this chapter. In addition, you can rearrange open windows by using the tile and cascade functions.

Sizing Windows

The Workplace Shell provides several ways to size windows on the computer screen so that you can work comfortably and efficiently. You may want to size individual windows or all windows so that you can work with their contents. The following sections describe several methods of sizing windows.

Drag Window Borders

To move one side of a window to make the window larger or smaller, follow these steps:

1. Place the mouse pointer on a window border so that the pointer changes into a double-headed arrow.

2. Press either the right or left mouse button and drag out or in the border.

3. Release the mouse button when the window is the size that you want.

To move two sides of a window to make it larger or smaller, follow these steps:

1. Place the mouse pointer on a window corner so that the pointer changes into a double-headed arrow.

2. Right-click and drag out or in the border corner.

3. Release the mouse button when the window is the size that you want.

Using the Maximize and Hide Buttons

You can make a window as big as possible (maximize it) or as small as possible (minimize it) using the size buttons on the right side of the window title bar. To enlarge the window so that it fills the entire screen, click the larger square on the far right. You also can maximize a window by double-clicking on the title bar.

When you maximize a window, the maximize button changes to a restore button. To restore a window to its previous size, click the restore button in the upper right corner of the window. You also can double-click on the maximized window's title bar to restore the window.

To hide a window so that it does not clutter up your desktop, click on the hide button, the smaller square with broken lines just to the left of the maximize button. The default action is to hide the window so that you cannot see it on the desktop. The minimized window is placed in the Minimized Window Viewer. To show (unhide) the window, press both mouse buttons simultaneously (called *chording*) to display the Window List, and then click on the name of the window.

You also can use the Window List to hide a window by following these steps:

1. Display the Window List by clicking both mouse buttons simultaneously on an empty space.

2. Move the mouse pointer over the title of the window you want to hide.

3. Right-click.

4. Choose <u>M</u>inimize from the menu that appears.

Instead of hiding windows one-by-one by clicking on the <u>M</u>inimize button, you can use the Window List to hide all open windows in one operation. To hide all open windows, follow these steps:

1. Display the Window List.

2. Click on the title bar icon to display the menu.

3. Select the arrow to the right of S<u>e</u>lect.

4. Click on Select <u>a</u>ll.

5. Move the mouse pointer over the title of one window.

6. Right-click to display the pop-up menu.

7. Choose <u>M</u>inimize

If you want to hide several windows that are listed one after the other in the Window List, you can use the swiping technique to select them.

Follow these steps:

1. Display the Window List.

2. Press and hold down the left mouse button.

3. Move the pointer over the window titles. All the titles swiped should be highlighted.

4. Release the left mouse button.

5. Move the mouse pointer to one of the highlighted titles.

6. Right-click to display a pop-up menu.

7. Left-click on <u>M</u>inimize. All the selected windows disappear.

To hide several windows not listed one after the other, follow these steps:

1. Display the Window List.

2. Point to the first window you want to hide.

3. Press and hold down Ctrl and then left-click.

4. Repeat for each window.

5. Point to the title of one of the selected windows.

6. Right-click to display the pop-up menu.

7. Choose <u>M</u>inimize.

To show the hidden windows, use the same procedure but click on <u>S</u>how instead of <u>M</u>inimize.

Customizing Window Actions

You can use the window settings to specify whether windows are minimized or hidden. You also can specify where to place the minimized windows.

A VGA screen is a poor platform for a GUI. A size of 640 pixels by 480 pixels is not enough space to spread out. Imagine, for example, trying to work on desktop that measures only 12 inches diagonally.

One way to manage screen space is to close one program before attempting to use another. This is not a good solution, however, because it defeats one of the purposes of OS/2: multitasking. It is time-consuming and annoying to have to completely open and close each program every time you want to use it.

To solve this problem, OS/2 provides the following three ways to "put away" a task without having to close it altogether:

- **Minimized on the Desktop.** If you have worked with Microsoft Windows in the past, then you are familiar with minimizing. When an application is *minimized,* only its icon is visible on the desktop.

- **Minimized to the Minimized Viewer.** Unlike Windows, you can choose to reduce your application to an icon and then put it in a folder designed solely to hold minimized icons.

- **Hidden.** Using this option, you can make an application simply disappear until you call it back. This process can be very convenient. For example, you can open up and hide your Drives folder, which shows the files on the hard disk. When you want it, bring up the Window list, choose drive C, and the drive window appears.

Minimizing Windows

You can specify whether minimized windows are placed in the Minimized Window Viewer or on the desktop. When you double-click on the Minimized Window Viewer, it opens to display icons for all windows that you opened and then minimized. Another alternative is to have minimized windows placed on the desktop so that you can access them easily. You can change window settings for the entire desktop, or you can change them for an individual object.

Minimize All Windows

To change the minimizing behavior for all windows on the desktop, change the settings on the **W**indow page of the System Settings notebook, shown in figure 3.2. The settings to change are Button appearance for windows and Minimized windows.

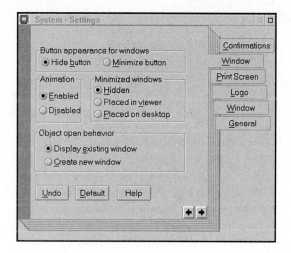

Figure 3.2:
Window Settings notebook page.

Follow these steps to change the Window settings:

1. Open the OS/2 System folder.

2. Open the System Setup folder.

3. Open the System folder. The Settings notebook is displayed.

4. Select the <u>W</u>indow tab.

5. Select <u>M</u>inimize Button Behavior for the button appearance.

6. Choose <u>H</u>ide window, Window to <u>v</u>iewer, or <u>W</u>indow to desktop depending on your preference.

Minimize an Object Window

To change the settings of an individual object so that its window is minimized rather than hidden, go to the Settings notebook of the object and follow these steps:

1. Right-click on an object. The pop-up menu displays.

2. Select <u>O</u>pen <u>S</u>ettings. The Settings notebook displays.

3. Click on the **W**indow tab.

4. Select **M**inimize for the button appearance.

5. Choose Minimize window to **v**iewer or Minimize **w**indow to desktop, depending on your preference.

6. Close the Settings notebook.

The changes take effect immediately. You do not need to save the changes.

Moving Windows

You can move windows in several ways. You can drag the title bar or use the title bar icon menu.

Drag by Window Title Bar

The easiest way to move a window on the screen is to place the mouse pointer on the window title bar, press and hold the right button (although the left button works as well), and drag the window to the new location.

Use Title Bar Icon Menu

You also can move an object by selecting the **W**indow **M**ove choice on the title bar icon menu, as follows:

1. Click on the title bar icon in the upper left corner of the window. The menu displays.

2. Click on **W**indow.

3. Click on **M**ove. An outline of the window appears.

4. Move your mouse (without pressing a button) to the place where you want the window.

5. Click either mouse button to drop the window in the new location.

Arranging Windows

You can arrange open windows by moving them individually with the mouse using the drag technique described earlier in this chapter. You also can have the system arrange the open windows by using the Window List.

Follow these steps to have the system arrange the open windows:

1. Display the Window List by moving the mouse pointer to an empty space on the desktop and then by clicking both the left and right mouse buttons simultaneously. The Window List is displayed with a list of all the windows you have opened.

2. Highlight the titles of the windows you want to arrange.

3. Right-click on one of the highlighted selections.

4. Click on either Tile or Cascade.

Tile

If you select Tile, the windows are arranged in quadrants, with each window completely visible, as shown in figure 3.3.

Tiling windows is useful if you want to see the contents of several open windows at the same time. You might, for example, want to see the clock, play a chess game, have your calendar open, and use your word processor all at the same time. Tiling windows also are helpful if you want to compare data in several spreadsheets, which you can arrange by tiling the windows.

The disadvantage of tiling, of course, is that you cannot see all the contents of the windows.

Figure 3.3:

Tiled windows.

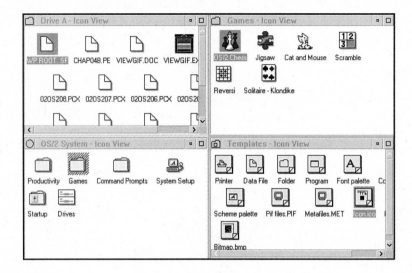

Cascade

If you select Cascade, the windows are stacked in a staircase arrangement, as shown in figure 3.4. To move a cascaded window to the top of the stack, left-click anywhere on the visible portion.

Arranging windows using Cascade is useful because it places the windows in an orderly arrangement, and you can easily identify them because you can see their titles. The disadvantage is that you can see the contents of only the top window.

Figure 3.4:

Cascaded windows.

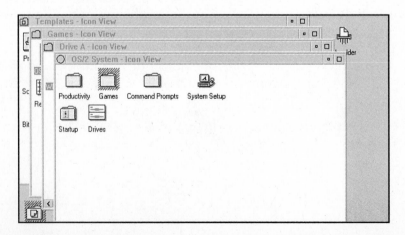

Closing Windows

To close a single window, double-click on the title bar icon at the top left of the window. Another technique is to pull down the title bar icon menu and choose <u>C</u>lose.

Remember to close windows as soon as you are finished working with them. The more open windows you have, the slower the system responds.

You also can use the Window List to close all open windows. To do this, follow these steps:

1. Highlight all window titles shown in the Window List, either by holding down Ctrl and dragging the mouse pointer across the titles or by opening the title bar icon menu and clicking on Select <u>a</u>ll.

2. Right-click on one of the titles to display the object's pop-up menu.

3. Click on <u>C</u>lose.

You can close several windows, but not all, by clicking on the titles of the windows you want to close, displaying the pop-up menu of one of them, and selecting <u>C</u>lose.

Arranging Icons

You can rearrange the icons on your desktop by dragging them and dropping them where you want them. You also can have the system arrange them.

Arranging Icons on the Desktop

To have the system place the icons in the default arrangement, follow these steps:

1. Move the mouse pointer to an empty space on the desktop.

2. Right-click to display the pop-up menu of the object whose window you are working with.

3. Choose **A**rrange.

 You can use the **S**ort option on context windows to rearrange the icons by name, date, and so on.

Arranging Icons in a Window

You can arrange icons in a window by using menus. The pop-up menu for an object, the title bar icon menu, and the view page of Settings notebooks enable you to arrange icons.

Using the Object Pop-Up Menu

1. With the window open, move the mouse pointer to an empty space in the window.

2. Right-click to display the pop-up menu of the object whose window you are working with.

3. Choose **A**rrange.

Using the Title Bar Icon Menu

You also can use the title bar icon menu to arrange the icons in a window:

1. With the window open, click the title bar icon in the top left corner.

2. Choose **A**rrange.

Using View Settings

To change the way icons are arranged in a window, follow these steps:

1. Open the Settings notebook for the object.

2. Click on the View tab.

3. Click on a radio button in the Format field to choose Flowed, Non-flowed, or Non-grid.

The View settings are shown in figure 3.5.

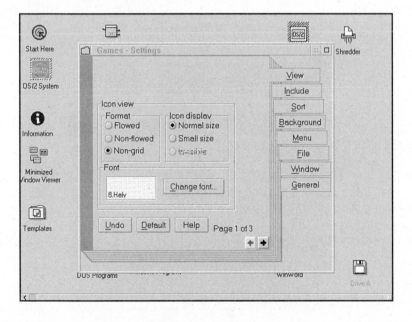

Figure 3.5:
View settings page.

If you select Flowed, the icons are placed in rows across the desktop. If you select Non-flowed, the icons are placed in one vertical column. If you select Non-grid (the default), the icons are placed randomly on the desktop.

Saving Screen Appearance

You can save the appearance of your customizedscreen so that the next time you start OS/2 2.0, the objects and windows are in the same place on your desktop and the same programs will be activated.

To save the screen in earlier versions of OS/2, you selected Shut down from the desktop pop-up menu. (To display this menu, right-click on an empty space on the desktop.) Now, OS/2 automatically saves new settings, and you no longer need to exit the program.

To shut down when you have windows open, follow this sequence:

1. Press Ctrl-Esc
2. Select OS/2 Desktop
3. Press Ctrl-\ (backslash)
4. Press Shift-F10
5. Select Shutdown

You should see a message that asks you to confirm the shutdown.

Using the Startup Folder

You can put objects into the Startup folder that you want started each time OS/2 2.0 is activated. This arrangement, however, is not recommended for large applications. Consider instead using the startup folder as the place for short batch routines, so that they run as part of the startup procedure.

 If you have an application that you use every day, make a shadow of it and put it in the Startup folder. Then each time you start your computer, that application will start automatically.

Securing Your Desktop

By using Lockup, you can have the screen go blank and the system lock up after a certain period of time so that other people cannot use your system. You also can set up a desktop password for yourself.

To use Lockup:

1. Display the desktop pop-up menu by right-clicking on an empty space on the desktop.

2. Select Open Settings. The Settings notebook opens.

3. Click the Lockup tab on the right side of the notebook.

Setting the Timeout

Three pages are for Lockup settings. The first page displays the Timeout settings, as shown in figure 3.6.

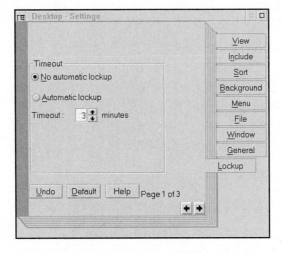

Figure 3.6:

Lockup settings notebook.

You can change the settings depending on whether you want an automatic lockup time. That is, when you are not interacting with the computer, do you want the screen to blank automatically? This feature is called *timeout*.

If you choose Automatic lockup, you need to set the amount of time to wait before the screen goes blank. The default is three minutes. You can change the setting by clicking on the up and down arrows that are part of the Timeout setting.

Notice the number of pages indicated at the bottom right of the notebook page. This information tells you how many settings pages there are for this feature.

Selecting the Wallpaper (image)

Click on the right arrow to go to page two. On this page, you can select the bitmap (picture) that is displayed after an automatic timeout occurs. Experiment with the available bitmaps to find the one you like best.

 The available bitmaps depend on your selection during installation. If you did not install bitmaps, only one choice is available, the OS/2 wallpaper.

Setting a Password

Click on the right arrow to go to page three. On this page, you can enter a desktop password. Use this password to unlock the desktop after an automatic timeout occurs.

If you forget your password, you have to turn off the computer (Ctrl-Alt-Del) and restart. Then open the desktop Settings notebook as described in this section and set a new password.

 If you want to lock up your desktop immediately rather than wait for an automatic timeout, choose Lockup now from the desktop pop-up menu.

Customizing Using System Setup Objects

The System Setup folder contains several objects, such as the Color Palette, that you can use to tailor the Workplace Shell desktop to your preferences and style so that it is your own personal workspace.

Using Settings Notebooks

Each Workplace Shell object has settings that are contained in aSettings notebook. As already described, you open the desktop Settings notebook by right-clicking over an empty space on the computer screen (the desktop). To open the Settings notebook of any other object, follow these steps:

1. Move the mouse pointer to an object and right-click. The object's pop-up menu displays.

2. Click on the arrow to the right of the **O**pen choice on the menu.

3. Click on **S**ettings.

NOTE The metaphor of the notebook is employed in other places in the Workplace Shell as well. The Master Help Index, for example, is a notebook with pages, tabs, and scroll arrows similar to the Settings notebook.

The settings, or properties, of the object are presented using a notebook format. Tabs on the notebook pages indicate the types of settings available for the object. Although each Settings notebook is created especially for a specific object, similar objects have similar settings. Program objects, for example, have pages with tabs for the following settings:

- **G**eneral—program title and icon

- Association—types or names of data files linked to this program

- **P**rogram—path, file name, parameters, and working directory of this object

- **S**ession—type of session the program is set to run in: OS/2, DOS, or Windows; window or full-screen

- **W**indow—behavior of hidden or minimized windows and arrangement of icons

Figure 3.7 shows the Settings notebook for one device object, a printer.

Figure 3.7:

Settings notebook for a printer.

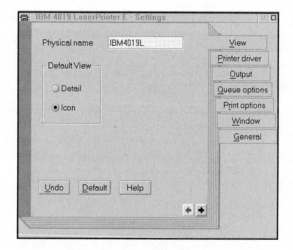

When you change a setting in the notebook, the change takes place automatically and immediately. You do not have to save the change. To undo a change, click on the **U**ndo button. To reset to the original default, click on the **D**efault button.

Using System Setup Features

The System Setup folder has features and tools that you can customize by changing their settings. The contents of the System Setup folder are shown in figure 3.8.

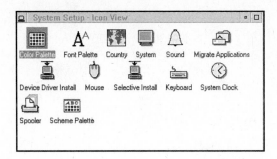

Figure 3.8:
Contents of
System Setup
folder.

System

You can change system-wide settings for **C**onfirmations, **W**indow, **P**rint Screen, **L**ogo, and **G**eneral.

Color Palette

You can change the color of window parts and the desktop using the Color Palette (see fig. 3.9).

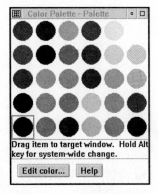

Figure 3.9:
Color Palette.

Select a color from the chart, drag the paint roller to the area you want to color, and release the mouse button. If the color does not suit you, you can edit the color. Click on the Edit color button to go to a color wheel to adjust the color.

Select a color from the chart, move the mouse pointer (now shown as a paint roller) to the area in the window or the desktop that you want to color, and release. The color change is made instantly. To make the color change system-wide, hold down Alt when you move the paint roller to a window. If a color does not quite suit you, you can edit the color. Click on the Edit color button to go to a color wheel to adjust the color.

Scheme Palette

You can use the Scheme Palette to select a color scheme from spring, summer, fall, and winter palettes, or you can create a new palette. The difference between Color Palette and Scheme Palette is that with the Color Palette you change one color at a time; with the Scheme Palette, you change a set of colors. The objects in the Scheme Palette window, shown in figure 3.10, each use a unique set of colors.

Figure 3.10:

Scheme Palette.

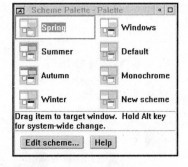

Similar to the Color Palette, in which you drag a color to a window, in the Scheme Palette you drag the scheme to the window you want to change. To make system-wide changes, hold down Alt as you drag the sample scheme to a window or the desktop.

If you want to adjust some of the colors in a sample scheme, choose the Edit Scheme button. In the Edit Scheme window, shown in figure 3.11, the parts you can change are shown on the left.

On the right is the title of this scheme, which you can edit. Below it is the field called *Window area*. This contains a pull-down menu of the names of the window parts. *Active Title Text* currently is displayed. If you click on the small arrow to the right of Active Title Text, a list appears to show the names of the window parts. You can scroll the list to find the part you want to change. Then, to edit the color of the part you have highlighted in the list, select the Edit Color button. A color wheel then displays so that you can select the shade you want.

Use the help buttons on these windows to get detailed instructions.

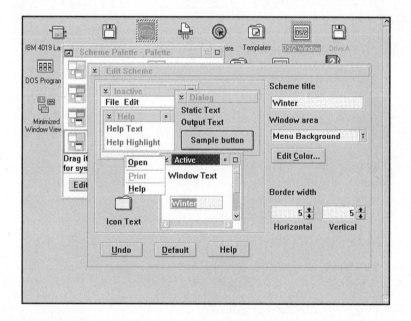

Figure 3.11:

Edit Scheme window.

Font Palette

Use the font palette to select a font in the typeface and size you want. You can select a font from the samples shown and drag it to the window where you want to use it. To make a system-wide change in the font, hold down Alt while you drag the sample. To type in the name of a font not shown, click on the Edit font button.

System Clock

The system clock is another highly customizable feature. You can set the clock or set an alarm. You can change the following settings:

- Information—show time, date, or both
- Mode—use an analog or digital display
- Color—change background and foreground colors
- Font—change the typeface for date and time

Sound

Only one choice is available. You use the Sound object to set the system's notification beep on or off.

Mouse

You can change the following mouse settings:

- Timing—how much time can pass between clicks in a double-click and still have the system recognize it as one action; how fast you can move the mouse and still have the system recognize the mouse movements
- Setup—for right-handed or left-handed use
- Mappings—which mouse buttons for dragging, displaying pop-up menus, editing title text
- General—object name and current icon

Keyboard

You can change the following keyboard settings:

- Timing—key repeat rate, repeat delay rate, cursor blink rate
- Mappings—keys for displaying pop-up menus and editing title text

- Special needs settings—features such as "sticky keys" and keyboard response adjustments for users with disabilities

 The customizing features of the special needs settings are designed to be used by those who have dexterity disabilities.

Spooler

The spooler manages the sending of print jobs to printers and the queues of jobs waiting to be printed. You can customize the spooler by changing the path to the location where files wait to be printed.

Country

To set the system to use date, time, numbers, and currency formats for certain languages, you can use the Country object.

The other three objects in the System Setup folder have to do with installation: Selective Install, Device Driver Install, and Migrate Applications.

You can use Selective Install to change mouse, display, or country information, or to add features you did not previously install. Perhaps you want to install more OS/2 productivity applications or more games. Maybe you have decided you need the command reference on-line. You can add these features without going through the entire installation procedure: just use Selective Install.

Device Driver Install is included so that you can use it to install a device, such as a memory card, that comes with a separate support disk. (Device Driver Install is not to be used to add a printer device driver that exists on an OS/2 installation disk.)

You can use the Migrate Applications object to create program objects for OS/2, DOS, and Windows programs installed on a hard disk. The objects you create then appear on the desktop in OS/2, DOS, or Windows folders.

You can change system-wide settings for confirmation messages, minimized window behavior, print screen enabling, presentation and timing of the logo, and the title and icon of the System object.

Changing Views of Objects

You can change the way the contents of an object are displayed by using the pop-up menu.

Move the mouse pointer to the object and right-click. If <u>O</u>pen is on the pop-up menu, an arrow is to the right. Click on the arrow to display the submenu. For folders, the submenu has these choices: <u>S</u>ettings, <u>I</u>con view, <u>T</u>ree view, and <u>D</u>etails view. <u>I</u>con view shows the objects in random order. <u>T</u>ree view shows the objects arranged in a hierarchy (a tree with branches). This view is similar to the directory tree in previous versions of OS/2. <u>D</u>etails view shows information about the objects, such as when they were created and what their sizes are.

Figure 3.12 shows the contents of the OS/2 System folder displayed in each of the three views.

At the top left is the icon view of the OS/2 System folder. Here the contents of the folder are presented as separate objects. The icons indicate something about the contents or function of the objects. When objects are in the icon view, they are easy to move around on the desktop.

At the top right is the tree view of the OS/2 System folder. A *tree view* is similar to an outline of directories (folders) and subdirectories (folders within folders) on a drive. It shows how the directories are organized.

At the bottom is the details view of the OS/2 System folder. The information in the columns includes, for each folder and file object, a miniature of its icon, the icon title, its real name in the operating system (if different from the icon title), its size, date, and time of last change and last access.

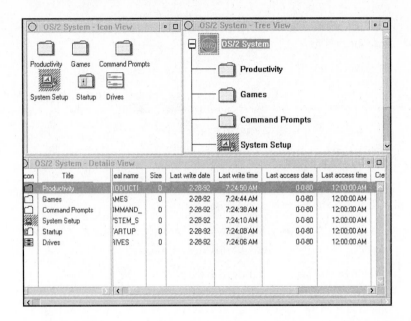

Figure 3.12:

OS/2 System folder opened in Icon, Tree, and Details views.

To the right, out of the picture, is other detail information: date and time of creation, and the flags (attributes): hidden, archive, read-only, and system. For more information on file characteristics and file systems, see Chapter 4.

Changing Object Names

You can change the name of an object on the desktop by changing the text itself, without having to go to a command line. The procedures for mouse and keyboard are somewhat different.

Permanently Changing an Object's View

By now, you have noticed that some objects open up in Icon view; others open up in Tree view or Details view. You can change the default view of an object because the OS/2 defaults are not always the best choices. For example, although the Tree view of drive C is helpful, the same view of drive A is not (floppy disks usually do not have subdirectories). For drive A:, the Icon view is usually a better choice.

To make drive A show the Icon view by default, use the Settings notebook for drive A by following these steps:

1. Open up the Settings notebook and click on **M**enu.

   A section called Available menus appears in the upper left hand corner of the Settings window, which contains two items: the Primary pop-up menu and ~Open.

2. Click on ~Open.

   The **S**ettings button becomes active.

3. Click on the **S**ettings button.

   A smaller window called Menu Settings appears. You see a drop-down box called Default action.

4. Pull down the Default action box.

   You see options for Details, Tree, and Icon view.

5. Click on Icon view to make it the default.

6. While still in the Menu Settings window, click on **O**K.

   The window closes.

7. Close the Settings notebook.

   Drive A appears in Icon view.

Using the Mouse

With a mouse, you can change the name of the object without using a menu. This action, called *direct name-editing*, is easier and more natural than using a menu or a command to rename an object. You can use direct name-editing to name an object that is a newly created copy. Follow these steps:

1. Press and hold down Alt.

2. Move the mouse pointer to the object whose name you want to change.

3. Left-click.

4. Release Alt.

5. Type the new name (use Del or backspace to erase unwanted characters).

6. Left-click on the icon.

Using the Keyboard

You can change the name (title) of an object on the General page of the Settings notebook for the object using the keyboard. Follow these steps to change the name of an object using the keyboard only:

1. Move the cursor to the object with the arrow keys.

2. Press the spacebar to select the object.

3. Press Shift-F10 to display the pop-up menu of the object.

4. Select the arrow to the right of **O**pen.

5. Select **S**ettings.

6. Change the name on the **G**eneral page of the Settings notebook.

 To use the keyboard fastpath, select the object and press Shift-F9.

Creating Objects

As you do your daily work, you need to create objects to add to the desktop, such as data file objects, printer objects, or icons. Perhaps you want to create a form for a specific purpose—say, a sales report that has to be filled out monthly. This is an opportunity to take advantage of the flexibility of the Workplace Shell.

You can create objects in several ways: make a copy including contents, make a copy without contents, make a shadow, or use a template. Which method would you use for your sales report form?

Make a Copy

Drag and drop is probably the easiest way to make a copy of an existing object. You can use drag and drop, for example, to put a copy of a data-file object on a disk. Follow these steps:

1. Point to the object.

2. Hold down Ctrl.

3. Hold down the right mouse button.

4. Drag the object to wherever you want it.

5. Release the mouse button and then the Ctrl key to drop the object.

 Remember that before starting a drag-and-drop copy, you must be able to see both the object you are copying and the location to which you are going to drag it.

You also can use the object's pop-up menu to make a copy of an object (a letter, for instance), including its contents. Follow these steps:

1. Right-click on the object. The pop-up menu displays.

2. Click on <u>C</u>opy. The Copy notebook displays as shown in figure 3.13.

3. Click on a tab depending on where you want to place the copy (the target of the operation).

4. Click on the <u>C</u>opy push button.

Create Another Object

You can use another pop-up menu choice, Create a<u>n</u>other, to make a duplicate of an object, but without its contents. The duplicate has the same settings as the original. To create another object, follow these steps:

1. Right-click on the object. The pop-up menu displays.

2. Click Create a<u>n</u>other or the arrow to the right to see the options, and then click on your choice.

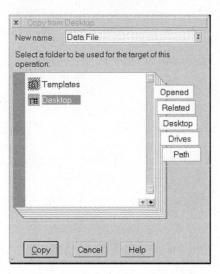

Figure 3.13:

Copy notebook page.

Use a Template

When you open the Templates folder on the desktop, you see various types of objects, such as data file, program, folder, and printer (see fig. 3.14).

You can make copies of these objects in the Templates folder when you need to create objects. You can then customize the templates you have created. You can, for instance, create a letterhead using a data-file template.

To peel off a template from an object in the Templates folder, simply point to the object and drag a copy to the desktop. You can use <u>C</u>opy or Create a<u>n</u>other from the pop-up menu of a template to place a copy in a closed object, such as a folder.

A duplicate of a template produces the same result as Create a<u>n</u>other on an object's pop-up menu.

Figure 3.14:

Contents of
Templates folder.

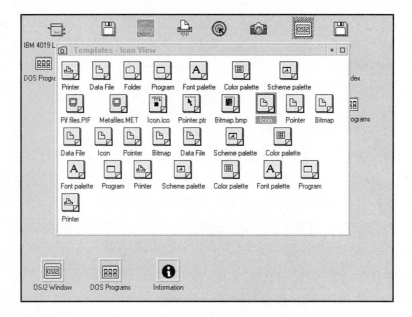

Create a Shadow

Some objects cannot be copied, such as the system clock. You can create a shadow of that object, however, and put it in another location.

For instance, you can have the system clock on the desktop and a shadow of it in a folder that you work with frequently where it would be convenient to have a second clock.

The data in the shadow is always the same as in the original object. That is, the time is the same in the shadow clock as in the original clock. You can change the name of the shadow and its icon.

Use either of these methods to create a shadow:

- Press and hold down Ctrl and Shift; then drag away a shadow of the object.
- Select Create shadow on the pop-up menu of an object.

Creating Work Areas

You might find it useful to create work-area folders for projects that involve working with several objects. Say, for example, you have several documents that you work with when you are getting ready to pay your income tax. You can keep them together in a work-area folder. This is a convenience for several reasons; perhaps the most important reason is that when you close the folder, all open objects inside it also are closed, and when you reopen it, all the objects reopen just as they were when you closed the folder. A work-area folder is displayed in the Window List as one object so that you can manipulate all involved objects with one action.

You must designate a folder as a work area to take advantage of the work area's special characteristics. To do this, follow these steps:

1. Open the pop-up menu of the folder.

2. Select **O**pen **S**ettings. The Settings notebook displays.

3. Click on the **F**ile tab.

4. Click on the **W**ork area check box.

Discarding Objects

You can remove an object from the desktop by dropping it on the Shredder or by selecting **D**elete on the pop-up menu of the object. The Shredder icon shows a sheet of paper being cut into small pieces rather than held in a trash can or wastebasket. This graphic helps to convey the idea that objects you place in the Shredder are discarded immediately.

You might want to move the Shredder to a convenient spot on your desktop away from other icons so that it is easily accessible. If the Shredder is not easily accessible, you can discard an object by using **D**elete on the object's pop-up menu.

Summary

This chapter has discussed many, but not all, of the ways in which you can organize and customize the desktop so that it is a comfortable and efficient place for you to work. As you explore, you will no doubt find even more opportunities to create your personalized workplace.

Chapter 4, "Managing Files with OS/2 2.0," shows you how the Workplace Shell makes your work easier by seeing and manipulating objects instead of having to remember a command language. It also illustrates the flexibility of OS/2 2.0 by introducing this operating system's two file systems.

Managing Files Using OS/2 2.0

A *file* is a collection of related information, such as a letter or a program, that the computer user stores as a unit. Each file has a name that the user assigns to it. Users can organize files into groups, and then store and retrieve the files using those groups. In DOS, users can organize files hierarchically by putting them into directories that they create. In the Workplace Shell, however, the structure changes: files and directories become objects and folders.

In the Workplace Shell, files are shown as *objects* on the computer screen. A *data file* is a data-file object such as a letter, a chart, or a spreadsheet. You can put data-file objects into a folder object, and then store and retrieve the data-file objects using that folder. A *folder* is simply a container that can hold a collection of objects. To better manage your work, you can put folders in other folders.

The Workplace Shell makes it easier for you to do your work because you see and manipulate objects directly without using commands. You simply point to an object and then work with it, using the mouse either to manipulate the object directly or to select actions from lists of menus. Nevertheless, underneath the Workplace Shell a command interface still is available. How to work with files using either the Workplace Shell or the underlying command interface is the subject of this chapter.

Introducing the OS/2 2.0 File Systems

OS/2 2.0 puts on a simple face for you. The easier a piece of software is for users, the more difficult it is to provide the necessary power and capabilities. An example of this phenomenon is the fact that OS/2 2.0 can use not just one, but two file systems.

Understanding File Systems

A *file system* manages the input, output, and storage of files. It works with file objects as you create them. A file system accepts the information you send, formats it, stores it in an organized fashion, and sends it back in the form you ask for.

OS/2 supports multiple file systems. One file system comes with OS/2. Users also can install another file system that comes with OS/2 2.0. Each storage device (hard disk or floppy disk) is managed by one file system, which is established when the disk is formatted. Each disk is assigned a designator (A, B, C, and so on) by the operating system. Disk drive A, for example, is managed by the built-in file system, and the hard disk drive C can be managed by the same or a different file system. Further, during installation of OS/2 2.0, you can divide your hard disk into *partitions*; each partition becomes a separate storage device and is assigned a letter and a file system. In a network of computers, each storage device in the server is assigned a character designation (the letter P, for example), so that users can access that remote storage device by using that letter.

The two file systems that OS/2 2.0 supports are the File Allocation Table (FAT) and the High Performance File System (HPFS). With OS/2 2.0, you do not have a choice of file systems for your disk drives; they can be formatted only with FAT. However, you do have the option of formatting your hard disk with HPFS.

Using the FAT File System

The personal computer operating system that preceded OS/2 is the Disk Operating System (DOS). Its file system uses a table to allocate storage of files on disks. This table-based file system is called the *File Allocation Table* (FAT). FAT uses storage space efficiently, although parts of a file may be scattered on the disk. It locates and chains together the parts of a file, as necessary, when the file is accessed. OS/2 2.0 comes with its own built-in version of FAT. It is an appropriate file system for a disk that has up to 60 megabytes (60M) of storage space—either a physical disk of that size or a disk partition of that size created by the user.

Both the OS/2 FAT and the DOS FAT file systems recognize file objects created by applications running either FAT file system because both work with the same structure of files and directories. What this means to the user, for example, is that if drive C is managed by FAT, the user can open either an OS/2 or a DOS command prompt to work with objects on FAT-managed drive A.

 A directory in FAT is the equivalent of a folder in the Workplace Shell.

Limiting Names to Eight Characters

Every file system has rules to follow for naming files. An important FAT rule is that you can give a file a name of up to eight characters plus, if you choose, a dot (period), and up to another three characters. TESTFILE.DOC, TEST06.DOC, or just TESTFILE are appropriate names. You can create extensions for your own files so that the file name is meaningful to you: for example, LETTER.SUE.

 A file with a file extension name of EXE, COM, CMD, or BAT is a special type of operating system or application file, whose name you should not change. If you do, the program might not run correctly.

Specifying Simple Attributes

The FAT file system maintains information about each file, including its current size, the date and time it was created, and the date and time it was last changed. You can see this information for the files in the directory you are working with by typing **DIR** at a DOS or OS/2 command line. In OS/2 2.0, you can select from a folder object's pop-up menu the **O**pen **S**ettings details choice to display these details about the object's files, as shown in figure 4.1.

Figure 4.1:

Details view of drive A.

Icon	Title	Size	Last write date	Last write time	Last access date	Last access time	Crea
	REXX	4,816	2-20-92	3:44:42 PM	0-0-80	12:00:00 AM	
	DOS	19,212	2-20-92	3:44:42 PM	0-0-80	12:00:00 AM	
	EGAFONT	23,604	2-20-92	3:44:40 PM	0-0-80	12:00:00 AM	
	SOFTERM	83,280	2-20-92	3:44:40 PM	0-0-80	12:00:00 AM	
	BIDI	32,380	2-20-92	3:44:36 PM	0-0-80	12:00:00 AM	
	EPM	46,700	2-20-92	3:44:34 PM	0-0-80	12:00:00 AM	
	WINENV	47,160	2-20-92	3:44:34 PM	0-0-80	12:00:00 AM	
	PMDIARY	58,508	2-20-92	3:44:28 PM	0-0-80	12:00:00 AM	
	FDISK	71,268	2-20-92	3:44:26 PM	0-0-80	12:00:00 AM	
	TIMES.BMP	95,076	2-20-92	3:44:24 PM	0-0-80	12:00:00 AM	
	LINK	07,884	2-20-92	3:44:22 PM	0-0-80	12:00:00 AM	
	REQUIRED	22,968	2-20-92	3:44:18 PM	0-0-80	12:00:00 AM	
	PMCHART	64,120	2-20-92	3:44:08 PM	0-0-80	12:00:00 AM	
	EA DATA. SF	2,048	3-20-92	10:33:42 AM	0-0-80	12:00:00 AM	
	WP ROOT. SF	224	3-20-92	10:33:32 AM	0-0-80	12:00:00 AM	

In addition, you can set the following simple attributes, or flags, for file or folder objects and directories:

- Read-only (can be read, but not changed)
- Archive (the commands BACKUP, RESTORE, COPY, AND XCOPY can be used)
- Hidden (will not be displayed)
- System (part of the operating system and should not be moved or renamed)

To change a file flag in the Workplace Shell, display the pop-up menu of the file object and select **O**pen **S**ettings. Then select the **F**ile tab from the settings notebook, as shown in figure 4.2. Click on the flag you want to set.

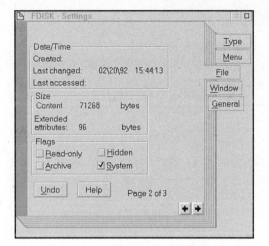

Figure 4.2:
File page in
settings notebook.

Using the High Performance File System

The High Performance File System (HPFS) comes as part of OS/2
2.0, but to activate it you must install it. Consequently, HPFS is
called an *installable file system*. HPFS uses high-speed buffer storage
(cache) to provide faster access than FAT does to large disks of more
than 60M of storage space. Up to 60M, FAT and HPFS are comparable in performance. If you have a 60M or larger hard disk or have
created a disk partition of at least that size, you should consider
installing HPFS.

HPFS has other advanced features, including multithreaded input
and output, strategic allocation of directory structures, and contiguous file allocation, which contribute to its high-performance
capability.

The directory structure of HPFS is different from that of FAT. DOS
cannot recognize objects created by HPFS-managed applications.
Consequently, if you start DOS from a disk or from a hard-disk
partition formatted with DOS, DOS does not recognize your other
disks formatted with HPFS. On the other hand, HPFS recognizes
objects created by FAT, which means HPFS drives do recognize
DOS-formatted drives.

Using Long File Names

When using HPFS, the length of file names is not limited to FAT's maximum of eight characters plus a three-character extension. You can have a file name of up to 254 characters, with any number of periods: for example, LETTER.TO.SUE.ABOUT.MY.VACATION.

Long file names are an advantage because you can assign more meaningful names to your files. This advantage, however, is not available for files that are created on disk drives or are transferred to disk drives. Disk drives can be managed only by FAT, which does not allow long file names. If you give a long name to a file on a disk drive, or if you transfer a long-named file to a disk drive, you receive a message saying that the file name is too long.

Applying Extended Attributes

HPFS can store much more information about a file than was previously possible. This information is called *extended attributes* (EAs). EAs can include file types such as icon or bit map, version, key phrases, notes, history, subject, and comments. EAs are used extensively in the Workplace Shell; OS/2 uses them to obtain additional information about objects, such as a description of the object's icon.

Users do not work directly with EAs; EAs are a tool for application developers. You can see some of the EA information, however, by opening a folder object in the details view. Figure 4.3 shows the details view of Drive C.

The file EADATA.SF in figure 4.3 shows that 829,440 bytes are taken up by EAs. You can only see the EADATA.SF file and its size when the partition has been formatted FAT, as in drive C in this example. With an HPFS partition, the extended attributes are stored with the individual files. Because FAT does not contain this capability, however, a FAT file system uses the EADATA.SF file to store the extended attribute. The space between "A." and "SF" makes it difficult to erase accidentally. As you can see, the details view shows a great deal more information than is available about files with a DOS DIR command. The columns of information display an outline of the icon of each object listed, its title on the desktop, its "real" name in the file system, its size, the date and time it was last changed, the date and time it was last accessed, the date and time it was created, and its flag.

Files can be flagged as *archive* (a saved copy for reference or recovery), *hidden* (not displayed in a directory tree or window), *read-only* (can be viewed, copied, or printed, but not changed), or *system* (part of the operating system).

Icon	Title	Real name	Size	Last write date	Last write time	Last access date	Last
▣	FALL'91.EXE	FALL'91.EXE	111,718	10-21-91	10:00:00 AM	0-0-80	
▤	OS2LDR	OS2LDR	30,720	2-18-92	2:13:48 PM	0-0-80	
▤	OS2LDR.MSG	OS2LDR.MSG	8,222	2-14-92	10:57:56 PM	0-0-80	
▤	HIMEM.SYS	HIMEM.SYS	11,304	5-1-90	3:00:00 AM	0-0-80	
▣	PRODIGY.BAT	PRODIGY.BAT	74	12-18-91	9:49:36 PM	0-0-80	
▤	AUTOEXEC.LZR	AUTOEXEC.LZR	54	11-15-91	3:28:38 PM	0-0-80	
▤	CONFIG.OLD	CONFIG.OLD	71	11-15-91	3:28:38 PM	0-0-80	
▤	WINA20.386	WINA20.386	9,349	5-9-91	12:00:00 PM	0-0-80	
▤	EA DATA. SF	EA DATA. SF	829,440	2-28-92	6:38:30 AM	0-0-80	
▣	IBMDOS.COM	IBMDOS.COM	37,378	5-9-91	12:00:00 PM	0-0-80	
▣	IBMBIO.COM	IBMBIO.COM	33,430	5-9-91	12:00:00 PM	0-0-80	

Drive C - Details View

Figure 4.3:
Details view of drive C.

Extended attributes can consume a significant amount of disk space. To see how much disk space is taken up by extended attributes in your OS/2 system, display the pop-up menu of the drive and click on Che**c**k disk, or open an OS/2 window or OS/2 full-screen session in the Command Prompts folder, and then type **CHKDSK**.

WARNING   Keep in mind that extended attributes can be lost if you transfer a file to a storage device managed by DOS or versions of OS/2 earlier than 1.2. Programs do not run correctly if they are transferred in this manner.

Using File Objects

Working with files in the object-oriented Workplace Shell means working with file objects. You can work with individual files or groups of files without having to know much about the organization of files or the file structure. If you use the pop-up menu of a data-file, such as a spreadsheet, you can change its settings, create another file with or without its contents, make it a template, move it, or delete it. A mouse or keyboard enables you to move a data-file object out of a folder onto the desktop or into another folder. You can create a folder, which then can contain files or other folders. You can move folder objects just as you do file objects. In addition, the Drives object displays the hierarchical structure of files and folders.

Seeing the File Structure

To see the file structure of the objects on the desktop, open the Drives folder in the OS/2 System folder (see fig. 4.4). When Drives is opened, you see an icon for each of the drives in your system: drive A, C, and so on.

Figure 4.4:

Contents of Drives folder.

For your convenience, a shadow of drive A is on your desktop at all times. When you want to copy files from or to drive A, you can use this shadow, instead of having to open the Drives folder.

To see how the files and folders on drive C are organized, open the drive C folder. By default, the file and folder objects are shown in a tree structure (see fig. 4.5). This format is similar to that in OS/2 1.3.

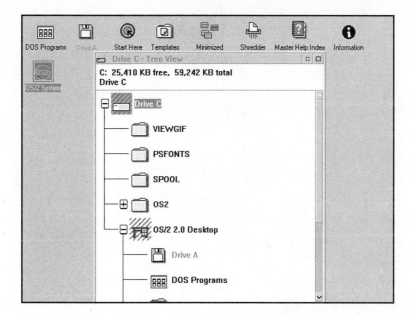

Figure 4.5:

Drive C tree structure.

The tree structure shows the hierarchical organization of the folders and the files inside the folders. A plus sign beside a folder means that other objects are inside it. Click on the icon to display the contents of the folder. A minus sign beside a folder means that all the objects inside it are displayed. By clicking on folder icons, you can collapse or expand the tree.

Navigating the File Structure

In the Workplace Shell, you can navigate the file structure by opening and closing objects in either the tree view or the icon view. Use expanded tree views to see the organization of files nested within folders within other folders, and so on. Icon view shows you one layer of objects at a time. To view the file structure of an entire drive, open the Drives folder, and then open the desired drive. Scroll up or down as necessary to find what you are looking for. To view the file structure of other objects, open them. You might have to enlarge the window to see all the file objects it contains, and then use **A**rrange to place the icons in an orderly fashion.

Using Find

Sometimes you cannot see a file or folder you want to work with because it is inside another object. In such cases, use Find. To start the Find process, right-click on a folder object to display a pop-up menu. Click on Find on the pop-up menu. The Find notebook page is displayed, as shown in figure 4.6.

Figure 4.6:

Find notebook page.

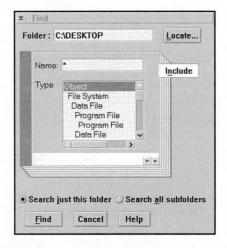

Fill in the necessary information on this notebook page, as follows:

1. If you know which folder the folder or file is in, you can type it in the Folder field or you can leave the default as drive C.

2. Click on Locate to display a notebook with tabs that you can use to specify where to start the search.

3. Fill in the Locate notebook page.

4. On the Find notebook page, type the name of the folder you are looking for in the Name field.

5. In the Type field, select the type of object you want to find.

6. Click on a radio button to specify whether to Search just this folder or to Search all subfolders.

7. Choose the Find button.

If you search only the current folder, Find creates a Find Results folder, which opens automatically on the desktop. If you search all subfolders, the Find Results folder displays the folders that contain the objects you are looking for.

Suppose you want to find all instances of the file COMMAND.COM on your C drive. The following steps enable you to find the file:

1. Open the pop-up menu of any window—for example, the Drives folder.

2. From the pop-up menu, select Find.

3. In the window that appears, click on the <u>L</u>ocate button on the top part of the window.

    A window that looks like the Settings notebook appears.

4. Click on the Path tab on that notebook.

    A field appears, labeled Enter physical path of desired location:, which prompts you for the path to search.

5. Enter **C:** and click on OK.

    The Locate window disappears, returning you to the Find window. <u>C:</u> appears in the Path field.

6. In the Name field, enter **COMMAND.COM**.

7. To search the entire drive, click on the Search <u>a</u>ll subfolders radio button, and then click on the <u>F</u>ind button.

    Eventually, a window appears, labeled Find results— COMMAND.COM—Icon view, which contains objects referring to all the COMMAND.COMs that it found.

Creating Folders and Files

In the Workplace Shell, folders and files are objects that perform in a consistent manner. You can create a new folder (sometimes called a *directory* in less graphical systems) in two ways:

- Display the pop-up menu of an existing folder and choose Create another. This action creates a folder with the same settings as the original.

- Drag a folder from the Templates folder. This action creates an empty folder, which you can then customize with settings.

These same techniques work for creating data file objects.

Copying Folders and Files

When you copy an object, the new object is a duplicate of the original, including its contents. To copy a folder, including the files and any folders it contains, follow these steps:

1. Right-click on the folder to display its pop-up menu.

2. Left-click on the Copy choice. The Copy notebook displays.

3. Select a tab corresponding to one of the following objects to which you want to copy:

   An open folder

   A related folder

   The desktop

   A drive

   A folder using a path statement

4. Fill in the fields on the appropriate notebook page.

Figure 4.7 shows the Copy notebook.

To copy an object to an open folder, follow these steps:

1. Type a new name on the Opened page.

2. Click on a folder shown on the page.

3. Click on the Copy button.

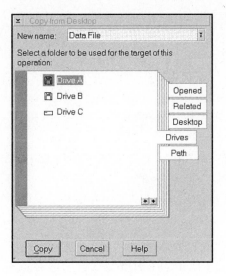

Figure 4.7:
Copy notebook.

To copy a folder or several folders from one drive to another, you can use the following dragging technique:

1. Open the Drives folder in the OS/2 System folder.

2. Open the drive object that contains the folders you want to copy.

3. Press and hold down the Ctrl key.

4. Left-click once on each folder.

5. Point to one of the highlighted folders.

6. Press and hold down the right mouse button and drag the folders to the appropriate drive object.

7. Drop the folders in the new location by releasing the mouse button.

The result of copying by dragging between drives is that copies of the original folders, including the contents, are in the new location.

These same techniques work for copying data file objects.

Moving Folders and Files

To move a folder or file object, you can either drag it with the mouse or use the object's pop-up menu.

The drag-and-drop technique is easiest when you can see the object and the place to which you want to move it. You may have to open some objects to use this technique.

When you have both the object you want to move and the destination in view, follow these steps:

1. Place the mouse pointer on the folder or file object.

2. Press and hold down the right mouse button and drag the object to the new location.

If you cannot see the folder or file object you want to move or the destination, you can use the Move choice from the object's pop-up menu. To do this, follow these steps:

1. Right-click on the folder to display its pop-up menu.

2. Left-click on the Move choice. The Move notebook displays.

3. Select a tab corresponding to one of the following objects to which you want to copy:

   An open folder

   A related folder

   The desktop

   A drive

   A folder using a path statement

4. Fill in the fields on the appropriate notebook page.

To move the object to an open folder, follow these steps:

1. Type a new name on the Opened page.

2. Click on a folder shown on the page.

3. Choose the Move button.

Deleting Folders and Files

To discard a folder or file object, you can either drag it to the Shredder or use the **D**elete choice from the object's pop-up menu. To drag a folder or file object to the Shredder, follow these steps:

1. Place the mouse pointer on the object.

2. Press and hold down the right mouse button.

3. Drag the object to the Shredder.

4. Release the mouse button to drop the object on the Shredder.

A window appears that asks you to confirm that you want to delete the object, unless you have previously changed the confirmation setting so that confirmations do not appear. Remember that the deletion is immediate. The Shredder cannot hold discarded objects. For this reason, make sure you want to discard an object before you click on OK.

To use **D**elete on the pop-up menu, follow these steps:

1. Place the mouse pointer on the object you want to delete.

2. Right-click on the object. The pop-up menu displays.

3. Click on **D**elete. A confirmation window appears.

4. Confirm the deletion. The object is deleted.

Checking Free Disk Space

Occasionally, you might want to see how much storage space is left on a disk. This information is useful when you use applications with graphical user interfaces because they tend to take up a lot of space. To check free disk space in the Workplace Shell, open the windows shown in figure 4.8.

Follow these steps to check for free disk space:

1. Open the OS/2 System folder.

2. Open the Drives folder.

3. Place the mouse pointer on the drive you want to check.

4. Right-click on the drive to display the drive's pop-up menu.

5. Left-click on Chec**k** disk.

6. Click on the **C**heck button. The report displays.

Figure 4.8:

Sequence of windows to check for free disk space.

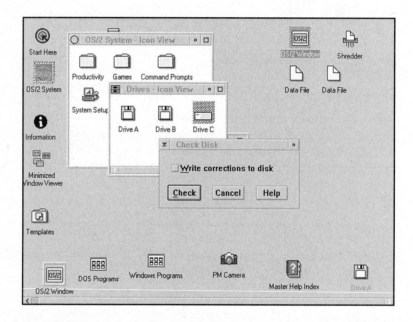

The report shows the type of file system on the disk, total disk space, space available on the disk, and current disk usage. The pie chart shows how much space on the disk is taken up by directories, user files, unusable areas, and extended attributes.

You can use this information to see whether enough storage space exists for an application you want to install on the disk.

Formatting Disks and Floppy Disks

To format a disk, follow the same steps as in checking disk space:

1. Open the OS/2 System folder.
2. Open the Drives folder.
3. Place the mouse pointer on the drive you want to format.
4. Right-click on the drive to display the drive's pop-up menu.
5. Left-click on Format disk.
6. Type a volume name (optional).
7. Click on the Format button.

The Format window is shown in figure 4.9.

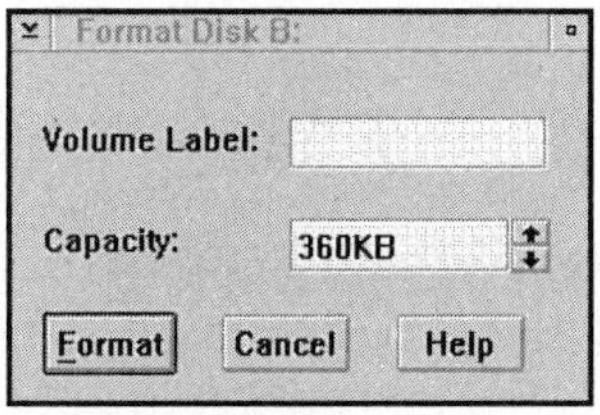

Figure 4.9:
Format window.

Because a shadow of drive A is always on the desktop, you can use a shortcut to format a disk on that drive. Follow these steps:

1. Put a disk in drive A.
2. Right-click on the Drive A object. The pop-up menu displays.
3. Left-click on Format disk.
4. Type a volume name (optional).
5. Click on the Format button.

Viewing File Contents

To view the contents of a data file, open the object by double-clicking on it or display the object's pop-up menu and choose **O**pen. If the file is associated with a program object, the program automatically starts when you open the file. If it is not associated with a program object, the file defaults to the System Editor, which starts when you double-click on the file. After the file opens, you can work with it as you wish.

 For more information on associating files with program objects, see Chapter 3.

You also can see the contents of a text file by using the command-line interface. See "Using TYPE To View the Contents of a File" later in this chapter.

Making Your Desktop More Useful

The following list contains suggestions to make your desktop more organized.

- **Use the small icons**. The icons that come with OS/2 applications are attractive and well-designed, but they take up a lot of space. Even the half-dozen icons that appear on your OS/2 desktop when you first install the system take up half the screen.

  Every object has large and small icons. You can tell your system to use the small icons by opening up the Settings notebook for the Desktop. On the first page of the Settings notebook, you see an option window labeled Icon display, which offers Normal size, Small size, and (perhaps grayed out) Invisible. This is a dynamic setting—click on Small size and the desktop changes; click on Normal and it changes back.

- **Flow the desktop**. In the Desktop Settings notebook, notice the area labeled Format. The options are Flowed, Non-flowed, and Non-grid. Click on Flowed; your icons then line up top-to-bottom on the left-hand side of your screen. If you keep your desktop in the small icons/flowed mode, it is much easier to work with.

- **Keep drive C opened, yet hidden**. Because opening up the C drive object takes time, it can be helpful to choose Shut down from the Desktop pop-up menu and leave the drive C object open. Then, the drive C object opens automatically the next time you start up your system. One disadvantage is that this procedure slows down the boot process a bit (OS/2 booting is so slow that you are probably used to getting a cup of coffee while the system starts).

- **Create a folder with the things you use most often**. It is often helpful to create a folder that contains the "stuff" you use most often—for example, the clock, the word processor, the system editor, Pulse, the Windows desktop, and so on—and keep it on the Desktop. (You can put the rest of the folders into a folder called Stuff, or some such). There are then fewer things visible on the desktop.

Using the Command-Line Interface

Occasionally you might want to use OS/2 2.0's command-line interface rather than the Workplace Shell.

To access a command prompt, follow these steps:

1. Open the OS/2 System icon.

2. Open the Command Prompts icon.

3. Open the icon for the command prompt you want.

The choices are shown in figure 4.10.

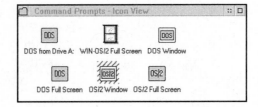

The Command Prompts window displays objects you open to use
command-line interfaces. Use DOS from Drive A to start DOS
versions from 3.0 to 5.0 from a DOS startup floppy disk. Use WIN-
OS/2 Full Screen to start a full-screen session in which you can run
multiple Windows programs in windows. Open DOS Window to
display the DOS command line in a window, or DOS Full Screen to
display the DOS command line in a full-screen session. Open OS/2
Window to display the OS/2 command line in a window or OS/2
Full Screen to display the OS/2 command line in a full-screen
session. You can open multiple instances of each of these command
prompts.

Using DIR To View File Structures

DIR is short for *directory*. The command shows the structure of the
files and directories (folders) in the specified part of the file system.
The OS/2 DIR command is equivalent to the same command under
DOS.

To view the file structure of a drive, follow these steps:

1. On the desktop, open the OS/2 System folder by double-
   clicking on its icon or by displaying its pop-up menu and then
   selecting <u>O</u>pen.

2. Open the Command Prompts folder.

3. Open an OS/2 Full Screen session.

4. At the command line, type **DIR** and press Enter.

If the list is too long to fit on one screen, add the **/P** switch to the **DIR** command to have the system pause when the screen is full. To continue, press any key and another screen displays.

The file structure of a hard disk resembles the file structure in figure 4.11.

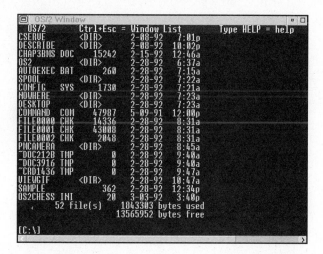

Figure 4.11:

File structure of hard disk.

Some files are listed individually. Others are in directories. Directories are marked (DIR). Other information includes sizes of files (but not directories), date and time of the last modification, number of bytes stored for a particular drive or directory, and number of free bytes.

To display this information for one file, type **DIR** *filename* or **DIR** *directoryname**filename* and press Enter.

To display this information for a group of files with similar names, use the asterisk (*) wild card in the generic file name. To display information for files in the current drive or directory that start with CHAP, type **DIR CHAP*** and press Enter.

To see the file structure of a drive without switching to it, type the letter of the drive, followed by a colon, and press Enter. If, for example, drive C is current and you want to see the contents of drive A, type **DIR A:** on the command line and press Enter. The contents of drive A display.

You can use the /O option to sort the contents of a directory list in one of several ways:

/ON	Alphabetizes by file name
/O-N	Reverse-alphabetizes by file name
/OE	Alphabetizes by three-character file name extension
/O-E	Reverse-alphabetizes by file name extension
/OD	Sorts by date, oldest first
/O-D	Sorts by date, most recent first
/OS	Sorts by file size, smallest first
/O-S	Sorts by file size, largest first

For example, to sort a directory by date with the most recent file first, type **DIR /O-D** and press Enter.

You can display files in a directory with the attributes you specify using the /A option, as follows:

/AH	Hidden files
/AS	System files
/AA	Files ready for archiving
/AR	Read-only files

To display hidden files in a directory, for example, type **DIR /AH** and press Enter.

Using MD To Create New Directories

In the command-line interface, a directory is the equivalent of a folder in the Workplace Shell. If you create a folder in the Shell, it appears as a directory in the command-line interface and vice versa. The purpose of a directory or folder is to keep together a group of related files.

To create a new directory, use the MD command (for Make Directory). For example, to create a directory named DIRECTORYNAME at the command line type **MD DIRECTORYNAME** and press Enter.

 Remember that the FAT file system allows file and directory names of up to eight characters only. If the drive you are using is formatted with HPFS rather than FAT, you can use up to 254 characters in a file or directory name.

Using CD To Navigate the File Structure

To move from directory to directory within the file system, use the CD command (for Change Directory). To go to a directory named CHARTS, for example, type **CD CHARTS** and press Enter. Keep in mind, however, that this process works only if the directory you want to access is the next level down in the file structure.

If the directory CHARTS is the next level up, change to CHARTS by typing CD followed by two dots (**CD..**).

If you are uncertain whether you need to go up or down in the file structure, you can always type the full path. In the preceding example, you typed **CD C:\DRAW\CHARTS**.

Using TYPE To View the Contents of a File

To see the contents of a file, use the TYPE command and follow these steps:

1. Open the Command Prompts folder in the OS/2 System folder.

2. Open an OS/2 or DOS window, as appropriate.

3. Use CD to move to the directory for the location of the file.

4. Type **TYPE** *filename* and press Enter.

In a DOS window, the text in the file is scrolled on the screen. In an OS/2 window, you can use the mouse to scroll the contents.

 TYPE enables you to view files only; you cannot work with their contents.

Using COPY and XCOPY To Copy Files

You can use the COPY command to copy a file or a group of similarly named files. The XCOPY command enables you to copy groups of files, including subdirectories. When you use XCOPY, you do not have to create a new directory at the destination: XCOPY does it for you. XCOPY is faster than the COPY command because it copies 64K of information at a time.

Using COPY

To copy a file from a directory to another directory, type the command, the path to the destination, and the file name. If the file you want to copy is in the CHARTS directory on drive C and this directory is current, enter the following command to copy the file CHART1 to disk drive A:

```
COPY CHART1 A:
```

If the CHARTS directory is not the current directory, enter the following command:

```
COPY C:\CHARTS\CHART1 A:
```

To copy all files beginning with "chart" in the CHARTS directory to drive A, enter the following:

```
COPY C:\DRAW\CHARTS\CHART* A:
```

If a CHARTS directory exists on drive A, and you want to copy all the charts to it, enter the following:

```
COPY C:\DRAW\CHARTS\CHART* A:\CHARTS
```

If you want to give the copied file a new name, include the new name in the COPY command. For example, enter the following:

```
COPY C:\DRAW\CHARTS\CHART1 A:\CHARTS\NEWCHART
```

Using XCOPY

To copy a directory and all of its files, type the command followed by the destination. For example, to copy the DRAW directory with all the files in it to drive A, type the following:

```
C:\DRAW XCOPY A:
```

If you are in the DRAW directory when you issue the command, enter the following:

```
XCOPY A:
```

To copy a directory and all of its subdirectories, add the /S switch to the XCOPY command, as follows:

```
XCOPY /S
```

To copy extended attributes of files (important in OS/2 2.0), add the /F switch to the XCOPY command, as follows:

```
XCOPY /F
```

For more information about XCOPY, see the OS/2 2.0 Command Reference. If you install the Command Reference (and you have not moved it), XCOPY information is in the Information folder. If you did not install it, you can add it at any time. Use the Selective Install object in the System Setup folder.

Deleting Files Using ERASE and DEL

You can use either ERASE or DEL (for DELETE) to discard files you do not need. Type **ERASE** or **DEL** and the name of the file.

To discard all files in a directory, type ERASE or DEL followed by two wild-card characters (asterisks) in place of the file name, as in **ERASE *.***.

The operating system asks you to confirm that you want to discard all files before carrying out your command. Respond to the "Are you sure?" question by typing **Y** or **N**.

Recovering Deleted Files

Occasionally, you can recover files you have mistakenly deleted or erased by using the UNDELETE command. An environmental variable, DELDIR, delays the removal of a file, which gives you the opportunity to retrieve a file before it is permanently deleted. DELDIR defines the path and maximum size of directories used to store deleted files. One DELDIR directory is specified for each drive and partition on your system. When you issue a **DEL** or **ERASE** command (or use the Shredder in the Workplace Shell), the folder or file is copied to the DELDIR directory for that drive. When you issue the **UNDELETE** command, the file is restored to its original location (path).

The syntax for the DELDIR statement in the CONFIG.SYS file is as follows:

```
SET DELDIR = drive:\path, maxsize; drive2:\path, maxsize
```

If DELDIR does not work correctly, check the CONFIG.SYS file to be sure it is written correctly.

If the deleted files exceed the specified maximum size, the excess is immediately deleted from the directory. If a REM statement is at the beginning of the DELDIR statement, erase REM so that you can use UNDELETE.

To recover a file, follow this form when typing the UNDELETE command on the command line in an OS/2 or DOS window or full-screen session:

```
UNDELETE drive:\path\filename
```

Drive and *path* specify the original location.

The following options are available with UNDELETE:

- **/L.** Lists recoverable files
- **/S.** Includes all files in the specified directory and all subdirectories
- **/A.** Recovers all deleted files
- **/F.** Removes files permanently (they cannot be recovered)

Defragmenting Files

Over a period of time, information on your hard disk tends to become fragmented; that is, parts of files are scattered on the disk. If you notice that the disk drive is taking a longer time than usual to read files from or write files back to the disk, you may want to speed up performance by reformatting the disk. Reformat the disk only if you suspect severe fragmentation because reformatting can take several hours. You first must back up your files so you can restore them to the disk after you have reformatted it.

To reformat a disk, use the FORMAT command and specify whether to format the disk for HPFS or FAT. To format drive D for HPFS, for example, type the following and press Enter:

```
FORMAT D: /FS:HPFS.
```

Another way to reformat is to use a software program that defragments the disk (see Chapter 11).

Monitoring Free Disk Space

You can find how much free disk space you have by using the CHKDSK command at a DOS or OS/2 command line. This might be important when you are considering adding an application. Find out the memory requirements of the application and how much is available in your computer before beginning installation of any application.

Backing Up Information

You might want to make backup copies of the information on your hard disk in case the original is lost or damaged. You must back up your data files before you install or reinstall OS/2 or reformat a disk. You also might want to back up some applications.

If you need to back up only some of your directories, you might want to use the XCOPY command instead of BACKUP. XCOPY is fast and flexible. You can directly access files backed up by XCOPY and select only those you want to work with. With BACKUP, you cannot access files directly. In fact, you cannot even see a list of them. BACKUP creates two files, BACKUP, which contains all backed-up files, and CONTROL, which saves paths, file names, and other information. When you are ready to copy your backed-up information to a disk, use the RESTORE command. RESTORE puts the information on the disk as it was originally.

If you are going to use BACKUP to back up your information to disks, you need several disks, and you must label and use them sequentially. When you use RESTORE to put the information on a disk, RESTORE asks you to insert the disks in the same order.

BACKUP cannot back up the COMMAND.COM and CMD.EXE system files, hidden system files, read-only files, or open dynamic link library (DLL) files. To save extended attributes, you must use an OS/2 command prompt to perform the backup.

You can use BACKUP to back up a single file or any group of files you specify. For example, to back up all the files in the Windows directory and all subdirectories to disks in drive A, type the following and press Enter:

```
BACKUP C:\WINDOWS\*.* A: /S.
```

To restore the Windows directory and all subdirectories on disks in drive A to the C drive, type the following, and press Enter:

```
RESTORE A:\WINDOWS\*.* C: /S.
```

For more information about BACKUP, see Appendix A.

Summary

This chapter described the two OS/2 2.0 file systems, FAT and HPFS, and compared their capabilities and features so that you can decide which to install on a hard disk. The techniques to manipulate the OS/2 2.0 file system objects (folders and data-file objects) were discussed. These techniques include using Find; creating, copying, moving, and deleting objects; checking free disk space; formatting disks; and viewing file contents. Similar topics were covered from the viewpoint of using the command-line interface instead of the Workplace Shell, including how to use some common commands.

II

Doing Business with OS/2

OS/2 Mini-Applications

OS/2 and DOS Programs

Running Windows Programs Under OS/2

A Sampling of OS/2 Applications

Working Smarter with OS/2

OS/2 Connectivity

OS/2 Mini-Applications

After you have become familiar with the new desktop metaphor and have a basic understanding of navigation, you are ready to begin exploring. In the last chapter, you viewed and started programs from icons. You also learned to open folders by double-clicking on an icon. OS/2 has a surprise for those who have used prior versions of the operating system. Included with this new release are some new and exciting "mini" programs called *applets*.

These applets, which are included free with OS/2 2.0, include general productivity programs and games. They are not intended to replace commercial full-featured programs, but sometimes a simple applet may be all that is needed.

 Although OS/2 applets were not found in prior versions of OS/2, you may be familiar with Microsoft Windows' mini-applications and games such as Write, Terminal, and Cardfile.

OS/2 version 2.0 is the first complete IBM version of OS/2 (prior versions were from IBM and Microsoft). The task for IBM's OS/2 is to expand on the idea of mini-applications and to provide more productivity-oriented applets. This expansion is necessary to position OS/2 as superior to Windows, instead of just a copy of it.

Although OS/2's applets are more robust than Windows' applets, games have not been forgotten. Games are still included and can be found in a folder called Games.

To access these productivity applets and the Games folder, open the OS/2 System folder by locating its icon (usually located at the top of the desktop). Figure 5.1 shows the OS/2 System folder icon with the mouse pointer next to it. After opening the OS/2 System folder by double-clicking with the left mouse button, the contents appear in a small window. This window contains the productivity, games, startup, command prompts, drives, and system set-up icons. Folders can contain many different objects including program and data icons, as well as additional folders.

Figure 5.1:

Choosing the
OS/2 System
folder icon.

Using OS/2 Productivity Applets

To view the OS/2 productivity applets, open the Productivity folder. To do this, select the Productivity icon by double-clicking on it with the left mouse button. A new window or folder opens, showing all the productivity applets included. Notice that several applets are included, which can be placed into three distinct groups: basic productivity applets, time-management applets, and utility applets. The following sections discuss these groups.

Understanding Basic Productivity Applets

The applets included in the basic productivity applet suite are PM Chart, PM Spreadsheet, PM Calculator, PM Database, PM Notepad, PM Sticky Pad, and PM Terminal. The new enhanced editor can be considered a basic business applet as a word processor, but it is included in the utilities section due to its limited feature set.

The letters *PM* stand for *Presentation Manager*, which is the interface used by OS/2 and is discussed in Chapter 1 and Chapter 2. The applets take advantage of the Presentation Manager; they should simulate typical functions you do at your desk. The applets may be shown in any order in the Productivity folder. If you are new to OS/2, start with a more familiar type of applet such as the PM Calculator.

PM Calculator

The first applet you may want to try is PM Calculator (hereafter referred to as Calculator), which is similar to a hand-held calculator. To start Calculator, double-click on the Calculator icon with the left mouse button. After a moment, the PM Calculator applet appears on the screen in a new window.

Notice the similarities to your calculator, including the key layout. In fact, only a few minor differences exist between the calculators. The first difference is that, by using Calculator, you can enter numbers in two ways (by pressing the keys on your keypad and by selecting numbers with the mouse). Another difference is the *paper tape*, which "prints" a record of the calculations. The *constant memory register* shows the current value of all your calculations. This is different from a hand-held calculator, which only shows the value after each command is executed. If you press the plus key (+) on a hand-held calculator, the total disappears and an entry screen appears. PM Calculator uses the paper tape for this and has a separate window that always shows your current total.

To enter figures into Calculator by using the keyboard, press the keys on the numeric keypad. If nothing happens, check to see that Num Lock is on. Notice the numbers appearing on the *tally roll* (tape). To add this number to another number, either click on the plus key or press the plus key on your keyboard. This inserts a new line with a plus sign at the left of the display. The plus sign indicates that the next number will be added to the number above. You can continue adding numbers in this manner, even after the numbers go off the screen.

As is the case with a paper tape, you can review all previous numbers and functions by using the scroll bar, which enables you to move from the beginning to the end of the tally roll. This is helpful when using Calculator to add long series of numbers, and it is intended to be an audit trail of your work. The tally roll can also be printed by selecting <u>T</u>ally from the menu bar and by selecting <u>P</u>rint from the pull-down menu.

An important feature of Calculator is its shutdown command, which closes all applications and applets, turns off your computer, and automatically saves the amount until the next time you start the Calculator. (Other OS/2 professional applications have this feature as well.)

Other functions, such as those that determine colors and font size are accessed from the <u>C</u>ustomize menu. It is probably a good idea not to change the font size—it is preset, based on the type of display adapter you have. Other font sizes can be chosen for larger or smaller windows and text. Remember that the font was set automatically during the install process. You can also customize colors to suit your taste. Experiment to see what you like best—colors can always be set back to their defaults.

Included with each applet is a help function, which can be selected from the menu bar. A product information selection also is available, which gives version and copyright information. Of special interest is key information. For example, you can print a list of the functions of Calculator keys (and their shortcut keys) from the <u>H</u>elp menu.

One problem with Calculator is that it cannot use cut-and-paste features with other PM applications and applets. Thus, once you have arrived at a value after entering several figures, you cannot copy that information to the Clipboard and then paste it into a word-processing document or other non-math application. Likewise, you cannot copy a value from an accounting package to the Clipboard and then paste it into the PM Calculator. These functions are reserved for more full-featured applications such as Lotus 1-2-3, Microsoft Excel, and Describe Word Processor.

PM Calculator is not a replacement for sophisticated calculators, such as those from Hewlett Packard, but it provides 90% of the important functions of most conventional calculators.

PM Sticky Pad

Another applet you can recognize by its icon is PM Sticky Pad (hereafter referred to as Sticky Pad). The equivalents on your desk are Post-it brand notes, which you use to write notes and then to peel off and attach to something. The major differences between conventional Post-it notes and Sticky Pad is that you use the mouse to peel and place *sticky notes*, and you stick these notes to objects on your desktop. These notes are then minimized to small icons and placed on objects or the desktop.

To create a sticky note, double-click on the Sticky Pad icon in the Productivity folder. The Sticky Pad applet appears in a window on your desktop. Sticky notes are always visible on the desktop, even if they are placed on a document. If you shut down your computer and then restart it, the sticky notes do not appear until you run the Sticky Pad program again. (This problem hopefully will be solved in a future release.) In any case, while Sticky Pad is running, it is always easy to locate and view reminders to yourself.

After the Sticky Pad applet is running, you can type in your message. The first thing you notice is that the time stamp is embedded on the first letter you type. This time stamp can be reset to the current time stamp by pressing Ctrl-T or by selecting Edit from the menu bar and then choosing Reset time stamp from the pull-down menu. Each sticky note can contain eight lines-by-29 characters, and a total of ten sticky notes can be placed at any one time. Each sticky note has an identifying number from zero to nine. While the sticky note is open, the word `sticky`, followed by the number, shows in the title bar. When it is minimized, only the number shows. If you delete a sticky note, that number is immediately available for the next sticky note to use.

Sticky Pad supports the following editing features: undo, cut, paste, clear line, clear note, delete line, insert line after, insert line before, reset time stamp, and graphics. All of these editing functions can be accessed by selecting Edit from the menu bar and then choosing the appropriate function. Accelerator keys are also available for most functions. These editing functions and accelerator keys are similar to the editing functions in the new enhanced editor, which is also included in the suite of applets.

You can print sticky notes by selecting Print from the menu bar. As mentioned earlier, Sticky Pad also supports copy-and-paste functions. Suppose you are reading something important in a document and you want to remember it. You can copy that information and put (paste) it on a sticky note. Likewise, you can take information from a sticky note and copy it to the Clipboard, locate a spot for it in another document or note, and then paste it in. The only limitation Sticky Pad imposes is that it only accepts text from the Clipboard. Graphics have to come from the 32 graphic symbols included with the applets.

To access and place a graphic symbol into your sticky note, select Edit from the menu bar, and then choose Graphics from the pull-down menu. A new window appears, showing the available graphic symbols. To include a graphic, select the graphic symbol you want and then click on the Select button, which places the graphic symbol at the previous position of your cursor. Remember that the copying-and-pasting capability supports text only, not graphics. If you try to copy a graphic symbol, you see strange letters instead.

The Customize option enables you to save the pad position, change the colors, change the font size, and specify to which corner the minimized sticky note will stick. The optimal font has been pre-selected for you. The minimized icons can be set to any corner of the current object or desktop (the default is the bottom left corner). To select a different corner, select Customize and then choose Icon. A pull-down menu appears with sections for bottom left, top left, top right, and bottom right. The last choice is Set default, which over-writes the bottom left default. Positioning can also be set by using Ctrl-1 for bottom left, Ctrl-2 for top left, Ctrl-3 for top right, and Ctrl-4 for bottom right.

PM Notepad

PM Notepad (hereafter referred to as Notepad) is another handy application that is included in OS/2 2.0's suite of applets. The Notepad, as indicated by its name, is the OS/2 implementation of the paper notepad on your desk. Instead of writing notes on paper, you can type them into the OS/2 Notepad. The primary function of Notepad is to simulate (and possibly replace) the paper notepad on your desk. Although Notepad is not a substitute for a word processor, it can be used for jotting down your thoughts quickly.

Notepad is different from Sticky Pad in several subtle ways. The important conceptual difference is that Sticky Pad is used as a reminder to yourself, and it can be placed on the desktop or on an object. These sticky pads are peeled off and placed in different locations like Post-it notes. Notepad, however, is a collection of information and ideas that are kept in a pad in one place.

There are limits to the amount of information that Notepad can store. It is 180 characters wide, 25 lines high, and five pages deep. The pages in the notepad are cascaded on the screen. To access the pages behind the front page, press Tab. You can go directly to a page by selecting it with the mouse, which swaps the current front page with the one you select.

You can also access other pages by selecting <u>V</u>iew from the menu bar, and then by choosing the page you want from the pull-down menu. Also available is the back page selection, which enables you to use Notepad without a mouse. (It is much more efficient to use the mouse, however.) After you have used the five pages, you cannot add additional pages. If you need more pages for additional data, consider using the System Editor or Enhanced Editor included in the OS/2 applets or your own word processor.

Notepads can be saved to the hard disk on your computer by using <u>F</u>ile <u>S</u>ave. These notepads can then be retrieved later for modification and review by using the open menu selections file, as you did with Sticky Pad. Like Sticky Pad, Notepad only supports text and the graphic symbols included with the applets. It also supports copying-and-pasting text between applications. This operation is the same as in other applications—all advanced graphical interfaces implement some sort of cut, copy, and paste capability.

The menu bar in Notepad is similar to that in other PM applications. The File menu selection enables you to open a new notepad, open an existing notepad file, and save the current notepad. Also available on the File menu is the Print selection, which enables you to print either the top page of the notepad or all pages.

In addition to the cut-and-paste functions previously mentioned, the Edit menu also supports line editing and graphics. The line functions include inserting a line before or after the current cursor position and deleting lines. Notepad also supports the same graphics symbols available to other applets. These graphic symbols can be inserted anywhere in a text letter; they add conceptual information to your sentences.

 Remember that graphic symbols cannot be copied to the Clipboard because it does not support them.

The View menu option enables you to move to other pages. The options from the pull-down menu are not the most efficient way to switch to other pages, but they are provided as an option. The Customize menu option enables you to change the default colors to suit your taste. As in Sticky Pad, the font for the notepad is already set, based on the display capabilities. You can change it, but the optimal viewing font has already been selected for you.

PM Spreadsheet

Software companies such as Lotus have made millions of dollars solely on spreadsheets. In fact, the number one use for PCs today is for electronic spreadsheets. OS/2 has included an applet called PM Spreadsheet (hereafter referred to as Spreadsheet). Of all the mainstream business applications, Spreadsheet attracts the most attention and is the most easily misunderstood. The temptation for professionals is to compare Spreadsheet to 1-2-3, Excel, and Quattro, which are professional strength spreadsheets. This is not a valid comparison because Spreadsheet is intended for light use and may serve to define what you look for in a professional spreadsheet (its inclusion in OS/2 is a great leap forward for operating systems).

You may find the functions in Spreadsheet sufficient for your needs. For instance, this spreadsheet is sufficient for simple sales reports and budgets. The function of a spreadsheet is similar to simple business journals and column-oriented math. What-if type calculations can also be accomplished with relative ease. The math functions are limited, but provide the base function.

 Spreadsheet has its own file format and does not import or export Lotus files (or any other common file formats) at this time.

Before you become discouraged by its lack of mainstream functions, remember that this spreadsheet is a free basic productivity applet, and it is not intended to compete or replace a professional spreadsheet. If it does not meet your needs, use its deficiencies to define your requirements for a more robust program. To help you understand its capabilities, consider a monthly budget project.

To create this spreadsheet (and to enter these or your own numbers), you must create a new file. To do this, start the Spreadsheet program by opening the System folder, then open the Productivity folder and double-click on the Spreadsheet icon. After a moment, the Spreadsheet applet appears in a new window. Select File from the menu bar and then choose Save as. Type in **budget.$$S**. Notice that the title bar now shows BUDGET - SPREADSHEET. Notice also the three fields at the top: Current Cell, Value, and Formula. The cursor should be flashing in the Value cell and the current cell should have A1 in it.

The spreadsheet has 26 columns (A through Z) across the top and 80 rows down (1 through 80). A1 indicates that you are in the upper leftmost row and column. A *cell* comprises a row and column coordinate. The data you enter in the Value cell is placed in this cell. You can move around the spreadsheet by using your mouse to select the cell directly or by pressing the arrow keys to move one cell at a time, vertically or horizontally. If you press Ctrl-Home, the cursor moves to the top left cell (or A1) of the spreadsheet.

In the Value cell, you can enter either words (labels) or numbers (values). If you need to enter formulas, use the Formula field (located below the Value field). For now, move your cursor to cell B1 by pressing the right arrow key or by selecting the cell directly with your mouse. The current cell field should now show B1. Type **January** in the Value field and press Enter. The word January should appear in cell B1, as shown in figure 5.2.

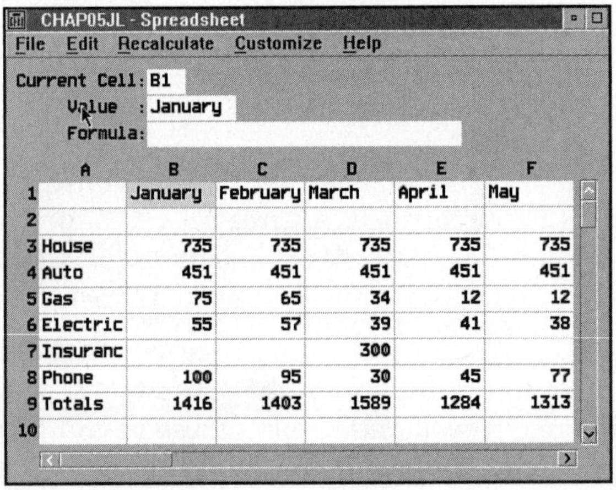

Figure 5.2:

Monthly budget spreadsheet, showing January in the Value field.

Move the cursor to cell C1 and enter **February**. Continue with cells D1 through F1. This should give you a row across the top showing January through May, as shown in figure 5.2.

Next, move your cursor to A3 and enter **House**. Continue moving down the left edge of the spreadsheet and enter **Auto**, **Gas**, **Electric**, **Insurance**, and **Phone**. Move the cursor to cell A9 and enter **Totals**. After each entry, you must either press Enter or select another cell. At this point, the months should appear across the top and the categories should appear down the left column. If not, go back and try the steps again.

To begin entering monthly figures into the cell, move the cursor to cell B3. Enter **735**. Numbers can be entered as whole numbers (such as 5) or as integers (such as 3.7 or 345.9212). Move to cell C3 and again enter **735**. Assume that this is the monthly amount—enter **735** in each cell on row 3. Move to cell B4 and enter **451**. Again, enter this same amount for February through May. Move to cell B5, which is the Gas line. For January (cell B5), enter **75**. For February (cell C5), enter **65**, and so on. Continue adding the information from figure 5.2 until you get down to the Totals column.

Place your cursor in cell B9. This time, instead of entering a number, enter a formula and let the spreadsheet do the math for you. This is the base function of a spreadsheet. You can then go to any cell, change the number, and the total changes to reflect the new total. If you have a sales application, this is useful for what-if applications.

To make the spreadsheet do math for you (recalculate), you must understand how to enter formulas. Enter formulas in the Formula field by selecting it with the mouse or by pressing Tab. Spreadsheet supports the basic math functions: addition (+), subtraction (–), multiplication (*), division (/), and area summation(@). You can use left and right brackets([]) to change the order of calculation. All formulas operate from left to right, meaning that 5+2*3 equals 21, not 11. To have the multiplication operate first, enter **5+[2*3]**, which yields 11.

In your budget application, add the figures in column B. This can be accomplished in two ways. First, move to cell B9 and make sure you are in the Formula field. Enter **B3+B4+B5+B6+B7+B8**, which places the value 1416 in cell B9 (assuming you used the numbers provided). If you enter your own numbers, you see the total of your numbers in cell B9.

The other way to accomplish the same thing is to enter **B3@B8** in cell B9. This formula is called *area summation*, and it says to sum the range or area from B3 to B8. (In Lotus, this formula reads +@sum(B3..B8); in Excel the same formula reads =sum(B3:B8).) The area summation is not limited to one row or column. To sum your first quarter expenses, move to an empty cell, tab to the Formula field and enter **B3@D8**, which yields the total of all expenses from January through March. In the case of the budget in figure 5.2, the formula yields 4408.

You can tell the spreadsheet when and how often to recalculate. You can also instruct the spreadsheet to calculate the current cell only or to recalculate all cells automatically. The Recalc current cell only option is more important with large spreadsheets that have long formulas.

To print your budget spreadsheet, select File from the menu bar. A pull-down menu appears, showing New, Open, Save, Print and Print formulas/cell data. Select Print to print your spreadsheet as it appears on your screen. If you want to print the formulas, select the Print formula/cell data from the pull-down menu. You can now save your work using the Save option. If you forget and try to close the spreadsheet, you are asked if you want to save the changes you have made.

As with the other applets, Spreadsheet offers cut-and-paste options from the Edit menu. Also included are Clear input line and a selection to place your cursor in cell A1. The Customize menu option functions as it does with the other applets. Selections also are available that enable you to change the colors, fonts, graphics, and screen size. (Again, the font setting should prove satisfactory in its current setting.)

A context-sensitive on-line help system is available, which includes a list of key assignments available from the Help menu. Spreadsheet provides the base functions required for entry-level spreadsheet use and is a welcome addition to the suite of basic productivity applets. The next applet, PM Database, is a general-purpose flat file database, which is simple to use and shares the same interface and menus you have learned from using the other applets.

PM Database

PM Database (hereafter referred to as Database) is straightforward and simple to use. The database shares most of the same menu options found in other applets. You should already know how to use most of the features. Like Spreadsheet, Database is not intended to replace full-featured third-party products like Paradox or dBASE (see fig. 5.3).

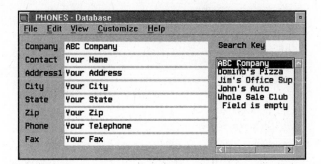

Figure 5.3:

Database screen.

This applet has a special feature suited for a common desktop function—a computer-based Rolodex. Although many uses are possible, Database's best use is for contact management. Even with the addition of a professional database, you still need the contact list and Rolodex combination capabilities of the PM Database. The feature that provides this capability is the *auto dialer*, which enables your computer to dial a number located somewhere in the current record.

The database also supports searching through all records by field for any word you type. Two views of your data are simultaneously supported. Viewing by records takes up the majority of the screen and shows all information pertaining to the current record. A smaller accelerator window is on the right side of the screen for moving quickly between records (see fig. 5.4).

Each record can contain eight fields—each having 30 characters. Database files are limited to 5000 records. As an introduction to the database, you create a computer-based Rolodex. You can store retrieval information for 5000 clients or contacts and keep eight pieces of information on each. If your needs exceed these limits, you may need a professional contact-management package such as Conductor Software's ACT package.

Figure 5.4:

View by fields and View by records.

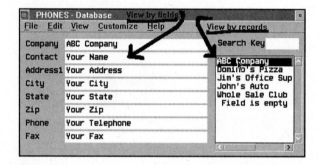

To begin the Rolodex project, start Database, which is located in the Productivity folder. Double-click on the Database icon. After a moment, the Database applet appears in a new window on your screen. The title bar shows the applet name Database. If a database file is open, the title bar also includes the file name.

To begin the Rolodex project, select New from the File menu. You now have an eight-field database file with no records. The field view area indicates field is empty. If any records with data exist, the field view area would show the contents of a field for each record.

All databases have one record at the start—the blank record you see when you begin. Again, this first record currently has no information in it (notice eight blank vertical fields in the record area). These fields comprise that first record.

Before you begin entering data, tour the menus. You have to define the types of information to be entered and tracked. To become comfortable with the database, review the options of the pull-down menus. The following main menu items should become familiar to you: File, Edit, View, Customize, and Help. Also available from the File pull-down menu are Open, Save, Dialing function, Print, and

Print list format. The options with trailing periods(..) indicate that additional information is required and you will be prompted for it. Each submenu is explored in greater detail.

The Edit pull-down menu offers the following choices: Restore record, Copy, Paste, Clear line, Clear all lines, Delete current record, cancel edit, Graphics, Edit line headings, and Add a new record. The View menu offers Lines 1-8, Display statistics report, and Print statistics report. The Customize menu has three choices: Dial setup, Colors, and Font size. The Help menu has the same options as in all the applets—context-sensitive help, key stroke shortcuts, and general OS/2 help.

The last portion of the screen is an area called the Search Key field, which is shown in figure 5.5. In this field, you can enter words or numbers you want to find.

Figure 5.5:
Search Key field.

Now you can begin your project. The first thing to do is to define the data you want to track. For a Rolodex project, use the following fields: Company, Contact, Address, City, State, Zip, Phone, and Fax. These are the line headings (maximum of eight characters) located at the left of the eight data fields allowed per record.

To add these new line headings to your database, select Edit line headings from the Edit menu. Your cursor is then placed in a white area to the left of the fields where you type in the eight-character line headings. Type **Company** and press Enter, to place your cursor on the next blank line. Type **Contact** and press Enter. Continue for all line headings.

After you have entered all line headings, your cursor stays in the Fax field. To save these changes, choose Save from the File menu.

You should now see the new line headings for each field. All of your database design work is done (you can still change the colors and font). Two other functions to configure are the dial setup and print list formats, which are discussed later.

The database is complete. You are viewing the first record, which is currently blank. To enter your first record, move the cursor to the Company field, enter **ABC Company**, and then press Enter. The entry is accepted, and your cursor moves to the Contact field. Continue entering information into the other fields until you get to the Phone field.

Remember that the same graphic symbols available to you in other applets are available to you in your database. If you intend to use the auto dialer, you must enter the number as you would dial it from your phone. For example, if the number is long distance, you need to enter a 1- and the area code before the number; if it is local, just enter the number as you normally dial it without an area code. After you enter the phone number and the fax number, your cursor remains in the Fax field.

No record is entered into your database until you save it to the database by selecting **S**ave or by pressing Ctrl-S. This fills in the first blank field.

 Do not delete this first record or your database may be destroyed. Use the **D**elete current record option from the Edit menu only if you have more than one record.

After you have saved the record, you still only have one record in your database. Notice that the field view area of the database now shows ABC Company. It does not show any other fields in the first record because the purpose of the field view is to show you a selected field of each record in your database. After additional records have been added, you will see other company names appear. You can change the field displayed in the field view by selecting the field by which you want to search from the **V**iew menu. For example, if you want to see all records by state in field view box, select **S**tate from the pull-down menu. The state you entered for company ABC appears.

For now, select the company name from the **V**iew menu. Adding additional records to your database is easy—first select **A**dd a new record from the **E**dit menu. Your screen now looks like the first record did when you entered information for ABC Company. Add the following records to your database:

Company

John's Auto
Domino's Pizza
Jim's Office Supply

Contact

John Wells
Driver
Jim Peterson

Address

123 Burn St.
2 East Main
34 Harding St.

City

Fort Wayne
Fort Wayne
Indianapolis

State

IN
IN
IN

Zip

46808
46825
46023

Phone

1-219-482-8656
422-7394
1-317-735-9659

Fax

1-219-483-3330
422-7393
1-317-735-9943

After you enter these into your database, you have five records. Notice that the names of the companies were automatically sorted for you by company name. To have the records sorted by contact name, select **C**ontact from the **V**iew menu. You now see the contact name for each record in the field view window. To understand how the search key field works, move your cursor to that field and begin typing the name **jo**. Did you notice that the cursor moved to Jim's Office Supply when you entered the j and then to John's Auto when you pressed the o? Match your results with those of figure 5.6.

Figure 5.6:

Sorting example for PM Database.

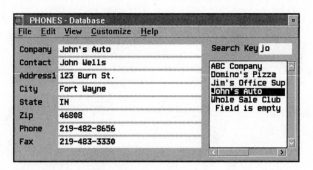

In this manner, you can search and find the record you are looking for by narrowing the list with each letter you type. This works for all other fields, including phone numbers. The Record view also changes as you narrow the list, giving you positive feedback on your searches. To print a list of your Rolodex, select **P**rint. There are two choices: Current Record Only and All Records. If you select All Records, the printout should appear as follows:

```
Database  : ROLODEX - 23:22:47 - 5 February 1992
Company : ABC Company
Contact    : Your Name
Address1  : Your Address
City         : Your City
State        : Your State
Zip          : Your Zip
Phone       : Your Telephone
Fax          : Your Fax

Company : Domino's Pizza
Contact    : Driver
Address1  : 2 East Main
City         : Fort Wayne
State        : IN
Zip          : 46825
Phone       : 422-7394
Fax          : 422-7393

Company : Jim's Office Supply
Contact    : Jim Peterson
Address1  : 34 Harding St
City         : Indianapolis
State        : IN
Zip          : 46023
Phone       : 1-317-735-9659
Fax          : 1-317-735-9943

Company : John's Auto
Contact    : John Wells
Address1  : 123 Burn St
City         : Fort Wayne
State        : IN
Zip          : 46808
Phone       : 1-219-482-8656
Fax          : 1-219-483-3330
```

You can get a table-style printout of your information by selecting Print list format from the File menu (see fig. 5.7). Depending on the width of your printer, you can show one to eight fields on your report. Use the spin bars to report on company, contact, and phone.

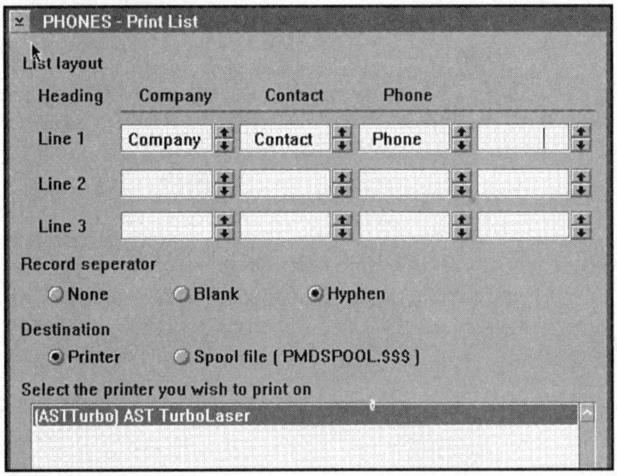

Figure 5.7:

Report menu for PM Database.

Your printout should look like the following:

Database: PHONES - 23:29:13 - 5 February 1992

Company	Contact	Phone
ABC Company	Your Name	Your Telephone
Domino's Pizza	Driver	422-7394
Jim's Office Supply	Jim Peterson	1-317-735-9659
John's Auto	John Wells	1-219-482-8656

Now that you have learned to create and print your Rolodex, it is time to set up the database to use the auto dial feature. This feature is only available if you have a modem attached to your computer on your serial port or if you have a modem inside your computer. The first thing you must know is the communications port (serial port) the modem is using. The database supports COM1 through COM4. You also must know the dial control text and hang up control text, which can be found in the modem manual. To set up this feature, choose **D**ial setup from the **C**ustomize menu. A new menu appears, as shown in figure 5.8.

Figure 5.8:
Dial Setup menu.

If your modem is connected to serial port 1, left-click on COM1. If you are not sure if you have a modem (or which port it is connected to), contact the place from whom you purchased your computer. If you are using a Hayes-compatible modem, type **ATDT** in the Dialing Control Text field. Next, type **+++ATH0** in the HangUp Control Text field. (The 0 is a zero, not the letter O.)

If you have a special asynchronous or non-Hayes compatible modem, refer to your user's manual for the correct strings. When you are finished, select the **S**et button. Your dialing functions are now set up.

To use the auto dialer, locate the record on your Rolodex and select **D**ialing Function from the **F**ile menu. A new menu pops up on your screen showing all numbers in the record. Study the numbers carefully—no line headings tell you which number is the telephone number. For instance, if you try to auto dial the phone number for Jim's Office Supply, four numbers appear (see fig. 5.9).

Figure 5.9:
Numbers found
for Autodialer.

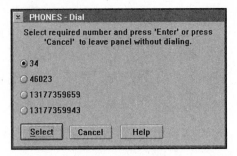

The third number is the phone number you want (13177359659). Select this number by clicking on the button next to it with your mouse. When you click on **S**elect, the database automatically begins dialing that number for you. Be sure you have a hand set ready to listen for the phone to ring. After you have verified that the phone is ringing, press Enter.

Be careful not to press Enter until you are sure the number has been completely dialed.

You will find many other uses for PM Database. Like Spreadsheet, it does a good job of meeting basic and simple application needs. They also are helpful for determining additional requirements you might have in a professional application. The auto dial feature found in the database is only one use for a modem. The addition of a modem opens vast new resources to your computer.

In addition to dialing numbers for you, the next applet, PM Terminal, enables your computer to communicate with other computers. This capability enables you to send files to and from other systems, and look up information not kept in your computer. You can get weather reports, read stock quotations, book airline reservations, send electronic mail, shop at Sears, and even play games with others across the country. To do these things, you need a communications package. The communications applet, Softerm, is a surprisingly sophisticated package.

PM Terminal

PM Terminal (Softerm) is a communications package that enables your computer to communicate over telephone lines by using a modem. Softerm is more advanced than the terminal package included with Windows—it is a full-featured communications package.

To launch this applet, double-click on its icon as you have done with the other applets. After the initial introduction screen disappears, the Softerm Session Manager screen appears, as shown in figure 5.10.

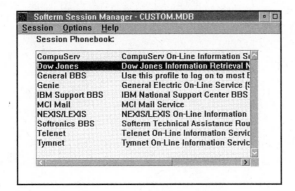

By using Softerm, you can enter a fictitious BBS and number and add it to Softerm. To add an entry into the Session Manager, select **A**dd from the file **s**ession menu. An Add Session input screen appears. Enter the information, as shown in figure 5.11.

If you do not have a Hayes 2400 section, you can add that later. Select **S**etup Profiles; the Setup Profiles window appears, as shown in figure 5.12.

If you are calling from an intercompany phone system, you may need to access the Telephone option to enter a prefix or suffix. If not, the only option you need is the Connection Path Profile Module, as shown if figure 5.13.

Figure 5.11:

Add Session input
screen.

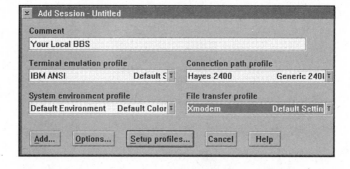

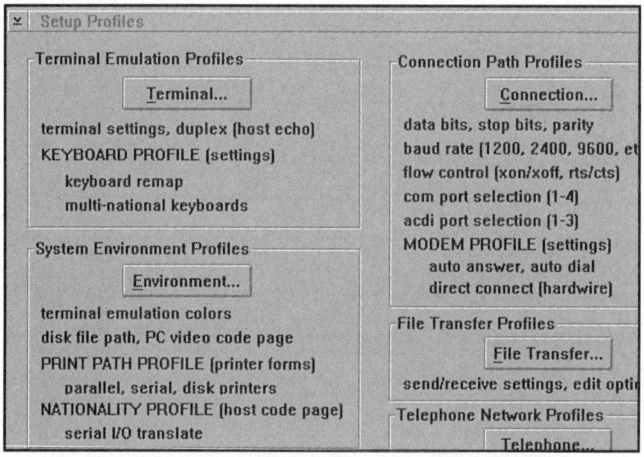

Figure 5.12:

Setup Profiles
window.

Figure 5.13:

Connection Path
Profile Module
screen.

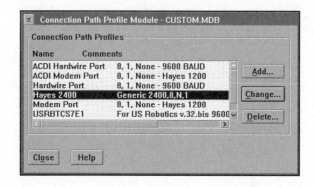

In this module the Hayes 2400 profile is set up for 2400 baud, 8 characters, 1 stop bit, and no parity. Select **A**dd and enter the above information into the prompts. Be sure to use COM1 or COM2, not the ACDI mode. Select Cl**o**se and then choose OK. The next pop-up window to appear is the Admittance Data dialog box, as shown in figure 5.14. The default data is a [CR]. By itself, this information alone will not dial the modem. Use the cursor to place the I bar in front of the [and enter **ATDT 123-4567**.

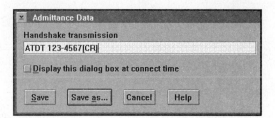

Figure 5.14:
Admittance Data dialog box.

ATDT is a Hayes command that represents ATtention Dial Tone; the number 123-4567 is a fictitious number. If you know the number of a local BBS number, insert it here. If you need to dial a long distance number, remember to use 1-AREA CODE before the number. When you save your work, the Softerm Session Manager window looks like figure 5.15.

To launch your new entry, double-click on the MyfirstBBS option. The Softerm communications window appears, as shown in figure 5.16.

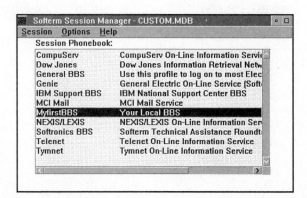

Figure 5.15:
Completed Softerm Session Manager window.

Figure 5.16:

Admittance Data
dialog box.

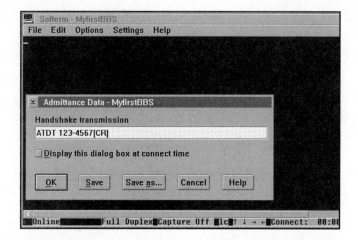

Select File from the main menu and choose the Dial option. The Admittance Data dialog box appears. You can press Enter to accept this dialing information. The number should dial (if you included a real number, you will connect with the BBS). The BBS describes what to do next (most of the time you need to press Enter after the connect message).

Logging on usually consists of giving your first and last name, and then entering a password. Some BBSs require you to have this approved ahead of time. You can create a number of these options in Softerm. Softerm supports a number of different protocols for sending and receiving files from the BBSs. After you instruct the BBS that you want to download (receive) a file and tell it what protocol you use (Xmodem), select Receive from the File menu. A new dialog box appears, as shown in figure 5.17.

The file is then transferred to your hard disk, to the specified directory and file name.

As you can see, Softerm has many options available, and it can be difficult to use the applet. Technical support on this product is available from the manufacturer. Like other OS/2 applications, Softerm can be run in the background. This means that while you are receiving a file in the background, you can do other work. If you intend to use modem communications, you may want to use a communications package that is easier to configure and use, such as ChipChat from Cawthon Software. You can also order a version of Softerm that is even more advanced.

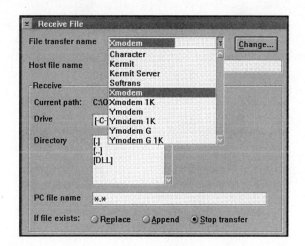

Figure 5.17:
Receive File dialog box.

PM Chart

PM Chart is not a simple applet—it is a limited version of a full-featured OS/2 PM application. PM Chart is available from Micrografx, Inc., a company known for its presentation products. Like Softerm, IBM has made arrangements with Micrografx to include this limited version of the product in the OS/2 applets.

PM Chart is used to create charts and other graphical presentations of your data. The types of data PM Chart accepts are the following: GRF (Micrografx Charisma Graphic), DAT (Micrografx Charisma Data), DRW (Micrografx Draw), DIF (Data Interchange Format), WRK (Lotus 123 version 1.*x*), SPC (Space Delimited ASCII), SLK (Microsoft Symbolic Link), XLS (Microsoft Excel) and WK1 (Lotus 1-2-3 version 2.*x*). DAT, DRW, and GRF files can be opened directly. DIF, SPC, SLK, WK!, WKS, and XLS files are imported and entered into the PM Chart spreadsheet.

The obvious omission is PM Spreadsheet data files, which is a minor limitation (Micrografx's product was not designed with PM Spreadsheet in mind). Charts in PM Charts can be saved in either GRF or DRW formats. For the PM Chart project of this book, you will use a Lotus 1-2-3 version 2.01 spreadsheet. (If you do not own this Lotus version, most other programs can export a *.WK1-compatible file. This chapter shows you how to create a 3-D graph of the budget spreadsheet created earlier in the PM Spreadsheet section. To start the PM Chart applet, open the Productivity folder and double-click on the PM Chart icon (see fig. 5.18).

Figure 5.18:

PM Chart icon.

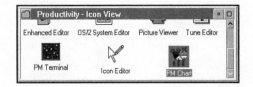

After a moment, the PM Chart applet starts as shown in figure 5.19.

Figure 5.19:

PM Chart begins.

After the title and copyright information displays, your screen should be blank. Before continuing this project, you should have created a spreadsheet in Lotus, as shown in figure 5.20.

Figure 5.20:

Spreadsheet in Lotus 1-2-3.

If you have not yet created the BUDGET.WK1 file, do so now by switching to DOS full screen and create this file in your favorite application. As in all applets, before you begin the project, it is important to become familiar with the basic menu selections. It is not the intent of this project to detail and exercise all options and features of this applet. The purpose is to introduce PM Chart and to guide you through the process of creating your first chart.

Under the File menu, the following options appear: New, Open, ClipArt, Save, Save as, Print, and Printer setup. Use the New option to begin a new chart; use the Open option to either open an existing chart or a data file that you want to import. The ClipArt menu selection enables you to import Micrografx clip art files not included with OS/2 (these clip art files can be purchased separately).

Use the Save option to save the current chart to your hard drive or a floppy disk. If your chart already has a name, it is saved under the default name and file format. If this is the first time you have saved your chart, the Save as function is initiated instead. This option prompts you for the place, file name, and file format (either GRF or DRW). The last two options enable you to print the chart and to select which printer to print to. When you choose Print, you are asked whether you want to print the current view, the first page, or all pages.

The Edit option has the following selections: Undo, Cut, Copy, Paste, Clear, Remove, Block Select, Select all, and Symbol name. The Undo, Cut, Copy, Paste and Clear functions are the same Clipboard functions found in most PM applications and applets, as well as in most Windows applications. Use the Remove option to remove currently selected objects or entire charts from the chart or all overlays. Block Select enables you to select a group of items using your mouse. Select all selects all the items on the current chart for manipulation. The last option, Symbol name, gives a name to the currently selected figure or text. When you name a symbol you can use it in the future as a clip art symbol. You can use this feature to create your own symbol library for use in future charts.

The next main menu option, **C**hange, offers new functions specific to PM Chart. These new options include: **A**lign, **C**ombine, **D**uplicate, **F**lip, Mo**v**e to, R**o**tate, S**m**ooth, U**n**smooth, and Color/**S**tyle. The **A**lign function offers control over the alignment and attachment to the current chart image. Use the **C**ombine function to make the currently selected group of objects one object or to ungroup previously grouped objects. Also supported is the grouping of symbols into one symbol for complex symbols; disconnecting these symbols is also enabled. The **D**uplicate function enables duplication of the currently selected object.

Use the **F**lip option to flip the currently selected object vertically or horizontally over an axis. The Mo**v**e to option moves the currently selected object to the front or back layer of objects on your chart. The R**o**tate function rotates the selected symbol on an axis. This is important if you want a symbol or text to be on a slant (or even upside down). The S**m**ooth and U**n**smooth options smooth (or unsmooth) the currently selected object. Color/**S**tyle enables the custom coloring of the chart and background. This option is also available from the toolbar.

The **P**references menu option varies from other applets included with OS/2, even though it shares the same name. It does not offer a screen font selection because this is a complete PM application that fully exploits the PM interface. Fonts are based on Presentation Manager, not on the display adapter as for other applets. Most of the applets are quick text to PM port; therefore, they are font-specific. Micrografx' applet was a PM applet from the ground up, and therefore relies on PM to manage its text displays.

The options on the **P**references menu are Cross**h**airs, Pa**g**es, Ru**l**ers/Grid, and Screen **c**olor. The Cross**h**airs option adds a vertical and horizontal line on your screen that intersects at the cursor, which helps to align the mouse for the placement of objects. The Pa**g**es option sets the page size, borders, and orientation. The Ru**l**ers/Grid option enables rulers to be placed along the top and left side of your screen. You can also create a line on the ruler to show the current cursor position. The **S**nap to rules function forces the cursor to move in intervals stipulated by the ruler, either in inches or centimeters. The grid is also configured here. Screen color sets the screen color.

The Help main menu option is the same as in all other applets. It offers the following suboptions: Help index, General Help, Using help, Keys help, and Product information. The Product information option is interesting: instead of having only version and copyright notification, Micrografx has included in it a group of advertisements. If you like PM Chart, for example, this is where you can find more information about the full-featured retail version, as well as other companion products from Micrografx.

The latest productivity enhancement that is included with most applications is a *toolbar*, which is a line of boxes with pictures that represent menu shortcuts. These are visual representations of a series of menu selections. The PM Chart toolbar is located along the left side of the screen, as shown in figure 5.21.

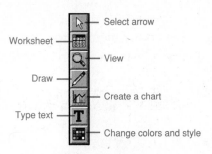

Figure 5.21:
PM Chart toolbar.

The select arrow is used to restore the cursor to an arrow if you are in another mode. The worksheet option is used to create or edit a worksheet you have imported (it is where you highlight the area of the spreadsheet you want to graph). The magnifying glass symbol represents the viewing options. When you select this option, a new toolbar extends horizontally to the right, enabling different views of your chart or charts.

The pencil represents the drawing functions. From a new toolbar, you can select box, circle, and line drawing tools. The chart option enables you to choose the type of chart you want to create. You can create line, bar, and pie charts. 3-D and other effects are supported. The capital T represents the text type. From this new toolbar, you are able to select style, size, and alignment. All normal text controls are available here, such as bold, italic, and so on. The last option is the colors and style option. With this basic tour of the menu and toolbar you are now ready to begin the following project.

The objective of this project is to chart the budget spreadsheet you created earlier. To begin, open the System folder and the Productivity folder. Start the PM Chart applet by double-clicking on its icon. The PM Chart applet starts and fills the entire screen. To have PM Chart import your BUDGET.WK1 spreadsheet, select File from the main menu and then choose Open. Use your mouse to select the data type WK1 and type BUDGET.WK1 in the path, as shown in figure 5.22.

The path assumes that the file BUDGET.WK1 is in the apps sub-directory of the OS/2 directory. If your budget spreadsheet is in a different directory, substitute the displayed path for the path where your file is located. Press the Open button. Your spreadsheet does not show on the screen. To view it, select the spreadsheet icon on the toolbar.

Figure 5.22:

Import options for PM Chart.

Another means of displaying the current spreadsheet in memory is to right click the mouse. Your spreadsheet appears with all data selected. Use your mouse to select cells A1 to F7. This highlights all months and the rows through Phone, as shown in figure 5.23.

*	A	B	C	D	E	F
1		January	February	March	April	May
2	House	735	735	735	735	735
3	Auto	451	451	451	451	451
4	Gas	75	65	34	12	12
5	Electric	55	57	39	41	38
6	Insurance			300		
7	Phone	100	95	30	45	77

Figure 5.23:
PM Chart spreadsheet showing highlighting.

Close this worksheet by double-clicking on the box in the upper left corner of the worksheet. Select the create a chart icon from the toolbar (the toolbar icon with the picture of a chart). A number of chart types appear in the new horizontal toolbar. For this exercise, select the first choice, the column chart. A new window opens, enabling you to add additional information about the chart you will create. Select the 3-D and legend boxes, and you see check marks appear verifying their selection. Now select New to place a new chart on the screen. Your chart should look like figure 5.24.

This chart is unreadable. To improve it, you need to move the legend to the upper right of the chart. To do this, move your mouse to the border of the legend and left-click. This adds small squares to the corners of the legend. To move the legend, move your mouse to the center of the legend and press and hold the left mouse button. Drag the legend to the upper right of the graph until you think you can see all columns in the spreadsheet. When you release the mouse button, the screen redraws the chart and all the data are present except the text along the bottom.

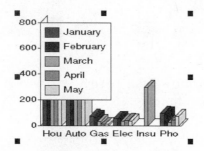

Figure 5.24:
Chart pasted from a Lotus spreadsheet.

To make room for all the text, the chart must be stretched horizontally. Notice that eight black filled boxes surround the chart. These are the *control points*. To reshape the chart, left-click on one of the points. Now drag the control to reshape and stretch the chart. Drag the left center control to the left and the right center control to the right. You should now be able to see all the text at the bottom.

The finishing touch for this project is to add a title to your chart. First, choose the style of letter you want by selecting the text option from the toolbar. A new window opens, offering a selection of typefaces. For the sake of conformity, select HELV and bold. The size should be set at 18. Next, select the text option from the toolbar again. This time, use the text insert option. The I bar now replaces the cursor. Move the I bar to the point where the title should begin. Left-click the mouse button to anchor the beginning point for your text. If you make a mistake, do not worry—you can move the text later by selecting it and dragging it to the desired location. Enter the following text: **1992 Budget Chart**. To end text insert mode, choose the select arrow from the toolbar. Your finished chart should look like the one in figure 5.25.

Figure 5.25:

Completed chart.

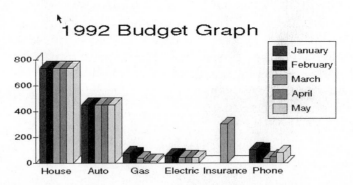

Many other options are available, such as coloring backgrounds, importing pictures, rotating objects, drawing tools, and others. You can experiment with these other features to enhance this chart. To save your chart, select Save **a**s, enter a name, and choose the graph type.

PM Chart is a powerful applet for which you will find many uses. Its inclusion in OS/2 increases the overall value of the operating system.

Understanding Time Management Applets

The time management applets can be put into one group. For the purposes of this chapter, a folder has been created and called Time Management. The following applet objects have been dragged out of the Productivity folder and placed into the new Time Management folder. The contents of this new folder are shown in figure 5.26.

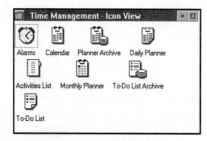

Figure 5.26:

Time Management folder contents.

From the contents of the folder, you can see why these applets are called the time management applets. Included is a daily journal, a monthly pert chart, a calendar view, an activities list, a To-Do list, and two applets used for archiving your completed tasks. With the exception of the To-Do List, all the applications are tied to a common database, which is created and updated through the Daily Planner (the primary application you work with in this section).

Because the Daily Planner is the program you use to enter information into the time database, all other time management applets are dependent on it and are fed information from it. The alarm clock is instructed when to go off by it; the monthly planner is nothing more than a month at a view of your Daily Planner, and so on. The only applet not affected by the Daily Planner is the To-Do list.

For the companion time management applets to get information from the Daily Planner, they must be instructed to use the same database. The database file uses the following naming convention: FILENAME.D. The project in this section uses the time management database name JWL.D. You can have as many separate databases as you like.

If you are using a network, you can keep a number of different database files in one location so that several users can view and update these database calendars. Although these applets are not multiuser networking applets, they are compatible with ones used by one person at a time. (This person can be anyone on the network with rights to that place on the file server.) For now, the assumption is that you will keep the database stored on your local machine.

PM Daily Planner

If you have not done so, open the folder called Time Management. If you did not create this folder and move the applets into it, open the Productivity folder and start from there. Once the Daily Planner has been launched, it appears blank, as shown in figure 5.27.

To use the Daily Planner and create the database file, choose **N**ew from the **F**ile menu. Enter the file name **JWL.D**.

Figure 5.27:

Blank Daily Planner.

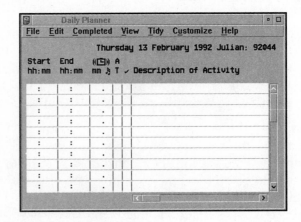

Seven options are on the menu bar: File, Edit, Completed, View, Tidy, Customize, and Help. The File option offers New, Open, Save, and Print. These options work the same as in all other applets.

The Edit menu has basic editing selections: Undo, Copy, Paste, Clear line and Clear all lines. In addition to these basic editing functions, some application-specific options are available: Activity type, Graphics, Select alarm tune, and Propagate/delete lines. The Activity type selection enables you to highlight or mark a line in a special way. The Graphics option enables you to place a graphic symbol to give additional visual feedback on the purpose of a meeting. Select alarm tune specifies the alarm tune that plays when this time entry occurs. The last edit menu option is Propagate/ Delete lines. Consider the following task: you have a branch meeting every Thursday at 8:00 am. It is time-consuming to type in this meeting every Thursday. Instead, highlight the item to duplicate to other weeks (propagate), and then select the option from the Edit menu. A new window appears (see fig. 5.28).

Select Daily and check Thursday. Make sure the Number of times to perform action field has a value of 10 or higher and that Propagate is selected (Delete removes these entries). You can use this capability for any recurring activity.

Another handy feature is the biweekly feature. If you are paid every two weeks, for example, you can enter your pay date, propagate it weekly, and select every two weeks. To enter this for a whole year, propagate it 52 times.

The next main menu selection is the Completed menu option, which gives you marking and archiving capabilities. From this menu, you can mark a line as complete, unmark lines, add lines to archives, and delete completed lines. The options on the completed menu are the following: Mark line as completed, Mark line and add to archive, Add line to archive then delete, Unmark line as completed, Mark all lines as completed, Mark all lines and archive, Mark all lines, archive then delete, Unmark all lines as completed, Archive all completed lines, and Archive all completed lines then delete. These options offer a good definition of their functions. Keep in mind that any archived entry can be revealed and restored.

The <u>V</u>iew menu option has four submenu selections: <u>V</u>iew complete entry, Ne<u>x</u>t day, <u>P</u>revious day, and Return to <u>t</u>oday. These entries offer ways to switch the days you want to view or edit.

The next menu is <u>T</u>idy. As you may have guessed, this menu is used to "tidy up" your planner by removing unwanted entries. Its four selections are: <u>D</u>elete all earlier entries, D<u>e</u>lete completed earlier entries, <u>A</u>rchive then delete all earlier entries, and A<u>r</u>chive then delete completed earlier entries.

The last two main menu selections are the same as in the other applets. <u>C</u>ustomize offers colors and font size; <u>H</u>elp offers the standard help submenus.

As a planner, suppose you are in an office environment and that you are a busy executive who goes from meeting to meeting. You will create a planner database file to be shared by the other time applets, called JWL.D.

If you have been following this chapter with your computer, you should already have the PM Daily Planner open (and the file name JWL.D). This file is the sole link between all the time management applets. If you enter an appointment into the Daily Planner, it is automatically updated to the other applets when you save the last changes to the PM Daily Planner file JWL.D.

For this exercise, suppose that today's date is Monday, February 17, 1992. Figure 5.29 shows your busy schedule. To start, enter the information as shown in the figure (be sure to add a zero prefix to single-digit hours). The mm field indicates the number of minutes before the appointment that the alarm clock will notify you (for this project, five minutes is used). Allow more time when necessary. The tune icon specifies which tune plays at the alarm time (use one for all alarms in this project). The check mark indicates completed appointments or tasks. The description is scrollable—more information is available than can be viewed at one time.

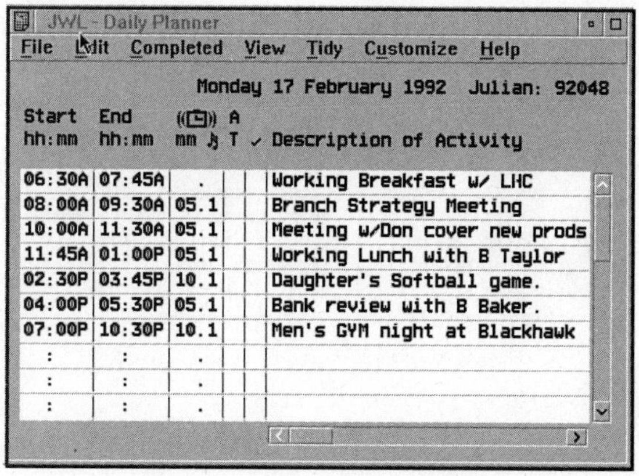

Figure 5.29:

Daily Planner for Monday, February 17, 1992.

Feel free to use the sample descriptions provided or to specify your own. After you have completed this day's entries, save your work. Next, select Day from the main menu view selection. A new blank daily worksheet appears. Enter the appointments for the next day (shown in fig. 5.30).

The final day for this project is Wednesday, February 19, 1992. Enter the information in figure 5.31 after saving the information from the previous day.

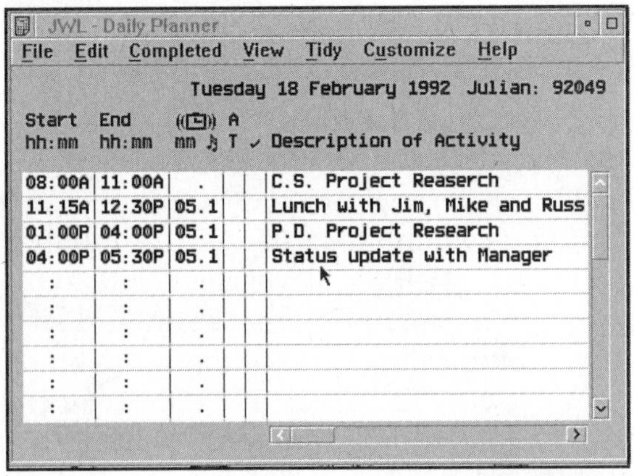

Figure 5.30:

Figure 5.30:

Daily Planner for Tuesday, February 18, 1992.

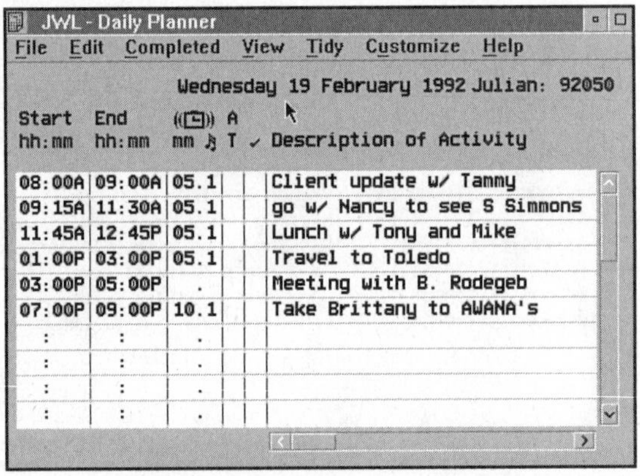

Figure 5.31:

Daily Planner for Wednesday, February 19, 1992.

Notice that the Monday branch meeting is a weekly meeting. You can use the Propagate option to indicate a weekly occurrence for the Monday morning meeting. You can also print a daily schedule by using the quick report menu in Daily Planner. To print out today's activities, choose Print from the File menu. Set the number of days to 1 for this report. When your report prints out, it looks similar to the following:

Daily Planner - JWL - - 20:30:12 - 16 February 1992

17 February 1992 Monday	06:30A	07:45A			Working Breakfast w/ LHC
	08:00A	09:30A	05	1	Branch Strategy Meeting
	10:00A	11:30A	05	1	Meeting w/Don - new prods
	11:45A	01:00P	05	1	Working Lunch with B Taylor
	02:30P	03:45P	10	1	Daughter's Softball game
	04:00P	05:30P	05	1	Bank review with B Baker
	07:00P	10:30P	10	1	Men's GYM night - Blackhawk

If you need to remove or mark an appointment, remember to select that time slot first and then choose an option from the Completed or Tidy menus. For now, leave the appointments as entered.

 The Alarm does not have any of the appointments or alarms you have set; it only shows alarms for today's date (not the day of this exercise).

This exercise has given you a general introduction to creating a PM Daily Planner database and adding appointments to it. You use this same database in the PM Monthly Planner.

PM Monthly Planner

The PM Monthly Planner is the monthly view of the time management database. The Daily Planner gives you a daily interface to the file "JWL.D." The Monthly Planner uses the same "JWL.D" file, but displays in a format similar to a pert chart.

This month-at-a-glance view is useful for quickly locating time available in your schedule. Monthly Planner can use more than one database, but it can use only one at a time. To use the time database created previously for the Daily Planner, you first must open it by selecting Open from the File menu. The monthly planner then appears (see fig. 5.32).

Figure 5.32:

PM Monthly
Planner.

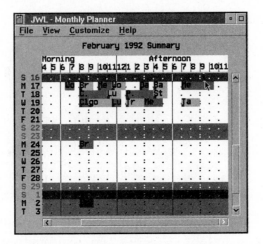

Take a moment to examine the figure. Weekends are shown in dark gray, and time during the week that is not used is white. If any portion of the next month is shown, as is March 1st through March 3rd, then those days are in a duller color.

Any alarms that are set are indicated by a small red dot in the lower left corner of each scheduled time slot. Scheduled time slots are illustrated by a light or dark gray block with the first two characters of the description. Colors alternate for clarity. If you used the Propagate command, as instructed in the previous section, you see that Br appears in the 8:00am slot every Monday.

Menu selections in the Monthly Planner are the same as those in the Daily Planner. To see a detailed view of a week, double-click on it to bring up Daily Planner. This process enables you to locate free times in your day. You can then enter the new appointments, save your work, and exit. Monthly Planner reflects these changes, showing that time as booked.

Notice that the current date is in a different color. Also note the current time indicator, which tells you where you are in your schedule.

If you use a graphic symbol as the first character in your description for a Daily Planner entry, that graphic will show up on the Monthly Planner viewing screen.

PM Calendar

PM Calendar is like PM Monthly Planner, in that it is a front end to the time management database. The calendar offers less information than does PM Monthly Planner—it is used as a smaller, more compact monthly viewer (this applet is suited only for a monthly view). Calendar's basic look is shown in figure 5.33.

Figure 5.33:
PM Calendar.

To make Calendar reflect the appointments and schedules set up in the time management database JWL.D, you must first open the file. The days that have appointments are marked with a red box around them. Like the Monthly Planner, you can see details of any day by double-clicking on that day. The Daily Planner applet starts and then opens that day.

The only difference in menus is the addition of two options that enable you to move back or ahead one year at a time. This applet offers a more compact view of your schedule—not much detail, but it shows which days are free. (Use Monthly Planner for details on an hourly level.)

PM Activities List

Also tied into the time management database is the PM Activities List applet. Like the other time management applets, Activities List supports multiple time management databases. You must open the file you want to use (in this case, JWL.D). After you open it, the applet should look like figure 5.34.

The concept and purpose of this applet is simple—it is a view of the PM Daily Planner file entries for all day. Sorting is also available in a limited fashion. The sort options are shown in figure 5.35.

A Find command is included to locate specific information. Keep in mind that this applet has a list of information from beginning to end (it has every Monday morning branch meeting and every other

Friday payday you have entered). When you print out the file, all these appointments print.

The major difference between this and other applets that use the same time management database is the lack of a day filter. PM Activities List shows any and all appointments. PM Daily Planner shows empty time slots (even empty days). PM Activities List does not show blank time slots, but it shows all others. The PM Activities List applet is best used for time management tasks other than keeping and viewing your personal schedule. To get this level of detail, you are better served by PM Daily Planner.

PM Planner Archive

Two archive applets are available: Planner Archive and To-Do List Archive. (Archives are for historical review and retrieval purposes.) These databases are similar to the other time management databases. They keep the data that you have completed and removed from the regular databases. The only time you use these applets is to go back and review past appointments or to restore an accidentally removed appointment or to-do task. It is important to note that items erased are not placed here; only those items you specifically archived from the appropriate applet are placed here. Options enable you to mark or remove and add to these archives.

PM Alarm

When you type a scheduled event and enter 05 in the time warning, an alarm clock called PM Alarm is automatically loaded and set. You tell PM Alarm which database to monitor as the master database (in this case, JWL.D), and all events with alarms are loaded. When the time arrives (for example, five minutes before your appointment), a window appears, as shown in figure 5.36.

The PMDiary alarm screen will appear accompanied by the chosen tune. In this case, it is tune 1. In the figure, Alarm indicates that you have set an alarm to go off at 9:15 pm and reminds you that you have some personal research to do. You can select **S**nooze or Set **n**ew alarm (a new time for the alarm to go off). PM Alarm is smoothly integrated into the Planning series of time management applets.

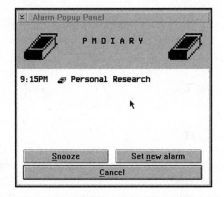

PM To-Do List

PM To-Do List has its own archive because it does not use the same database as the planning series of applets. This applet is a stand-alone database containing entries to be done. To-Do List uses the *Filename*.T format (instead of the *Filename*.D format used by the other time management applets.) To-Do List does not attach to PM Alarm.

The following project is used to illustrate the functions of PM To-Do List. Create a new database file called HOME.T (remember to use T—not D, as used earlier). Enter the tasks shown in figure 5.37 in any order you choose.

You can now sort tasks by priority, date, or description. Notice that the things to be done today or earlier are shown in red; tasks to be done later are shown in black. The menu options are basically the same as other applets. The options dealing with removal and archiving are the same as the PM Daily Planner. One menu option that is different, however, is the **M**ark and Mark **i**tem and date stamp option. This option enables you to mark an item as being done and also stamps the date on it.

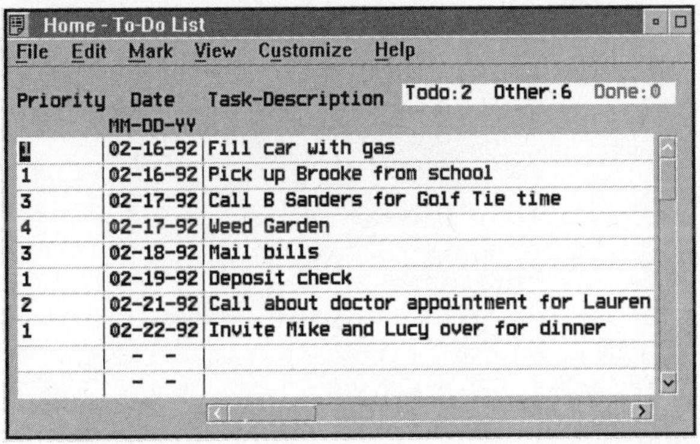

Figure 5.37: PM To-Do List.

The status area in the upper right side of the screen shows current statistics for completed tasks, current tasks, and tasks to be done (other), as shown in figure 5.38.

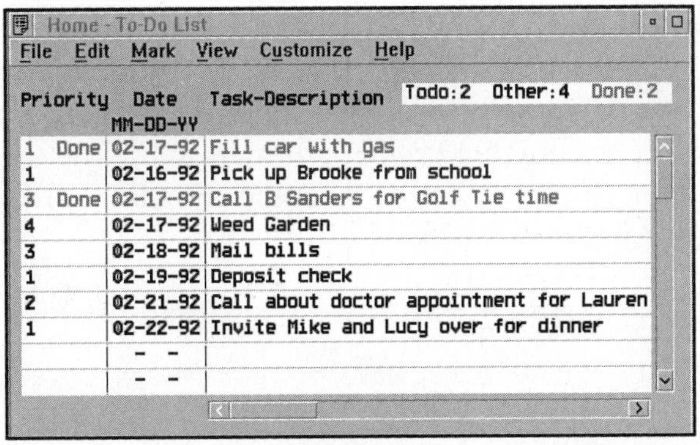

Figure 5.38: To-Do List with two finished items.

Items can be removed and archived after they are completed. To see a detailed view of a to-do task, select View Complete Entry from the View menu. Figure 5.39 shows the complete entry for the third task.

If your description is too long to be shown on the main screen, it is shown here in its entirety. This applet replaces the paper to-do list found on your desk. You can print a complete printout to carry with you, pass out to others, or mark up. If you already use a to-do list, you will find PM To-Do List a welcome addition to your automated desktop.

Figure 5.39:

Completed task.

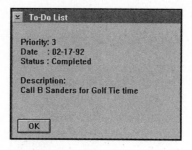

Assorted Utility Applets

PM Tune is one of many OS/2 2.0 utility applets that function as an editor, enabling you to modify or create tune files, which are supported by some OS/2 2.0 applets. You can add notes and adjust them intuitively and easily.

Several tunes are available on CompuServe. To access them, type **GO IBMOS2** after you are logged on to CompuServe. If you have musical talent, create your own tunes. The **P**lay menu contains options to play the current tune or all tunes in the file. A PM Tune file can support 36 tunes. To see what the song Reveille looks like, refer to figure 5.40.

Figure 5.40:

Reveille.

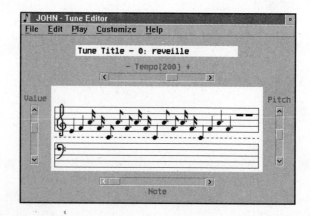

Although Tune is nice for editing tunes to attach to the applets, the real power of OS/2's music capabilities is found in multimedia extensions and those applications that support it. PM Tune requires no special equipment or drivers—it uses the speaker found in your computer and offers a simple way to add short tunes to liven up your PM applets.

PM System Editor

The PM System Editor is the same graphical editor found in previous versions of OS/2. It offers the basic text editing functions of DOS and then expands on them by adding the capabilities of cut-and-paste, font selections, word wrap, and a find utility. This utility is mainly used to view Read Me files, edit system files, and create new basic text files. This is the default editor for the PM Seek applet. If your needs for a text editor are more complicated, you may need to use EPM, the Enhanced Editor included with OS/2 2.0.

PM Enhanced Editor

The Enhanced Editor (EPM) originally was an IBM internal-use only text editor for OS/2 that is now finally available to the public. EPM is a feature extension of the System Editor. To understand the extent of the enhancements, the following sections describe the menu options, as was done for the previous applets.

The File menu is the same, except for the addition of two options: Import text file and Rename (see fig. 5.41).

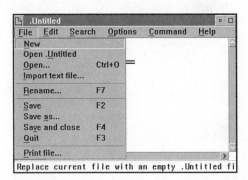

Figure 5.41:
File menu options.

The Edit menu shows the differences between EPM and the System Editor. You see that EPM is clearly intended for heavier editing (see fig. 5.42). Although EPM is not a professional word processor, it provides most word-processing functions.

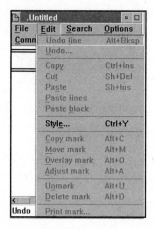

The Search menu enables you to search for characters and groups of characters. You can also set bookmarks, as shown in figure 5.43. The Bookmarks feature is handy for longer documents because you can give a name to a specific point in your document. For instance, if you are writing a long REXX file, you can place bookmarks at critical points or at the start of major routines.

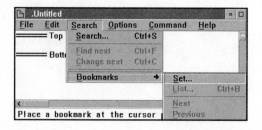

EPM also includes a replace feature and control mechanism, as shown in figure 5.44.

Figure 5.44:
Search and
Replace menu.

The **O**ptions menu is the menu from which you set defaults,
autosaving, and preferences. Save options are also set from the
options menu, as shown in figure 5.45.

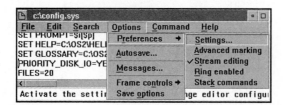

Figure 5.45:
Option menu
options.

The **C**ommand menu is used for entering macros and EPM
commands.

The most important menu selection is the **Q**uick Reference option,
which is available on the **H**elp menu. This option contains a list of
all the editing keystrokes and commands available to EPM.

EPM is the editor you will probably use instead of the System
Editor. It provides all functions required for general-purpose text
editing. Text and tune editing are not the only types of editing
available—you can also edit OS/2 icons, as described in the following section.

PM Icon Editor

OS/2 now includes the much-needed PM Icon Editor, which enables you to change or create icons for applications. Icon Editor acts like a paint package.

After you have saved your icon, it should have an ICO extension so that other applications recognize it. If you have a program that does not have an icon, and you want to use one to launch it, first create the icon. If you have created the icon and located it in the same directory as the executable file, that icon is automatically used. Be sure to give the icon the same name as the executable file name. For example, if you have an application called DATABASE.EXE, name your icon "DATABASE.ICO."

 When you create an icon, take advantage of the color called screen color. It is transparent and gives your icon a professional look.

A utility is available on CompuServe called CVTICO.ZIP, which converts Windows 3.0 icons to OS/2 2.0 icons. These icons can then be read into Icon Editor and modified. Icons are an intuitive way to start programs and a visual means to identify what the program is or what it does. Icon Editor gives you an easy way to enhance your desktop's look and productivity.

PM Picture Viewer

The Picture Viewer (Picview) is a simple applet for viewing the following types of pictures: MET, PIF, and SPL. Of special interest is the SPL (Spool Files Support), which is the format of spooled files waiting to be printed. You can set your print spooler to hold all print jobs, and then look at the contents through the picture viewer. Picview is a utility, not a real productivity application.

Clipboard Viewer

The Clipboard Viewer (Clipview) is not a full-featured applet—it is mainly used to view the contents of the Clipboard, which is where all the data goes when you issue the Cu<u>t</u>, <u>C</u>opy, and <u>P</u>aste options in the <u>E</u>dit menu.

Clipview can also be used to render a PCX file of the current picture or text in the Clipboard. Some limited importing and exporting is supported.

Another program that is used with the Clipboard is DDE-Super-Agent (see fig. 5.46). This is a special utility that enables the PM Clipboard to exchange data with the Windows Clipboard. On the Windows side is a special Windows DDE agent.

Figure 5.46:
DDE-Super-Agent icon.

Pulse

The Pulse applet utility is a visual tool for monitoring CPU utilization. Pulse does not produce an MIPS rating or any figures; it provides a graph that, by nature of its height, indicates the utilization. The colors of both the chart and the background can be set from two menu choices: <u>O</u>ptions and <u>H</u>elp. The graph can either be outlined or filled and, to review the utilization, the pulse can be frozen. In figure 5.47, you see peaks and flat points. The peaks represent places in time when, for a moment, more processing power was used. Another use for Pulse is when nothing happens on the screen for awhile. The Pulse program gives you positive visual feedback that your program is doing something. Programs such as Pulse have been available on other platforms for some time.

PM Seek

PM Seek, called Seek and Scan Files in the Productivity folder, is a utility you will probably use often. The main job of PM Seek is to locate files for you. There are two ways to launch PM Seek: by clicking on Seek and Scan Files or by typing PMSEEK from an OS/2 prompt. Once PM Seek is launched, a number of fields can be filled. PM Seek allows a case-insensitive search. You can also search for text in all files.

Figure 5.47:

Pulse screen.

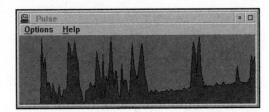

The most impressive feature of PM Seek is its capability to search for any characters in a file name by using multiple wild cards (such as *tr*.,*c, or bu*t.w?1). You can tell PM Seek to search subdirectories. PM Seek also has a field for your favorite text editor (the default is E.EXE). After a search is completed, the file that is clicked on launches the editor and retrieves the selected file. As your directory structure becomes more complicated and the amount of files increases, so does the value of PM Seek.

Entertainment Applets

IBM has included six games in this release of OS/2. The concept of games was popularized by the success that Microsoft had with its games. The following sections describe these games.

Reversi

Reversi works like the board game. The object of the game is to surround your opponents' circles with your color. The winner is the player who has the most circles.

Scramble

Scramble is like the hand-held Scramble game. The object is to unscramble the numbers.

Solitaire

Solitaire is the blockbuster game that made Windows' games popular, and it may still be the most-used Windows application. The OS/2 version, Klondike, offers the same features to make it an instant hit. Several enhancements have been added, including animation and the cheat option. Solitaire has possibly taught more people to use a mouse and a graphical user interface than any other application or teaching aid.

Jigsaw Puzzle

Jigsaw Puzzle, also called Jigsaw, accepts an OS/2 PCX file and then slices it up into a jigsaw puzzle. You then use your mouse to reassemble the pieces into a complete picture.

OS/2 Chess

The OS/2 Chess game is surprisingly well done. It offers a 3D perspective and network support. The network support is what really sets this game apart. You can play anyone (even across the country).

Cat and Mouse

Cat and Mouse, also known as NEKO, has a kitten that chases your "mouse" around the screen. The kitten's speed and play time can be set.

Summary

Chapter 5 has provided a glimpse into OS/2 2.0's new productivity applets. Most of these applets provide enough functions for simple tasks, while others offer functions rivaling full-feature commercial packages. Only you can determine if the applets meet your needs or if you require a professional version of the applet. The benefit is that these applets are provided free for you to use and evaluate.

The OS/2 2.0 applets are significantly more powerful than their Windows counterparts. In several cases, Windows has no comparable applet. The power of the OS/2 applets go well beyond what has been shown. As you use them, you will find additional uses. You may not use all of them, but at least one is bound to appeal to you. Several applets have been included to meet the diverse needs of OS/2 users.

Chapter 6 expands on OS/2's support for DOS programs and gives additional detail as to how OS/2 supports DOS sessions. In addition, OS/2 programs are explained.

OS/2 and DOS Programs

As you have seen, OS/2 provides a platform for building powerful graphical programs, programs that can exceed the old memory limits, multitask, and use the power of the Workplace Shell to bring the ease of a GUI to today's programs. But the older versions of OS/2, versions 1.0 through 1.3, offered those things also; and yet their sales languished, outstripped by operating system products like DOS 5.0, Windows 3.0, and Quarterdeck's DesqView product. The reason why the more powerful OS/2 1.X was overshadowed by less powerful offerings is simple: a lack of backward compatibility on OS/2's part. People just are not willing to leave behind the comfortable tools that DOS provides.

In this respect, OS/2 2.0 shines. It provides a level of DOS emulation that is like an enhanced version of DOS 5.0. In fact, during the first few months, you may use OS/2 more as a DOS multitasker than as a platform for your OS/2 programs.

In this chapter, you see how to use DOS emulation to the fullest. You learn how to create program objects that enable you to activate your DOS programs with just a double-click. You see how to run multiple copies of DOS, right on your OS/2 desktop. And, most importantly, you learn how to use the many DOS Settings options to customize OS/2 for any DOS program.

Creating a DOS Session

You start out learning about DOS support under OS/2 by taking the DOS support "out for a spin." The first step in using the DOS support is to create a new program object for use in accessing the DOS prompt.

Building the DOS Object

1. Open the OS/2 System folder.

2. Inside the OS/2 System folder, open up the Command Prompts folder.

3. On your Desktop, open the Templates folder.

4. Click and hold the right mouse button on the Program object. Drag the Program object to the Command Prompts folder. Because the program object is a template, you can peel off a program object using this method.

 The procedure described in step 4 copies the Program Object template to the folder.

5. You see a window that looks somewhat like figure 6.1.

Put an asterisk (*) in the Path and File name: field. Do not put anything in the Parameters: or Working directory: fields. Click on the Session tab to get a screen like the one in figure 6.2.

Currently, the OS/2 Window radio button is clicked. Click on DOS Window. Notice that the DOS Settings button, which was formerly grayed out, is now enabled. Do not select this button yet—you do plenty with that later on. Click on the General tab and enter **Practice DOS session** in the Title: field and close the window. You should now have a program object with the name Practice DOS session in your Command Prompts folder. (Close the Templates folder because it is not needed for the rest of this chapter.)

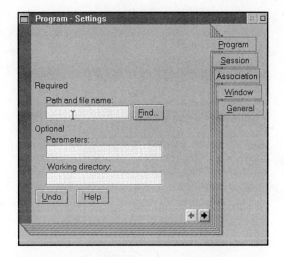

Figure 6.1:
The Program Settings screen for a new program object.

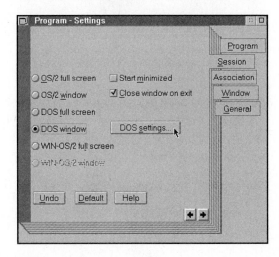

Figure 6.2:
The **S**ession tab in Program Settings.

Starting the DOS Object

Double-click on your new object and you get a windowed DOS session, as you see in figure 6.3.

Figure 6.3:

A windowed DOS session.

To try out this DOS box, type **mem**, the memory status report command. You may know it if you have used DOS version 4.0 or later. Look at the number before the largest executable program size: a number like 618272 is not unusual. (Yours should be a bit different, depending on the number and size of device drivers and TSRs loaded.) It means that your DOS session has over 603K of free space, not a bad start at all. (618272=603K because 1K=1024, not 1000, and 618272/1024 equals a bit over 603.) If you also see references to XMS and EMS memory, do not worry about them right now. Later in this chapter, you learn how to make the amount of free space actually exceed 640K.

The DOS session is now windowed, but you can make it a full-screen session just by pressing Alt-Home. Try it. Return to windowed status by pressing Alt-Home again.

Modifying DOS Object Settings

Suppose you want to change this object so that it does not start up as a windowed DOS session, but starts up instead as a full-screen DOS session? You have seen that double-clicking on the object starts the session up; to change settings, click on the object once with the right mouse button. The menu appears. Click on Open, and then on Settings. The Settings screen returns.

If you find that you use this object quite a bit—that is, if you find that you use windowed DOS sessions a lot—you might consider dragging the object from the Command Prompts folder onto the Desktop. That way, it is right where you can find it as soon as you start up the computer for the day. Better yet, just use Shutdown with the DOS window active, and a DOS window starts up every time you activate OS/2.

Creating a DOS Object for a Program

Now that you have your DOS prompt, you could start up a program by typing its name at the prompt, as is normally done under DOS. To start up WordPerfect for DOS, for example, you just type **wp**. But that is tedious; it would be much more convenient to have a program object that you could simply click to start up WordPerfect. You learn how to do that in this section.

 This example assumes that you have WordPerfect version 5.1 for DOS in a subdirectory named C:\WP51.

1. As you did before, create a new DOS object from a template. On your Desktop, open the Templates folder, and then click on the Program object with your right mouse button. Drag the Program object to the Desktop. This copies the Program Object template to the Desktop. Close the Templates folder.

2. In the Path and file name: field, enter **c:\wp51\wp.exe**. Put that value in the Working directory: field also and leave the Parameters: field empty for the moment.

3. Click on **S**ession, and then click on the DOS wi**n**dow radio button.

4. Click on **G**eneral, and then replace the word "Program" in the Title: field with **WordPerfect 5.1**.

5. Close the Program Settings window by double-clicking on its close box.

Now, you can try out your WordPerfect object. Double-click on the object's icon. In a minute or two, WordPerfect should start up in a window. Maximize the window.

Move the mouse around and you see an immediate problem: WordPerfect has a mouse cursor, but it is offset from the actual OS/2 cursor. The two cursors look like they are flying in formation. This is remedied easily, however.

1. Pull down the control menu for the WordPerfect session. It looks like figure 6.4.

Figure 6.4:

The control menu for the WordPerfect session.

Click on DOS Settings, and you see a formidable set of options, as depicted in figure 6.5.

> **TIP** Because you use the DOS Settings options throughout this chapter, make the DOS program a window using Alt-Home. Do this by clicking on the control icon in the upper left corner of the window, and then clicking on DOS Settings.

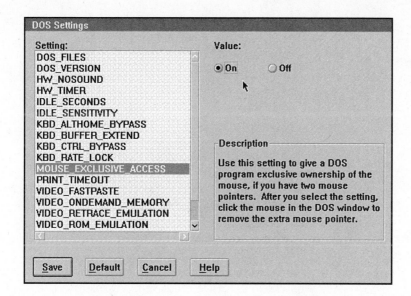

Figure 6.5:
A DOS Settings
dialog box.

To fix the WordPerfect problem, click on MOUSE_EXCLUSIVE_ACCESS, and then select ON, and **S**ave. The dialog box disappears. Just click the mouse cursor anywhere in the WordPerfect window and the OS/2 cursor vanishes, leaving only the WordPerfect cursor, which now behaves quite nicely. Press Alt, and you get the OS/2 cursor back.

What you have just done is the first step in a process called *tuning* an application. OS/2 offers dozens of options, all designed to enable OS/2 the flexibility that it needs to run the wide variety of DOS programs that are available today. You learn about some of the items in the DOS Settings dialog box in the course of this chapter.

Terminating Runaway DOS Applications

Suppose you are running a DOS application, and for some reason, it locks up—that is, it no longer responds to the keyboard. What do you do?

Under DOS, there is nothing to do except press Ctrl-Alt-Del and do a warm reboot. But OS/2 offers another way that does not require terminating all other activities. Just pull down the control menu, and you see the option Close. Click on it, and you see a dialog box, like the one in figure 6.6.

Figure 6.6:

A dialog box, confirming whether you want to abnormally terminate a program.

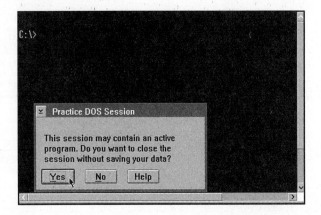

This option is a last resort because any files that are open at the time of termination are generally lost. Some of the files may become lost clusters and some may disappear altogether. In any case, data loss may result. One example of such a file loss occurs if you abnormally terminate WordPerfect. Start up the program again, and WordPerfect asks `Are other copies of WordPerfect currently running? (Y/N)`. WordPerfect generates this prompt because it uses some disk space as temporary storage. That is, it creates files when it starts and cleans those files up as it exits. But that is only if you exit the program normally (by pressing the F7 or "exit" key). Once WordPerfect is restarted, it sees the files and is programmed to erase them. But it first must check with you to be sure that there is not another copy of WordPerfect running on the PC at the same time. If it erases those temporary files, it damages the other copy of WordPerfect.

NOTE Although WordPerfect was written for DOS, an operating system that does not multitask, the fact that WordPerfect checks before erasing those files is a real tribute to the foresight of its programmers.

Determining when OS/2 is not the Right Platform for DOS Programs

You have seen how to start up a DOS program and how to create a program object for any given DOS program. The rest of the chapter shows you how to tune OS/2 to support your DOS programs better than DOS itself. You can tune OS/2, for instance, so that it gives the DOS program faster operating-system services and enables the DOS program to multitask. Although there are not many cases, there are a few instances in which OS/2 does not serve a DOS program well.

OS/2 Runs DOS Programs More Slowly than DOS

Because OS/2 is a multitasking operating system, it handles multiple tasks in a fashion. The PC still has only one processor, however. (At least, this is true for most PCs. A few multi-CPUs do exist, but they are somewhat rare and fairly expensive.) Dividing the CPU's attention inevitably results in each task running more slowly than if each task had the undivided attention of the CPU. To see this, run a DOS speed-testing program, like the SYSINFO program that comes with Norton Utilities, or run the benchmark programs included with diagnostic packages like QAPlus or Checkit. In all cases, the CPU operates slower than it would under DOS. This also is the case, by the way, with other multitaskers like Microsoft Windows, Quarterdeck DesqView, or UNIX.

Not All DOS Programs will Run

Some DOS programs are so firmly wedded to a real mode, I-am-in-control-of-the-whole-system design, that they can never run under any multitasker. The most likely candidates for trouble are the following:

See Chapter 1 for a discussion of the 8088-based real mode versus the 286-based and 386-based protected modes.

- **Some games.** The popular arcade-type game *Lemmings* has trouble running under Windows or OS/2 because of its out-of-date copy protection scheme, which this game shares with a number of other games. All is not bad news in this department, however. It is perhaps an odd distinction, but OS/2 seems more capable of accommodating video-intensive games than Windows.

NOTE These days, it seems that the best test of PC compatibility is a game from Origin called *Wing Commander*. (The game also is more addictive than the lotus flowers of Homer's *Odyssey*, so do not buy a copy to have around the office unless you have iron self-control.) *WC* runs under OS/2, but not under Windows 3.0. If you can find a game that runs under OS/2, there is even an additional bonus: you can shut off the sound with the HW_SOUND setting.

- **Disk diagnostic programs.** Under no circumstances should you run a program like *Norton Disk Doctor*, *Disk Technician*, or *SpinRite* in a DOS session under OS/2. Under the best of circumstances, such programs realize that something very odd is going on and just terminate themselves. Under the worst of circumstances, they actually do some damage to your data. Run these programs only under real DOS.

- **DOS communications programs.** These programs are much easier to run under 2.0 than they were under OS/2 1.x, but they are still touchy. Test a communications program in a DOS box before you depend on it.

- **Some graphical programs.** Graphical programs that rely on special features of a particular video board may experience trouble when they are switched to and from the background. Happily, however, OS/2 has a set of video-control commands that can eliminate most problems.

Tuning DOS under OS/2: An Overview

The next few sections show you how to modify OS/2's support of DOS programs to solve compatibility problems and to improve performance of DOS programs under OS/2, in other words, how to "tune" DOS.

First, you can do the majority of DOS tuning from the DOS Settings window. There are, however, a few commands that are not controlled by DOS Settings; instead, they reside in the CONFIG.SYS or AUTOEXEC.BAT files.

Second, be prepared for a bit of a ride. A lot of the detail presented here applies to hardware specifics under DOS that you have either taken for granted or have never wanted to "mess with." Some DOS settings must be changed before starting up a particular DOS session; others can be changed "on the fly" while the DOS program is running. In either case, the procedure is the same.

Explaining all the ins and outs of memory structures, video, and communications, would take a book or many books, so the following is a somewhat condensed overview of the relevant hardware topics. If you need more information about how the parts of the PC fit together, there are many good books on the market that can help you.

If the DOS program is not running yet, click on the DOS program's program object with the right mouse button, and then click on Open and Settings. Then click on the **S**ession tab, and finally click the DOS Settings button.

If the DOS program is already running and if it is not in a window, switch from full screen to windowed mode by using Alt-Home. Click on the session's control icon, and then choose DOS Settings from the menu that drops down.

Table 6.1 lists all of the DOS settings, notes which settings you can change while a DOS session is active, and summarizes what the settings do.

Table 6.1
DOS Settings

Command	Summary of Command Function
COM_HOLD	Helps OS/2 stay out of DOS's way on COM ports
DOS_BACKGROUND_EXECUTION*	Enables/disables running a DOS program when it is switched to the background
DOS_BREAK	Tells how often to poll for Ctrl-Break
DOS_DEVICE	Enables selective loading of device drivers
DOS_FCBS	Sets aside space for DOS 1.x file support
DOS_FCBS_KEEP	Restricts opening of FCBs by network programs
DOS_FILES*	Sets aside space for DOS 2.x+ file support
DOS_HIGH	Loads DOS above 1024K addresses
DOS_LASTDRIVE	Designates highest drive letter
DOS_RMSIZE	Restricts conventional memory size
DOS_SHELL	Specifies an alternative command shell or adjusts environment size

Command	Summary of Command Function
DOS_STARTUP_DRIVE	Boots an actual copy of DOS, rather than the OS/2 emulator
DOS_UMB	Enables support for upper memory blocks
DOS_VERSION*	Deceives applications about DOS version
DPMI_DOS_API	Designates how DOS extender should access DOS
DPMI_MEMORY_LIMIT	Restricts memory available to DOS extender
DPMI_NETWORK_BUFF_SIZE	Controls size of network translation buffer
EMS_FRAME_LOCATION	Places support memory area for LIM manager
EMS_HIGH_OS_MAP_REGION	Controls support for LIM 4.0
EMS_LOW_OS_MAP_REGION	Controls support LIM 4.0 memory backfilling
EMS_MEMORY_LIMIT	Restricts LIM (expanded) memory size
HW_NOSOUND*	Disables sound generation
HW_ROM_TO_RAM	Copies ROM data to RAM, speeding up I/O
HW_TIMER*	Designates actual or emulated timer circuit
IDLE_SECONDS*	Controls detection of DOS program idleness

continues

Table 6.1 Continued

Command	Summary of Command Function
IDLE_SENSITIVITY*	Controls detection of DOS program idleness
KBD_ALTHOME_BYPASS*	Disables window/full-screen switch key
KBD_BUFFER_EXTEND*	Enables extended keyboard buffer support
KBD_CTRL_BYPASS*	Disables task-switching hot keys
KBD_RATE_LOCK*	Defeats application attempts to alter keyboard delay and repeat rate
MEM_EXCLUDE_REGIONS	Indicates areas in upper memory to be avoided by memory-manager software
MEM_INCLUDE_REGIONS	Indicates areas in upper memory available to memory-management software
MOUSE_EXCLUSIVE_ACCESS*	Temporarily disables mouse support from OS/2
PRINT_TIMEOUT*	Helps OS/2 determine when DOS printed output is ready for printing
TOUCH_EXCLUSIVE_ACCESS	Temporarily disables touchscreen support from OS/2
VIDEO_8514A_XGA_IOTRAP	Tells OS/2 that programs only use AI interface

Command	Summary of Command Function
VIDEO_FASTPASTE*	Enables alternative keyboard-pasting method
VIDEO_MODE_RESTRICTION	Disables full VGA capabilities in return for an extra 96K of conventional memory
VIDEO_ONDEMAND_MEMORY*	Tells OS/2 to pre-allocate storage area for video images
VIDEO_RETRACE_EMULATION*	Solves potential problems with super VGA disappearing when placed in background
VIDEO_ROM_EMULATION*	Improves text video support
VIDEO_SWITCH_NOTIFICATION*	Solves potential problems with super VGA
VIDEO_WINDOW_REFRESH*	Tells OS/2 how often to update the image in a windowed DOS session
XMS_HANDLES	Restricts maximum number of areas to be allocated under XMS memory management
XMS_MEMORY_LIMIT	Restricts memory available under XMS
XMS_MINIMUM_HMA	Keeps programs from using HMA, unless they exceed a certain size

Note: Items noted with an asterisk (*) can be changed in an active DOS session; other items can only be changed before starting the session.

The commands roughly fall into seven categories:

- Memory allocation and support

- Keyboard access

- Video access

- Access to sound

- Helping OS/2 share the mouse, touchscreen, and printer with DOS programs

- File input/output handling

- DOS version control

Getting More Memory for DOS Sessions

You saw previously that a simple DOS session easily gets access to 603K with no special adjustments. Lots more is possible, however, with just a few tweaks to the DOS program's object and to the CONFIG.SYS file. To understand how these changes work, however, you need to know how memory is structured under DOS.

While the PC is running DOS, it is in a processor mode referred to as "real mode." In real mode, a 286 or later processor mimics an 8088 processor. Any discussion of memory must begin with the basic 1024K. As you see in figure 6.7, this is the "canvas" on which the DOS memory architecture is drawn.

Building a computer with a given chip is like designing a new town. There is space to work with, but the town cannot just develop haphazardly if it is to work well. Town planners must allocate some acreage to residential areas, to commercial shops, to industrial areas, to schools, to fire and police departments, to public parks, and so on. A computer designer must look ahead to the future, leaving enough room for growth of user programs' memory requirements, but reserving enough room for the use of the system.

Conventional Memory

When IBM designed the PC in 1980, it left the first 640K for user programs. That area has become known in the PC world as *conventional memory*. Figure 6.8 places it in the first 1024K.

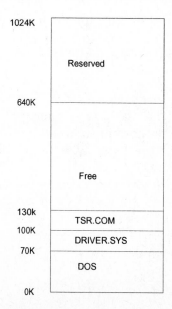

Figure 6.8:
Conventional memory under DOS in the 8088.

Notice in figure 6.8 that not all of the memory is available for user programs; DOS inhabits the bottom part and takes up to 70K of space, depending on the DOS version. Over the years, DOS has increased its girth. DOS 1.0 took about 11K of memory space, but DOS 5.0 takes about 70K of space.

Directly above DOS are system "helper" programs called *device drivers* and *terminate and stay resident (TSR)* programs. DOS device drivers support special hardware functions. The most common examples are support for a piece of hardware that DOS does not directly support, like a tape drive, an optical disk, or some other non-standard input/output device; or support of a new function for an old piece of hardware. Two examples of the latter kind of device driver are ANSI.SYS under DOS, which enables the video board to respond to a new set of programming commands that are consistent with an international standard for screen control, and memory manager software, such as that found with DOS 5.0's EMM386.EXE and HIMEM.SYS. *Memory manager software* enables the extended memory found in the 386 and later CPUs act like another kind of memory called expanded memory. (You learn more about expanded memory later in this chapter.)

TSRs exist under DOS to do three things:

- Support an unusual device, much as a device driver does. In fact, the question of whether to build device support as a device driver or as a TSR is largely the option of the hardware's designer.

- Run a program in the background. Although DOS never directly supports multitasking or context-switching, TSR programs enable programmers to work around that. Examples are the DOS PRINT program, which prints files in the background, or the SideKick suite of programs. SideKick offers such desktop accessories as a notepad, calculator, and calendar that you can access while still inside an application by pressing Ctrl-Alt or Ctrl-Shift. Of course, under OS/2 there is no need for this. OS/2 supports many programs running at once, and they are just a keystroke or two away.

- Redefine a device like a keyboard or a video screen. Keyboard macro programs have been around for years and enable you to take a long string of characters, like "Acme Manufacturing Corporation" and assign that string to a key sequence like Alt-A. That way, if you type "Acme Manufacturing Corporation" many times per day, you need only press Alt-A, and the words appear as if you had typed them.

The need for TSRs has largely disappeared under OS/2, as has the need for device drivers under DOS; most device drivers can load from OS/2 itself, not from a DOS application. But there may still be a few TSRs or device drivers from DOS that you want to run because their functions have not yet been duplicated in OS/2. So, for many examples in the remainder of this chapter, the DOS memory maps contain one prototype device driver called DRIVER.SYS (no relation to the device driver by that name that comes with DOS) and a prototype TSR called TSR.COM. TSR.COM and DRIVER.SYS are, for example's sake, 30K in size each.

As you saw in figure 6.8, after DOS, the device driver, and the TSR load, 130K of the initial 640K has been used up, leaving 510K for DOS programs.

How OS/2 Provides More Free Conventional Memory

An OS/2 DOS session frees up considerably more than 510K, however. Why? First, understand that OS/2 is not running DOS—it is running a program that behaves like DOS, as far as a DOS program is concerned. That program takes much less space than DOS does because OS/2 is doing most of the work of an operating system, enabling this DOS-like program to mainly call on OS/2 for vital system functions. Calling on OS/2 to get a job done takes a lot less code than doing the job would. Second, recall that the example DOS session had a 30K TSR and a 30K device driver. Your system probably does not have either of those, so you got an amount of free memory around 600K. (If your free memory values do not match the ones in this book, do not worry. Your programs may require TSRs or device drivers that chew up some of your DOS space.) Assuming that you have a 30K device driver and a 30K TSR, however, you see a memory map like the one in figure 6.9.

Figure 6.9:
Conventional memory map under OS/2 DOS session.

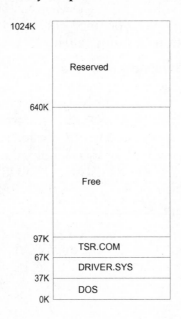

Compare figure 6.9 to figure 6.8, and you see that the OS/2 DOS emulator immediately gives you more memory than DOS. Rather than 70K, it takes about 37K.

OS/2 has a DOS setting, DOS_RMSIZE, that restricts conventional memory. Since OS/2 1.X, there has been a CONFIG.SYS command called RMSIZE. It took a value from 0 to 640K and restricted the amount of conventional memory available in a DOS session. You can still use RMSIZE in CONFIG.SYS, although there is no need to. The DOS_RMSIZE setting enables you to set any value from 0 to 640K by going to the DOS settings dialog box. The default is 640K, and although you will probably never need it, it is here for the sake of completeness. This setting might be of value if you are running OS/2 on a very memory-constrained PC, and you do not need every

DOS box to be at least 640K in size. Another use of this setting is for testing DOS programs in memory-constrained environments.

The Reserved Area

640K through 1024K is called the *reserved area*. Why do DOS programs only get access to the first 640K?

- Some devices in the PC need addresses for their own reserved memory, like the video board. The video board requires memory space to hold the current on-screen image.

- Some devices require a small amount of Read-Only Memory (ROM) that contains software that those devices need in order to be of use to the rest of the computer. Virtually everything in the PC is served directly or indirectly by software in ROM.

Video RAM and the VIDEO_MODE_RESTRICTION Setting

The first area above 640K is a large area used by the video board. PC video boards all use a set of memory addresses from 640K through 768K to place memory that holds the current video image. That 128K of addresses is not always fully used, but, because it is still allocated, normal DOS programs are shut out of that entire area. A closer look at the 128K shows how you can grab 96K more RAM for DOS programs. Figure 6.10 illustrates how that memory area is used by the most popular video boards.

Notice that the bottom 64K of the area (addresses 640K through 704K) is only used by DOS when displaying graphics on an EGA-type video board or more advanced (EGA+, for this discussion) video board. Although an EGA+ board operates in text mode, it does not touch that area and works only in the range from 736K through 768K. (An EGA+ board never uses the range from 704K through 736K. That means that if you know that you are not going to use the video mode on a program, you can safely move the top of DOS's conventional memory from 640K to 736K, resulting in a memory map like the one in figure 6.11

Figure 6.10:
How video RAM areas are used by the PC.

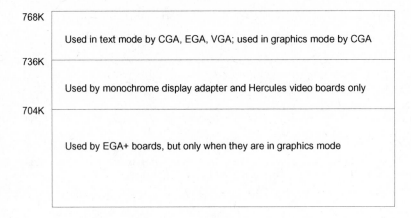

768K

Used in text mode by CGA, EGA, VGA; used in graphics mode by CGA

736K

Used by monochrome display adapter and Hercules video boards only

704K

Used by EGA+ boards, but only when they are in graphics mode

Figure 6.11:
Memory map for computer with only CGA.

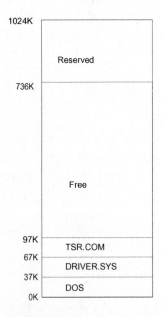

1024K

Reserved

736K

Free

97K
TSR.COM

67K
DRIVER.SYS

37K
DOS

0K

OS/2 enables you to build a DOS session with only those characteristics. Try it out on your Practice DOS session.

1. First, open its Settings screen. Do this by right-clicking on the Practice DOS session object. Click on Open, and then on Settings.

2. You now see a window entitled Practice DOS session - Settings. Click on the **S**ession tab, and then on the DOS **s**ettings button. You see a DOS Settings window, as shown in figure 6.12.

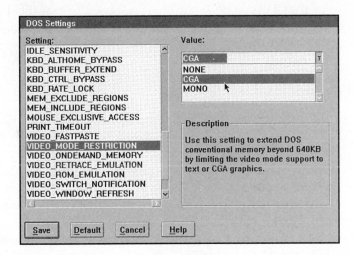

Figure 6.12:
DOS Settings window.

3. In figure 6.12, the Setting: window has already been scrolled down a bit to show the VIDEO_MODE_RESTRICTION setting. Pull down its menu, and you see three options—NONE, CGA, and MONO. Select CGA.

4. Click on **S**ave to return to the Practice DOS session - Settings window and close the window. If you have forgotten how to close a window, double-click on the box in the upper left corner of the window.

 There is no OK button to signify that you are done modifying the settings.

5. Start up the Practice DOS session by double-clicking on its object. You again get a windowed DOS session. Type **mem**. On a machine running basic OS/2 without any device drivers or TSRs, you get 722,752 bytes free (705.8K). In our hypothetical

DOS session with a 30K TSR and a 30K device driver, you have 645K free, which is not a bad total compared to the 510K that you started with.

If you know that a given program does not use the graphical video modes, it is a good idea to activate the video mode restrictions to gain a free 96K.

The ROM Reserve Area

The other part of the reserved use area from 640K through 1024K is the range from 768K through 1024K, an area devoted largely to ROMs. There are two kinds of memories on a PC, RAM (Random-Access Memory) and ROM. RAM is the ordinary memory that people are talking about when they say, "I've got a 386 with four megabytes of memory." RAM is the memory that can be read from or written to. OS/2 is resident in RAM when the system is running, as are any operating programs. RAM is very fast (a byte of data can be fetched from RAM in less than one millionth of a second), but this memory is *volatile*, meaning that when the PC's power is shut off, the contents of the RAM disappear. That is why your computer has a hard disk—hard disks are considerably slower than RAM, but they are not volatile.

ROM also is not volatile. ROMs are a special kind of memory chip that can only be written to with a device called a *ROM programmer*. Once the data has been written, however, it remains forever—powering down the PC has no effect on the data.

 Actually, data in ROM does not remain forever. Static electricity, extreme power surges, or high-intensity ultraviolet light can damage ROMs. But under normal conditions, "forever" is a good enough characterization.

ROMs are used by hardware manufacturers as repositories of small programs. A typical video card, for example, has a ROM on it that contains the programs needed by the PC to put characters on the screen, activate the board's graphics modes, and support whatever other features the video board has. The main circuit board in the PC, the *motherboard*, has a ROM on it that contains software called the system BIOS. The *BIOS*, or Basic Input/Output System, is a collection of dozens of small programs that control the keyboard, disk drives, parallel ports, and other devices integral to the PC.

No matter what a ROM's function is, it is a form of memory, albeit an unusual one. Memories all must have addresses in order to be accessible to the system, and that is why the addresses from 768K through 1024K have been set aside for ROMs.

Recall the analogy of computer design to planning a town. Town planning is a tough job; knowing how much space to set aside for schools requires knowing how many school-age children the town will have in the future. IBM, as "town planner," did a fairly good job, but it could not foresee that it set aside too little space for conventional memory, and too much space for ROMs. Very rarely does a PC run out of address space to accommodate ROMs, but running out of conventional memory is easy because of TSRs, DOS, device drivers, and applications programs competing for the 640K. That is where UMBs come in.

UMBs (Upper Memory Blocks) refer to unused addresses in the ROM reserve area. To see what they do, consider the following hypothetical PC memory map, as depicted in figure 6.13. The figure depicts the same hypothetical situation discussed so far: DOS, a 30K device driver, a 30K TSR, and some ROMs. Note that DOS stays out of the 128K video RAM area.

Note also that there is an item that is not a ROM, but a small RAM buffer used by the token ring board (a local area network interface). You see this on some expansion boards. Although the ROM area predominantly contains ROMs, there are a few odd boards that tuck in a little RAM. You can see that there is plenty of room in the attic with the ROMs, but not too much downstairs in the conventional area. If you could load the TSR and device driver into the unused space in the ROM area, that would free up conventional memory.

Figure 6.13:

Memory map for a hypothetical PC.

The unused ROM reserve area can be filled with RAM and used for TSRs and device drivers under OS/2. This configuration results in a memory map looking like the one in figure 6.14.

Figure 6.14:

Memory map when programs are loaded in Upper Memory Blocks (UMBs).

How do you load these programs into UMBs? First consider how they are loaded in the first place. Suppose your 30K device driver is called DRIVER.SYS. You would then have a line in your CONFIG.SYS file that looks like the following:

```
device=c:\os2\mdos\driver.sys
```

Note, by the way, that although OS/2 device drivers are written differently than DOS device drivers, both are loaded with the `device=` statement. OS/2 can sense, when loading the driver, whether it is a DOS or OS/2 device driver. Suppose further that the 30K TSR is called TSR.COM. It would be loaded from your AUTOEXEC.BAT file with the following line:

TSR

The name of the TSR stands by itself on a line in the AUTOEXEC.BAT.

That is how these files are loaded into low conventional memory. Loading them into a UMB requires the following steps:

1. In CONFIG.SYS, look for a line that starts with `DOS=`. Replace it with the following:

   ```
   DOS=UMB
   ```

2. Also in CONFIG.SYS, locate the `device=` line that loaded the driver. (In the example, it is called DRIVER.SYS, but it can be any device driver.) Replace `device=` with **`devicehigh=`**. That way, the system knows to load that particular device driver high if possible. Not all drivers load high properly.

3. As you have done before, examine the DOS Settings of your program objects that run DOS programs. The setting DOS_UMB should be on (the default value). Check to see that it is actually enabled.

Save CONFIG.SYS and reboot. Open up the DOS program object and run **mem** again. The result: greatly improved conventional space. Assuming that you are running a text-only program, you can add the video mode restriction and gain another 96K of RAM.

Because OS/2 device drivers serve both DOS and OS/2 in an automatic dual-mode fashion, there are very few DOS device drivers that you still need to use under OS/2. In addition, the expanded functionality of OS/2, when compared to DOS, removes the need for most TSRs, so you may find yourself never loading them. Nevertheless, it is nice that the designers of OS/2 included a solution to the old DOS memory problem of TSR and device driver "memory hogs."

The DOS_DEVICE DOS Setting

Most device drivers can be loaded quite nicely from CONFIG.SYS. Use the device= command, and then OS/2 sorts out whether it is an OS/2 device driver or a DOS device driver. If you have a device driver that you only want to load during particular DOS sessions, DOS_DEVICE is what you need. To selectively load a device driver only during a particular session, do not include it in CONFIG.SYS. Rather, open the DOS Settings box for the particular DOS session that needs the device driver and type its name into the field provided.

Restricting UMB Space with MEM_EXCLUDE_REGIONS and MEM_INCLUDE_REGIONS

A UMB is an unused part of memory between 768K and 1024K. How does the DOS memory manager know which areas are used and which are unused? Two DOS settings answer that question: MEM_EXCLUDE_REGIONS and MEM_INCLUDE_REGIONS. In the vast majority of the cases, the DOS memory manager has no trouble sniffing out the free and unused areas. Now and then, however, you see a PC expansion board with some RAM or ROM on it that the memory manager does not catch. The DOS memory manager then unknowingly opens up some UMB space right over an existing ROM or RAM buffer, causing the board with the ROM or RAM buffer to stop working or causing the board's

ROM/RAM to overwrite whatever TSR or device driver is in that particular UMB.

If you have a device that does not work in DOS under OS/2, upper memory conflicts are one possible reason. Check it out by temporarily disabling DOS_UMB, which keeps DOS from loading anything into a UMB. If that makes the problem go away, you have an upper memory conflict. Fix it in the following fashion:

1. Examine the documentation for your PC's add-in boards or, if you do not have the documentation, contact the manufacturers of those boards. Find out whether the board has a ROM or RAM situated between 768K and 1024K. Get the addresses of the ROM/RAM in hexadecimal. That is usually how the documentation states it, and that is how OS/2 needs it. A token ring RAM buffer, for example, might be in the range C800-CBFF. It might be expressed in five-digit addresses, like C8000-CBFFF; if so, just drop the rightmost digit.

2. Open the Settings window of the program object for the DOS program that is malfunctioning. Reenable DOS_UMB and click on MEM_EXCLUDE_REGIONS. The window has space in which you can type the range found in step 1.

3. Click on Save and close the Settings window. The program should run now. If not, consider the possibility that the manufacturer has misdocumented the addresses. Sometimes, it makes sense to exclude the whole UMB area (C000-FFFF). That should work because there cannot be a UMB conflict when the system is not allowed to use any of the UMB. (If the problem persists after you have excluded C000-FFFF, you are not experiencing an upper memory conflict.) If this is the case, try lower addresses until the problem reappears; in this way, you can ferret out the required exclusions.

There also is a MEMORY_INCLUDE_REGIONS setting, which you can use if the DOS memory manager is not using some potential UMB location. You should probably never have to use this feature. Consult a book on memory management for a more in-depth discussion of memory management.

Shadow RAM with HW_ROM_TO_RAM

Another DOS setting is worth examining here. Some PCs for years have offered something called *shadow RAM*. OS/2 has a similar command called HW_ROM_TO_RAM. RAMs are faster than ROMs. When a PC reads from ROM, it often must slow itself down compared to the speed with which it can read RAM. So some PCs offer the option to copy the ROMs to RAM and then make RAM mimic a ROM. Such a process is called *shadow RAM*. OS/2 copies ROMs to RAM for you if you like. Just set HW_ROM_TO_RAM to ON.

In general, however, shadow RAM does not offer much in the way of rewards because most DOS programs address hardware like video boards and keyboards directly, bypassing the ROMs. The driver programs that you have seen for DOS programs like WordPerfect, Windows, and 1-2-3 are essentially replacements for the ROMs that are intended to contain the programs that control the PC's peripherals.

The High Memory Area (HMA)

As if video mode restriction and UMBs were not enough, OS/2 has yet another trick up its sleeve that you can use to squeeze out a few more K of conventional memory.

Earlier, you saw that the top of memory for an 8088-based system was 1024K and that the IBM designers worked within that constraint when designing the PC. Further, you have seen that the constraints of the 8088 haunt PC users to this day because the DOS operating system, as well as PC applications, were written to exist within those constraints. Recall that when a 286 or later CPU (call them 286+ chips here) runs DOS programs, it does so in real mode. Because real mode copies the behavior of an 8088, the top of real mode memory should be 1024K. But when mimicking an 8088, a 286+ chip sees a slight improvement of the top memory-addressable value. Instead of a limit of 1024K, the 286 and later chips have a real mode limit of 1088K—an extra 64K.

DOS_HIGH

Perhaps an extra 64K does not sound that useful because it sits atop the system BIOS, and PC programs need all of their memory in one place in the conventional area. But OS/2 can place DOS itself into that area; this is called loading DOS high and requires just two steps:

1. In the CONFIG.SYS file, locate the line that starts DOS=. Type **HIGH** in front of the command. It will look like the following:

   DOS=HIGH,UMB (indicates that OS/2 should load DOS high and use UMBs).

   or

   DOS=HIGH,NOUMB (indicates that OS/2 should load DOS high but not use UMBs).

2. Once again, check your DOS Settings window. Click on the DOS_HIGH setting and be sure that ON (the default) is selected.

Try a DOS box with and without DOS loaded high. You should see a difference of about 23.5K.

XMS_HMA_MIN

Why not load DOS high all the time? An occasional program cannot work with DOS loaded high. Perhaps IBM tried to be conservative by not loading DOS high. Nevertheless, make this adjustment one of your first permanent changes to your OS/2 configuration. You will probably never run into trouble. If a DOS program ever refuses to run under OS/2, load DOS low again and see if that fixes the problem. You need not change CONFIG.SYS to load DOS low. Just temporarily modify the DOS Settings window.

One other reason not to load DOS high is that only one program can live in HMA. HMA has, as you have seen, a total of 64K, and DOS takes up 23.5K. Thus, 40.5K of HMA is being wasted. There are a few (very few) DOS programs that can alternately live in HMA. If this is the case, you are better off not loading DOS high; instead load an HMA-aware DOS program.

Worse yet, a few programs sniff out HMA and steal it if it is available, without even asking permission. Then, when you try to load a program high, you get an error message, indicating that HMA is not available. That is annoying because you like to control what program uses HMA. Although this is not a very common problem, OS/2 has a command to give some extra control of HMA: it is called XMS_HMA_MIN, and it is set to a value between 0 and 64. This value refers to a threshold memory requirement that a program must satisfy before OS/2 loads that program into HMA. For example, suppose there is a 16K program that insists on loading itself into HMA, denying you access to HMA for a larger program. Set the XMS_HMA_MIN to 17; and OS/2 does not allow any program smaller than 17K to load into HMA. The default value is 0, meaning that there is no restriction by default.

Getting the Most Memory

You have seen that there are three approaches to gaining more memory for DOS programs:

- Restrict video mode and take 96K of addresses from the video RAM area, giving those addresses to the conventional memory area. Do not attempt it if your DOS program ever enters EGA+ graphics modes. (It still works in CGA graphics modes, but these graphics look terrible.)

- Load TSRs and device drivers into Upper Memory Blocks between 768K and 960K. This is effective under actual DOS, but not relevant for OS/2.

- Load DOS into the High Memory Area above 1024K, which nets you another 23.5K of memory.

Ignoring any benefits from UMBs, loading DOS high and restricting the video mode yields a DOS session with 729K of free space.

Enabling DOS Programs To Use Extended (XMS and DPMI) Memory

Normally, DOS programs are restricted in their use of memory to real mode's 1024K or 1088K because DOS was built to work on the 8088, and the 8088 has no memory above 1024K. The 286 and later chips can address memory beyond 1024K. This memory is called *extended* memory.

Many programmers wanted to be able to give their clients access to the extended memory that came with virtually every 286, 386, and 486 purchased after 1988. OS/2 offered the promise of getting to the extended memory, but OS/2 1.x's market troubles made programmers grow weary with the waiting. Some companies began offering programming tools called to fill in the gap until OS/2 arrived. A DOS extender is, as its name implies, a programming tool that enables programmers to build DOS programs that can use extended memory. Two standards have been developed to enable developers to build programs that use DOS extenders and remain compatible with operating systems that use extended memory like Windows and OS/2.

DPMI_DOS_API

DPMI_DOS_API is a DOS setting that controls who translates or reflects DOS requests from a DOS extender. Actually, getting to the extended memory is not terribly difficult. DOS programs rely upon DOS to perform services like reading and writing files, and this is where the problem arises. DOS itself can only be called by a processor that is in real mode; recall that an 8088 processor only had real mode, and that 286 and later processors only have real mode for purposes of backward compatibility with the 8088. Thus, a program created with a DOS extender requiring DOS's help in doing some kind of input/output must first return to real mode before making a service request of DOS. The process of shifting the processor from protected to real mode and reissuing a program's DOS requests to real mode is called *reflection*.

The DPMI specification was designed to accommodate a wide variety of approaches to DOS extending. Newer DPMI-compliant programs handle the translation themselves. In this case, set this value to AUTO. If, on the other hand, the program expects the operating system to do the reflection (Windows is one example), set the value to ENABLED. The majority of DOS programs do not use DOS extenders; in that case, just set the value to DISABLED. If you have an application that uses DPMI (Lotus 2.3 is one example), check with the product's manufacturer for guidance on this setting. If you do not know, leave it at the default, AUTO.

DPMI_MEMORY_LIMIT

DPMI_MEMORY_LIMIT specifies how much memory to make available to DPMI-using programs. Set it to zero if your program does not use DPMI. Setting it to zero speeds up program loading a bit because OS/2 does not have to get ready to provide the DPMI memory that is never requested.

XMS Commands

XMS (eXtended Memory Specification) is a similar standard developed by major PC manufacturers for programs that need extended memory. XMS manages extended memory, in that it keeps track of what program is using each part of extended memory. It also answers queries from programs that want to know how much extended memory is available.

XMS_HANDLES

Each block of memory allocated to a program by the XMS memory manager is pointed to by a handle. XMS_HANDLES is a DOS setting that tells the XMS memory manager the maximum number of handles a program can have. You should almost never have to change this value.

XMS also manages the UMBs that DOS uses to load device drivers and TSRs into, as well as the High Memory Area (HMA) that DOS loads itself into, freeing up conventional memory.

XMS_MEMORY_LIMIT

Most extended memory needs no care, but there is an XMS_MEMORY_LIMIT value that sets an upper limit on the amount of XMS memory that can be allocated to any one DOS application. If you know that a DOS program does not need XMS memory, it is a good idea to set this value to 0. That way, OS/2 does not have to pre-allocate memory to meet the potential need indicated by the default XMS_MEMORY_LIMIT of 2048K, two megabytes. In the process, your programs load faster.

Enabling DOS Programs To Use Expanded (EMS or LIM) Memory

Before extended memory, PC manufacturers needed some way out of the 640K straitjacket imposed by DOS's conventional memory. The problem became most evident when Lotus 1-2-3 version 2.0 was released. The new release was larger than version 1A, and programs that had fit into 640K would not fit into version 2.0.

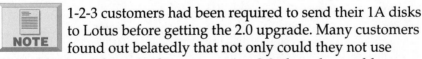

1-2-3 customers had been required to send their 1A disks to Lotus before getting the 2.0 upgrade. Many customers found out belatedly that not only could they not use their old spreadsheets in the new version 2.0; they also could no longer use version 1A because Lotus had the required disks. (People were so mad about it that Lotus contemplated a "downgrade" offer, wherein you could get your old 1A disks back for $25.)

To address this problem, EMS (Expanded Memory Specification) memory was first developed by Lotus, Intel, and Microsoft in 1985, leading to its alternate monicker, LIM memory. *Expanded memory* is a scheme whereby DOS programs can access memory beyond the normal 640K. Many programs can use this memory, including Lotus 1-2-3 version 2.x and WordPerfect version 5.1. It works by putting a 64K RAM buffer somewhere between 768K and 960K in the upper memory area. That buffer area then acts as a window to a special expanded memory board. The DOS memory manager places the 64K buffer in some location between 768K and 960K, but if you wish to place the buffer yourself, you can do that by using the EMS_FRAME_LOCATION DOS setting.

EMS_MEMORY_LIMIT

EMS_MEMORY_LIMIT specifies how much EMS memory should be made available to a DOS program. Specifying a large number forces OS/2 to find extra memory resources for a DOS program, probably slowing down the whole system. Do not specify a large number here unless it is necessary.

EMS_HIGH_OS_MAP_REGION and EMS_LOW_OS_MAP_REGION

The two remaining EMS support commands EMS_HIGH_OS_MAP_REGION and EMS_LOW_OS_MAP_REGION refer to some special features of the latest version of LIM (LIM 4.0). The low value controls a capability to backfill conventional memory, meaning to fill in any areas of the low 640K with expanded memory. While that was nice on an XT with only 512K of memory, there is no real use for it on an OS/2 machine with at least 4M of RAM. The high value enables resizing the 64K page frame area, a particularly bad idea. Whereas the LIM 4.0 specification allows a page frame of any size, 99 percent of the LIM-aware programs expect behavior consonant with the earlier LIM 3.2 specification, which mandated a 64K-page frame.

Controlling How OS/2 Shares the Computer with DOS

The next group of commands works around a fundamental problem for OS/2: how to share a computer with DOS programs that do not know how to share.

PRINT_TIMEOUT

PRINT_TIMEOUT tells OS/2 when a DOS program is finished with the printer. OS/2 programs are designed to share system resources, and the printer is no exception. Because each DOS program behaves as if it is the only program running in the system (which is generally true when running under actual DOS), the DOS program does not know that it must alert the operating system when it is finished using the printer.

When printing under OS/2, a DOS program's printed output does not go directly to the printer; rather, it is redirected to a disk file called a *spool file*. While the DOS program is printing, the output goes to the file, and all is well. But how does OS/2 know when the DOS program is finished printing? There are two methods. First, the user can press Ctrl-Alt-Prtsc combination, telling OS/2 that it is okay to send the spool file to the printer ("flush the spool" is the term). Second, OS/2 can deduce, after a certain amount of time with no printer activity, that the DOS session is completed. PRINT_TIMEOUT sets the amount of time that OS/2 waits. The default value is 15 seconds.

COM_HOLD

DOS communications programs running under OS/2 1.x sometimes would not work because the extra overhead of the operating system's polling of those communications ports would slow down communications processing so much that data would be dropped from the communications ports, usually dropping communications connections or crashing the DOS program. OS/2 1.x included a command called SETCOM40 to avert that problem. You type **SETCOM40 COM2 ON** to essentially detach COM2 (in this example) from OS/2's sight. The process is reversed when you type **SETCOM40 COM2 OFF**.

OS/2 2.0 has a similar problem, although for a different reason. Suppose you want to hand off a communications session from one DOS program to another. You cannot, normally. Once you terminate a DOS session, all of its attached hardware resources (files, COM ports, and the like) are closed. All communications sessions are terminated along with the DOS session. Similarly, upon opening a new DOS session, the COM ports not currently in use by an OS/2 program are reset, an action that also drops any active communications session.

The answer is COM_HOLD. Set it to ON, and any active communications sessions remain active, even though you close the DOS session that created them. COM_HOLD set to ON also keeps any OS/2 programs from grabbing the port. Unless you need the capability to transfer communications from one session to another, however, leave it OFF: generally, OS/2's automatic close of active communications sessions is more of a plus than a minus.

Keeping DOS from Wasting Time: IDLE_SENSITIVITY and IDLE_SECONDS

Efficiency is a necessity for a multitasking operating system. The actual amount of CPU shared with the running programs is woefully scarce—you have probably never said to yourself, "Gosh, this program is running quickly! What can I do to slow it down?" Ideally, OS/2 would like every single microsecond of the CPU's time engaged in useful pursuits.

DOS programs, on the other hand, waste tremendous amounts of time. Take an average DOS word processing program. What does it spend most of its time doing? Waiting; waiting for a keystroke.

When a program like WordPerfect is idle, it just checks the keyboard repeated for any keystrokes.

Although OS/2 was built to multitask with DOS programs, it does not want a DOS program to waste time, any more than it wants an OS/2 program to waste time. OS/2 tries to detect when a DOS program is just polling the keyboard. Detecting keyboard polling is not a straightforward task; it is hard to tell the difference between a routine read of the keyboard and an idle polling. So OS/2 keeps track of the percentage of the application's time spent polling the keyboard.

IDLE_SENSITIVITY is a DOS setting expressed as a percentage from 0 to 100. It means "If you find the application spending more than X percent of its time reading the keyboard, assume that it is idle and stop wasting CPU time on it." OS/2, in that case, greatly reduces the CPU time that the application gets, slowing down the application (which does not care because it is idle anyway) and freeing up CPU time for the other programs running in the PC at the moment. A value of 75, then, tells OS/2 not to consider an application idle until it is spending 75 percent of its time reading the keyboard. A value of 100 turns off idle detection, saying to OS/2, "Don't consider this application idle until it is spending 100 percent of its time reading the keyboard."

IDLE_SECONDS is the other OS/2 multitasking tuning parameter. Every time the application receives a keystroke, OS/2 can be certain that it is not idle because the user is clearly interacting with that application. Because monitoring the program for idleness requires some time on OS/2's part, it would be nice not to have to burn up too much CPU time performing a monitoring role. IDLE_SECONDS tells OS/2 to not bother monitoring until Y seconds have passed from the previous keystroke. Zero seconds is the IDLE_SECONDS default setting. The bigger the number, the longer the time before OS/2 can consider lowering priority.

It is worth mentioning that OS/2 cannot always detect that an application has received keyboard input, so you may sometimes see an application slow down in the middle of a session for no apparent reason. In that case, try setting IDLE_SENSITIVITY to 100 and IDLE_SECONDS to a large number.

DOS_BACKGROUND_EXECUTION

The idea behind the OS/2 approach to disabling idle programs is a good one. But why not use a more straightforward approach to recovering CPU time that is usually wasted on idle DOS applications—to shut them down in the background. When most DOS applications are in the background, they are not doing anything. This is not always true—a recalculating spreadsheet would be a counter-example, as would any communications program or an application that is busy printing, but it is usually the case that when a DOS application is not interactive with a user, it is not doing anything. You can tell OS/2 to temporarily suspend any DOS application while it is in the background by setting DOS_BACKGROUND_EXECUTION to OFF. The default value is ON. This setting is one that can be turned on or off for an active window, or it can be permanently set for a program object.

Sharing Mice and Touch Screens

MOUSE_EXCLUSIVE_ACCESS has already been discussed in this chapter. It is another command that makes DOS and OS/2 share an input device—in this case, a mouse. TOUCH_EXCLUSIVE_ACCESS does the same thing for a touch screen, such as the one that IBM sells with the PS/2 model 57 Ultimedia multimedia PC.

DOS Settings for Keyboard Control

A few commands control the way that OS/2 enables DOS programs to communicate with the keyboard. You can enable or disable certain hot keys, keep DOS programs from messing with the keyboard interface, and speed up the capability of DOS programs to cut-and-paste among themselves.

KBD_ALTHOME_BYPASS and KBD_CTRL_BYPASS

You use KBD_ALTHOME_BYPASS and KBD_CTRL_BYPASS when your DOS program needs a keystroke that OS/2 is snatching away for itself. As you know, the Alt-Home key combination switches a DOS session in full screen or windowed mode. That means that OS/2 is monitoring every single keystroke that you feed to DOS, checking to see if it is a keystroke that is meant for OS/2 before handing it over to your DOS application. Besides Alt-Home, the Alt-Esc and Ctrl-Esc combinations have meaning to OS/2; they force a switch away from the DOS program to the next active program (Alt-Esc) or to the OS/2 Task Window (Ctrl-Esc).

What if you have a program that needs one of those keystrokes? Many terminal-emulation programs use Alt-Esc or Ctrl-Esc to switch from one terminal session to another. If OS/2 snatches those keystrokes away, then the DOS-based terminal emulator never sees them, making it unable to switch between terminal sessions.

If you are faced with a problem like this, take a look at the KBD_ALTHOME_BYPASS or KBD_CTRL_BYPASS DOS settings. Set to ON, you can tell OS/2 to ignore Alt-Home (KBD_ALTHOME_BYPASS) or the Alt-Esc and Ctrl-Esc combinations (KBD_CTRL_BYPASS).

 If you bypass all three control combinations, you are unable to return to OS/2 from inside your DOS program until you exit the DOS program. That means that if the DOS program crashes—its keyboard no longer responds to user input—you have no choice but to warm reboot your system, possibly losing data in your other active OS/2 and DOS sessions.

KBD_BUFFER_EXTEND

Once you have used a PC for a while, you see that the PC has a type-ahead buffer of 15 characters. If the PC is busy doing something like a disk read, you can type up to 15 characters. After the PC is done, it sees what you have typed and acts upon it. That is convenient because it means that you need not wait for the PC to finish whatever it is doing before issuing a short command. But the buffer is only 15 characters long; if you type any more, the PC chirps at you. OS/2 improves the DOS session's type-ahead buffer by increasing its size to 128 characters. If, on the other hand, you want to restrict the size of the type-ahead buffer to the normal 15 characters used by DOS, click on the KBD_BUFFER_EXTEND setting in the DOS Settings window. By default, it is ON. If your keyboard input is garbled, try changing the value of KBD_BUFFER_EXTEND to OFF. It is not clear why a large buffer could cause a problem, but IBM added this option just in case.

KBD_RATE_LOCK

The introduction of the AT made a radical change in the way the system communicates with the keyboard. For one thing, the responsiveness of the keyboard can be controlled in software on most 286 and later systems. The 8042 keyboard controller chip accepts software commands to modify the repeat rate and the delay time of keystrokes. Setting the delay time low and the repeat rate high makes for a very fast and responsive keyboard. One of the items in the OS/2 System Setup folder enables you to control the responsiveness of your keyboard. If you have not taken the time, experiment with keyboard speeds to improve your productivity.

Now and then, however, you come across a DOS program that seems determined to reset your keyboard controller to some ideal setting envisioned by the program's designer. OS/2 gives you a DOS setting in this case that you can use to defeat the DOS program's attempt to adjust your keyboard delay and repeat rates: set KBD_RATE_LOCK to ON.

Cutting-and-Pasting between DOS Applications and Using VIDEO_FASTPASTE

It may not sound like it, but VIDEO_FASTPASTE controls a keyboard option, not a video option. After you have a DOS text screen in a window, you can click on the window's pop-up menu and select Mark. By holding down the right mouse button and dragging the cursor, you can mark an area, as you see in figure 6.15.

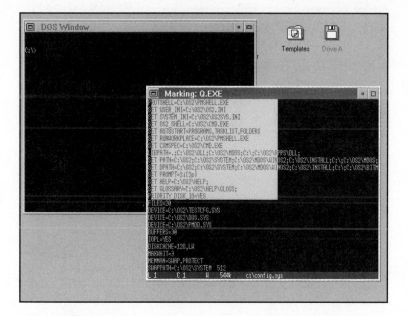

Figure 6.15:
Marking an area in a DOS window to copy to the Clipboard.

Figure 6.15 shows QEdit, a simple ASCII text editor, that has been opened to examine CONFIG.SYS. Open the pop-up menu again, click on Copy, and OS/2 sends the marked text to the Clipboard. Alternatively, you can open the pop-up window, click on Copy **A**ll, and all of the visible screen is copied to the Clipboard. To paste, open the pop-up menu of the DOS session that you intend to paste the text into, and click on **P**aste, as illustrated in figure 6.16.

The second DOS window also is running a copy of the QEdit ASCII text editor. After the paste is finished, the screen looks like figure 6.17.

You can even paste the information from a DOS window into an OS/2 program like the OS/2 System Editor, if you like.

Nevertheless, the OS/2 cut-and-paste does work for some applications, and you may find it valuable, although it is kind of slow. Copying 50 lines of text from one DOS screen to another in one test took 16 seconds on a 20 Mhz 386SX. On a character-by-character basis, that is a pasting rate of about 140 characters-per-second, which is why there is the VIDEO_FASTPASTE alternative.

Figure 6.16:

Choosing Paste
from a DOS
window's pop-up
menu.

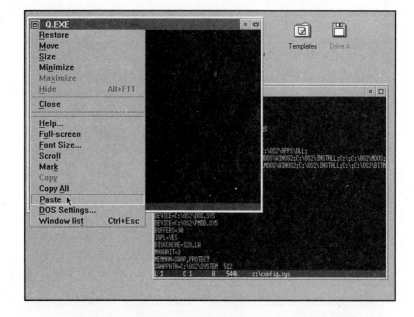

Figure 6.17:

The result of a
paste to a text
editor.

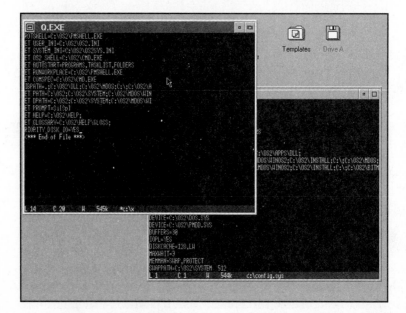

A keystroke gets to an application through a multistep process. First, you press the key. The CPU notices that the key has been pressed and transfers the keystroke information to the keyboard buffer. (This is the area that is 15 bytes long under DOS, but that can optionally grow to 128 bytes under OS/2's DOS emulation.) Finally, DOS or the application examines the keystroke and acts on it. VIDEO_FASTPASTE bypasses the keyboard by stuffing the pasted text right into the keyboard buffer. The paste test mentioned before was rerun with VIDEO_FASTPASTE enabled, and what took 16 seconds without fast pasting took a mere 4 seconds with fast pasting enabled.

The fact that OS/2 enables you to cut-and-paste between DOS applications seems pretty improbable, even if it does work. Although DOS programs have no notion of cut-and-paste, the way that OS/2 pulls this trick off is by first capturing any marked text on the screen from the cut application to be the Clipboard, and then simulating the text being keystroked into the paste application. It may not work because OS/2 only inserts carriage returns at the ends of lines. For instance, consider what happens if you cut a column of figures from WordPerfect and paste the column to 1-2-3. OS/2 simulates the process of typing number after number with a carriage return between them. With 1-2-3, however, this does not work. You need a carriage return followed by a down arrow, and there is no way to make Paste add a down arrow. The result is that OS/2 types each number into the first 1-2-3 cell, overwriting the previous number.

Of course, this cut-and-paste process does not work everywhere. Some DOS programs never look in the keyboard buffer, preferring to grab the keystrokes directly from the keyboard. Fast pasting does not work for them.

Controlling Sound with HW_NOSOUND

PC users have long asked "Is there a way to shut off the sound on one of those obnoxious programs that insists on beeping, whistling, and chiming?" Because sound support has never been handled by a well-defined interface, up to now the answer has been no. The reason has to do with the method whereby software communicates with the speaker. Other PC input/output operations, like disk reads and writes, keyboard reads, and screen writes can be handled by a software interface called an *interrupt*. For example, INT13 (interrupt 13) is the software interface to the disk drives. That does not mean that programs addressing the drives must use INT13, but many do. Having a central interface to a piece of hardware makes adding value to that hardware easy. A disk-cache program under DOS, for example, can work for virtually all PC programs, without the complicity of the programs, because all the cache needs to do is attach itself to INT13. Because the applications programs use INT13 to address the drives, these programs do not notice that the cache program is hooked to INT13—unless they notice that the disk is suddenly running a lot faster.

If sound had a single interrupt, programmers could write a program that would monitor that interrupt, stopping all attempts to produce sound. But, because sound does not have an interrupt, all sound-producing programs must write their own program code to manipulate the speaker. And because there is no central depot for sound requests, there is no central point for a "no sound" program to monitor.

OS/2 solves this problem simply with the HW_NOSOUND DOS setting. How is it that OS/2 succeeds where DOS fails? OS/2 runs DOS programs by creating an image of an 8088-based PC. When putting data on the screen, for example, DOS programs do not communicate with the video board. They communicate instead with a virtual image of a video board. The way OS/2 disables sound is to simply leave the speaker out of its virtual image of an 8088. To disable sound, then, open your DOS settings window, click on HW_NOSOUND, and select ON. The default is OFF, so unless you tell it otherwise, OS/2 includes sound support in its DOS emulation.

Video Support for DOS Programs under OS/2

DOS has never directly supported much of the PC's video capabilities, and that portion of the video that DOS does support has not done well, which has made the task of video support under OS/2 a tough one.

In 1981, when DOS first appeared, the DOS programmer's reference (which was included in the DOS user manual, perhaps because most users then were programmers) included sample programming code that demonstrated how a programmer could use DOS to display information on the screen by using a programming construct called INT 21. Many programmers followed IBM's and Microsoft's advice and employed the INT 21 interface.

The INT 21 interface was not written by Microsoft to be very fast, so early programs that followed IBM/Microsoft's advice found programs with very slow screens. The original version of a then-popular word processor, WordStar, used INT 21. So programmers began designing their programs to bypass DOS's INT 21, directly putting video information on the screen. Microsoft and IBM warned that such programming practices lead to poorly behaved programs that might not work in future versions of DOS and might not work on all PC compatibles. Programmers were not happy about the situation, but they really had no choice: who would buy unusable software? Today, almost no commercial software uses INT 21 to put data on the screen—every program on the market bypasses DOS to show text.

This effect is exacerbated by INT 21's lack of completeness. PC video boards can do many things that are not supported by INT 21—graphics of any kind, the 43-line text mode of the EGA, or the 50-line text mode of the VGA.

 OS/2 supports various graphics modes, however. To see a 50-line screen under VGA, type **mode co80,50** in any command-prompt screen, whether windowed or full screen.

Consequently, there are many programming practices that form a kind of informal standard that programmers use when manipulating display screens, and OS/2 needed some DOS settings to cope with those practices. You can use them to speed up your video screen or to solve a compatibility problem, such as when the screen blanks itself for no reason or when the colors on your screen change inexplicably when you put a DOS program into the background and then bring it back to the foreground. The following sections give you the details on the video DOS settings.

VIDEO_ONDEMAND_MEMORY

VIDEO_ONDEMAND_MEMORY controls how OS/2 allocates memory for a DOS program's video image. When you tell OS/2 to shift a DOS program into the background, OS/2 stores the current screen image somewhere in memory, so that OS/2 can restore that image when you tell OS/2 to bring the DOS program back to the foreground. How much memory does OS/2 need to save a DOS screen? As table 6.2 illustrates, different video modes require different amounts of RAM.

Table 6.2

Memory Requirements of Various Video Modes

Mode	Memory Required (K)
80 x 25 text	4
80 x 43 text (EGA+ only)	7
80 x 50 text (VGA+ only)	8
any CGA graphics mode	16
EGA graphics	256
VGA graphics	256
super VGA	256-1024
XGA	1024

A simple DOS text screen requires no more than 4K of memory to store and retrieve data. A super VGA or XGA screen, on the other hand, can require as much as 1024K of RAM to store and retrieve data. Many programs spend some time in text (low RAM requirement) mode, and some time in graphics mode. If you switch away from a program in graphics mode, OS/2 must then find more memory to save that video image than it would have if you switched away when in text mode. That does not mean that you should not switch away from DOS programs when they are in graphics mode, but it does imply that there is a greater memory requirement for graphics.

If, for example, OS/2 is memory constrained at the time you switch away from a graphics program, what does it do? When OS/2 runs out of actual RAM, it conscripts disk space to serve as RAM. This use of disk space to substitute for RAM is called *virtual memory*. If you switch away from a DOS program, and the hard disk drive light suddenly comes on, do not be alarmed. It just means that OS/2 was getting low on memory and it moved some of the DOS program temporarily to disk. (OS/2's virtual memory method of temporarily moving RAM to disk is called *paging*.)

What does this have to do with the VIDEO_ONDEMAND_MEMORY setting? When you tell OS/2 to load a DOS program, it first locates enough free RAM to load the program, then it loads the program into that RAM, and then it executes the program. By default—when VIDEO_ONDEMAND_MEMORY is ON—OS/2 puts off the problem of finding enough memory to store the video image until you actually switch away from the DOS program.

 Where does the video image stay until you switch from the DOS program? There is memory right on the video board itself; while the image is on-screen, the image stays in the video RAM.

OS/2 puts off finding the space for the video image until it absolutely needs the space. This is a good idea, because ferreting out 1M of RAM (in the case of super VGA or XGA) can take some time and limit OS/2's memory-management options. Besides, you may terminate the DOS program before you ever switch away from it, rendering the appropriation of extra storage space a waste of the system's resources.

On the other hand, when you switch away from the DOS program, OS/2 must then find the space for the video image, and that may take time, making you wait. Worse, in some situations, OS/2 may not be able to find sufficient space for the video image either in RAM or on disk; in that case, the program's screen image is probably damaged by the switch.

VIDEO_8514A_XGA_IOTRAP

Related to the VIDEO_ONDEMAND_MEMORY setting is VIDEO_8514A_XGA_IOTRAP. When IBM introduced the 8514A video coprocessor, and its successor, the XGA coprocessor, it also established a set of programming standards to control these boards, called the *Application Interface* or, as it is known among programmers, the AI. Not all programs use the AI; some programmers write directly to the video hardware, as in the case of earlier video boards. That is a fast way to address the video board, but it requires OS/2 to set aside 1024K of RAM to buffer video images. Set to OFF, the system assumes that the program uses the AI interface, rather than direct memory writes. If it works, it frees up 1024K of memory. If it does not, you get incomplete screens when you switch into and out of the background, altered color palettes, or blank screens.

VIDEO_RETRACE_EMULATION

The next video control setting is VIDEO_RETRACE_EMULATION. When CGA video was popular, programmers learned that bypassing INT 21 and directly modifying the video memory can put data on screens quickly, but this process is not without drawbacks.

Video and television screens use an electron gun to hit the picture tube with a stream of electrons, illuminating parts of it and producing a picture. Programmers soon found that programs writing directly to the video board should only do so during *retrace periods*, times which are when the electron gun inside the monitor is briefly switched off. Because OS/2 puts a layer of device drivers between the DOS program and the actual video hardware, there is no longer any need to look for the retrace signals. The DOS programs do not know that, however, because they are totally unaware that they are running under anything but DOS.

The VIDEO_RETRACE_EMULATION, when set to ON, simulates retrace signals. Turning it ON or OFF does not affect most programs, but it is worth playing with because it may actually speed up some programs. On the other hand, it also may cause some other programs's screens to be totally blank when switched into and out of the background, or the color palette may end up altered. This is a dynamic switch—you can change it at run time—so experiment if you are getting a blank screen on a DOS application in full screen mode.

VIDEO_SWITCH_NOTIFICATION

Another DOS video setting, VIDEO_SWITCH_NOTIFICATION, has a default of OFF, and you should probably leave it there. When you ask OS/2 to switch a DOS program to the background, you are asking OS/2 to save a copy of the current screen in memory. But OS/2 only knows how much information to save if it understands your video board. If your system has a super VGA or another unusual board, OS/2 may not save all information needed to refresh the board's image when you return the DOS program to the foreground. To combat this potential problem, some programs written specifically for those boards support switch notification, whereby they rebuild their screens when notified that they had been switched away. Although no major programs support this feature, try this command if the screen disappears when you switch a DOS program into the background and then bring it back into the foreground.

VIDEO_WINDOW_REFRESH

VIDEO_WINDOW_REFRESH is only relevant to windowed DOS sessions. Because the Workplace Shell has a large number of things to worry about—there are probably a number of programs simultaneously active that share the OS/2 desktop when you have a DOS window open—Workplace Shell must know how often to redraw the DOS window. The value is in tenths of seconds, and the default—1—means that the screen is redrawn ten times-per-second. Setting the value lower makes the system faster overall, but it does fewer redraws, making the screen look jerky. Because the differences between different values for this parameter are most easily seen in graphics mode, you can enter a short QBASIC program that tests the speed with which OS/2 puts graphics on a VGA (or more advanced) video board under DOS.

To check out this feature of OS/2, do the following:

1. From a DOS command prompt, type QBASIC.

2. Press Esc to clear the opening screen.

3. Enter the following QBASIC program:

```
a = TIMER
SCREEN 12
FOR i = 0 TO 300 STEP 30
 x = 50 + i
 y = 50 + i
 CIRCLE (x, y), 100, 1
 PAINT (x+28, y+28), 1, 1
NEXT
b = TIMER
PRINT "Time required="; b - a; "seconds."
```

4. Save the program by clicking on File, and then on Save As in the QBASIC menu. When prompted for a file name, use GRAFTEST.BAS. You may find that QBASIC does not respond to mouse clicks on its menu when running on some computers; in that case, set MOUSE_EXCLUSIVE_ACCESS to ON, as you have seen earlier in this chapter.

5. Press F5, and the test briefly runs. At the top of the screen, GRAFTEST reports the number of seconds that the test took to complete. You may get a number that seems too small, but that is normal, because OS/2 is a multitasking operating system. Just because you waited 15 seconds for the program does not mean that the program took 15 seconds; some of those 15 seconds were taken up in OS/2 housekeeping.

Try the test under several circumstances in the following fashion:

1. First, start from a full screen. There is no difference in performance, no matter what you set VIDEO_WINDOW_REFRESH to.

2. Switch from full-screen to windowed mode with the Alt-Home key combination.

3. Click on the DOS window's pop-up menu, as you have done before, and click on DOS Settings. Remember that you are not making a permanent change to the DOS settings; VIDEO_WINDOW_REFRESH is one of the dynamic commands that you can change on the fly. Click on VIDEO_WINDOW_REFRESH and note that the value is 1. Click on Save.

4. Run the GRAFTEST program again with an F5. Note that it is now taking a bit longer.

5. Change VIDEO_WINDOW_REFRESH from 1 to 30; that is, tell the system to only update the window every 30 tenths of a second, or every three seconds. Run the test again.

What you probably saw in the last step were two things. First, the circles do not appear on screen smoothly, but in a choppy fashion. Second, it took less time than the program did with the smaller refresh rate. The first result was as expected: fewer screen updates means choppy output. The second result makes sense also: fewer screens displayed means less CPU time devoted to displaying data. You get a faster display system, but at the price of discomfitting output.

Another interesting side effect of the video refresh is its effect on the mouse. If you have turned MOUSE_EXCLUSIVE_ACCESS to ON, turn it OFF. Set the refresh rate high, and you find that the mouse does not work very well. You expect to see a change in the menu—an item on the screen—whenever you click the mouse. Less frequent refreshes mean that the menus become sluggish or seem to disappear altogether. So avoid high refresh rates with mouse-driven programs.

File I/O Control

If you are familiar with DOS, you have probably noticed that most CONFIG.SYS files include the line FILES=, and the line FCBS=. Those commands remain to this day, even in OS/2. PC applications make heavy use of files, so there are DOS settings to control how DOS applications handle files. DOS_FILES, DOS_FCBS, and DOS_FCBS_KEEP are included in OS/2's DOS support so that OS/2 can even support programs written for DOS 1.0.

Under DOS 1.0, a program that needs to read a file did so by creating a small (128 byte) area in memory called a *File Control Block* or FCB. The FCB contained information like the name of the file, the size of the file, where the program was currently reading from in the file, and other information needed by DOS and the application to get the job done. Under DOS 2.0, Microsoft restructured file input/output to use *file handles*. A file handle is a "porthole" through which an OS/2 or DOS program can read or write a file. File handles are numbered. A program accesses a file by first asking the operating system to connect the file to a file handle, and then the program reads or writes through that handle. You need not worry about the differences between FCBs and file handles; understand that programs are either written to use FCBs or file handles. The vast majority of DOS programs on the market today, and in fact those that have been on the market since 1985, use file handles; FCBs are only used by the DOS ERASE command.

The OS/2 DOS emulator does not use FCBs.

You tell a DOS session how many FCBs to leave space for the DOS_FCBS DOS setting. If a program needs more FCBs than you have enabled DOS to have, DOS closes the FCB that has not been used for the longest time—the least recently used FCB. DOS is allowed to recycle FCBs, forcing a program using an FCB to reopen it if DOS has recycled the FCB. That is where DOS_FCBS_KEEP comes in. It tells DOS how many FCBs not to recycle. Default values for DOS_FCBS and DOS_FCBS_KEEP are 16 and 8, respectively. If you set the values to 3 and 3, you have no compatibility problems and also save a little memory.

Miscellaneous DOS Settings

There are a few DOS settings that do not really fit in anywhere. That does not mean that they are not important, however.

DOS_BREAK

You know that the Ctrl-Break key sequence sometimes stops a process dead in its tracks. But you probably also know from experience that the Ctrl-Break key sequence does not always work. To understand the reason why, you need to understand how DOS or OS/2 uses the Ctrl-Break sequence. Ordinarily, the operating systems only monitor the keyboard for a Ctrl-Break sequence when writing text to the screen or when accepting input from the keyboard. Thus, you can use the Ctrl-Break sequence, but it is ignored by the operating system while it is reading the disk or sending output to the printer. You can, however, optionally tell the system to monitor the keyboard for a Ctrl-Break whenever the application requests something of the system—every time the application sends output to the printer, reads the disk, or requests more memory. Ctrl-Break is still ignored by the application itself, but the frequency with which the OS checks for Ctrl-Break increases, making it more likely that your frantic "Stop!" request is heeded. The one disadvantage to this extra Ctrl-Break checking is that is slows the system down.

The DOS_BREAK setting controls how frequently the system checks for Ctrl-Break. Set to OFF, it causes the system to only check for Ctrl-Break when doing video output or keyboard input. Set to ON, it instructs the system to check for Ctrl-Break whenever the application makes a request of the operating system. The default is OFF. By the way, you may know the DOS CONFIG.SYS statement BREAK=. This is the direct analog of that command.

DOS_STARTUP_DRIVE

It was not until the 386 chip that DOS multitasking was truly feasible. Since then, many DOS multitasking operating systems have been made available. Perhaps the most interesting DOS multitasker was VM/386 from IGC. VM/386 did all the things that you expect DOS multitaskers to do, and something else besides. Every other DOS multitasker could do multitasking of a single copy of DOS. Once you had settled on DOS 3.3 as your DOS baseline, you could spawn as many DOS 3.3 sessions as you liked. What made VM/386 unique was that you could run different versions of DOS all at the same time. For a long time, it was the only multitasker that could do that—until OS/2 2.0 came along.

As you know, you can partition a hard disk into several logical disk drives. A 300M hard disk, for example, can be divided into a 100M C: drive, a 100M D: drive, and a 100M E: drive. Ordinarily, you would not make any of those drives bootable, except for drive C:, but with OS/2 you can make any of those disks bootable, and all with different versions of DOS. DOS 3.31 could go on drive D, and DOS 4.01 could go on drive E:. Then you can specify that a particular DOS session should boot from D: or E:. The impact of this is that you are not running the DOS emulator but an actual copy of DOS. You accomplish this with the DOS_STARTUP_DRIVE DOS setting.

Just put the drive letter into its edit field, and that DOS session only starts from the specified drive. If you only need this capability once in a while, you can specify drive A:, the floppy drive. Then, when you want to run this special session that requires an actual version of DOS rather than the emulator, you can insert a bootable floppy containing the desired version of DOS.

Why would you use an actual copy of DOS rather than the DOS emulator? You may find that certain rare DOS programs do not run under the emulator. In that case, an actual copy of DOS may be all that works.

DOS_VERSION

Some DOS programs may refuse to run under OS/2's DOS emulator because they insist on a particular version of DOS, such as version 3.3 or 4.01. You may not have to go to the trouble of running such programs under actual DOS with DOS_STARTUP_DRIVE, however. The setting DOS_VERSION may save the day. Open the DOS Settings window, click on DOS_VERSION, and you see a screen such as the one illustrated in figure 6.18.

Note the lines of program names that you can see in the right-hand list window. One such line says `IBMCACHE.SYS,3,40,255`. It is in four parts, each separated by a comma. The first item is the name of the executable program file, IBMCACHE.SYS in this case. Whenever it queries the DOS emulator about what version DOS it is currently running under, the DOS emulator is instructed to respond, "DOS version 3.40," as indicated by the next two numbers—"3" and "40". The "255" is mandatory, meaning, "No matter how many times this program asks you what version DOS this is, insist that it is version 3.40." You can add as many lines to the DOS_VERSION list box as you like. Be careful, of course, because the DOS_VERSION is essentially telling OS/2 to "lie" to the DOS program in question; the program may not be stable if run under any version of DOS but the one that it insists on—and there may be a good reason for that. Use this program with some care. This is the analog of the SETVER command found under DOS 5.0.

Figure 6.18:

The DOS_VERSION setting.

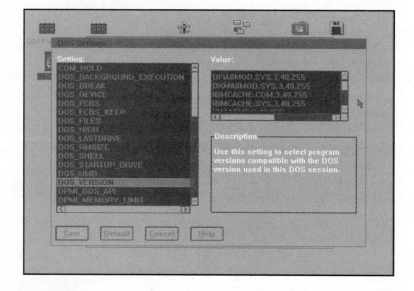

HW_TIMER

The DOS setting HW_TIMER, when ON, gives a DOS program direct access to the PC's 8253 timer port. It is not necessary for most programs, but the simulated timer that OS/2 provides is not as precise as the actual 8253 timer signal. Perhaps the emulated timer does not work for your application because the emulated timer includes some system overhead. Potentially affected programs include communications programs, low-level disk tester programs (which should not be run under OS/2 in any case), and benchmark programs. Communications programs are the most likely potential trouble spots.

DOS_LASTDRIVE

The OS/2 analog to the LASTDRIVE statement in the DOS CONFIG.SYS, DOS_LASTDRIVE sets a maximum drive letter visible to a DOS session. Although you may not find this a particularly useful setting, you can shield a particular DOS program from certain network drives—usually the drives with the higher letters—with this command.

DOS_SHELL

As you will see in Chapter 11, the DOS COMMAND.COM program and the OS/2 CMD.EXE programs are operating system *shells*, which are programs that accept user input and provide responses. It is COMMAND.COM that displays the C:\> prompt, for example. Some vendors have offered replacements for this operating system shell over the years, like QDOS, 4DOS, and Norton's Batch Enhancer. If you use these shells, or if a particular DOS program requires an alternative shell, use this DOS setting. You do not need to specify a shell for every DOS session because there is a CONFIG.SYS shell= statement that sets the default DOS shell. Yours probably looks like the following:

```
SHELL=C:\OS2\MDOS\COMMAND.COM C:\OS2\MDOS /P
```

If you replace your DOS shell with another on a wholesale basis, do not change the DOS_SHELL DOS setting. Change the CONFIG.SYS file instead.

DPMI_NETWORK_BUFF_SIZE

This setting controls the size, in kilobytes, of the network translation buffer for the DPMI applications in this session.

Summary

In this chapter, you have learned about the wide breadth of capabilities of OS/2 for supporting existing DOS programs. You have learned how to create a DOS program object, as well as how to change its DOS settings to customize the program object's session for that particular program.

You also have learned about the 45 DOS settings, which are a complete toolbelt for DOS emulation. The settings control multitasking, memory, sound, timer support, and assist DOS in providing support to programs that read and write files. There is special support for video boards and video-using programs, as well as a provision to run multiple versions of DOS simultaneously. Perhaps there is something to IBM's claim that OS/2 2.0 is a better DOS than DOS.

The OS/2 emulation of DOS has generated a lot of interest. Even more attention has been paid to its graphical adjunct—Windows. In the next chapter, you will learn how to use Windows programs under OS/2.

Running Windows Programs under OS/2

For many OS/2 enthusiasts, the most exciting news about OS/2 2.0 is its capability of running Windows programs. That is, OS/2 now "does Windows." Under an agreement with Microsoft, IBM has included a modified version of Windows 3.1 in OS/2. This means not only that OS/2 is compatible with Windows applications, but also that users no longer have to purchase Windows in addition to OS/2 if they want to run Windows programs. OS/2 now is compatible with Windows versions 3.x and 2.11, and can even run all versions of Windows at the same time.

OS/2 now truly is the integrating platform for DOS, Windows, and OS/2 programs. The Windows environment has been implemented seamlessly under OS/2. This means that Windows applications can run on the same desktop with other programs. A Windows application, for example, can run in a window next to an OS/2 PM application. Several Windows programs can run with other programs, all in view at the same time.

This chapter shows you how OS/2 supports the Windows operating environment and describes the manner in which Windows is implemented in OS/2, including OS/2's memory allocation for Windows sessions. You learn how to install Windows applications and the various methods of launching Windows applications from OS/2. You then explore performance issues affecting Windows applications under OS/2 and learn some of the basic OS/2 options that help you fine-tune your Windows applications. This chapter closes with a discussion of Windows' popular OLE and DDE features, and shows you how well they work under OS/2. Specifically, this chapter covers the following topics:

- Interfacing Windows memory management with OS/2
- Windows operating modes supported by OS/2
- Installing Windows applications
- Starting Windows programs under OS/2
- Anticipating performance differences
- Tuning Windows applications
- Using OLE and DDE between Windows applications

Portions of this chapter are provided as architectural background, while other portions are tutorial.

Interfacing Windows Memory Management with OS/2

OS/2 enables you to run Windows applications in Standard mode as well as in real mode. Windows originally was designed to operate in real mode because the original IBM PC used the Intel 8088 microprocessor, which can run only in Real mode. In Real mode, the processor can directly access 1M of memory, with 640K of that memory set aside for applications, DOS, and Windows. As applications became more complex, however, they soon ran out of memory.

With the introduction of the Intel 80286 processor, however, things changed. The 80286 microprocessor includes a "protected" mode, which can address 16M of RAM. When used with an 80286 processor, Windows 3.0 switches the system from Real mode to protected mode. Because DOS is strictly a Real-mode operating system, it is not able to take advantage of protected mode by itself; Windows must accomplish this task. In Windows, this mode is called Standard mode. Almost all Windows applications written today require *Standard* mode. The capability to implement Windows in Standard mode was the major design task for IBM in developing OS/2.

When running under OS/2, the only form of memory management not available to Windows is 386-enhanced mode. Because OS/2 is a 32-bit operating system and runs in 386 mode, no other operating system can run under it in that mode. Developers may someday find a way around this by emulating 386-enhanced mode, but not in this version of OS/2.

Even so, the lack of Windows' enhanced-mode operation should not create any major problems, except in the most unusual cases. Very few Windows applications actually require 386-enhanced mode under Windows. Windows 386-enhanced mode is designed primarily for executing multiple DOS programs under Windows and for providing a crude virtual DOS environment. OS/2 already excels in this area, and provides far superior DOS multitasking to Windows 386-enhanced mode. OS/2 also provides critical protection between these DOS sessions.

Figure 7.1 shows an example of several applications running under OS/2's memory-management scheme. Session 1 is an OS/2 application. Session 2 is a DOS application. This DOS application could very well be using DOS Protected-Mode Interface (DPMI) or eXtended Memory Specification (XMS) memory. Session 3 shows a Windows 2.11 application running in Real mode. Session 4 shows three Windows 3.x applications all running under one copy of Windows in Standard mode. The last session, session 5, shows one application running its own copy of Windows in Standard mode.

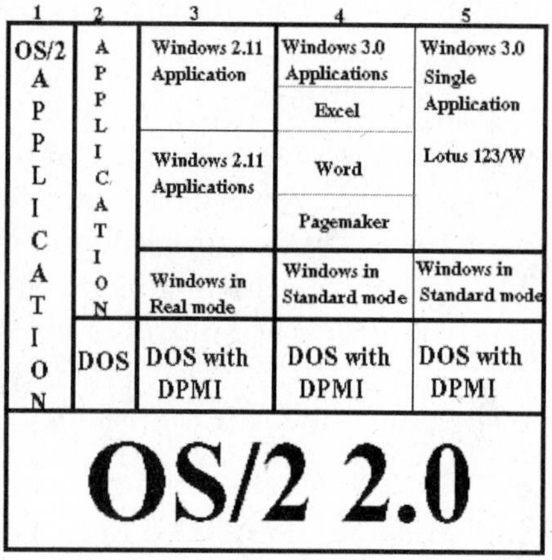

Figure 7.1:

Several sessions running on top of an OS/2 foundation.

1	2	3	4	5
OS/2 APPLICATION	APPLICATION	Windows 2.11 Application	Windows 3.0 Applications Excel	Windows 3.0 Single Application
		Windows 2.11 Applications	Word Pagemaker	Lotus 123/W
		Windows in Real mode	Windows in Standard mode	Windows in Standard mode
	DOS	DOS with DPMI	DOS with DPMI	DOS with DPMI

OS/2 2.0

The last two sessions illustrate the difference between running several programs under one copy of Windows and running a single program under one copy of Windows. Session 5 has the greatest system tolerance for application failure. If session 5 fails, no other tasks are affected. In the case of session 4, however, if one of the Windows tasks fails, the other applications sharing that copy of Windows also are terminated.

OS/2 2.0 now provides limited 80286 emulation, which is required for Windows Standard mode as well as other applications that must access extended memory. One such application is Lotus 1-2-3 version 3.1.

NOTE OS/2 now also features a virtual HIMEM.SYS, which allows the DOS compatibility box to load DOS in high memory, a feature found in DOS 5.0. This frees almost 640K of memory for DOS programs. The DOS Protected-Mode Interface (DPMI) is the memory server chosen by Microsoft for Windows. Under DOS, Windows uses EMM386.EXE to provide this function. Under OS/2, DPMI has been virtualized and is available to each DOS session. Not all applications use DPMI. In those cases, DPMI can be disabled for that session. Disabling DPMI conserves resources and improves performance.

See Chapter 6 for more information about setting up sessions to support non-Windows DOS applications.

The Windows included in OS/2 has been modified to use OS/2 as its DPMI server. Any program that runs under DPMI on an 80286 should run under OS/2 2.0.

OS/2's capability to emulate the Windows 3.x environment is evident in its capability to simulate various DOS versions. The DOS 5.0 SETVER command enables you to specify the version of DOS that is reported to an application. OS/2 2.0 offers this same capability on a session-by-session basis. Some applications need to be told they are running on DOS 3.30, 4.01, or 5.0 even if they are not. This bit of trickery is necessary due to continuing changes in the operating systems arena. With this basic understanding of how OS/2's DOS is emulated, it is now easier to understand how Windows Standard mode is implemented under OS/2.

Windows Operating Modes Supported by OS/2

In OS/2, you can interact with the Windows environment in two ways: by running Windows either in full-screen mode or in an OS/2 window. The full-screen mode is the OS/2 default when running Windows, and will be familiar to seasoned Windows users. When OS/2 runs Windows in full-screen mode, the Windows Program Manager, icons, and other Windows objects occupy the entire screen. OS/2 remains in the background ("behind" Windows); you can bring the OS/2 interface to the foreground by pressing Ctrl-Esc.

The new seamless integration of Windows into the OS/2 environment enables Windows applications to coexist with DOS and OS/2 applications. This is likely to become the most common way to run Windows applications under OS/2.

Task protection has long been touted as one of OS/2's greatest benefits. Just as OS/2 protects one OS/2 application from having problems when another application crashes, it also provides protection in the DOS/Windows environments. Most Windows 3.0 users have experienced an Unrecoverable Application Error (UAE) and know first-hand about the disagreeable situation of losing data and having to restart the computer. Windows has received a lot of unwanted notoriety for its instability and routine UAEs. The robust task-protection mechanisms provided by OS/2 minimize UAEs and offer a reasonable solution to this problem.

Each Windows session runs under OS/2's task protection. If a Windows application should terminate or crash during use, only that task is ended. All other sessions and programs continue to run in the background and are immune to a particular session's disaster. Only the crashed session needs to be ended and restarted. If, however, multiple Windows programs are running under that one Windows session, they also must be restarted.

Installing Windows Applications

The first question to ask when deciding to run Windows programs under OS/2 is how to install them. One way is from within Windows itself. To do this, just start a full-screen Windows session from the OS/2 Command Prompts folder. When the familiar Windows desktop starts, just follow the instructions that came with your software. You can even install Adobe's Type Manager in this manner. In most cases, you select Run from the File drop-down menu selection of Program Manager. This is the standard means of installing Windows programs under the pure Windows environment and is by far the best way to install Windows programs under OS/2.

You also can accomplish the same thing by typing the following command at a full-screen DOS prompt:

```
WINOS2 A:\INSTALL
```

Note that under OS/2, WINOS2 is equivalent to running Windows 3.x under DOS. When running Windows under DOS, you would type the following command:

```
WIN A:\INSTALL
```

Working with a full-screen Windows session is the best way to install Windows applications for several reasons. First, this is the environment that the Windows installation programs expect to encounter when they start. These programs are written and tested to install in this manner. All applications, for instance, have icon and program groups available each time you start any Windows desktop. These icons and program groups usually cannot be created under any other environment and may cause an installation failure if not used in this manner. Second, by starting a full-screen Windows session, you ensure that Windows' INI files are properly updated. This, in turn, ensures successful operation under any Windows session.

Some Windows programs, such as WordPerfect for Windows, do not use the **R**un menu option and require additional setup. Such programs run from a DOS prompt, so you need to tell them where to find Windows. In such cases, give the program the following path to find Windows:

```
C:\OS2\MDOS\WINOS2
```

Installation at the Operating System Prompt

Because DOS and Windows are run as a task or service under OS/2, installation is not limited to installation from within a full-screen Windows session. OS/2 enables you to install programs in other ways as well. If you type **A:\INSTALL** under a full-screen DOS or OS/2 prompt, OS/2 examines the file and determines if it is a Windows program. If the program is a Windows program, OS/2 automatically launches Windows and then runs the program under Windows.

Not all installation programs, however, work in this manner. In fact, this technique seems to work better from OS/2's full-screen mode than from a DOS screen. 1-2-3 for Windows is a good example. Under a full OS/2 screen, OS/2 starts the Windows desktop and usually proceeds as if you started the full-screen Windows environment yourself. If you attempt to install 1-2-3 for Windows under

DOS, on the other hand, the outcome is unpredictable; the installation program may respond that Microsoft Windows is required to install this program.

Installation through the OS/2 Desktop

The last method of installing Windows programs is the most interesting. You may have noticed, as illustrated in figure 7.2, that when OS/2 is installed, an icon representing drive A appears on the OS/2 desktop.

Drive A

Figure 7.2:

The drive A icon is automatically loaded to the desktop.

If you double-click on the drive A icon, a new window opens. At this point, you can double-click on the folder in the drive A window to fill the window with an icon representing all files in the drive A root directory. Scroll through the icons until you locate the IN-STALL file. Double-click on this file to launch the installation program.

 Note that some programs install by means of a file called SETUP rather than INSTALL.

The interesting thing here is that now the program is being installed under the new OS/2 PM desktop rather than the full-screen Windows desktop. You can install 1-2-3 for Windows in this manner. 1-2-3 displays an error message stating that the icon and program group cannot be created. This is because Windows program groups and their icons are services provided by the full-screen Windows desktop—not OS/2's desktop. In this case, 1-2-3 is installed completely, but the new group and icon are not created. The bad news is that when you start a full-screen Windows desktop, the group and icon do not appear. The program is installed but it is not listed in the Windows full-screen groups.

You can add the group and icon manually, if you like. In most cases, Windows applications are launched from the OS/2 PM desktop and not from a full-screen Windows desktop. Under the OS/2 desktop, Windows program icons can be placed out on the desktop or in any folder you create. If you install OS/2 on top of a system that already contains DOS, Windows, and some Windows programs, then a Windows PM group or folder is created for you. You may decide to create any number of folders yourself and move the icons around to suit your taste and work environment.

 Chapter 2 shows you how to add program icons to your OS/2 desktop.

Starting Windows Programs under OS/2

You can launch Windows programs under OS/2 as easily as you can start them under DOS and Microsoft Windows. In fact, you can launch your Windows programs in several different ways:

- From the OS/2 desktop
- From the Windows desktop
- From the OS/2 or DOS command line
- From the STARTUP.CMD file
- From a new type of folder called Startup

The following sections briefly describe each of these methods.

Launching from the OS/2 Desktop

The preferred method for launching any program—whether it is an OS/2, DOS, or Windows program—is from the OS/2 desktop. To start the program, simply double-click on its icon. The program then starts in a new session. The type of session is determined by its settings. To view these settings, move the cursor over the icon and press the right mouse button. A window appears with an arrow to the right of the Open line. Select this arrow, and then choose Settings. The windowing selections are found under the Session tab.

Launching from the Windows Desktop

The second method of starting Windows applications is from the Windows full-screen desktop. To launch a program in this way, you need to start a full-screen Windows session and then double-click on the program icon as you normally would under Windows. OS/2 provides this technique to maintain the Windows look and feel, but this is not the operating system's ultimate design goal. As mentioned earlier, it is best to launch your applications from the OS/2 desktop.

Launching from a Command Prompt

The third way to launch a Windows program is from a command prompt. To start the program, enter the following command at either the OS/2 or DOS command prompt:

```
WINOS2 C:\PATH\FILENAME.EXT
```

You do not always need to use the WINOS2 command but, as a general rule, you should routinely use it to cover the few programs that require it. In most cases, OS/2 determines that the program is a Windows program and starts Windows automatically. To launch the program in a separate background session, enter the following command at the command prompt:

```
START WINOS2 C:\PATH\PROGRAM
```

This command launches the program but does not tie up the current session.

Launching from the Startup Facility

The last two program-launching methods—the STARTUP.CMD file and the Startup folder—are quite similar. The STARTUP.CMD file contains a series of commands that are executed each time you start your system. If you want a Windows program to launch automatically when you turn on your computer, include the following command in STARTUP.CMD:

```
START WINOS2 C:\PATH\FILENAME.EXT
```

You can achieve the same effect by dragging the desired program's icon into the Startup folder, which is located in the system folder. All programs located in this folder start automatically once the OS/2 desktop has been initialized. This program-launching technique provides a simple means of adding and managing the programs you want to start automatically.

If you want to launch two programs under the same Windows session, you can add statements to the same line, such as the following:

```
WINOS2 C:\123W\123W C:\WINWORD\WINWORD
```

This command launches 1-2-3 for Windows and Word for Windows in the same Windows session. If your system's memory is tight, this technique may offer the best Windows performance.

 Launching multiple Windows programs under the same Windows session has some drawbacks. As mentioned earlier, OS/2 protects one session from another. But this is true only when each application runs in its own session. In the preceding example, 1-2-3 and Word share the same session. If the Word application crashes, it also brings down the 1-2-3 session.

The solution is to start each program in its own session with its own copy of Windows (by using the WINOS2 command). To do this, you can first start one program (in this example, Word for Windows) by entering the command **WINOS2 C:\WINWORD\WINWORD**.

Then you can start another program (in this example, 1-2-3 for Windows) by entering the command **WINOS2 C:\123W\123W**. In this case, if the 1-2-3 session crashes, the Word session remains unaffected.

This multiple-program-launching technique does, however, require more memory resources and processing power. Remember that OS/2 is now running six programs rather than four: two copies of DOS, two copies of WinOS2, and two applications. If you run everything in one session, OS/2 must run one copy of DOS, one copy of Windows, and two applications. The tradeoff is speed versus integrity. Even though WinOS2 is more stable than Windows, the Windows 3.0 or WinOS2 environment itself is prone to UAEs. For this reason, you may want to run each program in its own Windows session.

Anticipating Performance Differences

Before you begin running multiple Windows applications under OS/2, you need to examine some of the performance issues that arise when Windows applications run under OS/2's Windows environment. How much performance must you sacrifice to gain all this flexibility?

The stated design goal for OS/2 2.0 is to be a "better Windows than Windows." This means that, under OS/2, Windows applications should run as well as or better than they do in a native DOS and Windows environment. In reality, however, the issue is not as simple. The fact is that some applications run a little more quickly and some run a little more slowly in the OS/2 environment. The average performance of Windows programs under OS/2 2.0 should be close to their performance under Windows 3.0.

Which Applications Run Better?

OS/2's 32-bit graphics engine makes most Windows 3.x programs run faster than they do under Windows. For example, the

PC Magazine WINBENCH program reports 6.4 million WinMarks under OS/2's Windows and only 4.5 million WinMarks under Windows 3.x.

Not all programs are faster under OS/2, however. Some disk-intensive programs run more slowly, as do applications that use multimedia.

Under OS/2, other issues affect a program's performance that do not apply under Windows itself. You can, for example, run several copies of Windows concurrently in OS/2. The fastest way to execute a Windows program under OS/2's Windows environment is to run just one copy in a full-screen session. This approach approximates a Windows environment running one program, and performance is very acceptable under these conditions. As you add programs under this one Windows session, performance degrades, just as it degrades under native Windows if you run more than one Windows program simultaneously under Windows.

OS/2's Seamless Operating Mode

Sometimes this decline in performance is not linear. Every program is different and requires different amounts of resources. Remember that Windows 3.0 does task-switching with no preemption or task-scheduling. Windows programs, therefore, run more quickly in full-screen mode than they do in a windowed environment. When Windows programs are running in a windowed environment on the PM desktop, you can see the OS/2 desktop and other tasks as well. This type of operation is called *seamless mode*; many users have asked IBM to include such a mode to make OS/2 2.0 more usable. This mode frees you from hot-keying back and forth from Windows to OS/2.

Seamless mode also forces you to run each Windows program under its own copy of WinOS2. This means that for each Windows program you are running, you also are running a copy of Windows (WinOS2). As you might suspect, this also slows things down. The more programs you run, the more processing power and memory are required.

Consider what would happen to performance if you ran two copies of DOS 5.0 and two copies of Windows 3.x and then two programs on a DOS machine. Under this hypothetical environment, your programs would run half as fast. This is not strictly true under OS/2 (the programs would run much better than half as fast), but all that code still requires some overhead. OS/2 is designed to handle this type of load; DOS is not.

Other Performance Considerations

If you are not interested in a strict comparison between OS/2 and DOS and Windows, other considerations affect the performance of Windows applications under OS/2. These considerations also affect all the other programs you run.

RAM and Hard Disk Speed

A computer with 16M of memory performs better than a machine with just 4M of memory. What your computer lacks in available system memory can be made up for with available hard disk space. OS/2 emulates RAM on your hard disk in a special file called SWAPPER.DAT. This file grows dynamically to meet your memory requirements. A system with only 4M of memory makes extensive use of a hard disk, and a computer with 16M of memory uses the disk considerably less. Because a hard disk is dramatically slower that RAM, however, the 16M machine operates much better.

If you intend to run several applications at once, consider increasing your machine's RAM to at least 8M if it does not already have that much.

As you may have guessed, the speed of your hard disk is very important as well. The faster your hard disk, the faster your system runs. A faster hard disk also means that your applications run better. This is true under Windows 3.0 as well as OS/2.

Microprocessor Speed

The speed of the microprocessor is another important factor. A 66MHz 80386DX2 runs programs quite a bit faster than a 16MHz 80386SX. Think of the MHz rating as the speed at which the microprocessor executes instructions. The faster the MHz rating, the faster your programs run.

The type of microprocessor also has direct bearing on performance. An 80486 will outperform an 80386 running at 25MHz due to differences in the processors' internal designs.

Graphics Capability

Another significant performance component is the type of graphics card and display you are using. Some graphics cards are faster than others. IBM's XGA adapter, for example, is faster than IBM's VGA adapter.

The other component of the graphics system is the resolution under which you run OS/2 or Windows. Generally, the higher the resolution, the slower the performance. This is because higher-resolution displays require OS/2 or Windows to do more work to move images around the screen. Higher-resolution displays also use more pixels to represent objects and provide greater detail. Most people prefer the highest resolution they can get to produce sharper images on the screen. Further, some high-performance display adapters running high resolutions such as XGA actually run faster than lower-resolution adapters running standard resolutions such as VGA. To get the best image and performance, buy a high-performance, high-resolution adapter that is supported by OS/2. Currently, VGA is the standard graphics adapter shipped with most systems, and looks and performs satisfactorily.

Tuning Windows Applications

The performance of your Windows programs also is affected by the DOS or Windows settings, which you can adjust to meet your needs. You can change these settings for each Windows session you run. To change the DOS/Windows settings, locate the icon that represents the session you want to tune. As an example, assume you are tuning 1-2-3 for Windows so that it can run under OS/2 in a seamless window. For this exercise, you have already installed 1-2-3 for Windows; an icon already exists on your PM desktop. The icon should look like the one shown in figure 7.3.

Figure 7.3:

The standard icon for 1-2-3 for Windows.

Lotus 123/W

Right-click on the icon. A new pop-up window appears. The first menu option is the word **O**pen with an arrow box to its right. Left-click on the arrow. A second menu appears, displaying the two options shown in figure 7.4.

Figure 7.4:

The 1-2-3 icon's pop-up menu.

Next, left-click on **S**ettings. A new, larger window appears showing the settings notebook for 1-2-3 for Windows, as shown in figure 7.5. Notice the tab selections on the right side of the pages. For this exercise, you need to use only the **S**ession tab.

To access the session settings, left-click on the **S**ession tab. This turns the notebook to that page (or causes the **S**ession settings page to come to the foreground), as shown in figure 7.6.

Take a moment to look over this page of the Settings notebook. Because OS/2 has already identified this as a Windows program, all but two program types have been grayed out. Here you determine whether the Windows program operates in a full-screen session of its own or in a seamless window on the PM desktop. For this example, set the application to operate in a seamless window on the

OS/2 desktop. As discussed earlier, this also means that the program will run under its own copy of WinOS2. The button in figure 7.6 already shows the WIN-OS/2 window selected. If the program is not already set this way on your settings page, left-click on the WIN-OS/2 Window button.

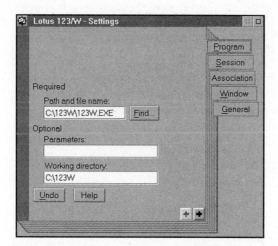

Figure 7.5:

The first page of settings for the 1-2-3 for Windows icon.

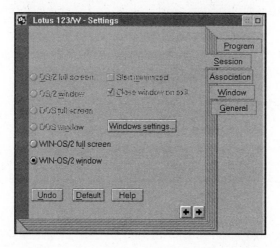

Figure 7.6:

The **S**ession settings page for the 1-2-3 for Windows icon.

Now you can define the session settings. Open the Windows settings by left-clicking on the Windows s**e**ttings box. This opens the window shown in figure 7.7.

Figure 7.7:

Pop-up settings for the 1-2-3 for Windows icon's windows settings.

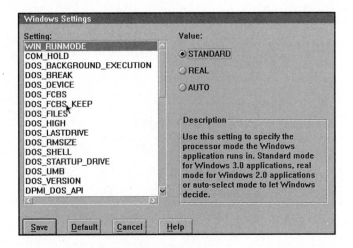

The Windows Settings window enables you to tell OS/2 what resources to make available to your applications. The first setting, WIN_RUNMODE, determines whether a Windows application runs in Standard mode or Real mode. You can select AUTO and let OS/2 decide, but you should specify the mode if you know which mode you want to use. This is because some Windows 2.11 applications do not run properly in Standard mode, and some Windows 3.1 applications require Standard mode.

Other settings can enhance performance. The first of these settings is DOS_BACKGROUND_EXECUTION. This setting should be turned on for most Windows programs—especially if you are going to use Windows DDE or if you intend to let computations run while you are working on other programs. Your settings page should now look like the one illustrated in figure 7.8, with the On button selected.

Next, select DPMI_MEMORY_LIMIT from the settings menu. The default value is 2. Lotus recommends this be set to at least 3. Remember that the SWAPPER.DAT file grows in direct proportion to this setting—a value of 3 adds 3M to your SWAPPER.DAT file. You can use the scroll bar to adjust this value. To do this, place the mouse point on the square slider bar, then press and hold down the left

mouse button. Move the mouse to the right to increase the value.
When the desired number appears in the value box, release the
mouse button. For this exercise, use a value of 3. Refer to figure 7.9
to verify your work.

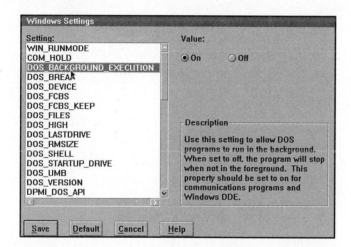

Figure 7.8:

The proper
settings for
background
execution of
1-2-3 for
Windows.

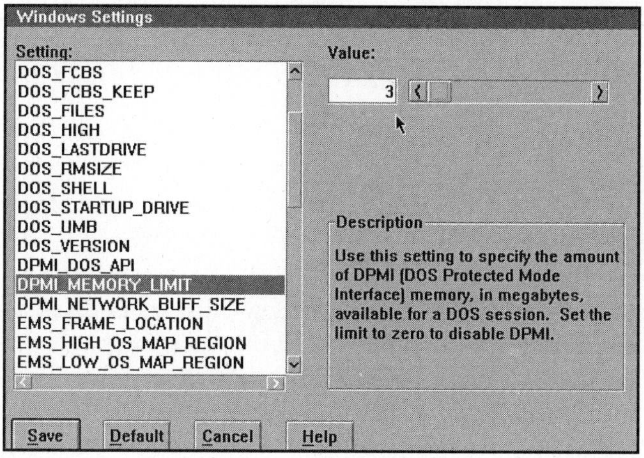

Figure 7.9:

The DPMI Limit
set to 3, as
recommended
by Lotus.

The next setting, IDLE_SENSITIVITY, dramatically affects response
time. The default is 75. To improve performance, increase this value

to 90. To change this setting, use the slider bar as you did for the DPMI memory-limit setting. Figure 7.10 shows the default value of 75.

Figure 7.10:

Setting the default idle sensitivity for all DOS sessions.

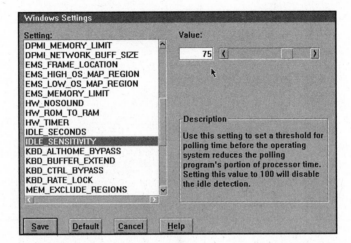

VIDEO_FASTPASTE allows faster pasting between sessions. Turn on this option if you plan to use the clipboard in Windows or to transfer data between sessions. This setting applies to DOS programs as well, but its most dramatic effects are demonstrated in Windows applications. For most Windows applications, set this button as shown in figure 7.11.

To save these settings, choose the **S**ave box at the window's lower left corner. When you are finished editing the session settings for 1-2-3 for Windows, select the icon box in the upper left corner of the menu bar and then choose **C**lose. This completes the basic tuning for 1-2-3 for Windows. Other applications may require additional setting changes.

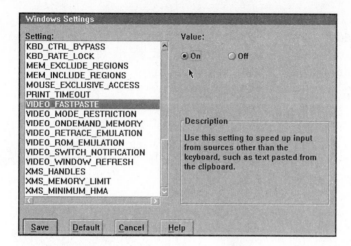

Using DDE between
Windows Applications in OS/2

Windows 3.0 includes the Dynamic Data Exchange capabilities that
have made Windows so popular. DDE enables data in one program
to be updated by data from another session. To set up this automatic data-updating process, you must establish a DDE link between the two programs. This is nothing more than establishing a
conversation or reference between the two programs. As an example, create a spreadsheet in 1-2-3 for Windows and then link it to
a document in Word for Windows 2.0.

To begin, launch both 1-2-3 and Word. Figure 7.12 shows the icons
for both programs. If you try to launch the programs from Windows
full-screen mode, your icons may appear in their respective groups.
This exercise assumes that you are running both programs from the
OS/2 PM Desktop. You can launch both programs by double-
clicking on the icons.

After both applications have been started, switch to 1-2-3 by pressing Ctrl-Esc. A Windows List appears, showing you which Windows applications are available. From the list, select 1-2-3 for

Windows. To provide a simple example with data already provided by Lotus, use the spreadsheet INVEST.WK3. (This file is located in the SAMPLE directory under the directory in which you installed 1-2-3. If you accepted all the defaults when installing 1-2-3 for Windows, then the path for this file is C:\123W\SAMPLE\INVEST.WK3.) To load this file into 1-2-3, select **F**ile from the main 1-2-3 menu. Next, choose **O**pen, and when asked for the path, enter the appropriate path (in this case C:\123W\SAMPLE\INVEST.WK3). This loads the INVEST spreadsheet into 1-2-3.

Figure 7.12:

The 1-2-3 for Windows and Word for Windows icons.

Move your mouse pointer to cell G3, then press and hold down the left mouse button and drag the mouse down to cell G12. This highlights or outlines the cell range G3-G12 as shown in figure 7.13. Do not worry if your screen does not look exactly like the one shown in figure 7.13. The important thing is that you highlight the correct range.

Now you want 1-2-3 to copy this information to the clipboard so that the data is available for other applications. Select **E**dit from the main 1-2-3 menu, and then choose **C**opy from the **E**dit pull-down menu. This procedure copies the information from cells G3 to G12 to the clipboard.

The next step is to activate Word so that it can receive the clipboard data. To switch to Word, press Ctrl-Esc to access the task list. From this list, choose Microsoft Word - Document1.

Document1 represents a new blank file. If you have inadvertently saved a file by this name, you see Document 2, 3, and so on. For this example, you do not need to create text with the word processor or perform any complex or lengthy formatting. Instead, you just paste the 1-2-3 data into Word and see what happens when the data is changed. Most Windows programs implement DDE but sometimes in different ways. This example shows only the manner in which Word implements DDE.

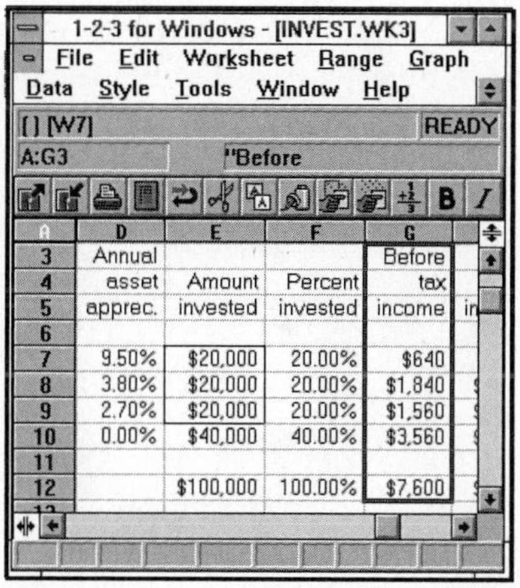

Figure 7.13:

Selecting the range G3 through G12.

To copy the spreadsheet data into Word, you must paste it in. Here is where DDE is slightly different from typical pasting. If you simply paste the data into Word, the data in Word is identical to the data in 1-2-3. The problem is that if you then change the data in 1-2-3, the data is not updated in Word. The secret is to use Paste Special rather than Paste. Figure 7.14 shows the new window that appears after you choose Paste Special from the Edit menu. In the Paste Special window, note the Source field. This shows 1-2-3 as the source application and the file and range just as you selected it in 1-2-3. Here, choose the Paste Link box rather than Paste.

The Paste Link option not only pastes the data into Document1 but also establishes a link between the two applications and data files. This means that if any of the numbers or text changes in the pasted range (INVEST.WK3 A:G3..A:G12) in 1-2-3, that data is automatically updated in the Word file Document1. Figure 7.15 shows the pasted data after it is pasted into the Word document.

To understand how this works dynamically, switch back to the 1-2-3 window and enter **10000** in cell E7. Notice that the $640 in cell G7 is recalculated and changes to $320. Because you have set up a DDE link between that cell and Word, the $640 value in the Word document also automatically changes to $320. DDE enables a non-1-2-3 application to use 1-2-3 data. You can imagine the many useful applications of the DDE feature: budgets, sales reports, investment mailings, and many more.

Figure 7.14:

Paste Special menu options in Word for Windows.

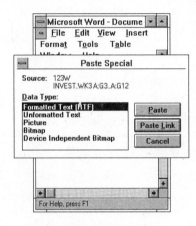

Figure 7.15:

The pasted range from 1-2-3 for Windows in Word.

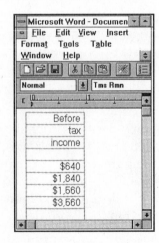

Using OLE between Windows Applications under OS/2

Object Linking and Embedding (OLE) existed under a few Windows 3.0 applications, although this capability was not fully implemented in Windows until Windows 3.1. Simply stated, OLE is an extension to DDE. The main difference is that OLE includes other information along with the pasted data. This information contains the source file's name and the application that created it. To use OLE, an application must contain a piece of code called an *OLE server*. Word for Windows, for example, is an OLE server and therefore can launch source applications directly.

OLE adds even more ease of use to the Windows environment. With OLE, not only are your documents automatically updated, but you can launch the data's source application from within the destination document. To illustrate, assume that you need to change the formula in cell G7. Obviously, Word is not a spreadsheet, and you cannot write and edit 1-2-3 formulas in Word. OLE, however, enables you to make this change easily by including information about the source application in the embedded data.

Look back at the source field in figure 7.14. This is all the information Word needs. To edit the formula in cell G7, just double-click on the pasted area. The OLE code embedded in Word launches 1-2-3 and reads INVEST.WK3 into it. Now you can edit the cell and write in its native spreadsheet format. When you have made all the changes, just save the changes and exit from 1-2-3. All the changes are automatically repasted and updated in Word. As you can see, DDE and OLE provide powerful pasting and communications tools for WinOS2.

 You also can utilize the DDE feature with OS/2 applications and between Windows and OS/2 applications. This technique is covered in Chapter 9.

You can sometimes speed up Windows applications under OS/2 by closing the Clipboard application, which creates overhead that slows down Windows programs.

Summary

The addition of Windows 3.0 operations represents a major enhancement to OS/2 2.0. OS/2 now can exploit memory and enable the Standard mode of Windows operation—two tasks that once were thought to be impossible. Not only is Standard mode possible under OS/2 2.0, but you also can concurrently run multiple copies of Windows in Standard mode. The fact that OS/2 runs Windows applications in Standard mode legitimizes OS/2 2.0 in the minds of many. By providing users the option of running any program written for DOS, Windows (2.11 and 3.0), and OS/2 (16-bit and 32-bit), OS/2 2.0 provides an outstanding environment for application integration.

This chapter has explained how Windows is implemented in OS/2 and how your Windows applications can exploit OS/2's memory-management and multitasking capabilities. This chapter, however, is only a WinOS2 primer. Many more features and options are available under OS/2 as the operating system attempts to live up to its title of "the integrating platform."

A Sampling of OS/2 Applications

In the past, computer users asked why they should switch to OS/2 when so few applications were available for that operating system. Occasionally, the answer was that the OS/2 environment was needed to develop multitasking applications. If you were looking for off-the-shelf applications, however, your choices were limited. Today, the situation is different.

Although the plethora of applications that are available for DOS or Windows still does not exist for OS/2, the number of OS/2 applications available today is growing. Programs for OS/2-based word processing, graphics and design, databases, spreadsheets, and communications utilities are plentiful. A host of tools are available for developing OS/2 applications, and many programs have been written for specialized industries (such as health, finance, construction, law, manufacturing, and human relations).

In this chapter, you are introduced to some of the many applications available today for OS/2. Figure 8.1 shows a typical array of office productivity applications. One of these applications, the DeScribe Word Processor, was used to write this chapter. Another program, PrntScrn, was used to capture the screens.

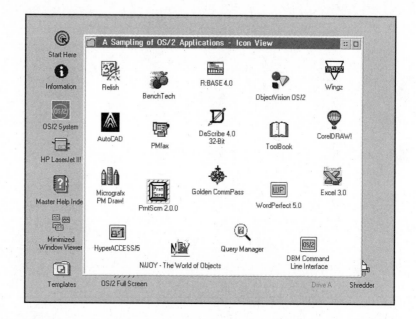

Exploring OS/2 Word Processing and Office Systems

The advent of relatively inexpensive computer systems and powerful word processing software revolutionized the art of writing. The combination of lower cost hardware and sophisticated software brought the power of word processing to the general population and put PCs on most desks in corporate America.

After PCs were placed on those desks, however, they assumed other tasks and ran other programs. For the moment, though, consider some of the word processors that are available for OS/2.

DeScribe Word Processor

Many of today's word processors contain some desktop publishing features. DeScribe provided many of these features with its very first version of the program. DeScribe uses hierarchical style sheets that are attached to each document. The program provides style sheets for common business letters, memos, and reports. [ ] Scribe enables you to control fonts and sizes, create or import gr... hics, and link spreadsheet data into your documents. DeScribe also adds kerning, leading, set width, and letter spacing to its text-enhancement features.

DeScribe version 4.0 provides extensive icon palettes. The main editing screen displays a row of icons that give you quick access to fonts, sizes, and other common editing options. There are also icon palettes for the drawing tools that are included with DeScribe.

Figure 8.2 shows an example of the icon palette. If you place your mouse pointer over an icon and press the right mouse button, a box appears over the icon explaining its use.

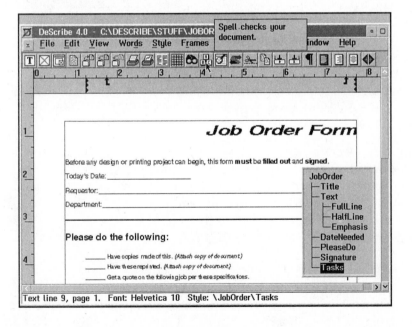

Figure 8.2:

DeScribe uses an icon palette and style sheets.

Figure 8.3 shows the View menu. This menu offers you the choice of viewing the document in draft, outline, or WYSIWYG mode. This menu also allows you to toggle the display of any icon palette on or off.

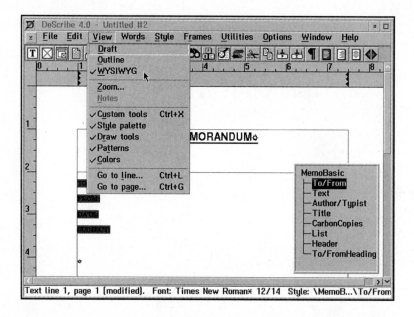

DeScribe offers some advanced features that you do not find in other word processors. One of these features, for example, is a multilingual spell checker. In addition, you can perform SEARCH and REPLACE on two strings at once. DeScribe also has an unlimited UNDO feature.

You can program keyboard macros to automate simple tasks or to write scripts. These macros can be assigned to DeScribe's menus or to keyboard combinations. With DeScribe's powerful macro language, you can call data from other programs, create dialog boxes, and perform complicated jobs with a single keystroke.

WordPerfect 5.0 for OS/2

WordPerfect 5.0, perhaps the best-selling word processor, has been available for OS/2 in a character-based format. WordPerfect's graphics features enable you to integrate text and graphics and make it easy to produce any type of document that requires figures, diagrams, logos, or pictures. WordPerfect is compatible with most graphics programs, and the graphics included in your documents can be sized, scaled, and rotated.

The Style feature enables you to combine text and codes to create a specific text appearance, such as chapter headings or subheadings. Because you easily can insert styles into a document, they are particularly useful for reproducing frequently used formats. Styles also can be edited and moved from one document to another.

Fonts can be mixed and changed at random without affecting margins or columns. WordPerfect supports up to 24 side-by-side columns in newspaper or parallel arrangement.

Figure 8.4 shows a typical WordPerfect editing screen. Text is entered and formatted from the editing screen, but it does not display exactly as it is printed. WordPerfect for OS/2, like the DOS version, includes the Print View function so that you can see what your documents look like before you print them.

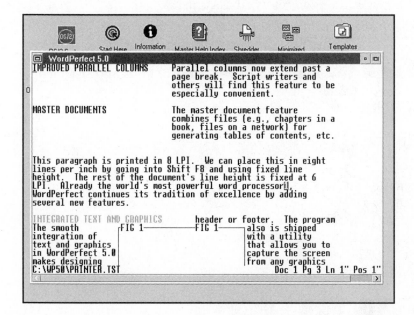

Figure 8.4:
WordPerfect 5.0 is character-based.

WordPerfect easily handles sophisticated document production. A Master Document combines individual files (like book chapters) and generates tables of contents, indexes, page numbers, and more. You can combine or separate documents as needed.

WordPerfect Corporation is working on a new version of WordPerfect for OS/2 that takes full advantage of the graphical interface of the WorkPlace Shell. (No release date has been set for this new product.) In the meantime, WordPerfect Corporation says that owners of WordPerfect 5.0 for OS/2 who want to work in a graphical word processing environment can upgrade their existing copies to the current Windows version (version 5.1) for the cost of the diskettes only.

Microsoft Word for OS/2

Word is a full-featured word processor designed for earlier versions of OS/2. Word uses advanced graphical formatting aids, such as the Ribbon and Ruler, to reformat documents with the click of a mouse. The Ribbon contains icons for the most commonly used features of the program; the Ruler controls the document formatting as a whole. Text, graphics, images, and data can be combined on the same screen. Word supports a full array of fonts and sizes that appear on screen in a WYSIWYG format. It also supports the HPFS file structure and long file names of OS/2.

Microsoft says that this version of Word, as well as its OS/2 version of Excel, were produced in the days when Microsoft and IBM were working together on OS/2. The two companies have gone their separate ways, as far as OS/2 is concerned, and Microsoft no longer writes separate versions of its products for OS/2. Microsoft admits that Word for OS/2 may be difficult to find, and suggests that customers choose Word for Windows instead, which works well with OS/2.

N/JOY the World of Objects

N/JOY the World of Objects is a document-production tool that enables you to use any combination of data from its integrated word processing, spreadsheet, and graphics applications. With N/JOY you can produce form letters, lists, and reports by linking and importing data from external data bases, such as the OS/2 Database Manager, dBASE, Lotus, and other formats.

N/JOY does not use menus. Instead, common tools and procedures that you use to create documents are represented as objects within a room. You enter the room by double-clicking on the opening screen, which is a picture of an office building (see fig. 8.5).

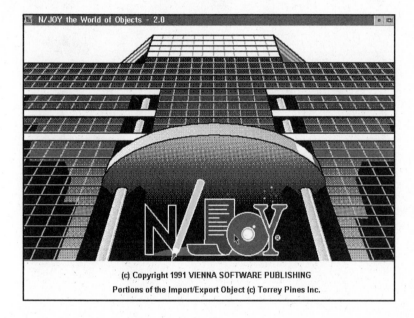

Figure 8.5:
Enter the World of Objects.

Once in a room, you can select from a catalog of objects. You select a text-pad object, for example, to create text-based documents. You select pencil objects to change fonts and styles. You can place other objects within any document, such as a spreadsheet, graphic, or a link to a database. You can even create door objects that open into other rooms, either yours or someone else's. Rooms can even exist on a network, and mail can be sent from one room to another. Figure 8.6 shows some of the objects available in N/JOY.

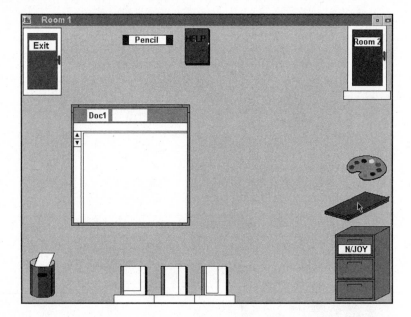

N/JOY is a sophisticated and intuitive program that does not limit
you to what menus provide. It enables you to work on your computer the same way you work at your desk—with tools such as
pencils, a calculator, and a copier. Once you are familiar with the
concepts of using objects instead of menus, N/JOY is a fun program
to use and a real productivity booster.

PMfax

PMfax is an application that enables you to fax documents from any
OS/2, DOS, or Windows application simply by using a Print command and a fax/modem. You set up your printer object on the
OS/2 desktop to send print requests to the PMfax program instead
of to your printer. When you open the Settings menu for your
printer object and select the Printer driver tab, you see the screen
shown in figure 8.7. Simply click on the PMfaxD icon to enable your
print requests to go to PMfax.

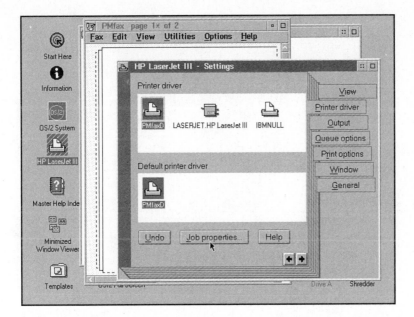

Figure 8.7:
Select the PMfaxD driver to enable applications to print to fax.

Once you are in the PMfax application, sending the document is easy—just view the document on screen and edit it if necessary. Attach a cover sheet, as shown in figure 8.8. Then, send the document to a fax number from your phone book or enter the fax number directly from the screen.

With PMfax you receive fax documents on your computer; you do not have to print them out, edit them, and fax them again. You can edit and fax documents directly in the PMfax application; and you can add notes, drawings, and even charts from other documents. You also can store the document in a number of image formats for later retrieval and editing with other OS/2 applications.

Create a cover sheet for your fax document.

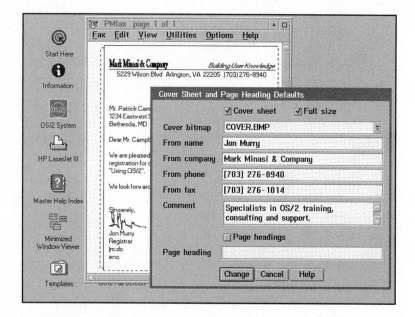

Exploring OS/2 Time-Management Programs

Time-management programs enable the individual user or group to schedule appointments, meetings, and other to-do items. These programs can contain databases, phone dialers, calculators, and other useful desktop productivity tools.

Relish

Relish is a time-management and information-organization program that stores schedule information as a database of notes. These notes can describe meetings, appointments, phone calls, or to-do items. You can customize Relish to run a program, such as a backup program, at a certain time. Reminders for scheduled events display on-screen, even though Relish may not be running at the time.

Once notes are entered, they can be displayed in a variety of ways. For example, Relish displays appointments, meetings, phone calls, notes, and to-do items. With a click of the mouse, Relish displays information for any day or month. The to-do list can be displayed with all items collected together.

The new 32-bit version of Relish has greater capability than earlier versions. For example, figure 8.9 shows the Relish telephone directory. You access the directory by clicking on the telephone icon in the Relish window. Select the name, click on **D**ial, and Relish dials the phone for you.

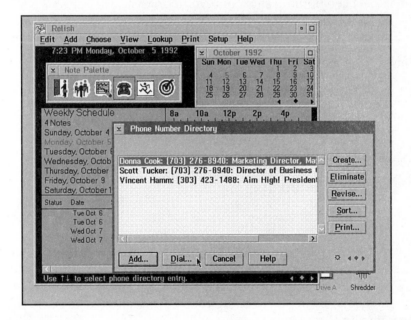

Figure 8.9:

Relish can dial a number from the telephone directory.

Relish Net

Relish Net expands a scheduling capability to the workgroup when it is installed on a local area network. Individual calendars can be searched for free time, and events can be scheduled tentatively on these calendars. Events are not officially scheduled until they are accepted. Security and privacy are maintained; others can only see what you allow them to see. As with single-user Relish, reminders of scheduled events are displayed even when Relish Net is not active.

Exploring OS/2 Spreadsheets

Some claim that spreadsheets, single-handedly, are responsible for the success of the personal computer. These claims may be exaggerated, but the impact of spreadsheet programs on business management has been nothing short of revolutionary.

Spreadsheet programs have changed significantly since the creation of VisiCalc, which was the first PC spreadsheet. Most users are no longer satisfied with a simple spreadsheet that contains columns of data—they want spreadsheets that contain graphics, fonts, and even colors. Spreadsheet programs do not just calculate and sort anymore; they publish as well. The following sections give you a brief look at some sophisticated spreadsheet programs.

Lotus 1-2-3 for OS/2

The 1-2-3 for OS/2 program exploits the graphical environment of OS/2 to the fullest, while maintaining compatibility with previous versions of the program. 1-2-3 supports both the "slash key" interface as well as pull-down menus. Multiple worksheets can be linked, formatted, and manipulated simultaneously. Worksheets can be displayed in 3-D, with up to five worksheets being viewed in a single window.

One of 1-2-3's functions is that of a database manager. Lotus databases are represented as tables of data, and can contain up to 8,192 records and 256 fields (the number of rows and columns in a 1-2-3 worksheet). Databases can have up to 255 sorting keys. Statistical and mathematical operations, from simple averages and counts to data extracted into computed and aggregated columns, can be performed on this data.

The data contained in external databases, including OS/2's Database Manager, is readily available to 1-2-3 via the DataLens technology, which is an add-in program that creates links to external databases.

Complex mathematical problems can be solved easily with 1-2-3 for OS/2 by using Lotus' Solver and BackSolver. The program even generates reports on the solutions, such as an answer table, how it is solved, what-if limits, differences, inconsistent or unused constraints, and unused cells.

1-2-3 for OS/2 is a powerful program when used for the creation of high-impact business graphics. Graphs created in 1-2-3 can be pasted into the worksheet, along with bitmaps, metafiles, and clip art from other sources. Graphs are created and edited on a separate draw layer, and easily can be moved anywhere on the page. 1-2-3 contains a gallery of 64 basic graph types. To change graph types, select the graph and apply a different graph type. You can view the resulting graph with real data in a sample window before you actually make the changes. You can rotate, scale, make three-dimensional, and use a wide array of colors and patterns to fully customize your graphs. In fact, 1-2-3 can map colors to black-and-white patterns for printing on a non-color printer.

Lotus did not stop at creating pretty spreadsheets; it went one step beyond to also give you a powerful macro programming language. 1-2-3 for OS/2 uses the familiar Lotus macro language and adds specific macro commands for the WorkPlace Shell environment. Users can even create customized @functions and macro commands by using C language.

The OS/2 version of 1-2-3 maintains compatibility with all earlier versions of 1-2-3. The OS/2 version can read and write files from 1-2-3 for DOS and 1-2-3 for Windows in WK1 and WK3 format. It also reads WYSIWYG formats (FMT and FM3), and can even read Symphony files.

1-2-3 for OS/2 is fully integrated with other OS/2 applications using Dynamic Data Exchange (DDE) links. It supports all DDE formats, including text, rich text, metafiles, ASCII, and DDE

Execute. 1-2-3 can also be used on all OS/2-compatible local area networks.

Microsoft Excel for OS/2

Microsoft Excel for OS/2 is another Microsoft product that may no longer be available. If you already own this program, however, you will be pleased by its performance with OS/2 2.0. Excel boasts an intuitive outlining of worksheets, automatic data consolidation, and the trademarked Toolbar, which is an on-screen feature that enables you to perform analytical functions, charting, and formatting in a single step. One of the most useful tools on the Toolbar is Autosum, which instantly adds a range of numbers with one click of the mouse.

You can consolidate information from several worksheets automatically, regardless of the structure or format of the worksheets. Excel contains many built-in auditing tools that keep track of where the data comes from and how it is used.

Worksheets go from plain to pretty with the help of Excel's easy-to-use publishing tools. Fonts, shading, borders, custom number formats, and even colors combine to make memorable worksheets.

Excel contains 68 chart types, many of which are available in 3-D versions. Highlight a range, click on the Charting tool, and a chart like the one shown in figure 8.10 is instantly added to the worksheet. Double-click on the chart to open a chart editing window; enhancements are easy to make. The chart is a separate object that you can place anywhere on the worksheet. Charts are also linked to their data—when the source data changes, so does the chart.

With Excel, you can create graphic objects directly on the worksheet with drawing tools such as lines, rectangles, ovals, and arcs. You can also import graphics as pictures from other applications to enhance worksheets. You can even draw macro buttons that run macros when you click on them.

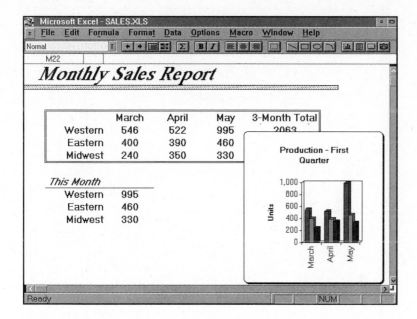

Figure 8.10:
In Excel, charts
can be placed
anywhere on the
worksheet.

You can use Excel as a database manager for simple, single-file applications. A unique feature known as the data form makes the database easy to maintain. Figure 8.11 displays an Excel screen that uses a data form.

A *data form* is a dialog box that displays the field names and their contents; and provides a simple way to view, change, add, or delete records from the database. The data form also can be used to define search criteria for a selection.

Excel has many other features that were built specifically with OS/2 in mind. For example, Excel can use the HPFS file system and supports long file names. Excel is fully integrated with other OS/2 applications and uses Dynamic Data Exchange for information sharing. Excel also offers access to external databases such as OS/2's Database Manager, dBASE, Microsoft's SQL Server, and text files using the trademarked Q+E system.

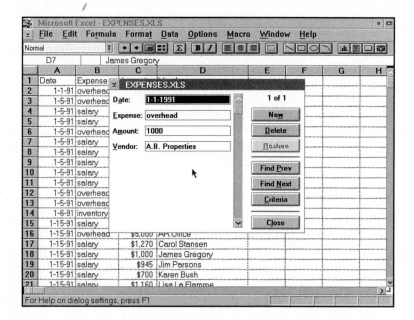

WingZ

WingZ, available from Informix Software, Inc., is an easy-to-use,
high-performance graphical spreadsheet program for business and
technical professionals. In its basic format, WingZ is a powerful
analytical tool with worksheet linking and auditing features, 32,768
rows by 32,768 columns (more than any other spreadsheet program), and more than 140 functions.

Numbers, words, charts, and graphic images can be combined on a
single page to produce presentation-quality graphic worksheets.
Although some other spreadsheet programs have this capability,
WingZ provides some of the most sophisticated graphs ever used in
a spreadsheet program. WingZ supports three-dimensional graphs
with rotation, elevation, and variable perspective. This is impressive
when working with the contour, surface, or wire frame graph types,
such as the one shown in figure 8.12. You also can combine graphs

on the screen to produce several views of the same data. And you can further enhance worksheets by including clip art or graphic images imported from the Clipboard or from other programs.

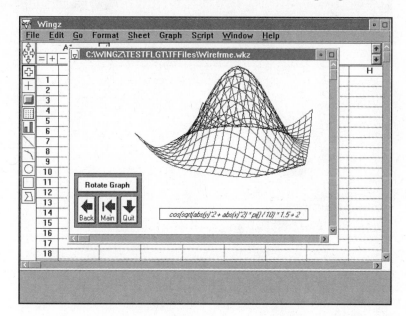

Figure 8.12:

WingZ can create contour, surface, and wire frame graphs.

You can create completely unique applications by using the HyperScript programming language included with WingZ. Unlike other macro languages, HyperScript is a fully functional, event-driven command language used to build custom applications using graphical control elements such as buttons, slide bars, and menus.

Figure 8.13 shows a screen from the WingZ "Test Flight." In this figure you see the way buttons are placed to navigate through the tutorial. When you click on the Europe button, for example, a script runs that displays a linked worksheet. Other buttons move from one screen to another in this automated application.

Figure 8.13:

WingZ includes HyperScript for creating customized applications.

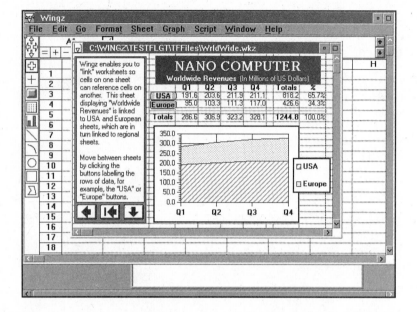

Exploring Accounting and Financial Management

In addition to the spreadsheet programs for creating financial, accounting, or technical applications, a number of custom applications written for the OS/2 environment also exist. Many of these applications support local area networks and mainframe or mini-computer access. The following list is a sampling of the types of features that you may find in these applications:

- **General Accounting**. Many vendors offer accounting software in modular form, so that a business can choose only those modules it needs. The most popular are general ledger, accounts receivable and payable, payroll, sales order entry, inventory, and purchasing. Several vendors offer programs for tracking cash receipts and disbursements. Time and billing programs are also available, and even a specialized program for oil and gas accounting is available.

- **Banking and Financial Services**. This category includes the many applications that are available to track banking transactions, credit-card services, financial planning, customer services for financial institutions, and loan processing. Stocks, bonds, mutual funds, and other financial instruments can be tracked and maintained with custom programs. Fiduciary accounting systems are available for estates, trusts, and guardianships. A program for signature verification also is available that scans, stores, and displays images of signatures from bank signature cards.

- **Sales**. Many applications are written specifically for point-of-sale situations. Some of these include inventory, price look-up, commissions, and accounting functions. Several of the programs available are specific to a certain sales industry, such as soft goods, packaging and shipping, or amusement parks. Many programs support interfacing with cash registers or other point-of-sale terminals that may be connected on a network in the store, across the country, or around the world.

Exploring OS/2 Databases

Database-management programs enable you to computerize record systems that you previously maintained manually. With database-management software, you can computerize virtually any type of filing or record system.

Once a form or structure is defined for a database and the data is entered, it can then be sorted, searched (the popular new term for this is *queried*), and collected together in any number of report formats.

Many PC database-management programs offer interfaces to large mainframe or minicomputer-based databases. Some programs use familiar commands or query statements; others contain their own programming languages for extremely sophisticated database operations.

R:BASE for OS/2

Microrim, the makers of R:BASE, have recently announced a new version of their database program. R:BASE 4.0 continues to offer ease-of-use, yet adds powerful new features that include an application debugger. R:BASE's new features enable you to focus on your work instead of worrying about how to make the database give you what you want.

R:BASE makes all the essential database elements—databases, tables, views (queries you save), forms, reports, and applications—available in one step. Everything you need is on the main screen in visual, pull-down menus (see fig. 8.14). Highlight what you want, click on the mouse button, and you have the information instantly. The pull-down menus "cascade" and stay on the screen as a road map until you get the results you want.

Figure 8.14:

R:BASE has intuitive pull-down menus.

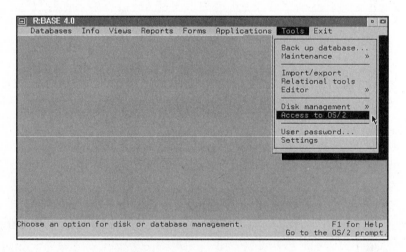

R:BASE is a true relational database system with some sophisticated features. The number of databases it can handle is limited only by your hardware. Each database contains up to 800 fields and greater than two billion records. You can give your fields meaningful names of up to 18 characters, and you can create up to 400 indexes for a database. You can choose from nine different data types when you define your database, including text/character, note, currency, numeric/decimal, integer, real, double/float, date, and time.

With R:BASE, you can create custom forms used to enter new data or edit existing data. Choose from three types of forms: quick, custom, or variable. All the forms you create appear on pull-down menus, which makes them easy to access.

Once the forms are created, you can search easily for records. Use the pull-down menu system to guide you through the process. You can see what R:BASE is doing as you cascade through different menus until you arrive at your destination.

Figure 8.15 shows a typical journey through the menus to access the *Condition Builder*. To locate records to edit in the database, select a field from the list, then choose an operator (such as "equals" or "less than"). Enter the information you want R:BASE to search for, and press F2. Your record then appears, using the custom form you created (see fig. 8.16).

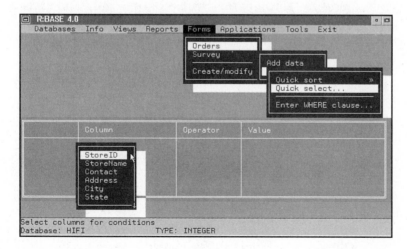

Figure 8.15:

Cascading menus show you the route to the Condition Builder.

R:BASE displays the record using your custom data form.

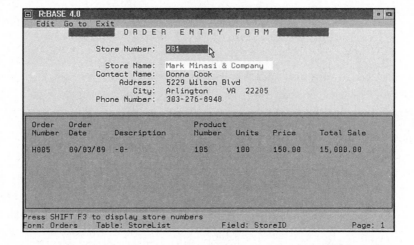

With R:BASE, you can use *query-by-example* to find and list the information you need. By using query-by-example, you do not have to memorize a lot of operators and complex commands; pop-up windows guide you through the process of setting up and executing the query. You can do queries on multiple linked databases as easily as you can with one. Queries can be saved and reused at a later time.

For more advanced users, R:BASE has a fully integrated *Structured Query Language (SQL)*. SQL is a high-level data definition and manipulation language. SQL is easy to learn and is powerful enough to express complex queries. R:BASE's SQL is embedded, which means you can use R:BASE and SQL commands interchangeably, without translation.

R:BASE is 100% read/write-compatible with dBASE III, III+, and IV. You can use R:BASE and dBASE on the same network and can simultaneously access the same dBASE files. dBASE files are handled just like R:BASE tables. This enables you to perform the same ad hoc queries and editing as if they were native R:BASE databases. You can even use R:BASE reports and forms on dBASE files.

R:BASE databases are inherently network-ready. *Concurrency Control* allows all users to get the data they need without slowing things down. Records are automatically protected, and other users are instantly updated about any changes made to records. Even getting on the network is easy; you simply choose a selection from a menu.

Extended Services Database Manager

IBM's Extended Services Database Manager is a relational database system developed for OS/2's client-server environment. Information in the database is contained in tables, which are simple rows and columns. You access data directly from the tables, so you do not have to understand complex data structures and access methods. Database Manager accomplishes this by using its Structured Query Language.

Database Manager consists of several modules. The first module, *Database Services*, provides the basic functions of the program. You work with the database by using SQL statements that create, manage, and access your data. You can retrieve data from single or multiple databases located on your workstation. Database Services offers some simple built-in functions for summation, grouping, ordering, and basic statistics.

If you need help using SQL, Database Services provides a prompted interface called *Query Manager*, which enables you to access and manipulate data by using menus and screens with context-sensitive help. You can even create a customized menu interface for your database application using Query Manager. Figure 8.17 shows an example of a prompted query.

Another method of accessing your database is to use the *Command Line Interface (CLI)*. You issue SQL statements directly from the command line prompt. The CLI also enables you to maintain a history of commands, and to redirect output to a printer or file.

Figure 8.17:

Database
Manager's Query
Manager provides
an SQL interface.

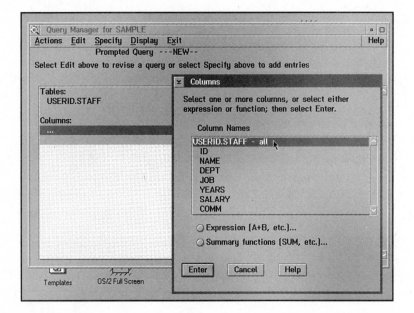

Database Manager provides you with additional features that are useful for managing a database in a client-server environment. These include the following:

- **Database Tools.** Use these tools to allocate resources to a database, back up and restore a database, and manage a database catalog.

- **Remote Data Services**. Used by multiple workstations to access a common database or by a single workstation to access a database at a remote workstation. When you select this option, you are working with OS/2's Communications Manager to provide the necessary communications services.

- **DOS and Windows Database Client Support**. Used to provide support for developing DOS and Windows database client applications.

- **Distributed Database Connection Services/2.** Used to access and update information in other relational databases. It is purchased separately.

Exploring OS/2 Graphics and CAD

You have already seen the way spreadsheet programs can create charts and graphs based on the data they contain, and the way word processing programs can create and incorporate graphics. Although both spreadsheet and word processing programs have relatively simple graphics capabilities, sometimes the graphs or charts created are inadequate for a strong presentation. When this is the case, you can use a dedicated graphics program.

Today's graphics programs enable you to create graphic elements and then include them in other programs' data files. You can create a simple graphic, such as a corporate logo or a bit of clip art, and incorporate this graphic into a word processing document or spreadsheet report layout. A complex drawing can be included in a technical manual, or you can create an entire brochure or flyer out of a collection of pictures.

Specialized graphics programs help artists and engineers produce technical drawings electronically. These programs, called *computer-aided design (CAD)* programs, have revolutionized many technical industries such as electronics, construction, automotive, and aerospace, which rely heavily on this type of drawing.

CorelDRAW!

CorelDRAW is a fun, fast, and powerful graphics program. It offers superb drawing power and stunning special effects in one program. CorelDRAW is perfect for anything that involves graphics, including publishing, presentations, technical illustrations, and graphic design.

With CorelDRAW, you can create and edit your own typefaces and symbol libraries. You can mold text to any shape. Even graphic elements can be placed in "envelopes" and molded and shaped in surprising and unpredictable ways.

Objects can take on some interesting 3-D effects, such as perspective and vanishing point. You can blend one object into another one, and show the transformation steps in between. You can even stretch and scale objects.

Freehand drawing is easy with CorelDRAW. You simply turn on the on-screen grid for visual alignment, set rulers and guidelines anywhere on the page, select from a number of available color palettes, and begin to draw. You can create drawings like the one in figure 8.18 by using simple tools that you choose from CorelDRAW's handy tool palette.

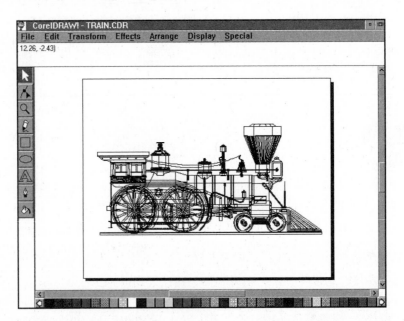

Figure 8.18:

CorelDRAW! can create simple or complex drawings.

CorelDRAW contains more than 750 clip art samples in 14 categories, and it contains more than 3000 symbols in 36 categories. Both the clip art samples and the symbols are selected visually—you no longer must guess what the clip art or symbol actually looks like. You can also create custom symbols that can be added to the existing symbol libraries.

Corel contains a few related programs that are accessed separately from CorelDRAW, but are included with the program when purchased. These include the following:

- **MOSAIC** is a visual file manager that enables you to see and perform operations on whole directories of CorelDRAW files.

- **CorelTRACE** enables you to trace color bitmaps; the program then fills the traced image with colors.

- **WFN BOSS** is an Adobe Type I export that was added to create downloadable PostScript fonts. This program can be used with the customized typefaces that CorelDRAW creates.

Micrografx Designer

Designer is a precision illustration package for OS/2 that provides an unmatched combination of powerful tools and ease of use.

With Designer, you can create, modify, and control type with any of the 41 included Bezier fonts. The output is WYSIWYG, regardless of your printer. Any Bitstream or URW typeface can be used. Rich text support enables you to edit font styles, types, and sizes within the same line.

Professional design and technical illustration features, such as layers, dimensioning, snap-to-grid, and object snap provide precise control over object placement, creation, editing, and manipulation. Any shape can be drawn—arcs, curves, parabolas, polylines, ellipses, rectangles, pies, and freehand drawings. Any text or graphic can be reshaped using Bezier curve editing. During an editing session, you can use Show Preview to view the work in color or in "wire frame" for quicker redraw time.

Designer includes over 1700 clip art symbols and a clip art management tool to select and preview multiple clip art symbols before you import them. Color objects that were scanned can be traced and automatically converted into full-color editable Bezier curve line art.

Over 16 million custom colors can be created with RGB, HLS, and CMYK custom mixing palettes. You can save any palette. Designer even has an optional PANTONE palette available.

Designer also includes the following free utilities:

- **SlideShow**. Creates on-screen presentations, complete with special fade-and-wipe effects.
- .**TeleGrafx**.Sends files via modem to slide service bureaus.

Files created with Designer can be output as SCODL or PostScript slides using drivers that Micrografx provides with the program. In addition, Designer can import or export files of DRW, CGM, DXF, GEM, TIFF, WMF, HPGL, PCX, EPS (export only), and Macintosh PICT I and II file formats.

Micrografx PM Draw!

PM Draw, which is available from Micrografx, is a spectacular drawing program. With PM Draw, the novice or expert can create professional-looking drawings for publications. The program is easy to learn and fun to use, and has some impressive extras such as gradients, patterns, text along a curve, and a lot of clip art.

Clip art symbols (about 2600) can be searched for within the clip art catalog or within a specific subject in the catalog. You can preview the symbols before you paste them into your drawings, you can edit and save existing clip art, and you can even create symbols of your own to add to the clip art catalog.

The clip art used with PM Draw is some of the best in the software industry. It was created with Micrografx's Designer product, which produces *vector-based* objects. Vector-based means that no matter what you do to the art—stretch it, pull it, twist it, or rotate it—it keeps the same shape and proportion that it had to begin with. Curves remain curves rather than becoming ugly jags or steps (which can happen with clip art created with paint programs). Vector-based objects also print true to design, no matter what type of output device you use, from dot-matrix printers to PostScript imagesetters.

With PM Draw, you can create objects that consist of lines, curves, polylines, and rounded rectangles; you can reshape any object by using the Bezier reshape tool. Objects can have simple color or complex gradient patterns, and they can be blended, rotated, slanted, and sized exactly the way you want.

Text attributes include fully scalable fonts from Bitstream and URW. PM Draw supports rich text format, which enables you to change font styles, sizes, and types anywhere on the page, even on the same line. You can curve text around another object, or you can convert text to a symbol for reshaping or adding gradients and pattern fills. Figure 8.19 shows some of the text enhancements you can do with PM Draw.

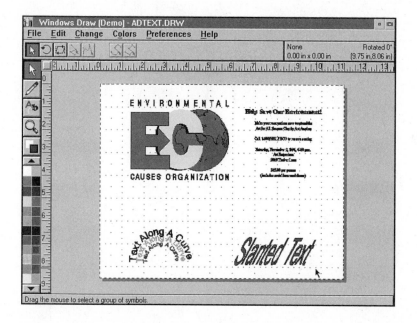

Figure 8.19:
PM Draw! from Micrografx is fun, fast, and friendly.

PM Draw includes filters to import and export to AI, TIFF, TXT, WPG, and many other formats. Draw supports file and clipboard compatibility with Micrografx Designer and Charisma, PageMaker, Ventura Publisher, and many other PC programs. Draw is compatible with Adobe Type Manager and Adobe TypeAlign, and can convert Adobe Type I fonts to curves.

AutoCAD

AutoCAD, from Autodesk, Inc., is the world's most popular design and drafting program for technical designers. AutoCAD offers a wide variety of commands and features to speed up repetitive drawing tasks and simplify drawing revisions.

AutoCAD Release 10 provides design professionals with some impressive features that include full three-dimensional design capability (see fig. 8.20). Program options include the capability to create and edit any AutoCAD entity in any 3-D orientation, user-defined coordinate systems, and 3-D surface modeling capabilities. Release 10 contains a feature called the *Advanced User Interface* that offers pull-down menus and dialog boxes to guide you through command selections and icon menus for 3-D objects and other display options.

Figure 8.20:

AutoCAD can create 3-D drawings.

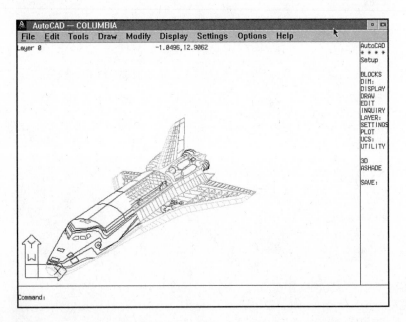

AutoCAD's open architecture, embedded high-level programming language, and capability to create customized drivers for input/output devices make it a flexible and versatile graphics standard for nearly every discipline. AutoLISP, which is an implementation of the popular LISP programming language, offers a powerful means to create individualized menus and commands. This capability helps you to execute frequently used functions and to customize your environment. With the *Autodesk Device Interface,* you can configure AutoCAD to operate with virtually any peripheral.

AutoCAD continues to support the Autodesk Drawing Interchange File (DXF) and Initial Graphics Exchange Specification (IGES) formats, which enable you to transfer drawings to and from most CAD programs. Release 10 also supports AutoCAD's binary file format, which provides access to files between different makes of computers running DOS, Macintosh, UNIX, AEGIS, and VMS operating systems without the need for file conversion.

Because AutoCAD is a standard in the design industry, AutoCAD drawing files are an efficient way to exchange information within a company and between organizations. For example, an architect can use AutoCAD to draw the overall design of a building, then pass the drawings to individual subcontractors who design the construction, electrical, mechanical, and plumbing phases of the project. In figure 8.21, you see an example of the type of drawing that the construction contractor creates.

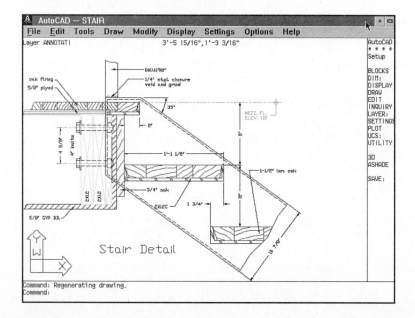

Figure 8.21:

AutoCAD is used to design building components.

Exploring Application Development Tools

OS/2 ships with a program development system known as REXX. (You are introduced to REXX in Chapter 11 and explore it further in Chapter 13.) For now, consider that you can use REXX to develop powerful batch procedures and programs for OS/2.

ToolBook

ToolBook is a software construction set you can use to develop your own OS/2 applications. To create applications (called *books*) with ToolBook is easy because its graphical user interface and object-oriented programming features make building applications as simple as using a draw program.

A *book* is a collection of individual pages. The pages of a book are stored together as an OS/2 file. To build a book, you create pages and link them together, then you create a script. The script carries out the actions the book is to perform. Using Author mode in ToolBook to create books, the books are then placed into the ToolBook Bookshelf, which is the opening screen you see when you start the program (see fig. 8.22).

In ToolBook, information is presented graphically, which is more effective than presenting it as text alone. Drawings, scanned images, color, and even animation and sound can be used to enhance books.

ToolBook makes it easy to use the applications that were created. A single command puts ToolBook into "Reader" mode, which provides commands for using the application. The book is viewed one page at a time in a ToolBook window—you move through the book by displaying different pages in the window.

ToolBook is an object-oriented development system. The objects that ToolBook uses are buttons, fields, and graphics, which have distinct properties associated with them. An author easily can change any of the properties of an object. Objects also have scripts associated with them, which describe the way the object behaves in a program.

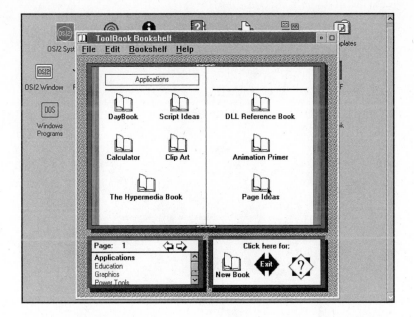

Figure 8.22:
Toolbook
applications are
started from the
Bookshelf.

Objects are placed on *pages*. ToolBook offers a wide selection of predefined pages to use as backgrounds, or you can create your own custom backgrounds. Figure 8.23 shows the selection of pages that are included with ToolBook.

Programmers can create complete ToolBook applications that consist of one or more books designed for a particular purpose and linked together. The applications created with ToolBook can include a simple collection of information, an interface to another application, or a self-contained system.

ObjectVision OS/2

ObjectVision from Borland International has been around for Windows for quite some time. Now, Borland has a new version for OS/2. The two versions are similar, although the OS/2 version has significant enhancements to exploit the OS/2 environment. These enhancements include full 32-bit capabilities for high performance, multithreading, integrated support of IBM's Database Manager, and close ties to the REXX macro language.

Figure 8.23:

ToolBook's predefined pages.

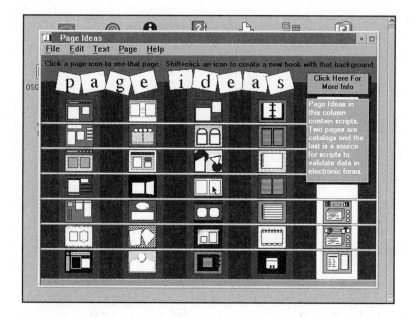

Applications are created in ObjectVision in three basic steps: you must design the program interface, define the business rules (the logic of the program), and connect to an external database.

The *program interface* is the part of the program that you see when you run the program. To design the interface in ObjectVision, you must place building blocks, called *objects*, on a blank screen. You can also modify one of the many sample screens that comes with the program.

Objects are laid out in ObjectVision by using a WYSIWYG format. That is, to create the form on the screen you use objects from the Object Bar and place them anywhere you like. You can choose from several different kinds of objects, including text, graphics, lines, patterns, and value fields. Figure 8.24 shows the way objects are placed to create an order entry form.

The most powerful objects—*value fields*—are like cells in a spread-sheet. They can contain text, numbers, dates, formulas, and expressions, and they can reference values in other cells. Value fields also can be represented by check boxes, selection lists, or tables.

All objects have *properties* assigned to them, which define how an object looks and behaves. For example, figure 8.25 shows the possible choices available for the value field "tax."

One of the properties you can assign to an object is a *value tree*, which produces a conclusion based on conditional logic and data values that are provided by the user, external sources, other fields, or the conclusions of other value trees. Essentially, these are calculated fields. The only difference is that instead of simple calculations, values are derived from the evaluation of *decision trees*.

Decision trees are a visual and logical representation of a decision-making process. ObjectVision applications take you through the decision-making process automatically—with prompts for needed information at just the right time and in just the right sequence, based on the decision tree logic.

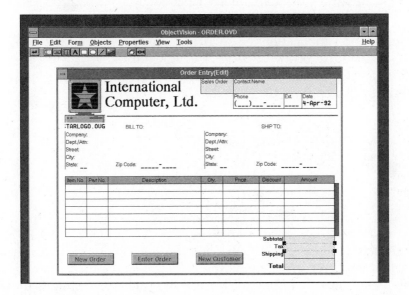

Figure 8.24:

Objects are placed to create custom forms.

If your application requires access to external databases, then the final step in creating your application is to establish links between fields in the application and fields in the database.

Figure 8.25:

Properties associated with objects.

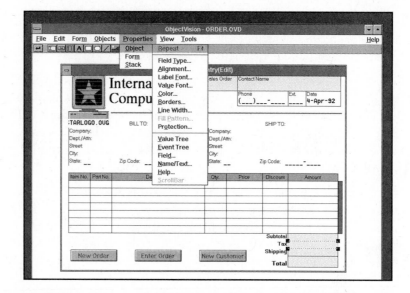

ObjectVision applications easily connect to your corporate database files in Paradox, Btrieve, dBASE, and ASCII formats. ObjectVision is all you need to read and/or write directly to the database, with full multiuser access over OS/2-compatible networks.

Btrieve may require Novell's XQL software.

Exploring Communications Programs

Communications programs enable you to connect your PC to another PC, a minicomputer, or a mainframe by using a modem and normal telephone lines. You may want to connect to these computers for purposes of viewing information stored there or to transfer information to and from the computer. If you are a writer, you can transmit drafts of your work to your editor. You can access data services or bulletin boards for the latest news, airline schedules, or to download the latest game. To do any of these tasks, you need a communications program.

Golden CommPass

Golden CommPass is a program designed to automate access to the CompuServe Information Service. CommPass provides access to CompuServe's electronic mail, forums, and libraries by setting up logon scripts that work in the background. You simply tell CommPass which CompuServe forums and libraries you access regularly (see fig. 8.26). The first time you use CommPass, it dials the service, creates a user profile for each forum, and hangs up. Subsequent communications are done by using the profile CommPass created.

You create electronic mail messages by filling out screens in CommPass. CommPass holds all your messages in a file until you are ready to send them. You then connect to CompuServe by selecting one of the options. Access is established, your electronic mail messages are sent, and any forums you selected are searched for messages. If any messages are found, they are downloaded to your computer for viewing off-line. This procedure can be running in the background while you are doing other work on your computer.

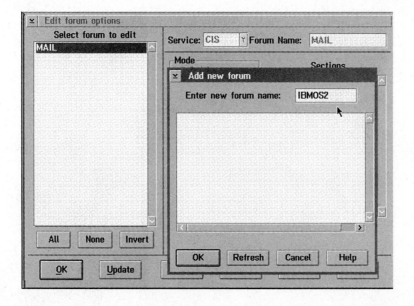

Figure 8.26:

Select CompuServe forums that you use often.

Inside the Golden CommPass package, you find an introductory membership to CompuServe. The membership includes one month of basic service and a $15 usage credit for extended and premium services. This is a great way to get started with CompuServe if you are not already a member.

HyperACCESS/5

HyperACCESS/5 is a modem communications program built specifically for OS/2. When you first start up the program, you see an interface that consists of "sliding" windows. Going from one function to another is simple in this program—you just select from among the choices listed on the opening screen menu. When you do, the next screen slides up.

Figure 8.27 is the main menu screen of HyperACCESS/5. Although it appears somewhat simple, it is a powerful program that handles multiple communications sessions with ease. You easily can adapt this interface to suit your own purposes and redefine keys to suit your needs.

Figure 8.27:
HyperACCESS/5 main menu.

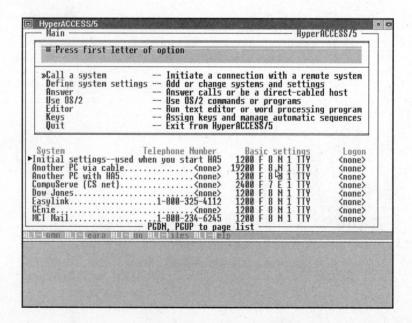

You can automate the things you do frequently without being a programmer. HyperACCESS/5 executes your commands in the three following ways:

- By using *macros* to repeat simple sequences of keys or characters.

- By using *commands* that duplicate your selections from HyperACCESS/5's menus.

- By creating *scripts* to automate the use of remote systems. Scripts are compiled automatically for fast execution and are encrypted to keep your passwords secret

HyperACCESS/5 stores dialing information, on up to 250 systems, which you can sort three different ways (by frequency of use, recentness of use, or alphabetically). Dialing information is simple to set up. Choose Define System Settings from the main menu, and select a system to define. The screen displayed in figure 8.28 slides up. Next, enter or edit the system information.

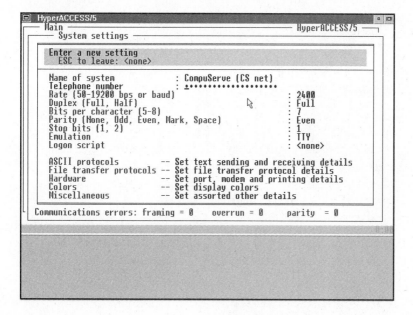

Figure 8.28:

Dialing settings are easy to change.

The program automatically redials busy numbers and can place automated and unattended calls. The program also logs the time, date, and duration of every call. You can even queue calls for accessing several systems.

Once you are connected, the program gives you excellent terminal emulation and extremely fast data-transfer rates. HyperACCESS/5 uses on-the-fly data compression to give you one of the fastest transfer times (and lowest data-transfer costs) of all communication programs on the market.

Exploring Utilities

There are a number of specialized programs that are available to assist you with system maintenance. The following section discusses an assortment of helpful utilities that you may want to use.

PrntScrn

PrntScrn is a screen-image utility that captures OS/2 screens in one step. It's easy to capture a screen—just press the PrntScrn key. The screens can be captured to a LAN-attached or local printer, to the OS/2 clipboard, or to a disk file.

You can select the type of disk file to create, along with other settings, from the Options window. You can also choose to capture the full screen or any portion of it. Color screens can also be mapped in several ways. Figure 8.29 gives you an idea of the type of control you have with this screen-capture program.

PrntScrn also provides a screen blanking function. When activated, this function works for both the WorkPlace Shell desktop and all your OS/2 full-screen sessions.

Screen blanking occurs after a specified time of no keyboard or mouse activity. You can also choose Blank Screen Now from the main menu or press the screen blanker "hot key." When the program detects that you have moved the mouse or a window appears on the desktop, screen blanking is canceled.

While the screen is blanked, a message appears to remind you that the screen blanker is active. You can customize the message any way you want. The program can even move the message around on the screen for you, or display it in more interesting ways such as Ricochet, Centipede, or Fireworks. The characters that make up the message also create the display.

Finally, PrntScrn can place a small window that shows the current date and time anywhere on the desktop. The information in this window is formatted according to the settings you chose in the OS/2 Control Panel/Country Settings screen. This window not only keeps you informed of the current time and date, but also stamps your screen prints with the current date and time.

BenchTech

BenchTech is an OS/2 performance-measurement tool that contains 25 different 32-bit benchmarks. These programs are designed to measure differences between systems that run OS/2. Some of the tests BenchTech uses may already be familiar to you—the Dhrystone test and Towers of Hanoi, for example. In addition to the basic tests, there are eight video tests and two application tests that use real applications (DeScribe and Excel) to evaluate performance. A third application-oriented test measures the time it takes to load applications.

The BenchTech interface resembles the familiar OS/2 notebook. The first page of the notebook contains a window that displays the results of the tests, as shown in figure 8.30. The tests are grouped together by function, with one page of the notebook dedicated to each function. You access the pages of the notebook, and the tests they contain, by clicking the tabs at the bottom of the notebook.

Figure 8.29:

Options available
with PrntScrn.

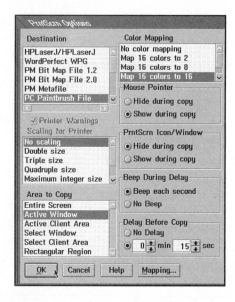

BenchTech contains an extensive program reference on-line. The
reference describes each of the tests in detail. There is a user's guide
included with the program that provides a general description of all
of the tests, along with considerations for publication of the results.

Figure 8.30:

BenchTech
displays results of
performance
tests.

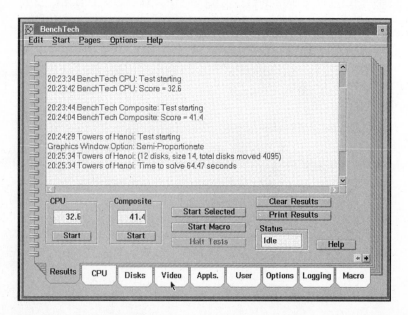

File Encrypt

File Encrypt uses a full implementation of the Data Encryption Standard (DES) algorithm to protect sensitive data. The program runs in OS/2 protected mode and automatically senses its environment. File Encrypt uses multiple threads for maximum efficiency in protected mode.

Keeptrack Plus for OS/2

Keeptrack Plus is a full-featured backup and restore utility that features high-speed backups to diskettes and other devices. Keeptrack uses visual representations of directories and files to make it easy for you to identify which files you want to back up. For example, you can determine which files to back up based on date, marking, or directory. Keeptrack also can do *exception file handling*, which enables you to strip out the files you do not want included in the backup.

MaynStream for OS/2 Systems

MaynStream high-performance tape backup software provides state-of-the-art information storage and retrieval for OS/2 systems. MaynStream supports both FAT-based and HPFS-based filing systems, both locally and on local area networks.

MaynStream supports the complete line of Maynard tape backup devices, from 60-M to 2.0-G 4mm DAT, up to 2.2-G 8mm drives.

Summary

This chapter introduced you to some of the many applications available for OS/2. As you can see, you can use OS/2 for all your computing requirements, and not just for specialized multitasking applications.

Working Smarter with OS/2

OS/2 2.0 provides vast improvements in personal productivity by changing the way you work. Historically, work done on personal computers was accomplished one task at a time. With OS/2, however, you can transform your single-tasking PC into a multitasking PC.

Although many attempts have been made to add multitasking capabilities to DOS, DOS was designed to be a single-task floppy drive-based command line interpreter, not a full-fledged operating system. DOS does not have preemption, protection, task scheduling, or memory exploitation. When IBM introduced the first PC, one megabyte address capability seemed an enormous amount of memory. Because DOS was designed for the Intel 8088 processor, DOS memory was limited to 640K of address space for programs and DOS to use. The additional 384K of memory was reserved for the BIOS, BASIC, and the adapter cards.

With the introduction of the Intel 80286 processor and the development of more sophisticated applications, the limitations of DOS became apparent. The 80286 included a new mode called *protected mode*. Protected mode enables the physical addressing of up to 16M of RAM instead of the 1M supported by the 8088. IBM and Microsoft introduced OS/2 1.*x* to operate in this new mode, as you learned in Chapter 1. Intel then introduced the 80386, which offered a new mode called *virtual DOS machines* or *virtual 86 mode*. This mode enables the emulation of several 8088/6 processors inside one processor, the 32-bit 80386.

The 80386 processor is the first Intel chip to expressly support multitasking and protection. All that was needed was an operating system to exploit these inherent capabilities. OS/2 2.0 is designed specifically for 32-bit processing. The combination of a 80386 or 80486 processor and OS/2 2.0 enables you to multitask DOS, Windows, and OS/2 applications. This enables you to work smarter and increase your productivity. The integrity limitations of multitasking on a single-tasking operating system are gone. Previous microprocessors had no means of switching modes or emulating an 8086 environment—all of this was done in the software. To switch the 80286 from protected mode to Real mode, the processor had to be stopped and restarted in Real mode. The 80386 has a built-in function to emulate Real mode while still in protected mode.

Now that you are able to multitask applications, you must identify those tasks that can benefit from this capability.

Multitasking Ideas

OS/2 2.0 provides many features that do not necessarily emphasize its multitasking capabilities, such as memory over commitment and solid program protection. *Memory over commitment* capability means that space on your hard drive can be used to implement main memory when you run out of real RAM. This is important when you have limited RAM installed in your computer, such as a system with only 4M of main system RAM. These capabilities are covered in more detail in other chapters. The focus of this chapter is to target those tasks that can best be accomplished while other tasks are being performed. Some obvious candidates are background printing, sending and receiving files in the background, copying disks, backing up your hard drive, and detaching commands.

Printing with OS/2

If you have ever printed a long document and wished you could work on other things while you were printing, OS/2 is a welcome addition to your computing environment. OS/2 provides a complete printing subsystem called the Print Manager. The *Print Manager* is a multitasking application that sits in the background and manages your print jobs. When you send a document to the printer, the Print Manager grabs the print job and takes over. Your application or other tasks are free to continue working. The Print Manager submits your document to the printer in the background and shares time on the processor with all the other applications that are running. You can send multiple documents to the Print Manager from one or any number of different applications that you have running.

In a single-tasking environment, such as DOS, when you print a document you must wait for it to finish before you can do anything else on your system. If you want to print another document in another application, you must exit the first application and then start the new application and print from it, waiting for it to finish before starting a new task. This can be time-consuming when you need to print large documents from many applications.

The Print Manager in OS/2, on the other hand, is a spooler and scheduler, enabling it to accept output from many sources. It spools all the print jobs and then schedules them for printing. You do not need to wait for one print job to finish before sending the next document for printing. You might, for example, start printing a long document from your word processor, switch to your spreadsheet and send a worksheet to the printer, then switch to an accounting system and print an account receivable report. All three of these jobs are spooled, scheduled, and printed one after the other. You do not need to worry about the first document being interrupted by the second or third because the Print Manager spools and schedules each print job for you. The Print Manager even enables you to access the Print Spooler and change the order in which your print jobs are printed.

The Print Manager also supports printing to multiple printers at one time. You can have multiple printers attached to one queue, enabling the first document to print to the first available printer and the second document to print to the next available printer in the queue. You can set up the third document so that it goes to a specific printer on another queue. The main benefit of the Print Manager for most users is the capability to continue working while a document is being printed. If you print a larger number of documents, this will be a vast improvement in productivity. Any task that does not require your immediate attention and monitoring is a candidate for background processing.

Using Modems with OS/2 2.0

Another area that you might consider multitasking is in the use of modems. Modems are becoming almost as commonplace as printers in the computer environment. Similar to printing, sending and receiving files (called *uploading* and *downloading*) over the modem is a task in which you normally wait and watch as the files are sent and received.

OS/2 was designed with communication in mind. Inherent in the advanced task scheduling system in OS/2 is the capability to communicate as a background task. All of the traditional problems associated with the processor not paying enough attention to the modem are removed from OS/2 2.0. Communication applications receive special priority in OS/2's task scheduling and get the appropriate amount of the processor to maintain communication integrity. What this means to you is that you can do other work without worrying about losing data. You can, for example, download a large file over the modem, print a large document, and continue to work with your word processor all at the same time. OS/2 sacrifices the performance of the word processor and printer in favor of a successful file transfer.

As your time becomes more complicated these background capabilities become requirements. If you communicate on your modem only sporadically, you still benefit from OS/2's support for communications. If you are a regular user of a modem, the benefits of OS/2 will make you all that much more productive. Again, the main benefit of OS/2's multitasking capability applies to tasks that currently tie up your computer and do not require your constant interaction.

Formatting and Copying in the Background

Another routine task that usually requires the full attention of your computer is the formatting and copying of floppy disks. Although these are necessary procedures, they are tedious and inconvenient. The typical routine for formatting floppy disks in a single-tasking environment is to stop all the tasks that you are performing, shell out to the command prompt, and issue the FORMAT command. This means that while you are formatting disks, you cannot perform any other tasks. You just sit and watch. If you have several disks to format, this can mean a great deal of unproductive time. OS/2, on the other hand, enables you to format disks in the background while you perform other tasks in the foreground.

Some DOS-based multitasking solutions have resulted in formatting failures, resulting in unreliable data storage. OS/2 gives enough processor attention to the FORMAT utility to ensure a successful format. OS/2 provides several ways that you can format floppy disks. The first is similar to DOS formatting. You switch to the OS/2 command prompt and then issue the FORMAT command. You then can use hot keys to switch to another session and continue working. Another procedure is to use the PM Desktop's drive A icon. After you select the drive A icon, you see a menu option for formatting disks. When the PM Format command window appears, follow the instructions.

Another common task that requires the full attention of your computer under DOS is disk copying. Disk copying is used to create an identical copy of a floppy disk. OS/2 offers two disk-copying benefits over DOS. OS/2 enables you to do one-pass copying and perform disk copying as a background task.

The formatting method preferred by most OS/2 users is to use a third-party PM utility available on CompuServe. The PMFORMAT.EXE utility is similar to the PM FORMAT command included with OS/2, but offers additional features and more control. This utility enables you to format two disks at the same time (if you have two floppy disk drives), but this is not recommended. Because of limitations in the floppy drive controller's data transfer rate, not limitations in the OS/2 operating system, you probably should not try to format two disks at one time. You can, however, receive data over your modem and format a floppy disk at the same time.

Similar to the FORMAT command, you can switch to the OS/2 command prompt and issue the following command to duplicate a disk:

```
DISKCOPY A: A:
```

OS/2 reads the entire source disk into memory before writing it to a blank floppy disk. After the process starts, you can switch to another task, such as word processing or running Windows or DOS program.

 Similar to formatting utilities available on CompuServe, third-party floppy disk copier utilities also are available. PMDSKCPY, for example, enables you to copy disks from a PM interface and offers you more features than the OS/2 DISKCOPY command, such as read-once write-many.

You also can perform many other commands in the background while you do other work in the foreground. You can, for example, perform long XCOPY commands, start connection procedures to a host system, and perform any other automated tasks not requiring continual interaction from you. You also can run the STARTUP.CMD file that automatically runs each time the system starts in the background.

OS/2 does have special considerations for commands that are run in the background. If background commands need additional instructions from you, they will suspend and wait for your input. The DETACH command does not allow any keyboard, screen, or mouse input or output after it is launched in the background. Therefore, only certain kinds of applications can be detached. A good example of using the DETACH command is compiling programs in the background. The final output can be redirected to the printer. Redirection is the only output form supported, as mentioned in the previous section. Screen I/O is not supported.

 When you run commands in the background, you must consider what tasks you are performing. You might, for instance, run a backup program in the background as you work on a word processing document. Be aware, however, that the document that you are working on in the foreground may not be backed up in the background. This is because most tape backup programs do not back up open files.

Some differences exist between starting files in the background and detaching them. Both methods provide a means of launching background processes. The DETACH command does not allow any interaction and cannot be viewed or closed. Also, tasks started with the DETACH command are not listed on the task list. Use the DETACH command for any background task that does not require any further interaction and can be done entirely in the background. If you need status or output from the DETACH command, add redirection with a statement like the following one to the end of the DETACH command:

```
Detach DIR > LPT1
```

The syntax and examples for the preceding syntax can be found in the Command Reference in the Information folder.

The START Command is different from the DETACH command in many ways. First, it starts a new command interrupter and a new session regardless of whether it is DOS, DOS and WINDOWS, or

OS/2. The purpose of START is to start a program in another session. The START program was developed for the STARTUP.CMD file. The STARTUP.CMD file is similar to DOS' AUTOEXEC.BAT file, but is designed specifically for launching applications. The AUTOEXEC.BAT file in DOS, on the other hand, generally is used for setting up the environment, path, and other nonlaunch functions. Programs to be launched in other sessions begin with the START command. You can specify whether the session is full-screen, windowed, PM, Foreground, Background, Maximized, Minimized, and so on. You also can give the session a name by enclosing one in parentheses.

With the START command, you can switch to other sessions and interact with the programs running in them. Tasks that require input from you can be started and then you can switch to that session and answer the prompts. When you start the FORMAT command in the background, for example, you might want to specify a volume label for it. To do this, use the command **START "FORMATTING FLOPPY IN A:" FORMAT A:**. This instructs OS/2 to start formatting in a background session. To make this operation a foreground session, use the /F switch in the command, such as in the following command:

```
START "FORMATTING FLOPPY IN A:" /F FORMAT A:
```

The START command can be used to launch applications in the background and, while these applications are loading, return you to the command prompt. This is useful if the launched application takes a long time load or if the application needs to run for a while without needing further interaction from you. You can launch several applications or commands by using START and then call up the task list and select the one that you want to switch to. Because OS/2 supports applications that launch and process in the background, you should become comfortable using the START command. The START command will help you work smarter and more efficiently.

Running Network Applications on a Local Workstation

OS/2 also enables you to start and process applications on a file server and have them appear as if they were running locally on your machine. In this way, the file server's CPU resources are used instead of your machine's. This is important if your file server has processing resources to spare and your workstation's CPU already is being taxed.

Multitasking System and Diagnostic Utilities

The capability to process tasks in the background opens up a whole new category of applications and possibilities. You can, for example, run a virus protection program in the background to constantly monitor changes to current files and scrutinize existing files. If a virus is found in a current file or in the file currently being downloaded, a message immediately displays. The capability to monitor changes in all sessions would be required for this to really be effective. You also can run diagnostic and performance tuning utilities as background tasks to monitor system activity and to make changes or report on the status of your system.

Using DDE and OLE

Another type of background processing that helps you work more efficiently in the foreground is Dynamic Data Exchange (DDE). A program called a *DDE agent* runs in the background and enables two programs to exchange data dynamically between themselves and other applications. This means that you can instruct the DDE agent to update your Lotus 1-2-3 for Windows chart to change every time you change a number in a Microsoft Excel document. DDE exchanges can be set up easily. See your application's documentation to help you set up DDE for OS/2.

OS/2 supports DDE in a variety of ways. You can use it in OS/2 applications that support DDE, Windows programs running in OS/2, and programs to link data from OS/2 to Windows. You might, for example, set up Lotus for OS/2 so that it charts the stock market status through a communications package. To do this, you need a communications package that supports DDE, such as ChipChat. You can set up your system so that your communications package has a DDE link to Lotus for OS/2 to read an on-line stock quote system. Each time the price of certain stocks change, you can have the DDE link update your Lotus graph.

You also might have your desktop publishing program linked through DDE to other applications. You can, for example, have text, a spreadsheet, and a graph run as foreground applications, and then have a word processor, a spreadsheet, and a graphing program run in the background. You then can link all these applications together with a DDE link. If you switch to the spreadsheet and change a few numbers, for example, then the desktop publishing document is dynamically updated with the new numbers from the spreadsheet.

DDE also enables you to update multiple documents. You can, for example, change your data in one application and then link it to a closed document. The next time you open the closed document, the data that you changed previously is updated through DDE. Not all software supports updating to closed documents, so you may need to open the documents that you want updated and have them run as background tasks. See the documentation that comes with your application to see if it supports updating data to closed documents.

A new specification from Microsoft is called Object Linking and Embedding (OLE). OLE extends DDE by storing an *object* and its source application information in the linked document. When you select the object, such as a graph, the application in which the graph was created launches and the currently selected graph is read in and is ready for editing. The only limit to OLE is when the document is transferred to a computer that does not have the OLE source applications used to create the embedded objects. The objects still are in the document, but you cannot edit them.

Currently the Windows portion of OS/2 2.0 supports OLE. This OLE support is inherent in WinOS2 (IBM's rewritten version of Microsoft Windows) because it is built into the Microsoft Windows 3.1 source code, which is built into OS/2 2.0. Both DDE and OLE provide background processes that yield foreground productivity enhancements. As you begin to do more multitasking, you probably will run into tasks that need to work together and exchange data dynamically.

Understanding and Using Client/Server Technology

One benefit of OS/2 that has been touted from the beginning is the way OS/2 exploits client/server technology. The basic concept of client/server is that a *client process* requests a task and a *server process* performs the task and returns to the client the results of the task. Under OS/2, you not only can have multiple tasks being performed in one processor, but you can have tasks divided and executed on multiple processors. Not all client/server applications are split over multiple processors. Two separate packages, a client package and a server package, can be executing on the same system and divide a task between themselves. DDE, SQL (Structured Query Language), EIS (Executive Information Systems), and Data Collection Systems are implementations of client/server computing.

A simple example of a DDE client/server application is a DDE link between AutoCAD and Excel. Suppose, for example, that Excel is the client component and AutoCAD for OS/2 is the server component. You can then construct a project drawing by entering dimensional measurements into Excel. By using a DDE link, Excel sends the measurements to AutoCAD, which interprets the numbers as drawing commands. AutoCAD processes the changes to a predefined drawing specification, regenerates the drawing, and then returns a paste-linked image to the Excel document. The client component (Excel) displays the input (measurements) and the output (the drawing). The AutoCAD application runs in the background and does not need any additional input after the initial DDE links have been defined and established. When you enter data in Excel, you do not need to interact with AutoCAD or even know that it is running in the background and processing the drawing. The only interfacing required from the user is the entering of measurements and the viewing of the results in picture form.

The preceding example is a client/server process that is performed on one CPU and one operating system. In this case, all the computations are split between two applications. The AutoCAD server component does the majority of the computing and Excel acts mainly as the data-entry point.

Structured Query Language (SQL)

When most users think of client/server technology, they automatically think of SQL. This is because SQL is the most commonly used example and most generally understood usage of the client/server technology. SQL is the most popular database language on larger systems. Specifically, SQL is a database language in which a series of instructions are run against a data file or number of data files on an SQL server.

The major difference between SQL on a mainframe and SQL implemented on an OS/2 LAN is the presence or absence of processing on the client component. In the past, the client on a mainframe usually was an unintelligent workstation (terminal). Now, however, the role of the mainframe client is changing because of the implementation of intelligent workstations (PCs) by the LAN SQLs. More and more clients on mainframes are emerging as PCs.

SQL can be implemented in several ways. The most common way is by setting up the system so that all the processing is done on the host CPU resources. A series of SQL commands are entered into a file called a *program*. The program then is executed and the execution is monitored on the terminal. The terminal provides a view or window into the process and does no computing of its own. It is merely a means of entering requests and viewing the results. Operations of this nature generally are text based and offer no graphics.

You can contrast the preceding scenario with the graphical high-powered workstations on the front end of today's SQL databases. Today's client/server environment consists of a distributed processing platform. The mainframe or server acts more as a peer than a master. Some processing is done locally on your machine. Requests, in the form of SQL instructions are then sent to an SQL engine. The SQL engine processes the instructions, and returns the results to the client. As more stations are added to the network, the traffic becomes a problem.

An SQL does not require a mainframe or another computer at all; SQL can be implemented on a single PC. This form of using an SQL database is not generally considered client/server but in the broadest definition it qualifies. The reason is that an OS/2 session can act as a client to another session (the server). OS/2 Extended Services comes with an SQL database that can be run in this way. The most common implementations of SQL, however, are implemented on a mainframe or across a network. SQL has an advantage over other forms of databases in that only instructions and results are transmitted over the network. Most databases now pull the entire data file across the network to process instructions locally. This decade may see the end of this type of networked database and text-based interfacing with client/server applications. The move to graphical interfaces has been going on for some time and seems finally to be gaining momentum.

Executive Information System (EIS)

Executive Information System (EIS) consists of distributed processing and graphical front ends. EIS came from the need for executives to begin to harness the power of computers and the wealth of information contained in them. Usually, executives do not have the time to master many advanced computer techniques. The goal of EIS is to create an environment that is easy to use and does not require recoding background processes. Accounting systems and SQL applications are good areas for EIS use.

One of OS/2's early success stories was that it was and still is a superior platform for developing and running the EIS systems. EIS systems can incorporate a touch screen and the OS/2 PM shell and menuing system. Instead of presenting the user with a normal query screen, a GUI (graphical user interface) screen that has a limited number of choices can be presented to make the system appear friendly. This stresses the notion that EIS is intended to make users work smarter, not harder. EIS systems based on OS/2 offer programmers the capability to create intuitive front ends for noncomputer personnel, enabling them to reap the benefits of a graphical environment. The following is a short list of development tools for creating executive information systems:

- EASEL
- AM/2
- CASE:PM
- ObjectVision for OS/2

Not only are these systems easier to use, they also are becoming easier to program. Look for EIS to continue as a high growth area for OS/2 in this decade.

Data Collection Applications

Another area in which OS/2 shines is in data collection applications. Intermec, IBM, and others offer solutions based on OS/2 for accurate and fast data collection. OS/2 has superior communications handling and the capability to act on the acquired data in the background.

Suppose, for example, that you own a manufacturing company that has an AS/400 midrange computer and a large number of employees. You notice that employees take too long to clock in on the time clock. After the time cards are collected, they then are keyed into a payroll system on the AS/400. Not only are there many handwritten changes on the time cards, but because of the nature of this process, you notice the information keyed in to the AS/400 often contains typing mistakes.

The solution to these problems is to automate the process. You can issue each employee a bar-coded ID card. You then can place bar code readers around the plant and at the entrances. The bar code readers then can be connected to an OS/2 system. The OS/2 collection system is, in turn, connected to the AS/400 over a Token Ring network. As the employees arrive at the plant, they run their badges across the bar code reader, which is polled by the OS/2 collection system. The OS/2 collection system then passes the data onto an AS/400 entry screen as if the data was being entered directly.

Bar coding is reliable and offers a secure means of collecting data when it is combined with OS/2's communication strengths. The OS/2 machine in this example also can do messaging to the data and provide feature checking (such as employment status) and check to see if the person already is clocked in. OS/2 can run this as a background task. The OS/2 collection system also can pass information to the reader from the AS/400 and vice versa. This feature is useful if you want the employee's name and other status returned and displayed on the reader's screen after their badge has been read. This provides visual feedback to the employee. This whole process is accomplished on top of OS/2. Data collection is possible on DOS, but is not as robust and reliable. OS/2 not only makes it work, but makes it work more efficiently than DOS.

Troubleshooting OS/2 Problems

Powerful as it is, OS/2 still suffers from some problems now and then. The following sections include suggestions for keeping the system running and what to do when OS/2 fails to work.

Testing the System

This advice is better late than never. Test your system thoroughly before installing OS/2. In particular, you should always run a thorough test of your hard disk drives and your memory.

Test the hard disk drives with a program such as Gibson Research's SpinRite II 2.0 or Prime Solutions' Disk Technician Gold. Although both programs take a long time to test a disk (SpinRite required a whole night to test a 60M disk on a notebook computer), you only have to test this thoroughly once a year, and it is good insurance.

Test the RAM with a memory tester that has a "slow" mode (the quick testers are essentially useless). The memory testers that find virtually all memory problems include Checkit, available from Touchstone Software, and QAPlus. As in the case of disk testers, a thorough memory tester requires a significant amount of time to do its work (three hours for a 16M system), but you need not test often, and it is time well spent.

OS/2 relies on RAM and disk for its data integrity. When something goes wrong with either subsystem, OS/2's typical response is to emit a TRAP error and lock the system up. You can avoid system locking by using good preventive testing.

OS/2 assumes that the RAM and disk in your system are 100 percent reliable. If that assumption is not correct, the system does not offer the dependability that you require from an operating system.

When the Desktop is Damaged

Sometimes you can boot OS/2 and see a blank gray desktop or a desktop that is missing some important pieces. Although you can use the MAKEINI program to rebuild the desktop, there is an easier way. Follow these steps:

1. Rename your STARTUP.CMD to another file name (the desktop rebuild procedure does not work if you have a STARTUP.CMD file).

2. Reboot the system.

3. Before the OS/2 logo comes up, hold down the Alt-F1 key combination.

4. Hold the keys down until you see a message from OS/2 about copying configuration files (you can't miss this message because it does not ordinarily appear).

 Remember that all customization is lost when you perform the preceding procedure.

Your system now has a desktop that is restored to the state that it was in when you first set up OS/2.

There is, however, one slightly tricky part: when to press Alt-F1. If you wait too long, Alt-F1 is ignored; if you press the keys too early, you interrupt the boot process (and you are greeted with annoying beeps.)

What you want to do is to press Alt-F1 just before the OS/2 logo appears, but that is not very helpful advice. (Remember the joke about the kid in the strange city who responds to your question "Which stop is for Elm Street?" with the answer "Just get off at the stop before the one I get off, mister.") It is probably better to be too early than too late. If the beeping begins, ease off for a second, then resume pressing Alt-F1.

Black Icons

If you have modified an icon for one of your objects, the icon may show up in solid black. There is a kernel fix for this from IBM, but here is an instant workaround: when an icon shows up black, just re-install it. The second time's a charm, and the icon will look fine from this point on.

You can either get the fixed kernel program from IBM's bulletin board directly (there is information in your OS/2 package about accessing this bulletin board system) or in IBM's IBMOS2 forum on CompuServe.

Windows Video Problems

OS/2 has two common video problems. The first one appears when you run Windows programs under OS/2 on a system using a video board based on the Tseng Laboratories' ET4000 chip set. Examples of such boards are the Diamond Speedstar, the Orchid Pro Designer II or IIs, the Orchid Fahrenheit 1280, and many "local bus" video systems.

IBM has a replacement VSVGA.DRV driver file that solves this problem. The replacement driver file is available either from IBM's bulletin board or on CompuServe.

General Video Problems

OS/2 has drivers both for standard VGA and super VGA adapters. Sometimes, however, it thinks that a standard VGA adapter is a super VGA adapter, and it tries to use the super VGA drivers on a standard VGA adapter.

You can fix this by changing two lines in your system's CONFIG.SYS file. If OS/2 is currently installed for super VGA on your system, you see the following two lines:

```
SET VIO_VGA=DEVICE(BVHSVGA,BVHVGA)
DEVICE=C:\OS2\MDOS\VSVGA.SYS
```

Change the lines so that they look like the following:

```
SET VIO_VGA=DEVICE(BVHVGA)
DEVICE=C:\OS2\MDOS\VVGA.SYS
```

Reboot, and the system then works just fine.

Just for Fun

You may have seen the *gang screens* in Windows and Windows applications, which are screens that only appear when you press a few "secret" keystrokes. These screens give credit to the Windows designers.

OS/2 also has a gang screen. To see it, follow these steps.

1. Click anywhere on an empty part of the Desktop.

2. Hold down Ctrl, Alt, and Shift.

3. While still holding those three keys down, press "O" (capital "oh").

4. Release the keys. The credits roll!

5. Quit the screen by pressing Esc.

Summary

OS/2's communications strengths are explored in more detail in Chapter 10. OS/2 was designed from the ground up for easy-to-use mission-critical line-of-business applications. OS/2 can be used as an EIS system, a data collection platform, a client/server platform, or just as an operating system for performing multiple tasks in the background while you continue to work in the foreground. This increases your productivity and creates an environment in which you do not need to be burdened by mundane tasks, such as copying and formatting disks.

OS/2 Connectivity

If OS/2's advanced scheduling and preemption capabilities are manifested anywhere, it is in the communications arena. OS/2 was designed from the ground up with communications in mind.

Taking advantage of mature technologies, IBM built advanced network administrative utilities, file and device-sharing facilities, and other sophisticated LAN capabilities into OS/2.

OS/2's capability to multitask processes enables truly seamless network access to shared devices, such as printers and disks, while delivering unparalleled reliability and efficiency.

Comparing OS/2 and DOS Connectivity

OS/2 can communicate in every way that DOS can. DOS-only communications, as well as DOS versions 3.30, 4.01, and 5.0, are supported in the DOS box. DOS device drivers are supported in the MVDM compatibility boxes under OS/2 2.0.

Under OS/2, none of the communications servicing problems that occur under DOS are present. OS/2 supports task scheduling and true preemptive multitasking. Any communication problems under DOS are experienced only if you attempt multitasking on top of DOS.

The classical communications problem occurs with task switchers. A simple task switcher enables you to load more than one program at one time. If you want to switch from one program to another, you simply press the appropriate key combination and switch to the next program session. In most cases, this action suspends the initial session. If, however, the initial session was communicating in any way, whether on a LAN or over a modem, the communication ends in an error and the connection is broken.

A more sophisticated task switcher is a timeslicer. A *timeslicer* differs from the task switcher in that the program in the background continues to receive processing cycles from the processor as the control program (the timeslicer) allows.

As an example of this configuration, consider the following tasks associated with downloading a file over a modem and formatting a floppy disk. To begin, you start a DOS timeslicer program with two sessions, such as Windows 3.0 or DesqView. In the first session, run a communications program and begin to download a large file from a remote computer. After you begin this process, switch to the second session and make sure that you do not have a disk in drive A. Then type **FORMAT A:** and press Enter. Session two (running the format command) monopolizes the processor and causes the communications session to timeout. In most cases, the timeout terminates the downloading process and causes the session to fail.

In this scenario, the communications session fails. Although both sessions have access to the processor, no operating system function is in place to preempt the formatting task and service another session based on its task type (in this case, communications with the remote computer).

A communications connection must be serviced on a consistent and time-sensitive basis to remain active. Failure to service this connection results in a disconnection. Unlike DOS, OS/2's scheduler maintains the connection by halting processing of other tasks momentarily to service the communications line as needed. In the case of the floppy disk formatting procedure in this scenario, OS/2 continues to properly service the communications package while attempting to access a drive in drive A. Eventually, an error message is returned to the formatting session, but the download session continues without error in the background.

Because of OS/2's scheduler, OS/2 has been praised for its communications support. IBM has mandated full Systems Network Architecture participation for OS/2. SNA is IBM's connectivity blueprint for all of its hardware and software platforms. SNA specifies support for hardware such as token ring, Advanced Program to Program Communication (AAPC), Logical Unit (LU) 6.2, LU 2.0, PU 2.1, TCP/IP, NetBIOS, and others. This communications support built into OS/2 applies to mainframe communications, Asynchronous communications, and Local Area Networks (LANs).

Supporting Communications Types

OS/2 supports several physical connection types: Synchronous, Asynchronous, 5250 Direct Attach, 3270 Direct Attach, and X.25 support. Support for all of these physical media is necessary to provide the robust connectivity requirements of modern operating systems. OS/2 supports all major connectivity platforms except Macintosh's AppleTalk.

 The most popular connection medium available today is the LAN.

Principal Local Area Networks

What exactly is a LAN? A Local Area Network is a foundation or medium for delivering communications. If your company has a mainstream LAN in place, OS/2 can be introduced and used as a node on that network. OS/2 operates as a node in a Novell, LAN Manager, LAN Server, Banyan Vines, and TCP/IP Network environment. OS/2 also can be used as a server.

A LAN is made up of hardware, software, and a delivery system. The hardware consists of the computer and a network adapter.

The software includes drivers for the adapters, protocols, and a resource sharing/using package. The delivery system is either bound (a cable of some type) or unbound (radio or infrared signal). The most common form of delivery in offices today is bound.

LANs are used to connect computers so that they can share both physical and application resources. This includes micro, midrange, and mainframe computers. In a microcomputer environment, a LAN allows workstations to utilize such area resources as hard drive space, printers, modems, faxes, and mass storage archiving. This environment is generally made up of one or more workstations (also called *nodes*) and a server. Servers can be file servers, print servers, modem servers, fax servers, application servers, and so on.

 A LAN allows a workstation to have access to costly resources not contained in the workstation.

Servers usually are a combination of several shared resources. The benefits of a LAN server stem from cost savings and increased productivity through shared data and resources. An electronic mail system can reside on a server and enable all users who operate attached workstations to leave messages and pass files to each other. In another case, an expensive color laser printer that is part of a LAN enables all users access and negates the need to purchase several such printers. A centralized database on a server provides a structured and centralized point of resource control for updating and record searching. OS/2 even allows a single interface to multiple databases located on several different database servers.

OS/2 was designed for LAN use and is uniquely suited for this environment. DOS, on the other hand, was originally designed for floppy disk drive support only. Local Area Network support was added later, not designed into DOS from the beginning.

If your company has a midrange or mainframe computer, you can use a LAN to access resources and information. The number of LAN-attached workstations today is growing at an astronomical rate. OS/2 is qualified to excel in this environment due to its multitasking, scheduling, and preemption capabilities. With OS/2 you can LAN-attach to a host and use its printers and mass-storage devices. You also can emulate a terminal through software. PCs attached to a host provide new function in the work environment so that some processing can occur on the PC and some on the mainframe. This configuration is the predominant trend in the industry today.

OS/2 supports the most popular LAN connections in today's business environment, the exceptions being AppleTalk and ARCnet typologies. Nevertheless, these typologies can be integrated by means of a bridge in a network where OS/2 is being used. Figure 10.1 illustrates several ways in which AppleTalk and ARCnet nodes can function on a network that also supports OS/2 clients.

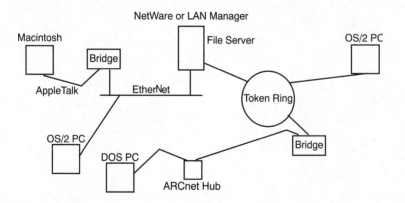

Figure 10.1:

AppleTalk and ARCnet networks connected to an OS/2 LAN through bridges.

Supported adapters include: EtherNet, Token Ring, IBM PC Network, and 3174 Peer Communications Network. The majority of connections under OS/2 on a LAN are anticipated to be EtherNet and Token Ring.

EtherNet compatibility is supported by means of the ETHERAND standard using Digital-Intel-XEROX (DIX) Version 2.0 and IEEE 802.3 protocols. Adapters compatible with this standard include

IBM's PS/2 Adapter for EtherNet, Ungermann-Bass, Western
Digital's Ether Card Plus series, and 3Com's 3c503 Ether Link series.
Token Ring support supplied is for IBM's 4 and 16/4 Megabit
adapters as well as the new Bus Mastered Token Ring adapter.
Support also is supplied for IBM's PC Network II and Baseband
adapters. Peer communications is provided through IBM's 3270
adapter for 3174 Communications.

EtherNet

EtherNet support for OS/2 was implemented in the maintenance
release of OS/2 1.2 and is fully supported in OS/2 2.0.

EtherNet is a linear bus topology as opposed to Token Ring, which
is a star-wired ring topology. Linear bus topology is like a one-lane
road that allows traffic to flow one way at a time. Two cars starting
at opposite ends cannot pass in the middle and must back up and
travel one at a time. Computer nodes on a linear bus have the same
constraints; only one session can communicate at a time. EtherNet
transmission is so fast that all conversations appear to be occurring
at the same time.

EtherNet is based on a Carrier Sense Multiple Access with Collision
Detection (CSMA/CD) technology, also known as *Contention-Based*
technology. CSMA/CD is currently the most commonly installed
LAN medium.

The basic structure of an EtherNet network is as follows: All stations
on an EtherNet network have equal access to the *bus* (the cabling
communication medium—the EtherNet cards and the cable). Any
station that wants to communicate listens to the bus to see if anyone
else is talking on it. (This process is defined as *carrier sense*.) If
another station is communicating, the station waits; if not, it proceeds to talk. *Multiple access* means that any station can communicate when the bus is not being used. If two stations are waiting to
talk and both sense inactivity, both may try to talk at the same time.
This action causes a *collision*, which is invisible to you but *detected* by
the EtherNet implementation and corrected.

This detection and correction is important and necessary for reliable transmission of your data. If you are the only one talking at that split second, the other sessions must wait for your request to finish before they can sense an idle bus and begin to communicate.

Because EtherNet is contention-based, collisions are common, although of minimal consequence. As stated earlier, collisions are transparent to the user because both (or all) communicating stations detect the collisions and issue a jamming command. All stations then back off, generate a random number, and try again later. This process takes place in fractions of seconds. This last phase is the Collision Detection (CD) portion of CSMA/CD.

Due to the inherent design of EtherNet, it is more advantageous to send larger frames as opposed to smaller frames. Smaller frames mean more traffic, and thus, potentially more collisions. Most software used in offices, such as dBASE, use small frames. Although smaller frames may sound inefficient, because of the speed and size of most small offices, collisions are not noticeable.

Although EtherNet is contention-based, it is very fast in most environments. In fact, EtherNet has a theoretical speed limit of 10Mbit (10 million bits per second). Speed on networks, measured in Mbits also is known as *bandwidth*. The band is the delivery mechanism (adapter and cable), and the width is the amount of data that can pass by one point in one second.

Of course, 10Mbit is never achieved on EtherNet because there is overhead, idle time, error correction, and collisions to be accounted for as well as the computer's capability to fill that bandwidth. Most computers cannot attach and detach from a network fast enough to meet the 10Mbit limit. As the number of stations on a network increases, the available bandwidth is filled to the point of diminishing returns. EtherNet's 10Mbit bandwidth, however, is sufficient for most office needs. OS/2 completely supports EtherNet transmission.

EtherNet, or derivatives of EtherNet, are common on DEC, SUN, and other hardware platforms and form the bulk of installed LANs. This gap is rapidly losing ground to Token Ring, but for now, EtherNet is the reigning king. Figure 10.2 illustrates EtherNet's linear bus topology.

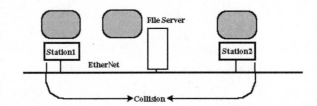

EtherNet support was added to the basic LAN support in OS/2 by means of an interface mapper. This interface mapper was included for addressing the MAC (Medium Access Control) layer generically. The generic MAC programming interface in provided by means of Network Driver Interface Specification. NDIS allows the OS/2 Communications Manager to talk to non-IBM network adapters.

The NDIS drivers are adapter-specific; therefore, OS/2 does not need to contain the code to support all cards on the market. The NDIS layer sits between the 802.2 API and the physical adapter. To gain support for non-IBM supported EtherNet adapters, the manufacturer's card must be compatible with the DIX 2.0 standard, or the manufacturer must supply its own MAC-NDIS software.

One benefit of controlling an adapter in this manner is to gain the support of Communications Manager functions, such as Host communications and LAN Server Support. If your EtherNet network is supported by Communications Manager, it can act as a node, a server, or an SNA gateway to a host with the inclusion of the appropriate adapter on the host side.

NDIS under the MAC layer sets the foundation for Emulator High Level Language Application Programming Interface (EHLLAPI), Advanced Program to Program Communications (APPC), and NetBIOS sessions to communicate over the EtherNet adapter. The protocols currently supported over EtherNet are: NetBIOS, IPX, Named Pipes, APPC, and TCP/IP.

These protocols are implemented in several ways. The most common communications software to seasoned OS/2 users is the Communications Manager, previously only available from IBM in the fashion of OS/2 Extended Edition. Novell has made its version of

NetBIOS and IPX available in the form of NetWare Lan Requester for OS/2. IBM and others have provided TCP/IP support.

APPC and NetBIOS support is found in the Communications Manager function of Extended Services 1.0 and also is available from a few manufactures.

OS/2's support for EtherNet is robust, functional, and growing. Support for additional EtherNet adapters and even direct support for 10baseT is imminent. If not from IBM, this support will be provided from the manufacturers.

 If your adapter is not listed, check with the manufacturer or your computer dealer to find out if a driver is available or if it is compatible with IBM's standard requirements, DIX 2.0.

Token Ring

OS/2 first supported Token Ring transmission, and Token Ring still remains the most widely used transmission medium for OS/2. Token Ring is IBM's network strategy for at least the near future. Computers—PCs to mainframes—connect through Token Rings. First with a bandwidth of 4Mbit and now 16Mbit, IBM intends to make this connection medium a more broadly accepted standard.

Token Ring was the first network connection supported under OS/2 and remains the favorite choice for most OS/2 shops. IBM chose this topology for its reliability, robustness, and intrinsic peer-to-peer support. Token Ring is not an IBM technology, and IBM is only credited with the topology's popularization and growth. Other companies such as DCA, Proteon, Ungermann-Bass, Thomas Conrad, StarTek, Olicom, Madge, and Intel have helped to spur it to today's current level. Analysts predict that Token Ring will overtake EtherNet in sales in the near future, but exactly when is still disputed.

Although dominant in IBM's world, Token Ring is just now catching on in other manufacturer's environments. EtherNet dominates the rest of the market today and perhaps will retain that top spot a little longer due to the IEEE adoption of the 10BaseT EtherNet standard.

So what makes Token Ring so desirable? For one thing, it is not contention-based. Token Ring uses a token-passing architecture. Only one conversion is allowed on the ring at a time. Each workstation that wants to communicate must grab the token when it is free. No two stations can talk on the network at the same time. When a station wants to communicate, it waits for a free token (one without data in it), and then grabs it. The workstation then adds data to the token, thereby changing it into a frame. This frame is then sent on to its destination. Any other workstation that wants to communicate notes that this is a frame, not a token, and does not attempt to use it. Thus, collisions never occur.

The benefits of this data transmission scheme are manifested in larger networks where network traffic is a problem. The Token Ring continues to pass data in a consistent manner unobstructed by collisions. The number of attached clients on this type of network does not effect transmission speed, but rather response time. In small departmental networks, EtherNet has similar and sometimes even better performance. The advantage of midrange and main-frame support for the Token Ring makes this method even more attractive in larger, host-oriented environments. The downside, however, is the greater overhead required for idle token passing.

Token Ring, as its name implies, is implemented on a ring. The ring is not wired in a physical ring, or loop, but rather is wired in a logical ring. A Token Ring is actually wired as a star-wired ring. Though logically a ring as shown in figure 10.3, it is wired as a star-wired ring as shown in figure 10.4.

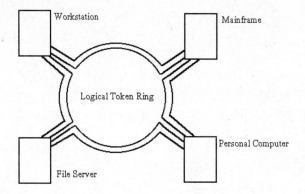

Figure 10.3:
The star-wired topology of a token ring network.

This arrangement also is known as a structured wiring system. In a star-wired ring or structured cabling system, each node is connected physically to a central point, a Multi-Station Access Unit (MAU).

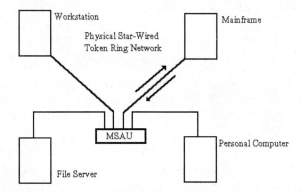

Figure 10.4:
A star-wired ring or structured cabling system.

IBM's MAU, also known as an 8228 or concentrator, is a passive device. Several versions of MAUs are on the market. Some are quite famous, like Synoptics and Cabletron, both founded in EtherNet roots. More versions appear on the market every day.

The MAU has several functions. Its premier design function is to provide structure to the cabling system by supplying a central control point. The MAU also provides ease of attachment or detachment. If any station fails, it is disconnected from the ring at the MAU automatically. Many concentrators provide diagnostics and signal regeneration inside the MAU. This feature is especially important in large networks with long runs. These runs from the MAU to the workstations are known as *lobes*.

In an EtherNet network implemented over coaxial cable, if one station fails, it can bring the network down. Likewise, a cable break can bring the network to a halt. Recently, EtherNet has adopted a structured-wiring system, similar in layout to Token Ring, to avoid this shutdown. This wiring system is 10baseT and has been spearheaded by Synoptics and others.

To further enhance transmission speed over Token Ring, the early token release was implemented on a 16Mbit ring by IBM. This version allows a second token to be issued after a frame has been passed to its final destination. A workstation that is waiting to receive a token does not have to wait until the frame has been received and converted to a token from the destination of the frame. This feature is available only in the 16Mbit implementation of Token Ring. A 4Mbit Token Ring operates as outlined earlier.

IBM, the IEEE Committee, and all the other Token Ring manufacturers are currently working on a 100Mbit that operates over a shielded twisted-pair medium. This model will raise the bandwidth stakes considerably. After this version is released, it will be only a matter of time before OS/2 will support it. The same protocols supported over EtherNet are supported over Token Ring. In fact, in some cases, the protocols were first supported over Token Ring and then EtherNet. This first-support attention makes Token Ring an "early adopter's" choice for a communication medium.

IBM plans to add EtherNet and fiber optics support for most of its strategic platforms. For now, Token Ring remains the favorite choice for LAN communications under OS/2 and in the IBM world.

Synchronous Connections

Synchronous communication is available under OS/2 through IBM's Extended Services add-on to OS/2 base services. Other third-party solutions also provide this capability, such as the Microsoft/DCA OS/2 Communications add-on. If your environment requires synchronous transmission to connect to a midrange or mainframe computer, OS/2 can be added to your environment with ease.

Synchronous communication is rooted in the midrange and mainframe world. It is the native way some host systems were designed to communicate. Your company may use a transmission technology called Binary Synchronous Communication (Bisync). Bisync was developed in the 1960s. It is similar to Synchronous Data Link Control (SDLC), but is character-oriented rather than bit-oriented like SDLC. Bisync has been replaced by Synchronous communications. OS/2's support for host communications is limited to those devices that can talk synchronously as well. Bisync is being phased out in today's MIS departments and should not pose a problem for integrating OS/2 in your environment.

Asynchronous communication is the native manner in which PCs communicate. For your PC to communicate synchronously, a synchronous adapter must be added to your system. The most common synchronous adapters are the Synchronous Data Link Control (SDLC) and Multiprotocol Adapter/A for Micro Channel machines.

Synchronous transmission is generally faster than asynchronous transmission and yet slower than LAN transmission. Synchronous communication sends large blocks of data and relies on sophisticated clocking instead of start and stop bits. All the timing and error correction is carried out in the modem, communication devices, and software.

Data sent synchronously is surrounded by control characters and is sent in large groups. Transmission throughput is very fast. Even though synchronous communications equipment is expensive, the speed at which it can transmit data may actually make it the more economical approach.

Almost all permanent synchronous attachments are done over leased lines (also known as data lines). The reliability afforded by leased lines, along with their transmission speeds, make synchronous connection the choice of most IBM host connections. OS/2 is a full participant in IBM's SAA platform.

Although synchronous transmission is usually associated with remote attachment, 3270 and 5250 emulation adapters that directly attach to host systems employ synchronous transmission. For remote communication to a host system, several components are necessary. You need a PC, a synchronous adapter, software, a synchronous modem, and—almost always—a leased line for best results.

 If you plan to purchase a modem, contact the MIS staff at the host location and find out the exact modem they are using. Purchasing a modem on your own can lead to great difficulty and incompatibility.

Also worth mentioning is the cable to connect the modem to the SDLC adapter in your computer. In most cases, this cable must be special-ordered. You must match this cable to the modem and the card in your computer. Because synchronous communication is not standard in most PCs, research your host environment and equipment needs with your MIS department, PC dealer, or an outside consultant to help eliminate installation failure and intermittent problems down the road.

OS/2 supports synchronous transmission through the OS/2 Communications Manager. The OS/2 Communications Manager is now packaged separately in OS/2 Extended Services 1.0. In previous versions of OS/2, you purchased OS/2 and Extended Edition together in one package. Because Extended Edition also contained the OS/2 Database Manager, those who only wanted communications were forced to pay a higher price. OS/2 Extended Services 1.0 only includes the Communications Manager. The OS/2 Communications Manager supports synchronous transmission through a gateway over SDLC, LAN, 3270, 5250, and EtherNet adapters. Although synchronous transmission is the language of the host world, the workstation (both PC and RISC) has standardized on asynchronous transmission.

Asynchronous Connections

Asynchronous communication capability is built into most PCs today by means of a serial port. OS/2 fully supports asynchronous communications through the serial port on your PC and even supports asynchronous communications over other multiport serial boards. These boards most likely need a special driver, which is usually supplied with the multiport card from the manufacturer.

Asynchronous communications also is known as *start-stop transmission*. This name is due to the way asynchronous transmission is carried out. In order for a receiving machine to determine where a character begins and ends, a start and a stop bit are framed around the character. This framing differs from the clocking approach used in synchronous transmission.

Almost all computers support asynchronous transmission in one form or another. OS/2 can use the serial port in your computer to communicate with mainframes (through a protocol converter), midrange computers (through a protocol converter), other PCs over modems, bulletin board services, ASCII data collection devices, and direct connection to another PC by means of a null modem cable.

Under OS/2, you can run your favorite DOS communications packages like ProComm Plus and CrossTalk. Windows communications packages also are supported under OS/2 2.0. If your computer has three serial ports, you can have ChipChat connected to a VAX mini over one telephone line, ProComm in a DOS session downloading a file from CompuServe, and the OS/2 Communications Manager reading bar code entries in another session all at the same time. The type of machine, modem, and adapters define how fast each session can effectively communicate, but the configuration is possible with OS/2 2.0.

X.25 Protocol

OS/2 supports packet-switched networks by way of its X.25 implementation in the OS/2 Extended Service 1.0. X.25 is a Wide Area

Network (WAN) protocol defined by the CCITT. X.25 was designed to allow communications over Packet Switching Networks (PSNs). A Packet Assembly Disassembly device (PAD) or Network Interface Module (NIM) can be used to allow asynchronous devices to converse on packet-switched networks.

PDN networks are available to the general public. PDNs contain numerous paths to any one location. Data is sent over PDNs one packet at a time. No permanent direct connection is established between the sender and receiver. At the time a packet is sent, the most efficient path is chosen based on traffic and location. A different path may be used for the next packet sent by that same terminal depending on current conditions. The path dynamically changes to meet current conditions.

Because no one direct route is tied up between two end points, a greater number of devices can use a PDN, reducing the cost of transmission for all. OS/2 enables you to dial out onto a PDN through a DOS, Windows, or OS/2 session. (You need software to do so.) OS/2's Extended Services includes X.25 support. Other software packages are available from several sources for DOS, Windows, and OS/2 support. Figure 10.5 illustrates an X.25 environment.

Figure 10.5:

An X.25 environment.

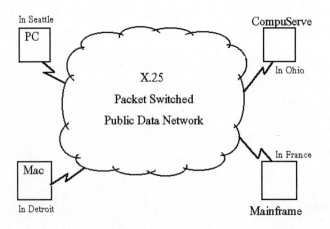

Introducing the OS/2 LAN Connection

OS/2 includes extensive LAN support. This section explains which LANs are supported and how they are supported. Additionally, figures help explain the connection mechanism and protocol stacks. NetWare, LAN Server, LAN Manager, Banyan-Vines, TCP/IP, and communications protocols support are explained. This section also discusses supported environments and gives you a general idea of what that support entails.

Novell NetWare and OS/2 Workstations

Novell NetWare is the dominant network operating system today. Novell owns roughly 70 percent of the network market. OS/2 2.0 supports NetWare versions 3.11 and higher through use of Novell's NetWare Requester for OS/2. If your corporation has a Novell network installed, you can add OS/2 clients to your existing network. NetWare has support for OS/2's High Performance File System (HPFS) through use of a name space on the server.

Novell's NetWare support for OS/2 was recently enhanced due to changes in OS/2 2.0's NDIS support. In previous versions, the NDIS interface supported only a limited list of Token Ring and EtherNet adapters. Under OS/2 2.0 the NDIS specification is more generic and allows the use of additional adapters and protocols. Novell and IBM have announced several partnerships to integrate OS/2 with NetWare. Eventually the NetWare server program will run on top of OS/2.

Currently, OS/2 machines are supported as clients on a traditional NetWare network. The capability to attach OS/2 clients to a NetWare network is made possible through Novell's Open

Data-Link Interface (ODI) specification. Novell also works with IBM's NDIS layer mentioned earlier. If you are just attaching to one server, a NetWare server, then you only need Novell's ODI support. If your environment calls for connection to an IBM LAN server on host, then you need to use both ODI and NDIS. The NDIS support software is replaced during Novell's install process to include a more generic version supplied by Novell. The new NDIS software is completely compatible with IBM's and does not affect IBM communication functions.

To better understand the way in which NetWare is implemented under OS/2 2.0, figure 10.6 demonstrates the configuration of protocol stacks. This figure in particular shows the layers connection in a Novell-only environment.

Figure 10.6:

The configuration of protocol stacks.

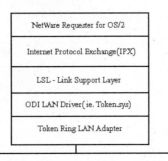

In an environment in which connection is required for LAN servers, the protocol stack is different. Novell replaces IBM's NDIS MAC Driver. Novell implements its own ODI layer and driver as shown in figure 10.7. To allow multiple protocols to be sent across one adapter, ODI creates a logical network board. In this manner, all protocols can be transmitted as if all are communicating over their own adapters.

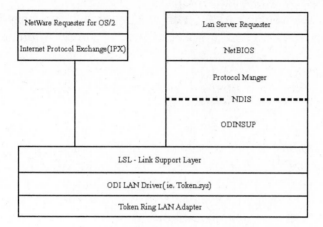

Figure 10.7:
Implementation of
Novell's ODI layer
and driver.

The NDIS MAC driver, IBMTOK.OS2, is replaced by LSL.SYS, TOKEN.SYS, and ODINSUP.SYS during the NetWare for OS/2 installation. This replacement is needed because when IBM OS/2 LAN support is installed, a LAN-adapter specific NDIS LAN driver is placed in the CONFIG.SYS. In order for NetWare to pass its IPX protocol over, it must be modified. The last protocol stack example showed the stack in a mixed connection environment. As an example, say your requirements are to allow simultaneous connection to an SNA host, OS/2 LAN Server, and a Novell network. Your protocol stack will look like the one in figure 10.8.

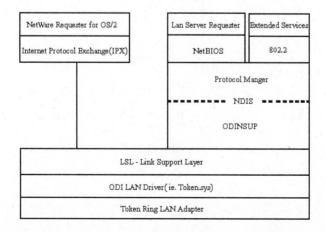

Figure 10.8:
Simultaneous
connection to an
SNA host, OS/2
Server, and a
Novell network.

In this environment you can maintain simultaneous connection to a PROFS session on a mainframe, a Lotus notes application on an IBM LAN Server, and access files and printer resources on your Novell NetWare Network. This versatility is another reason OS/2 2.0 is called the Integrating Platform. OS/2 offers full application support over Novell's NetWare operating system.

Under Novell's NetWare Requester for OS/2, two session environments are available: full system-wide redirection and session-specific redirection. In the system-wide support, which is the default, all sessions running on top of OS/2 and NetWare share one environment and have global system mappings, for instance. If you have captured a printer, all applications you start have access to that printer. Likewise, if a resource was mapped in NetWare's Login Script, all sessions started also have access to that drive. Figure 10.9 illustrates a captured printer and mapped drive in this environment.

Figure 10.9:

A captured printer and mapped drive.

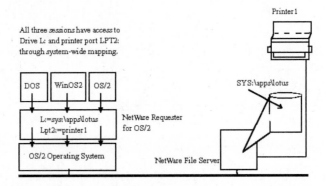

You may have mapped drive L to point to a directory on the server that contains Lotus 1-2-3 system files. This mapping may have occurred in the System Login Script or in your User Login Script. In either case, each session you open under OS/2—whether it be DOS, Windows, or OS/2—will have access to an L drive. This command in the Login Scripts looks something like this:

```
MAP L:=SYS:\APPS\LOTUS
```

Check with your network administrator for your mapping environment.

In the second case, a session-specific redirection, a NetWare session is created in a DOS MVDM session. You must select MVDM Support during the NetWare for OS/2 install process. Under DOS sessions, change the last drive setting to the last physical driver. If you also are connecting to an OS/2 LAN Server Network, be sure to allow for all LAN server redirected drives.

If, for example, you have redirected G, H, and I, the last drive statement should be set to I. The J drive becomes your login drive. To load a session-specific version in a DOS MVDM session, you must execute the NETX.COM program first, and then log into the Novell NetWare Network. If you have a global version of NetWare already running, an additional connection to the NetWare server is initiated. Figure 10.10 illustrates an environment where a global and session-specific NetWare session have been implemented.

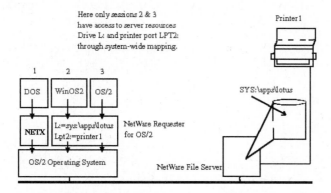

Figure 10.10:

Implementation of a global and session-specific NetWare session.

If you want to use system-wide NetWare resources mapped in the OS/2 Login Script, do not execute NETX.COM in the DOS MVDM session. If you do, all system-wide redirections will not be available in this session. The benefit of loading the DOS NETX.COM redirector in a DOS session is the support for the NetWare # command, which executes external commands and supports NetWare drive Map Management utilities.

NetWare is packaged in a red box from Novell and from IBM in a blue box. IBM and Novell have an agreement that gives IBM the rights to market Novell in their own packaging. Both versions of the software are the same. The only differences are the color of the boxes and the location of technical support. IBM's NetWare opens up acceptance in traditional IBM-only MIS departments and allows MIS departments to mix and integrate NetWare and OS/2.

Overall, OS/2 provides extensive support for Novell NetWare. If you have NetWare or are planning to install a NetWare network, OS/2 can be integrated with benefits not offered by DOS alone.

LAN Manager with OS/2 as a Server

Microsoft's LAN Manager Version 2.1 is an OS/2-based Network Operating System (NOS). LAN Manager (LANMAN) is the result of joint 3COM, Microsoft, and IBM efforts. Microsoft has taken over all development from 3COM and occasionally borrows from IBM as needed, based on their joint development agreement.

The LANMAN server program sits on top of an enhanced version of IBM/Microsoft OS/2 version 1.3. This version of OS/2 has been rewritten to run on a greatly increased number of machines. Microsoft has certified over 250 machines for LANMAN.

Almost any $80x86$ system will work if the appropriate amount of RAM and hard disk is present. Microsoft recommends 9M of RAM and an appropriately sized hard drive greater than 60M. LAN Manager is shipped in one package (NOS and OS/2) with two service add-ons—LAN Manager for Macintosh services and LAN Manager Remote Access Services. With these two add-ons, LAN Manager is now the most viable NOS Microsoft has offered to date. The joint Microsoft DCA Communications Server can be added to round out the offering, providing SNA and APPC functions. This puts LAN Manager in an equal playing field with Novell's NetWare NOS. The recent enhancements to LANMAN are the new protocols now supported. LAN Manager 21 supports five protocols with the inclusion of the two add-ons. The five protocols supported for LAN Manager access are the following:

- NetBEUI
- AsyncBEUI
- IPX
- TCP/IP
- AppleTalk

These new protocols enable you to integrate DOS, OS/2, UNIX, and Macintosh environments. This integration changes the scope of environments LAN Manager can fit into. Today, more and more environments are multiplatform. The requirement for a single protocol (NetBIOS or IPX) LAN is disappearing. TCP/IP networks and backbones are gaining mainstream acceptance rapidly. The Macintosh has made major inroads in corporate America and must be included in the network architecture. LAN Manager now has the power to do this.

The new surprise in LAN manager is AsyncBEUI. AsyncBEUI is Microsoft's asynchronous implementation of NetBIOS. AsyncBEUI is used for remote access and supports NetBIOS Emulation over telephone lines. AsyncBEUI allows a remote workstation to act as if it is locally attached even though a modem and serial port is used instead of a network adapter. This should be especially exciting to organizations that want to connect field sales personnel to their network.

AsyncBEUI provides additional security options. Most notable is a dial-back function. Though AsyncBEUI is an exciting and powerful addition, there are some practical limitations. Locally attached machines communicate on the network at a theoretical speed of 10 megabits. Remote workstations using AsyncBEUI over standard Asynchronous dial-up line access resources at 2400–14400 bits per second.

Even at 14,400 bits per second, remote access is nearly 700 times slower than local connection. A baud rate of 2400 is unbearable, and a rate of 14,400 is a reasonable approach for occasional attachment.

Client/server applications are different. Because client/server applications typically exchange only queries and responses, performance is acceptable in all but the most complicated and demanding situations. The remote workstations can be DOS- or OS/2-based. No support is included for UNIX or Macintosh clients.

The TCP/IP support in LAN Manager is a long-standing "known requirement." As TCP/IP gains acceptance, lack of support for it greatly limits the acceptance of LAN Manager in the environment. As in NetWare, an OS/2 or DOS workstation can attach to a LAN Manager server by use of TCP/IP. No other protocols need to be run. The benefit of this is demonstrated in environments on which SUN, RS/6000, HP, or other UNIX systems are used on the same network. A single DOS or OS/2 workstation can connect to all resources at once through one protocol, TCP/IP.

AppleTalk support in LAN Manager was inherited from 3COM's efforts, which have been turned over to Microsoft. AppleTalk is supported on System 6.0.3 through System 7 and OS/2. The AppleTalk protocol can be used over Token Ring, EtherNet, or LocalTalk adapters by means of the new and improved NDIS interface. No support is currently available for DOS clients that use AppleTalk.

IPX support is important to LAN Server environments that require access to NetWare Servers as well. LAN Manager 2.1 now supports simultaneous access to both servers, and is installed during LAN Manager installation. During this process, setup prompts you for NET5 and NETX and then generates an NDIS version of IPX. This IPX driver is actually compatible with the new NDIS specification compatible with both Token Ring and EtherNet from one IPX driver. Currently IPX support is for DOS only.

Figure 10.11 illustrates the possible connections available under LAN Manager 2.1. LAN Manager also supports IBM LAN Server's Domain concept, managing a series of servers as one collection of resources through a single interface.

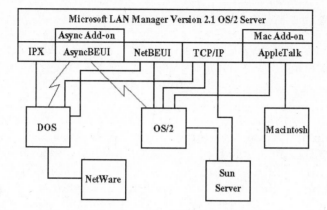

Figure 10.11:
The possible connections available under LAN Manager 2.1.

LAN Manager with OS/2 as a Workstation

Although OS/2 as a client was introduced earlier, several enhancements and features are available only to OS/2 workstations. OS/2 on a workstation has advantages inherent to OS/2, such as multitasking, multithreading preemption, and task scheduling, as well as its roots in LAN Manager. OS/2 is the only client operating system that allows Console Management, whether local or remote. Also available only to OS/2 clients is Print Queue Monitoring and direct use of LANMAN's serial ports for modem communications. The Print Queue Monitoring is especially interesting because an OS/2 workstation can monitor print jobs for LAN Manager as well as AppleTalk. Print streams from one interface connection to LAN Manager through the AppleTalk protocol is available only to OS/2 PCs and System 6.0.3 through 7.0 Macintoshes.

The last major benefit to OS/2 machines is the way AsyncBEUI is supported. Due to OS/2's superior handling of asynchronous communications, you can efficiently carry out multiple tasks while using AsyncBEUI. Under DOS, all other tasks seem to crawl if you execute applications over AsyncBEUI. DOS has no means of scheduling a communications application or preempting another to service the AsyncBEUI session. OS/2 excels where communications of any kind are required.

LAN Server with OS/2 as a Server

IBM OS/2 LAN Server 2.0 represents IBM's latest LAN operating system offering. As its name suggests, the LAN Server operating system runs on top of OS/2. In this environment, OS/2 is both the client and the server operating system. LAN Server also supports DOS and Windows clients. Version 2.0 of LAN Server has major changes. Extended NDIS Support, 386 HPFS, Coprocessor support, OS/2 RIPL, Fault tolerance, Mirroring, Duplexing, Operator Privilege, Windows 3.0 Client Support, RIPL over EtherNet, and Off-LAN Administration are just a few of the new features available in IBM's new OS/2 LAN Server 2.0. Before reviewing a few of the new features, a list of some differentiating features of LAN Server is covered. OS/2 LAN Server and LAN Manager from Microsoft support a control concept called *Domains*.

Domain Server/Additional Server

A *domain* is a server or collection of servers and all the nodes attached to it logically. You can have several servers on one physical network all belonging to different domains, or all the servers can be part of the same domain. Figure 10.12 shows three servers on a network with two domains: Domain1 and Domain2. Each domain is logically separate and shares bandwidth on the same physical network. Each domain requires one special server called a *Domain Controller*. The Domain Controller can be the only server or it can coordinate the efforts of several servers. In figure 10.12, the Sales1 server is the Domain Controller and Sales2 is an Additional Server. Both servers are members of Domain1. Server Account1 belongs to Domain2 even though it is physically on the same network.

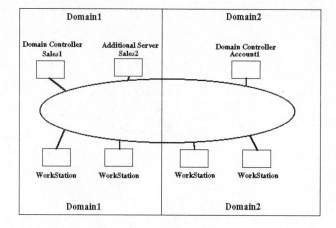

Aliases

Aliases are nicknames given to LAN server resources. An alias is used to name file, printer, and serial devices. Aliases are used in conjunction with LAN Server's Universal Naming Conventions. Figure 10.13 shows a typical server with file, printer, and serial resources available.

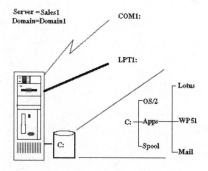

As an example, you want to share COM1, LPT1, the Lotus, WP51, and Mail directories. Under LAN Server, these resources can be shared by using the NET SHARE command, which conforms to the universal naming conventions.

Universal Naming Conventions

The universal naming conventions that you can use are as follows:

NET SHARE Modem	//Server1/Com1
NET SHARE Laser	//Server1/LPT1
NET SHARE Lotus	//Server1/C:\APPS\LOTUS
NET SHARE WP	//Server1/C:\APPS\WP51
NET SHARE Mail	//Server1/C:\APPS\MAIL

You must be a network administrator to perform these tasks and must be currently logged onto the server. A Net Access command must also be issued to indicate which users can access these resources. Issue the following Net Access command for a group of users:

```
Net Access Lotus /Add Sales:CDRW
```

or for one user, issue the following command:

```
Net Access Lotus /Add Rhonda: CDRW
```

Now that the resource has been shared and the appropriate people have access to it, a NET USE command must be issued to assign those resources. To assign the resources locally and begin using them, the following commands must be executed from a DOS or OS/2 prompt:

```
NET USE COM1:  //Server1/Modem
NET USE LPT2:  //Server1/Laser
NET USE L:     //Server1/Lotus
NET USE W:     //Server1/WP
NET USE M:     //Server1/Mail
```

This command sequence assigns the server's COM1 port to your COM1 port. In this case, the LASER alias is assigned to your LPT2 port, which leaves your LPT1 port free for local printing. Lotus can be accessed on the L drive, word processing from the W drive, and Mail from the M drive. This process does not need to be done in this manner each time you connect. In most cases, all of the resource assignments are done from menus, only once, by a system administrator. Each time a person logs onto the network, LAN Server looks at the NET.ACC file and the Domain Control DataBase (DCDB) file and issues all commands automatically.

 Modem support is only available under OS/2. DOS users can only use the server's COM ports for serial printing.

386 HPFS

Version 1.0 to 1.3 of LAN Server relied on the basic OS/2 file subsystem support for hard disk access. Even with HPFS, access times lagged considerably behind market leader NetWare. One of the main reasons for the differences in speed is due to the ring at which the file systems ran. NetWare runs its file system at ring zero, giving it equal footing with the operating system itself. Versions 1.0 to 1.3 of LAN Server run the file system at ring three. This means that each disk request must be passed to the kernel at ring zero to be processed. The trade-off was speed for protection.

With the introduction of IBM's OS/2 LAN Server Advanced Edition, a new file system called 386 HPFS is available. This is a replacement file system for the standard HPFS included with OS/2. 386 HPFS runs at ring zero, the same priority as the OS/2 kernel. With 386 HPFS installed, performance against NetWare 3.11 is very favorable. 386 HPFS offers speed gains beyond ring zero implementation. It permits a 32-bit path to the file system. Included with 386 HPFS is a new network-aware Installable File System (IFS). The new IFS has been optimized for common cache and contiguous file allocation mechanisms. The first release of LAN Server 2.0 Advanced with 386 HPFS only runs on OS/2 1.3. Support for OS/2 2.0 will be added shortly thereafter. OS/2 2.0 clients can attach to a file server running 386 HPFS and gain the throughput benefits, as can DOS, Windows, and OS/2 1.3 clients.

Coprocessor Support

Going hand-in-hand with the new 386 HPFS is the new support in place for a second processor. Coprocessor support allows some of the system software and processing to be off-loaded to the co-processor to run alongside the main processor. This also is known as implementing loosely coupled processing. This feature will be available when loosely coupled processing is available under OS/2 2.0. LAN Server code has been redesigned in 2.0 to support this software/hardware feature when available.

Why is this important to your network strategy? The most compelling reason is in the area of client/server computing. As an example, consider an SQL Database Manager application running on OS/2 LAN Server 2.0. With 386 HPFS and coprocessor support, the 386 HPFS code could run on the second processor, leaving the main processor free to run the Database Manager. In this manner, a processor has main support for a function, enhancing transaction throughput in a two-fold manner. OS/2 should eventually support tightly coupled processing, which will enhance performance even more.

Coexistence

This topic could be placed in the Novell section as well as this section. IBM and Novell have worked out the kinks in their network operating system environments to allow peaceful coexistence between NetWare and LAN Server. Release 2.0 of LAN Server expands on these changes to make the coexistence even more stable. If your environment calls for access to both NetWare and LAN Server, you can attach to both with either DOS, Windows, or OS/2. Novell or IBM can provide a document called COEXIST.TXT with additional details on this joint support. Under an agreement with IBM, Novell has committed to developing an OS/2 version of NetWare. This will take coexistence to a higher level of intraoperability.

Installation

Because OS/2 LAN Server uses much of the standard OS/2 code, the OS/2 LAN Server program comes on very few disks. Also included with the server code is a migration disk, DLR, LSP, and OS/2 Requester software. DOS LAN Requester (DLR) is the support software for DOS and Windows clients. LAN Support Program (LSP) is the series of IBM-supplied adapter and NetBIOS drivers for DOS and Windows clients. Installation time runs from 10 minutes to 3 hours depending on what features you load. A straight installation on a standard PC with all disk-based DLR machines will be the quickest to install.

RIPLing DOS

OS/2 LAN Server provides a service for booting diskless workstations over a LAN. This is known as *Remote Initial Program Loading* or RIPLing. RIPL is supported over token ring and EtherNet networks. In order for RIPL to work, two components are necessary: a boot PROM on the network adapter and an Image Server. The boot PROM is used to broadcast a request for a boot image. This boot image is a binary file representation of a bootable disk. This emulates placing a DOS system disk in your PC's A drive. The second component is the image server. An OS/2 LAN server performs this task. After a boot PROM broadcasts an image request, the image server downloads the binary boot image to the diskless machine's main memory. OS/2 diskless workstations are handled a little differently.

RIPLing OS/2

OS/2 is a much more sophisticated operating system requiring significantly more disk resources for booting. A functional OS/2 machine cannot be booted from a floppy disk alone. OS/2 requires a fixed disk of at least 30M to boot. This poses a problem for RIPLing.

If RIPLing was implemented in the DOS image structure, there would be at least two major problems. The first is the sheer hard-disk requirements of holding several 30M images. The second is that OS/2 uses a SWAPPER.DAT file and INI files that must be written to. For these reasons, OS/2 RIPL does not use an image to download for diskless OS/2 workstations. Instead, a new mini-file system is used. Under this environment, a connection is initially established as under DOS RIPL, and then a mini-file system is used instead of down-loading an entire Operating System Image.

After the DOS bootstrap has been established, this connection is used to download the critical OS/2 loader files. These files over-write the DOS in the PC's memory. Because some OS/2 files are required for all OS/2 workstations, these files are made available in a read-only shared directory for all RIPLed OS/2 workstations. A separate, private area is established for each OS/2 RIPL workstation for its SWAPPER.DAT and other files which need to be updated exclusively by that system. This arrangement allows each OS/2 RIPL machine to maintain its own customized environment and helps to reduce the hard disk requirements for supporting OS/2 RIPL systems while allowing each OS/2 RIPL machine to maintain its own uniqueness. The only penalty to OS/2 RIPL is the perfor-mance loss inherent in constantly accessing the SWAPPER.DAT over the LAN. This can be offset by increasing the RAM on the workstation, thereby reducing dependency on a SWAPPER.DAT file. OS/2 RIPL capability adds to an already robust network oper-ating system.

LAN Server with OS/2 as a Workstation

OS/2 is the premier client in an OS/2 LAN server network. A great deal of attention has been given to OS/2's communications capabili-ties. In this book, LAN client support is no exception. An OS/2 Requester can access all DOS and OS/2 applications on an OS/2 LAN server network. OS/2 offers capabilities as a node that are not available to DOS workstations, such as server administration and named pipe support. Named pipes, explained earlier, are built into

OS/2. Server administration capability is available only to an OS/2 client. This means that the administrator will either have to have an OS/2 workstation or have to use the server itself to perform those tasks.

The capability of a workstation to use a modem attached to a LAN server is available only to OS/2 workstations. With an Arctic card, up to eight modems can be available in a shared pool for OS/2 clients. Likewise, only OS/2 workstations can view and manage the server's print queue because only an OS/2 workstation incorporates the OS/2 print manager. DOS workstations, on the other hand, have no multitasking print queue. Another benefit of an OS/2 Requester is the capability to reliably perform other tasks in addition to the LAN connection. Examples have been given throughout this book. LAN connection now is provided by the OS/2 Requester Software included in the OS/2 LAN Server software.

In the past, IBM required that you purchase the Extended Edition of OS/2 to get the LAN Requester component. This proved very costly for those only needing the LAN code. OS/2 Extended Edition included the communications manager, Database Manager, and LAN Requester. With release 2.0 of the LAN Server program, the requester portion was removed from Extended Edition and included in OS/2 LAN Server. The resulting Communications Manager and Database Manager now are packaged in Extended Services 1.0. Just as OS/2 provides the foundation for OS/2 LAN Server, it also provides the broadest and most complete support as a client of an OS/2 LAN server network.

Banyan-Vines with OS/2 Workstations

OS/2 supports Banyan-Vines networks through Vines Support for OS/2, provided by Banyan-Vines. In a Vines network, an OS/2 workstation acts as a client to the Banyan-Vines server. If your company currently uses a Vines network, then you can add an OS/2 workstation to that network. Vines OS/2 client support must be purchased separately and includes all the software necessary to enable an OS/2 client to communicate with the Vines server.

Banyan-Vines includes an install program called VCLIENT. VCLIENT copies all the necessary files to a directory on the hard drive of your OS/2 machine and alters your CONFIG.SYS file. A new redirected drive, Drive Z:, is added to your search path. This drive is where OS/2 locates Banyan-Vines software on the Vines server. The LIBPATH statement is updated to include Vines-specific Dynamic Link Libraries (DLLs). Vines for OS/2 supports named pipes, mail slots, and the OS/2 Print Manager. OS/2 Extended Attributes also are supported. Vines even supports files created by using the OS/2 HPFS (High Performance File System).

Vines rides on top of the NDIS layer, which was introduced earlier in this chapter. Vines can support ARCnet if a vendor provides you with the appropriate NDIS driver. Some ARCnet vendors currently are working on NDIS drivers, although a release date has not been set. ARCnet support is not available under standard OS/2 and is not supported by IBM. The only LAN access mediums supported by IBM at this time are Token Ring and EtherNet. These drivers are readily available. If your company uses ARCnet, contact the manu-facturer to obtain release dates.

As you saw earlier, the VCLIENT program is used to select and install LAN drivers and client software. All LAN drivers must be written to the NDIS specification. NDIS enables vendors to write drivers that support their LAN adapters. Banyan-Vines needs to address only the NDIS interface, leaving adapter support up to the manufacturer of the adapter. Although VCLIENT is used to install Vines software and load adapter drivers, PCCONFIG must be used to configure the adapter for use. If you are using adapters not provided by Banyan-Vines, then the following parameters apply:

- You cannot use the VCLIENT and PCCONFIG to set up the adapter. This must be done manually according to manufacturer's instructions.

- The adapter must be compatible with the PROTMAN.OS2 version 1.1 and version 2.0.1 or the NDIS specification.

To get Banyan-Vines up and running on your system, you must first run the VCLIENT program and then run PCCONFIG. Finally, boot

up your system. The installation manual from Banyan-Vines provides a clear and easy-to-use set of instructions for installation. It is
full of pictures and diagrams to assist you.

After you install Vines support for OS/2, the Vines requester is
started by running a program called BAN. This process can be
automated by placing this command in your STARTUP.CMD file.
As discussed earlier in this book, the STARTUP.CMD file is a file
containing one or more commands to enter each time the system is
started. This file is located in the root directory of your boot drive. If
you do not currently have a STARTUP.CMD file, you can create one
by typing **E STARTUP.CMD** from an OS/2 full-screen command
prompt. Add the following commands to the file:

```
CD\VINES
BAN
```

Banyan-Vines starts each time your system starts and places you at
the login screen. From this point, Banyan-Vines acts as it does under
DOS, yet also offers you all the benefits of OS/2 and a multitasking
environment. When using a natively supported adapter such as
Token Ring or EtherNet, Banyan-Vines supports multiple protocols
to be shared over the same adapter.

Banyan-Vines also supports more than one adapter at one time.
Suppose, for example, that your company needs to access data on a
Banyan-Vines server and resources on another Banyan-Vines server
or IBM LAN server. These connections can be based on 802.2,
named pipes, or NetBIOS. This can be on the same machine or on
different OS/2 machines on the same network. Mail slot and named
pipes support must be selected during VCLIENT'S installation
process for these services to be available. OS/2 fully supports
connection to a Banyan-Vines network through the Vines for OS/2
support provided by Banyan-Vines. It provides an effective way to
integrate OS/2 into your current network scheme.

UNIX with TCP/IP

The test for a truly connection-oriented operating system, such as
OS/2 2.0, is TCP/IP (Transmission Control Protocol/Internet

Protocol). TCP/IP was designed for the military and has been widely embraced by the UNIX community. TCP/IP is intended for nonproprietary networking among mixed environments. TCP/IP support under OS/2 is provided by a program called TCP/IP for OS/2. TCP/IP for OS/2 supports the following:

- File transfer
- Remote login
- Network file sharing
- Electronic mail
- Remote printing
- Network management
- Terminal emulation
- Security functions
- Server functions

Of major interest is TCP/IP for OS/2's support for Sun's NFS (Network File System), RPC (Remote Program Call), and MIT's Xwindows. Several vendors of UNIX packages have standardized on NFS and Xwindows, such as SCO's UNIX and IBM's AIX. With TCP/IP for OS/2, your OS/2 workstation can connect, log on, and share data and applications with these UNIX servers. TCP/IP for OS/2 communicates over ETHERAND DIX 2.0 (EtherNet), IEEE 802.3, and Token Ring connections.

If your UNIX system connection requirements are not LAN-based, then you can use a terminal emulation package to communicate using the serial port on your PC in one session. The LAN-based solution provides a richer environment that offers multiple sessions and background transfers. The RPC function enables distributed processing over a LAN, enabling processing to occur on a machine better fit for a particular task.

If you are a programmer, TCP/IP for OS/2 provides APIs to address various sockets. The following three socket interfaces are supported:

Stream socket interface

Datagram socket interface

Raw socket interface

The stream interface is the most secure, providing error checking and flow control. Datagram is the connectionless interface NFS is built on. The raw socket interface, as its name implies, is the base-level interface. A popular utility called PING is implemented at the raw socket interface. TCP rides on the stream interface and has no length limits. The stream interface is best suited for moving large chunks of data. It is the slowest socket interface because of its overhead relating to error correction. Datagram and raw sockets are faster, but lack integrity checking. Datagram data transfer in packets of 2048 bytes of less. Error correction may be carried out above the socket level as in NFS.

If you are using programs and not doing the actual programming, these actions are invisible to you. An example of a multivendor environment that is using TCP/IP under OS/2 might help you understand the power of OS/2. Suppose, for example, that your company has an engineering department that is using Sun workstations to provide client information. Your company also might have a Novell NetWare server that has PC applications stored on it. Your task is to integrate this information into a customer presentation. You might have AutoCAD for the Sun to create your CAD drawings on the Sun workstations. Your database is in dBASE on the IBM LAN server. You use PageMaker for OS/2 on your machine. PageMaker is located on the NetWare server. Your network hardware is EtherNet. The layout of your system may look like the one shown in figure 10.14.

Figure 10.14:

OS/2, NetWare
3.11, and UNIX
coexisting on a
LAN.

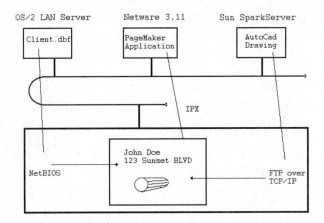

In this example, the client information is accessed on the LAN
server network by using NetBIOS. The PageMaker application,
located on the NetWare file server, is accessed by the IPX for Novell.
The drawing on the Sun server can be transferred to your machine
by using the File Transfer Program (FTP). All of these diverse
environments can be accessed by using objects on the OS/2 PM
desktop. The FTP transfer can be started by an icon and then simply
prompt you for the file to transfer. All of this can be set up and
automated by a network engineer.

The actual connections to the servers generally are established at
system startup. Multiprocessing and multiple connections are tasks
generally exploited and available only under OS/2. TCP/IP for
OS/2 provides basic support for UNIX environments and includes
most industry standard protocols and APTs. OS/2 in your environment is an effective means of integration with existing and future
UNIX connection.

OS/2 Communications Protocols

OS/2 supports two types of pipes: named pipes and unnamed pipes
(simply called *pipes*). Pipes were introduced in OS/2 version 1.0 as a
means for two related processes to communicate in the same machine. Technically, pipes are not transport protocols, but are an

application programming interface to the OS/2 operating system. Named pipes appear as a transport protocol because the results look the same.

Pipes, as mentioned earlier, were introduced with OS/2 1.0 to provide simple one-way intraprocess communication. Each end of the pipe is called a *handle*. One end is for receiving and the other is for sending. The pipe layout appears as a pseudofile in RAM. Any child process that is spawned from a parent process can read from the pipe handle. Figure 10.15 illustrates the pipe concept as a lead pipe with data thought of as water traveling through the pipe.

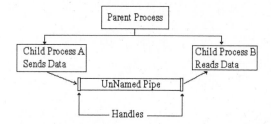

Figure 10.15:
The pipe concept.

Data traveling through the pipe is managed in a first-in, first-out access method. When the pipe is filled with data, no additional data can be fed through it until enough data has been read out. Data can be read only once from the receive handle. After a piece of data has been read, it is removed from the pipe. The pipe API was fine for light data passing between closely related processes, but lacks two-way transmission and intra-PC application communication.

With the introduction of OS/2 Version 1.1, named pipes were introduced. Named pipes offer many advantages over pipes. *Named pipes* provide a variable length, duplexed message pipe, enabling clients to send and receive from a handle. Named pipes are structured in a client/server manner. The server creates the named pipe and then advertises it. A client process then can grab the named pipe and establish a connection. The server then hands the pipe off to a tread and creates a new named pipe.

Over twenty named-pipe functions are available to control the communication providing robust intraprocess communication.

Named pipes excel over NetBIOS networks because of their high-level interface and support for Virtual Circuit abstraction. One of the major benefits of named pipes over the previous pipe API is the support for pipe connection between applications on different computers. Previously, the process had to be on the same machine. In today's networking environments this is a significant advantage. Figure 10.16 provides a simplistic flowchart of the server side of named pipes. This is not a complete list and shows no support code. The flowchart merely provides you with a general idea of what goes on.

Figure 10.16:

Flowchart of the server side of named pipes.

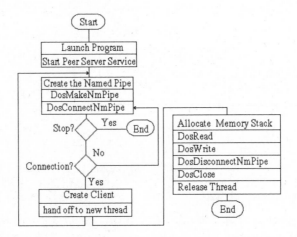

Although this is a simplistic example, it is quite a bit simpler than a NetBIOS application. Named pipes provide client services for both DOS and OS/2. The server portion is available only to OS/2. OS/2's multitasking capabilities make client/server applications based on named pipes a powerful and easy-to-implement platform. This is especially true as the named pipes API is built into the OS/2 operating system itself.

APPC

Advanced Program-to-Program Communications (APPC), is an application-programming interface enabling programs to communicate in a Systems Network Architecture (SNA) environment. OS/2 is a full participant in IBM SNA master plan. The SNA umbrella can be a misnomer, as APPC applications do not necessarily require use of a network. APPC is a program interface and can be used on one machine between two PM applications. APPC is not even an OS/2 programming interface. APPC was designed by IBM to enable programs to communicate on various platforms, whether they are mainframe, mini, RISC, or PC.

APPC/PC is a software package that enables DOS programs to integrate into an APPC conversation. You can think of APPC/PC as one program capable of talking to another program regardless of the platform it is on. The strongest multiplatform APPC communications exist between IBM's AS/400 midrange computer and OS/2 on a PC. APPC is available on mainframes as well.

To help explain why APPC was developed, a brief synopsis of IBM's Logical Unit (LU) types needs to be covered. In the past, IBM used the mainframe to control the network. All other devices attached were subservient to the mainframe, not peers. APPC does not require the mainframe to control the LU-to-LU conversation unless the mainframe is directly involved. This opens up the peer-to-peer status of all nodes involved. IBM recognized the growing trends of downsizing and distributed processing. This is best evidenced in client/server applications. For distributed processing work, the platforms must be peers. APPC's session layer interface is different than IPX or NetBIOS, as it implements a set of protocols called Logical Unit 6.2 (sometimes abbreviated LU 6.2). Where NetBIOS was developed to allow programs to communicate over a pure LAN environment, APPC was designed to allow multi-platform communications. The following lists the common LU types defined by IBM:

Common LU Types	Description
LU 0	Defines Transmission and Data Flow Control
LU 1	Defines a 3270 printer and supports the SNC Character Set (SCS) or Document Content Architecture (DCA) data streams
LU 2	Defines a 3270 terminal using the 3270 data stream

continues

Common LU Types	Description
LU 3	Defines a printer as does LU 1 and uses the 3270 data stream
LU 4	Defines a terminal for 5250 connections
LU 6.2	Defines a program-to-program communications protocol and is a peer-to-peer multiplatform implementation
LU 7	Defines a terminal session as does LU 4

These LU types provide end-user access connection to an SNA host resource. The LU session can be implemented in software, hardware, or a combination of both. LU type 1 provides both SNA and non-SNA connection, while LU types 2, 3, 4, and 7 must connect with an LU of the exact same type on the other end to function. Only LU type 6.2 provides the capability of communication between different LU types and platforms. LU 6.2 is network independent and can be used as a bridge or backbone for an SNA network of similar or dissimilar platforms. These platforms do not need to be IBM. This change represents IBM's strategy for future connection and communications for current and future product releases.

LU 6.2 is a transport, network, and session interface. IBM's AS/400 manages all communications through APPC. This is only the beginning of things to come. APPC support is provided by IBM's OS/2 Extended Services 1.0 and Extended Edition 1.1 through 1.3. APPC also is supported by other non-IBM hardware. OS/2 APPC software also is supplied by Microsoft, DCA, and others. As mentioned earlier, APPC is a programming interface and requires that a program be written to use it. Support for APPC alone is not enough. The major problem with APPC is its lack of portability. APPC is difficult to program to and uses different control blocks, which are specific to the platform being used. This is not a problem if you are in an IBM shop, but in a mixed environment, this poses a significant problem. In mixed environments, NetBIOS is a better choice. The combination of OS/2 and its Presentation Manager, APPC support, through Extended Services and the Data Base Manager, provides developers with a strong foundation for creating advanced client/server applications.

Understanding NetBIOS

Network Basic Input/Output System (NetBIOS) is a defacto LAN-to-application program interface standard. NetBIOS is the interface that communicates with firmware located on Network adapter cards. It is to Networks what IO.SYS, IBMBIOS.COM, and the OS/2 kernel are to your PC hardware and system BIOS.

NetBIOS was designed by IBM and Sytek, Inc. to enable applications to communicate over a network. As its name implies, NetBIOS was designed for Network communications—not dial-up modem or other non-LAN communications. OS/2 supports NetBIOS for DOS and OS/2 programs and sessions, and it can be used over a modem when communicating LAN to LAN, as in the case of a bridge. Nevertheless, NetBIOS is not a LAN operating system. NetBIOS is used by LAN operating systems to allow the operation system to talk to the network adapter card. In fact, NetBIOS can be used when no network operating system is being used. Some examples of this are network remote control packages such as Close-up LAN and Carbon Copy LAN. OS/2 uses NetBIOS for Remote Data Services and other SQL Data Base programs. The list of Network Server Operating Systems that support NetBIOS is extensive: Microsoft LAN Manager, IBM LAN Server, Banyan-Vines, Novell NetWare, and many others can use NetBIOS or are completely based on it.

NetBIOS is the most common means for applications to link up over a network for whatever reason. The NetBIOS interface is used in many different situations. IPX, which is used by Novell NetWare, is mainly confined to Network Operating System functions. NetBIOS can be used in conjunction with NetWare to open NetWare up to NetBIOS specific applications. In the case of NetWare, NetBIOS emulation is supplied and IPX is the transport mechanism.

Figure 10.17 illustrates how a NetBIOS application communicates over an adapter using various transport methods.

Figure 10.17:

NetBIOS
communication.

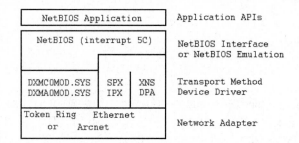

In reference to the ISO model, NetBIOS is located at layer 5, the session layer. The original implementation called for NetBIOS to cover layers 6 and 7 as well. Today, NetBIOS is mainly used at layer 5 and DOS; OS/2 Network Operating System software handles layers 3, 4, 6, and 7, as shown in figure 10.18.

Figure 10.18:

Historical
comparison of
NetBIOS.

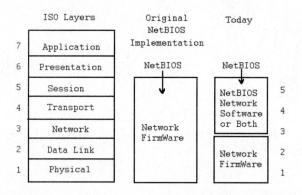

It is important that two aspects of NetBIOS are differentiated— the NetBIOS API and the NetBIOS protocol. NetBIOS can be used as an API only as in NetWare or a complete protocol and API as used in Remote Data Services and application programs such as Close-up LAN. The differences are the OSI layers NetBIOS provides. In conjunction with a Network Operating System the purpose of the NetBIOS interface is to present resources or communication to a program as if they are local. NetBIOS is not the Network Operating System, but is used by the Network Operation System.

OS/2 provides NetBIOS support through a program called NetBIOS.OS/2 or NetBIOS.OS2, which is loaded in the CONFIG.SYS file. Under OS/2, the NetBIOS interface is available to every DOS or OS/2 session started. The two most popular NetBIOS applications for OS/2 are IBM LAN Server and Remote Data Services. Any NetBIOS application, whether DOS, Windows, or OS/2, can be supported under OS/2 when NetBIOS for OS/2 support has been added.

Understanding Novell's IPX Protocol

Internetwork Packet Exchange (IPX) and Sequenced Packet Exchange (SPX) are the native protocols used by Novell's NetWare Network Operating System (NOS). IPX is an adaptation of XNS, the Xerox Network System protocol. These protocols can be used by an OS/2 or DOS requester to communicate with a NetWare server. NetWare 3.11 also supports other protocols, such as NFS, through its Open Protocol Technology (OPT). Although NFS connection is a possible means of connection with OS/2, IPX is still the most common choice for OS/2-to-NetWare communications. IPX is not adapter dependent, as the Open Data Link Interface (ODI) bridges the IPX to LAN adapter gap. IPX operates at ISO layer three; layers one and two are handled by the ODI and firmware. This differs from IPX's implementation on NetWare versions prior to 3.*X*, in which IPX was adapter-specific and addressed layers one through three. Figure 10.19 shows where IPX fits into the ISO model.

Novell's native client and server protocol is the NetWare Core Protocol (NCP). NCP is similar to Server Message Block (SMB) used in Microsoft LAN Manager and IBM LAN Server. NCP interfaces with IPX, which gains access to the Network Card through the ODI layer. IPX is based on datagrams and does not require an acknowledgment for the packets it sends. For this reason, it is known as *connectionless transmission*. The transport layer is handled by NetBIOS, SPX, NCP, SAP, or RIP. Refer to figure 10.19 to see how all the protocols fit together.

Figure 10.19:

Interworkings of protocols.

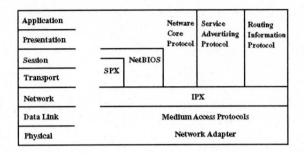

Application					Netware Core Protocol	Service Advertising Protocol	Routing Information Protocol
Presentation							
Session		SPX	NetBIOS				
Transport							
Network		IPX					
Data Link		Medium Access Protocols					
Physical		Network Adapter					

The MAC protocols used are dependent on the network topology used (that is, Token Ring, EtherNet or ARCnet). IPX is located on top of the appropriate ODI support software for each type of adapter. IPX can support a total of two adapters, and provides the node and network addressing. This is analogous to the street address for your home. Figure 10.20 provides an IPX packet, and a correlation to a house address.

Figure 10.20:

IPX packet and its correlation to a house address.

IPX Packet Structure		Your PC		Your House	
Checksum		Error Checking			
Packet Length		Size		Length of Letter	
Transport Control	Packet Type	Control	Information	FedEX	Letter
Destination Network		Your Network Segment		Your City	
Destination Node		Your Computer		Your Street	
Destination Socket		Your Application		Your House	
Source Network		Server Network Segment		From City	
Source Node		Server Machine		From Street	
Source Socket		Server Process		From House	
DATA		The Requested Data		Content of the Letter	

This IPX packet can be contained inside an 802.3 EtherNet or 802.5 Token Ring packet. OS/2 can send IPX, NFS, APPC and other packets inside these 802.X packets concurrently, providing you with several communication options at the same time.

IPX support is critical to OS/2's success as Novell NetWare currently dominates the network market. Again, IPX—not NetBIOS or NFS—represents the bulk of NetWare connection access protocols.

OS/2 fully supports IPX through Novell's NetWare Requester for OS/2 software. This software is available from IBM, Novell, or your local Novell dealer.

Reviewing OS/2 Host Connection

This next section covers OS/2's advanced connection options to midrange and mainframe computers, also known as *host systems*. Host systems are older than personal computers and are found in mid-to large-size corporations. The capability to attach to these host systems has been a requirement beginning with DOS and the original PC.

The ordinal PC was not designed for host connection. A special adapter and software must be used to allow a PC to emulate a host terminal. The first implementations were merely that, terminal emulators. Today PCs do much more than just emulate terminals. Peer-to-peer status has been granted to advanced PCs, offering distributed processing and resource sharing. It was the PC that first brought computing power to the common person.

The power of host systems has escaped the general public due to their high cost. Several vendors, including IBM, MicroSoft, DCA, Attachmate, and others, have introduced hardware and software that allow varying degrees of conversation and resource utilization. IBM's offering is called OS/2 Extended Services Version 1.0. Extended Services enables an OS/2 workstation to attach to IBM's 370 systems (mainframes) and 3/X systems (midrange).

The first host systems were called mainframes. For an OS/2 PC to connect to a mainframe, 3270 emulation is required.

Using 3270 Emulation

OS/2 provides a firm foundation for host communications due to its multitasking capabilities and IBM heritage. A host system is characterized as a large computer capable of supporting a large number of users. Host systems are typically fast and expensive. In a host environment, almost all processing is done on the host processor or processors. Most large host systems have multiple processors that divide up tasks and carry them out concurrently.

Host systems predate today's personal computers. One of the design requirements was superior 370 host support. This was originally provided by IBM's Extended Edition and now Extended Services. Microsoft and others also provide Terminal Emulation and other host services. Terminal Emulation is also provided in the DOS sessions under OS/2 2.0.

Connection to a mainframe is available over several mediums. With the appropriate software and hardware, you can connect to a host over a LAN, asynchronous or synchronous modem, coax line, or an X.25 network. A gateway enables several PCs to connect to a host over a LAN. Figure 10.21 illustrates various connection types.

Figure 10.21:

Multiple connections to a LAN.

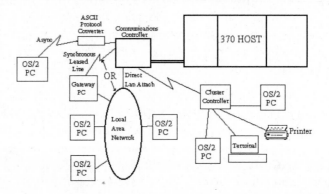

Figure 10.22 shows the possible connections in a more complete manner. Though not all possible methods are shown, figure 10.22 list the most common networking connections.

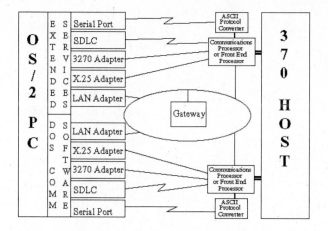

Figure 10.22:
Common networking connections.

Host session-pass-through, EtherNet, Fiber Optic, TCP/IP and other hardware/software combinations are possible. OS/2 2.0 has enhanced and expanded the list of combinations due to its MVDM support. In the past, 370 connection was only supported by using OS/2 software. OS/2 2.0 has greatly enhanced DOS support, enabling DOS programs to perform communications even while in the background. 3270 communications packages are specifically listed as supported in the OS/2 2.0 documentation.

Even though 3270 emulation is supported in a DOS session, this is not the best choice. Under OS/2, multiple programs can use one adapter for different purposes. OS/2 also provides better support for communications than DOS. This is due to OS/2's task scheduling, preemption, and true multitasking. DOS is structured for handling one task or session at a time. Typically, but not always, this means one task over one adapter. Mainframe environments usually consist of a host and a LAN.

Under OS/2, you can attach to the Network Server, the mainframe, and other services. OS/2 was designed for this environment—DOS was not. In a DOS session (MVDM), the same restrictions apply. Figure 10.23 illustrates an OS/2 environment making several connections over one adapter.

Figure 10.23:

An OS/2 environ-
ment that makes
several connec-
tions over one
adapter.

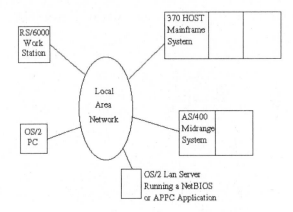

In this example, OS/2 can maintain conversations with a variety of platforms. If your company has all the systems shown, you can use an OS/2 application to read data from the 370 and AS/400 and update data on the OS/2 LAN server with an APPC application. This sophistication is not possible under DOS.

Many benefits are made available to OS/2 2.0 that are only possible by using a DOS program in an OS/2 MVDM. DOS has been around much longer than OS/2. During that time, hundreds of companies have developed software and hardware specific to DOS. In these cases, no OS/2 software equivalent exists. If OS/2 is capable of running these programs, it is a major boost to the operating system. One such example is Attachmate's Extra Software, which provides touch screen/mouse drivers for its 3270 Emulation software. Extra implements the "cursor select" function, which is a known require-ment for OS/2 based Emulation packages (it is not available at the time of this writing). A few other examples are available, but in the bulk of environments, OS/2 excels as the operating system for any communication application.

One area of host communications that OS/2 leads is front-ending host emulation. The Easel Corporation provides an ideal program-ming platform for developing Executive Information Systems (EIS). EIS was developed to provide an easy-to-use graphical front end to mainframes. An EIS application communicates with a text-based 3270 session running in the background. EIS systems are now being introduced to the DOS world, which still dominate the PC world.

OS/2 Extended Services, a communications add-on product for OS/2, provides OS/2 with several terminal types for host terminal emulation. A host system communicates with terminals, printers and PCs as Logical Units (LUs). OS/2 supports LU types 0, 1, 2, 3, and 6.2.

LU 0 defines flow control and transmission. LU 1 supports printer control and supports the SNA character set and Document Control Architecture data streams. LU 2 supports 3270 terminal data streams. LU 2 historically made up the bulk of terminal types. LU 3 is an enhanced version of LU 1. It is used to allow host applications to drive host or host-emulated printers. LU 6.2 is IBM strategic communications architecture. LU 6.2 supports both terminals and printers. LU 6.2 is a peer-to-peer based protocol and differs from previous LU types in that the host is no longer in charge. LU 6.2 is implemented on all IBM platforms from micro to mainframe architectures.

OS/2 is a full participant in IBM's peer-to-peer distributed processing vision. OS/2 also supports non-IBM host communications. Due to OS/2's support for DOS with OS/2 software support, it offers the broadest connectivity solution available today. If your organization has a RISC-based workstation, midrange, mainframe, or PC LAN environment, OS/2 provides unmatched support and integration.

The next type of host environment supported by OS/2 is the midrange family of computers. Midrange computers, like their mainframe ancestors also are powerful and expensive. To attach to an IBM midrange system, a 5250 emulation hardware and software package is needed

Using 5250 Emulation

OS/2 2.0 provides extensive connection options for connecting to the IBM midrange family. IBM's midrange family consists of the S/34, S/36, S/38, and the new AS/400 platforms. With each new platform released, additional microsystems support has been added. This section will focus on the newest member of the system 3/X environment, the AS/400. The AS/400 represents IBM's first full participant in its SAA strategy.

OS/2 provides you with a plethora of connection mediums. Connections to the AS/400 are available in two basic types: single-session and system-wide connection. PC Support/400 for OS/2 is provided in version 2, release 1 of the OS/400 operating system of the AS/400. Access to an AS/400 under OS/2 is provided using TWINAX, Token Ring, SDLC, or ASCII (via a protocol converter).

In a single-session implementation, a DOS Emulation (WSF) package is used running in a DOS box or VDM (Virtual DOS Machine) session. If you currently use DOS to access a 5250 session on a S/36, S/38, or AS/400, the same software will work under OS/2 2.0. This connection can be made over any of the previously mentioned connection types. Keep in mind that OS/2's native communication support is better than that of DOS.

Under DOS, both emulation and PC Support are supported by OS/2. Although DOS 5250 software is supported, OS/2 Extended Services is the best choice for this connection. Under OS/2, the connection is managed by OS/2, which does not tie up that adapter to one session. Under OS/2, that same adapter can be used to communicate with multiple destinations. As an example, you can have a 5250 session and OS/2 LAN server connection over just one Token Ring adapter.

OS/2 also can reliably communicate over multiple adapters. You can have an AS/400 session over a 5250 card and a Novell NetWare connection over an EtherNet adapter at the same time, without having to worry about time-outs or data loss. DOS was never designed for this environment. OS/2, however, excels in this situation because of its innate preemption and task scheduling capabilities. The PC Support/400 software for OS/2 provides critical data transfer, shared folders, and organizer support.

The organizer support is necessary to use the word processor on the AS/400 and for launching PC-based applications from an AS/400 menu. Shared folders provide an emulated drive on the AS/400 for storage. This drive is usually accessed as drive I. Through OS/2 Extended Services, AS/400 terminal emulation is provided, which gives you access to five sessions, which can comprise any combination of terminal sessions and printer sessions. The printer sessions can be LAN based, Local, or AS/400 system printers. All communications to an AS/400 are APPC based. The OS/400 Operating System uses APPC to manage these sessions. Figure 10.24 illustrates the connection methods.

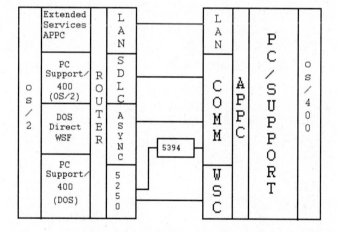

Figure 10.24:

Connection methods with AS/400 terminal.

Figure 10.24 shows OS/2 direct support and indirect support through DOS emulation. Extended DOS support is not supported under OS/2 2.0 as it is based on VCPI (Virtual Control Program Interface) instead of DPMI (DOS Protect Mode Interface), which is the preferred method for addressing memory under DOS and OS/2. DPMI, as stated earlier, is better because as it has superior memory management in multitasking environments. OS/2 is a multitasking operating system. OS/2 was designed for multiple connections in a multitasking environment. 5250 emulation and midrange resource sharing is just one option afforded to OS/2 users. If your organization has a 3/X system, you can enjoy the vast support provided by IBM for the environment.

Understanding OS/2 Communications in a Client/Server Context

Client/server is one of the industry's favorite buzz words. *Client/ server* is the division of an application between two or more processes. These processes may be in the same machine or in separate machines. Everyone claims to support it, but few deliver. OS/2, however, is a good example of a program that does have this technology. Client/server is not only possible under OS/2, but it also functions properly.

Client/server is the result of the industry's trend to down-size and distribute processing on a more affordable platform. Problems facing the PC platform in the past stemmed from integrity and mainframe control mechanisms.

Client/server applications differ from typical PC networks in several ways. Networks often focus on file and peripheral sharing— client/server platforms focus on application cooperation and processor sharing. LAN Operating Systems and applications designed for them are typically platform-specific (that is, PC-to-PC).

Client/server allows for a coherent environment-distributing application process over a variety of platforms. This offers a flexible mix-and-match approach enabling you to select the right processor for a particular task. This mix-and-match approach also provides a seamless integration for PCs. By using a PC to act as a client, you can use a graphical front end to a mainframe application instead of a green text screen.

This section mainly discusses a client/server architecture over a Local Area Network. The server piece runs an SQL Database. Keep in mind that the server could just as easily be an AS/400 or mainframe. PCs represent the bulk of today's downsizing trend and offer the most "bang for the buck."

Before diving into an OS/2 application for its client/server capabilities, a little more information is necessary. As mentioned before, *client/server* is the division of an application between two or more processes. These processes may be in the same machine or in a separate machine. The machines may be connected by a LAN or a leased line.

Most client/server applications are broken into two components: a Client (or requestor) and a Server. This server piece is not a file server, though it may be incorporated into one. The server is actually a program that accepts instructions from a client and processes them for the client. An example of a server is an SQL Database Server or DB2 application running on a host system. The sole purpose of the server is to process requests. The client issues the requests and is responsible for the interface. Today, this interface is usually graphical and hides most of the complexity inherent in advanced client/server environments. The client system typically runs a program, which as needed, sends requests to a server to be processed there, and then accepts the results.

One significant advantage to client/server is the reduction in network traffic. Because only the request and the answer are transmitted over the LAN, traffic is kept to the bare minimum. Contrast this with a typical PC File Server environment in which traffic is not so light. Most PC-based LAN applications require an entire file be sent over the LAN to the workstation to be processed locally. This increases network traffic and reduces efficiency. File servers share files over a network as opposed to client/servers which send only the requested records.

OS/2 can act as the client operating system and the server operating system. OS/2 provides a superior platform for client/server applications by saving development time and supplying multitasking. Much has already been said about OS/2 advanced communications capabilities. A number of protocols are supported by OS/2 as well as the most common physical connections. OS/2 supports TCP/IP, APPC, and NetBIOS, which is the default. Token Ring, EtherNet, and SDLC hardware connections are supported. Figure 10.25 shows a LAN and SDLC connection example.

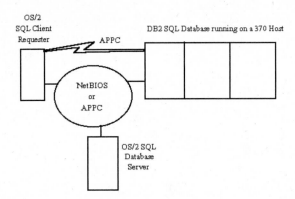

The most common example of client/server computing is an SQL database application. Structured Query Language (SQL) was invented by E.F. Codd at the IBM San Jose Research Center. This was the result of the System R Project, which concluded in 1984, although SQL is continually being updated and enhanced. SQL is considered simple to learn yet powerful and robust. The actual storage, computation, and access methods are far more complex than the simple query and presentation interface. If you program in C or Fortran, you will be amazed at what can be accomplished by one SQL statement.

An *SQL statement* is one instruction that a client sends to the server application. Several related SQL statements can be grouped together into a *transaction*. SQL statements are constructed in two forms: *Dynamic* and *Static*. Static SQL statements are hard coded into applications and never change.

A precompiler is used to convert the SQL statements into the application's native language. Static SQL is used when the same request must be issued on a constant and continual basis. Dynamic SQL, as its name suggests, is interactive and can be changed as needed. Dynamic SQL is interactive and is compiled as it is submitted instead of precompiled as in Static SQL. Dynamic SQL is slower yet flexible. The command line and Query interfaces are Dynamic.

Use Dynamic SQL when you only occasionally issue a command or need to modify a request.

Many software packages are available that enable OS/2 to be the client in a client/server application. In addition, several applications, such as Gupta, Sysbase, and IBM use OS/2 as the server operating system. As an example IBM offers the OS/2 DataBase Manager. The DataBase Manager provides both client and server pieces. The DataBase Manager also provides access to host databases, eliminating the need for a minicomputer.

Another benefit of OS/2-based SQL servers is that the DataBase Manager was designed from the ground up for PC support. Mainframe databases, such as DB2, were designed specifically for the host. PC access was added later as an afterthought. OS/2 fully supports seamless PC to mainframe communications in an SAA environment.

 Mainframe communications require the use of APPC as the protocol instead of the default NetBIOS.

Now that you know more about SQL client/server technology, examine its language. This example does not include all the necessary code and is merely provided as an overview. In most cases, a programmer incorporates the SQL instructions into an application and uses a graphical interface to hide its complexity. For this example, you are the company communications director. Your task is to retrieve employee names from the company SQL database and create invitations to the company golf outing. The employee database appears as in figure 10.26.

EMPLOYEE database

Lastname	Firstname	Address	City	State	Zip	Code
Smith	Dan	8376 South Clinton	Ft. Wayne	IN	46815	G
Carter	Bill	378 Maplewood	Ft. Wayne	IN	46825	S
Culbert	Bobby	48 Ennis	Ft. Wayne	IN	46805	G
DeBender	Jim	128 Volvo Rd	Ft. Wayne	IN	46810	G
Hartzog	Russell	987 Vance Ave	Ft. Wayne	IN	46805	S
Quillin	Mike	3402 S. Michigan	Huntington	IN	46811	G
Nowlan	John	4745 Converse Dr.	Ft. Wayne	IN	46835	T
Allison	Don	RD 1 , St Rd 3	Albion	IN	46845	B
Drewery	Tony	P.O. Box 311	Ft. Wayne	IN	46815	S
Zonker	Tammy	4894 W. Palm	Angola	IN	46853	G

Figure 10.26:

The employee database.

Because you will be mailing these invitations, they need to be sorted by zip code and then by last name. To do this, you must be logged onto the database and have authority to access the database. Use the Query Manager component of IBM's DataBase Manager to enter dynamically the following commands:

```
SELECT FIRSTNAME, LASTNAME, ADDRESS, CITY, STATE, ZIP FROM
➥EMPLOYEE
WHERE CODE = ANY (SELECT CODE FROM EMPLOYEE WHERE TYPE = "G")
ORDER BY ZIP ASC, LASTNAME ASC
```

In the above example the SELECT command was used to indicate which fields you want to include in the result table. The WHERE command tells the SQL server to include only those records that have a "G" for Golfer in the result. The last command ORDER BY provides the sorting criteria. The result table looks like figure 10.27.

Figure 10.27:

Sorting criteria table.

Resulting Table

Firstname	Lastname	Address	City	State	Zip
Bobby	Culbert	48 Ennis	Ft. Wayne	IN	46805
Jim	DeBender	128 Volvo Rd	Ft. Wayne	IN	46810
Mike	Quillin	3402 S. Michigan	Huntington	IN	46811
Dan	Smith	8376 South Clinton	Ft. Wayne	IN	46815
Tammy	Zonker	4894 W. Palm	Angola	IN	46853

The PHONE and CODE fields are not necessary for the invitation or mailing label and, therefore, were not "SELECTED." After the query has been run, you can use the export capability to send the data to an ASCII comma-delimited file to be imported by your favorite desktop publishing software or word processor to create the invitation and mailing labels. This represents a simplistic example and does not include all the necessary commands. The intent is to give you a preview of SQL commands. Your queries can be much more sophisticated and you can select data from multiple databases. An application may have most of the necessary instructions hard coded into the application. To understand the client/server benefits of this example, figure 10.28 shows the client/server traffic versus a file server-based implementation.

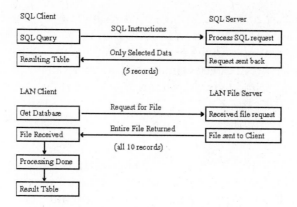

Figure 10.28:

Client/server traffic versus a file server-based implementation.

As you can see the client/server application required half the traffic. In reality, the file server environment generates significantly more traffic than the two-to-one example. The client will also be required to do all the processing instead of client/server's distributed approach. Again, this is only one approach on one platform. Client/server computing is supported over the entire SAA and other company platforms. OS/2 enables you to mix-and-match environments that are platform independent. Figure 10.29 show OS/2 connection options.

PC Based Client		Various SQL Server Platforms	
OS/2 Based PC	OS/2 DataBase Manager	OS/2 DataBase Manager	Personal Computer
		SQL/400	AS/400
		SQL/DS	370 Host
		DB2	370 Host
		Other SQL Applications	Various Platforms

Figure 10.29:

OS/2 connection options.

Summary

OS/2 provides a sophisticated yet easy to use means of implemented client/server applications into your environment. OS/2 provides both front and back processes of the client/server model.

OS/2's superior communications, multitasking, and protected mode operation form the foundation for building mission critical line-of-business applications. In the era of downsizing, OS/2 provides the most robust and cost effective means of reliable client/server implementation. PC prices for midrange power make OS/2 a sure success. With OS/2's full participation in IBM's SAA strategy, you can count on future support and enhancements. OS/2 is the integration platform for the 90s.

This chapter discussed OS/2's vast scheduling capabilities in regards to communications. You learned that OS/2 was designed from the ground up with communications in mind.

DOS and OS/2 were compared, and you learned why OS/2 is the superior product when it comes to communications. IBM built advanced network administrative utilities, file and device-sharing facilities, and other sophisticated LAN capabilities into OS/2.

OS/2's capability to multitask processes enables truly seamless network access to shared devices, such as printers and disks.

The next chapter discusses the command-line interface. After you know your way around the OS/2 screen, you may find it quicker to use the command line. As you become more proficient in OS/2, the command line opens the door to more advanced topics.

III

Using OS/2's Power

*Using the Power of the OS/2
Command-Line Interface*

Optimizing OS/2

Writing Batch Programs Using REXX

Using the Power of the Command-Line Interface

As you read in Chapters 2 and 3, OS/2 has a powerful graphical user interface that simplifies most tasks by enabling you to click on objects or fill in a dialog box. In this way, OS/2 resembles other graphical user interfaces, such as the Apple Macintosh or Commodore Amiga computers. Further, OS/2 has another, less visible, component that you read about in Chapter 3. That is, OS/2 retains the command-line interface (CLI) that DOS has used for years.

The DOS CLI has received more than its share of abuse in print since 1981, but "power" users know that they can get more done with the CLI than they can with a graphical user interface. (For some operations, however, a GUI is preferable.) In addition, you can use the command-line interface to write batch files that simplify normal tasks.

If you have a "slow" PC (with a microprocessor whose operating speed is less than 25 MHz), the OS/2 command-line interface is much more responsive than the Presentation Manager. A machine that responds sluggishly to the mouse and objects is faster when the command line interface is used.

In this chapter you learn the following:

- When the CLI is preferable to the GUI
- How to activate the OS/2 CLI
- How the OS/2 CLI actually executes commands
- How to use "redirection" from the CLI
- How to use the CLI as a recovery tool when OS/2 does not boot

Once you have learned more about the CLI and its advantages, you probably will use it more often in your work.

Understanding the Command-Line Interface

OS/2 users that work only with the GUI may find the CLI mysterious and uninviting. Although many beginners feel that the CLI is not as powerful and user-friendly as the Presentation Manager, all of OS/2's power is contained in the command-line interface. Suppose, for example, that you want to erase a file in OS/2. If you use the GUI, you must perform the following steps:

1. Locate the folder that contains the file.
2. Double-click on the folder to open it. The file is probably several folders deep, requiring even more effort.
3. Use the right mouse button to select and drag the file to the Shredder.
4. Release the mouse button while the object is over the Shredder.
5. Click on **OK** when the dialog box asks you to reconfirm the action.

To perform the same deletion in the CLI, you simply type the following command:

> **ERASE** *filename*

In this generic syntax, *filename* is the name of the file to be erased. Although the preceding example is basic, it supports studies showing that a command-line-based system can be considerably more productive than a GUI.

Although CLIs can be more productive than GUIs, they also require more initial training. GUIs are a good interface for programs used only occasionally, but some kind of command-line approach is a desirable option. Many graphical OS/2 programs offer GUI and CLI options that use menus and "speed keys." An experienced Word-Perfect user, for example, can create text quickly because he or she has learned all the odd key combinations. The same tasks can be performed with less training through the WordPerfect menus, but this approach takes more time.

The OS/2 command-line interface is the best (or only) interface to use in the following situations:

- When you must diagnose and recover from OS/2 boot problems

- When you need quicker access to the power of OS/2, as seen in the preceding example

- When you need to use batch files (small programs that simplify complex or repetitive tasks)

Starting with the Command Line

Open a windowed command line by opening the System folder and then the Command Prompts folder. Double-click on the OS/2 Window object. The screen should appear as shown in figure 11.1.

As you can see from the figure, the CLI is not an inviting interface. The following elements make up the screen:

- The help banner at the top of the screen shows you how to return to the Workplace shell (press Ctrl-Esc)

- The prompt indicates that you currently are in the C:\OS2 subdirectory

Figure 11.1:

An OS/2 win-dowed command prompt.

Understanding Command Prompt Operation

Many people have used DOS for years, but some still do not know why an error message appears after they enter a mistyped command. OS/2 command prompt users have the same problem, one that can be fixed quickly by understanding the error messages (you read about these messages in the following sections). To see how the command prompt works, type **BANANA** or another nonsense command at the OS/2 C:\ prompt. An error message appears as seen in figure 11.2.

What happens when you type a command? When you type a command at the command prompt, your keystrokes are read by a program called CMD.EXE, which is the OS/2 version of the COMMAND.COM program in DOS. CMD.EXE accumulates the line that you typed into a buffer, then divides the line into parts. This process is called *parsing*. Figure 11.3 shows how the command **DISKCOPY A: B: /V** is parsed by CMD.EXE.

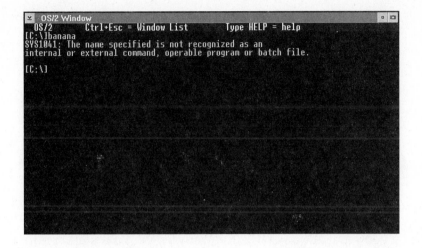

Figure 11.2:
OS/2 command-line error message.

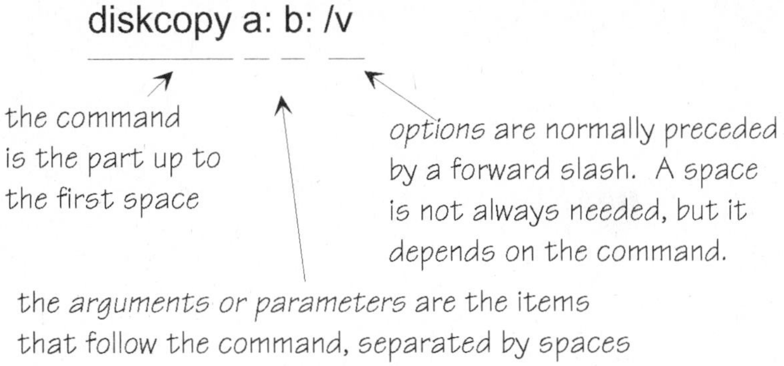

diskcopy a: b: /v

the command
is the part up to
the first space

options are normally preceded
by a forward slash. A space
is not always needed, but it
depends on the command.

the arguments or parameters are the items
that follow the command, separated by spaces

Figure 11.3:
CMD.EXE parsing a command.

OS/2 parses input by first examining spaces and the forward slash. As the figure shows, CMD.EXE assumes that the first string of characters up to the first blank to be the user's input command. Later in this chapter you learn more about parameters, arguments, and options; for now, consider the command and what CMD.EXE does with it.

After CMD has separated a command from a command line, it performs five steps:

1. CMD.EXE checks to see if the command is an *internal command*, one whose program is contained wholly inside CMD.EXE. If so, it executes the internal command.

2. If the command is not internal, CMD.EXE looks for a file with the command's name, and the COM extension. If a COM file exists, CMD.EXE loads the COM file and executes it.

3. If no COM file exists, CMD.EXE looks for a file with the command's name and the extension EXE. If an EXE file exists, CMD.EXE loads the program and executes it.

4. If neither a COM nor an EXE file is found, CMD.EXE looks for a file with the command's name and the extension CMD. If such a file exists, CMD.EXE loads the file and executes it.

5. If none of the preceding file extensions are found, CMD.EXE searches the path.

When you type DIR or COPY, for example, you execute a command internal to CMD.EXE. When you run the Klondike program that comes with OS/2, you run an external program file called KLONDIKE.EXE. The following section discusses these five steps used by CMD to execute your commands.

Interpreting Internal CMD.EXE Commands

The main job of CMD.EXE is to interpret and execute the commands of the user. CMD.EXE also processes *internal commands*, which are commands incorporated into CMD.EXE. Unlike commercial programs and larger OS/2 utility programs, which are contained in external COM and EXE files, internal commands are incorporated in CMD.EXE. When you type the DIR command, for example, CMD.EXE compares the DIR request to an internal table of familiar commands. Because DIR is listed, CMD.EXE knows how to respond to the request. Table 11.1 lists OS/2 2.0's internal commands.

For more information on OS/2 2.0's internal commands, see the Command Reference at the back of the book.

Table 11.1
CMD.EXE Internal Commands

Command	Function
DIR	Shows information on a file directory
COPY	Copies and merges files
CD	Changes the current subdirectory
MD	Creates subdirectories
RD	Deletes subdirectories
DEL	Erases files
ERASE	Erases files
IF	Batch command for decision-making
FOR	Looping command
REM	Allows remarks in batch files
ECHO	Controls how much information OS/2 shows on-screen
BREAK	Tells OS/2 how often to check for Ctrl-C
CALL	Calls one batch program from another
CHCP	Changes code pages or reports current code page
CLS	Clears the screen
DATE	Displays the date or allows user to change date
EXIT	Closes the CMD.EXE session
GOTO	Batch command
PATH	Changes the program search path
PAUSE	Makes OS/2 display the message Press any key to Continue...
PROMPT	Changes the command prompt
REN/RENAME	Renames a file or group of files

continues

Table 11.1 Continued

Command	Function
SET	Creates or displays environmental variables
SHIFT	Moves the relative position of the parameters in a user command
TIME	Like "date," displays or changes system time
TYPE	Copies a file to the screen.
VER	Displays OS/2 version number
VOL	Displays disk volume ID

Each internal command is a program, which accounts for CMD.EXE's size of 87K. Although CMD.EXE is a large program, internal commands are beneficial for the following reasons:

- Many commands, like DIR and COPY, are essential. These commands are always available because they are part of CMD.EXE.

- Many of these commands require only small programs. A file that supports the vol command, for example, requires no more than 40 bytes. If this file were separate, however, it would actually take 2048 bytes because the minimum space allocated to many disks is 2K.

- Unlike an external command, which first must be loaded before it executes, an internal command is already loaded in memory and executes more quickly.

- If an internal command existed under DOS, inertia has made it remain an internal command under OS/2. Memory space is not as critical as it was under DOS, which means more internal commands can benefit OS/2 with their greater execution speed.

Interpreting External Commands: COM and EXE Files

If CMD.EXE does not find an internal command that corresponds to your request, it looks for a file with the same name as the entered command and the extension COM or EXE. In the BANANA example, CMD looks for a file called "BANANA.COM;" if it finds a file by that name in the current directory, it loads that file into memory and instructs OS/2 to execute the instructions now in memory. If it finds no file by that name, CMD.EXE looks next for a file called "BANANA.EXE." If the EXE file exists, it is loaded into memory and executed.

What are EXE and COM files? Professional software developers use tools called "compilers" and "link editors" to create computer programs. The programmer first writes the program in a computer language, such as C, COBOL, BASIC, Pascal, or FORTRAN, and then feeds the program into a compiler program. The compiler is written for the language you use to write your program. The compiler feeds its output to a link editor, which oversees the linkage of the programmer's program to other programs in the system. The output of the link editor is then an EXE file or a COM file. Either type file is a "machine language" file, which is a set of commands built with the processor's native language. These machine language commands are a set of *opcodes*, which are operation codes that mean nothing to programmers without the help of another program called a "debugger." To see this code, type **TYPE CMD.EXE**; the computer will list output that, to you, seems to be gibberish.

COM and EXE files are files containing the basic machine language that makes the PC operate. Whenever you buy a commercial software package, the software includes at least one COM or EXE file that contains the program.

What are the differences between COM and EXE files? DOS differentiates between a COM file and an EXE file. OS/2, however, considers all EXE and COM files to be EXE files. The only reason why the COM extension still exists is for backward compatibility to DOS. The disk maintenance program CHKDSK.COM, for example, has always been a COM file in PC-DOS. The CHKDSK.COM file, which is part of OS/2, still can be called CHKDSK.COM although it is read as an EXE file. CHKDSK.COM loads and executes correctly in OS/2 even though a DOS-type COM file could not run under OS/2.

OS/2 considers a machine language program file an EXE file whether it has an EXE or COM extension. Regardless, OS/2's CMD.COM still searches for files in a particular order (COM and then EXE).

 CMD.EXE's search method created some problems for DOS and OS/2 programs. One case happened under DOS with the database program dBASE III.

After dBASE is installed on a system, it is activated by entering the dBASE command. This command is not internal, which means the dBASE executable command must be either DBASE.COM or DBASE.EXE (it could be DBASE.BAT under DOS or DBASE.CMD under OS/2, but ignore those possibilities for the moment). The first version of dBASE III, version 1.0, was shipped as a COM file. Version 1.0 contained a number of *bugs*, or operational problems. Ashton-Tate, the dBASE vendor, soon released an update, dBASE III+ 1.1, which installed over the old version of dBASE. When the new release was installed, however, the update refused to work citing a violation of copy protection. The new dBASE was shipped as an EXE file, and its installation program did not erase the old COM file. As a result, the dBASE subdirectory contained every file in version 1.1, including DBASE.EXE, and one remnant from version 1.0—DBASE.COM.

You now can see what happens if you try to run dBASE III+ 1.1: the operating system (DOS) first finds DBASE.COM, which loads but cannot run because all of its support files are all gone. Although this problem seems major, you can fix it easily—simply erase DBASE.COM.

NOTE The relationship in DOS between COMMAND.COM and EXE and COM files was exploited by a computer virus called "Aids II" (or "Companion"). Any EXE file could be infected, but in such a way that the EXE file was left unchanged.

The virus created a hidden COM file with the same file name. If a particular subdirectory contained a program called XYZ.EXE, Aids II would create a file called XYZ.COM, then hide the file. Hidden program files run even though they are hidden, which means that when CMD.EXE (or its DOS counterpart, COMMAND.COM) attempted to execute "XYZ", it would see XYZ.COM first, and then execute it. The program would display a viral message, then the XYZ.COM program would load and execute the XYZ.EXE program. Because the XYZ.EXE program is started by the XYZ.COM program, control passes back to the XYZ.COM program when the user exits XYZ.EXE. The XYZ.COM program then puts a "farewell" message on the screen, and exits.

Interpreting Command Files

If no internal command matches the user's request, and no EXE or COM files exist, CMD.EXE looks in the current directory for a file with the extension CMD. If it finds such a file, CMD.EXE executes the file, line by line. Note that CMD.EXE executes the file instead of loading it into memory and passing control to OS/2. CMD.EXE executes a command file (also called a batch file) because it is more a super command line than a program. In other words, a CMD file consists of prestored commands that CMD executes one at a time, just as if you type them into the command line yourself. You learn more about command files later in this chapter.

If CMD.EXE does not find BANANA.COM or BANANA.EXE for the BANANA request, for example, it looks for a file called BANANA.CMD. If this file exists, CMD.EXE loads it and executes it.

Searching the Path

If the current directory yields no matching files—no BANANA.COM, BANANA.EXE, or BANANA.CMD—then CMD.EXE may be looking in the wrong place. Suppose, for example, that you type the command WB to start a word processor called Word Blaster. The system should load and execute a file called WB.EXE. WB.EXE is located in the C:\WORDBLIST subdirectory. WB is located in the C:\WORDBLST subdirectory, and your documents have their own subdirectory called C:\DOCS, from which you usually invoke the WB command. If Word Blaster is not in the directory from which you invoke WB, how do you load the program? You can load WB.EXE in one of two ways.

The first way is to specify the entire command, including the subdirectory. Instead of typing WB to load the program, you can type C:\WORDBLST\WB. The second way involves an important part of OS/2 called the path.

The *path* is a list of subdirectory names that are separated by semi-colons. A path statement can look like the following:

```
PATH C:\OS2;C:\OS2\SYSTEM;C:\OS2\MDOS\WINOS2;C:\UTILS
```

This path statement directs OS/2 to perform the following search: if OS/2 finds no COM, EXE, or CMD files in the current directory, it looks for COM, then EXE, then CMD files in the C:\OS2 subdirectory. If no files are found in that directory, OS/2 searches C:\OS2\SYSTEM, then C:\OS2\MDOS\WINOS2, and then C:\UTILS. If no EXE, COM, or CMD files are found, OS/2 displays an error message.

You can see how a long path can potentially slow down OS/2. The maximum line length for a path is limited to 128 characters, however, to ensure that paths do not become too long.

As you can see from the previous sections, when you invoke a command that OS/2 does not recognize, it searches extensively before displaying the following message:

```
SYS1041: The name specified is not recognized as an
internal or external command, operable program or batch
file
```

If you mistype a command such as BANANA, CMD.EXE performs the following search before displaying its error message:

1. It looks for an internal command named BANANA.

2. CMD.EXE then looks in the current subdirectory for a file called BANANA.COM.

3. Next, CMD looks in the current subdirectory for a file called BANANA.EXE.

4. CMD then repeats the search process by looking in C:\OS2 for a file called BANANA.COM.

5. The search path repeats for each directory that CMD searches. If no EXE, COM, or CMD files are found, the preceding error message appears.

Occasionally, a legitimate OS/2 command may not work. If a command does not work, it might require programs that OS/2 cannot find because the programs are not on the path. In that case, the commands only work when you're situated in the particular directory that contains the files that the commands need to execute or when you use the fully qualified path name.

Troubleshooting with the Command Line

When trouble occurs or when backups are necessary, even the most dedicated GUI user resorts to the command-line interface. OS/2 uses many megabytes of files to boot properly—if just one file becomes corrupted, you must boot from a floppy disk. Even if disaster does not strike, you have to boot from a floppy to back up the entire disk.

 Some of CHDKSK's disk maintenance operations do not work unless you boot OS/2 2.0 from a floppy.

Booting the System

At one time or another, you may have tried to boot OS/2 and instead were greeted with a screen full of hexadecimal numbers, a reference to a TRAP 000d, and the message internal processing error. Although these messages seem cryptic, the final message speaks volumes:

```
the system has stopped.
```

This message is perhaps the greatest understatement in the PC world. Sometimes it means your system has stopped for good. Other times, this message means nothing more than to turn off the PC's power, count to five, and then turn on the PC again. In fact, the first thing that you should do when your machine has trouble booting is perform a *cold* reboot: turn it off and then wait. A warm reboot (Ctrl-Alt-Del) does not "clean out" the system completely.

Many PCs have reset buttons. A number of computer users think that pushing the reset button is the same as a cold reboot. They fear that turning the PC off and then on again stresses the computer and that using the reset button is less harmful to the PC's components. Although these fears are accurate, you cannot avoid a cold reboot if a system has stopped error appears on-screen. The reset button only resets the main CPU. Other CPUs exist in the PC, such as the keyboard CPU, a serial port CPU (on more complex PCs such as the IBM ARTIC board), the video board (the video coprocessor or the IBM XGA), and the hard disk controller (any caching and bus mastering hard disk controller or both). OS/2 can even make the keyboard controller crash because many PCs need the keyboard controller to talk to memory above 1024K in addresses. Such a crash cannot be fixed by using the reset switch; you must cycle the power (perform a cold reboot) to fix the problem.

Performing an Emergency Floppy Boot

If cycling the power switch does not solve your system's boot problems, try running CHKDSK. Obviously, CHKDSK is difficult to run if the operating system does not boot. Follow these steps to perform an OS/2 emergency boot:

1. Turn off the PC.

2. Insert the *OS/2 Installation Disk* in drive A.

3. Turn on the PC.

4. Put the *OS/2 System Disk 1* in drive A and then press Enter.

5. After a minute or two, the OS/2 greeting screen (with the big "IBM") displays. Press Esc, rather than Enter.

   The floppy runs for a bit, and then you see an OS/2 command prompt.

Now that the emergency boot is complete, run CHKDSK from the floppy drive.

1. Put a blank floppy into drive A, and type `COPY C:\OS2\CHKDSK.COM A:` to copy the CHKDSK program to the floppy in drive A.

   You must copy CHKDSK to drive A because no programs can be running from drive C when you use CHKDSK with the "/F" option.

2. Now that CHKDSK.COM is on drive A, type `CHKDSK C:/F;` the /F switch means "FIX."

3. CHKDSK runs for a while and may prompt you to convert lost cluster chains to files.

4. When CHKDSK finishes, remove the floppy disk from drive A and reboot the system.

Rebuilding OS2.INI and OS2SYS.INI

OS/2 mainly consists of programs, help files, and device drivers that do not vary from computer to computer. Five files, however, are specific to each PC:

- **OS2.INI.** Backs up your desktop and the options saved from an OS/2 application

- **OS2SYS.INI.** Tells OS/2 what kind of equipment your system uses

- **CONFIG.SYS.** Sets system options

- **AUTOEXEC.BAT.** Specifies startup options for the DOS sessions

- **STARTUP.CMD.** Optional file that contains startup commands for OS/2 that cannot be included in CONFIG.SYS

CONFIG.SYS, AUTOEXEC.BAT, and STARTUP.CMD can be manipulated easily because they are ASCII files with no sharing restrictions. Any text editor can modify these files, and they can be backed up or restored without trouble.

The two files with the "INI" extension are not ASCII, which means you cannot fix them with an ASCII text editor if they become damaged. In addition, OS2.INI and OS2SYS.INI remain open throughout each OS/2 session, which makes copying them almost impossible. If you try to copy either of these files, or restore them from a backup, the following message appears:

```
SYS0032: the process cannot access the file because the
file is being used by another process
```

In other words, the message says you cannot modify this file because OS/2 is using it.

It is not clear exactly why OS2.INI is so hesitant about interacting with anything but OS/2. OS2.INI contains all your user-defined settings and the arrangement of your desktop. Every time a setting is changed, OS2.INI must be opened. OS2.INI also is open when no settings are changed. The reason for this is not clear, and IBM is not telling. Because it is open at all times, even when no settings are being changed, OS2.INI and its hardware-specific partner, OS2SYS.INI, almost cannot be backed up.

The only way to back up OS2.INI and OS2SYS.INI is to boot from a floppy disk. If you do so, the Workplace Shell is not activated, which means the two INI files are never opened. You can copy or replace these files with no interference from the operating system.

Suppose that before you back up the INI files, OS2.INI or OS2SYS.INI is trashed by some errant process, such as a hardware failure. If this happens, you probably want to start again with a basic pair of INI files. You can do that easily using a program called MAKEINI.EXE, which ships with OS/2. MAKEINI.EXE builds a new set of INI files, which might fix certain OS/2 boot problems. Follow these steps to run MAKEINI.

1. Boot from the floppy, as described in the previous steps.

2. Type `C:`, and then `CD\OS2` to access the C drive and the OS2 subdirectory.

3. If you want to rebuild the OS2.INI file, type `MAKEINI OS2.INI INI.RC`. If you want to rebuild the OS2SYS.INI file, type `MAKEINI OS2SYS.INI INISYS.RC`.

   The process takes a few minutes.

4. After MAKEINI reports its success, try rebooting the system.

   If the system boots properly, be prepared for a long wait; a number of files must be rebuilt that can take up to 20 minutes. For this reason, if you see on-screen only a blank desktop with a mouse pointer and perhaps the Tutorial program, do not worry—just wait for the hard disk light to go off.

If you still cannot boot the system, you must reinstall OS/2, which is an involved process.

> **TIP** Before you reinstall OS/2, boot from DOS or the Installation disks, erase the existing OS/2 files, and then defragment the disk. For some reason, OS/2 does not install well on a fragmented disk (that is, one with fragmented empty space). Even a mildly fragmented disk can cause OS/2 to run through the install process without complaint, but then fail when it first boots.

If you do not use the High Performance File System, you can use one of many DOS-based file defragmentation programs. Remember that you do not want to defragment the files; you want to defragment the empty space.

The SpeedDisk program that is part of the Norton Utilities enables you to defragment empty space.

Backing Up Files

In addition to OS2.INI and OS2SYS.INI, a number of files are open during a typical OS/2 session. None of those files can be backed up while OS/2 runs. The only way to back up these files is to use the same procedure for backing up INI files: boot from the installation disks and then run your backup program.

Which backup program should you run? The OS/2 BACKUP command provides only basic backup functions. Iomega's Bernoulli Box products offer fast, reliable cartridge backup devices. SyTOS has been available under OS/2 for years, and supports a wealth of tape drives. You probably will find either product preferable to BACKUP. If you work on a LAN, you can use the LAN server as a central backup point.

One word of caution when picking a backup program. Remember that you might need to boot from the floppy to back up every file. If you boot from a floppy, you cannot access the Workplace Shell. For this reason, make sure that your backup program runs from the command line, and that it is not a graphical. Otherwise, you will not be able to run the program when the command prompt appears. Additionally, there are some backup programs that can back up open files.

Stacking Commands

Occasionally, you may want to put more than one command on the command line so that you can issue several commands, press Enter, and walk away.

OS/2 has supported *command stacking*, which is the capability to specify multiple commands per line, since OS/2 1.0 in 1987. To stack two commands, use the ampersand character (&). Suppose, for example, that you want to copy a file named FILES.DAT from a subdirectory named C:\ONE to a subdirectory named D:\TWO, and then erase the original copy of the file. You can perform both operations in just one line:

```
COPY C:\ONE\FILES.DAT D:\TWO&ERASE C:\ONE\FILES.DAT
```

The preceding command is a little dangerous, however. The copy operation could fail and then your file would be erased. You can stack two commands so that CMD.EXE only executes the second command if the first one succeeds by using the double ampersand (&&). Using the previous example, the command would be:

```
COPY C:\ONE\FILES.DAT D:\TWO && ERASE C:\ONE\FILES.DAT
```

In some cases, however, you might want to run a second command only if an operation fails. Suppose, for example, you have a program called BEEP that makes the computer emit a beep (you learn how to write such a program later in this chapter). You might then instruct the computer to beep if the copy fails. The command stacker you use is the double vertical bar (¦¦). The command would be entered as follows:

```
COPY C:\ONE\FILES.DAT D:\TWO ¦¦ BEEP.
```

If you want to combine the preceding commands to erase something or beep if the erase operation fails, put the ampersands (&&) before the vertical bars (¦¦):

```
COPY C:\ONE\FILES.DAT&&ERASE C:\ONE\FILES.DAT¦¦BEEP
```

 See the section "Using Redirected Output" for information on using the greater-than (>) and less-than (<) characters in command lines.

Finally, multiple commands can be grouped using parentheses. Suppose you had one program that made one beep—call it "ONEBEEP"—and another program that made two beeps, named

"TWOBEEP." You want two beeps to sound if every command succeeds, or one beep if not. You can group the ERASE command with the TWOBEEP command using parentheses, as in the following commands:

```
COPY C:\ONE\FILES.DAT&&(ERASE
C:\ONE\FILES.DAT&TWOBEEP)¦¦ONEBEEP
```

 If you want to perform more complex operations, you probably need to use batch files, which are discussed later in this chapter and in Chapter 13.

Including Command Characters in File Names

As you read in previous sections, the OS/2 command interpreter uses the characters "&," " |," " (," and ")". If you want to use any of these characters in a file name, how do you do so without confusing OS/2?

The easiest solution is not to use these characters in your file names. Avoid using those characters because they can cause trouble with some applications. If you need to name a file <>|&().DAT, however, you need to use another important character.

Any "special" character can be prefixed with the *circumflex*, or escape character (^, Shift-6 on most keyboards). You must prefix each special character with the escape character. The file <>|&().DAT, for example, is specified as ^<^>^|^&^(^).DAT. The big problem with using one of these characters is that you may forget one of the circumflexes.

Understanding Virtual Devices

The discussion so far in this chapter has been concerned largely with files and paths on the PC's disks. This is to be expected, as most of an operating system's responsibilities are with storage devices. Other kinds of input and output devices exist on a PC, and those devices also are managed by the operating system. In particular, OS/2 must control the following devices:

- The screen
- The keyboard
- The serial ports
- The parallel ports

Some operating systems treat each device on a computer differently from other devices. OS/2's management of devices is based on UNIX, the system from which OS/2 was developed. UNIX introduced the term "virtual devices" to the mainstream operating system market. *Virtual devices* are devices treated as files by the operating system. The printer is treated as a file to which you can write, the serial ports are read-and-write files, the screen can only be written to, and the keyboard only read. Virtual devices simplify the command structure because everything is incorporated into the operating system in file terms. In OS/2, for example, you do not need a special command to print an ASCII file; simply COPY the file to the printer. To print the CONFIG.SYS file, enter the following command:

```
COPY C:\CONFIG.SYS PRN
```

PRN is the name of the generic printer device.

 If you have a laser printer, it will not print until you take the printer off-line and then press the form feed button.

Using Virtual Devices

Table 11.2 lists the names of the OS/2's virtual devices and their functions.

Table 11.2
Names and Functions of OS/2 Virtual Devices

Device name	Description
LPT1	First parallel port
LPT2	Second parallel port
LPT3	Third parallel port
COM1	First serial port, if present
AUX	First serial port, if present
COM2	Second serial port, if present
COM3	Third serial port, if present
COM4	Fourth serial port, if present
PRN	First parallel port
KBD$	Keyboard
CLOCK$	System clock device
NUL	The null device
CON	The screen (for output)
CON	The keyboard (for input)
MOUSE$	The pointing device

Many of those devices are accessible only to programmers, but the COM*n*, LPT*n*, NUL, and CON devices are useful in a number of situations. First, the preceding print-the-file example is a handy way to print a file. In addition, modems are controlled with a programming language first created by Hayes Microcomputer Products for their original Smartmodem product. Smartmodem commands are all in uppercase, and all start with AT. One such example is the command ATT, which instructs the modem to use touch tones when it dials. The alternative is ATP for pulse dialing. Suppose, for example, that you have a modem connected to the COM2 serial port. This modem works best using a string of commands like ATTM0E0 (dial with tone, turn off the modem's speaker, and do not echo commands). You can store the ATTM0E0 string in a file (call it MODEM), and then just type the following command before you start the modem:

```
COPY MODEM COM2
```

Another common usage of virtual devices is the COPY CON command. Try these steps to learn more about COPY CON:

1. Type **COPY CON TEST.TXT**, and press Enter.

2. Type **I am now creating an ASCII file.** and press Enter.

3. Press Ctrl-Z, and then press Enter.

A message similar to the following appears:

```
1 file(s) copied.
```

You just created a file called TEST.TXT. Look at your disk's directory to confirm this new addition. Type **TYPE TEST.TXT**, and you will see the line that you typed.

What happened? You copied from the "console" device (the keyboard) to a file called TEST.TXT. As you typed, the contents of the "file" (whatever was typed from the keyboard) was dumped into TEST.TXT. Anything you type goes into this file. To stop the process, use the Ctrl-Z sequence. Ctrl-Z has been the "end of file" marker for operating systems for years—from CP/M in the late 1970s to MS-DOS in the '80s and '90s, and now for OS/2. Every time you create a text file with a text editor, the text editor appends a Ctrl-Z to the end of the text file when the file is saved to disk.

As mentioned before, CON is a dual-purpose device. When used as input, it represents the keyboard. When used as output, it represents the screen. Type **COPY TEXT.TXT CON** to display the file on-screen.

The NUL device is the "do nothing" device. Sending output to NUL essentially eliminates it. If a program insists on creating some kind of report that you do not want, tell the program to write the report to the NUL device—you can substitute NUL in any location that you would put a file.

Copying a file to NUL does not produce any copies, but the action does force OS/2 to read the file before realizing that the file is not going anywhere. That means that you can use NUL as a simple floppy disk tester. For example, put the floppy disk that you want to test in drive A, then type **COPY A:*.* NUL**. Although the process creates no files, the system must read every sector that has a file in it. (This process does not read sectors that contain no files.)

By the way, you also can get some odd results by typing, copying, or listing the contents of virtual devices. Just for fun, try these commands:

1. `TYPE CLOCK$`

2. `DIR CLOCK$:`

3. `DIR CON:`

4. `COPY KBD$ CON`

Understanding and Using Input and Output Redirection

OS/2 followed UNIX with the use of virtual devices. UNIX also originated a related idea known as *redirection*. Consider the following question: when you type DIR, to what device does CMD.EXE send the output? Most people answer "on the screen, of course." This answer is true to a degree. When the IBM programmers wrote the DIR command, they did not write the program to put its output on-screen; they wrote the program to put its output on the *standard output device*, or as programmers refer to it, STDOUT. The program enables the operating system to determine the standard output device. By default, STDOUT is the screen—the output from the DIR command usually shows up on the screen. Try typing this command:

```
DIR >DIROUT.TXT
```

You will not see any output on the screen because >DIROUT.TXT instructs OS/2 to change the definition of STDOUT to a file named DIROUT.TXT. Type **TYPE DIROUT.TXT** to see what looks like normal directory output captured in an ASCII text file.

From the operating system's point of view, applications have one input, called STDIN (standard input), and two outputs, called STDOUT (standard output) and STDERR (standard error). Think of it as pictured in figure 11.4.

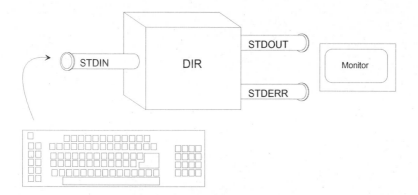

Figure 11.4:
Standard inputs and outputs in an OS/2 program.

The DIR program's default input device is the keyboard. DIR's standard output device and standard output stream for error messages is the monitor screen. By redirecting DIR's output, you create a situation such as that depicted in figure 11.5.

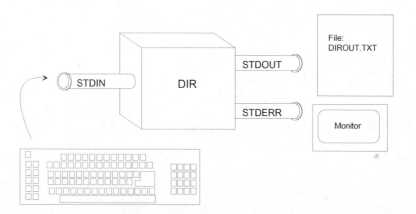

Figure 11.5:
DIR's output redirected to a file.

Using Redirected Output

Many uses exist for output redirection. For example, after the output of the DIR command is captured to a file, you can include it in documentation: "After you install Word Blaster, you will have a directory with the following files included in it..." You also can use the virtual devices with redirection, as in these examples:

- `DIR >PRN`

- `COPY X Y >NUL`

- `ECHO ATTM0E0 >COM2`

In the first example, you redirect the output of the DIR command to the printer to print the current directory. Make sure that you have a printer attached before trying this, or OS/2 prompts that your printer is out of paper.

The second example, `COPY X Y >NUL`, copies from X to Y. If you are an OS/2 support person, you might write this command as part of a batch file for other users. If these users are confused by such output messages as `one file(s) copied` when they run the batch file, you can get rid of the message. Send the standard output of the COPY command off to the NUL device, which acts as OS/2's "black hole."

Recall in the section "Using Virtual Devices" the discussion about using virtual devices to program a "smart" modem. A smart modem may require the setup string ATTM0E0, a sequence that tells it to dial touchtone, shut off the speaker, and suppress command echoing. Rather than create a file and copy the file to COM2, a simpler method is to use the ECHO command.

What happens when you type **ECHO HELLO**? Your reaction may be to say, "ECHO puts 'hello' on the screen." This is true but not completely accurate. ECHO puts "hello" on the *standard output device*, which is, by default, the screen. ECHO can be redirected to any virtual device. If you type the following line, the printer prints "Hello, there" on-screen:

```
ECHO HELLO, THERE > PRN
```

When ECHO is redirected, it is a powerful tool. For example, you probably know that laser printers require a full page of data before they print; they are full-page printers. Until a laser printer receives a full page, it holds the partial page in memory. If a partial page exists in the printer, you can force it to eject the page by taking the printer off line, pressing the Form Feed key, and putting the printer back on line. Another simpler method is to type the following command from the command line (type "^L" as Ctrl-L, not Shift-6,L):

```
ECHO ^L>PRN
```

This command forces your printer to perform a form feed.

Using Input Redirection

Another valuable use of redirection is *input* redirection. Just as the output of a program can be sent to a file, you can make a program look in a file for input it normally receives from the keyboard. If you try to erase an entire directory called \X using the command **ERASE *.***, the following message appears:

```
\X\*.*, are you sure (y/n)?
```

You must press **Y** to finish the erase.

Input redirection enables you to accomplish the same task in one step. Try this command by first creating a directory that you will erase.

1. Open an OS/2 command line prompt, either full screen or windowed.

2. Enter **MD\JUNK**.

3. Enter **XCOPY\OS2\JUNK**.

4. Enter **CD\JUNK**.

   You need a file that contains the letter "Y" to act as the response for the prompt "are you sure?". Use the COPY CON trick illustrated earlier in the virtual devices section to create this file:

5. Type **COPY CON RESPONSE**.

6. Type **Y**, and press Enter.

7. Type Ctrl-Z, and press Enter. You now should have a file called RESPONSE that contains a "Y".

8. Type **ERASE *.* <RESPONSE**. The message \JUNK*.*, are you sure (y/n)? appears, but is answered automatically using the "RESPONSE" file.

   No files are left in the directory, except for the RESPONSE file: OS/2 does not erase it, because it is used in the ERASE process.

9. Enter **ERASE RESPONSE** to erase the RESPONSE file.

10. Enter **CD **, and then enter **RD \JUNK**. The JUNK directory is erased.

 You also can use the new "/N" option introduced with OS/2 version 2.0 to erase a directory. These exercises assume that this option is not available.

Using Error Redirection

If the system displays an error message like SYS0002: The file could not be found, it does not display it on the standard output device. The system displays it on another output device called the "standard error device", or STDERR. For example, consider the sample run illustrated in figure 11.6.

First, the command DIR BANANA fails because no file or directory is called "banana." The second command, DIR BANANA 2>ERRORS.TXT enables OS/2 to show the drive, directory, label, and volume serial number, but the error message does not appear. If you use the TYPE command to list the contents of the ERRORS.TXT file, the error message is listed in this file.

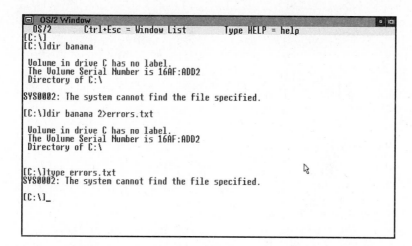

Figure 11.6:

Illustration of standard error redirection.

Why would you redirect error messages? Programmers primarily use this capability. Large job compilations produce large amounts of error information, far too much to fit on a single screen. Redirecting the errors to a file enables programmers to examine the errors at another time.

Using Append for Redirection

What if you redirect output to a file that already exists? The current information in that file is erased. Suppose, for example, that you want to run three programs, PROG1, PROG2, and PROG3, one after the other, and you want to capture the output of each to a file called OUTPUT.TXT. The following commands run these programs:

```
PROG1>OUTPUT.TXT

PROG2>OUTPUT.TXT

PROG3>OUTPUT.TXT
```

After you run these programs, the only output that appears in the OUTPUT.TXT file is that produced by PROG3. Each separate redirection command began by erasing existing files named OUTPUT.TXT.

To avoid this problem, you need to append new output. Rather than use the ">" character, use the double ">>" symbol. The append character redirects output to a file, but does so starting at the end of the file. The following commands substitute the append symbol:

```
PROG1>OUTPUT.TXT

PROG2>>OUTPUT.TXT

PROG3>>OUTPUT.TXT
```

Notice that the first line still uses ">". You do not want anything currently in OUTPUT.TXT to be part of your output (assuming the file exists).

The append symbol also is useful for batch files. If you have a battery-powered laptop, for example, and you want to find out how long it will run on a full charge before it runs out of power, use the following TIMETEST.CMD REXX command file:

```
/* */
call RxFuncAdd 'SysLoadFuncs', 'RexxUtil', 'SysLoadFuncs'
call SysLoadFuncs
r=lineout('response','')
"TIME<RESPONSE >START.TXT"
do forever
"TIME<RESPONSE>>ETIME.TXT"
call SysSleep 60
end
```

 Batch files and REXX files are discussed in Chapter 13.

The command file performs the following functions:

1. The first three lines just do some setup housekeeping, loading some REXX progrms that this file will use.

2. The command TIME <RESPONSE >START.TXT uses the basic OS/2 TIME command to place the current time into a file called START.TXT.

3. The system appends the current time into a file called ETIME.TXT, and then the line SysSleep 60 forces the system to remain idle for 60 seconds.

4. The program returns to step 3 and continues this loop until the PC's power has been completely run down.

As you can see from the preceding example, the append operator ">>" is useful if you need to send information to a "logging" file—in other words, a file that continually logs information.

Using Pipes

OS/2 programs have input and output "sockets" called STDIN, STDOUT, and STDERR. Those sockets normally attach to input and output devices, such as the keyboard and screen, but they also can be redirected to files or virtual devices. *Pipes*, on the other hand, enable two programs to connect their input and output sockets (see fig. 11.7).

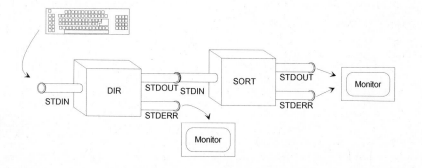

Figure 11.7:

Connecting ("piping") the output of one program to the input of another program.

To pipe the output of one file to the input of another, use the pipe character (|). To pipe the output of program X into the input of program Y, for example, type **X|Y**. The following example shows you how to use pipes.

The DIR command usually lists files in an unorganized manner. STDOUT, an abbreviation for "the standard output device," goes to the monitor. Another OS/2 program is called SORT.EXE. To use

SORT, type **SORT** and feed it a few lines. It will sort those lines and display them, as in the following example:

1. At any OS/2 command prompt, type **SORT**.

2. Type a line of text, and press Enter. Similar to the COPY CON command, anything that you type now goes into the SORT program.

3. Type several more lines and press Enter between each one.

4. After you finish, press Ctrl-Z, and then press Enter.

    Recall that Ctrl-Z is the "end of file" marker, which signals to SORT the end of input.

The preceding steps display output similar to that in figure 11.8.

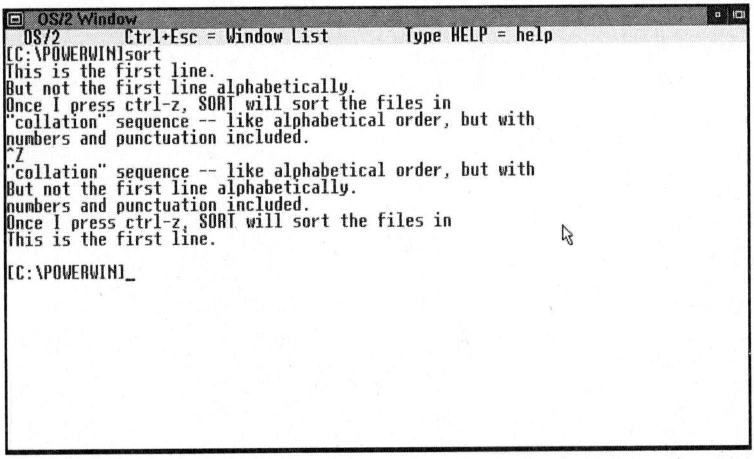

Figure 11.8:

A sample run with SORT.

```
□ OS/2 Window                                                    □  □
  OS/2      Ctrl+Esc = Window List       Type HELP = help
[C:\POWERWIN]sort
This is the first line.
But not the first line alphabetically.
Once I press ctrl-z, SORT will sort the files in
"collation" sequence -- like alphabetical order, but with
numbers and punctuation included.
^Z
"collation" sequence -- like alphabetical order, but with
But not the first line alphabetically.
numbers and punctuation included.
Once I press ctrl-z, SORT will sort the files in
This is the first line.                              ⍚

[C:\POWERWIN]_
```

All the lines are organized alphabetically, or to be more specific, in collation sequence. *Collation sequence* is an organization method using character ASCII codes. These codes range from 32 to 126. The capital "A," for example, has code 65, the lowercase "a" has code 97, the digit "0" as code 48, and the "space" character has code 32. SORT orders file entries according to their codes. Lines that start with digits precede lines starting with capital letters, which precede lines starting with lowercase letters.

When SORT is used by itself, it is not that helpful. When you pipe the output of another program like DIR into SORT, however, its usefulness increases. Such programs (called *filters*) are valuable add-ons that give new powers to pre-existing programs. OS/2 comes with three filter programs:

- **SORT.** Puts lines of data in collation sequence

- **FIND.** Looks for matches with a particular sequence of characters

- **MORE.** Stops a program for every screen's worth of output and displays the prompt — More — -

FIND matches a stream of input against certain character strings. Suppose, for example, that you wanted to find every BASFDEV statement in the CONFIG.SYS file. Pipe the statements into FIND using the TYPE command:

```
TYPE C:\CONFIG.SYS¦FIND "BASFDEV"
```

Only the lines with "BASFDEV" in them display on-screen.

You also can use FIND to determine which files have not been backed up. To do so, first consider the ATTRIB command. Type the command **ATTRIB *.***. The screen should look like figure 11.9.

```
┌─ OS/2 Window                                                    · □┐
 OS/2          Ctrl+Esc = Window List    Type HELP = help
            C:\powerwin\06U0S212.PCX
            C:\powerwin\06U0S207.PCX
 A          C:\powerwin\11U0S208.DRW
            C:\powerwin\11U0S201.PCX
            C:\powerwin\11U0S202.PCX
            C:\powerwin\11U0S203.PCX
 A          C:\powerwin\DDETEST.SAM
 A          C:\powerwin\A.CMD
            C:\powerwin\11U0S204.PCX
            C:\powerwin\11U0S205.PCX
 A          C:\powerwin\DIRPIPES.DRW
 A          C:\powerwin\DIRPIPES.BAK
 A          C:\powerwin\PIPEENDS.DRW
            C:\powerwin\11U0S208.PCX
            C:\powerwin\11U0S210.PCX
 A          C:\powerwin\11U0S209.DRW
            C:\powerwin\11U0S209.PCX
            C:\powerwin\11U0S211.PCX
            C:\powerwin\11U0S212.PCX
 A          C:\powerwin\11U0S211.DRW
 A          C:\powerwin\PIPEEX.DRW
 A          C:\powerwin\CHP11STF.SAM

[C:\POWERWIN]
└─────────────────────────────────────────────────────────────────┘
```

Figure 11.9:

Sample output from the ATTRIB command.

Notice that some files have an "A" next to them. Those files' "archive" bits are set, meaning they have not been backed up since the last time they were updated. Type the following FIND command to pick out the files that have not been backed up:

```
ATTRIB *.*¦FIND " A "
```

The output lists only the files with an "A" next to them, as you see in figure 11.10.

Figure 11.10:

Using the FIND command to filter ATTRIB output.

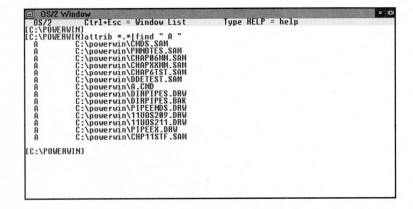

In addition to FIND, the MORE filter adds useful features to programs. You probably have seen the output of a DIR command scroll off the screen, losing the information at the top of the directory. The OS/2 program PSTAT, for example monitors system status. If you type **PSTAT** from a command prompt, several screens of data zip by too fast to read. If you type **PSTAT | MORE**, however, every PSTAT screen stops and waits for you to press a key.

The "/P" option also pauses the DIR command after each screen of information.

Filters come from the UNIX world. UNIX includes filters that spell check, perform complex search-and-replace operations on files, and even compress a file to a smaller size. Although filters have been available on the PC since 1983, they have never been popular in the PC world. Even if you rarely use filters and redirection, you can see that they are a powerful addition to the command-line interface.

Understanding Batch Programs

The greatest power of the command line is its programmability, which involves batch files. *Batch files*, also known as *command files*, use a simple and easy to use programming language. You do not need any programming tools, only the text editor that comes with OS/2. Batch files can simplify and automate any task you perform repeatedly.

Although GUIs (Graphical User Interfaces) are easy to use, most of them lack programmability. Suppose, for example, that logging onto a network involves three steps:

1. Load a program that enables your PC to recognize a *protocol stack*, which is the language a network uses to communicate internally. Name the stack **STACK.EXE**.

2. Load a program that serves as a network monitor, which reports constantly on network status as an icon at the bottom of the Workplace screen. Call that program **MONITOR.EXE**.

3. Load the network shell program that accepts user inputs and attaches you to system resources. Call it **SHELL.EXE**.

Every day you have to double-click on the "stack" program's object, then double-click on the "monitor" program's object, and then double-click on the "shell" program object. If you perform these operations from the command line, you have to type **STACK**, then wait for the command prompt to return, and then type **MONITOR**, then **SHELL**.

The command processor makes life easier by enabling you to combine all three commands into a single command. Simply follow these steps:

1. Use the OS/2 text editor to create a file called NET.CMD. It uses the following five lines:

```
@ECHO OFF
ECHO NOW ATTACHING TO THE NETWORK...
STACK
```

```
MONITOR
SHELL
```

2. Save the file.

3. Open an OS/2 window and type **NET**. The commands flash by, and then you are in the network. From this point on, you need only type **NET** to get into the network.

If you like to use GUIs, you do not even need to open an OS/2 window to benefit from this batch file. You can just as easily create a program object for it.

Using the ECHO Command

ECHO is a batch command that is actually three commands in one. ECHO can be used to put messages on the screen. From an OS/2 command line, try typing **ECHO HELLO, THERE**. The computer responds HELLO, THERE. The second line of the preceding batch file is another example of ECHO; the line places the message Now attaching to the network... on-screen.

Another use of ECHO is as an instruction to CMD.EXE about *command echoing*, not message echoing. ECHO ON and ECHO OFF tell the command processor whether to show a command before executing it. Command echoing is most easily demonstrated using two batch files—B1.CMD and B2.CMD:

The batch file B1.CMD contains the following statements:

```
@ECHO ON
ECHO HELLO, THERE
```

B2.CMD contains the following statements:

```
@ECHO OFF
ECHO HELLO, THERE.
```

Figure 11.11 shows the results of running the B1.CMD and then B2.CMD batch files.

Notice that when the first batch file is run, the "ECHO HELLO, THERE" line appears on-screen before the actual "Hello, there."

This is the default situation for CMD.EXE; unless it is told otherwise, CMD.EXE displays a line of a batch file before actually executing it. In the second example, B2.CMD, you see that CMD.EXE executed the "ECHO HELLO, THERE" command without showing the command. In general, the command **@ECHO OFF** will be the first line of all your batch files. The at symbol (@) at the front of this command keeps it from echoing.

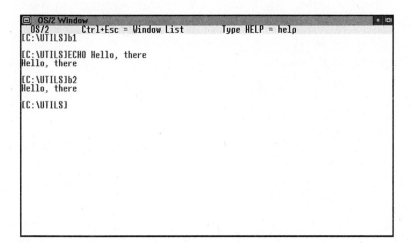

Figure 11.11:

Sample runs of two batch files demonstrating the use of ECHO ON and ECHO OFF.

Instead of including ECHO OFF at the beginning of every batch file, suppress command echoing by invoking a batch file with the /Q (quiet) option. Type **A /Q**, for example, to invoke the A.CMD batch file. Command echoing will be turned off because you included the /Q switch.

A third way to use ECHO is by itself to list the status of command echoing. Type **ECHO** and CMD.EXE probably will reply echo is on, unless you have already explicitly shut it off.

Do not shut off echo when you work from the command line—it produces strange-looking command screens.

ECHO is useful if you start your batch files with the command **@ECHO OFF** and use ECHO to put simple text messages on-screen.

Using ECHO To Build BEEP.CMD

Occasionally, you may want to use a program to make the computer emit a beep. The Ctrl-G character is the "bell" character, named for old teletype machines that rang a bell. Try this two line batch file whenever you need your computer to emit a beep:

```
COPY CON BEEP.CMD
@ECHO OFF
ECHO ^G
^Z
```

 Remember that to enter the ^G character, you must press and hold down the Ctrl key, then press G. The ^G character appears on the screen. In the System Editor, enter ^G as Alt-Z.

Try out this simple file, but not too much—the people in the room next to you may not like it.

Detecting Errors in OS/2 Batch Files

The network logon batch file may have looked useful, but actually it is limited. The "stack" program may not work properly if the network is not available immediately and at all times. Before you created the batch file, you kept trying to get into the network by typing **STACK** until you succeeded. You followed a plan that looked like this:

1. Load the protocol stack.

2. If loading the protocol stack failed, repeat step 1. Otherwise, go to step 3.

3. Load the network monitor.

4. Load the user shell.

This process can be a real pain in the neck and is just the kind of repetitive task that computers were built for. How does a batch file know whether the "stack" program fails? OS/2 programs (and DOS programs) return a number to the operating system called a return code A *return code* is a number from 0 to 255 (integers only) that indicates whether the program was successful. In general, a value of 0 means everything went well. What would a nonzero value like 1, 20, or 255 mean? That depends on the program. Some programs do not bother returning values other than 0, rendering the return code useless; other programs offer a number of return codes. Table 11.1 displays documented return codes for two representative OS/2 programs.

Table 11.3
Return Codes for Some Representative OS/2 Programs

BACKUP Return Code	Meaning
0	Normal completion.
1	No files were found to back up.
2	Some files or directories were not processed because of file errors.
3	Ended by user.
4	Ended because of error.
5	Not defined.
6	BACKUP was unable to process the FORMAT command.

CHKDSK Return Code	Meaning
0	Normal completion.
3	Ended by user.

continues

Table 11.3 Continued

CHKDSK Return Code	Meaning
4	Ended due to error.
6	CHKDSK was unable to execute file system's CHKDSK program (a separate version of CHKDSK exists for HPFS and FAT).

You can see that some OS/2 programs give information to the system about why they failed. The next section shows you how to exploit that information in your batch files.

Decision Making and Branching in OS/2 Command Files

Suppose that the "stack" program produces a return code of 0 if the network connection is successful or 1 if the connection is unsuccessful. OS/2 includes a batch command, IF ERRORLEVEL, that can test the return code of a program. The syntax for IF ERRORLEVEL is as follows (the *command* variable represents any OS/2 command):

```
IF ERRORLEVEL n command
```

This batch command executes the specified *command* if the return code from the previous program is equal to or greater than *n*. If the return code is less than *n*, IF ERRORLEVEL does nothing. You can write a batch file called CHECK.CMD, for example, that runs CHKDSK and reports on the results. This batch file might contain the following lines (a major problem exists with this program, but it is a good start):

```
@ECHO OFF
CHKDSK A:
IF ERRORLEVEL 6 ECHO ERROR: COULDN'T RUN THE FILE
SYSTEM'S CHKDSK.
IF ERRORLEVEL 4 ECHO CHKDSK ENDED DUE TO ERROR.
IF ERRORLEVEL 3 ECHO TERMINATED BY USER.
IF ERRORLEVEL 0 ECHO CHKDSK RAN NORMALLY.
```

The objective is to run CHKDSK and then to detect return codes and report the results of these codes. You can try this batch file on a new floppy disk. The results should resemble the output in figure 11.12.

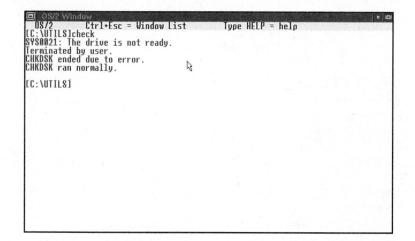

Try this batch file again without a floppy disk in the drive; you should see results similar to those in figure 11.13.

Why does the output for the run display all the messages? Each ERRORLEVEL statement responds if the return code is the requested value or higher. The high number error code from the failed CHKDSK run triggered all the ERRORLEVEL statements. If a floppy disk is not in the drive, the system generates a return code of 4, which is greater than 0 and 3. How can you fix this? Use the GOTO command with the following syntax:

```
GOTO labelname
```

The *labelname* parameter is a line in the batch file with only a colon (:) and the labelname. Use the GOTO command in the following batch file, appropriately-named FOREVER.CMD:

```
@ECHO OFF
:TOP
ECHO HELP! I CAN'T STOP!
GOTO TOP
```

Press Ctrl-Break to stop the preceding batch file. Apply the GOTO command to the CHECK batch file:

```
@ECHO OFF
CHKDSK A:
IF ERRORLEVEL 6 GOTO ERROR6
IF ERRORLEVEL 3 GOTO ERROR3
IF ERRORLEVEL 4 GOTO ERROR4
IF ERRORLEVEL 0 GOTO ERROR0
:ERROR6
ECHO ERROR: COULDN'T RUN THE FILE SYSTEM'S CHKDSK.
GOTO END
:ERROR4
ECHO CHKDSK ENDED DUE TO ERROR.
GOTO END
:ERROR3
ECHO TERMINATED BY USER.
GOTO END
:ERROR0
ECHO CHKDSK RAN NORMALLY.
:END
```

Now the program works fine. Notice the order in which the ERRORLEVEL commands must appear, from higher numbers to smaller numbers. This order is necessary because of the "greater than or equal to" nature of ERRORLEVEL. The same method can be applied to the network program, although it is simpler: a return code of 0 for "all clear," and 1 for "did not work."

```
@ECHO OFF
:TRYAGAIN
STACK
IF ERRORLEVEL 1 GOTO TRYAGAIN
MONITOR
SHELL
```

Finding OS/2's Undocumented Return Codes

Now that you know some OS/2 commands have return codes that can be used to control batch files, you may be disappointed when you look in the OS/2 manual. The manual lists only ten commands with return codes other than zero: BACKUP, CHKDSK, COMP, EAUTIL, FORMAT, RECOVER, REPLACE, RESTORE, UNPACK, and XCOPY.

Nevertheless, OS/2 includes a number of undocumented return codes. The odd thing about these codes is their inconsistency. If you try to perform an operation on a nonexistent file, the CD, RD, and COPY commands generate a return code of 1; the DIR command generates a code of 18; and PRINT generates a code of 255. Although it is almost impossible to find every undocumented return code, a tool does exist for this purpose.

Building the "Return Code Sniffer"

Recall that the previous CHECK.CMD file used a series of IF ERRORLEVEL statements to isolate particular return codes. To find undocumented return codes, start with a batch file that tests for each of the 256 possible return codes. The batch file resembles CHECK.CMD, but is much larger. It might look something like this:

```
@ECHO OFF
%1 %2 %3 %4 %5 %6 %7
IF ERRORLEVEL 255 GOTO ERROR255
IF ERRORLEVEL 254 GOTO ERROR254
IF ERRORLEVEL 253 GOTO ERROR253
 . . .
IF ERRORLEVEL 2 GOTO ERROR2
IF ERRORLEVEL 1 GOTO ERROR1
IF ERRORLEVEL 0 GOTO ERROR0
:ERROR255
ECHO FOUND ERROR CODE 255
GOTO END
:ERROR254
ECHO FOUND ERROR CODE 254
GOTO END
 . . .
ECHO FOUND ERROR CODE 0
:END
```

The purpose of the second line of the preceding batch file, %1 %2 %3 %4 %5 %6 %7, is discussed in the next section on replaceable parameters.

The size of the batch file for the return code sniffer will be about 20K, which would be a pain to type in. Fortunately, most of the program uses a short QBASIC program. QBASIC is the built-in BASIC interpreter loaded as part of the DOS support—you have to load DOS support to run this program. Follow these steps to build the QBASIC batch file:

1. Open a DOS full-screen session.

2. Type **QBASIC \OS2\SEECODES.BAS** and press Enter. The QBASIC editor is activated.

3. In the editor, type in the following program exactly as you see it:

```
OPEN "\OS2\SEECODE.CMD" FOR OUTPUT AS 1
PRINT #1, "@ECHO OFF"
```

```
PRINT #1, "%1 %2 %3 %4 %5 %6 %7"
FOR I = 255 TO 0 STEP -1
 PRINT #1, "IF ERRORLEVEL "; I; " GOTO ERROR";
MID$(STR$(I), 2)
NEXT
FOR I = 255 TO 0 STEP -1
 PRINT #1, ":ERROR"; MID$(STR$(I), 2)
 PRINT #1, "ECHO FOUND ERROR CODE "; I
 PRINT #1, "GOTO END"
NEXT
PRINT #1, ":END"
CLOSE
```

4. Press F5. The screen changes and the program runs for a minute or two. When the message Press a key appears, press any key to return to the QBASIC editor. If you get an error, double-check that you typed the program exactly as it appears—one misplaced comma can keep the program from running.

5. Exit QBASIC by pressing Alt-F, and then X. You are prompted to save the BASIC file.

6. Press Enter to save the file. QBASIC then exits.

7. Type **EXIT**, and your DOS full-screen session is terminated.

If you followed these steps correctly, you now have a program called SEECODE.CMD in the OS2 subdirectory.

Running the Sniffer

Use the return code sniffer on a simple command such as CD, the change directory command. Suppose, for example, that you try to issue CD for a drive that is not ready. What return code appears? Follow these steps to see:

1. Open an OS/2 windowed or full-screen session.

2. Make sure that no floppy disk is in the floppy disk drive.

3. Type **SEECODE CD A:**\ (or another drive letter), and press Enter. Drive A (or the specified drive) runs for moment, and then a

popup error message appears similar to the message in
figure 11.14.

Figure 11.14:

Change Directory
error message for
floppy drives with
no disk.

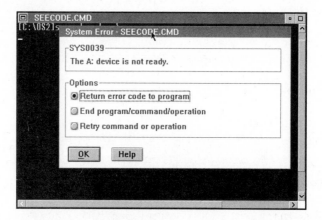

4. Click on `Return error code to program` and then click OK. CD
announces that it cannot fulfill the request, displaying system
error code SYS0021 (see fig. 11.15).

Figure 11.15:

Result of
SEECODE
command file.

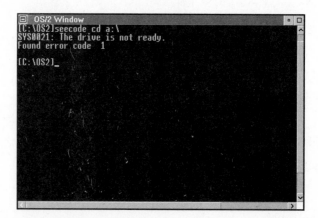

SEECODE reports that CD's response to a "drive not ready" is an
error code of 1, which also is CD's response to an attempt to change
to a nonexistent directory.

Use SEECODE if you must work with an error condition caused by a particular set of circumstances. Type **SEECODE** and then, on the same line, the command from which you want the return code. Armed with specific return code information, you can build powerful command files.

Using Variable Parameters in Command Files

In the previous section, you probably noticed the second line in the batch file, %1 %2 %3 %4 %5 %6 %7. These numbers are *replaceable parameters*, and they can help you build powerful, flexible batch files.

Creating a Batch File That Makes and Uses Subdirectories

When you receive a floppy disk full of information, your natural reaction is to create a subdirectory for the floppy disk and then copy its contents to the subdirectory. The commands for this sequence resemble the following:

```
MD \NEWSUB
CD \NEWSUB
COPY A:*.*
```

Occasionally, you may forget to change to the new subdirectory when you issue these commands. If you forget, the data copies to the disk, but not into the new subdirectory. It would be nice if a command performed the operation of MD and CD in one step, as in the command MCD \NEWSUB. You can write a batch file that creates and moves to \NEWSUB:

```
@ECHO OFF
MD \NEWSUB
CD \NEWSUB
```

This batch file, however, only creates a subdirectory called NEWSUB. What if you want a subdirectory called SUB2? The batch file would be as follows:

```
@ECHO OFF
MD \SUB2
CD \SUB2
YOU SEE THE PATTERN EMERGING: THE BATCH FILE LOOKS LIKE
@ECHO OFF
MD [SOME SUBDIRECTORY NAME]
CD [THAT SAME SUBDIRECTORY NAME]
```

As mentioned before, it would helpful if you could write the
MCD.CMD batch file so that the system associates the command
MCD \NEWSUB with the \NEWSUB directory and the MD and
CD commands. Fortunately, you can create this short cut using
replaceable parameters. The following example demonstrates one
use.

```
@ECHO OFF
MD %1
CD %1
```

The %1 is the replaceable parameter. You read earlier in this chapter
how CMD.EXE parses a command line, but the discussion did not
cover everything. After CMD.EXE recognizes that it is executing a
batch file, it takes each parameter or argument and puts it into
temporary holding spaces called *replaceable parameters*. These spaces
are numbered from 1 though 9. If you have a command file called
ABC.CMD, for example, and you type the following line:

```
ABC DOG LINCOLN HOUSE JUSTICE
```

The command parser executes ABC.CMD and passes to it the
parameters %1="DOG", %2="LINCOLN", %3="HOUSE", and
%4="JUSTICE". Parameters %5 through %9 receive the "null," or
empty argument.

NOTE More than nine replaceable parameters are available
using an OS/2 batch command called SHIFT. This
command is not used often, however, and its operation
is too extensive to cover in this edition.

Understanding the Command Parser and Parameters

If you are using MCD.CMD and you type the command MCD \NEWSUB, the command parser performs the following steps:

1. The command parser puts \NEWSUB into the parameter %1 and activates MCD.CMD.

2. The first line of MCD.CMD is @ECHO OFF; the second line is MD %1. The command parser first must resolve the replaceable parameter variables before it executes the line. It looks up "%1," and finds \NEWSUB. The parser then reassembles the command so that it is MD \NEWSUB and executes it.

3. The third line again contains a "%" variable. The parser converts the %1 parameter to \NEWSUB, and reassembles the command so that it is CD \NEWSUB. The batch file is finished.

To see in more detail how replaceable parameters work, type in this batch file (call it SEEVARS.CMD):

```
@ECHO OFF
ECHO THE FIRST REPLACEABLE PARAMETER (%%1)=%1
ECHO THE SECOND REPLACEABLE PARAMETER (%%2)=%2
ECHO THE THIRD REPLACEABLE PARAMETER (%%3)=%3
ECHO THE FOURTH REPLACEABLE PARAMETER (%%4)=%4
```

To try out the new batch file, type **SEEVARS LOG DOG BOG FOG**, and **SEEVARS SHERPA DOPPELGANGER**. The output should resemble figure 11.16.

As you can see in figure 11.16, the ECHO statements put messages on the screen. The messages vary from run to run because the replaceable parameters are inserted in place of the "%1," "%2," and so on by CMD.EXE before the ECHO statements are actually executed. The third and fourth variables in the second example are empty because you only entered two parameters. This is not an error because the parameters %1 through %9 always exist, even if they are empty.

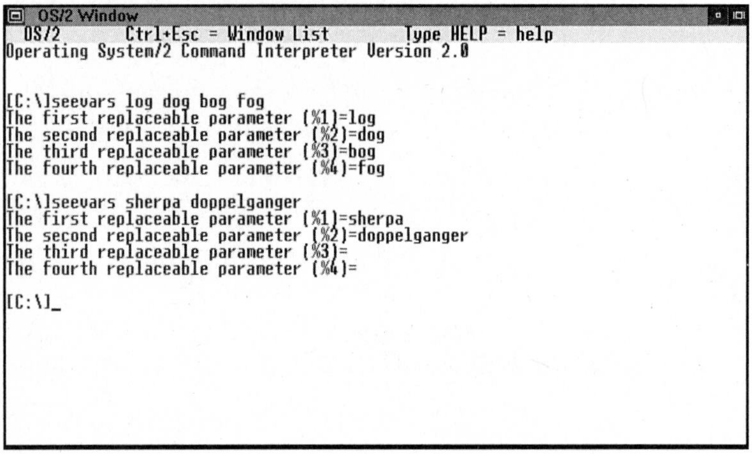

Figure 11.16:

Sample output from SEEVARS.CMD.

```
┌─────────────────────────────────────────────────────────────────────┐
│ ▣  OS/2 Window                                                  □ │□│ │
│    OS/2       Ctrl+Esc = Window List        Type HELP = help        │
│ Operating System/2 Command Interpreter Version 2.0                   │
│                                                                      │
│ [C:\]seevars log dog bog fog                                         │
│ The first replaceable parameter (%1)=log                             │
│ The second replaceable parameter (%2)=dog                            │
│ The third replaceable parameter (%3)=bog                             │
│ The fourth replaceable parameter (%4)=fog                            │
│                                                                      │
│ [C:\]seevars sherpa doppelganger                                     │
│ The first replaceable parameter (%1)=sherpa                          │
│ The second replaceable parameter (%2)=doppelganger                   │
│ The third replaceable parameter (%3)=                                │
│ The fourth replaceable parameter (%4)=                               │
│                                                                      │
│ [C:\]_                                                               │
│                                                                      │
│                                                                      │
│                                                                      │
└─────────────────────────────────────────────────────────────────────┘
```

Checking for Replaceable Parameters

Now that you know how to use replaceable parameters, you might encounter a potential problem. That is, if you write a batch file that needs replaceable parameters, it must have replaceable parameters. Consider what happens to MCD if you forget to type in replaceable parameters. The second line, MD %1, becomes MD because nothing exists in %1. The MD command issued by itself creates an error; the operating system does not know what directory to make. The CD command executed by itself produces the name of the current subdirectory.

To ensure that your batch files contain replaceable parameters, use the IF command. You used IF ERRORLEVEL in an earlier section to check return codes. Another version of IF, the "evaluation" IF, uses the following syntax:

```
IF firstitem == seconditem command
```

The *firstitem* and *seconditem* parameters are any string of characters; *command* is any batch command, such as GOTO END or ECHO HELLO. The double equal sign (==) means "is equal to." OS/2 does not use a single equal sign (=) probably because it was written by programmers using the C language, which uses == to test for

equality. In the following example of IF ==, the SECRET.CMD batch
file instructs you to guess a secret password:

```
@ECHO OFF
IF %1==SWORDFISH GOTO RIGHTANSWER
ECHO YOU DIDN'T GET IT THIS TIME!
GOTO END
:RIGHTANSWER
ECHO CORRECT!
:END
```

Try it with **SECRET OPENSESAME, SECRET PASSWORD**, and
SECRET SWORDFISH. Because SWORDFISH is the correct password, the first two entries should produce the output you see in
figure 11.17.

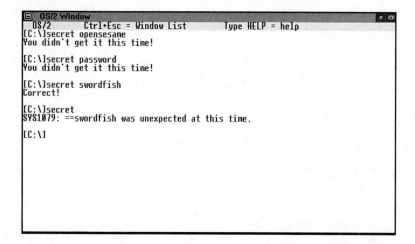

Figure 11.17:

Sample output
from
SECRET.CMD.

Try it without a parameter, and the error message at the bottom of
figure 11.17 appears. The problem stems from the comparison,
%1==SWORDFISH. The batch file only works if something exists on
both sides of the line; if you do not supply a parameter, nothing
appears on the left-hand side of the command. How do you protect
your command files against this kind of "user input" problem? Use
the following program, named INPUTTST.CMD:

```
@ECHO OFF
IF %1A==A GOTO NOGOOD
```

```
ECHO GOOD — YOU ENTERED A PARAMETER!
GOTO END
:NOGOOD
ECHO YOU DIDN'T ENTER A PARAMETER. TRY AGAIN, BUT THIS TIME
ECHO TYPE "INPUTTST PARAMETER," WHERE "PARAMETER" IS ANY
ECHO COMBINATION OF CHARACTERS.
:END
```

INPUTTST.CMD "traps" user errors. Either the user types a parameter, or he or she does not. Suppose that the user types a parameter X. CMD.EXE substitutes X for the %1 parameter and the comparison becomes IF XA==A. This comparison fails because the character sequence XA differs from the character sequence A. If the user does not type anything, the test becomes IF A==A—the %1 parameter is empty and no difference exists between the two sides of the test. This test succeeds when the user does not enter a parameter. The batch file produces an error message, or, as programmers sometimes call it, "a nastygram."

Apply input checking to MCD.CMD to make the file resemble the following:

```
@ECHO OFF
IF A%1==A GOTO NOGOOD
MD %1
CD %1
GOTO END
:NOGOOD
ECHO ^GERROR: PLEASE USE THIS PROGRAM LIKE SO:
ECHO MCD SUBNAME
ECHO WHERE "SUBNAME" IS THE NAME OF THE SUBDIRECTORY THAT YOU
ECHO WISH TO CREATE.
:END
```

 Write your batch files so that they are as "bulletproof" as possible—that they anticipate and respond to a variety of situations—to ensure that users do not become confused if they do something wrong. Bulletproof batch files also are helpful if you forget the batch file's purpose.

Remember that ^G in the error message is typed as Ctrl-G. This makes the system beep to get the user's attention.

Understanding and Using Environment Variables in Command Files

Replaceable parameters are one kind of a larger class of programming tools called *environment* variables or *batch* variables. *Variables* are places in memory that programmers use to hold transient information. Think of variables as temporary "scratchpad" areas. Earlier sections described how the MCD.CMD batch file would be inoperable without replaceable parameters. Some programs also would not work without variables.

A variable is named by any string of characters with a percent sign (%) at the front of it. The name must start with a letter: %F, %MYDATA, or %VARNAME are usable names—%7 is not, nor is %4DATA, because it is confused with replaceable parameters.

Variables are stored in a section of CMD.EXE called *the environment*. Your system already contains a few variables in the environment. To see them, open an OS/2 prompt and type **SET**. The output should resemble the one in figure 11.18.

```
┌─ OS/2 Window                                                        ─□─┐
│  OS/2      Ctrl+Esc = Window List      Type HELP = help               │
│ Operating System/2 Command Interpreter Version 2.0                    │
│                                                                       │
│ [C:\]set                                                              │
│ USER_INI=C:\OS2\OS2.INI                                               │
│ SYSTEM_INI=C:\OS2\OS2SYS.INI                                          │
│ OS2_SHELL=C:\OS2\CMD.EXE                                              │
│ AUTOSTART=PROGRAMS,TASKLIST,FOLDERS                                   │
│ RUNWORKPLACE=C:\OS2\PMSHELL.EXE                                       │
│ COMSPEC=C:\OS2\CMD.EXE                                                │
│ PATH=C:\OS2;C:\OS2\SYSTEM;C:\OS2\MDOS\WINOS2;C:\OS2\INSTALL;C:\;C:\OS2\MDOS;C:\O │
│ S2\APPS;C:\UTILS;                                                     │
│ DPATH=C:\OS2;C:\OS2\SYSTEM;C:\OS2\MDOS\WINOS2;C:\OS2\INSTALL;C:\;C:\OS2\BITMAP;C │
│ ;\OS2\MDOS;C:\OS2\APPS;                                               │
│ PROMPT=$i[$p]                                                         │
│ HELP=C:\OS2\HELP;                                                     │
│ GLOSSARY=C:\OS2\HELP\GLOSS;                                           │
│ KEYS=ON                                                               │
│ DELDIR=C:\DELETE,5;                                                   │
│ BOOKSHELF=C:\OS2\BOOK;                                                │
│                                                                       │
│ [C:\]_                                                                │
└───────────────────────────────────────────────────────────────────────┘
```

Figure 11.18:

Displaying environment variables.

Figure 11.18 shows a number of prestored environment variables. They are used by the operating system for various purposes. USER_INI, for example, tells the operating system the name and location of the file that contains the user setup information, which in this figure, is the default file C:\OS2\OS2.INI. That information is in an environment variable for OS/2 programs that want to store user setup information. The programs know where to find OS2.INI if it is in a variable, which is the place where they are supposed to store the setup information. The next variable obviously identifies the name and location of OS2SYS.INI. Not all the variables are documented, and no way exists for you to know what they all do. The following list provides a partial overview, however, of each of their functions:

- **OS2_SHELL.** Identifies the name and location of the command-line shell (CMD.EXE can be replaced with a third-party replacement, but none exist).

- **RUNWORKPLACE.** Identifies the program that actually provides the Workplace Shell.

- **COMSPEC.** Identifies the command-line shell, as does OS2_SHELL, but is used at a different time in the process of running OS/2. OS2_SHELL directs OS/2 to load the shell at boot time; COMSPEC helps OS/2 find it later when user programs overwrite some of CMD.EXE should the programs need more memory space. After the overwriting program finishes, OS/2 must reload the overwritten part of CMD.EXE— COMSPEC provides this function.

- **PATH.** Holds the current value of the path. You learned about PATH in the section "Searching the Path."

- **DPATH.** Functions similar to PATH, but for data. The DPATH statement helps D system find D data. Like PATH, you specify a list of subdirectories in which to look for data files, separating each subdirectory's name with a semicolon.

- **PROMPT.** Controls which user prompt you see. The [C:\] prompt is presented by OS/2, and is controlled by this environment variable.

- **HELP.** Functions as a PATH for help files. OS/2 looks for a program's help files wherever HELP points. Like DPATH and PATH, this is a list of subdirectory names.

- **GLOSSARY.** Points to the Master Help file. GLOSSARY is another list of subdirectories.

- **KEYS.** Instructs CMD.EXE whether to recall previous keystrokes for recall with the up arrow. This is known as the "command history" feature. OS/2 keeps 64K worth of previous commands in this command history.

- **DELDIR.** Tells OS/2 where to keep deleted files for undeletion, and how many deleted files to keep.

- **BOOKSHELF.** Points to the on-line documentation supplied with OS/2.

These environmental variables (and any new ones that you define) are accessible immediately from inside batch files: simply surround the variable's name with percent signs, and CMD.EXE substitutes the value inside the variable for the variable's name. Suppose, for example, that you want a batch file that reports the status of the command history feature. Type **SET**, and then look to see whether KEYS is equal to ON or OFF. What if you want the output to be more user-friendly? You can write a short batch file called HIST.CMD.

Before you enter the following batch file, note that each line is preceded by a number. Do not include the numbers when entering this program. The numbers are for explanation in the following paragraphs.

```
(1)@ECHO OFF
(2)IF %KEYS%==ON GOTO KEYON
(3)IF %KEYS%==OFF GOTO KEYOFF
(4)ECHO ^GKEYS VARIABLE SHOWED AN ODD VALUE: CONTAINED
"%KEYS%"
(5)GOTO END
```

```
(6):KEYON
(7)ECHO COMMAND HISTORY IS ENABLED.
(8)GOTO END
(9):KEYOFF
(10)ECHO COMMAND HISTORY IS DISABLED.
(11):END
```

 When you type this file, be sure to type the "ON" and "OFF" in uppercase. The "==" operator is case-sensitive, and it will not see that "ON==on."

HIST.CMD performs the following functions:

Line 1 is the usual @ECHO OFF that keeps CMD.EXE from displaying every command before executing it.

Line 2 tests the value inside KEYS—hence the %KEYS%—against the value ON. If it matches, the command processor proceeds to the line with the label KEYON. Otherwise, it proceeds to line 3.

Line 3 tests against the only other expected value of KEYS, OFF. Note that the only way the program can move to the next line is if KEYS is neither ON nor OFF.

Line 4 displays the value in KEYS if it is not ON or OFF, and then jumps to the end of the batch file in line 5.

Line 6 is the label for the section that reports that KEYS was ON, line 7 prompts that KEYS was on, and line 8 jumps to the end of the file.

Lines 9 and 10 report that KEYS is OFF, and line 11 is the end of batch file label.

To see just how %KEYS% is substituted for an actual value, remove the @ECHO OFF line, and then run the batch file. If KEYS=ON, the program should run similar to the one in figure 11.19.

The second line in figure 11.19, which says IF ON == ON goto keyson is interesting because no line exists in the original batch file that says "... ON == ON ..." CMD.EXE must first resolve variables before it executes a line. For this reason, %KEYS% disappears, and ON is put in its place before the line gets executed.

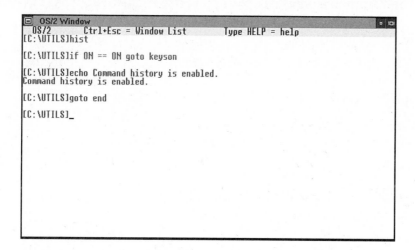

KEYHIST without ECHO OFF displays environment variable use.

The following pair of batch files enables you to modify your path "on the fly." The first, called ADDPATH, enables you to add a subdirectory to your path temporarily, without making you retype the entire PATH statement. The second batch file deletes the temporary element that was added to the PATH.

```
ADDPATH LOOKS LIKE
@ECHO OFF
IF %1A==A GOTO MESSUP
SET OLDPATH=%PATH%
SET PATH=%1;%PATH%
GOTO END
:MESSUP
ECHO PLEASE USE THIS BATCH FILE WITH THE SUBDIRECTORY THAT
ECHO YOU WISH TO ADD TO THE PATH, AS IN "ADDPATH C:\WP"
:END
ITS TWIN, DELPATH.CMD, IS SIMPLER.
@ECHO OFF
SET PATH=%OLDPATH%
```

ADDPATH first checks for a parameter. If no parameter exists, it issues an error message. At the same time, ADDPATH stores the current path to a new environment variable called OLDPATH. OLDPATH is kept around so that it is easy to restore the path to its pre-ADDPATH state.

DELPATH uses that information to then return PATH to its former state: set PATH=%OLDPATH% takes the value in OLDPATH and copies it into PATH.

Complex command files can be built using environment variables. You learn more about them in Chapter 13 on REXX files.

Adding Comments to Batch Files

An earlier section discussed the importance of adding error checking and messages to batch files. These additions safeguard against accidental misuse of a batch file and serve as a reminder of the purpose of the batch program. Good programmers usually document their work. You should include sentences inside the program to help others who are trying to figure out what you did in the program. The batch language enables you to add lines to a program that do not execute. These statements are prefixed with the word REM, which stands for remark. A typical REM statement might be as follows:

```
REM This next line tests for user input.
```

The line does not do anything except make your life easier when you cannot remember what the line does. Fully commented, the MCD.CMD batch file might resemble the following:

```
@ECHO OFF
REM DIRECTORY MAKER AND CHANGER
REM WRITTEN BY: MARK MINASI 10 MARCH 1992
REM COMBINES THE FUNCTIONS OF "MD" AND "CD"
REM
REM THE NEXT LINE CHECKS THAT THE USER ENTERS A PARAMETER
IF A%1==A GOTO NOGOOD
REM IF YOU GOT TO THIS LINE, THE USER USED A PARAMETER; NOW
```

```
MAKE REM THE DIRECTORY, AND CHANGE TO IT.
MD %1
CD %1
REM NOW JUMP OVER THE ERROR MESSAGE.
GOTO END
:NOGOOD
REM EXPLAIN WHAT WENT WRONG, WITH SUGGESTIONS FOR NEXT TIME.
ECHO ^GERROR: PLEASE USE THIS PROGRAM LIKE SO:
ECHO MCD SUBNAME
ECHO WHERE "SUBNAME" IS THE NAME OF THE SUBDIRECTORY THAT YOU
ECHO WISH TO CREATE.
REM EXIT POINT
:END
```

Big batch files need comments. Use them in small batch files and eventually they will become an integral part of all your batch files.

Summary

The OS/2 command line provides a compact, powerful way to direct OS/2 to perform a number of operations, rivaling the capabilities of OS/2's Workplace Shell. CMD.EXE, the command shell, accepts and interprets your commands and parses them into pieces. CMD.EXE searches itself and the disk for the information it needs to satisfy those commands.

The command line also gives you access to the power of virtual devices and redirection. Nevertheless, the greatest power of the command line lies in its programmability, or the power to store commands in batch files. Batch files enable you to take a repetitive task and automate it, which makes you more productive.

In the next chapter, you explore other ways to flex OS/2's muscle by tuning the performance of OS/2's multitasking engine, its memory

Optimizing OS/2

OS/2 is more advanced than DOS. Once OS/2 is on your machine, you are not just working with a PC; you basically have a mainframe on your desk. In fact, OS/2 is so powerful that many users feel, at one time or another, that their system must have power that they are not even aware of.

Consider printing, for example, which, at one time, was a relatively simple procedure. Under DOS, printing involved no more than selecting a printer driver and downloading fonts. An OS/2 system offers many printer options, including print drivers, queue managers, the spooler, and the spool-viewer programs.

As another example, look at the multitude of OS/2 multitasking options. When you make a computer perform several tasks at the same time—even a very fast computer—the tasks are done slowly. The real power of OS/2 is that it makes multitasking easy to understand and enables you to fine-tune the multitasking process.

Printing and OS/2

The ultimate output of most computer programs is some kind of hard copy or a printed result. Whether they are dealing with a bill, a check, a contract, or a written job offer, people do not really believe it is true until they "see it in black and white." OS/2 features highly flexible printer support, but with OS/2's added power comes the necessary evil of its complexity.

Understanding the Print Management System

When you start to understand how OS/2 uses printers, you may be intimidated by the operating system's apparent complexity. This complexity is suggested by the fact that OS/2 has the following three programs associated with printing:

- A spooler
- A queue driver
- A print driver

Figure 12.1 helps you understand how these three programs interact. In this example, three OS/2 programs—P1, P2, and P3—are running. The PC that has two parallel ports—LPT1 and LPT2—which are connected to a LaserJet printer and to a plotter, respectively. Each application provides commands that you can use to direct output to one port or another. In this example, P1 and P2 print to LPT1 (the laser printer) and P3 prints to LPT2 (the plotter).

Figure 12.1:

How the Print Manager works.

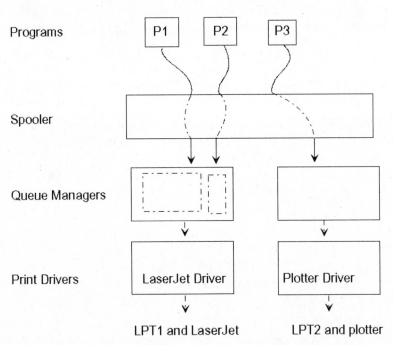

If all three programs try to print at the same time without any help from OS/2, they can create havoc on the laser printer. Each printed page is a mixture of the outputs from P1 and P2. The spooler, queue drivers, and printer drivers solve this potential problem.

The Spooler

First, the spooler takes the output intended for LPT1 or LPT2 (or any other printer interface) and redirects it to a file. If P1 and P2 both try to print to LPT1 at the same time, you want OS/2 to print all of P1's output before it prints any of P2's. Both sets of output are temporarily sent to files in preparation for the next step. The spooler deals only with redirecting print output to disk files; the queue driver follows with the next step.

Queue Drivers

After the spooler has the output in a file, the queue driver or drivers keep track of which print output files (or *spool files*, as OS/2 calls them) go to which output ports. The queue driver orders the output files and sends them, one by one, to the print driver.

Printer Drivers

To this point, the information in the spool files has been printer-independent, meaning that the information has not yet been formatted for any particular type of printer. A particular kind of text formatting, such as underlining a word, requires different instructions on different printers. To initiate underlining with an Epson dot-matrix printer, for example, a program sends a specific code before the text that the program wants underlined. A Hewlett-Packard laser printer, on the other hand, requires a different code to start underlining. Because so many types of printers are available, developers have had to implement printer-driver programs.

When you print from an OS/2 word processor, the word processor program itself does not deal with underlining the actual text; its print output simply includes a generic command that tells the printer to "underline this part." The spooler's output still contains that generic command, and the queue driver passes that command to the printer driver. The printer driver then must convert the generic command to the specific codes that your printer needs. Thus, each printer driver is tuned to the specifics of a particular printer's language.

By now, you may wonder who writes the printer drivers. The four parties most interested in high-quality printer drivers include:

1. **IBM.** If OS/2 performs badly, you will not want to use it, and printer drivers determine a great deal of a printer's performance.

2. **Printer vendors.** If a company, such as Hewlett-Packard, sold inferior printer drivers, users would not use HP printers because of their bad performance.

> **NOTE** One of the largest barriers to OS/2 1.*x*'s acceptance was the lack of HP LaserJet drivers. Microsoft claimed that HP was responsible for developing the drivers, and HP claimed that it was Microsoft's responsibility. The HP drivers did not appear until the OS/2 version, ultimately hurting all parties involved. Fortunately, OS/2 2.0 is fairly well-stocked with printer drivers.

3. **Software vendors.** These manufacturers desperately need good printer drivers. The software developers at WordPerfect Corporation can build terrific word processing software, but that software cannot work without printing, and printing requires a good driver.

4. **Users.** End users need good drivers to get the full return from their hardware investment. If the drivers from IBM, HP, and Aldus are bad, then all is not lost: some wily programmer will write a good set of HP drivers for OS/2, put them on the market, make a bundle of money, and make life easier for OS/2 users.

Together, these four players keep up the pressure needed to create high-performing printer drivers.

Installing and Changing Printer Drivers

Suppose that you want to install a new printer driver or to use an updated printer driver. Hewlett-Packard pursues good drivers, so it is a good idea to check CompuServe's HP forum now and then for new drivers. One printer driver upgrade in the past sped up printing by 30 percent—not bad for a new driver that requires only a few minutes to download and a few more to install.

Before you can install a driver, you must have a printer object. A *printer object* contains both the queue driver and the printer driver for a particular interface/printer pair. The following pages show you how to install a printer driver.

First, create a printer object. Open up the Templates folder, as shown in figure 12.2. Drag the printer object onto the desktop and release it. The Create a Printer window appears, as shown in figure 12.3.

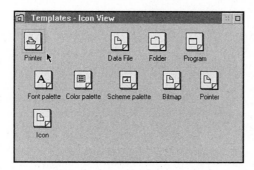

Figure 12.2:

The Templates folder with the printer object selected.

Figure 12.3:

The Create a
Printer window.

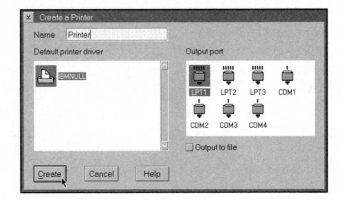

Note the seven printer interfaces depicted on the right side of the
window, and notice that LPT1 is shaded. On the left side of the
window, the available printer drivers are displayed. Even if you
choose not to install the default printer when you install OS/2, the
installation program still installs a "null" printer driver, called
IBMNULL. The Output to file option enables you to permanently
send print output to a file rather than the printer. You might do that
if you want to send a file with print output to someone, or if you
print on a different machine from the one that you are currently
working on.

Click on the Create button. OS/2 asks if you want to load a driver
for the Windows support under OS/2 also, as shown in figure 12.4.
If you run Windows programs under OS/2, click on Yes. OS/2
prompts for the Presentation Manager's Device Driver 1 disk, as
shown in figure 12.5.

Figure 12.4:

Prompting for
Windows printer
support drivers.

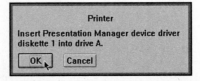

Figure 12.5:

Prompting for the
Device Driver 1
disk.

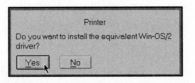

Insert the disk, click on OK, and the printer object appears on your
desktop, as shown in figure 12.6.

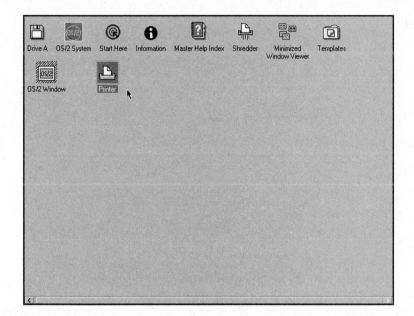

Figure 12.6:

The new printer
object on the
desktop.

Open the printer object's Settings window by right-clicking on the
printer object, and then clicking on **O**pen and **S**ettings. Your screen
should resemble figure 12.7.

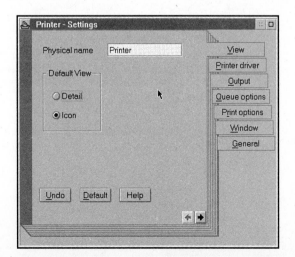

Figure 12.7:

The Printer
Settings screen.

Now install a new printer driver. Left-click on **P**rinter driver and you see a screen like the one shown in figure 12.8.

Figure 12.8:

The **P**rinter driver page of the Printer Settings notebook.

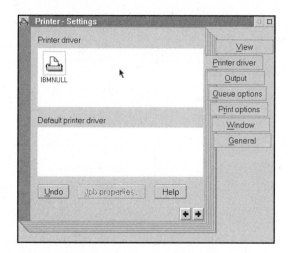

Note the existing IBMNULL printer driver. (You may have others in your notebook if you already have installed other drivers.) You are going to install a new printer driver, but the control to do that is in a nonintuitive place: the pop-up menu of the printer driver that is already installed. Right-click on IBMNULL (or any other printer driver you already have), and a small pop-up menu appears, as shown in figure 12.9.

Figure 12.9:

The pop-up menu from a printer driver object.

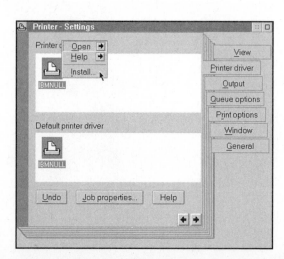

Click on **I**nstall, and another window appears. As figure 12.10 shows, the new window does not seem to contain anything useful.

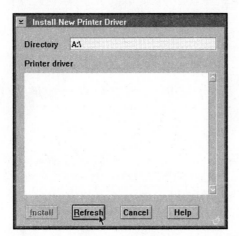

Figure 12.10:
The initial screen
for installing a
new print driver.

This screen expects you to insert a disk containing the printer driver in drive A, and then click the **R**efresh button. *Refresh* means to refresh the display; because the display shows printer drivers, the net effect is to make OS/2 reread the floppy drive in search of drivers. Insert the Device Driver 1 disk, and click on **R**efresh. The screen should resemble figure 12.11.

 If you have drivers somewhere else, perhaps on drive B or on a hard disk, you can change the driver letter.

You then see a list of print drivers that you can scroll through in the window. Device Driver Disk 1 contains the drivers for PostScript printers, LaserJets, and the IBMNULL driver. You may have to insert several of the Device Driver disks, click on **R**efresh each time, and scroll through the choices before you find the driver for your printer. Figure 12.11 shows the driver for the LaserJet III highlighted. Click on **I**nstall, and the driver is copied to the hard disk. A confirmation screen appears, like the one shown in figure 12.12.

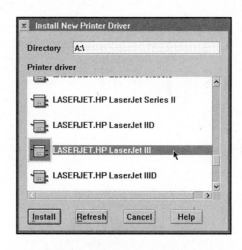

The window of driver choices returns. Click on Cancel, and you
return to the Printer Settings window (see fig. 12.13).

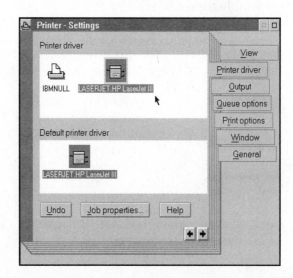

Click on the HP LaserJet III driver object, and it appears as the
default printer driver in the bottom part of the window. Close the
Printer Settings window; as figure 12.14 shows, the new printer
object appears on the desktop.

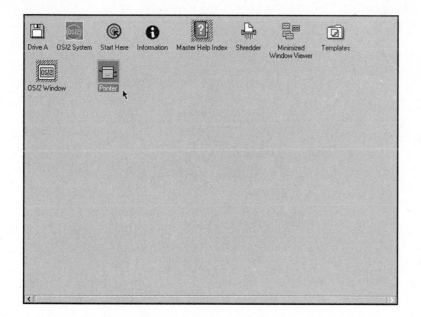

Figure 12.14:

Desktop with HP
LaserJet printer
object.

Deleting Printer Drivers

Earlier, you learned that major printer vendors release interim
updates of their OS/2 printer drivers, and that you may benefit
from installing those upgrades. It is, however, often a good idea to
first delete the old driver version before installing a new version,
rather than trying to install a new version on top of the old.

Before you can delete an existing printer driver, however, you must
have another driver installed and ready to take its place. Look back
at figure 12.9; in the pop-up menu for IBMNULL you notice that
there is no **D**elete option. This is because the print object contains
only one driver, and the print object must have at least one printer
driver. If you add another printer driver, the **D**elete option appears
on the pop-up menu.

It is a good idea to keep IBMNULL loaded as a printer driver. Your printer objects then have at least two printer drivers (the one corresponding to your printer, and IBMNULL), and so you can delete the old print driver for your printer before installing a new print driver for that printer.

Further, even if you have already installed a driver for a printer, the print driver installer (figures 12.10 and 12.11) does not show that driver to you. It is as if the driver did not exist on the Device Driver floppy disk. If you loaded the LaserJet series III driver, try running the print driver installer on the Device Driver 1 disk. You see a screen like figure 12.15.

Figure 12.15:

The printer driver installer without a LaserJet III driver.

Previously, the series III driver was located between the IID and IIID drivers, but now it is gone. The driver is still on the disk, but the print driver installer is designed not to show you the drivers that you already have on disk. To conclude, remember to do the following:

- Delete old drivers before installing new ones.

- Keep the IBMNULL printer driver in your print objects so that you can delete old drivers.

Modifying Queue Options

In general, you do not worry much about the queue manager. It is not printer-specific, so you do not need to change it when you change the printer driver. But the queue manager does feature a few options that are worth discussing.

Open your printer object's Settings notebook and you see a screen like the one in figure 12.7. Last time, you clicked on the <u>P</u>rinter driver tab. This time, click on <u>Q</u>ueue options, and you see a screen like the one shown in figure 12.16.

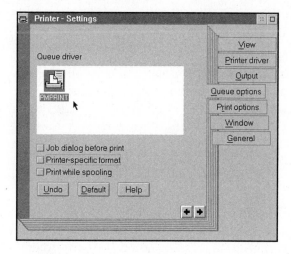

Figure 12.16:

The <u>Q</u>ueue options tab in the Printer Settings notebook.

The Job dialog before print Option

In the printer driver, you can set options that are specific to your printer. If, for example, you use a printer with dual paper trays, you can open up the printer driver options and direct subsequent print jobs to a particular paper tray. You also can set your laser printer to print in landscape mode.

What if you need to direct job output to particular trays or resolutions on a job-by-job basis? Check the Job dialog before print box. When you do, a pop-up window should appear between each print job, enabling you to change print options for each job. Suppose that you print documents that contain high-resolution graphics, which take a long time to print. Check this box so that you can temporarily set your laser's resolution down to 75 dots-per-inch. Your draft prints are not as crisp as the final results, but they print much more quickly. When you are ready to print final copies of your graphics, change the laser resolution back to a higher setting.

The Printer-specific format and Print while spooling Options

The process of printing from the program to the printer was briefly discussed earlier in this chapter. Figure 12.17 provides a more detailed look at this process.

As you saw before, OS/2 programs can call on OS/2 to draw figures, use fonts and font attributes, and generally support all the functions of a graphical user interface. The part of OS/2 that supports those functions is collectively called the *Graphical Programming Interface (GPI)*. Programs can make dozens of requests of the GPI, through commands that start with the prefix *GPI*. In the diagram in figure 12.17, the program is requesting that the GPI draw a circle on the paper. The command to draw a circle is GPIBOX. This command is printer-independent. The "printed" output is grabbed by the spooler, whose job is to collect the output in a file, which is then routed to the queue driver. That file is called *nnnnn*.SPL, in which *nnnnn* is a sequential number assigned by the spooler: 00001.SPL, 00002.SPL, and so on. This file contains the GPI commands.

Next, the file containing the output of the program is put in the queue for the particular printer that the program requested. The file is still in the printer-independent GPI command set.

Finally, when the spool file is at the head of its queue, the file and its set of GPI commands are read by the printer driver, which converts the GPI commands into printer-specific commands.

Look back at figure 12.16, and you see a check box labeled Printer-specific format. When you check that box, the whole sequence changes. You see the next sequence of events in figure 12.18.

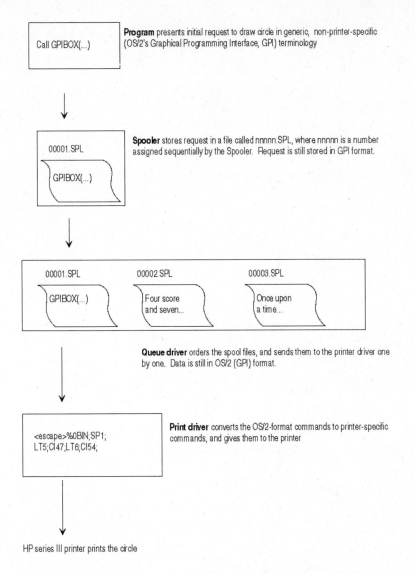

Figure 12.17:
The normal flow
of information
from program to
printer.

Call GPIBOX(...)

Program presents initial request to draw circle in generic, non-printer-specific (OS/2's Graphical Programming Interface, GPI) terminology

00001.SPL

GPIBOX(...)

Spooler stores request in a file called nnnnn.SPL, where nnnnn is a number assigned sequentially by the Spooler. Request is still stored in GPI format.

00001.SPL

GPIBOX(...)

00002.SPL

Four score and seven...

00003.SPL

Once upon a time...

Queue driver orders the spool files, and sends them to the printer driver one by one. Data is still in OS/2 (GPI) format.

<escape>%0BIN;SP1;
LT5;CI47;LT6;CI54;

Print driver converts the OS/2-format commands to printer-specific commands, and gives them to the printer

HP series III printer prints the circle

Figure 12.18:

The flow of information from program to printer.

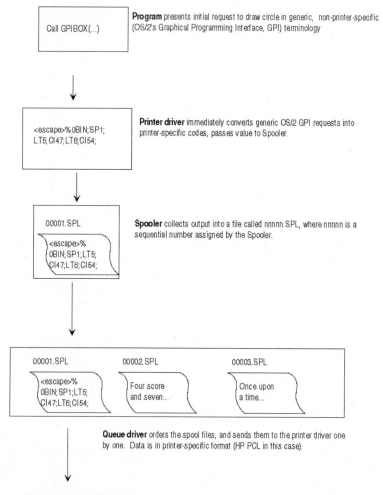

Call GPI BOX(...)	**Program** presents initial request to draw circle in generic, non-printer-specific (OS/2's Graphical Programming Interface, GPI) terminology
`<escape>%0BIN;SP1; LT5;CI47;LT6;CI54;`	**Printer driver** immediately converts generic OS/2 GPI requests into printer-specific codes, passes value to Spooler.
00001.SPL `<escape>% 0BIN;SP1;LT5; CI47;LT6;CI54;`	**Spooler** collects output into a file called nnnnn.SPL, where nnnnn is a sequential number assigned by the Spooler.

00001.SPL	00002.SPL	00003.SPL
`<escape>% 0BIN;SP1;LT5; CI47;LT6;CI54;`	Four score and seven...	Once upon a time...

Queue driver orders the spool files, and sends them to the printer driver one by one. Data is in printer-specific format (HP PCL in this case).

HP series III printer prints the circle

The print driver is immediately invoked and produces the specific code, which is spooled to a file, queued, and sent to the printer.

Why should you choose Printer-specific format? If you do, OS/2 can print faster in some cases. Or you may want to just take the SPL files and copy them directly to a printer on another machine. If, for instance, you have a computer without a printer attached to it, you can print from your program as you would normally, and your output ends up in the *nnnnn*.SPL files. If the files are in GPI format, there is not much you can do with them. If the files already are in a specific printer-driver format, however, you can copy those files to a floppy disk and place them in a machine that is attached to a printer. You then copy the files to the printer—you learned that this is possible in the last chapter—and get your printed output. Best of all, the machine with the printer does not even have to be running OS/2.

The last reason to choose Printer-specific format is that it enables you to choose Print while spooling. When you check this option, the spooler and queue manager become much less important, and you print your jobs in considerably less time.

OS/2 spools in order to handle multiple programs printing at the same time and to handle different jobs printing to different printers on different interfaces. Spooling is good for OS/2 in its role as a platform for building server products, but the typical user has only one printer and probably prints from only one application at a time. If this is your situation, the extra CPU time required by the spooler and queue manager considerably slows down printed output. You should, therefore, choose the Printer-specific format and Print while spooling options. Because the spooler/queue manager options are in the background, they stay out of the way and your printing should be faster.

Because the temporary spool files no longer contain GPI commands, they are bigger: Hewlett-Packard's HPPCL, for example, is a more verbose language than GPI. Make sure that you have 1M or 2M of free memory on your hard disk.

Controlling the Spooler

You do not have to do much with the spooler, but you should follow one piece of advice when you run the spooler. As you just learned, the printing process creates files on the disk, so the spooler needs disk space in which to create those files. If you open the

Spooler Settings notebook (the spooler is in the System Setup folder, which is accessed from the OS/2 System folder), you see a one-page notebook like the one shown in figure 12.19.

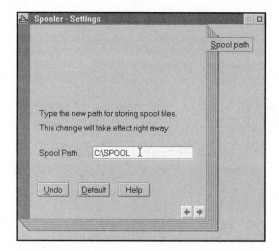

If you have a multiple-drive system (such as a large hard disk that has been partitioned into several logical disk drives), instruct the spooler to send its output to the disk drive with the most free space. This setting prevents OS/2 from terminating your program—which can happen if the program runs out of disk space on which to save spool files—and makes printing faster because the spooler does not search as hard to find the space that it needs for the SPL files.

If you need to, you can disable the spooler altogether; the printer driver is then the only software working with the program and the printer.

Printing without a Printer

Hard-copy output is important in the computer world, but it is not always possible to have a printer at hand. If you do a lot of work on a laptop, or if you share a printer, you cannot always wait for a printer before you can get down to work. OS/2's print-management system enables you to see what you are going to print before you print it.

First, right-click on the printer object, left-click on Change status, and click on <u>H</u>old, as shown in figure 12.20.

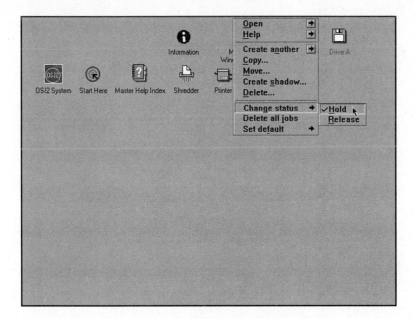

Now you can print to your heart's content, and the output goes to a file. Once you are connected to a printer, change the Change status back to <u>R</u>elease, and all the output is printed.

NOTE The spooler must be enabled for this procedure to work. If you have disabled the spooler, reenable it, or the Change status item does not appear on the printer object's pop-up menu.

Getting a Print Preview

You may be able to preview your print job by using the printer object.

Assume that you have just told the system to print a file called
BITMAP.BMP, and then pressed PrntScrn to get a "snapshot" of
how the system looks at a particular point in time. Because the print
jobs are held, nothing happens on the printer. Where are the two
print jobs? In the printer object. Open it to see the jobs, as you see in
figure 12.21.

Figure 12.21:

Printer object with
two print jobs.

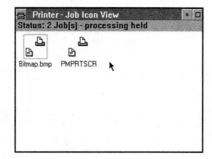

Each print job is an object in itself and has a pop-up menu. Right-
click the bit-map job and you see a pop-up menu, as shown in
figure 12.22.

Figure 12.22:

The pop-up menu
for a print job
object.

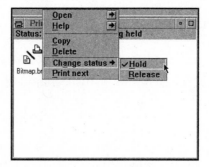

You see a Change status item, showing that you can release particular jobs. You also can see from the menu that you can delete this
print job or move it to the head of the print queue by choosing the
Print next option.

Finally, if you have forgotten what a particular job is, double-click on it. Although this technique does not always work, you can often see a "print preview" of what you have routed to the printer. Finally, you can eliminate all jobs from the print object's pop-up menu. Simply click on the <u>D</u>elete all jobs option, and all print jobs disappear.

Understanding and Controlling Multitasking

One of OS/2's big three benefits is multitasking. (The other two are access to extended memory and the graphical user interface.) Chapter 9 explores some of the ways that you can work better by using OS/2's multitasking capabilities. You can work even smarter when you understand how multitasking is actually accomplished. How, exactly, does OS/2 perform multiple tasks at the same time? After all, your PC contains only one main CPU; how can it multitask?

Many people think that OS/2 does not really multitask; rather it performs simple context switching. *Context switching* means loading several programs at once, but running only one at a time. In this way, for example, you might load 1-2-3 and dBASE. When you press a key to bring dBASE to the foreground, the CPU only executes the dBASE program. The 1-2-3 program, although loaded, does not run at all; a spreadsheet awaiting recalculation waits and waits. Then, once 1-2-3 is brought to the foreground, that spreadsheet starts getting CPU time and the recalculation commences. OS/2, however, does not perform this simple kind of multitasking; whether a program is in the user's view or not, it receives CPU time. A simple batch file proves this point.

Open an OS/2 full-screen session. The program object for OS/2 full screen is in the Command Prompts folder, which is in the OS/2 System folder.

Type the following four-line command file (call it ANNOY.CMD):

```
@echo off
:top
echo ^G
goto top
```

Do not forget that the "^G" is typed "Ctrl-G."

Start the program by typing **ANNOY**.

The program beeps continuously (hence the name). Put the program in the background by pressing Ctrl-Esc. The Workplace Shell screen returns, but the beeping continues. This is because OS/2 is a true multitasker. You can stop ANNOY by switching it into the foreground and pressing Ctrl-C or Ctrl-Break.

Levels of Multitasking

OS/2 is a true multitasking operating system; it has three levels of multitasking:

1. OS/2 divides your PC into multiple sessions or screen groups.

2. Each session contains one or more processes.

3. Each process is composed of one or more threads.

The following sections examine each of these levels of multitasking.

Sessions

Sessions or *screen groups* (the former term appeared in IBM OS/2 1.x literature, the latter in Microsoft OS/2 1.x documentation; both terms are used equally) are the top level of OS/2 multitasking. This is the level that you see most directly as a user. When you create an OS/2 full-screen session or start a program that does not work directly through the Workplace Shell—such as the OS/2 command-line commands or a DOS or Windows program—you cause OS/2 to spin off a separate session.

Sessions are like separate virtual PCs. Each session has control of a single entire screen, as well as a virtual keyboard, printer, and whatever other resources the PC owns, except for nonshareable things like the modem. You switch from session to session by pressing either Alt-Esc or Ctrl-Esc. Alt-Esc takes you round-robin from one session to the next, and Ctrl-Esc takes you to the Workplace Shell session and opens the Task List.

A simple demonstration reveals how separate the sessions are. Open two OS/2 full-screen sessions. While you are in one, set the screen to 50-line mode by using the command **mode co80,50**. In the other session, press Caps Lock. Notice that the Caps Lock LED is lit up on the keyboard. Now switch back to the first session and notice that the Caps Lock light goes out. OS/2 actually remembers the state of the keyboard for each session. Notice that the screen is still 50 lines, even though the other session is only a 25-line screen. Switch back to the Caps Lock session, and the Caps Lock light comes back on.

Once the system is powered up, OS/2 starts two sessions. The first is the Workplace Shell's session. The second is a session you never see—the "detach" session. OS/2 sends processes that you have detached to this session.

Processes

Most of the multitasking you have seen in this book has not been multisession work. There has been plenty of multitasking, but it is all taking place in the Workplace Shell. How does the WPS fit into this model of multitasking?

Remember that OS/2 sees multitasking as a three-level process. Sessions are only the top level. Moving down from the session level, OS/2 can multitask within a session. Each session has at least one program running in it, but there can be more. In OS/2 terms, actually, there are no programs—they are called *processes*. Basically, anything in a COM or EXE file is a process. But here is the interesting part: one process can run one or more other processes. As a matter of fact, all full-screen sessions use at least two processes: CMD.EXE and whatever program is running.

OS/2 starts up a copy of CMD.EXE with every full-screen session. You learned in Chapter 11 that CMD.EXE interprets and executes your commands. You also learned that CMD loads a file into memory and instructs OS/2 to execute the instructions in the file. Technically, what is happening is that CMD.EXE spawns a process. Whenever one program starts another program running, it is said to have *spawned* that program. (Spawn is a term borrowed from UNIX.)

Actually, process spawning has been going on in PCs since the early 1980s because the COMMAND.COM command interpreter under DOS spawned DOS programs when executing user commands. What OS/2 brings that is new and different is the idea of *asynchronous spawning*. Ordinarily, after the command interpreter loads and starts up a process, the command interpreter remains in memory but does not receive any CPU time. This is called *synchronous spawning* in OS/2 terminology, and it makes perfect sense when discussing the command interpreter example: the command interpreter is said to be the *parent process*, and the program that it starts up is called the *child process*. What about a case in which one program may want to spawn another and still remain active? Examples of this situation might include the following:

- A printing program that is part of a word processor

- A file-format conversion program, such as one you would use to convert a file from one graphics format to another

- An editing program, such as one that has always been incorporated in dBASE and is used to edit programs before dBASE executes it

- A program that monitors disk activity, user input, or anything that must be viewed "from the outside"

Threads

The newest and most foreign of the OS/2 multitasking terms is the notion of *threads*. The threads concept brings the capability of multitasking from the operating system down to the application.

A thread of execution is a particular sequence of instructions within a program: "Do A, then do B four times, then see if any work is left; if so, do C until you are finished." Developing a flow of execution is the central part of designing a program, and creating an efficient flow of execution is much harder than actually writing the program. Programmers develop programs by first laying out a sequence of operations to get a job done, and then converting that sequence of operations into a particular computer language. The sequence of operations for a particular program is called that program's *algorithm*. To illustrate, the following sequence of operations finds the square root of a number:

1. Call the number that you want to find the square root of N. Use two variables, named X and Y, to develop ever-improving guesses of the square root that you want.

2. Set X so that it is equal to N/2. This is the initial guess for N's square root.

3. Compute Y = N/X.

4. If Y is very close to X, then X times X equals N, which means that X is the square root. Otherwise, keep going.

5. Compute a new X that is halfway between X and Y. The new X equals (the old X + Y) / 2.

6. Go back to step 3.

To see how this thread of execution works, compute for the square root of 8. Set N=8. Then, as step 2 dictates, set X=8/2=4. Step 3 says to compute Y=N/X=8/4=2. Step 4 says to compare X and Y to see if they are close in value, and 2 and 4 are fairly far apart. For example, suppose that "close" is defined as "being within 0.1 of each other in value." The new X is halfway between the old X and Y. Halfway between 4 and 2 is 3, the new value of X. Back to step 3, Y=8/3, which is approximately 2.67—hold this to two decimal places to keep it from becoming too messy. Step 4 compares the values (3 and 2.67) again, and finds them too far apart. Step 5 computes the new value for X as halfway between the current X value of 3 and the current Y value of 2.67, which is 2.83. Back up to step 3, the new Y value equals 8/2.83, or 2.83. X is now within 0.1 of Y; you are done.

Although the preceding algorithm may look a bit complex, notice that, at any point in time, the CPU was doing only one thing at a time. This little sequence is much the same as some of the most complex computer programs in existence—they may be big and ugly, but they do only one thing at a time. And therein lies their problem in a GUI environment.

GUI programs currently offer so much, and they are so interactive that waiting for something to finish now becomes much more onerous than it was in the old command-line environment. At this moment, for example, the author is writing text with a word processor that offers the usual pull-down menus and a tool bar that enables easy access to dozens of fonts, features, and files. Yet, when the spell checker is active, the hourglass appears on the screen, and nothing else can be done. This is annoying when you realize that the base operating system, OS/2, can multitask if permitted. But within the word processor, any single subtask—such as repagination, the spell checker, the thesaurus, or a search-and-replace—gets the full benefit of whatever time OS/2 gives to the word processor. Although the operating system understands multitasking, the application does not. That is because the program is single-threaded: it is designed to do only one thing at a time.

Under OS/2, there is no reason for a program to follow one thread of execution. OS/2 is by its nature multithreaded, enabling many algorithms to exist simultaneously within the fabric of a single program. The trouble is, most OS/2 programmers do not understand multithreading. Newer languages, such as Modula-2, Ada, and Smalltalk support multithreading, but there are not nearly as many programmers adept in those languages as there are that work in the more traditional languages.

Examples of single-threadedness are easy to spot. If you cannot keep editing while a search-and-replace is happening, you are experiencing single-threaded architecture. You should not have to wait while saving or printing a file. Many applications display the hourglass when repaginating, such as when you change the font that a document will be printed in. Other programs freeze temporarily when you resize the window they are working in. None of these situations is acceptable in the OS/2 framework. Consider backups, too: most backup programs stop at problem files and wait for advice before going further. It would be more expedient if they would back up the files that do not offer any trouble, and then present you with a list of the problem files, enabling you to direct the program to either cancel backups for the files that do not copy, to retry, or whatever.

When you are buying OS/2 software, observe how the software multitasks; make your motto "Stamp out hourglasses in our time."

Figure 12.23 summarizes what you have learned about the levels of OS/2 multitasking.

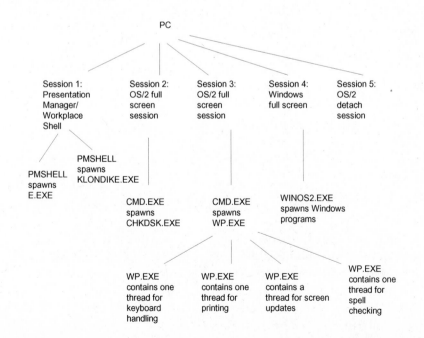

Figure 12.23:

An example of OS/2 multitasking.

Figure 12.23 shows a single PC divided into multiple sessions. The first session is the Workplace Shell, which has spawned two processes: the System Editor and Klondike Solitaire. Both the System Editor and the Klondike game are single-threaded, so you do not see separate threads diagrammed under them. Next is an OS/2 full-screen command prompt session running CHKDSK (CHKDSK is single-threaded). After that, another full-screen session shows a hypothetical word processor called WP.EXE. WP is threaded; one thread collects and executes keyboard commands, another thread prints, another thread handles the screen, and a fourth thread runs the spell checker in the background. The next session is the OS/2 Windows full-screen session. The last session is the one that detached programs go into.

All programs are, to OS/2's eyes, merely threads of execution. The maximum number of active simultaneous threads is determined by the THREADS= parameter in CONFIG.SYS. The maximum allowable value is 4095. Imagine a normal PC performing more than four thousand tasks simultaneously. The default is 64 if no THREADS command exists in CONFIG.SYS, and most users probably do not need to change that setting.

How OS/2 Divides CPU Time

Because there is only one CPU in most PCs, OS/2 must make it look like there are many CPUs in your PC. OS/2 accomplishes this by the following:

- Timesliced multitasking
- Event-driven multitasking

You can fine-tune the timeslicing method with a few CONFIG.SYS commands; OS/2 handles the event-driven function. There is a rich amount of control that a good OS/2 programmer can take advantage of to help OS/2 multitask well. Even if you are not a programmer, the following discussion enables you to see why some programs run better than others.

Round-Robin Multitasking

In its simplest form, timeslicing works by alternately giving small amounts of time—called *timeslices*—to applications. Suppose you are running three programs: a word processor called WP, a database called DB, and a spreadsheet called SS. WP is in the foreground, meaning that it is the program that you are currently using. DB is in the background, sorting a database file. SS also is in the background, recalculating a large spreadsheet.

Suppose the timeslice is one second long. For the first second, the CPU gives its undivided attention to WP, the word processing program. In that second, DB and SS receive no CPU time. In that first second, the word processor is responsive because it grabs your keystrokes and handles them immediately.

In the second second, DB gets the CPU's attention. It works at sorting the database for that second. In that second, you do not see any response from WP: your keystrokes are accepted and stored by OS/2, but you do not see the result of those keystrokes on the screen. SS does not get any CPU time.

The third second goes to SS. DB's sorting gets put on hold, and your word processing keystrokes are stored, but unused for the moment.

In the fourth second, control goes back to WP. Your earlier, saved-up keystrokes are put on the screen, producing an effect that looks as if the keystrokes are "squirted" onto the screen. The fifth second goes to DB, and the sixth to SS, and so on.

If this were actually the way OS/2 operated, you would soon stop using it because it would "feel" terrible. With the timeslice set to one second, you would experience one second of responsiveness separated by two seconds of inactivity. Your input would seem to "squirt" onto the screen at semiregular intervals. If you think that two seconds is not a long time to wait, consider that even a slow typist produces about four characters per second. This means that you would see at least eight characters per squirt, and that you would wait longer than you can type, reducing your productivity.

Instead, the operating system can use a smaller timeslice, one-millionth of a second, for example. That way, WP gets OS/2's full attention for one-millionth of a second, then DB for a millionth, SS for a millionth, and back to WP, all within three-millionths of a second. You never notice that OS/2 has neglected you.

You also may notice that OS/2 is painfully slow because the operating system takes time to switch from one task to another. That time is a fixed amount, totally independent of the length of the timeslice. Consider what happens with one cycle of WP-DB-SS:

1. Do one timeslice's work with WP.

2. Save the system state: copy the contents of the CPU's registers, the stack, and other important information somewhere in memory.

3. Find the location in memory where the registers from the previous DB timeslice are located, and reload them in the CPU.

4. Do one timeslice's work with DB.

5. Save the system state for the next DB timeslice.

6. Locate and load the system state for the SS program.

7. Do one timeslice's work with SS.

8. Save the system state for the next SS timeslice.

9. Locate and load the system state for the WP program.

10. Go back to step 1.

Six of the steps involve shuffling the information that the CPU needs to pick up where it left off on a task. You probably do something like this every day when you come to work. You enter your office, open up your "work-in-progress" folder and remind yourself what you were doing yesterday. That "switching time" takes a little of your workday, and it takes basically the same amount of time, whether you are at work for one hour or eight hours.

To exaggerate the situation for clarity's sake, imagine that the system takes one-tenth of a second to reload a program's state information. (The actual time is unknown, but it is a lot less than one-tenth of a second; it is more on the order of sub-milliseconds. The faster your computer is, the less time it takes to switch.) Set the timeslice to one second, and the system spends about one-tenth of its time switching from one task to another. Set the timeslice to one-tenth of a second, and it spends equal time switching and working. Set the timeslice to one-hundredth of a second, and it spends ten times as much time switching as it does working. This is like a person taking seven hours to reacquaint himself with his work each day, leaving only one hour for productive work.

An optimum timeslice exists for each system. This optimum timeslice is a compromise between a timeslice that is too large (which causes the system to appear choppy) and one that is too small (which causes the system to appear too slow).

You can experiment with timeslices by using the CONFIG.SYS parameter TIMESLICE. Just specify a numeric value, as in TIMESLICE=50. This number represents the length of the timeslice in milliseconds. Experiment with timeslices by running one or more programs at the same time under different timeslices and note which timeslice works best.

Prioritized Multitasking

OS/2 has a timeslicing system that is much more powerful. In addition to simple round-robin timeslicing, OS/2 overlays a system of priorities. This system includes a two-story hierarchy of priorities called *classes* and *deltas*. There are three classes, and they supercede deltas. OS/2 uses the following classes:

Class	Meaning
3	Urgent priority; break into normal operation to run
2	Normal priority
1	Low priority; run when nothing else is running

The dispatching algorithm here is simple: If there are any programs running with class-3 priority, share all the CPU time with those programs, giving none to the 2s and 1s. If there are no 3s, give all the CPU time to the 2s, ignoring the 1s. If there are no 3s or 2s, give all the CPU time to the 1s. Deltas provide a "fine-scaling factor" within classes, as you will see later.

Event-Driven Multitasking

If this system seems simplistic, it becomes powerful when linked with OS/2's next great strength—I/O-driven or event-driven multitasking. The insight of event-driven multitasking is that most GUI programs are highly interactive, and interactive programs spend most of their time waiting for I/O. For instance, word processing programs spend most of their time waiting for keystrokes, for the printer to finish printing, or for the operating system to retrieve a file or to save a file. In general, the slower the device that a program is waiting for, the higher priority it should be given. Here is an example. Suppose that you are running the three programs that you saw before—WP, DB, and SS. Also, suppose that you assign priorities as follows:

Program	Priority
WP	High-priority class 3
DB	Normal-priority class 2
SS	Low-priority class 1

Under the simple prioritized scheme, OS/2 gives all of the timeslices to the only class-3 program in the system, the WP program. The OS/2 scheduler program is blind to the class-2 and class-1 programs as long as there is an active class-3 program in the system. But OS/2's event-driven nature makes it notice that WP is just waiting for a keystroke. There is no point in wasting CPU time allowing WP to wait for a keystroke. Knowing that WP waits for an outside I/O event, OS/2 puts WP in a blocked state. The scheduler then no longer sees WP, leaving a class-2 program (DB) and a class-1 program (SS). The scheduler gives all the time to DB, which was sorting a file. But file sorting gets done a little at a time while the system alternately reads and writes pieces of the file that it is sorting. Consequently, DB also is soon waiting for the disk to finish reading or writing some data. Again, there is no sense in wasting CPU time waiting for the disk to read or write data, so DB gets blocked. This leaves the field to SS, a lowly class-1 program. It recalculates away, receiving all the timeslices until an I/O event occurs, either for WP (such as a keystroke) or for DB (such as the completion of a disk operation).

Event-driven multitasking is a remarkable approach to multi-tasking. Not a single CPU cycle is wasted. Consider how much CPU time has been wasted under DOS waiting for disk and print operations to get finished, and you have an inkling of how powerful OS/2's multitasking system can be. In the preceding example, the spreadsheet recalculates only when nothing else can be done, squeezing CPU power seemingly from out of the ether.

OS/2 further refines its priorities, however, through the deltas. This second layer of the priority system consists of 63 subclasses, "tie breakers," when the system finds multiple programs of equal class. The deltas range from –31 to +31. A program with a priority class of 2 and a delta of +1 gets all of the CPU time, to the exclusion of another program with a priority class of 2 and a delta of 0. Again, if the classes are different, the deltas are irrelevant. Deltas affect system performance only if there are a number of active, nonblocked programs with the same class. If there are several active, nonblocked programs with the same class and level, OS/2 does round-robin scheduling among those programs.

One flaw exists in this system, however: you cannot set the priorities. A well-designed OS/2 program enables you to alter the program's priority, but few programs do. Instead, most OS/2 programs rely on a CONFIG.SYS option called PRIORITY that enables OS/2 to set and reset priorities on a dynamic basis.

PRIORITY can take the value DYNAMIC or ABSOLUTE. The default is DYNAMIC. ABSOLUTE works as you have read so far, making priority decisions on the basis of program-set priorities. DYNAMIC works the same way, in that class distinctions cannot be bridged. No matter what, a class-3 program that is not blocked always steals from a class-2 program, but DYNAMIC adjusts the deltas dynamically. PRIORITY=DYNAMIC boosts the priority of a process if it is the foreground process or if it is doing a great deal of I/O. PRIORITY=DYNAMIC is assisted by one more CONFIG.SYS parameter, MAXWAIT.

OS/2 has a "watchdog program" that runs now and then, checking to see if any program has not gotten any CPU attention in a while. If the watchdog finds a program that has not gotten any CPU time since the last time the watchdog checked, OS/2 boosts the program's priority. The watchdog program runs every n seconds: the n variable is set by the MAXWAIT parameter. If your CONFIG.SYS specifies MAXWAIT=5, then the program runs every five seconds. You must use whole numbers, not fractions or decimals.

If the other program is a class-1 program, and class-2 programs are active, MAXWAIT's priority boost does not help the class-1 program at all. If there are two programs running that are both of the same class, but with different deltas, the program with the lower delta gets no CPU time. Every time the watchdog program runs and sees a CPU-starved program, it boosts that program's priority by one delta. Eventually, the program gets enough priority boosts to receive a timeslice. After that happens, the program returns to its original priority.

Consider, for example, the case of program A, with class 2 and delta 0, and program B, with class 2 and delta 3. Set MAXWAIT to one second, and here is what happens:

1. After one second, program A is apparently CPU-starved, and it is reprioritized to class 2, delta 1.

2. Program A still remains CPU-starved. After another second, it gets another boost, raising its priority to class 2, delta 2.

3. Program B still holds higher priority, and so it gets all of the timeslices in the next second. Program A is raised to class 2, delta 3.

4. Program A finally receives a timeslice, and is reduced in priority to its initial value, class 2 delta 0.

5. After one second, A has gone without any time, and is increased to class 2 delta 1.

The process continues like this: A creeps up for a while, receives a timeslice, and falls back to its initial position.

Consider what you accomplish by adjusting MAXWAIT: change it from 1 second to 10 seconds, and A gets only one-tenth of the CPU time that it got with the larger timeslice.

You have seen that you can adjust and fine-tune OS/2's multitasking process with several CONFIG.SYS parameters:

- THREADS sets the maximum number of simultaneous threads that the system handles.

- TIMESLICE sets the size, in milliseconds, of the unit used to dole out CPU time.

- PRIORITY sets the algorithm used by OS/2 to dynamically adjust process priorities.

- MAXWAIT, which is only relevant when PRIORITY=DYNAMIC, tells OS/2 how often to check for CPU-starved processes.

Experimenting with OS/2 Multitasking

The previous discussion seems a bit theoretical. To see the effects of these parameters, enter a REXX program that just counts numbers. The program (call it CNT1.CMD) looks like this:

```
/* REXX program */
if arg()=0
then countto=10000
else do
  arg x
  parse var x countto
end
a=time('r')
  line=1
do countto
  line=line+1
  say "Now at line " line
end
b=time('e')
tottime=b-a
periter=tottime/countto
say "Time required=" tottime "; time per iteration="
periter
```

Do not worry if you do not understand this program; you do not have to understand it to run it. Just be sure to type it as you see it (use the System Editor or equivalent), and call it CNT1.CMD.

Invoke this program with its name and a number—the number that you would like the program to count to. If you type **cnt1 1000**, for example, the program counts up to 1000. When the program is done, it reports how long it took in total, and how long it took per number counted (per "iteration"). Try it with cnt1 1000, and you see a screen that resembles figure 12.24.

To examine multitasking, open two OS/2 command windows and size them so they are side by side, as illustrated in figure 12.25.

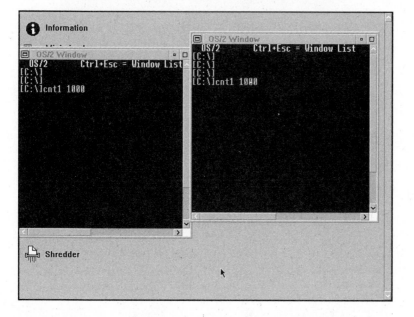

In the figure, you see that both commands have already been
typed—that is, the CNT1 1000 is in both windows, but Enter has not
been pressed in either window. Start the test by pressing Enter in
the first window, then quickly click on the other window and press
Enter. That starts up both programs. The result is a screen that looks
like figure 12.26.

Figure 12.26:
The result of the
speed test with
two windows.

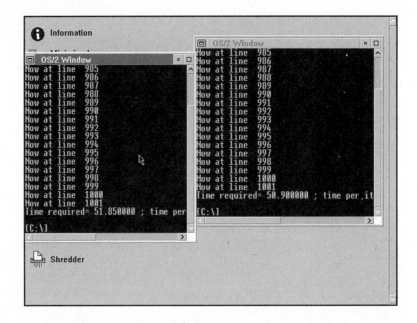

In the figure, you see that each program took about the same time,
around 50 seconds. What you cannot see is that both programs
shared the CPU fairly well: window 1 ran for about 100 lines, then
switched to window 2 for 100 lines, and back to window 1. Try
doing tests and changing the values of MAXWAIT, TIMESLICE,
and PRIORITY. Table 12.1 summarizes the results of some experiments on a 20 MHz 386SX. In this first set of experiments, neither
window has the focus. In table 12.2, the second program gets the
focus.

Table 12.1
Results of Some Multitasking Trials
(Neither Window Has the Focus)

Priority	Timeslice	Time for 1	Time for 2	Sharing?
Dynamic	Default	49.6	43.8	Well-mixed
Dynamic	32	45.0	48.5	Well-mixed
Dynamic	2000	49.6	33.8	Choppy; 1 almost finished before 2 started

Priority	Timeslice	Time for 1	Time for 2	Sharing?
Absolute	Default	41.9	49.5	Well-mixed
Absolute	32	36.0	44.7	Well-mixed
Absolute	2000	46.5	46.6	Choppy; program 2 getting the focus

Table 12.2
Results of Some Multitasking Trials
(Program 2 Has the Focus)

Priority	Timeslice	Time for 1	Time for 2	Sharing?
Dynamic	Default	44	24.9	Choppy; program 2 got all the time
Dynamic	32	43.1	24.9	Same
Dynamic	2000	49.1	35.5	Choppy, but better than 32

In the first set of dynamic and absolute experiments, the mouse was immediately clicked on the desktop background, so that neither OS/2 window had the focus. That is important because, as you have learned, OS/2 gives higher priority to the application in the foreground. Notice that the distribution of CPU time is scattered when neither program is in the foreground.

In table 12.2, the second program remains in the foreground, enjoys a remarkable increase in CPU priority, and ends up finishing its task much more quickly. A higher timeslice gives MAXWAIT more time to make its presence felt, so the distribution of CPU time is a bit more equitable when the timeslice is 2000. Experiment with other values for MAXWAIT and TIMESLICE, and you see dramatic differences in system performance.

Managing Memory under OS/2

Chapter 6 described the kinds of nightmares the 640K limit imposes on DOS—nightmares that led to the intricacies of memory management. OS/2's direct use of the 386 architecture's 4G workspace has spared us most of that, but there are still a few loose ends to tie up. OS/2 deals with the following two primary memory-management issues:

- Whether to allow memory defragmentation

- Whether to allow OS/2 virtual memory

Because OS/2 loads and unloads programs many times per day, the system can develop the problem of *memory fragmentation*. Suppose that you have loaded six programs into the system; call them A, B, C, D, E, and F, as you see in figure 12.27.

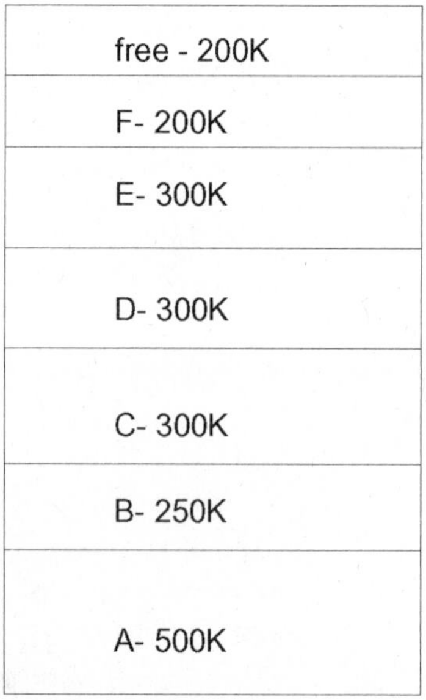

Figure 12.27:

Memory status after loading six programs in OS/2.

free - 200K
F- 200K
E- 300K
D- 300K
C- 300K
B- 250K
A- 500K

Now suppose that you exit from programs A, C, and E. The situation in figure 12.28 results.

This results in a less-than-desirable arrangement because you may not want a bunch of small empty spaces. If you want to load a large program, you need a single big space. That is what memory defragmentation is all about. After defragmentation, the memory looks like figure 12.29.

OS/2 defragments memory on an as-needed basis if you enable it to; this feature is controlled by part of the CONFIG.SYS command, MEMMAN. Your CONFIG.SYS may contain a line like this:

```
MEMMAN=SWAP,MOVE
```

MOVE (the default) empowers OS/2 to defragment memory. The alternative is NOMOVE, which disallows defragmentation. Why even consider specifying NOMOVE? The whole defragmentation process is a little tricky. Consider what is happening here: the system is moving memory blocks while the programs are using them. This is like tuning a car while it is traveling down the highway at 60 miles per hour. The task is possible, but it is fraught with risk. If a block of memory is moved at the wrong time, the system can crash.

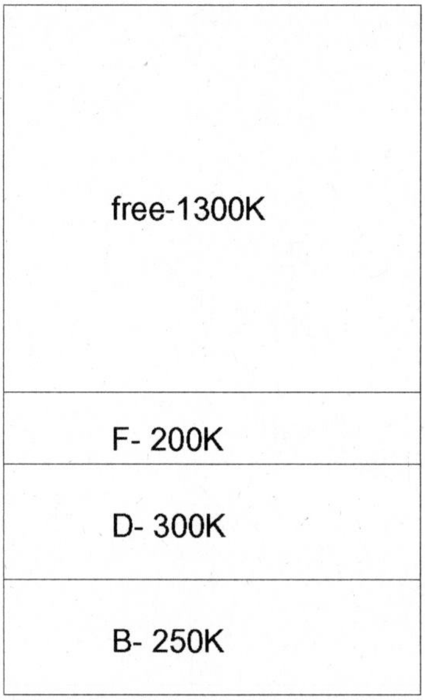

Figure 12.29:
Memory after
defragmentation.

```
┌─────────────────────┐
│                     │
│                     │
│                     │
│                     │
│     free-1300K      │
│                     │
│                     │
│                     │
├─────────────────────┤
│      F- 200K        │
├─────────────────────┤
│      D- 300K        │
│                     │
├─────────────────────┤
│                     │
│      B- 250K        │
│                     │
└─────────────────────┘
```

Further, defragmentation occurs at essentially random times; this means that the system might periodically slow down for no reason at all. If you have some process running that is very time-critical, the variation in run-time imposed by the background defragmentation process can be unacceptable. In this case, you can disable defragmentation by specifying NOMOVE.

The other option, SWAP, controls OS/2's use of virtual memory. *Virtual memory* means that when OS/2 runs out of RAM, it can utilize disk space as if it were RAM. As you saw in Chapter 1, this memory-enhancement technique is good because disk space is cheaper than RAM space, byte-per-byte; but it is also bad because disk space is much slower to read from and write to. If you are running OS/2 on a machine with heavily constrained RAM, however, you have few alternatives: running your programs on slow disk drives rather than fast RAM is better than not running the programs at all.

Here is how virtual memory works. Assume that you have several programs loaded into memory, including a word processor, a spreadsheet, communications programs, and several utilities. You have only about 512K of RAM left, and you try to load a graphics program that requires one megabyte of memory. To make space for that program, OS/2 looks at the currently loaded programs and asks, "Which program has not done anything recently?" Just because a program is loaded, after all, that does not mean that it is doing anything. For example, you may have loaded the communications program first thing in the morning to check your electronic mail, and then not used it since. OS/2 zips it off to disk, freeing memory for the graphics program. Remember that OS/2 is not unloading the program. The communications program icon is still shaded, and if you double-click on it, the window for the communications program opens up, and you see that you are wherever you left off. OS/2 moves data to and from the hard disk for you.

Virtual memory is controlled by the SWAP or NOSWAP parameter in the MEMMAN command. Use SWAP, and virtual memory is enabled. Use NOSWAP, and OS/2 is not allowed to employ virtual memory.

You can see virtual memory in action if you load several large programs onto OS/2. Suppose you had a word processor loaded with a very large word processing document and a spreadsheet program loaded with a very large spreadsheet (so large that it would be impossible to load both into RAM simultaneously). Assuming that you have allowed OS/2 to use virtual memory with MEMMAN=SWAP, you see some disk activity every time you switch the focus from the spreadsheet to the word processor or vice versa. That is because OS/2 recognizes that both applications are getting a lot of use, but since there is not enough room for both of them, OS/2 must constantly swap data to and from disk. In extreme situations like this, OS/2 spends virtually all of its time swapping, slowing system performance to a crawl. Programmers call such a situation *thrashing*.

MEMMAN is, then, a two-part command. It both controls memory defragmentation and virtual memory. Use it like so:

```
MEMMAN=virtual memory,memory defrag
```

The variable *virtual memory* is either SWAP or NOSWAP, and the variable *memory defrag* is either MOVE or NOMOVE.

Once you have decided that it is okay for OS/2 to use virtual memory, where should the swapped data go? You control that with another CONFIG.SYS command, SWAPPATH. Like MEMMAN, SWAPPATH does two things in one line.

First, SWAPPATH controls where the swap files are kept. You can specify a drive and path name, as in

```
SWAPPATH=D:\SWAPSTUF
```

The preceding example puts all of the swapped memory contents in a file (called SWAPPER.DAT) in a subdirectory called \SWAPSTUF on drive D.

TIP   To get the best performance from SWAPPATH, place the SWAPPER on the least-used disk, and in the most-used partition on that disk. Many people make a separate partition for their swapper on a well-used disk, which does not help. It may, in fact, hinder performance. Do not use a network drive for swapping. If you do, it slows down the entire network.

SWAPPATH also takes an extra, numeric parameter. This extra parameter tells OS/2 how much space to leave free on the disk when swapping. A SWAPPATH statement, for example, might look like the following:

```
SWAPPATH=D:\SWAPSTUF 1024
```

This statement tells OS/2 to put the swapping file SWAPFILE.DAT on the drive D and the \SWAPSTUF subdirectory. It also says that if there is a lot of swapping going on, SWAPFILE.DAT will grow. This swap file can grow so much that there is no space left on the D: drive, except for the 1024 "free space" parameter. 1024 means "SWAPFILE can grow, but not so much that there is not at least 1024K of free space on drive D."

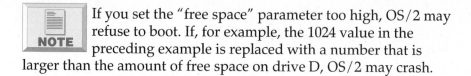 If you set the "free space" parameter too high, OS/2 may refuse to boot. If, for example, the 1024 value in the preceding example is replaced with a number that is larger than the amount of free space on drive D, OS/2 may crash.

If OS/2 refuses to load, boot from a floppy disk, as explained in Chapter 11, and then check the "free space" parameter on the SWAPPATH statement. If that number is larger than the amount of free space on the drive pointed to by SWAPPATH, then you have found the culprit. Lower the "free space" number below the amount of current free space, reboot, and all will be well.

Using Video under OS/2

One feature that makes the Workplace Shell really stand out is the way it interacts with your screen. OS/2 has come a long way from the days of OS/2 1.1. Windows 3, for example, lets you choose a default color scheme from a wide array of color combinations like "Autumn," "Spring," and "Winter." Earlier versions of OS/2 offered only a default color scheme, which was best called "less than beautiful."

OS/2 was clearly designed with the VGA in mind—but with the VGA as the base-level machine. The VGA has a wonderful color potential. Even though VGA is capable of over a quarter of a million colors, it can only display 16 of those at any time, and generally they are the defaults of white, bright white, gray, black, and the light and dark versions of blue, green, red, yellow, purple, and cyan.

Newer VGAs—the so-called Super VGAs (SVGAs)—offer greater numbers of colors. Many SVGAs can display 256 colors simultaneously, again chosen from 262,144 different possibilities. Standard VGA also is characterized by a particular screen resolution—that is, a particular number of dots (or pixels) visible on the screen. Standard VGA displays 640 pixels across the screen and 480 pixels down the screen. How good is that? Compare it to graphics capabilities of previous and succeeding graphics adapters (see table 12.3).

Table 12.3
Graphics Board Capabilities

Adapter	Resolution	Total Pixels	Max Colors
CGA	640×200	130K	2
EGA	640×350	210K	16
VGA	640×480	307K	16
Super VGA	1024×768	780K	256
XGA	1024×768	780K	256

Older adapters, like CGA, are limited in their display capabilities. But the super VGA adapters available today are remarkable in their capabilities; for example, many 486 clones today are shipped with Orchid Designer IIs, a super VGA board that can support resolutions of up to 1024×768 and up to 32,000 colors. If you use such an adapter with OS/2, you can use the full power of that adapter—provided that you have the proper driver software. The same is true for IBM's high-resolution XGA adaper.

Look at the "Total Pixels" column, and you understand a real problem with the newer video boards. When running in CGA mode, OS/2 must only recompute and update 128,000 pixels. That same copy of OS/2, when running with a VGA, must recompute and update 307,200 pixels—about two and a half times as many pixels to handle. This increased amount of pixel handling slows down OS/2's response time noticeably, and handling the almost 800,000 pixels of the super VGA or XGA causes windows to appear to roll up and down, rather than to simply open and close. The processor now is incredibly burdened.

Choosing Video Mode

If you have VGA, you do not have much choice about what video mode to use for OS/2—you either run in 640×480×16 color mode or in 640×480 monochrome mode. What if you have an SVGA system?

Consider a typical mid-range performance SVGA board, the Orchid ProDesigner II. It has options for three resolutions: 640×480, 800×600, or 1024×768. Each of those resolutions also is available in a 16- or 256-color mode, except 1024×768×16. (This mode requires that you run the highest resolution with 256 colors.) You choose the video mode by changing video drivers, and the drivers are not shipped with OS/2: you get them from Orchid or you can find them on CompuServe. The Orchid VGA board is, like other VGA boards, built around the Tseng Labs' ET4000 chip, so any ET4000 drivers work fine for the Orchid. Table 12.4 shows the results of a quick-and-dirty video benchmark test when run in different resolutions and numbers of colors. The times are "time to complete bench-mark," and they are in milliseconds. Larger numbers mean slower performance.

Table 12.4
Graphical Benchmark Results

Resolution	Colors	Speed
640×480	16	48.76
640×480	256	132.31
800×600	16	66.43
800×600	256	217.28
1024×768	16	91.18
1024×768	256	308.52

As you might expect, higher resolutions lead to slower perfor-mances. But, as table 12.4 demonstrates, the effect of going to 256 colors dwarfs the effect of higher resolutions.

The moral of the story is that if you can avoid the 256 color drivers, avoid them. They slow down graphics by a factor of about three. Use them only when running the infrequent OS/2 application that can benefit from a full 256 colors—most OS/2 applications do not use more than 16 colors.

What about higher resolutions? Higher resolutions also slow down the system, but the slowdown may be an acceptably small one, and there is a very important reason for using higher resolutions. At 640×480, you see only the top three-fifths of a page on a word-processor screen. At 1024×768, you see the entire page; that is important when it comes to productivity. Imagine the improvement in Excel when you can see a much larger spreadsheet.

Speeding Up Video

How do you solve this problem: I'd-like-better-resolution-but-I-need-speed? Two ways: video coprocessors and faster drivers.

The speed of OS/2 is largely dependent on the quality of its video drivers. A fast video board, coupled with inefficient video drivers, equals a sluggish and unresponsive screen. Although no one has done it yet, someone will no doubt re-engineer the OS/2 video drivers to add some spark to a VGA's performance. For years, there has been such a market for alternative drivers for AutoCAD, Windows, 1-2-3, and similar packages; so it is reasonable to believe that we will see them for OS/2 soon. In the meantime, however, try loading the OS/2 driver for monochrome VGA. It supports as many pixels as normal VGA, but supports only two colors, meaning less color information to have to manipulate.

In the future, more and more applications will use both 256 colors and higher resolutions. What's the answer? Video coprocessors.

You may already know about the sockets for math coprocessors, which are found on the motherboards of most PC compatibles. A *math coprocessor* is a special-purpose CPU, that is designed only to do floating-point math, but to do it much more quickly than a general purpose CPU like your 80386. In fact, the coprocessor for the 80386—a chip called the 80387—can compute sines, cosines, and logarithms twenty times faster than the 80386.

Video coprocessors are another kind of special-purpose CPU. As you might expect, they are designed to move pixels around quickly. Your math coprocessor is a single chip; video coprocessors take up entire circuit boards.

Inside a Video Coprocessor

A video coprocessor board generally consists of the following basic parts:

- Video CPU

- Special high-speed "video" RAM (VRAM)

- On-board programs in a Read-Only Memory (ROM) area

- Feature connector to your VGA

Most video coprocessors cannot stand alone in your system; they act as a "helper" to your VGA board. Notice the edge connector on the top of your VGA board. It is called the *VGA feature connector*, and it is intended to be connected with a ribbon cable to a video coprocessor board. The CPU is generally either a Texas Instruments TI34010 or TI34020 CPU. VRAM is required on most coprocessor boards, and it is, as you might expect, expensive.

The biggest change in the way your system works after installing a video coprocessor is how it manipulates the screen. Previously, it handled the screen pixel by pixel. If a program needed to, draw a circle, the system would have to do the following things:

1. Compute the locations of every dot on the circle, an operation that requires computing of sines and cosines.

2. Check that the video hardware is ready to be modified.

3. Change each pixel so that the circle appears on the screen.

With a video coprocessor, however, the system says, "Coprocessor board, draw a circle at such-and-such location, such-and-such size, and such-and-such color," and the video coprocessor handles it. It handles it quickly: the on-board CPU on some coprocessor boards runs at 60 MHz or faster.

IBM's Coprocessors: PGA, 8514, and XGA

You might wonder why IBM has not come out with a video coprocessor. It turns out that they have, three times in the past. The first two video coprocessors, however, had problems; the third one was introduced in February 1991.

In 1984, IBM offered a slew of new products, including the EGA—which is fairly well-known—and the PGA (Professional Graphics Adapter)—which is not well-known. The PGA had a computer (a fairly slow 8080, but any processor is better than nothing) right on the board, qualifying it as a video coprocessor board. The processor was a general-purpose CPU chip that was a direct ancestor of the 8088, 80286, and 80386 CPUs that computers use today.

The PGA was not a bad idea, but the price was out of most users' range: $3000 for the board and $3000 for the monitor. The resolution was 640×480×256 colors.

In 1987, the VGA was announced, with the general introduction of the PS/2 line. Another video coprocessor also was announced: the 8514/A. 8514 offers a special-purpose video coprocessor whose real strength is in *vector* operations, which are operations that manipulate simple shapes like lines, circles, arcs, and the like. For people who used vector-oriented applications like Computer Aided Design and Drafting (CADD), 8514 was a good answer. 8514 is not only fast (at vector drawing) but also offers high resolution: 640×480 resolution×256 colors or 1024×768×256.

8514 has some real problems, however, which have slowed its acceptance in the market. First, as a video coprocessor board, it must exist in the system beside a VGA, requiring an extra slot in the computer. Second, the $3,000 price tag for the board and $3,000 for the monitor has further prevented this system from competing with other systems.

Another problem appeared when, in order to save money on the monitor, IBM cut a corner on the system and interlaced the monitor when in 1024×768 mode. One way to get higher resolution out of a cheaper screen is to "refresh" it less often. The electron beam in the back of a video monitor must repaint the screen at least 60 times-per-second, or your eye perceives flicker. The 8514 does not refresh 60 times-per-second but rather at 43 times-per-second. This slower refresh of interlacing rate can cause eyestrain headaches. In general, try to avoid interlaced video systems.

If you have an interlaced monitor, there are a few things that you can do to reduce the effects of flicker. First, you see flicker better with your peripheral vision because the center of your vision is built around low-resolution color receptors (called *cones*) on your retina. Surrounding the cones are high-resolution monochromatic receptors, called *rods*. Peripheral vision images fall on the rods. Sailors know this because when searching for a ship on the horizon, they do not look right at the horizon—they look below it, so the horizon falls on the high-resolution rods. In any case, the closer you are to your monitor, the more of its image falls on the cones, which are less flicker-prone.

You can demonstrate the flicker phenomenon with any monitor. Stand so that your monitor is about 60 to 80 degrees to your left: if you are facing 12 o'clock, the monitor should be at about 10 o'clock. Hold a piece of paper in front of you and read the text on it. Notice that you are seeing the monitor out of the corner of your eye and that it is flashing. This also suggests that you should buy a small monitor because a large image falls more on your rods.

Glare screens also reduce flicker, as does lighting: brighter environmental lighting reduces flicker by closing your pupils and restricting the light to the rods.

The newest IBM offering, XGA, may be a solid contender. It supports higher colors—up to 65,536 colors at 640×480 resolution—as well as 8514's 1024×768 resolution. But it is a single-board solution and is fully backward VGA compatible. And you can have up to eight XGAs in a system.

XGA is a coprocessor like 8514, but it is a coprocessor with a different mission. Recall that 8514 is good at drawing lines and arcs. That is important for OS/2, but more important is a process called bit blitting, more commonly written as bitblt. *Bitblt* means "Take some pixels from one part of the screen and move them to another part of the screen." This is of vital importance under OS/2: every drop-down menu is a bitblt, every window move is a bitblt, and so on. 8514 is pretty weak at bitblt, as is VGA. But XGA was built to bitblt.

XGA currently has the following problems:

- XGA is a bit expensive: $1100.

- XGA is available only for Micro Channel machines.

- XGA is still interlaced at 43 refreshes per second.

IBM will soon offer a non-Micro Channel version of XGA, as well as a noninterlaced one.

Coprocessor Problems: Promise and Reality

There is another general drawback to pixel-based boards—their speed when communicating with the computer. Plug-in boards on PC compatibles only run at a speed of eight MHz. Even if you own a 386-based or 486-based PC that runs at 33 MHz, that 33 just represents the speed of the CPU. Plug-in boards only run at eight MHz, so whenever your system is updating the screen—a lengthy process under VGA in any case—it is then running at only eight MHz.

Coprocessor boards also slow the system down because all plug-in boards force the system to run at eight MHz whenever one of those boards is accessed. The number of commands that must be sent to a coprocessor board is much smaller than the number of commands that must be sent to a pixel-based board, as you saw in the example of drawing a circle.

Although coprocessors are still expensive—coprocessor boards tend to be in the $1000+ range—prices are coming down, thanks to the popularity of Microsoft Windows.

Speeding Up Your OS/2 Disk

Next in this tour of hardware speedups is your system's major mass storage device—the hard disk. The three approaches to speeding up a sluggish disk are as follows:

- Run a disk-cache program

- Defragment the files on disk

- Adjust the sector interleave of the disk

How Caches Work

The most demanding mechanical activities for a disk drive are starting up in the morning and moving the head throughout the day. You can avoid the first stress by leaving your machine on all the time. You can avoid the second stress with a cache program because a cache minimizes the number of head movements that the disk must do. In the process, it also makes the system work more quickly. Bug-free disk caches make the disk do less work and offer speed as a side effect.

Disk caches rely on one basic fact—that transfers from memory to memory are much faster than transfers from disk to memory. Disks locate or seek information in milliseconds. In a given machine, however, reading memory takes a much shorter amount of time—generally around 1/5 of a microsecond, which is a fraction of a millionth of a second. That makes a memory seek over a thousand times faster than a disk seek. Data transfer rates—the rate at which data can be shuffled from one part of memory to another—can be up around 5 M/second, which is still about four times faster than the fastest ESDI.

Caches also are built on several assumptions, the first being that when you read from or write to the disk, chances are you will read it again soon. This is the principle of *locality*—once you start working in an area, you tend to stay in that area. For example, whether you realize it or not, part of CMD.EXE gets reread after you exit any large program. CMD.EXE is a file, and rereading a file requires disk activity. If you have ever noticed a quick flash of the hard disk light when you exit from a large program, you have seen the CMD.EXE reload. Rather than firing up the disk and moving the head to re-read CMD.EXE, it would have been better if the computer had kept a copy of the file somewhere in memory and reread CMD.EXE from memory, rather than from disk.

The second assumption that caches are built on is that when a program reads one sector on a disk, it usually ends up reading the next sector shortly thereafter. This implies that when OS/2 fires up the disk to read sector X, it may as well read X+1, X+2, and so on because it is the seek time that takes the lion's share of the disk reading time. Those extra sectors that have not been requested yet, but probably will be, go in the cache.

Whenever you tell a program to read in a file, no matter if it is a word processing file, spreadsheet, or database, and you make changes, you soon thereafter tell the system to rewrite the file. But you probably have not changed that much of the file, so rewriting the whole file is silly—but DOS does it anyway.

Therefore, the final assumption wherein a cache can speed up disk activity is in the disk-write process. Some caches check a sector-to-be-written against the sector as it currently exists on disk. If there is no change, the cache tells OS/2 not to rewrite that particular sector.

NOTE Many hard disk drives and hard disk controllers have a small, 32K cache right on them. Being much smaller than the suggested 256K to 512K, this cache is not adequate for assisting Windows. Go ahead, therefore, and use the OS/2 cache even if your disk has a small cache right on it.

On the other hand, some advanced controllers have tremendous amounts of cache—16 M, in the case of the UltraStor controller for EISA-bus systems. If you have one of those, do not bother running an OS/2 cache because there is no point in doing an extra level of caching and wasting memory.

Caching Disk Writes

What if cached data is sitting in memory and the computer is powered down? Will data be lost? In general, no, at least if the cache works as described so far. As you have seen, a cache does not cause the system to run any faster with the initial disk read. Its value appears when you reread an area on disk. Because the necessary data is already in cache, it gets transferred from the cache (one part of memory) to the program (another part of memory.) What does the cache do during writes? Anything written to disk should be copied into the cache in the process of reading the data. After that, there are two possible courses of action.

- Most caches are write-through caches, meaning that any disk writes occur instantly—the cache keeps its hands off the operation, except to keep a copy of the written data in its memory. When the operating system reports to an application that a file is written, it is indeed written.

- Other caches—including OS/2, if you let it—use a faster, somewhat riskier approach called *lazy writes*. In this approach, the cache program copies the data to be written to its cache memory, as before. It then instructs OS/2 to tell the application that the file has been written normally. Then the cache program monitors the system until the cache detects that the system is inactive and uses that idle time to actually do the disk write. This seems quite a bit faster because something like a file save operation seems to occur instantaneously.

 Lazy writes are risky. Consider what can happen if WordPerfect under OS/2 reports to a user that the user's document has written normally to disk.

That user might then feel safe in shutting down the system before the file has actually been written. Suppose you start editing a new document, but when the cache actually gets around to writing the data to disk, there is a disk error. The operating system reports the error, but it is too late—you have already flushed the document out of WordPerfect's memory, and there is no way to get it back; you thought it was safely written to disk.

Controlling Caching in OS/2

The solution to the preceding problem is to disable the lazy writes under OS/2's cache. That is easy because caching is controlled in CONFIG.SYS. The statement looks like this:

```
diskcache=size,lw,threshold value,AC:drive letter
```

Size refers to the amount in memory, in K-byte increments, that you want to devote to disk caching. More cache makes your system's disk faster, but limits your system's memory for programs. The default is 64K, but a value of 256K to 512K markedly speeds up disk access. The `lw` parameter, if included, enables the OS/2 cache to use lazy writes. Omit it—that is, replace `lw` with nothing between commas (,,)—and the system does no lazy writes. The `lw` parameter is there by default, so modify CONFIG.SYS if you want to eliminate lazy writing. The *threshold value* tells OS/2 whether or not to bother caching a piece of data on the disk. It is set by default to 32K and probably is best left that way. The last parameter, `AC`, tells the system to run CHKDSK every time the system is powered up. Although the idea of running CHKDSK every time you start the system may sound like overkill, the designers of OS/2 included this feature because of OS/2's multitasking nature and some common side effects. Because of the lazy writes and system lockups, half-written files may be lying around the disk, taking up space, and perhaps confusing OS/2, if they are program files. The idea of running CHKDSK on startup is to clean up any inconsistencies in the file system before setting up the OS/2 housekeeping for this session.

The DISKCACHE command only controls caching on FAT volumes; on HPFS volumes use the RUN=CACHE.EXE command, as is documented in the Command Reference at the end of this book.

Defragmenting Files

Running out of disk space? It is a pain to constantly remove one thing in order to put another on a disk. Worse yet, there is a nasty side effect of doing that: your files get fragmented. A *fragmented* file is one that is physically scattered all over a disk. Fragmentation occurs to almost-full disks because, when you try to create a file on disk, the system cannot find enough space to put it all on one place: rather than possessing a single five-megabyte lump of space, the disk may have a two-megabyte empty space in one place, and three one-megabyte spaces scattered all over. OS/2 tries to write files that are not fragmented, but that is not always possible because of the arrangement of free space on the disk. Reading fragmented files is undesirable because the disk head must move to and fro, requiring more time than is necessary otherwise and causing more wear and tear on the disk head.

Software vendors have come out with a slew of programs that defragment the data on your disk. Unfortunately, however, they are all DOS programs, so you have to reboot under DOS to run them. The Big Three disk utility packages (Norton, Mace, and PC Tools) all contain defragmentation programs; any one is acceptable for your needs. The one shipped with Norton Utilities is called Speed Disk, PC Tools has Compress, and Mace has Unfragment.

There is a disadvantage to having to use DOS programs to defragment your disk. If you have formatted your disk to HPFS, DOS does not recognize the drive, so the DOS defragmenter does not work. Fortunately, HPFS volumes are designed to fragment less than FAT volumes fragment.

You can find out which files are fragmented on your disk with the multifaceted CHKDSK program. Just type **CHKDSK *.***, and you see the usual CHKDSK output, followed by a report on which files are fragmented.

What Not To Worry About: Disk Interleaves

If you have read anything about disk optimization, you have probably heard of the notion of setting the right interleave for your drive. *Interleaving* refers to the process of arranging sectors on a track in such a way that the entire track can be read quickly. PC experts used to worry about how to interleave a disk, largely because the period from 1983 through 1989 saw vendors selling computers with incorrectly interleaved disks. You do not need to worry about disk interleave, for two reasons.

First, today's drives are already interleaved in such a fashion that they provide data-transfer rates far in excess of older drives. The original XT's hard disk could not provide data to the system at a rate any faster than 80K-per-second. Hard disks currently can transfer data at rates of around 1200K-per-second and up, so there is no point in trying to improve speed by tinkering with the interleave. Second, today's drives tend to use a technology called Imbedded Drive Electronics. IDE packs a lot of drive into a small and inexpensive package, but, in order to do it, a few corners must be cut; one of them concerns reinterleaving.

> **TIP** You can permanently damage some IDE drives by re-interleaving them, so do not get an interleave program off your local bulletin board and start messing with your drive. If you really want a program that adjusts interleaves, but that can first determine whether or not it is safe to adjust them, get SpinRite II from Gibson Research.

> **TIP** If you run a defragmentation, do not necessarily take its advice as to the best interleave factor. The extra overhead of multitasking makes OS/2 read a disk a bit more slowly than does DOS. That means that your system may speed up if you space the sectors farther apart than would be optimal for DOS. Thus, a larger interleave factor than the interleave fixer

programs recommend may be correct. So, assuming that you have a drive that can be reinterleaved, try increasing the recommended interleave by one. If SpinRite says that your best interleave is 1:2, try 1:3. Do a simple test, like reading a big file into a word processor, at both 1:2 and 1:3, and time the results. You may find that the larger interleave is faster.

To speed up your disk, defragment your disk. Then spend some cash on more memory so you can spend some of the extra memory on some cache.

Summary

OS/2 is software that demands a lot from your hardware. You can make sure that you get the best performance from the software by tuning the hardware. In this chapter, you have seen how to modify printing, multitasking, memory management, screen access, and disk performance. No one can tell you how best to set up your system because every system is different. Experiment to find the best CONFIG.SYS settings. Document your successes and failures. And—perhaps the most important advice—be sure to have the OS/2 boot floppies nearby, in case you disable the system with your experiments.

Now that you have tuned your system's performance, you are ready to learn how to extend its capabilities. The next chapter shows you how the powerful REXX/2 language gives you programming power without the typical programming problems.

Writing Batch Programs Using REXX

In the second half of Chapter 11, you were introduced to batch programming, a tool that extends the power of the command line and enables you to build small "programs" that automate or simplify a computer task. OS/2 adds an even more powerful tool in the REXX programming language. In this chapter, you are introduced to some of the fundamentals of REXX programming, specifically REXX programming under OS/2. This chapter is not a comprehensive guide to REXX programming. Entire books are available that discuss this topic. This chapter is intended to be an *invitation* to REXX programming, giving you a first exposure to the power of REXX. In this chapter, you are introduced to some of the many built-in REXX functions. You also write a game to learn how to write complete REXX programs.

The batch language that is discussed in Chapter 11 is the basic DOS batch language, called DBL, that has been available on microcomputers since the 1983 introduction of DOS 2.0. REXX has been around longer than DBL, but only on mainframes; you could use REXX on microcomputers only by using an add-on product that costs extra money. IBM's inclusion of REXX as a free inclusion to

OS/2 is a step forward for support people, or for users who want to experiment with a programming language.

Examining REXX Programs

To become familiar with REXX programs, the following is a short program that says "HELLO, THERE." This program demonstrates how to create a REXX program, how to run a REXX program, and how a REXX program must be structured.

In the System Editor, create a file called HELLO.CMD. Place the file in a subdirectory on your path, or add the subdirectory to the path, or execute it from the subdirectory in which it is located. (See Chapters 4 and 11 for more information on the path.) Enter the following lines in the HELLO.CMD file:

```
/* FIRST REXX PROGRAM */
SAY "HELLO, THERE"
```

Save the file and open up a command line. At the command line, type **HELLO** and press Enter. The file displays the following message:

```
HELLO, THERE
```

In Chapter 11, you learned that all command files or batch files—and REXX is a type of batch file—must have a file name ending in CMD. Further, the file must be a simple ASCII file created by a text editor, such as the System Editor. Do not try to create a REXX program with a word processor unless the word processor offers a file format with a description such as simple ASCII. If your word processor offers such a file type, you can use that word processor. After you create the REXX program, you invoke it by typing its file name.

In the HELLO.CMD file, the first line is a comment, just like the statements preceded by REM in programs written with DBL. Any time that you surround a line with /* and */, that line is ignored by the system. You must have a comment on the first line of each REXX program to help CMD.EXE determine whether the command file is a REXX program or a DBL program when the program is first executed. If a REXX comment is on the first line, the rest of the program is interpreted as REXX. Otherwise, the program is treated as DBL.

The second statement in the HELLO.CMD file is a SAY statement. SAY is the basic output command of REXX, similar to the ECHO statement in DBL. You can use the SAY statement for both variables and quoted statements in a single statement, as in the following:

```
SAY "THE CURRENT VALUE OF THE X VARIABLE EQUALS " X
```

The output from the preceding line shows the actual value of X after the SAY statement.

Displaying Information with REXX

The first batch program that you saw in Chapter 11 was intended to solve a hypothetical problem of network logons. In that program, you had three commands to run—STACK, MONITOR, and SHELL. You wrote a program that logged you onto the network without typing all three of the preceding commands. The following output shows the way that program looks in REXX:

```
/* NETWORK LOGON PROGRAM */
SAY "NOW LOGGING ONTO THE NETWORK..."
STACK
MONITOR
SHELL
```

In REXX, the initial ECHO OFF statement usually is unnecessary, because REXX does not display commands before it executes them (except for internal OS/2 commands). The first statement in the preceding file is the comment line, which is required. On the second line, the SAY command replaces the part of the ECHO command that places information on the standard output device. Unlike the ECHO command, the SAY command requires quotation marks around the items that you want to display on-screen. The third, fourth, and fifth lines in the preceding file are the commands that start the network.

Using the PARSE PULL Command

So far, REXX does not seem to look like much of an improvement over DBL. REXX, unlike DBL however, enables you to create programs that enable users to interact with the program. The PARSE PULL command allows your program to solicit input from the user. Use the following command, called TRYPULL.CMD, to see the way PARSE PULL works:

```
/* REXX CONVERSATIONALIST */
SAY "HELLO, I'M REXX. WHAT'S YOUR NAME?"
PARSE PULL USERNAME
SAY "WHY, HELLO THERE, " USERNAME ". NICE TO MEET YOU."
```

A sample run of the preceding program might look something like the one shown in figure 13.1.

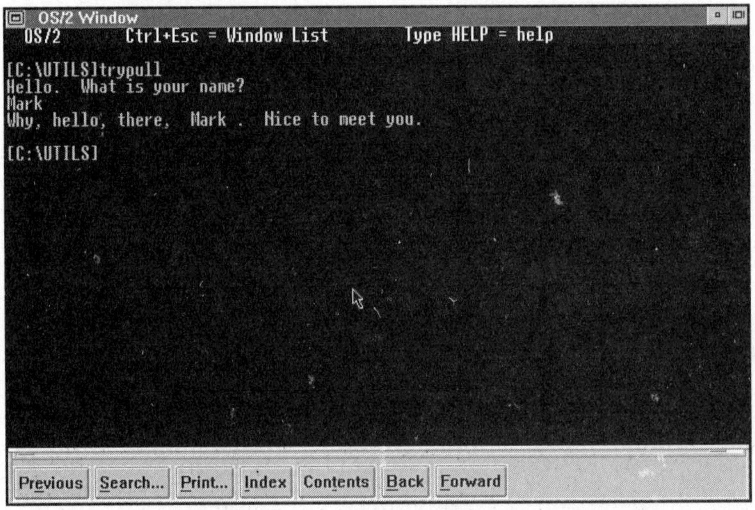

Figure 13.1:

Sample run of TRYPULL.CMD.

When you run the TRYPULL program, OS/2 displays the greeting Hello on-screen and then asks for a name. In figure 13.1, the user typed in **Mark** and TRYPULL stored that name in the variable called "USERNAME". The name can be any string of characters, but, as with any program that asks for user input, you should use descriptive names to help you remember what a batch file does.

Using Variables in REXX

Chapter 11 introduced variables and showed you the way to use them to provide run-specific information in a DBL program. You also were shown how other variables in DBL store information, such as the current state of the path, prompt, or other system-specific information. REXX, on the other hand, has a richer set of capabilities for using variables.

In REXX, a variable can be named with any string of characters that starts with a letter and continues with letters or numbers. The names TOM, DICK27, or H78ARRY are examples of variables that you can use. Names should not start with numbers or include special characters that have other meanings to the operating system. The names 123X, TOMDICK&HARRY, or <WOW>, for example, cannot be used because the first example starts with numbers, the second has an ampersand "&" embedded in it, and the third has redirection signs "<" and ">" in it. (Redirection is discussed in Chapter 11.) See the REXX documentation that comes with your copy of OS/2 for more details on naming variables.

Variables can store numeric or text information. Text information usually is referred to as *string* information by programmers, so that is how you will see the documentation refer to it. You assign values to variables in programs that contain the = operator, as in *variable=value*. String information must be surrounded with quotation marks. The following statements, for example, are legal REXX operators:

```
a=3
```

or

```
MYNAME="MARK MINASI"
```

In the preceding statement a=3, the variable named a receives the numeric value 3. (The 3 is not surrounded by quotation marks because it is a numeric value. Only character strings require quotes.) In the second statement, MYNAME="MARK MINASI", the variable named MYNAME gets the string value "MARK MINASI".

You also can do arithmetic with variables, as shown in the following:

```
/* SMALL REXX ARITHMETIC PROGRAM */
A=3
B=4
C=A+B
SAY "C NOW EQUALS" C
```

When you run the preceding program, the response c now equals 7 displays. REXX supports the four basic arithmetic functions (+, -, *, and /).

In the REXX conversationalist program in the last section, the line PARSE PULL *username* contains the variable *username*. In that situation, the name of the variable is replaced by the input value that the user types in.

REXX can compare numbers and trigonometric and logarithmic functions. Consult the on-line REXX help for more information.

Making Decisions and Detecting Errors in REXX Programs

You saw in Chapter 11 that you should check the return code for each crucial step in a batch program before you go on to the next step. The IF ERRORLEVEL statement is used in DBL to check the crucial steps of batch programs. As you saw, IF ERRORLEVEL is a little annoying in that it does not detect only one value for a return code; IF ERRORLEVEL detects the target value and any greater ones. If, for example, your program is designed to do only a particular function on seeing a return code of 16, the program also does that function for any return code value equal to or more than 16, unless you provide some extra programming to get around the problem.

In REXX, however, you can correct the problem much easier. REXX has a built-in variable called RC (short for *return code*). You can test this RC function by using the REXX IF statement, although the IF statement that REXX knows is different from the DBL IF statement. The following example is a REXX program that issues a CD command and reports on its success:

```
/* REXX CD PROGRAM; SILLY, BUT IT ILLUSTRATES A POINT */
/* TRY TO DO A CD TO A SUBDIRECTORY THAT DOES NOT EXIST */
CD JUNKDIR
IF RC=0 THEN SAY "SUCCESSFUL!"
ELSE SAY "IT DID NOT WORK."
```

When you run this program, the screen displays the screen report It did not work. unless you have a subdirectory named JUNKDIR, in which case the system says Successful!. The hard-working part here is the RC variable. The last two lines of the program, the line that starts with IF and the line that starts with ELSE, actually are one command. REXX syntax, however, requires that you write it as separate lines. The REXX IF command looks like the following:

```
IF condition THEN action
ELSE action
```

In the preceding syntax, the condition statement is what you test for and the action statement is what you do in response. You also can write out this command in three lines (many IBM manuals do):

```
IF condition
THEN action
ELSE action
```

You cannot, unfortunately, write it as one large line.

Grouping Commands in REXX Programs

Suppose, for example, that you want to put more than one command into the THEN or ELSE part of an IF statement. As explained so far, this appears impossible. If, for instance, in the preceding simple example you want to echo a number of statements rather than just one statement, you can group commands with the words

DO and END. This technique is shown in the following modified version of the IF/THEN example program:

```
/* REXX CD PROGRAM; SILLY, BUT IT ILLUSTRATES A POINT */
/* TRY TO DO A CD TO A SUBDIRECTORY THAT DOES NOT EXIST */
CD JUNKDIR
IF RC=0 THEN
DO
 SAY "SUCCESSFUL!"
 SAY "THE CHANGE DIRECTORY COMMAND WORKED FINE."
END
ELSE
DO
 SAY "IT DID NOT WORK."
 SAY "THE CHANGE DIRECTORY COMMAND WAS UNABLE TO COMPLETE
➡CORRECTLY."
END
```

DO and END act somewhat like right and left parentheses that keep a number of commands together from REXX's point of view. You can put as many commands between DO and END as you want. Notice that the SAY statements used if the CD is successful are all indented. The SAY statements that execute if the statement is unsuccessful are indented also. The computer ignores any extra blanks in the beginning of a line; the indents are to help you to determine what a program does.

In summary, whenever REXX expects a single statement, but you want to insert multiple statements, you can use DO and END to make a group of statements that act like a single statement. You can write the network logon program to look like the following:

```
/* REXX logon program with decision-making */
SAY "Now logging onto the network"
stack
IF rc=0 then
DO
 monitor
 shell
END
ELSE SAY "The STACK process failed; try a logon later.
```

This program first announces that it is going to attempt a network logon with a SAY command, as in the previous versions. Then it tries to load the stack program. The IF rc=0 statement tests the return code.

Remember that a return code of zero means that all is well; anything else means the stack program failed.

Next, the program branches off in two directions: what to do if the stack succeeds and what to do if stack fails. The statements between DO and END specify what to do if the stack is successful; ELSE tells what to do if stack fails. Between DO and END, you see the "monitor" and "shell" commands. The ELSE clause reports failure with a SAY command.

Looping under REXX

The previous network logon program does not duplicate the function of the original DBL program. The original DBL program was built on the premise that the stack only failed when the network experienced a timeout, and that persistence got you on the network. The logic of the program is something like the following:

1. Try to log onto the network.

2. If you are unsuccessful, repeat step 1.

3. Load the monitor and shell programs.

This process assumes that a looping structure exists in steps one and two. You built that looping structure with the DBL by using the GOTO statement, but REXX does not have a GOTO statement. Instead, REXX offers a number of looping structures built on DO and END. They include the following:

- A simple infinite loop built with the command DO FOREVER.

- A loop that only runs while a particular condition occurs, built with either DO WHILE or DO UNTIL.

- A loop that runs a specified number of times with DO *n*. The *n* statement is a number or variable.

Each loop structure has a different use in REXX.

The Infinite Loop

The simplest REXX loop is the DO FOREVER loop. The following sample program (called DONTSTOP.CMD) demonstrates the infinite loop:

```
/* DEMONSTRATES DO FOREVER */
DO FOREVER
 SAY "HELP! I CANNOT STOP!"
END
```

Create the file DONTSTOP.CMD, then type **DONTSTOP**. The message is printed over and over; press Ctrl-C to stop the program.

A program that runs forever is not very useful; therefore, another REXX command, LEAVE, tells REXX to break out of a loop. You can, for example, write the network logon program as follows:

```
/* REXX VERSION OF NETWORK LOGON PROGRAM WITH ERROR
➡CHECKING */
SAY "NOW LOGGING ONTO THE NETWORK..."
DO FOREVER
 STACK
 IF RC=0 THEN LEAVE
END
MONITOR
SHELL
```

The sequence of commands looks much like before, but now the stack program runs inside a loop. After executing the stack, REXX checks the return code. If the return code is zero (that is, if the logon was successful), REXX leaves the loop and executes the monitor and shell programs.

DO FOREVER can do many other things. You can, for example, use it to build a command file that waits for a particular time of day. You can use this to make a backup program wait until after hours, such as after 6 p.m. The program is as follows:

```
/* WAITS UNTIL 6PM, THEN CLEARS THE SCREEN. */
DO FOREVER
 IF TIME('H')>17 THEN LEAVE
END
CLS
```

To understand this program, you need to understand the REXX language's built-in math function, TIME. The TIME function times how long things take to finish. The TIME function also reports the number of seconds since midnight, the number of minutes since midnight, or the current hour of the day, depending on the configured options. The H option that is used with TIME reports the hour of the day in 24-hour format. 12 midnight is 0, 1 a.m. is 1, 12 noon is 12, 1 p.m. is 13, and so on. The preceding loop checks the time over and over again, and as soon as it exceeds 17—when the hour value passes 5 p.m.—REXX exits the loop.

TIME also accepts several options, which are listed in table 13.1.

Table 13.1
Options for the TIME function

Call	Result
TIME()	Reports the current time
TIME('R')	Resets the clock prior to timing an event
TIME('E')	Reports how many seconds have elapsed since the clock was last reset
TIME('S')	Reports the current time in seconds past midnight
TIME('M')	Reports the current time in minutes past midnight
TIME('H')	Reports the current time in hours past midnight

NOTE For more information on the REXX language, open the REXX documentation in the Information folder on the OS/2 desktop. The on-line REXX manual covers REXX syntax more comprehensively than is possible in a single chapter.

If you want to try out the TIME function or any other REXX command, use the REXXTRY command. Simply open a command line window and type **REXXTRY** followed by the command with which you want to experiment. One of the most irritating parts of learning any programming language is trying all its capabilities. Working with a language quickly becomes annoying if you have to write a program every time you want to see if a line works. The REXXTRY command eliminates this inconvenience.

REXXTRY is a REXX command file that runs single lines of REXX commands. You run it by typing **REXXTRY** followed by the command you want to try. Open a command line window and try this command by typing **REXXTRY SAY "HELLO"**, and you see HELLO appears on-screen.

You can see the results of REXXTRY with the TIME function invoked with various options in figure 13.2.

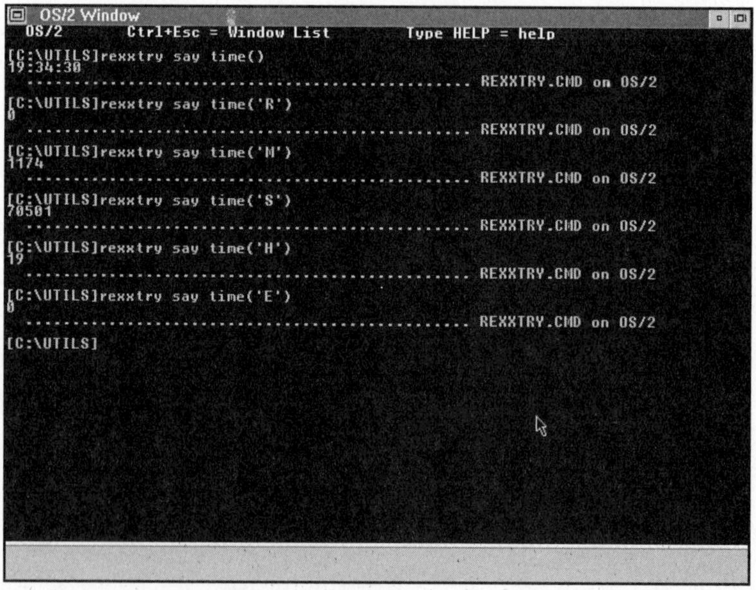

Figure 13.2:

Examples of the REXXTRY command.

```
OS/2 Window
 OS/2        Ctrl+Esc = Window List      Type HELP = help
[C:\UTILS]rexxtry say time()
19:34:30
.................................................. REXXTRY.CMD on OS/2
[C:\UTILS]rexxtry say time('R')
0
.................................................. REXXTRY.CMD on OS/2
[C:\UTILS]rexxtry say time('M')
1174
.................................................. REXXTRY.CMD on OS/2
[C:\UTILS]rexxtry say time('S')
70501
.................................................. REXXTRY.CMD on OS/2
[C:\UTILS]rexxtry say time('H')
19
.................................................. REXXTRY.CMD on OS/2
[C:\UTILS]rexxtry say time('E')
0
.................................................. REXXTRY.CMD on OS/2
[C:\UTILS]
```

In figure 13.2, you first see the TIME function called with no arguments—that is, nothing between its parentheses. TIME used by itself only reports the time, which in this case is 7:34 p.m. and 30 seconds. Next, you see the result of resetting the elapsed timer, which always returns a zero. You cannot experiment too much with the elapsed timer because REXXTRY sees each REXX statement as a separate program. In contrast, the timer only works within a single program. Resetting the timer and then reading it does not do anything when you use REXXTRY. You saw an example of using the elapsed timer in the last chapter when you used TIME('E') to time how long it took to perform a simple loop to test the multitasking capabilities of OS/2. The command TIME('M') reports that 1174 minutes passed since midnight, which makes sense because 60 minutes are in an hour and 1174 minutes are in 19.56 hours, or a bit past 7:30 p.m. Seconds are similar. The value 70501 makes more sense when you consider that 3600 seconds are in an hour, which yields 19.58 hours, or a bit past 7:30 PM.

The following guessing game program, called GUESS1.CMD, illustrates loops, which you create by using the command DO FOREVER:

```
/* REXX NUMBER GUESSING GAME */
N = RANDOM(1,100)
DO FOREVER
 SAY "I AM THINKING OF A NUMBER. WHAT DO YOU THINK IT IS?"
 PARSE PULL GUESS
 IF N=GUESS THEN LEAVE
 ELSE DO
 IF GUESS<N THEN SAY "NO, IT'S BIGGER THAN THAT."
    ELSE SAY "NO, IT'S SMALLER THAN THAT."
 END
end

SAY "EXACTLY RIGHT!"
```

This program uses the following logic when you run it:

1. REXX picks a random number between 1 and 100.

2. You make a guess about the number.

3. If you are right, the program tells you that you are right, and stops.

4. If you were not right, the program tells you whether you were too high or too low.

5. The program returns to step two.

You can see a sample run of this program in figure 13.3.

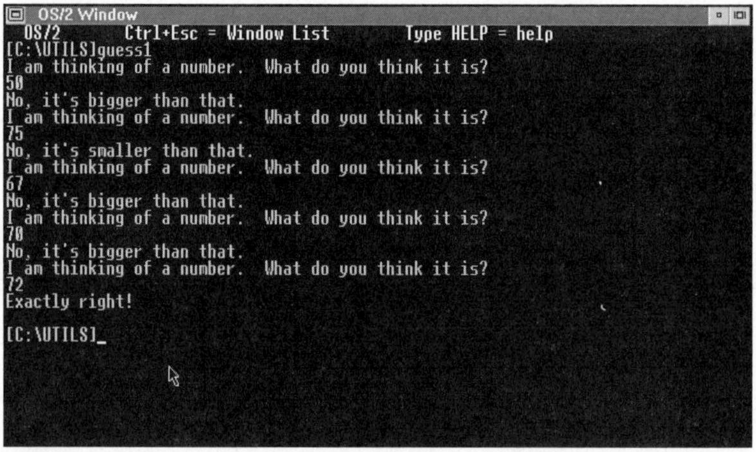

Figure 13.3:

Sample run of GUESS1.CMD.

```
┌─┐ OS/2 Window                                              ┌─┐┌─┐
   OS/2      Ctrl+Esc = Window List       Type HELP = help
[C:\UTILS]guess1
I am thinking of a number.  What do you think it is?
50
No, it's bigger than that.
I am thinking of a number.  What do you think it is?
75
No, it's smaller than that.
I am thinking of a number.  What do you think it is?
67
No, it's bigger than that.
I am thinking of a number.  What do you think it is?
70
No, it's bigger than that.
I am thinking of a number.  What do you think it is?
72
Exactly right!

[C:\UTILS]_
```

TIP Did you know that you can always guess the number within seven guesses? Make 50 your first guess. If the first guess is too high, guess 25; if too low, guess 75. The final five guesses follow the same pattern.

The program starts with the obligatory REXX comment. The second line N=RANDOM(1,100) begins the program and is a built-in REXX function. It returns a randomly generated number chosen between the two numbers presented to it as arguments, in this case 1 and 100. The variable N then is set to a random value between 1 and 100. Next, the DO FOREVER loop begins.

Every DO command needs a matching END command. A good way to read a program is to find immediately the END command that matches a DO command. You can find the END command easier if the program uses indented lines. Everything from the DO FOR-EVER down to the second-to-the-last line is indented at least two spaces. All those statements are inside the DO FOREVER loop. Take a look at the statements that fall inside the loop:

```
SAY "I AM THINKING OF A NUMBER. WHAT DO YOU THINK IT IS?"
PARSE PULL GUESS
IF N=GUESS THEN LEAVE
ELSE DO
 IF GUESS<N THEN SAY "NO, IT'S BIGGER THAN THAT."
    ELSE SAY "NO, IT'S SMALLER THAN THAT."
END
```

First is the SAY command that asks for a guess. SAY asks for a guess, but the PARSE PULL line actually gets the guess from the user. PARSE PULL patiently waits for the user to type a number and then to press the Enter key. PARSE PULL then puts the number into a variable called GUESS. Again, the variable could have been named anything, but GUESS is descriptive. Next, the big test: was the user's guess correct? If it was, leave the loop immediately. If not, the ELSE gets stretched out to another DO ... END sequence, except that in this case, the DO ... END commands do not cause looping—instead, they act as "bookends" for a set of statements. The first statement is IF, which checks to see whether the guess was too small; whether the guess was too big, the ELSE statement triggers.

The last statement, SAY, tells you that you guessed right. This line executes only if you exited the loop.

The DO FOREVER loop is a simple way to represent any kind of program behavior that repeats itself. The DO WHILE and DO UNTIL loops, however, are much more capable.

Using DO WHILE and DO UNTIL

When you use the DO FOREVER command, you periodically need to test inside the loop for some kind of condition that enables the program to leave the loop. If the condition is successful, you tell the program to LEAVE. Another way to perform the same function is to use DO UNTIL and DO WHILE, which have "is it time to leave yet?" tests built right into them. These commands use the following syntax:

```
DO WHILE condition
 ... commands in the loop go in here ...
END
DO UNTIL condition
 ... commands in the loop go in here ...
END
```

A DO WHILE loop works as follows:

1. Check the "condition." If it is false, jump to the first statement after the loop—exit the loop.

2. If not, perform the commands in the loop.

3. Go to step one.

A DO UNTIL loop works as follows:

1. Execute the commands in the loop.

2. Check the "condition." If it is false, jump to the first statement after the loop—exit the loop.

3. Go to step one.

A DO WHILE loop checks at the top of the loop to see whether you should stay in the loop. The DO UNTIL command checks the condition after you execute the statements inside the loop. WHILE checks at the top of the loop; UNTIL checks at the bottom of the loop. You can use DO UNTIL to build the network logon program, as in the following example:

```
/* REXX NETWORK LOGON PROGRAM */
SAY "NOW LOGGING ONTO THE NETWORK"
DO UNTIL RC=0
 STACK
END
MONITOR
SHELL
```

Notice that the "condition" on this loop is RC=0, which means the loop runs until a return code of zero appears from the stack program. The DO UNTIL loop is a better choice than DO WHILE because the program does not try to load the protocol stack with the "stack" program the first time in the loop. For this reason, no useful value is gained from loading the stack in RC. The DO UNTIL command ensures that the program executes at least once. DO WHILE skips the loop if zero is in RC when the loop is first entered.

The timer program can be rewritten by using a DO UNTIL loop, as follows:

```
/* WAITS UNTIL 6 PM */
DO UNTIL TIME('H')>17
END
```

Simpler, hmmm? That is a pure loop—no statements inside it. The "condition," in this case, is "TIME('H')>17". The guessing game can be recast, also:

```
/* GUESSING GAME WITH DO WHILE */
N = RANDOM(1,100)
DO UNTIL N=GUESS
 SAY "I AM THINKING OF A NUMBER. WHAT DO YOU THINK THE
 ➥NUMBER IS?"
 PARSE PULL GUESS
 IF N<GUESS THEN SAY "NO, IT'S LARGER THAN THAT."
 ELSE IF N>GUESS THEN SAY "NO, IT'S SMALLER THAN THAT."
END
SAY "YOU GOT IT EXACTLY RIGHT!"
```

The guessing game program you created earlier has not changed much with this rewrite. The loops need to run until a particular event occurs. Some loops must run a specific number of times, hence the arithmetic loops.

Using Arithmetic Loops

Sometimes you need a loop that runs a specific number of times. The arithmetic loop, which uses the following syntax, performs this function:

```
DO variable=smallest_value to largest_value
 ... statements ...
END
```

The *variable* parameter specifies any variable name. The loop runs once for each value from *smallest value* to *largest value*. The following example uses the DO *variable* loop:

```
/* SIMPLE EXAMPLE OF ARITHMETIC LOOPING */
DO I=3 TO 8
 SAY "NOW AT I=" I
END
```

If you run this program, the output appears as follows:

```
Now at i= 3
Now at i= 4
Now at i= 5
Now at i= 6
Now at i= 7
Now at i= 8
```

If you incorporate arithmetic loops into the multitasking program you created in Chapter 12, its commands would appear as follows:

```
/* REXX PROGRAM */
IF ARG()=0
THEN COUNTTO=10000
ELSE DO
 ARG X
 PARSE VAR X COUNTTO
END
A=TIME('R')
DO LINE=1 TO COUNTTO
 SAY "NOW AT LINE " LINE
END
TOTTIME=TIME('E')
PERITER=TOTTIME/COUNTTO
SAY "TIME REQUIRED=" TOTTIME "; TIME PER ITERATION="
PERITER
```

Do not worry about the parts that do not make sense. Look at the section that starts with DO COUNTTO and ends with the following END. That is an arithmetic loop. Extracted, it looks like this:

```
DO LINE=1 TO COUNTTO
 SAY "NOW AT LINE " LINE
END
```

In the first arithmetic loop in this section, the largest and smallest values were numbers, but in the preceding loop, the smallest number is a number (1) and the upper value is a variable. The program is written that way to make it more flexible.

You now know enough REXX to understand more of the counting program. Ignore the part in the beginning of the program and look at a simplified version. Note that the numbers in parentheses on the left side of the line are for explanation; do not include them in the program.

```
(1) COUNTTO=10000
(2) A=TIME('R')
(3) DO LINE=1 TO COUNTTO
(4) SAY "NOW AT LINE " LINE
(5) END
(6) TOTTIME=TIME('E')
(7) PERITER=TOTTIME/COUNTTO
(8) SAY "TIME REQUIRED=" TOTTIME "; TIME PER ITERATION="
PERITER
```

Line one puts the value 10,000 in the "countto" variable to make the computer count to 10,000. Line two gets the initial time and resets the elapsed time counter, which is the R parameter in the TIME function. Lines three to five tell the program to count to 10,000, which puts 10,000 lines on-screen. Line six determines the elapsed time in seconds and puts it into the TOTTIME variable. The program places this figure in TOTTIME so that it can report how long it took to count the 10,000 lines. What if you want to know the average time it took to execute each single line? In other words, how much time did the computer take "per iteration," which is per each of those 10,000 lines? This figure is computed in line seven, which divides the entire time by the number of lines displayed. Finally, line eight reports the total time and the per-iteration time.

Computing Square Roots by Using Looping Commands

Now that you know of some of the tools necessary to build actual programs, recall that in Chapter 11 you learned about algorithms, which are step-by-step procedures. Developing an algorithm is the first step in writing a program, which is a step-by-step process of refinement. Consider the algorithm that you saw in Chapter 11, which demonstrates how to compute the square root of a number. The algorithm uses the following method of computation:

1. Call the number that you want to find the square root of "N." Two variables named X and Y are used to improve guesses of the desired square root.

2. Set X equal to N/2. This is the initial guess for N's square root.

3. Compute Y = N/X.

4. If Y is close to X, then X times X equals N, which means that X is the square root. Otherwise, keep going.

5. Compute a new X that is halfway between X and Y. The new X equals (the old X + Y)/2.

6. Go back to step three.

REXX cannot "go to" places—there is no GO TO command to jump to a particular location in the program. You must recast the algorithm in terms of DO loops. Fitting the algorithm to the programming language often is the most difficult part of program development. You can rewrite the algorithm so that it performs as follows:

1. The user enters a number from which he or she wants the square root. Call the user's number "N." The program uses variables X and Y to improve guesses of the square root of N.

2. Set X equal to N/2.

3. Set Y equal to N/X.

4. Until X is close to Y, compute a new X that is halfway between X and Y. The formula appears as X=(old X+Y)/2.

5. After the step four loop exits, report the value of X that your program computed.

The next step in program development is to refine the algorithm so that unclear parts are eliminated. Step one is only a SAY and a PARSE PULL statement. Steps two and three also are straightforward. Step four, however, is confusing; what exactly does "X is close to Y" mean? It means that the X value should be no more than a certain distance from Y. What is that distance? Set an arbitrary value, such as 0.01. You always can change it if you need to. How do you test to see whether X is within 0.01 of Y? The algorithm appears as such:

Difference=Y–X

X and Y are close if Difference is negative and greater than –0.01 or if Difference is positive and less than 0.01.

This logic is confusing—fortunately you can use the ABS() function to simplify the algorithm. ABS() returns the absolute value of a number—it basically "strips off" the number's sign. With ABS(), the algorithm is easier to understand:

Difference=ABS(X–Y)

X and Y are close if Difference<0.01.

Rewrite the algorithm with the refinements so that it now looks like this:

1. The user enters a number from which he or she wants the square root. Call the user's number "N." The program will use variables X and Y to improve guesses of the square root of N.

2. Set X equal to N/2.

3. Set Y equal to N/X.

4. Until ABS(X–Y)<0.01, compute a new X that is halfway between X and Y. The formula for this is X=(old X+Y)/2

5. After the step four loop exits, report the value of X.

This algorithm is fairly easy to implement in REXX. The program appears as such:

```
/* COMPUTES SQUARE ROOTS */
SAY "WHAT NUMBER SHALL I FIND A SQUARE ROOT OF? "
PARSE PULL N
X = N/2
Y = N/X
DO UNTIL ABS(X-Y)<0.01
 X=(X+Y)/2
 Y=N/X
END
SAY "SQUARE ROOT OF " N " EQUALS " X
```

Debugging REXX Programs

Suppose, for example, that the square root program does not work? How do you determine what happens in the program? Use the TRACE RESULTS function, which enables you to track the progress of a program by adding a few commands. Tracing displays the intermediate steps that a program goes through step by step. Seeing how a program executes often helps when debugging it. You can see these commands in the following modified version of SQROOT.CMD (called SQTRACE.CMD):

```
/* COMPUTES SQUARE ROOTS WITH TRACE */
SAY "WHAT NUMBER SHALL I FIND A SQUARE ROOT OF? "
PARSE PULL N
TRACE RESULTS
X = N/2
Y = N/X
DO UNTIL ABS(X-Y)<0.01
 X=(X+Y)/2
 Y=N/X
END
TRACE OFF
SAY "SQUARE ROOT OF " N " EQUALS " X
```

Try this program to find the value of the square root of 34. Figure 13.4 displays the correct output.

What good is traced output? For one thing, it shows you the progress of your algorithm. You can see how X progresses in value toward its goal: first it calculates 17, then 9.5, then 6.54, then 5.87, and finally 5.83. You can check the progress of the algorithm. Imagine if the value of X went from 17 to 2 to 17 to 2 and so on. If you ran the program, it would run forever. When you trace the program, however, you quickly know whether X converges on an answer or cycles between two numbers.

The TRACE function does have one problem: its output is a bit wordy. Even if you set your screen to a 50-line mode, you are likely to lose traced output as it scrolls off the screen. That is why IBM includes PMREXX.

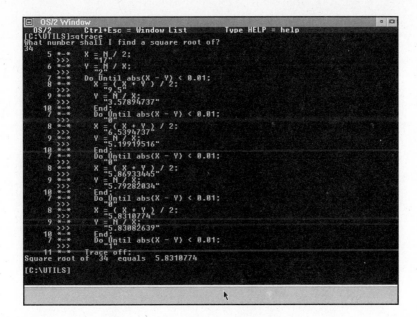

Passing Values to REXX Programs

PMREXX is a Presentation Manager program that runs REXX programs and saves their screen output to a PM window. A PM window can save hundreds of lines, enabling you to scroll and review the output. To call PMREXX, use the usual program invocation and add "PMREXX" to the front. Type **PMREXX SQTRACE**, for example, and an opening screen appears (see fig. 13.5).

In the figure, SQTRACE needs the initial program value, which you type in the Input: window. Press Enter, and the output shown in figure 13.6 appears.

Use TRACE R (short for TRACE RESULTS) in any section of a program that is not working properly, and the trace output helps you find the "bug" in the program. Simply type **TRACE R** at the beginning of the part of the program that you want to trace, and **TRACE OFF** at the end.

Figure 13.5:

PMREXX
prompting for
input values.

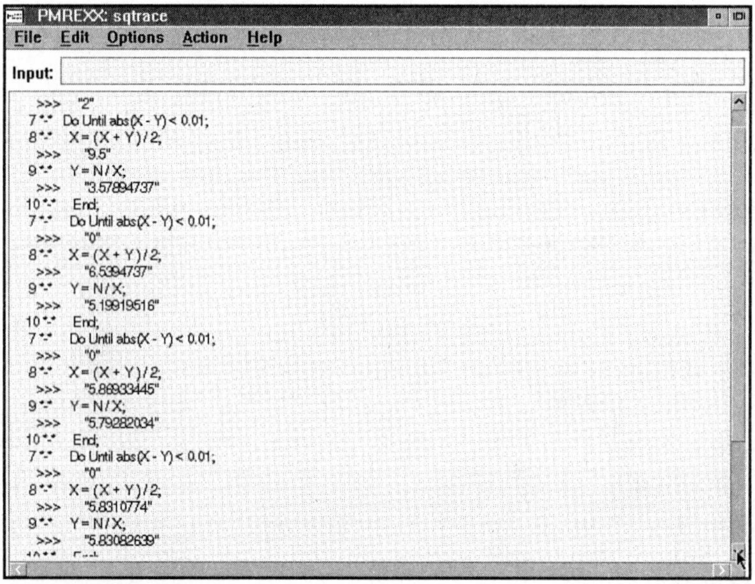

Figure 13.6:

PMREXX trace
output.

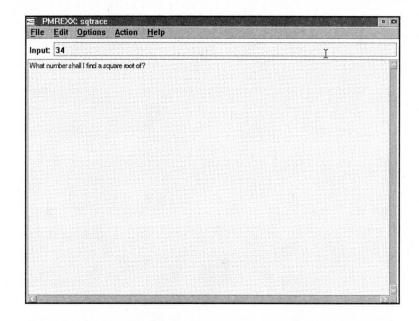

Passing Values to REXX Programs

In Chapter 11 you read that it often is useful to pass values, also known as *arguments* and *parameters*, into command files. The batch file MCD.CMD took an argument that was a subdirectory name, made a directory by that name and then made that directory the default directory. It relied heavily on the nine built-in batch variables %1 through %9.

Unlike DBL, REXX does not have predefined variables (except for RC, which is the variable for return codes). When you use REXX, you create variables as you need them. The values of the passed parameters are communicated from the command line to the REXX procedure with a built-in REXX function called ARG() and its alternate syntax, ARG.

Detecting Passed Values

You can determine whether any passed values exist with the ARG() and WORDS() functions by using the following REXX program (called COUNTARG.CMD):

```
/* REXX PROGRAM TO REPORT NUMBER OF PASSED VALUES */
ARG X
SAY "THIS PROGRAM WAS CALLED WITH" WORDS(X) " VALUES
➥PASSED TO IT."
```

You can see a few sample runs in figure 13.7.

First, COUNTARG gets called with no arguments and reports this value. Next, COUNTARG is run with four arguments; you can see that it detects the two arguments. This use of the ARG() function eliminates the need to determine whether the user forgot to enter some parameter required by a command file.

Separating Passed Values

After a program has detected passed values, the next step is to
capture those parameters. You do that with the ARG statement,
which uses the following syntax:

```
ARG variable1 variable2 variable3 ...
```

The variables *variable1*, *variable2*, and so on can have any name
you like. These variables act as receptacles for the values passed to
the command file, one by one. Try out ARG with this simple REXX
command file, called SEEARGS.CMD:

```
/* DEMONSTRATES USES OF ARG */
NUMARG = ARG()
IF NUMARG=0 THEN SAY "HEY! YOU DID NOT ENTER ANY
ARGUMENTS!"
ELSE DO
 ARG X1 X2 X3
 SAY "FIRST ARGUMENT=" X1
 SAY "SECOND ARGUMENT=" X2
 SAY "THIRD ARGUMENT=" X3
END
```

Try running this program without an argument by typing
SEEARGS, then try it with a few arguments, such as **SEEARGS**

APPLE PEAR DONUT. The arguments break up (*parse*, as programmers say) into their separate pieces and are assigned to the variables X1 through X3.

The OS/2 multitasking test program from the last chapter, CNT1.CMD, used the ARG() function for considerable flexibility. A design goal for CNT1 was to run a specific number of loops if an argument was present, or to run 10,000 times if no argument was included. That means that CNT1 10 runs 10 loops, CNT1 1000 runs 1000 times, and CNT1 runs 10,000 times. To see how that flexibility is built into CNT1, take a look at the first part of the program:

```
/* REXX PROGRAM */
IF ARG()=0
THEN COUNTTO=10000
ELSE ARG COUNTTO
```

This part of the program sets COUNTTO to 10,000 if no arguments exist. If arguments exist, COUNTTO is set to the input argument. You can use this to build considerable flexibility into your programs.

Working with String Variables

Addition, subtraction, division, and multiplication are familiar operations. Chapter 11 showed you that variables also can contain letters and other characters. These "string" variables seem not to need operations because you cannot add, subtract, multiply, or divide words and phrases. Nevertheless, a few valuable operations exist that you can perform on strings.

Performing String Concatenation

The most important string operation is concatenation. *Concatenation* is the process of putting together two strings. The concatenation operator is formed by two file separator characters(| |). If you run the following short REXX program, for example, the output is
`Concatenated value=HI HOW ARE YOU?`:

```
/* SHOWS CONCATENATION */
TOGETHERVALUE = "HI" ¦¦ " HOW ARE YOU?"
SAY "CONCATENATED VALUE=" TOGETHERVALUE
```

Using Substrings

Occasionally, you may want to take strings and modify them or extract them. Suppose, for example, that you want a simple "yes" or "no" response. The piece of code might look something like this:

```
/* SOLICITS RESPONSE OF YES OR NOT */
SAY "DO YOU WANT TO CONTINUE?"
PARSE PULL RESPONSE
IF RESPONSE="YES" THEN {DO SOMETHING}
ELSE {DO SOMETHING}
```

The problem with this plan is that you are testing the response against "yes," but the user may not type exactly that sequence of letters. If, for example, the user types any uppercase letters, the plan does not work. Furthermore, a "Y" does not do the trick. The program is more flexible if the procedure responded to "Y," "y," "yes," "Yes," and other permutations and possibilities. The following functions enable you to solve this problem:

- **TRANSLATE().** Converts all characters to uppercase. The function TRANSLATE('abcde'), for example, is translated to ABCDE.

- **SUBSTR().** Extracts part of a string—the "substring." SUBSTR needs three arguments:

```
SUBSTR(input string,start position, end position)
```

The *input string* variable is the string value from which you want to extract a substring; *start position* is the location of the start of the substring; and *end position* is the location of the end of the substring. Only the first character is important for the user input—this first character should be "Y" or "N."

Combining those two functions, you can recast the earlier code segment in the following manner:

```
/* ROBUST REXX INPUT CHECKING ROUTINE */
SAY "DO YOU WANT TO CONTINUE?"
PARSE PULL RESPONSE
X = TRANSLATE(SUBSTR(RESPONSE, 1,1))
IF X="Y" THEN {DO SOMETHING}
ELSE {DO SOMETHING
```

SUBSTR has another form, one with just two arguments. When you omit the third argument, SUBSTR returns the contents of the input string from the position indicated by the second argument to the end of the string. SUBSTR("ABCDEFG",5), for example, returns EFG, which is everything in position five and later.

Two other substring functions, LEFT() and RIGHT(), also are useful. The following is the syntax for LEFT():

```
LEFT(string name,number of positions)
```

This function extracts the leftmost *number of positions* positions from the string *string name*. LEFT("abcdef",3), for example, returns abc, the leftmost three characters in "abcdef." RIGHT does about the same thing, except that it takes characters from the right. The statement RIGHT("abcdef",3) returns def, the rightmost three characters in the string. You also can write the previous code fragment in the following manner:

```
/* ROBUST REXX INPUT CHECKING ROUTINE */
SAY "DO YOU WANT TO CONTINUE?"
PARSE PULL RESPONSE
X = TRANSLATE(LEFT(RESPONSE,1))
IF X="Y" THEN {DO SOMETHING}
ELSE {DO SOMETHING ELSE}
```

Using the String Length Function

You often find that you need to know the length of a character string—in other words, the number of characters in the string. REXX has a string length function called LENGTH. Use the following REXX program called SEECHARS.CMD to demonstrate the LENGTH function:

```
/* SHOWS THE STRING CHARACTER BY CHARACTER */
SAY "PLEASE ENTER A MESSAGE? "
PARSE PULL RESPONSE
/* DETERMINE LENGTH SO THAT YOU SEE HOW MANY CHARACTERS
➧TO PROCESS */
X=LENGTH(RESPONSE)
DO I=1 TO X
 A=SUBSTR(RESPONSE,I,1)
 SAY "CHARACTER " I "=" A
END
```

A sample run should look similar to the one shown in figure 13.8.

Figure 13.8:

Sample run of
SEECHARS.CMD.

Searching String Functions

Much of string processing involves matching things. What is the
most common use, for example, for a database? Databases are
commonly used to answer questions, such as "How many people
live in Peoria and make more than 500,000 dollars per year?" Two
useful REXX functions that search and report are POS and WORDS.
WORDS is easy to describe: it reports the number of words in a
string. Examine the following command:

```
SAY WORDS("Mary had a little lamb")
```

This WORDS line displays the numeric value "5." WORDS searches the string for blanks—it assumes that words are separated by blanks.

Like WORDS, POS does more than just search for blanks. You can use this function to look for any string inside any other string. POS() has two arguments: the string to look for, and the string to look in. Consider the following example:

```
SAY POS("sharon","krisdemiesharonjulie")
```

This line displays the numeric value "10" because the string "sharon" starts in the tenth position in the second string.

 Remember that you can try any function or REXX command by using the command REXXTRY.

Related to POS is LASTPOS, a version of POS that shows the location of the last occurrence of one string in another string. The line POS("a",""abcdab") returns 1 because an "a" is in the first location. LASTPOS("a","abcdab") returns 5 because the *last* occurrence of "a" is at location 5.

Using the STRIP() Function

When searching for something, or when processing a string, often it is useful to eliminate leading or trailing blanks. The STRIP() function uses only one input argument, which is a string variable that eliminates these blanks. The output is a string without any leading or trailing blanks. When you run this program, for example, you see that A is longer than B because it contains extra characters:

```
/* DEMONSTRATES STRIP */
A=" TEXT  "
B=STRIP(A)
SAY "LENGTH OF A=" LENGTH(A) " LENGTH OF B=" LENGTH(B)
```

Although a number of other string functions are available, the most often used are the ones discussed in the previous sections. Make sure you read the REXX documentation to learn about the other REXX string functions. Top-notch programmers always "go back to the books" and read their manuals. They know how easy it is to solve a particular class of problems with a basic knowledge of a language and to forget the language's total power. If you need a program that counts the number of words in a line, for example, you can write the program with just the POS and SUBSTR functions, as in the following COUNTWD.CMD program:

```
/* MIMICS THE WORDS() FUNCTION: UNNECESSARY, BUT
➥ILLUSTRATES STRING FUNCTIONS */
SAY "ENTER A SENTENCE?" PARSE PULL SENTENCE
/* X IS A TEMPORARY HOLDING SPOT FOR SENTENCE SO WE
➥CAN TAKE */
/* IT APART WORD BY WORD */
X=STRIP(SENTENCE)
/* NWORDS WILL COUNT THE NUMBER OF WORDS FOUND */
NWORDS=0
DO WHILE LENGTH(X)>0
 /* PULL OFF THE NEXT WORD */
 WORDENDS=POS(" ",X)
 NWORDS = NWORDS + 1
 /* NOW THAT IT'S COUNTED, DISCARD THE WORD */
 /* BUT IF POS=0, THEN THERE'S NO BLANK, AND SO
➥WE'RE DOWN TO */
 /* LAST WORD */
 IF WORDENDS<>0 THEN X = STRIP(SUBSTR(X,WORDENDS))
      ELSE X=""
END
SAY "FOUND " NWORDS " WORDS."
```

Although the preceding program is useful—it demonstrates a simple "parsing" operation—you can substitute these lines with simpler ones that use the WORDS() function. You might use this program to interpret commands that the user enters to a REXX program.

NOTE Many REXX programmers that need word count capabilities use the POS and SUBSTR functions because they are comfortable with them, and they probably have not cracked the REXX manual in a long time. For this reason, take a minute and reread the manual.

Using OS/2 Commands in REXX Programs

In the DBL discussion, you saw that most lines in DBL command files are just simple commands that you can enter at the command line. REXX, on the other hand, uses powerful REXX commands that are not simple command-line commands. Nevertheless, REXX enables you to insert OS/2 commands in a REXX program. You can tell REXX to perform a DIR command, for example, four times in a row with this short program:

```
/* DIRECTORY LOOP */
DO 4
 DIR
END
```

Although this program is silly, using OS/2 commands directly is helpful. Another way REXX enables you to control the command line is by enabling you to build a command in your REXX program "on the fly" and then execute it. To do so, you assemble the command into a string variable, and then put the variable on a line by itself. As with so many programming features, this is best explained with an example as follows:

```
/* COMMAND ASSEMBLY EXAMPLE */
SAY "PLEASE ENTER A ONE-WORD COMMAND, LIKE DIR, COPY, OR
➥ERASE:"
PARSE PULL C
SAY "NOW ENTER AN ARGUMENT FOR A COMMAND, LIKE *.*:"
PARSE PULL ARGS
/* ASSEMBLE THE COMMAND; DO NOT FORGET A SPACE BETWEEN
➥COMMAND */
/* AND ARGUMENT */
CMDLINE = C ¦¦ " " ¦¦ ARGS
/* NOW THAT IT'S ASSEMBLED, EXECUTE IT. */
CMDLINE
```

Try this, and you could get a run like this:

```
PLEASE ENTER A ONE-WORD COMMAND, LIKE DIR, COPY, OR
ERASE:
ERASE
NOW ENTER AN ARGUMENT FOR A COMMAND, LIKE *.*:"
A*.*
3 file(s) erased
```

This example assumes that you executed that command in a directory containing three files starting with "A." You can see the power of using OS/2 commands in REXX by building a disk installation program.

Occasionally, you might receive disks with OS/2 programs that are "packed up" in a single program called OS2.EXE. To use the programs, the user must follow these steps:

1. Create a directory called \UTILS on a drive with at least 2M of free space.

2. Copy the file OS2.EXE from the floppy disk drive to \UTILS.

3. Type **OS2** to make the program unpack itself. When it finishes, the user has a number of usable programs in the \UTILS directory.

This three-step process is necessary to decompress the files before the user can run the programs. Some people, however, do not always understand the preceding directions. This is a perfect job for a REXX command file. A good REXX program for this purpose enables the user to enter INSTALL and the directory. The program assumes that it should install from a specific drive (in this example, drive A) to the hard disk drive (C, for example). Consider how the new directory is made and how the files are copied from the source to the destination.

Suppose, for example, that the program already knows the source drive and the drive name is contained in a variable called SOURCE. The destination is a drive letter kept in a variable called DESTINATION. Do not worry about how that happens—you will see the entire command file in a minute. For now, consider the directory make and copy problems. The code fragment for this utility looks like the following one:

```
/* ASSEMBLE THE "MAKE DIRECTORY" COMMAND WITH A CONCATENATION
COMMANDSTR = "MD " || DESTINATION
/* THE NEXT LINE ACTUALLY ISSUES THE "MD" COMMAND */
COMMANDSTR
/* ASSEMBLE THE COPY COMMAND; RECYCLE THE COMMANDSTR VARIABLE
➡*/
/* ANOTHER CONCATENATION, THIS ONE'S A BIT BIGGER. */
COMMANDSTR = "COPY " || SOURCE || "*.* " || DESTINATION
COMMANDSTR
```

The program first must create a subdirectory. The first line assembles that command: MD plus the destination variable. The value is placed into the COMMANDSTR variable, which performs the actual MD operation. After the directory is created, files are copied to the directory in the second pair of lines. A copy command is assembled and placed into COMMANDSTR, and then COMMANDSTR performs the copy operation. The rest of the REXX program is fairly simple to write: get the command-line inputs and make sure meaningful information is in SOURCE and DESTINATION, then assemble and issue the commands.

As mentioned earlier, the following program enables you to unpack OS/2 applications from an OS2.EXE file on a floppy disk.

```
/* REXX PROGRAM TO INSTALL CLASS FILES */
/* FIRST, LOOK FOR ARGUMENTS.
IF ARG()=0 THEN
DO
 SOURCE="A:"
 DESTINATION="C:\UTILS"
END
ELSE
DO
 ARG SOURCE DESTINATION
 DESTINATION=DESTINATION || "\UTILS"
END
/* CLEAR THE SCREEN AND GET READY FOR THE "ARE YOU SURE?"
➡MESSAGE
```

```
CLS
SAY " --- OS/2 UTILITY PROGRAMS DISK -----------------"
SAY " --- MARK MINASI AND COMPANY --- (703) 276-8940 --------
➥-"
SAY "    >>> WARNING! <<<<<<"
SAY "YOU ARE ABOUT TO INSTALL OS/2 UTILITIES PROGRAMS FROM "
➥SOURCE
"TO" DESTINATION "." SAY "IF YOU DO NOT WANT TO DO THAT, TYPE
➥'N'
AND PRESS ENTER. OTHERWISE, PRESS ANY"
SAY "OTHER KEY AND PRESS ENTER?"
PARSE PULL RESPONSE
IF RESPONSE="N" THEN SAY "OKAY, I WILL NOT INSTALL THE
FILES."
ELSE DO
 /* MAKE THE DIRECTORY; NOTICE THAT YOU'VE GOT TO BUILD THE
COMMAND,
THEN SUBMIT IT */
COMMANDSTR = "MD " ¦¦ DESTINATION
 /* THE NEXT LINE ACTUALLY ISSUES THE "MD" COMMAND */
 COMMANDSTR
 /* ASSEMBLE THE COPY COMMAND; RECYCLE THE COMMANDSTR VARI-
ABLE */
 COMMANDSTR = "COPY " ¦¦ SOURCE ¦¦ "*.* " ¦¦ DESTINATION
 COMMANDSTR
 /* NOW EXPAND THE COMPRESSED FILE BY CALLING IT BY NAME */
 OS2
 /* ALL DONE NOW */
 SAY "ALL DONE. THE FILES ARE NOW UNCOMPRESSED ON YOUR HARD
DISK. "
END
```

As you can see, more comments are included in this program to help you understand each line.

Handling REXX Files

REXX is capable of inputting and outputting information to and from files using the LINEIN and LINEOUT functions. The syntax for LINEIN is the following:

```
LINEIN(source)
```

In the preceding syntax, *source* refers to the name of a file. This function returns the next line from the file. The first time that the following line is executed, for example, the variable A contains the first line of CONFIG.SYS:

```
A=LINEIN("CONFIG.SYS")
```

Another function similar to LINEIN is LINEOUT, which writes a line out to a file. A typical LINEOUT call looks like the following:

```
R=LINEOUT("MYFILE.TXT",A)
```

The preceding line writes out whatever is in the variable A to the end of the file MYFILE.TXT. The result of the operation goes into the variable R; this is not really a return code like the ones you have seen before, but it is similar. R either has the value 0 if the write is successful, or 1 if it is unsuccessful.

One of the most useful file utilities that you can write is a file copy routine. The algorithm for this operation looks like the following:

1. Get from the user the name of the file to be copied and new name for the copy. Call them SOURCE and TARGET.

2. Read a line from SOURCE into a variable and call it A, and write the line out to the TARGET. Continue this operation until the end of the file is reached or an error is generated writing data out to the target.

3. Report success or failure.

From the preceding example, you have all the tools to do this, except for the part about detecting when the program comes to the end of a file. The LINES() function enables you to do this. LINES(*filename*) returns the number of lines in a file that have not yet been read. If LINES() returns zero, the program has reached the end of the file. LINES also is useful for detecting nonexisting files: if the program receives a zero value from LINES the first time LINES looks at a file, the file does not exist. You can see the result of several LINES() commands in figure 13.9.

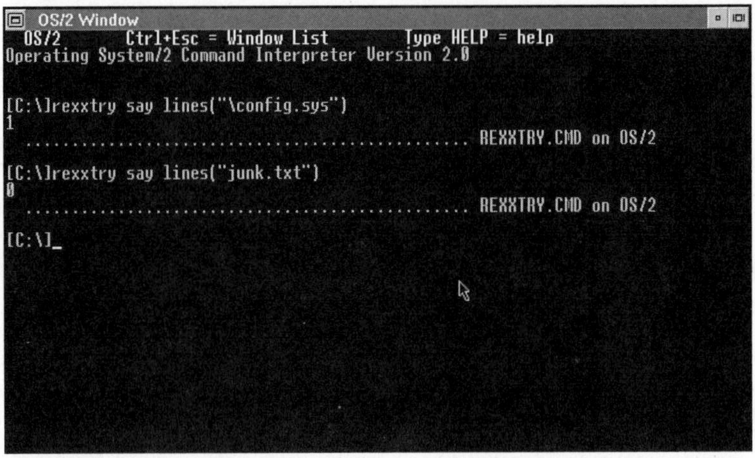

Figure 13.9:

Result of the
LINES() function.

```
OS/2 Window
  OS/2        Ctrl+Esc = Window List        Type HELP = help
Operating System/2 Command Interpreter Version 2.0

[C:\]rexxtry say lines("\config.sys")
1
.................................................. REXXTRY.CMD on OS/2

[C:\]rexxtry say lines("junk.txt")
0
.................................................. REXXTRY.CMD on OS/2

[C:\]_
```

Figure 13.9:
Result of the LINES() function.

A rough draft of a file copy program called REXXCOPY.CMD might
look like this:

```
/* FILE COPY ROUTINE */
/* FIRST GET SOURCE AND DESTINATION */
ARG X
PARSE VAR X SOURCE TARGET
J=LINES(SOURCE) /* "END OF FILE" FLAG */
R=0 /* "FILE WRITE FAILED" FLAG */
DO WHILE (J<>0) & (R=0)
 A=LINEIN(SOURCE)
 R=LINEOUT(TARGET,A)
 J=LINES(SOURCE)
END
IF R<>0
 THEN SAY "FILE COPY FAILED."
 ELSE SAY "COPY SUCCESSFUL."
```

The program starts by collecting the SOURCE and TARGET variables from the user. You can add code to check that the user included those parameters. Then REXXCOPY.CMD initializes J and R, two
variables that keep track of the "end of file" and "unable to write
information to target" conditions.

The main loop copies lines as long as the end of the file has not been
reached and as long as information continues to be written. The line

DO WHILE (J<>0) & (R=0) incorporates something that you have not seen before—the AND function. The way that you indicate AND, as in "do this if X and Y are true," is with the ampersand, "&." The following is the main body of the loop:

```
A=LINEIN(SOURCE)
R=LINEOUT(TARGET,A)
J=LINES(SOURCE)
```

The LINEIN line reads the next line, then the LINEOUT writes it out, reporting success or failure by using the variable R. Prior to the next read, LINES is invoked to ensure that another line is available to read. After REXXCOPY exits the loop, it reports success or failure.

This program works fairly well, but the following details some of the problems associated with it:

1. REXXCOPY does not copy the file to the target—it *appends* it to the target.

2. REXXCOPY does not first check to see if the SOURCE file exists.

3. REXXCOPY does not check to see if the user entered a SOURCE and DESTINATION argument.

None of these problems are fatal; recognizing them is just part of the refinement process of programming.

The first problem is the hardest to fix and stems from a peculiarity of the LINEOUT function. Most programming languages, when asked to write information to a file, erase any existing file with the same name before proceeding. The alternative, appending the data to the end of any existing file, usually is a separate option or operation. For some reason, however, that is the default situation with LINEOUT. To view this problem, use REXXCOPY to copy a file called "X" to a file "Y" more than once, then look at file Y. It now contains two copies of file X. REXXCOPY would be a better program if it first checked to see if the target file already exists and, if so, to erase it before copying. The algorithm for this sequence might work as follows:

1. Check to see if the proposed target file already exists.

2. If it does, ask the user if he or she would like to erase the target file.

3. If the user says **NO**, skip the copy procedure.

4. If the user says **YES**, erase the file and proceed.

The code for this procedure is as follows:

```
ARG X
PARSE VAR X SOURCE TARGET
/* CHECK TO SEE IF TARGET ALREADY EXISTS */
IF LINES(TARGET)<>0 THEN
  DO
  SAY "FILE " TARGET " ALREADY EXISTS. OVERWRITE?"
  PARSE PULL RESPONSE
  IF TRANSLATE(LEFT(RESPONSE,1))<>"Y" THEN EXIT
  ELSE DO /* ERASE EXISTING FILE */
  CMDSTRING="ERASE " ¦¦ TARGET
  CMDSTRING
  END
  END
```

First, the arguments get extracted, as you have seen before. Then the LINES function checks to see if any lines are in the TARGET (whether the file exists). If the file exists, a SAY statement informs the user, and then asks the user what they want to do. The "EXIT" command stops a REXX program by jumping directly to the end of the program. If the file is to be erased, the program first builds an ERASE command with concatenation, as you read earlier, and then issues the command. Unfortunately, the program does not work.

The program does not work because the target file is open while LINES() examines it. The file cannot be erased because the REXXCOPY procedure currently is using the file. OS/2 will not erase a file that is currently in use.

This program does not work unless the program first closes the target. For this reason, it is time to introduce another REXX function, STREAM(). STREAM() closes or opens a stream of information from a file. To close a file whose name is in the TARGET variable, use the command:

```
A=STREAM(TARGET,C,"CLOSE")
```

The **A** parameter accepts the return code of the close operation, but it is not a normal numeric code. If the process is sucessful, A contains READY:. The following is the copy routine (called RC2.CMD) with this fix:

```
/* FILE COPY ROUTINE */
/* FIRST GET SOURCE AND DESTINATION */
ARG X
PARSE VAR X SOURCE TARGET
/* CHECK TO SEE IF TARGET ALREADY EXISTS */
IF LINES(TARGET)<>0 THEN
 DO
 SAY "FILE " TARGET " ALREADY EXISTS. OVERWRITE?"
 PARSE PULL RESPONSE
 IF TRANSLATE(LEFT(RESPONSE,1))<>"Y" THEN EXIT
 ELSE DO /* ERASE EXISTING FILE */
 /* DISCONNECT IT FIRST */
 A=STREAM(TARGET,C,"CLOSE")
 IF A<>"READY:" THEN
 DO
  SAY "UNABLE TO CLOSE TARGET FILE; ABORTING."
  EXIT
 END
 CMDSTRING="ERASE " ¦¦ TARGET
 CMDSTRING
 IF RC<>0 THEN
  DO
   SAY "UNABLE TO ERASE TARGET FILE; ABORTING."
   EXIT
  END
 END
 END
J=-1 /* "END OF FILE" FLAG */
R=0 /* "FILE WRITE FAILED" FLAG */
```

```
DO WHILE (J<>0) & (R=0)
 A=LINEIN(SOURCE)
 R=LINEOUT(TARGET,A)
 J=LINES(SOURCE)
END
IF R<>0
 THEN SAY "FILE COPY FAILED."
 ELSE SAY "COPY SUCCESSFUL."
```

You can fix problems two and three fairly quickly. Before you do, however, notice that ERASE appears on the command line if the program requires it. You may recall that this was the case in DBL programs, which used the @ECHO OFF command to hide the display of the commands before they execute. You should be able to use @ECHO OFF in REXX files, but unfortunately there is a bug in OS/2's REXX interpreter that prohibits its use. You instead have to perform a somewhat roundabout approach to @ECHO OFF using the following lines:

```
COMMANDSTR = "@ECHO OFF"
COMMANDSTR
```

These lines work the same, but they are troublesome.

Back to adding erase prompts to REXXCOPY, first check to ensure that the source file exists. LINES() do that. The file with the fix (called RC3.CMD) is listed as follows:

```
/* FILE COPY ROUTINE */
COMMANDSTR="@ECHO OFF"
COMMANDSTR
/* GET SOURCE AND TARGET */
ARG X
PARSE VAR X SOURCE TARGET
/* CHECK TO SEE IF SOURCE EXISTS */
IF LINES(SOURCE)=0 THEN
DO
 SAY "ERROR: THE FILE " SOURCE "DOES NOT EXIST. ABORTING..."
 EXIT
END
/* CHECK TO SEE IF TARGET ALREADY EXISTS */
```

```
IF LINES(TARGET)<>0 THEN
 DO
 SAY "FILE " TARGET " ALREADY EXISTS. OVERWRITE?"
 PARSE PULL RESPONSE
 IF TRANSLATE(LEFT(RESPONSE,1))<>"Y" THEN EXIT
 ELSE DO /* ERASE EXISTING FILE */
 /* DISCONNECT IT FIRST */
 A=STREAM(TARGET,C,"CLOSE")
 IF A<>"READY:" THEN
 DO
  SAY "UNABLE TO CLOSE TARGET FILE; ABORTING."
  EXIT
 END
 CMDSTRING="ERASE " ¦¦ TARGET
 CMDSTRING
 IF RC<>0 THEN
  DO
   SAY "UNABLE TO ERASE TARGET FILE; ABORTING."
   EXIT
  END
 END
 END
J=-1 /* "END OF FILE" FLAG */
R=0 /* "FILE WRITE FAILED" FLAG */
DO WHILE (J<>0) & (R=0)
 A=LINEIN(SOURCE)
 R=LINEOUT(TARGET,A)
 J=LINES(SOURCE)
END
IF R<>0
 THEN SAY "FILE COPY FAILED."
 ELSE SAY "COPY SUCCESSFUL."
```

As you can see, the preceding program uses a simple application of the LINES() function. To finish the program, add lines that check for a SOURCE and TARGET. After the values have been parsed into the variables named SOURCE and TARGET, perform a simple test using the following line:

```
IF SOURCE="" OR TARGET="" THEN {ISSUE ERROR MESSAGES}
```

You must use a redirection symbol (|) to represent OR in REXX. The finished code, called RC4.CMD, appears as follows:

```
/* FILE COPY ROUTINE */
/* FIRST, TURN ECHO OFF */
X="@ECHO OFF"
X
/* THEN GET SOURCE AND TARGET */
ARG X
PARSE VAR X SOURCE TARGET
/* CHECK THAT USER ENTERED SOURCE AND TARGET */
IF SOURCE="" ¦ TARGET="" THEN
DO
 SAY "ERROR: PLEASE USE THIS LIKE SO:"
 SAY "RC4 SOURCEFILE TARGETFILE"
 SAY "WHERE SOURCEFILE AND TARGETFILE ARE THE FILE TO
COPY
AND THE PLACE"
 SAY "TO COPY IT TO, RESPECTIVELY."
 EXIT
END
/* CHECK TO SEE IF SOURCE EXISTS */
IF LINES(SOURCE)=0 THEN
DO
 SAY "ERROR: THE FILE " SOURCE "DOES NOT EXIST.
ABORTING..."
 EXIT
END
/* CHECK TO SEE IF TARGET ALREADY EXISTS */
IF LINES(TARGET)<>0 THEN
 DO
 SAY "FILE " TARGET " ALREADY EXISTS. OVERWRITE?"
 PARSE PULL RESPONSE
 IF TRANSLATE(LEFT(RESPONSE,1))<>"Y" THEN EXIT
 ELSE DO /* ERASE EXISTING FILE */
 /* DISCONNECT IT FIRST */
 A=STREAM(TARGET,C,"CLOSE")
 IF A<>"READY:" THEN
 DO
  SAY "UNABLE TO CLOSE TARGET FILE; ABORTING."
  EXIT
END
```

```
CMDSTRING="ERASE " ¦¦ TARGET
CMDSTRING
IF RC<>0 THEN
  DO
    SAY "UNABLE TO ERASE TARGET FILE; ABORTING."
    EXIT
  END
 END
 END
J=-1 /* "END OF FILE" FLAG */
R=0 /* "FILE WRITE FAILED" FLAG */
DO WHILE (J<>0) & (R=0)
 A=LINEIN(SOURCE)
 R=LINEOUT(TARGET,A)
 J=LINES(SOURCE)
END
IF R<>0
 THEN SAY "FILE COPY FAILED."
 ELSE SAY "COPY SUCCESSFUL."
```

Figure 13.10 shows some sample runs of this bulletproof file copy program.

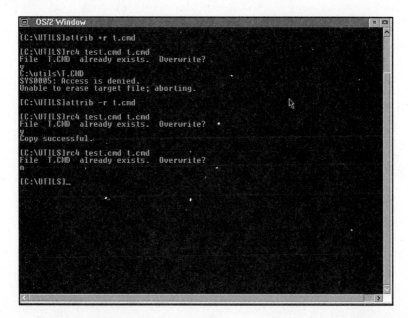

Figure 13.10:

Sample runs of the REXX file copy routine.

Summary

In this chapter, you were introduced to the major language elements of REXX. You now have enough knowledge to start building useful REXX files. You have seen how to handle numeric data as well as string data, how to manipulate files, and how to "user-proof" your REXX files so that they are reliable. If you want to know more about REXX, start with the on-line help that comes with OS/2. In addition, read IBM's REXX/2 manual called the *Procedures Language 2/REXX User's Guide*, available directly from IBM.

Few things are more rewarding than building a well-designed, useful program from scratch. Programming is similar to woodworking or auto mechanics without the mess. Document your work, do not be afraid to experiment, and you may find yourself bitten by the programming "bug."

IV

Appendixes

Appendix A: Installation

Appendix B: Current OS/2 Applications

Installation

The default installation program for OS/2 2.0 is interactive: the program presents options and asks questions. You simply respond by making choices. Installing the new operating system goes smoothly if you have the necessary equipment and understanding for the decisions you have to make. This appendix helps you select the appropriate hardware, make informed decisions about installation options, and step through the installation procedure.

Meeting OS/2 2.0 Hardware Requirements

To run OS/2 2.0, you need the following hardware:

- A personal computer with an Intel 80386SX CPU or higher microprocessor

- At least six megabytes of memory (RAM)

- 60M hard disk drive with 16 to 29M of free space

- 3 1/2-inch, 1.44M floppy disk drive

To use the graphical user interface (Workplace Shell), you need a two-button mouse or other pointing device, such as a track ball.

Planning for Memory

Graphical applications can use large quantities of memory. Your computer needs a large amount of memory if you want to take advantage of OS/2 2.0's capability to manage several applications. With 4M of memory, you can run one DOS application or one small OS/2 application, such as an OS/2 tool or game. If you plan to run Microsoft Windows applications, plan on an additional 1M of memory for each application you use concurrently. If you start a Windows word processing program, for example, and a Windows spreadsheet program, you need at least 6M of memory for acceptable performance.

For OS/2 full-function applications, you need 1M to 3M of memory for each one you run concurrently. Check the requirements of each application you intend to run with OS/2 2.0 to determine whether you need to upgrade your system. Remember that the amount of memory you need depends on the requirements of the applications you are running at the same time, not on the number of applications in your computer. In addition, keep in mind that memory requirements can be increased when applications are started and stopped, and when you use the print spooler.

Planning for Disk Storage Space

OS/2 2.0's requirements for disk storage space are 16 to 29 megabytes (M). You need 16M of storage if you install only the basic operating system; between 16 and 29M if you install additional features; and 29M if you install the full operating system (not including a local area network [LAN], OS/2 communications, or database extensions). You should have a hard disk drive with at least 60M of storage to accommodate OS/2 2.0 and your applications. An 80M or larger hard disk drive is preferable.

OS/2's disk storage estimates of 16 to 29M are only for the operating system. These requirements do not account for your applications.

To see how much free space you have on your hard disk drive, enter **CHKDSK** (for "check disk") at the DOS prompt or OS/2 command line. Look for the statement about free bytes or available disk space. If it says, for example, "16,200,000 bytes free," you have more than 16M of free disk space. As you proceed through installation, OS/2 2.0 checks free disk space and reports it to you. In many cases, it also tells you how much space various options take, so that you can make informed choices when deciding which features to install.

Backing Up Your System

Before you begin to install an operating system, back up files currently stored on the computer's hard disk. If you are installing OS/2 for the first time, you might want to format your hard disk during installation to install the High Performance File System (HPFS). If you format your hard disk, everything on it is erased.

If you use the BACKUP command to specify the parts of your system you want to back up, the system takes over the procedure and prompts you to insert and remove floppy disks as needed. Label each backup floppy disk with the date and the floppy disk number. Number the floppy disks consecutively so that you can feed them to the computer in order when you use RESTORE.

 Make sure you have extra floppy disks available before you back up the hard disk drive.

You need to decide whether to back up your entire hard disk or only portions of it. A backup of the entire system is helpful if in the future you decide to remove OS/2 2.0 and restore your previous system or another operating system. If you back up the entire hard disk, all operating system files, application program files, and data files are backed up.

To back up all the contents of drive C, for example, including all the directories and files, type the following command on a DOS or OS/2 command line:

```
BACKUP C:\*.* A: /S
```

The file structure of directory and file names is not listed on the backup floppy disks. Instead, the BACKUP command creates two files, BACKUP and CONTROL. The BACKUP file contains the files you have backed up, and CONTROL contains paths, file names, and other information.

Another way to back up the entire disk is to back up installed applications with the directories of user files. If you then install HPFS on the hard disk, you can restore the applications and files you had stored there before installing OS/2 2.0.

To back up an application and all its files using BACKUP, go to the application directory and enter the following:

```
BACKUP C: A:
```

If you decide to back up just your applications and data files, consider using the XCOPY command instead of the BACKUP command. Unlike BACKUP, XCOPY duplicates on floppy disks the file structure you see on the original disk.

 For more information on XCOPY and COPY, see Chapter 4.

To back up an application and all its files using XCOPY, go to the application directory and enter the following:

```
XCOPY C:\ A:\ /S
```

If you want to back up only your data files, you need to go through all your directories and select the desired files. When you format your hard disk during installation, you will have to reinstall your applications and restore your data files.

Installing One, Two, or More Operating Systems

With OS/2 2.0, you can run multiple operating systems and switch between them from the Boot Manager menu. Before you install OS/2 2.0, you should decide whether OS/2 2.0 is the only operating system you need to run.

Running DOS and Windows under OS/2 2.0

The standard installation of OS/2 2.0 is the operating system, which can run programs written for OS/2, DOS, and Microsoft Windows. Many DOS and Windows programs can run without modification under OS/2 2.0.

 A database is available inside OS/2 2.0 that contains information about DOS and Windows programs that have been tested for compatibility with OS/2 2.0. To read the database, enter at the C:\ prompt: **TYPE OS2\INSTALL\DATABASE.TXT**.

The database includes information about any settings for the tested programs that need to be changed so the programs will run correctly in OS/2.

The DOS version that comes with OS/2 2.0 is DOS 5.0; the Windows version is 3.0.

Some programs must run directly in DOS, rather than in an OS/2 2.0 DOS session (an emulation of DOS). Some games, for example, must be run directly under DOS. If this is the case, you can run DOS separately from OS/2 2.0, but still from the OS/2 Desktop. There are three ways to do this:

- Start DOS from a floppy disk drive after setting up a special DOS session in OS/2 2.0.

- Create a floppy-disk image of a DOS startup floppy disk and put it in the OS/2 2.0 partition on the hard disk. Then create a special DOS session that requires the floppy-disk image.

- Install DOS in a primary partition of a hard disk and OS/2 2.0 in the extended partition of the hard disk. Then set up a special DOS session in OS/2 2.0.

If you decide to use the first or second methods, perform the setup for it after you install OS/2. If you decide to use the third method, you should create the DOS partition during the installation of OS/2. This method does not require the installation of the Boot Manager, however, which presents a menu of operating systems each time you start the computer.

For most people, OS/2 2.0 is the only operating system they need because it can run DOS, Windows, and OS/2 programs. Nevertheless, you might want to look at the options of installing other operating systems, as described in the sections that follow.

Running OS/2 2.0 and DOS Separately

Another installation option is to install OS/2 2.0 and DOS with the capability to switch between them. The usefulness of being able to run DOS separately from OS/2 is that if you have applications that do not run well under OS/2, you can run them under DOS. Another advantage is that if you need some time to become accustomed to OS/2 2.0, you can run DOS and the programs you are comfortable with during the transition period.

The disadvantage of keeping OS/2 and DOS separate is that you have to start the other operating system each time you switch. If you are running OS/2, for example, and decide to switch to DOS, you must open the Command Prompts folder and double-click on the Dual Boot icon, shown at the upper left corner of the command prompts window in figure A.1.

The system asks you to confirm the switch, then shuts down OS/2 and starts DOS. To switch back to OS/2, type **OS2\BOOT/OS2** at the DOS command line. After getting your confirmation, the system shuts down DOS and starts OS/2.

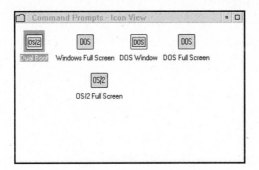

Figure A.1:
Dual Boot icon.

 Instructions for installing a dual boot configuration are given in a later section, "Setting up for Dual Boot."

Switching between Several Operating Systems

The third option is to run multiple operating systems. This option uses Boot Manager. With Boot Manager installed, you select the operating system you want to run from the Boot Manager menu.

A user might install, for example, DOS 4.0, OS/2 1.3, and OS/2 2.0. Boot Manager is especially useful for application developers, who might need the operating systems used in this example.

To set up for Boot Manager and several operating systems, you need to create partitions on the hard disk and install the operating systems in them, usually one operating system to a partition.

If you are not sure whether you need Dual Boot or Boot Manager, first install OS/2 2.0 in the standard manner. Work with the standard installation and see if you like this setup. If you have DOS or DOS and Windows installed on your computer, OS/2 is simply added to the existing setup during installation. OS/2 2.0 does not disturb your existing programs and data, and you do not have to create separate partitions on your hard disk.

If in the future you decide you want to install Dual Boot, you can do that without disturbing the programs and data on your hard disk. If you decide you want to partition your disk and add operating systems, you can use the FDISK or FDISKPM utility within OS/2 2.0. FDISKPM is the window version of FDISK, which is a full-screen program.

 Include FDISK/FDISKPM (the utility that the installation program calls "Manage Partitions") when you are installing OS/2 2.0, so that it will be available in case you decide to use it.

Setting up DOS for Dual Boot

The Dual Boot feature enables you to start either the Disk Operating System (DOS) or OS/2 2.0 and to switch between the two. To set up for Dual Boot, you must have DOS already installed on your hard disk before you begin installing OS/2 2.0.

To install the Dual Boot feature successfully, you must make changes to the AUTOEXEC.BAT and CONFIG.SYS files before you begin the installation procedure. First, make sure DOS is in a separate directory named DOS and not in the root directory. All the DOS files must be in this separate DOS directory. Second, use a text editor to add the following statements to the AUTOEXEC.BAT file:

```
SET COMSPEC=C:\DOS\COMMAND.COM
PATH C:\DOS
APPEND=C:\DOS
COPY C:\DOS\COMMAND.COM C:\ >NUL
```

If you are using DOS 5.0, put these statements before the C:\DOS\DOSSHELL statement. If these files already exist, make sure they are before the C:\DOS\DOSSHELL line.

Another addition you must make is to add the following statement to the CONFIG.SYS file:

```
SHELL=C:\DOS\COMMAND.COM /P
```

If you are using DOS 4.0 with the DOS shell, make sure the following DOS directory is specified in the DOSSHELL.BAT statement:

```
@CD C:\DOS
```

After you make the necessary changes, restart your DOS system to be sure it starts successfully. Do this before you begin OS/2 installation.

Considering Boot Manager

Another OS/2 installation option is Boot Manager, which enables you to install several operating systems and to switch between them. If you install Boot Manager, each time you start the computer the Boot Manager menu displays, from which you select the desired operating system. When you install Boot Manager, you set up multiple partitions on the hard disk and specify which operating system is to run in each partition. This procedure uses the FDISK (fixed disk) utility, which is a feature for experienced users.

You install OS/2 2.0 and set up a primary partition on your hard disk for each of the other operating systems you will use. In addition, you also set up a small partition of 1M for the OS/2 Boot Manager. You can put on a logical drive in the extended partition the system tools and applications whose data will be shared among the operating systems. After the OS/2 2.0 installation is complete, you install the other operating systems.

If you currently have only one partition for the entire hard disk and you decide to use Boot Manager, you must reformat the hard disk and then create multiple partitions. Before you reformat the disk, you have to back up data files onto floppy disks.

If you currently have multiple partitions on the hard disk, you may not have to reformat the entire hard disk. If some of the existing partitions are large enough, you may be able to save them. If the installation program sees that the existing partitions are too small during Boot Manager installation, it notifies you. If you have not already backed up the files you want to save, you must quit the installation, back up your files, and begin installation again.

The key to successful Boot Manager installation on the first try is to plan the partitioning of your disk beforehand. You can divide your disk into a maximum of four partitions. You can have up to four primary partitions, or up to three primary partitions plus one extended partition. The *extended partition* is an area outside the primary partitions in which you can create multiple logical drives. There can be only one extended partition on a hard drive. You do not explicitly create the extended partition; it is the space that is left over after you have created the primary partitions.

Usually, an operating system goes in a primary partition. OS/2 2.0 can reside in a primary partition or on a logical drive within the extended partition. You also can put the system tools and data in the extended partition that will be shared by the operating systems. Only information in the extended partition can be shared among the operating systems because only one partition can be active at a time.

Boot Manager needs a primary partition of its own of 1M. For this reason, you can have only three other primary partitions, each with an operating system in it, for a maximum of three operating systems. Each version of DOS needs a primary partition of 2M to 4M. A standard edition OS/2 version earlier than 2.0 needs a 20M primary partition; an earlier extended edition OS/2 needs a 30M primary partition. OS/2 2.0 requires a 16 to 29M partition (or logical drive within the extended partition), depending on the options you select during installation. AIX has a disk-utility program that creates a partition of an appropriate size.

All these recommendations for partition sizes are for the operating system only; you may need to increase the size of partitions so that they can accommodate your applications and data files.

Choosing a File System

Another choice you must make during the installation of OS/2 2.0 is which file system to use with this operating system. A file system manages input, output, and storage of files on your system. The OS/2 2.0 options are the File Allocation Table (FAT) and the High Performance File System (HPFS). FAT is an appropriate file system for hard disks with up to 60M of storage space; for hard disks with partitions larger than 60M, HPFS considerably improves their performance. If you start DOS from a floppy disk and then access information on the hard disk, the hard disk must be formatted for FAT because DOS does not recognize HPFS-formatted disks.

 For more information about the characteristics of the HPFS and FAT file systems, see Chapter 4.

If you have finished the following tasks, you are ready to install OS/2:

1. Backed up your data.

2. Decided whether to install OS/2 2.0, Dual Boot, or Boot Manager.

3. Decided whether to install the FAT file system or HPFS.

Using the Basic Installation Procedure

If you have decided that OS/2 2.0 is the only operating system you will use, the basic installation probably meets your needs. You can use the basic installation on a computer that does not have any operating system installed or on a computer with DOS or an earlier version of OS/2. Although OS/2 2.0 does not replace your existing DOS, you will not be able to run DOS separately from OS/2, unless you make the modifications described in "Setting Up DOS for Dual Boot." Unlike OS/2 1.2 and 1.3, no DOS "compatibility box" is included in OS/2 2.0. (You can run your DOS programs by opening

DOS windows or full-screen sessions.) If you have an earlier version of OS/2, OS/2 2.0 replaces it without disturbing your applications and data files.

Allow at least an hour for the installation. Simply inserting and removing floppy disks as the system requests them takes about 45 minutes, and you might need some extra time to read related information. Most of the instructions you need are displayed on-screen; if you need help, press the F1 key or a Help button.

Formatting the Hard Disk

The first part of OS/2's installation involves formatting the hard disk drive. This procedure does not use graphics because the components that provide graphics have not been installed. The screens have text on them (no graphics), and you respond by using your keyboard. Follow the on-screen instructions for inserting and removing floppy disks and making selections.

To begin installation, insert the installation floppy disk in floppy disk drive A, label side up and the metal piece toward the computer.

At a certain point, the installation program asks you whether you want to accept the default installation partition or set up your own partitions. If you accept the default and have no data on your hard disk, the installation program installs OS/2 2.0 on a partition that takes up the entire hard disk. If you accept the default and your hard disk already has partitions, the installation program tells you in which partition it installs OS/2. You can either accept this as the 2.0 partition or change it. If you do not choose the default partition, you next see a red screen that warns you to back up your data before continuing. You can remove this warning by pressing Esc. Following this is the FDISK utility screen, which you can use to specify hard disk partitions.

The FDISK screen shows you information about your existing partitions. At this point in the installation, a box displays in the center of the screen informing you that a partition of at least 23M must be set to Installable. OS/2 will be installed in the partition. If you choose not to change the existing partitions, you can ignore this message and exit FDISK.

> **NOTE** The FDISK command is used by experienced DOS users. If you want to continue the basic installation procedure without using FDISK, you can exit FDISK now by pressing the F3 key. For more information on FDISK, see "Installing Boot Manager."

If you are prompted with the message Cannot completely install Dual Boot because DOSSHELL statement is missing, ignore it unless you want to install Dual Boot. This message reminds you to make the necessary changes to the AUTOEXEC.BAT and CONFIG.SYS files, as described in "Setting Up DOS for Dual Boot."

Selecting a File System

If you are installing OS/2 on a new system, or if you have indicated you want to format an existing partition, the installation program asks you to choose either the File Allocation Table (FAT) or the High Performance File System (HPFS). Make sure you have read the available information before making the file system selection. You probably should select FAT unless you have a hard disk with at least 60M.

Now, the installation program prepares your hard disk. As files are transferred, a color bar fills up to show what percentage of the floppy disk has been transferred. When this process is completed, you see an instruction that tells you to restart your computer by pressing Enter.

The graphical part of the installation program now takes over. Information is presented in windows on the screen. Graphical progress indicators with the OS/2 logo replace the plain color bar. Pictures of floppy disks at the bottom of a window indicate which floppy disk you are currently installing, how many you have completed, and how many remain to be installed. In this graphical installation program, you can make selections either by clicking your mouse or by using the keyboard.

Making Setup and Installation Choices

The OS/2 Setup and Installation window presents a menu containing the following choices:

- Learn how to use a mouse
- Install preselected features (23M)
- Install all features (16M)
- Select features and install (16 to 29M)

To help you decide which features to install, the available disk space and the space needed for the features you have currently selected are displayed in a small box on the screen.

Learning How To Use a Mouse

If you have not used a mouse before and one is attached to your system, you might want to go through the mouse tutorial at this time. Then you will be able to use your mouse to make selections during the remainder of the installation. On the other hand, you can wait until OS/2 2.0 is installed and then go through the mouse section of the 2.0 tutorial. The mouse tutorial offered on this screen is the same as the one in the 2.0 tutorial. It is presented here for your convenience. If you go through the mouse tutorial at this point, at the end of it you return to this screen to make your setup and installation selection.

Installing Preselected Features

If you choose"Install preselected features," basic operating system features and a small set of additional utilities and programs are installed. This subset of features requires 23M of disk space.

The following features are not installed:

- CD-ROM (Compact Disk-Read-Only Memory) device support
- Command Reference (on-line version of the manual)
- REXX information (REXX programming language manual)

The following two fonts are the only fonts installed:

- System Proportional
- Helvetica

Other available fonts are Courier, System Mono-Spaced, and Times Roman; outline fonts include Courier, Helvetica, and Times New Roman.

The following utilities are not installed if you choose "Install preselected features":

- Display directory tree (show directory paths and files)
- Label floppy disks (create or change a floppy disk label)
- Link object modules (combine program modules into executable programs)
- Picture viewer (display or print picture files)
- PMREXX (REXX window)
- Recover files (retrieve files from defective disk sectors)

The utilities that are installed include backup hard disk, change file attributes, manage partitions, restore backed-up files, sort filter, and installation aid.

The following tools and games also are not installed:

- Enhanced Editor (creates and edits files)
- Terminal Emulator (communicates with other computers)
- PM Chart (creates graphical charts)
- Klondike Solitaire (plays a variation of the game)

- Reversi (captures opponent's game pieces)
- Scramble (reorders number pieces)
- Cat and Mouse (activates a cat that follows the pointer)
- Pulse (monitors system use with a graph)
- Jigsaw (puts together a puzzle)
- OS/2 Chess (plays against the computer or a person)

Installed tools include Personal Productivity and Search and Scan, such as an alarm, calculator, diary, and so on.

No optional bit maps are installed except for the OS/2 graphic.

Keep in mind that even if you do not install these features now, you can add any of them later by using the Selective Install object in the System Setup folder. Selective Install is convenient because you do not have to go through the entire installation procedure again just to install additional features.

 If you install all OS/2 2.0 features, you need 29M of disk space just for the operating system. After you choose this option, you cannot deselect features that you do not want to install.

Make sure your computer meets the requirements of OS/2 before you choose to install OS/2 2.0 features.

Select Features and Install

This custom installation takes 16 to 29M, depending on which features you select.

Custom installation is the most flexible install option. If you choose this option, you are shown lists of possible features and are assisted by information in OS/2's on-line help.

Selecting System Configuration

The System Configuration window presents mouse, keyboard, country, and display options, as shown in figure A.2.

The installation program shows you, in this window, the options it has found on your system. You can accept them by clicking on the OK button, or you can change any option by clicking on its check box.

If you select Mouse and then click on OK, you can change the pointing device attached to your computer:

- PS/2 ™ Style Pointing Device

- Serial Version

- Logitech ™ Serial Mouse

- IBM Touch Device

- Other Pointing Device for Mouse Port

- No pointing device support

If you check Keyboard and choose OK, you can select a keyboard layout from a list of 27 languages.

If you check **C**ountry, you can select a code page (character set) from a list of 31 countries.

If you check **P**rimary Display or **S**econdary Display, you can select from a list of six displays. If your display is not listed, select Other. Then, later in the installation process, when the Advanced Options window appears, check Install Device Support Diskette. You can then install the device driver for your display.

If you have two displays attached to your computer, make the one with the highest resolution your primary display.

Selecting Optional Features

If you choose "Select features and install," you see another OS/2 Setup and Installation menu, as shown in figure A.3.

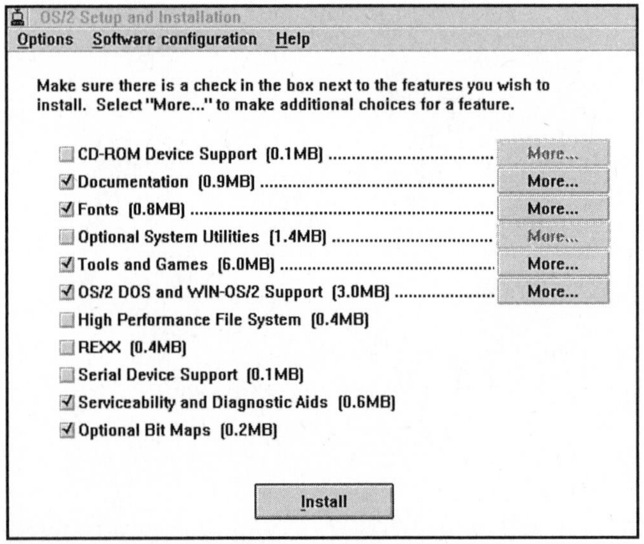

Figure A.3:

Optional features.

At first, all the features are checked, which means they will be installed unless you remove the check marks. To remove a check mark, click on it once with the left mouse button, or highlight it by moving the cursor to it, and then press the space bar.

Notice that to the right of each choice is the amount of disk space it needs. A More button to the right of a choice that is checked means a secondary menu exists. Make sure you examine the secondary menu to see if you want all the items on it to be installed. If you do not want to install an item, remove its check mark. The options for on-line documentation, for example, are shown in figure A.4.

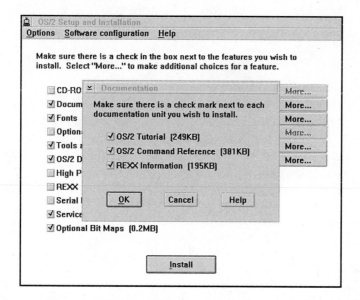

Figure A.4:

The secondary menu for the Documentation feature.

On the horizontal menu bar near the top of the OS/2 Setup and Installation window are the choices Options, Software configuration, and Help. The pull-down menu under Options contains Install, Format, and Command prompt. These choices are available in other places in the system, but they are presented here so that you can choose Install instead of using the button, or format a disk, or enter a command. The pull-down menu under Software configuration is for experienced users who want to change OS/2 or DOS parameters. Help is available to assist you in making decisions.

After you finish making selections, you can click on the Install button or choose Install from the Options menu.

After you insert and remove several floppy disks while the installation program copies files to the hard disk, the Advanced Options window appears.

You can use this window to perform the following:

- Install devices and their support floppy disks

- Configure a standard WIN-OS/2 desktop or one that resembles the Windows desktop you had before you installed OS/2

- Migrate installed DOS, Windows, and OS/2 applications

- Copy information from an AUTOEXEC.BAT or CONFIG.SYS file

When an application program is migrated, its object is displayed as an icon in an OS/2 Desktop folder. If you choose to migrate DOS, Windows, or OS/2 applications, a Find Programs window displays. If you select Find, the installation program searches those programs in a database of applications (C:\OS2\INSTALL\DATABASE.DAT). If your programs are listed in the database, OS/2 2.0 moves and places them in the appropriate DOS, Windows, or OS/2 program folder.

If the list displayed in the Migrate Programs window does not include some programs you have installed and need to use, select the Add Programs button. You then can select programs to add from a list of available programs. Keep in mind that this all-inclusive list probably contains programs that are eligible for migration and are already in your list of programs to migrate. For this reason, you do not need to select them here. After you finish selecting programs to migrate, click on the Migrate button. When migration is complete, choose the Exit button in the Find Programs window. After all the check boxes in the Advanced Options window are empty, choose OK. Now OS/2 setup and installation updates the system configuration.

You also can create your own database of programs by using the PARSEDB utility. This tool generates a binary database from a text file that you create.

Selecting a Printer

Now the system asks you to insert Printer drive floppy disk 1 into floppy disk drive A. If you do not want to set up a printer at this time, select **D**o Not Install Default Printer. If you want to set up a printer, find your printer in the list, highlight it, and then select a printer port. A *port* is a connector on a printer to which you can attach the printer cable. Check your printer documentation to see whether your printer is a parallel or a serial printer. Select another port if LPT1, the default, is not appropriate.

Now you are instructed to insert the floppy disks that contain the files for your printer. At the completion of this procedure, you receive a message saying OS/2 setup and installation is complete.

Completing the Installation

If you had applications on your machine before you installed OS/2, you should shut down your computer at this point and restart before using OS/2.

Remove the floppy disk in drive A and click on OK or press Enter to restart your computer.

While the OS/2 Desktop is being set up, the OS/2 Tutorial opens and displays on-screen. You can start the tutorial at any time.

Installing Dual Boot

If you have set up DOS for Dual Boot before you start the OS/2 2.0 installation, you do not need to do anything special during installation to install Dual Boot. See "Setting up DOS for Dual Boot" earlier in this appendix.

Installing Boot Manager

If you decide to install Boot Manager, select the second option when you are asked to accept the predefined installation partition or to specify your own partition. Check the information about your existing partitions, as shown on the FDISK screen. You might have to delete existing partitions to have enough room for the partitions you want to create. Delete any undesired partitions.

Next, create the Boot Manager partition. Make sure the Free Space line is highlighted. Press Enter to display the Options menu and then follow these steps:

1. Select Install Boot Manager from the Options menu.

   A location window appears. It asks you whether you want to create the Boot Manager partition at the start of free space or at the end of free space. The recommendation is to install Boot Manager at the beginning of the free space on the hard disk.

2. Select either Create at Start of Free Space or Create at End of Free Space.

The Boot Manager partition is automatically marked Startable in the list of partitions in the middle of the screen. If any other partition is marked Startable, you do not see the Boot Manager menu when you start your system. You see, however, the screen for the operating system you have marked Startable.

Next, create a primary partition for any DOS version you are going to install by following these steps:

1. Select Create partition from the Options menu.

2. Enter the size you want the partition to be (at least 2M for DOS 3.3; 3M for DOS 4.0; 4M for DOS 5.0).

3. Specify a primary partition.

4. Select Add to Boot Manager menu.

5. Enter the name of the partition as you want it to appear on the Boot Manager menu after you start the computer.

Follow the same steps to create a partition for each operating system. OS/2 Standard Edition before version 2.0 requires a partition of 20M; Extended Edition requires 29M.

Remember that four partitions is the maximum or three partitions and an extended partition. Create a primary partition of at least 23M or a logical drive within the extended partition for OS/2 2.0. Select Set installable for the 2.0 partition or drive.

Use the Assign C: partition choice to specify which partition will be active and visible when you restart the computer.

 For further details on using FDISK and setting options for partitions, refer to the OS/2 2.0 Installation Guide.

After you finish specifying the partitions for the hard disk, save the information and exit FDISK.

At this point, you are asked to insert the Installation disk again. The Installation program asks you whether you want to accept the drive shown for the installation of OS/2 2.0. If it is correct, choose Accept. If it is not the proper drive, choose the alternative, which is to specify partitions. This action accesses the FDISK screen again, from which you can adjust your partitions. Then continue with the installation, as described in the previous sections.

Adding and Changing Features

You can add or change many features after initial installation by using objects in the System Setup folder, such as Selective Install.

You can install device drivers on device support floppy disks by using the Install Device Driver object. Do not use this object to install device drivers, such as printer drivers, on the OS/2 floppy disks. To add a printer, create a printer object and install the appropriate printer driver (file) from the operating system floppy disks.

You also can migrate newly installed applications by using the Migrate Applications object. The choices are shown in figure A.5.

Figure A.5:
Migrate applications menu.

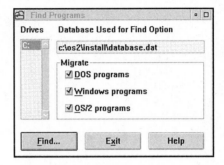

Changing Hard Disk Partitions

To add, change, or remove hard disk partitions, you can use FDISK full-screen or FDISKPM, the window version.

If you enter **FDISKPM** at an OS/2 window or full-screen prompt, the FDISKPM window displays, as shown in figure A.6.

Figure A.6:
FDISKPM window.

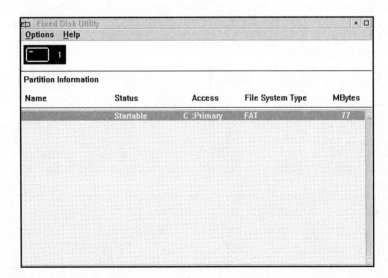

The Options menu, which you display by clicking on **O**ptions in the menu bar, contains the following choices (the same as in the full-screen version of FDISK):

- Install **B**oot Manager
- **C**reate partition
- Add to Boot Manager **m**enu
- Change partition **n**ame
- **A**ssign C: partition
- Set startup **v**alues
- Remove from Boot Manager **m**enu
- **D**elete partition
- Set **i**nstallable
- Make s**t**artable

Refer to the earlier section on "Installing Boot Manager" for information about using FDISK or FDISKPM to manage hard disk partitions.

Deleting Features After Installation

You can delete a feature with a mouse by dragging the object to the shredder. You also can use Selective Install and deselect any option you want to remove from your existing system.

You can remove OS/2 2.0 by using FDISK.

 If you plan to delete OS/2 2.0 from your hard disk, remember that you will not get another chance to confirm your decision; the deletion is immediate.

To delete OS/2 2.0 from your machine, follow these steps:

1. Open a DOS window or full-screen session.

2. Enter **FDISK** on the command line.

3. When the FDISK screen displays, select the OS/2 2.0 partition.

4. Press Enter to display the **O**ptions pull-down menu.

5. If you are certain you want to delete OS/2 2.0, choose **D**elete partition.

   The OS/2 2.0 partition is deleted.

Current OS/2 Applications

Literally hundreds of application programs are available for OS/2. Only some of them can be listed here, but this appendix gives you an idea of what is available. If you want a more complete list of available applications, refer to IBM's *OS/2 Application Solutions*, which is available from:

Graphics Plus, Inc.
640 Knowlton Street
Bridgeport, CN 06608
(800)786-PLUS

Application Development Tools

The following section includes a sampling of languages, code generators, and compilers.

Application Development Workbench

Knowledgeware, Inc.
3340 Peachtree Road NE
Atlanta, GA 30326
(404)231-8575

A suite of SAA-compliant CASE tools.

DESIGN/1 for OS/2

Andersen Consulting
69 West Washington Street
Chicago, IL 60602
(312)507-5161

A LAN-based set of integrated analysis and business tools.

The Developer's Business Graphics Toolkit

The Crossley Group, Inc.
P.O. Box 921759
Norcross, GA 30092
(404)751-3703

Integrates two- and three-dimensional graphics into business applications.

EASEL Workbench and EASEL/2

EASEL Corporation
25 Corporate Drive
Burlington, MA 08103
(617)221-3000

A visual development tool that is a strategic product in IBM's AD/cycle framework.

ObjectVision OS/2

Borland International
1800 Green Hills Road
Scotts Valley, CA 95067
(408)438-5300

An object-oriented program development system.

PM/FOCUS

Information Builders, Inc.
1250 Broadway
New York, NY 10001
(212)736-4433

A 4GL database application development system.

SAS/AF, SAS/ASSIST, SAS/CONNECT, SAS/GRAPH, SAS/IML, SAS/STAT

SAS Institute, Inc.
SAS Campus Drive
Cary, NC 27513
(919)677-8000

A complete set of application development tools, emphasizing database statistics.

Toolbook for OS/2 PM

Asymetrix Corporation
110 110th Avenue NE, Suite 717
Bellevue, WA 98004
(206)637-1500

A software construction set for building custom applications.

Zortech C++

Zortech, Inc.
4-C Gill Street
Woburn, MA 01801
(617)937-0696

A C++ compiler, which includes 16-bit and 32-bit extenders.

Software Utilities and Programming Aids

The following section lists programming utilities that perform specific tasks. These utilities can also be used with other development systems.

IBM SAA Personal Application System Development/2, Version 2

> IBM Corporation
> 3035 Center Green Drive
> Boulder, CO 80301
> (800)IBM-CALL

An application development tool designed to create custom OS/2 2 Presentation Manager applications that involve access to OS/2 relational Database Manager and mainframe applications.

AUTOSORT OS/2

> Computer Control Systems, Inc.
> Route 3, Box 168
> Lake City, FL 32055
> (904)752-6873

A sort/merge/select utility designed for large files that have fixed field lengths within fixed length records.

Spool+

> Ultinet Development, Inc.
> P.O. Box 34016
> Los Angeles, CA 90034
> (213)204-0111

Enables network users to share printers attached to local workstations on an IBM LAN Server network.

Accounting, Spreadsheet, and Financial Management

The following section lists custom accounting and finance applications, as well as several off-the-shelf spreadsheet programs.

AccountFlex

Infoflex, Inc.
875 Mahler Road, Suite 200
Burlingame, CA 94010
(415)340-0220

A modular accounting system that includes AR, GL, PR, AP, IN, and OE written in Infoflex, an SQL-based 4GL.

ACCPAC Plus Accounting

Computer Associates International
711 Stewart Avenue
Garden City, NY 11530
(800)645-2002

A complete accounting system operating in OS/2's protected mode. It is available in a network version.

Microsoft Excel for OS/2

Microsoft Corporation
One Microsoft Way
Redmond, WA 98052
(206)882-8080

A spreadsheet that combines advanced analytical and graphical features.

Oil and Gas Accounting

Dodson Programming Service
900 8th Street, Suite 500
Wichita Falls, TX 76301
(817)723-4481

Includes accounting functions unique to the petroleum industry.

WingZ

Informix Software, Inc.
4100 Bohannon Drive
Menlo Park, CA 94025
(415)926-6300

A spreadsheet program, as well as a self-contained program-development system.

Banking and Financial Services

The following section lists programs written for commercial and large-scale money management.

Advanced Property and Management Systems

Advanced Data Design, Inc.
184-08 Tudor Road
Jamaica, NY 11432
(718)380-0124

Property management of multi-unit residential buildings.

BranchTeller

Ampersand Corporation
128 S. George Street
York, PA 17405
(717)845-5602

A full-function teller automation system.

Cemetery Control and Management

Systems A.D.I.
8030 Cedar, Suite 226
Minneapolis, MN 55425
(612)854-1140

Includes property inventory, internments, contacts, and accounting.

Lotus 1-2-3 for OS/2

Lotus Development Corporation
55 Cambridge Parkway
Cambridge, MA 02142
(617)577-8500

The familiar 1-2-3 worksheet in the Presentation Manager environment.

Mutual Fund Trading System

DTS Management Corporation
6716 E. Desert Cove
Scottsdale, AZ 85254
(602)443-8054

A total solution for processing wire-order mutual fund trades.

PROBATE AS

Trust Service Co., Inc.
4033 Silver Bell Drive
Charlotte, NC 28211
(704)365-1417

A fiduciary accounting system for estates, trusts, and
guardianships.

Signature Verification

SQN, Inc.
65 Indel Avenue
Rancocas, NJ 08073
(609)261-5500

Scans, stores, and displays images of signatures from bank signature cards.

Industrial, Manufacturing, and Management

The following section lists some of the programs available for plant
management and job control systems.

C-PAK Manufacturing System

C-PAK Corporation
1495 Lafayette Parkway
LaGrange, GA 30240
(404)883-7664

Manufacturing control, including inventory and order entry, for job
shops, printers, and other discrete industries.

Job Costing

Computer Associates International
711 Stewart Avenue
Garden City, NY 11530
(800)645-2002

A cost-tracking system for any business that operates on a job or
project basis.

The Scheduler

STSC, Inc.
2115 E. Jefferson Street
Rockville, MD 20852
(301)984-5000

A decision support finite capacity system designed specifically for
process and high-volume repetitive manufacturers.

Tax Accounting and Legal

The following section is to be avoided (unless you are in this line of
work, of course).

Bankruptcy Management System and Forms Management

Integrated Software Technologies, Inc.
515 North Flagler Drive
West Palm Beach, FL 33401
(417)655-4550

Assists law firms practicing bankruptcy law, and automates federal
bankruptcy filing with convenient graphical interface and laser
printer output.

Juris

Juris, Inc.
151 Athens Way
Nashville, TN 37228
(615)242-2870

A comprehensive law office management system, including
Docket/Case Management and Time & Billing modules.

Insurance

The following programs help insurance companies keep up with the
growing demands of their businesses.

Claims Management System

Policy Management Systems Corporation
P.O. Box 10
Columbia, SC 29202
(803)735-4000

A full line of insurance management products, including Claims
Management, Client Information, Contracts & Commissions, and
Disbursement Management.

LABOR AS

Trust Service Company, Inc.
4033 Silver Bell Drive
Charlotte, NC 28211
(704)365-1417

Processes member records for union member benefits
administration.

Total Insurance Processing (TIPS)

Datamedic Corporation
20 Oser Avenue
Hauppauge, NY 11788
(516)435-8880

TeleClaim editor that provides paperfree access to hundreds of carriers, HMOs, and TPAs.

Government and Public Administration

The following section includes programs that are helpful for city governments.

DISPATCH/NET

GTE Government Information Services, Inc.
11150 Sunset Hills Road, Suite 320
Reston, VA 22090
(703)689-0001

A computer-aided dispatch system for law enforcement agencies, fire departments, and emergency medical agencies.

Voter Registration

Fundbalance
P.O. Box 1987
Ann Arbor, MI 48106
(314)677-0550

A computerized filing system for maintaining voter registration lists.

Public Utilities and Transportation

The following are applications for this specialized industry.

Cable Television Billing

El Dorado Softworks
2157 Bethel Road
Mt. Holly, AR 71758
(501)554-2300

A complete cable TV billing system. This company also provides Rural Electric Billing, Pest Control Billing, Water Utility Billing, Water/Gas/Electric Billing, and Waste Disposal Billing systems.

Electric System Mapping

Southern Engineering Company
1800 Peachtree Street NW
Atlanta, GA 30367
(404)352-9200

Applies Autodesk's AutoCAD to create electrical system maps.

Construction

The following lists applications for design, tracking, and cost of construction.

Contractor Business System

Carolina Computer Systems, Inc.
408 Russell Street
Orangeburg, SC 29115
(803)534-6742

A job-cost system for contractors.

Integrated 3D Structural Design

Engineering Software Company
2418 Cales Drive
Arlington, TX 76013
(817)861-2296

Sample solutions to complex frame and truss design problems.
This company also offers Integrated Beam Design and Analysis,
QuickCOLUMN, QuickFRAME 2-D, QuickFRAME 3-D,
QuickStress, and QuickWall programs.

Health

The following programs are likely to be found in your doctor's or
dentist's office.

Appointment Scheduling

Datamedic Corporation
20 Oser Avenue
Hauppauge, NY 11788
(516)435-8880

Appointment scheduling for a solo or group practice.

DENTPAC Dental Office Management System

Syscon, Inc.
94 McFarland Blvd. North
Northport, AL 35476
(800)543-3767

Automates the accounting function for single- and multiple-
provider dental offices.

Medical Office Management System

Systems Solutions, Inc.
1439 Riverside Drive NE
Gainesville, GA 30501
(404)535-1528

Provides all aspects of data processing needs for medical offices and mental health practitioners/clinics.

Scientific, Engineering, and Technical Computing

The following applications help technical professionals get their work done easier and with less time taken for revisions.

AutoCAD

Autodesk, Inc.
2320 Marinship Way
Sausalito, CA 94965
(415)332-2344

A general purpose design and drafting program for technical workstations.

LABTECH Notebook

Laboratory Technologies Corporation
400 Research Drive
Wilmington, MA 01887
(508)657-5400

An integrated, general-purpose program for data acquisition, analysis, and process control.

SPANS

Tydac Technologies Corporation
1655 North Fort Meyer Drive
Arlington, VA 22209
(703)522-0773

A family of stand-alone Geographic Information Systems.

SPSS for OS/2

SPSS, Inc.
444 North Michigan Avenue
Chicago, IL 60611
(312)329-3500

For statistical analysis, data management, and presentation.

Database, Expert, and Knowledge Based Systems

The following are database-management systems for tracking
information and for developing custom database applications.

KnowledgeMan

Micro Database System, Inc.
P.O. Box 6089
Lafayette, IN 47093
(317)447-1122

A relational database system that offers spreadsheet interface. It is
fully compatible with SQL.

R:BASE for OS/2

Microrim, Inc.
15395 SE 30th Place
Bellevue, WA 98007
(206)649-9500

A fully-relational database with intuitive graphic-style interface.

The SAS™System

SAS Institute, Inc.
SAS Campus Drive
Cary, NC 27513
(919)677-8000

An integrated application development system with a transparent link to mainframe SAS systems.

SYBASE

Sybase, Inc.
6475 Christie Avenue
Emeryville, CA 94608
(800)879-2273

An SQL-based relational database with client-server architecture.

Zip*Data

Melissa Data Company
32112 Paseo Adelanto
San Juan Capistrano, CA 92675
(714)661-5885

Provides nationwide zip code information for programmers, including the latitude and longitude for each zip code.

Word Processing and Office Systems

The most popular programs in use in today's businesses, these programs have changed the way you work.

DeltaImaging PM

Deltatech Corporation
8700 Georgia Avenue
Silver Spring, MD 20910
(301)588-2200

Index, retrieve, print, fax, and OCR documents.

DeScribe Word Processor

DeScribe, Inc.
4047 North Freeway Blvd
Sacramento, CA 95834
(916)646-1111

A word processor that has a multilingual spell checker, unlimited undo, and many other advanced features. It produces publishing-quality documents.

FaxPress Network Fax Server

Castelle, Inc.
3255-3 Scott Blvd.
Santa Clara, CA 95054
(408)496-0474

Self-contained network fax server for IBM LAN Server LANs.

IBM DisplayWrite

IBM Corporation
5 West Kirkwood Blvd.
Roanoke, TX 76299
(817)962-5385

An advanced text processor for the OS/2 environment. A good transition program from DisplayWriter.

Microsoft Word for OS/2

Microsoft Corporation
One Microsoft Way
Redmond, WA 98052
(206)882-8080

A full-featured graphical word processor with Ribbon and Ruler.

Relish™

Sundial Systems Corporation
909 Electric Avenue
Seal Beach, CA 90740
(213)596-5121

A time- and information-tracking system (network version also available).

WordPerfect for OS/2

WordPerfect Corporation
1555 North Technology Way
Orem, UT 84057
(801)225-5000

Character-based word processor with print preview, columns, and graphics.

Personnel and Business Management

The following programs assist with the staffing and reporting requirements of human resources departments.

Applicant Manager

Skopos Corporation
4966 El Camino Real
Los Altos, CA 94022
(415)962-8590

A tracking and requisition system that stores, retrieves, and matches applicants to specific staffing requirements. This company also provides Job Analyzer, Personnel Data Manager, and TotalComp programs.

Work Force/Job Group Analyst

PRI Associates, Inc.
1905 Chapel Hill Road
Durham, NC 27707
(919)493-7534

Processes required Affirmative Action plan information.

Publishing and Graphics

The following programs are used to create presentations, publications, and graphic objects to be used in other programs.

Aldus PageMaker for OS/2

Aldus Corporation
411 First Avenue South
Seattle, WA 98104
(206)343-4222

An advanced page-layout program.

Arts & Letters Composer

Computer Support Corporation
15926 Midway Road
Dallas, TX 75244
(214)661-8960

A comprehensive system containing more than 5,000 clip art images and 80 outline typefaces.

ClickArt

T/Maker Company
1390 Villa Street
Mountain View, CA 94041
(415)962-0195

Contains many clip art cartoons and graphics for business, sports, animals and nature, industry, and holidays.

CorelDRAW!

Corel Systems Corporation
1600 Carling Avenue
Ottawa, CN K1Z 887
(613)728-8200

An easy-to-use graphics program that produces stunning results.

Designer

Micrografx
1303 Arapahoe
Richardson, TX 75081
(214)234-1769

A precision drawing program.

PM Draw!

Micrografx
1303 Arapahoe
Richardson, TX 75081
(214)234-1769

A new product that enables you to do things such as place text along a curve.

Freelance Graphics for OS/2

Lotus Development Corporation
55 Cambridge Parkway
Cambridge, MA 02142
(617)557-8500

A program that creates presentations, from handouts to overheads.

Ventura Publisher for OS/2

Ventura Software, Inc.
15175 Innovative Drive
San Diego, CA 92128
(800)822-8221

A precision desktop-publishing and page-layout program.

Telephone and Communications

The following programs give you connectivity to other computers outside your home or office.

3270 Remote OS/2

Trisystems Corporation
74 Northeastern Blvd
Nashua, NH 03062
(603)883-0558

A 3174 emulation, enabling up to 32 sessions for IBM 30xx and 43xx over leased data lines. It also provides 5250 Remote and other emulation applications.

DaVinci eMAIL

DaVinci Systems Corporation
4200 Six Forks Road
Raleigh, NC 27609
(919)881-4321

An electronic-mail system.

HyperACCESS/5

Hilgraeve
111 Conant Avenue
Monroe, MI 48161
(800)826-2760

A communications program with multithreading for multiple sessions and script language with learning.

IBM DirectRoute/2

Voice Applications Solutions Development
100 Lake Forest Blvd.
Gaithersburg, MD 20877
(301)240-3302

An application for call centers, help desks, and service bureaus. It can retrieve caller profiles from the host computer.

Open+

Open+Voice, Inc.
13711 North Central Expressway
Dallas, TX 75243
(214)497-9022

Includes Open+Accel for interactive voice messaging; Open+Build for designing communications systems; Open+D, which is a script language for experienced developers; Open+Editor, which is an integrated voice prompt editor using the graphical interface of PM; Open+Entry for nonprogrammers to develop interactive response applications; and Open+Fax, which enables nonprogrammers to develop interactive fax applications.

REXXTERM Version 2.3

Quercus Systems
P.O. Box 2157
Saratoga, CA 95070
(408)867-7399

An asynchronous communications program for OS/2 that supports script writing with REXX.

File Utilities

The following are examples of programs used for backups and file protection.

File Encrypt™

Wisdom Software, Inc.
P.O. Box 460310
San Francisco, CA 94146
(415)579-7459

Protects your sensitive data with file encryption/decryption.

Keeptrack Plus for OS/2

The Finot Group
1504 Franklin Street
Oakland, CA 94612
(415)465-1100

A high-speed backup with advanced file-selection capability.

MaynStream for OS/2 Systems

Maynard Electronics, Inc.
36 Skyline Drive
Lake Mary, FL 32746
(407)263-3500

A high-performance tape backup for large tape capacities.

V

Command Reference

Command
Reference

Use this chapter as a reference to the 120 OS/2 and DOS commands available to you in OS/2 2.0.

Each command includes the following information:

- Name of command
- Type of command
- Syntax
- Switches (parameters that affect what the command does)
- Rules and Considerations
- Examples
- Notes and related commands, if any

The commands covered fall into several overlapping categories:

- Internal or external
- Command prompt, batch file, or CONFIG.SYS
- DOS or OS/2

Internal commands are built directly into the operating system kernel. External commands are separate programs. For external commands, the syntax statements assume that you have a copy of the program either in your current directory or in a directory and path included in your path statement.

Some commands can be executed directly from the command prompt; others work as part of batch files or in the CONFIG.SYS startup file. Some commands work in all contexts. Remember that statements included in your CONFIG.SYS file only take effect when you restart the system.

Because OS/2 was designed to be an evolutionary step beyond DOS, most DOS commands still exist under OS/2. Some commands work only in DOS sessions, however. Many other commands are new to OS/2, especially those that manage multitasking, virtual memory, and problem determination. The Type heading indicates whether the command works only in OS/2 2.0 sessions, or also in DOS sessions running under OS/2.

ANSI

Purpose

ANSI enables or disables extended keyboard and display support.

Type

OS/2 only

Syntax

ANSI

Switches

None

Rules and Considerations

With ANSI on, OS/2 can process ANSI control sequences. ANSI control sequences consist of a series of characters that begin with an escape character. They are often used to change your cursor, redefine keys, and change screen display colors. The KEYS ON command disables ANSI extended keyboard support.

Examples

To see whether extended keyboard and display support are currently enabled or disabled, type the following:

    ANSI

Type the following command to enable extended keyboard and display support:

    ANSI ON

To disable extended keyboard and display support, type the following command:

    ANSI OFF

Note

For extended keyboard and display support in DOS sessions, include the ANSI.SYS driver in your CONFIG.SYS file. (See DEVICE.)

See Also

DEVICE=ANSI.SYS
KEYS

APPEND

Purpose

APPEND tells the system where to look for a data file not found in the current directory. APPEND connects program and data files in one directory, while leaving related information elsewhere.

Type

DOS only

Syntax

APPEND *DRIVE: PATH; DRIVE: PATH*

Switches

/E	Restricts appended paths to the DOS environment
/PATH:*ON*	Searches appended directories, even if your file name specifies drives and/or paths
/PATH:*OFF*	Searches your specified drives/paths, or searches all appended directories if you have not specified drives or paths

Rules and Considerations

After you type **APPEND**, indicate the drives and paths of the directories to be connected.

APPEND first looks in a file's specified directory or your current directory. Next, it looks in the directories you have appended, unless you use the PATH:OFF switch and specify a drive or path.

Example

To define a search path that comprises all the files in the root directories of drives A, B, and C, type the following:

```
APPEND A:\;B:\;C:\
```

Note

APPEND is similar to the PATH command, except that you can use it with any kind of file, instead of only executable files. APPEND is a DOS command; see DPATH for a similar OS/2 command.

See Also

DPATH
PATH
SET

ASSIGN

Purpose

The ASSIGN command redirects disk I/O requests from one drive to another. This command is most commonly used with older programs that use only drives A and B, and it cannot work on a hard disk.

Type

DOS only

Syntax

ASSIGN *ORIGINALDRIVE=REPLACEMENTDRIVE*

Switch

/S   Tells whether any drives are currently reassigned

Rules and Considerations

After you reassign a drive, you are not able to use the source drive until you restore the original drive assignments.

You cannot reassign your hard disk.

When ASSIGN is in effect, the following commands do not work:

> CHKDSK
> DISKCOMP
> DISKCOPY
> FORMAT
> JOIN
> LABEL
> PRINT
> RECOVER
> RESTORE
> SUBST

Examples

To reassign drive A: to drive C, type the following:

> `ASSIGN A=C`

Type the next command to reassign both the A and B drives to your C drive:

> `ASSIGN A=C B=C`

To review current assignments, type the following command:

> `ASSIGN/S`

To restore the original drive references, type ASSIGN without additional parameters as follows:

> `ASSIGN`

See Also

JOIN
SUBST

ATTRIB

Purpose

The ATTRIB command displays or changes a file's attribute byte. By using ATTRIB, you can control whether a file is a read-only, archive, hidden, or system file.

Type

DOS and OS/2

Syntax

ATTRIB [+ATTRIBUTE/-ATTRIBUTE] FILENAME.EXT

Switch

/S   Shows archive and read-only bit settings for the
            file(s) you specify.

Rules and Considerations

You can use ATTRIB with BACKUP, RESTORE, and XCOPY to give you more control over copy and backup procedures. For example, the BACKUP command can be set to copy only the files that have the archive attribute set—in other words, files that have been changed. You can use ATTRIB to make sure that certain categories of files show an archive attribute (+A), while others do not (-A). This enables you to back up only the files you choose.

You also can use ATTRIB with XCOPY to copy your hard drive's contents onto floppies without losing your disk's structure. Mark all files to require a backup (+A), then use XCOPY and the /M switch to copy all files with the archive attribute.

As the files are copied, XCOPY clears their archive attributes. When you run out of room on your floppy disk, change to a new diskette, and issue XCOPY again. XCOPY begins where it left off, and copies the remaining files that still have an archive attribute.

The following attributes can be set or cleared by ATTRIB:

A   Archive

R   Read-only

H   Hidden

S   System

+   Sets an attribute

-          Clears an attribute

Examples

To change a file with the name FILENAME.EXT into a read-only file, type the following command:

```
ATTRIB +R FILENAME.EXT
```

The next command clears the read-only file attribute:

```
ATTRIB -R FILENAME.EXT
```

The next example clears the read-only file attribute and sets the archive attribute at the same time:

```
ATTRIB -R +A FILENAME.EXT
```

To make a file a hidden file, type the command as follows:

```
ATTRIB +H FILENAME.EXT
```

To clear the hidden file attribute, type the following:

```
ATTRIB -H FILENAME.EXT
```

Type the following command to view current attributes:

```
ATTRIB FILENAME.EXT
```

To view current attributes of all .doc files in the directory C:\oldfiles, type the following:

```
ATTRIB C:\OLDFILES\*.DOC/S
```

If FILENAME.EXT in subdirectory SUBDIR currently has archive and read-only attributes set, the display appears as follows:

```
A R     C:\SUBDIR\FILENAME.EXT
```

If neither attribute is set, you see the following:

```
C:\SUBDIR\FILENAME.EXT
```

To view current attributes on all subdirectories of your current directory, type the following:

```
ATTRIB *.*/S
```

To view current attributes on all directories on your hard disk, enter the following command:

```
ATTRIB C:\*.*/S
```

See Also

BACKUP
RESTORE
XCOPY

AUTOFAIL

Purpose

The AUTOFAIL command displays information about error conditions.

Type

OS/2 only

Syntax

AUTOFAIL=[NO | YES]

Switches

None

Rules and Considerations

When you install OS/2, the AUTOFAIL default is set to NO. If an error condition occurs, a window informs you. If you prefer an error code, enter **AUTOFAIL=YES** as a statement in your CONFIG.SYS file.

Notes

The AUTOFAIL command works only when included in CONFIG.SYS. Do not invoke it at the OS/2 command prompt.

BACKUP

Purpose

The BACKUP command copies one or more files from one disk to another.

Type

OS/2 and DOS

Syntax

BACKUP *SOURCEDRIVE: PATH FILENAME TARGET DRIVE*

Switches

/L:*FILENAME*	Creates a file—BACKUP.LOG—unless otherwise specified. This file states when, where, and what you are backing up.
/D:*MM-DD-YY*	Limits backup to those files created after the date you specify.
/T:*HH:MM:SS*	Limits backup to those files created after the time you specify. (Use with /D:.)
/M	Backs up only files that have been changed since your last backup.
/A	Adds new backup files to the files you already have on your backup disk (without overwriting previous versions).
/F:*XXX*	Formats target floppy disk before backing up. XXX sets number of kilobytes on target disk: 360, 720, 1200, 1440, or 2880.
/S	Backs up subdirectories beneath your current directory.

Rules and Considerations

If you back up to floppy diskettes, make sure you have enough disks available. If they are unformatted, include the /F:*XXX* switch. Track the order in which you create backup diskettes. If you use the RESTORE command later, you must load the diskettes in the same order.

Remember that BACKUP does not automatically back up all subdirectories unless you use the /S switch.

If you already have a BACKUP.LOG file, new entries are added to the current file as you continue to make new backups.

The BACKUP command works with hard drives and all standard floppy drives. If your source drive is a floppy, temporarily disable the write protection. BACKUP needs to clear the archive bit to indicate the file has been backed up.

Backed up files show up as two new files on your target diskette(s): BACKUP.XXX contains the files themselves, and CONTROL.XXX contains control information.

The BACKUP command does not back up the following files:

- System files (COMMAND.COM and CMD.EXE)
- Hidden system files
- Open dynamic link library (DLL) files
- Files marked Deny Read/Write

Examples

To back up all files on the C drive's root directory onto drive A:, type the following command:

```
BACKUP C: A:
```

Type the following command to add files in subdirectories:

```
BACKUP C: A: /S
```

The following command creates a log file called BACKUP.LOG:

```
BACKUP C: A: /S /L
```

To back up all files on the C drive's root directory that have been changed since April 1, 1992, at 9 am, type the following command:

```
BACKUP C: A: /D:04-01-92 /T:09:00:00
```

Enter the following command to add new backups from drive C to drive A without overwriting previous backups:

```
BACKUP C: A: /A
```

See Also

ATTRIB
RESTORE
XCOPY
Extended Attributes

BASEDEV

Purpose

The BASEDEV command loads the base device drivers that OS/2 requires upon startup before specific device drivers are loaded.

Type

OS/2 and DOS

Syntax

BASEDEV *FILENAME.EXT ARGUMENTS*

Switches

None

Rules and Considerations

When OS/2 is installed, CONFIG.SYS includes several BASEDEV statements that enable generic support for disk drives, printers, and other devices. If you install OS/2 on an Industry Standard Architecture system, for example, the following drivers are included in CONFIG.SYS:

PRINT01.SYS   For local printers on non-Micro
                                     Channel systems

IBMFLPY.ADD	For diskette drives on non-Micro Channel systems
IBM1S506.ADD	For non-SCSI drives on non-Micro Channel systems
IBMINT13.I13	Other device support for non-Micro Channel systems
OS2DASD.DMD	For disk drives

BASEDEV statements appear before device statements. If you need to add a third-party base driver, include it with your other BASEDEV statements. Because they appear before OS/2 can process path and drive information, include only the filename and extension. Copy the driver into your C:\OS2 subdirectory.

BASEDEV recognizes only files that have the extensions listed below. BASEDEV processes them in the order shown, not in the order you include them—unless more than one driver has the same extension.

SYS

BID

VSD

TSD

ADD

I13

FLT

DMD

Example

To add a third-party base device driver named NEWSTOR.ADD, include the following statement in your CONFIG.SYS file:

```
BASEDEV=NEWSTOR.ADD
```

Notes

IBM OS/2 also comes with several other base device drivers, which may be installed automatically depending on your system:

PRINT02.SYS	For local printers on Micro Channel systems
IBM2FLPY.ADD	For diskette drives on Micro Channel systems
IBM2ADSK.ADD	For non-SCSI drives on Micro Channel systems
IBM2SCSI.ADD	For Micro Channel SCSI adapters
OS2SCSI.DMD	For non-disk SCSI devices

See Also

DEVICE

BOOT

Purpose

BOOT switches between DOS and OS/2 operating systems both resident on drive C.

Type

OS/2 and DOS

Syntax

BOOT /02S|DOS

Switches

/OS2   Switches from DOS to OS/2

/DOS   Switches from OS/2 to DOS

Rules and Considerations

The BOOT command only works if you install DOS separately on drive C, and if you do not reformat your drive when you install OS/2. IBM or MS-DOS 3.3, 4.0, or 5.0 are recommended. BOOT supports only the FAT (File Allocation Table) file system; you cannot use HPFS on the C partition.

Before you invoke BOOT, complete all system operations and end all programs.

Examples

To switch from DOS to OS/2, type the following from the OS/2 subdirectory:

```
BOOT /OS2
```

To switch from OS/2 to DOS, close all programs and type the following command:

```
BOOT /DOS
```

BREAK

Purpose

The BREAK command causes DOS to check more often on the use of <CTRL>-<BREAK> to stop a program.

Type

DOS only

Syntax

BREAK=[ON | OFF]

Switches

None

Rules and Considerations

DOS normally monitors the use of <CTRL>-<BREAK> after standard I/O and keyboard operations. In most cases this is sufficient, but occasionally you may need to stop a program faster, especially if you are a program developer. When you set BREAK=ON, DOS checks for <CTRL>-<BREAK> before it executes any program requests.

You may set BREAK either at the DOS command prompt or in your CONFIG.SYS file.

Examples

To set DOS to check for <CTRL>-<BREAK> after every program request, type the following command:

    BREAK=ON

The following command limits DOS <CTRL>-<BREAK> checking to standard I/O and print operations:

    BREAK=OFF

Note

The BREAK command is only available in DOS; OS/2 always runs with BREAK set to ON.

BUFFERS

Purpose

The BUFFERS command allocates memory for the number of disk buffers you choose.

Type

OS/2 and DOS

Syntax

BUFFERS=X

Switches

None

Rules and Considerations

BUFFERS are 0.5K sections of RAM that briefly hold data on its way from the disk, so that the processor always has information available. When you install OS/2, the system defaults to 30 buffers. If you increase this number, you can improve performance sometimes, but this approach has a disadvantage. The more memory set aside for buffering, the less memory available for the programs themselves.

Example

To set the number of buffers at 40, include the following statement in your CONFIG.SYS file:

```
BUFFERS=40
```

Note

The maximum number of buffers is 100; the minimum is 1.

CACHE

Purpose

The CACHE command sets parameters for High Performance File
System (HPFS) caching.

Type

OS/2 and DOS (HPFS only)

Syntax

CACHE

Switches

/LAZY:*STATE*   Determines if cache contents are
                       to be written to disk immediately
                       (/LAZY:*OFF*) or when disk is other-
                       wise idle (/LAZY:*ON*)

Times for the following switches are in milliseconds:

/MAXAGE:*TIME*   Sets how long data waits before
                       moving to another cache level or to
                       disk

/DISKIDLE:*TIME*   Sets how long a disk must be idle
                       before accepting data from the cache

`/BUFFERIDLE:`*`TIME`*   Sets how long a buffer must be idle before its contents must be written to disk

Rules and Considerations

CACHE is only available if you format a hard disk partition to use HPFS.

The /LAZY switch is available at the OS/2 command prompt; /MAXAGE, /DISKIDLE, and /BUFFERIDLE must be included in run statements within your CONFIG.SYS file, as shown below.

If you reset /LAZY during an OS/2 command session and want to change it again without exiting the session, you must first invoke the DETACH command. For example, you must type the following:

```
DETACH CACHE /LAZY:ON
```

CACHE defaults are shown below:

/LAZY	ON
/MAXAGE	5000
/DISKIDLE	1000
/BUFFERIDLE	500

Examples

To set LAZY=OFF (so that all cache data is written to disk immediately), type the following at the OS/2 prompt:

```
CACHE /LAZY:OFF
```

To make LAZY=*OFF* your default, include this statement in your STARTUP.CMD file:

```
C:\OS2=CACHE.EXE /LAZY:OFF
```

To change any of the other defaults, include one of the statements in CONFIG.SYS, and reboot.

To change /MAXAGE from 5000 to 3000, type the following command:

```
RUN=C:\OS2\CACHE.EXE /MAXAGE:3000
```

To change /DISKIDLE from 1000 to 1500, type the following:

```
RUN=C:\OS2\CACHE.EXE /DISKIDLE:1500
```

Issue the following command to change /BUFFERIDLE 500 to 1000:

```
RUN=C:\OS2\CACHE.EXE /BUFFERIDLE:1000
```

See Also

IFS

CALL

Purpose

The CALL command runs a batch program from within another batch program, without stopping the first program. You can use it to create "master" or "parent" batch programs which incorporate many batch programs.

Type

OS/2 and DOS

Syntax

CALL *BATCHNAME % ARGUMENT*

Switches

None

Rules and Considerations

You may CALL as many batch files as you have RAM available. In DOS, batch files may CALL themselves; in OS/2, they cannot.

An argument parameter—% followed by a number from 1 to 9—enables you to pass information to the batch file you are calling.

Do not use piping or redirection with CALL.

Examples

To CALL a batch file named BATCH.CMD, include the following statement in your batch file:

```
CALL BATCH
```

To pass the third parameter to a batch file named BATCH.CMD, type the following command:

```
CALL BATCH %3
```

See Also

ECHO
ENDLOCAL
EXTPROC
FOR
GOTO
IF
PAUSE
REM
SETLOCAL
SHIFT

CD or CHDIR

Purpose

The CD or CHDIR command changes or displays the current directory.

Type

OS/2 and DOS

Syntax

CD *DRIVE:PATH*

Switches

None

Rules and Considerations

With CD, you can switch directories on your current drive, move to a subdirectory within your current directory, or change to the root directory or the parent directory from any subdirectory.

You can use CD or CHDIR interchangeably.

Examples

To change from your current directory to one named MAINDIR, type the following command:

```
CD \MAINDIR
```

The next command moves you into a subdirectory within your current directory. Notice that you type the name of the new subdirectory without the backslash:

```
CD SUBDIR
```

To change from your current subdirectory to subdirectory DIFFSUB in a different directory—DIFFDIR—on the same disk drive, issue the following command:

```
CD \DIFFDIR\DIFFSUB
```

Use the command as follows to change from your current subdirectory to a subdirectory in a different directory on a different drive:

```
CD C:\DIFFDIR\DIFFSUB
```

To move from a subdirectory to the root directory of your current disk drive, type the command that follows:

```
CD \
```

To view your current directory, type the following:

```
CD
```

See Also

DIR
MDRD
TREE

CHCP

Purpose

The CHCP command enables you to switch between the two code page character sets that have been prepared in CONFIG.SYS.

Type

OS/2 and DOS

Syntax

CHCP XXX

Switches

None

Rules and Considerations

In the United States, OS/2 defaults to the following two code page character sets:

437	United States
850	Multilingual

OS/2 can support several other code pages as shown below:

852	Latin 2 (Czechoslovakia, Hungary, Poland, Yugoslavia)
857	Turkish
860	Portuguese
861	Iceland
862	Hebrew-speaking (DOS support only available in certain countries)
863	Canada (French-speaking)
864	Arabic-speaking (DOS support only available in certain countries)
865	Nordic
932	Japanese
934	Korean
938	Republic of China (Taiwan)
942	Japanese
944	Korean (compliant with IBM System Application Architecture)
948	Republic of China (compliant with IBM SAA)

Code pages 932-948 require a special version of OS/2 and special hardware.

If you want to use another code page, you must first prepare it by using the CODEPAGE command. Then enter matching country and DEVINFO statements in your CONFIG.SYS file.

Examples

To switch from code page 437 to code page 850, type the following command:

```
CHCP 850
```

Enter the following command to view current code page:

```
CHCP
```

See Also

CODEPAGE
COUNTRY
DEVINFO
SPOOL

CHKDSK

Purpose

The CHKDSK command gives you a status report on the contents and format of your disk.

Type

OS/2 and DOS

Syntax

CHKDSK *DRIVE: PATH FILENAME*

Switches

/F	Fixes errors detected by CHKDSK
/V	Generates a verbose list of all files and directories on current drive

For High Performance File System only:

/C   Recovers files only if file system is in an inconsistent state when the computer is started—for example, if the computer was turned off or lost power without being properly shut down

/F:*N*	Specifies one of HPFS' four levels of recovery
/F:0	Analyze and display but do not repair
/F:1	Resolve inconsistent file-system structures
/F:2	Resolve inconsistent file-system structures and recover any recognizable disk structures not referred to by the file system
/F:"3	Go beyond /F:2 to scan the entire partition for recognizable file-system structures

Rules and Considerations

The CHKDSK command produces the following information:

- Type of file system
- Volume label
- Volume serial number
- Total disk space
- Bytes used by hidden files
- Number of hidden files
- Bytes used by directories
- Number of directories

- Bytes in user files

- Number of user files

- Bytes used by extended attributes

- Available disk space

- Bytes in each allocation unit

- Total allocation units

- Available allocation units

You can also use CHKDSK to check specific subdirectories or file names for fragmentation.

To request a list of all files by using CHKDSK/V is time-consuming.

Examples

To receive a status report on drive C, type the following command:

```
CHKDSK C:
```

Enter the following command to receive a status report on files in subdirectory SUBDIR:

```
CHKDSK C:\SUBDIR
```

Type the following to check all of drive C and fix any errors uncovered:

```
CHKDSK C: /F
```

Under HPFS, CHKDSK defaults to the /F:2 level of recovery. If you prefer level 3, type the following command:

```
CHKDSK C: /F:3
```

To list all directories, subdirectories, and files on the disk in drive A, as well as to check the status of that disk, type the following:

```
CHKDSK A:/V
```

Note

Under HPFS, CHKDSK /F places all recovered clusters in a
subdirectory—\FOUND.MMM. The extension *.MMM* is a unique
three-digit number.

CLS

Purpose

Type CLS to clear all information from the command interpreter
screen except the prompt and cursor. CLS stands for CLear Screen.

Type

OS/2 and DOS

Syntax

CLS

Switches

None

CMD

Purpose

The CMD command starts a new OS/2 command processor.

Type

OS/2 only

Syntax

CMD *DRIVE: PATH*

Switches

/Q	Starts new OS/2 command processor and overrides default for copying command line to standard output
/S	Tells new command processor to ignore <CTRL C> break requests
/K "string"	Passes string to new command processor for execution; stays in new command processor when complete
/C "string"	Passes string to new command processor for execution; returns to prior command processor when complete

Rules and Considerations

When used without a parameter, CMD starts another command processor that runs from the C:\OS2 subdirectory.

Use the /Q and/or /S switch before the /K or /C switch.

Examples

To start a new command processor located on the directory C:\MAINDIR, type the following command:

```
CMD C:\MAINDIR
```

Type the next command to start a new command processor, type the file EDIT.ASC onto the root directory and return to the previous command processor:

```
CMD /C TYPE EDIT.ASC
```

To start a new command processor that ignores break requests, issue the command, as follows:

```
CMD /S
```

To start a new command processor, pass it a string of commands—DIR A: >PRN—to execute, and remain in the new environment, type the following:

```
CMD /K "DIR A: >PRN"
```

(Notice that the quotation marks are required.)

To repeat the preceding procedure and also disable <CTRL><BREAK> in the new environment, type the following command:

```
CMD /S /K "DIR A: >PRN"
```

Notes

New command processor environments are completely independent of each other. If you make changes in one, it does not affect the others.

To close an OS/2 command processor environment, type **EXIT**.

See Also

COMMAND
EXIT
SET
START

CODEPAGE

Purpose

The CODEPAGE command prepares one or two code pages (alternate character sets) for code-page switching.

Type

OS/2 and DOS

Syntax

CODEPAGE=*XXX,YYY*

Switches

None

Rules and Considerations

You must insert the CODEPAGE statement in your CONFIG.SYS file. You must also include matching DEVINFO statements for keyboard, printer and video.

If you plan to use foreign code pages, make sure you do not use U.S.-only characters in your file and directory names. They may not be recognized properly.

Example

To prepare U.S. and multilingual code pages, insert the following statement in your CONFIG.SYS file:

```
CODEPAGE=437,850
```

Note

See CHCP for a list of code page defaults and available alternates. Not all printers support all code pages.

See Also

COUNTRY
DEVINFO

COMMAND

Purpose

COMMAND starts a DOS command processor.

Type

DOS only

Syntax

COMMAND *[DRIVE]: [PATH]*

Switches

/P	Makes the new DOS command processor permanent until you restart OS/2
/E:*X*	Sets the size of your new DOS environment, from 160 to 32768 bytes
/C STRING	Starts a DOS command processor, runs a command string, and returns to the previous command processor when finished
/K STRING	Starts a DOS command processor, runs a command string, and remains in new command processor when completed

Rules and Considerations

COMMAND expects to find the DOS command processor—COMMAND.COM—in the C:\OS2\MSDOS subdirectory. You can specify another place to look by adding a path and file name.

Note that /C and /K command strings do not require quotation marks.

When you run COMMAND from an OS/2 command prompt, the OS/2 window closes and a new DOS window opens. To end the DOS session and return to your OS/2 session, type **EXIT**.

Examples

To start a new DOS command processor from COMMAND.COM, type the following:

```
COMMAND C\SUBDIR
```

To start a new DOS command processor and make it permanent until OS/2 is restarted, issue the following command:

```
COMMAND /P
```

Enter the following command to start a new DOS command processor and allocate it 32000 bytes:

```
COMMAND /E:32000
```

To start a new DOS command processor, run a series of commands, and return to the previous DOS command processor, type the following:

```
COMMAND /C DIR A: >PRN
```

To repeat the preceding example but remain in the new DOS command processor when finished, type the command as follows:

```
COMMAND /K DIR A: >PRN
```

Note

COMMAND is available from both DOS and OS/2 command prompts. You can use COMMAND to create multiple DOS sessions if sufficient memory is available.

See Also

CMD
EXIT
SET

COMP

Purpose

The COMP command compares the contents of two files and specifies the first ten differences.

Type

OS/2 and DOS

Syntax

COMP *DRIVE: PATH FILENAME.EXT DRIVE: PATH FILENAME*

Switches

None

Rules and Considerations

You can use COMP to compare files on the same or different drives or directories. If the file names are identical, you only need to specify them once. You may use the wild cards * and ?.

Examples

To compare the files WORK.DOC and WORK2.DOC when both are in your current directory, type the command:

```
COMP WORK.DOC WORK2.DOC
```

To compare these same files when one is in the root directory on drive C and the other is on drive A, type the following:

```
COMP C:\WORK.DOC A:\WORK2.DOC
```

The next command enables you to compare WORK.DOC on drive C with another file with the same name on drive A:

```
COMP C:\WORK.DOC A:
```

Issue the following command to compare all files in directory DIR1 with all files in DIR2 on the C drive:

```
COMP C:\DIR1\*.* C:\DIR2\*.*
```

If you type **COMP** with no parameters, the system prompts you for file names:

```
COMP
```

See Also

DISKCOMP

COPY

Purpose

The COPY command copies one or more files. You can also use COPY to rename, merge, or append files as they are copied.

Type

OS/2 and DOS

Syntax

COPY *DRIVE: PATH FILENAME.EXT DRIVE: PATH FILENAME.EXT*

Switches

/A	Copies file as ASCII file, and stops just before first end-of-file character when used with source file. When used with target file, adds new end-of-file character at the end of file.
/B	Copies entire file, regardless of end-of-file characters that may appear partway through when used with a source file. When used with target file, does not add end-of-file character at the end of file.
/F	Halts copying if you try to copy a file with extended attributes onto a system that does not support them.
/V	Verifies that all sectors are copied correctly.

Rules and Considerations

You can copy files within the same disk or directory or between them.

You can use the wild card characters * and ? to copy multiple files sharing a common element.

You can also use the + character to merge, append, or combine multiple files.

Examples

To copy NEWFILE.DOC from drive C to drive B, issue the following command:

```
COPY C:\NEWFILE.DOC B:
```

The next command copies NEWFILE.DOC from drive C to drive B, and prints the file on your parallel printer at the same time:

```
COPY C:\NEWFILE.DOC B: /PRN
```

Enter the following command to copy all files on the subdirectory SUBDIR1 onto SUBDIR2:

```
COPY C:\SUBDIR1\*.* SUBDIR2
```

To copy OLDFILE.DOC to NEWFILE.DOC and also record the current date and time with the new file, type the following:

```
COPY OLDFILE.DOC /B + ,, NEWFILE.DOC
```

To merge two ASCII files—FILE1.DOC and FILE2.DOC—into a new ASCII file called FILE3.DOC, type the command as follows:

```
COPY FILE1.DOC + FILE2.DOC /A FILE3.DOC
```

To append FILE2.DOC onto FILE1.DOC, type the following command. Note that you do not use a target filename:

```
COPY FILE1.DOC + FILE2.DOC /A
```

Use the next command to combine two series of files with the same extension into a new series of files with a new extension:

```
COPY *.DOC + *.BAK *.REP
```

See Also

DISKCOPY
RENAME
VERIFY
XCOPY

COUNTRY

Purpose

The COUNTRY command customizes OS/2 for international use. COUNTRY establishes which defaults to use for date and time format, currency, decimal separators, and case conversions.

Type

OS/2 and DOS

Syntax

COUNTRY=*NNN,DRIVE: PATH FILENAME.EXT*

Switches

None

Rules and Considerations

COUNTRY must be included in your CONFIG.SYS file along with a statement that indicates where the system can find your COUNTRY.SYS file. You must also include an appropriate CODEPAGE statement and DEVINFO statements for your display, keyboard, and printer if your printer supports them.

Example

To set your COUNTRY code for Italy, and tell your system that the country file is in C:\OS2\SYSTEM, include the following statement in CONFIG.SYS:

```
COUNTRY=039,C:\OS2\SYSTEM\COUNTRY.SYS
```

Notes

The country codes supported by OS/2 are listed below. Notice that not all country codes are provided with OS/2's U.S. edition.

Country/region	Country code
Arabic	785
Asian English	099
Australia	061

Country/region	Country code
Belgium	032
Canada (French)	002
Czechoslovakia	042
Denmark	045
Finland	358
France	033
Germany	049
Hungary	036
Iceland	354
Israel (Hebrew)	972
Italy	039
Japan	081
Korea	082
Latin America	003
Netherlands	031
Norway	047
Poland	048
Portugal	351
Republic of China	088
Spain	034
Sweden	046
Switzerland	041
Turkey	090
United Kingdom	044
United States	001
Yugoslavia	038

Code pages for Japan, China, and Korea consist of 256 characters, rather than 128 characters. Both your software and hardware must support this "double-byte character set" capability.

See Also

CODEPAGE
DATE
DEVINFO
KEYB
SORT
TIME

CREATEDD

Purpose

The CREATEDD command creates a dump diskette you can use with the Stand-Alone Dump procedure to store an image of all of the physical memory in your system.

Type

OS/2 only

Syntax

CREATEDD *DRIVE:*

Switches

None

Rules and Considerations

You need several disks to complete the Stand-Alone Dump Procedure. Only the first disk must be created with CREATEDD. The others can be formatted with the FORMAT command. Make sure you label all dump disks in the order you use them. Label the disk you create with CREATEDD as Disk 1.

The CREATEDD.EXE file must be in your current directory or path.

Example

To create a dump diskette on drive A, type the following from an OS/2 command prompt:

```
CREATEDD A:
```

Note

The commands CREATEDD, TRACE, TRACEBUF, and TRACEFMT are advanced commands normally used with the support of a service technician or technical coordinator.

See Also

TRACE
TRACEBUF
TRACEFMT

DATE

Purpose

The DATE command sets the system clock.

Type

OS/2 and DOS

Syntax

DATE *MM-DD-YY*

Switches

None

Rules and Considerations

Months (MM) must be entered with the numbers 01 through 12. Days (DD) must be entered with the numbers 01 through 31. Years (YY) must be entered with the numbers 00 through 99. The numbers 00 through 79 represent the years 2000 through 2079.

Examples

To display the current system date and be prompted for a new date, type the following:

    DATE

Enter one of the following commands to set the system for June 1, 1992:

    DATE 06-01-92

or

    DATE 06/01/92

or

    DATE 06.01.92

See Also

COUNTRY
TIME

DDINSTAL

Purpose

The DDINSTAL command automates the installation of new device drivers.

Type

OS/2 only

Syntax

DDINSTAL

Switches

None

Rules and Considerations

Use DDINSTAL with your OS/2 Device Support disk. DDINSTAL uses information from that disk's device driver profile to revise your CONFIG.SYS file and copy support files into the correct locations.

Example

If you type **DDINSTAL** without a parameter, OS/2 prompts you throughout the installation process:

```
DDINSTAL
```

DEBUG

Purpose

DEBUG accesses the DOS debug environment designed to help you debug and then test binary and executable DOS files.

Type

DOS only

Syntax

DEBUG

Switches

None

Rules and Considerations

When you type **DEBUG**, your prompt changes to a hyphen and you enter the DOS debug environment, which accepts the following commands and accompanying parameters:

?	Lists debug commands
A *[address]*	Assembles 8086/8087/8088 mnemonics
C *[range address]*	Compares two areas of memory
D *[address]* or *[range]*	Displays contents of an area of memory
E address *[list]*	Enters data into memory, starting at an address you choose
F *range list*	Fills memory block with values you choose

G [=address1 address 2...]	Runs executable file in memory ("Go")
H value1 value2	Performs hexadecimal arithmetic
I value	Inputs and displays byte value from a specified port
L [address[drive record number]	Loads contents of file or disk sectors into memory
M range address	Moves a block of memory
N filespec1 [filespec2]	Specifies file for loading or writing, or specifies parameters for current file ("Name")
O value byte	Sends one byte value to output port
P [=address][value]	Executes a subroutine, program, loop, or interrupt ("Proceed")
Q	Quit DEBUG
R [register]	Displays or changes register contents
S range list	Searches portion of memory for specified pattern of byte values
T [=address][value]	Processes one instruction, then displays contents of all registers, status of flags, and decoded form of next instruction
U [address] or [range]	Disassembles bytes and displays source statements ("Unassemble")
W [address [drive record number]]	Writes file to disk
XA [count]	Allocates expanded memory

XD *[handle]*   Deallocates expanded memory

XM *[lpage] [ppage]*   Maps expanded memory pages
   [handle]

XS   Displays status of expanded memory

If you type **DEBUG**, followed by the name of an executable file, that file loads in memory where you can work with it.

Examples

To enter DOS debug environment, type the following command:

        DEBUG

Type the next command to enter DOS debug environment and begin debugging PROGRAM.EXE:

        DEBUG PROGRAM.EXE

DEL or ERASE

Purpose

The DEL or ERASE command deletes one or more files.

Type

OS/2 and DOS

Syntax

DEL *DRIVE: PATH FILENAME.EXT*

Switches

/P   Prompts you to decide whether to delete each file in a subdirectory.

/N   Deletes all files in a subdirectory without asking
`Are you sure (Y/N)?`

Rules and Considerations

DEL or ERASE deletes the contents of a subdirectory, but not the subdirectory itself. Use RD or RMDIR to delete a subdirectory.

Examples

To delete a file named DEADFILE.DOC from your current directory, type the following command:

```
ERASE DEADFILE.DOC
```

Enter the following command to erase all files in a current subdirectory on drive C:

```
ERASE C:\*.*
```

To erase the file DEADFILE.DOC in the SUBDIR subdirectory on drive C, type the command as follows:

```
ERASE C:\SUBDIR\DEADFILE.DOC
```

Note

Files deleted with DEL or ERASE can be recovered by using UNDELETE.

See Also

UNDELETE

DETACH

Purpose

The DETACH command runs an OS/2 program, such as a batch program, in the background while the OS/2 command processor continues to run in the foreground.

Type

OS/2 only

Syntax

DETACH *[PROGRAM OR COMMAND]*

Switches

None

Rules and Considerations

DETACH works with programs that require no input or output. Examples include batch files and OS/2 internal commands.

Example

To run the batch program BATCH.CMD in the background while the OS/2 command processor runs in the foreground, type the following command:

```
DETACH BATCH.CMD
```

DEVICE

Purpose

The DEVICE command installs the drivers OS/2 and DOS need to recognize ports, printers, video adapters, mice, touch pads, pointers, external drives, expanded memory, and other devices.

Type

OS/2 and DOS

Syntax

DEVICE=*DRIVE*: *PATH FILENAME ARGUMENTS*

Switches

Different switches apply to different drivers. The following switches apply to drivers included with OS/2:

ANSI.SYS (extended display/keyboard support):

/X	Redefines keys with extended key values as distinct keys
/L	Maintains number of rows specified through mode, regardless of application
/K	Disables extended keyboard capabilities

EXTDSKDD.SYS (external floppy drive support):

/D:*D*	Sets physical drive number, 0-255 (Drive A=0, B=1, D or E=2)
/T:*T*	Sets tracks per side, 1-999; (Default=80)
/S:*S*	Sets sectors per track, 1-99; (Default=9)
/H:*H*	Sets drive heads, 1-99; (Default=2)

/F:*F*	Sets floppy drive type, as shown below:

	0	360K
	1	1.2M
	2	720K
	7	1.44M
	9	2.88M

LOG.SYS (syslog error logging program):

/E:*N*	Sizes error-log buffer in kilobytes; (4-64)
/A:*N*	Sizes entry alert notification buffer; (4-64)
/OFF	Shuts off error logging after installation

VXMS.SYS (extended memory support):

/XXMLIMIT=*G,I*	Specifies system-wide maximum memory by using (G) and per-DOS session maximum (I)
/HMAMIN=*D*	Sets minimum request size for High Memory Area; (0-63, in kilobytes)
/NUMHANDLES=*N*	Sets number of handles per DOS session; (0-128)
/UMB	Creates upper memory blocks
/NOUMB	Does not create upper memory blocks

Rules and Considerations

OS/2 comes with most of the device drivers you need:

ANSI.SYS	Extended screen and keyboard support under DOS
COM.SYS	Serial port support
EGA.SYS	EGA video support
EXTDSKDD.SYS	External floppy drive support

LOG.SYS	System error logging (via SYSLOG utility)
MOUSE.SYS	Mouse support
PMDD.SYS	Pointer draw support under OS/2
POINTDD.SYS	Mouse pointer draw support
TOUCH.SYS	Touchpad support
VDISK.SYS	Virtual disk support
VEMM.SYS	DOS expanded-memory support
VXMS.SYS	DOS extended-memory support

Most likely, the appropriate drivers were included in CONFIG.SYS during your original installation. To install additional drivers, copy them into the directory of your choice (probably C:\OS2 or C:\OS2\MDOS). Then, add DEVICE statements to CONFIG.SYS, including the drive and path where the drivers can be found.

(You may prefer to automate the process by using the DDINSTAL command and the Device Support Diskette provided with your device.)

DEVICE statements load in the order you list them in CONFIG.SYS. After a device driver has loaded successfully, no DEVICE statement that appears later in CONFIG.SYS can take control of the same device.

- Serial drivers:

  When you load multiple serial port drivers, load COM.SYS last. The other drivers claim the serial ports they need. Then COM.SYS tries to claim each one, and reports back that it cannot access some of them—the ones you assigned elsewhere.

- Mouse drivers:

  To load a mouse, include both the POINTDD.SYS and MOUSE.SYS statements, in that order. Both of these statements, again, should load before COM.SYS.

- Virtual disk drivers:

  To load a virtual disk, include the VDISK.SYS statement after EXTDSKDD.SYS, and use the following syntax:

  ```
  DEVICE=VDISK.SYS DISKSIZE, SECTORS, DIRECTORIES
  ```

  DISKSIZE is the size of your virtual disk, in kilobytes from 16-4096 (Default=64.)

  SECTORS is the sector size, in bytes: 128, 256, 512 or 1024.

  DIRECTORIES is the number of entries in your directory, 2-1024.

- Expanded memory drivers:

  Load VEMM.SYS (expanded memory) before VXMS.SYS (extended memory). You can set the expanded memory available to each DOS session, as follows:

  ```
  DEVICE=VEMM.SYS NUMBER
  ```

  NUMBER equals any number of kilobytes from 0 to 32,768 (32M).

- Extended memory support:

  Load the extended memory driver VXMS.SYS after any other drivers that require upper memory blocks. VXMS.SYS requires sole access to all memory between 1M and 65M.

Examples

Each of these examples are to be included in CONFIG.SYS. Make sure that these drivers are located in the correct directories.

To load extended keyboard and display support, but to disable extended keyboard support, type the following command:

```
DEVICE=C:\OS2\MDOS\ANSI.SYS /K
```

(Use this command if your application cannot support extended keyboards.)

Use the following command to support an EGA monitor:

```
DEVICE=C:\OS\EGA.SYS
```

The following command accesses external drive A:

```
DEVICE=C:\OS2\EXTDSKDD.SYS /D:0
```

To log all system errors in a logfile of up to 16K, type the following command:

```
DEVICE=C:\OS2\LOG.SYS /E:16
```

Also include a statement to run the program LOGDAEM.EXE (see RUN).

To install a standard mouse on COM2, include the following two statements on separate lines, before the DEVICE=COM.SYS line within the CONFIG.SYS file:

```
DEVICE=C:\OS2\POINTDD.SYS
```

```
DEVICE=C:\OS2\MOUSE.SYS SERIAL=COM1
```

To create a 1M virtual disk with 128K sectors and 64 directory entries, issue the following command:

```
DEVICE=C:\OS2\VDISK.SYS 1024,128,64
```

See Also

ANSI
DDINSTAL
SYSLOG
RUN
PROTECTONLY

DEVICEHIGH

Purpose

The DEVICEHIGH command loads a DOS device driver into an upper memory block (UMB).

Type

DOS only

Syntax

DEVICEHIGH=*SIZE DRIVE: PATH FILE NAME ARGUMENT*

Switches

None

Rules and Considerations

Conventionally, DOS device drivers are loaded under 640K (low memory). If you have upper memory available, however, you can load them there instead. To do this, include a DEVICEHIGH statement in your CONFIG.SYS file.

You can optionally specify how much upper memory is required by the driver in hexadecimal bytes (size). Next, specify the drive, path, and complete name of the driver, including the extension. Finally, if your driver requires specific parameters or arguments, specify those.

Example

To load the driver DRIVE.SYS into upper memory from your C:\OS2\MDOS subdirectory, include the following statement in your CONFIG.SYS file and reboot:

```
DEVICEHIGH=C:\OS2\MDOS\DRIVE.SYS
```

Note

Sometimes DOS device drivers must be loaded "at the top"—that is, nothing can run in higher memory. As a practical matter, you can load them in lower memory, as close to 640K as possible.

See Also

LOADHIGH
DOS

DEVINFO

Purpose

The DEVINFO statement prepares keyboards, displays, and printers for the use of international character sets (code pages).

Type

OS/2 and DOS

Syntax

For displays use the following syntax:

DEVINFO=*SCR,DEVICE,DRIVE,PATH,FILE NAME*

The following syntax is for keyboards:

DEVINFO=*KBD,LAYOUT,DRIVE,PATH,FILE NAME*

For printers, use the syntax that follows:

DEVINFO=*LPT#,DEVICE,DRIVE,PATH,FILE NAME,ROM=(XXX,YYY)*

Switches

None

Rules and Considerations

To successfully adapt your system for use with a foreign character set, you must tell your keyboard, screen, and printer where to look for the required information. To do this, include one DEVINFO statement for each device in your CONFIG.SYS file.

DEVINFO=*SCR*	Prepares your display. Statement specifies display type (CGA, EGA, VGA, or "BGA"—IBM 8514A with expanded memory) and VIOTBL.DCP, a video font table that displays the foreign character set.
DEVINFO=*KBD*	Prepares your keyboard by specifying a keyboard layout ID (country and subcountry codes), and a file named KEYBOARD.DCP that translates keystrokes. Alternate keyboard layout parameters are listed under Notes.
DEVINFO=*LPT#*	Prepares your parallel printer. Statement specifies printer name and DCP file that contains the appropriate printer font table. Statement may also specify that system code pages are built into ROM (ROM=*NNN*) and indicate font IDs.

Examples

To set up a VGA display for a new code page, include the following line in CONFIG.SYS:

```
DEVINFO=SCR,VGA,C:\OS2\VIOTBL.DCP
```

To set up a Swiss French keyboard for a new code page, include the following line in CONFIG.SYS:

```
DEVINFO=KBD,SF,C:\OS2\KEYBOARD.DCP
```

Add the following line to CONFIG.SYS to prepare an IBM Proprinter Model II (device #4201) to print from LPT1:

```
DEVINFO=LPT1,4201,C:\OS2\4201.DCP,ROM=(437,0)
```

Notes

Alternate keyboard layout parameters include:

BE	Belgium
CF	Canada (French)
CS	Czechoslovakia
DK	Denmark
SU	Finland
FR	France
FR120	Alternate French keyboard
GR	Germany
HU	Hungary
IS	Iceland
IT	Italy
IT142	Alternate Italian keyboard
LA	Latin America
NL	Netherlands
NO	Norway
PL	Poland
PO	Portugal
SP	Spain
SV	Sweden
SG	Switzerland
TR	Turkey
UK	United Kingdom
UK168	Alternate UK keyboard
US	United States
YU	Yugoslavia

Check with your printer manufacturer about printer support for alternate code pages.

See Also

CHCP
CODEPAGE
COUNTRY
KEYB

DIR

Purpose

The DIR command lists the contents of a directory.

Type

OS/2 and DOS

Syntax

DIR

Switches

/W	Shows file names five-across on standard 80-column display
/F	Shows "fully-qualified" file names: drive letter, directory name, and file name
/P	Shows list of files, one page at a time
/N	Shows files that were formatted using FAT in the more detailed HPFS format
/A	Shows files with attributes you specify

/B	Shows files without heading information and summary
/O	Shows files in the sort order you request:

	N	Alphabetic
	-N	Reverse alphabetic
	E	Alphabetic by extension
	-E	Reverse alphabetic by extension
	D	Date and time, oldest first
	-D	Date and time, most recent first
	S	Size, smallest first
	-S	Size, largest first
	G	Directories grouped before files
	-G	Directories grouped after files

/R	Shows long file names, even under FAT
/S	Shows all copies of file in specified directory and all subdirectories
/L	Shows directory and file names in lowercase

Rules and Considerations

The DIR command displays the following information:

- File name
- Size (bytes)
- Date and time of last file change
- Disk volume label and serial number
- Total number of files
- Total bytes used
- Bytes left on disk

DIR does not show hidden system files.

If you type DIR without parameters, the system displays all files in your current directory.

You can use the * wild card to get a directory of all files with the same file name or extension.

Examples

To list contents of your current directory, type the following:

```
DIR
```

Type the following command to redirect output to your parallel printer:

```
DIR .PRN
```

To list contents of directory C:\MAINDIR, type the following command:

```
DIR C:\MAINDIR
```

To list all contents of C:\MAINDIR that have the DOC extension, issue the following command:

```
DIR C:\MAINDIR\*.DOC
```

To list file names only, five across so that more can fit on your screen, use the following command:

```
DIR C:\MAINDIR /W
```

Use the next command to list fully-qualified file names that show exactly where each file can be found, and to show no other information:

```
DIR C:\MAINDIR /F
```

The following command lists file names one page at a time, and pauses until you are ready for more:

```
DIR C:\MAINDIR /P
```

To list FAT files in the more detailed HPFS format, type the following command:

```
DIR C:\MAINDIR /N
```

Use the following command to list only files with the read-only attribute set to ON:

```
DIR C:\MAINDIR /A:R
```

To list files only, without a summary of disk information, type the following:

```
DIR C:\MAINDIR /B
```

To list files in alphabetic order, issue the following command:

```
DIR C:\MAINDIR /O:N
```

To list files with the most recent first, five across, type the following:

```
DIR C:\MAINDIR /O:-D /W
```

Use the next command to display long file names, even under FAT:

```
DIR C:\MAINDIR /R
```

To list all copies of the same file name on drive C, type the following:

```
DIR C: /S
```

Type the command that follows to list all names in lowercase:

```
DIR C: /L
```

See Also

CD (CHDIR)
MD (MKDIR)
RD (RMDIR)
TREE

DISKCACHE

Purpose

DISKCACHE allocates storage to your system's RAM disk cache.

Type

OS/2 and DOS

Syntax

DISKCACHE=*N,LW,T,AC:DRIVE*

Switches

None

Rules and Considerations

OS/2 sets aside a portion of RAM to act as a disk cache—which stores information on its way to and from your hard disk. Because RAM accesses information much faster than a hard disk, a RAM cache noticeably speeds up your system if you have enough RAM available.

A DISKCACHE statement included in your CONFIG.SYS file, controls four aspects of this process:

- The amount of RAM set aside (n)
- Whether the RAM cache must write immediately to disk or can wait until the disk is otherwise idle (this is called lazy writing, and is included in the statement as lw)
- The threshold for the number of sectors placed into cache (t)
- Whether the system automatically checks to see if the disk is in an inconsistent state at startup (ac:drive)

Not all of these statements must be included in your DISKCACHE statement. In fact, OS/2's CONFIG.SYS statement at setup is as follows:

```
DISKCACHE=128,LW
```

The threshold is set at the default of 4.

Examples

If you have an 8M system and wish to set disk cache to 256K, type
the following:

```
DISKCACHE=256
```

Use the following command to enable lazy writing:

```
DISKCACHE=256,LW
```

To also set the threshold at 32, type the command that follows:

```
DISKCACHE=256,LW,32
```

To check drive C for inconsistent states at startup, add the
following:

```
DISKCACHE=256,LW,32,AC:C
```

Note

In most cases, the more RAM you have, the more RAM you need to
set aside for disk caching. If you use the minimum OS/2 configuration of 3M, RAM, limit your disk cache to 64K. If you have 8M or
more, try a disk cache of 256K. IBM recommends that you set the
threshold at 32 in most cases.

DISKCOMP

Purpose

The DISKCOMP command compares the contents of two disks of
identical size and density.

Type

OS/2 and DOS

Syntax

DISKCOMP *SOURCEDISK: TARGETDISK:*

Switches

None

Rules and Considerations

DISKCOMP is available at both the OS/2 and DOS system prompts. To use DISKCOMP, indicate the location of the source and target disks you want to compare. You cannot use DISKCOMP to compare different types of disks, such as a 3.5" and a 5.25" disk, or a 720K disk and a 1.44M disk; you must use the COMP command instead.

You can compare two disks that use the same drive. Type the same drive name for both the source and the target, as in the following example:

```
DISKCOMP A: A:
```

The system prompts you to insert the source disk. Next you remove it, and insert the target disk.

If you type DISKCOMP without a parameter, the system walks you through the process of comparing two disks.

Examples

To compare the contents of a 3.5" 1.44M disk on drive A with another 3.5" 1.44M disk on drive B, type the following:

```
DISKCOMP A: B:
```

Use the following command to compare contents of two 3.5" 1.44M disks when drive B is your only 3.5" drive:

```
DISKCOMP B: B:
```

Note

DISKCOMP does not work with drives affected by the ASSIGN, JOIN, or SUBST commands.

See Also

COMP
DISKCOPY

DISKCOPY

Purpose

The DISKCOPY command copies the contents of one disk onto another disk of identical size and density. DISKCOPY also formats the target disk if necessary.

Type

OS/2 and DOS

Syntax

DISKCOPY *SOURCEDISK: TARGETDISK:*

Switches

None

Rules and Considerations

DISKCOPY is available at both the OS/2 and DOS system prompts. To use DISKCOPY, indicate the location of the source and target disks you want to copy. You cannot use DISKCOPY to copy differ-ent types of disks; such as a 3.5" and a 5.25" disk, or a 720K disk and a 1.44M disk. You must use the COPY command instead.

You can copy two disks that use the same drive. Type the same drive name for both the source and target, as in the following example:

```
DISKCOPY A: A:
```

The system prompts you to insert the source disk. The system then tells you to remove it and insert the target disk.

If you type DISKCOPY without a parameter, the system walks you through the process of copying two diskettes.

Examples

To copy the contents of a 3.5" 1.44M disk on drive A onto another 3.5" 1.44M disk on drive B, type the following:

```
DISKCOPY A: B:
```

Type the following command to copy contents from one 3.5" 1.44M disk to another, when drive B is your only 3.5" drive:

```
DISKCOPY B: B:
```

Notes

While you copy one disk to another, OS/2 prevents any other process from writing to either disk.

The DISKCOPY command does not work with drives affected by the ASSIGN, JOIN, or SUBST commands.

See Also

DISKCOMP

DOSKEY

Purpose

The DOSKEY command invokes the DOSKEY program, which recalls DOS commands, edits command lines, and creates macros.

Type

DOS only

Syntax

DOSKEY

Switches

/REINSTALL	Installs new copy of DOSKEY and clears buffer if one is already installed
/BUFSIZE=N	Establishes buffer size where DOSKEY stores commands and macros; minimum: 256 bytes; default: 512 bytes
/M	Lists DOSKEY macros
/H	Lists commands stored in memory
/OVERSTRIKE	Specifies that new text will replace old text
/INSERT	Specifies that new text will be inserted into old text

Rules and Considerations

The DOSKEY program gives you more flexibility than the standard DOS command line to edit DOS commands and macros. DOSKEY uses the following commands:

Up arrow   Recalls last DOS command

Down arrow   Recalls next DOS command

Page up   Recalls first DOS command of session

Page down   Recalls most recent DOS command

Use the following features to edit the command line:

Left arrow   Moves cursor back one character

Right arrow   Moves cursor forward one character

Ctrl-left arrow   Moves cursor back a word

Ctrl-right arrow   Moves cursor forward a word

Home   Moves cursor to start of line

End   Moves cursor to end of line

Esc   Clears command from screen

F1   Copies character from template (memory buffer) to command line

F2   Searches for next key you type

F3   Copies rest of template to command line

F4   Deletes characters, starting with first character in template

F5   Copies current command into template; clears command line

F6   Puts end-of-file character at end of command line

F7   Shows all commands stored in memory, with associated numbers

F8   Searches memory for any command you choose (type F8, then type beginning of command, and press F8 again)

F9	Asks for command number and responds with associated command
Alt-F7	Deletes commands stored in memory
Alt-F10	Deletes macro definitions

If you type DOSKEY without parameters, the program loads with default settings.

Macro creation

(Note: These DOSKEY commands are not case-sensitive.)

$g	Redirects output
gg	Appends output to end of file
$l	Redirects input
$b	Sends macro output to command
$t	Separates commands
$$	Specifies "$" character
$1-$9	Represents specific command-line information you specify when running a macro
$*	Represents a batch parameter that will be taken from command line input

To create a macro under DOSKEY, type DOSKEY, followed by the name of the macro, an equal sign, and the action you want the macro to take. For example, the following command creates a macro called DIRWIDE that lists the directory of drive A in wide format:

```
DOSKEY DIRWIDE DIR=A:\ /W
```

Examples

To enter DOSKEY, type the following:

```
DOSKEY
```

To recall the last command you typed, press Up Arrow.

To move the cursor to the beginning of a line, press Home.

To create a macro named WORDSTART that changes your directory to WORDPROG and then loads WORDPROC.EXE, type the
following:

```
DOSKEY WORDSTART=CD WORDPROG$TWORDPROC
```

To use the WORDSTART macro, type the following:

```
WORDSTART
```

Note

The OS/2 equivalent of DOSKEY is KEYS.

See also

KEYS

DOS

Purpose

The DOS statement in your CONFIG.SYS file determines whether to
place the DOS kernel in high memory and whether DOS or its
applications control upper memory blocks.

Syntax

DOS=*HIGH* | *LOW,UMB* | *NOUMB*

Type

DOS only

Switches

None

Rules and Considerations

The DOS command is included in the CONFIG.SYS file, not typed at the command prompt.

DOS=HIGH places the DOS kernel in high memory and prohibits DOS applications from using this space.

DOS=LOW places the DOS kernel in low memory (below 640K) and enables DOS applications to use high memory.

UMB gives the DOS operating system control over upper memory blocks. With UMB enabled, you can load DOS applications in upper memory, but those applications cannot themselves allocate upper memory.

NOUMB is the opposite of UMB. With NOUMB enabled, DOS applications can control the allocation of upper memory, but DOS cannot load these applications into upper memory.

OS/2's installation program defaults to DOS=LOW,NOUMB.

To use UMBs, also include a VXMS.SYS device statement in CONFIG.SYS, such as the following:

```
DEVICE=C:\OS2\MDOS\VXMS.SYS /UMB
```

Definitions:

High memory area (HMA)	The first 64K above 1M
Upper memory blocks (UMB)	Memory between 640K and 1M

Examples

To place the DOS kernel into high memory and enable your DOS applications to load into high memory, insert the following statement in CONFIG.SYS:

```
DOS=HIGH,UMB
```

To place the DOS kernel into conventional (low) memory and give your DOS applications control over the allocation of UMBs (but prohibit them from loading there), insert the following statement in CONFIG.SYS:

```
DOS=LOW,NOUMB
```

See Also
DEVICEHIGH
LOADHIGH

DPATH

Purpose
DPATH tells an application where to look for files outside its current directory.

Type
OS/2 only

Syntax
DPATH *DRIVE: PATH*

Switches
None

Rules and Considerations
You can include a DPATH statement in your CONFIG.SYS file that takes effect on startup. You can also set a DPATH for your current session at the OS/2 command prompt.

To see your current DPATH or to clear your current DPATH, type **DPATH** without a parameter.

Examples

To display your current DPATH, type the following:

```
DPATH
```

Type the next command to clear your DPATH:

```
DPATH;
```

To set DPATH in your CONFIG.SYS file, and to tell applications to search for files on your hard drive in DIR1, DIR2, DIR3, and DIR4, type the following command:

```
DPATH=C:\DIR1;C:\DIR2;C:\DIR3;C:\DIR4
```

See Also

APPEND
PATH
SET

EAUTIL

Purpose

The EAUTIL command enables you to split extended attributes from a file, store them safely while that file is used by other applications that do not recognize them, and then reconnect the extended attributes to the file.

Type

OS/2 and DOS

Syntax

EAUTIL *DATAFILE HOLDFILE*

Switches

/S	Separates extended attributes from data file and stores them in a hold file
/R	Replaces extended attributes in hold file with those in data file
/J	Reconnects extended attributes in hold file to data file
/O	Replaces extended attributes in data file with those in hold file
/M	Merges hold file extended attributes into data file extended attributes
/P	Copies extended attributes to/from data or holds files without deleting them from the source file

Rules and Considerations

Because not all programs and file systems understand OS/2 extended attributes, EAUTIL offers a way to store these attributes safely while you work with a file, and then rejoin them when you are finished.

The DATAFILE is the file you split the attributes from; the HOLDFILE stores the extended attributes. If you do not specify a HOLDFILE name, EAUTIL uses the same name as your data file, but places the HOLDFILE in a new directory called EAS.

Examples

To split extended attributes from FILE.DOC and enable EAUTIL to store the extended attributes in the FILE.DOC in the EAS subdirectory, issue the following command:

```
EAUTIL FILE.DOC /S
```

To copy extended attributes from FILE.D0C to a file called FILE.EASE, but not delete them from FILE.DOC, use the following command:

```
EAUTIL FILE.DOC FILE.EAS /P /S
```

The next command merges extended attributes from FILE.EAS (hold file) back into FILE.DOC (data file):

```
EAUTIL FILE.DOC FILE.EAS /M /J
```

To replace the extended attributes in FILE.DOC (data file) with the extended attributes in FILE.EAS (hold file), issue the following command:

```
EAUTIL FILE.DOC FILE.EAS /O /J
```

See Also

IFS

ECHO

Purpose

The ECHO command tells OS/2 whether or not to display batch file commands as they are run.

Type

OS/2 and DOS

Syntax

ECHO [ON | OFF | *COMMENT*]

Switches

None

Rules and Considerations

The ECHO command gives you control over which commands appear on-screen as you run a batch file. If you want users to see which commands are running, set ECHO to ON. If you want none of the commands to be visible, set ECHO to OFF. If you want to add messages—either for the user's information or as a prompt to evoke a response—use ECHO followed by the message.

Examples

To display all commands as processed, type the following:

    ECHO ON

Type the next command to turn off display of commands:

    ECHO OFF

To display the message DISPLAY THIS LINE with echo, type the following command:

    ECHO DISPLAY THIS LINE

To turn ECHO OFF without echoing the ECHO command when the batch file runs, use the "@" sign, as follows:

    @ECHO OFF

See Also

PAUSE
REM

ENDLOCAL

Purpose

In batch processing, the ENDLOCAL command works with SETLOCAL to restore all drive, directory, and environment variables to their original condition.

Type

OS/2 only

Syntax

ENDLOCAL

Switches

None

Rules and Considerations

Sometimes running a batch file changes some aspect of your environment in a way that inconveniences you after the batch file ends. To avoid this, OS/2 includes the SETLOCAL and ENDLOCAL commands.

Place SETLOCAL on a line by itself at or near the beginning of your batch file. SETLOCAL records the current drive, directory, and environment variables.

Place ENDLOCAL on a line by itself in the batch file when you want the original settings restored. If you do not use ENDLOCAL, SETLOCAL restores the original settings when the batch file completes processing.

Example

In the following simple batch file, SETLOCAL records the current environment, CD C:\EDITS changes the subdirectory, and ENDLOCAL restores the previous environment:

```
SETLOCAL

CD C:\EDITS

ENDLOCAL
```

See Also

SETLOCAL

EXIT

Purpose

The EXIT command closes a current command processing session, and returns to the previous session, or to the desktop.

Type

OS/2 and DOS

Syntax

EXIT

Switches

None

Rules and Considerations

End your current program(s) before you type EXIT. If no other OS/2 or DOS sessions are open, EXIT sends you to the desktop.

Example

To leave your current OS/2 or DOS session, type the following:

    EXIT

EXTPROC

Purpose

The EXTPROC command tells the system to use an external batch processor for a batch (CMD) file, instead of your standard command processor.

Type

OS/2 only

Syntax

EXTPROC *DRIVE: PATH FILE NAME ARGUMENTS*

Switches

None

Rules and Considerations

You may want to replace OS/2's standard batch processor with your own processor to run certain batch files. In this case, begin those batch files with the EXTPROC command, followed by the location of the batch processor you want to use.

Example

To tell OS/2 to use a batch processor called NEWBATCH.EXE located on the C:\OS2 directory, begin your batch file with the following command:

```
EXTPROC C:\OS2\NEWBATCH.EXE
```

FCBS

Purpose

The FCBS command tells DOS how many file control blocks can be open at once.

Type

DOS only

Syntax

FCBS=M,N

Switches

None

Rules and Considerations

File control blocks (FCBs) give information about a file to DOS. Some older programs use FCBs to manipulate files. Such programs may require you to adjust the number of FCBs that can be open at the same time. When DOS needs to open more FCBs than are available, it tries to close FCBs that have not been reused recently. You may want your program to protect some FCBs from being closed.

The FCBS command enables you to control either or both values through a statement in your CONFIG.SYS file.

In FCBS=M,N, the value M represents the number of FCBs DOS can open at once. The default is 4; the number can be as high as 255. The value N represents the number of FCBs DOS cannot close to make room for new FCBs. You can use a value from 0 to 254 (N must be less than M).

Unless program documentation requires you to change FCBS, you probably do not want to do so.

Examples

To allow DOS to open 12 FCBs at once, include the following statement in your CONFIG.SYS file:

```
FCBS=12
```

To also protect four FCBs from being closed, include this statement instead:

```
FCBS=12,4
```

FDISK

Purpose

FDISK enables you to display, create, or delete disk partitions.

Type

OS/2 only

Syntax

FDISK

Switches

FDISK PARAMETERS

/QUERY   Lists all partitions and free space.
                                /Creates primary partition or
                                logical drive

/DELETE	Deletes primary partition or logical drive
/SETNAME:*NAME*	Names primary partitions or logical drive; makes them bootable if name is included
/SETACCESS	Makes a primary DOS partition accessible and sets other primary DOS partitions off-limits
/STARTABLE	Sets a startable partition
/FILE:*FILE NAME*	Processes FDISK commands in a file set up for batching them

FDISK options limit FDISK and commands to the following:

/NAME:*NAME*	The partition name you specify
/DISK:*N*	A hard disk with a specific number
/FSTYPE:*X*	A partition of a specific file system type: DOS, FAT, IFS, Free, or other (not usable with /file and /set access)
/START:*M*	A specific partition starting location: t (top) or b (bottom)
/SIZE:*M*	A partition of a specific size (in megabytes)
/VTYPE:*N*	To specific partition type, from the following choices:

> 0 Unusable space
> 1 Primary partition
> 2 Logical drive (shared in extended partition)

/BOOTABLE:*S*	Partitions with a specific bootable status shown below:

> 0 Not bootable
> 1 Bootable

/BOOTMGR	The boot manager partition

Rules and Considerations

If you type either **FDISK** or **FDISKPM** without parameters, a menu-driven program loads that supervises your partitioning. Both must run under OS/2. The difference is that FDISKPM supports a mouse and other OS/2 conventions.

You also can manage the partitioning process from the command line, by using the parameters and limiting options already described. The parameter should appear before the limiting option.

Examples

To list your current partitions and free space, type the following:

```
FDISK /QUERY
```

Use the following command to create a logical drive on disk 2, place it in an extended partition, and name it USER2:

```
FDISK /CREATE:USER2 /VTYPE :2 /DISK?2
```

To make a disk startable, type the following:

```
FDISK /STARTABLE
```

Note

The FDISK command does not work with drives affected by the ASSIGN, JOIN, or SUBST commands.

See Also

FDISKPM
SETBOOT

FDISKPM

Purpose

Like FDISK, FDISKPM enables you to create, delete, or display partitions.

Type

OS/2 only

Syntax

FDISKPM

Switches

None

Rules and Considerations

FDISKPM loads an OS/2-compliant mouse-and windows-based program that manages the disk-partitioning process.

Example

To load FDISKPM, type the following command:

```
FDISKPM
```

See Also

FDISK

FILES

Purpose

The FILES command sets the maximum number of files that DOS can access at the same time.

Type

DOS only

Syntax

FILES=X

Switches

None

Rules and Considerations

When you install OS/2, FILES is set at 20. Some applications may require you to increase the number of files available. To do so, replace the FILES statement in your CONFIG.SYS file. You can theoretically set files as high as 255, though 20-40 is more typical.

Example

To set FILES to 30, include the following line in CONFIG.SYS:

```
FILES=30
```

See Also

BUFFERS

FIND

Purpose

The FIND command locates a specific string of text in a file or files.

Type

OS/2 and DOS

Syntax

FIND *"TEXTSTRING" DRIVE: PATH FILE NAME*

Switches

/V	Lists all lines that do not include the text string you specified
/C	States how many lines include the specified text string (/V counts the number of lines that do not include the text string)
/I	Ignores upper/lowercase differences in searching for the text string you specified
/N	Displays line numbers where text string appears

Rules and Considerations

The text string you are looking for must appear in quotation marks. The switch must appear before the text string. Unless you use the switch /I, FIND is case-sensitive. In other words, "word" does not match "Word.") FIND does not work with wild cards, such as * and ?.

Examples

To FIND the text string 2Q92 in the file FINANCE.DOC, type the following:

```
FIND "2Q92" FINANCE.DOC
```

The following command counts the lines that include the text string 2Q92, without displaying them:

```
FIND /C "2Q92" FINANCE.DOC
```

To find all references to 2Q92 and 2q92, issue the following command:

```
FIND /I "2Q92" FINANCE.DOC
```

The next command tells which lines include a match to the text string:

```
FIND /N "2Q92" FINANCE.DOC
```

To display all lines that do not include the line 2Q92, type the following:

```
FIND /V "2Q92" FINANCE.DOC
```

Use the next command to FIND all references to 2Q92 in both the files FINANCE.DOC and MONEY.DOC:

```
FIND "2Q92" FINANCE.DOC MONEY.DOC
```

FOR

Purpose

FOR repeats an OS/2 command for each file in a set of files.

Type

OS/2 and DOS

Syntax

From the command prompt, type the following:

```
FOR %VARIABLE IN (SET) DO COMMAND
```

From a batch file, the syntax is as follows:

```
FOR %%VARIABLE IN (SET) DO COMMAND
```

Switches

None

Rules and Considerations

The FOR command provides a way to run the same command on a set of files, devices, or system parameters. You can use the wild card characters * or ?.

Most commonly used from within batch files, the FOR command also is available at the OS/2 command prompt (note the slightly different syntax).

In the syntax shown above:

%VARIABLE and *%%VARIABLE* represent replaceable variables that are replaced sequentially with each item inset until processing is complete.

(SET) includes the item or items substituted for the replaceable variable. For example, *SET* can be a list of files—as in the case of C:*.DOC—all files in the drive C root directory with the DOC extension. *(SET)* must be typed in parentheses.

COMMAND is the OS/2 command repeated on each item.

Piping and redirection are available with the FOR command only under OS/2.

Example

Enter the following command from the command prompt to print all BAT files (on LPT1) from the root directory on drive C:

```
FOR %1 IN (*.BAT) DO PRINT /D:LPT1 %1
```

Note that the command includes the command parameter %1.

FORMAT

Purpose

The FORMAT command prepares your floppy or hard disk for use. FORMAT checks the disk for defects and then marks tracks, sectors, file allocation tables, and a directory on the disk.

Type

OS/2 and DOS

Syntax

FORMAT *DRIVE:*

Switches

/ONCE	Formats one diskette only, instead of asking you whether you wish to format another diskette
/4	Formats a 360K diskette in a 1.2M drive
/F:[*xxxx*]	Specifies how much data will fit on the disk to be formatted
/T:[*tracks*]	Specifies number of tracks when you do not wish to use the default value of 80 tracks

/N:[sectors]	Specifies number of sectors.
/V:[label]	Names disk (you may use up to 11 characters)
/L	Formats an unformatted IBM optical disk

Rules and Considerations

Remember that FORMAT erases any information that already exists on the disk being formatted.

The following table shows standard floppy disk sizes and formats:

Amount of Data	Diskette Size and Name	Tracks	Sectors
360K	5.25" DSDD	40	9
720K	3.5" DSDD	80	9
1.2M	5.25" HD	80	15
1.44M	3.5" HD	80	18
2.88M	3.5" EHD	80	36

When tracks and sectors are not specified, the FORMAT command defaults to the drive's maximum capacity.

Do not attempt to format floppy disks at higher densities than recommended; they may not work reliably.

If you format a 360K 5.25" (DSDD) disk in a 1.2M drive, remember to use that disk only in 1.2M drives thereafter. Because of limitations in 1.2M drive hardware, these disks cannot be reliably read or written to by a 360K drive.

/T:[tracks] and /N:[sectors] usually are used together. If you only use one, the other defaults to its standard value.

Once formatted, IBM optical disks do not require the /L switch in order to be reformatted.

Before attempting to format a hard drive, make sure an OS/2 partition has been established.

FORMAT does not work on network drives or on drives in which ASSIGN, JOIN, or SUBST are in use.

Examples

To format a 360K disk in a 1.2M floppy (B drive), issue one of the following commands:

```
FORMAT B: /4
```

or

```
FORMAT B: /T:40 /N:9
```

or

```
FORMAT B: /F:360
```

Note that /F:360K and /F:360KB are also acceptable.

See Also

IFS
LABEL
VOL

FSACCESS

Purpose

The FSACCESS command adds, removes, or changes access to the OS/2 file system from DOS sessions.

Type

DOS only

Syntax

FSACCESS DOSLETTER

Switches

None

Rules and Considerations

Typically, your DOS drive letters are mapped to the same drive letters for OS/2 drives. To check current mappings, type **FSACCESS** without a parameter.

To give a DOS drive access to the OS/2 file system, type **FSACCESS** followed by the drive name, as in the following:

    FSACCESS F

Type the following to prohibit that DOS drive from accessing the OS/2 file system:

    FSACCESS !F

You can also use the minus sign to specify multiple drives, such as drives A through D:

    FSACCESS A-D

You can use the equal sign to map a DOS drive to a different OS/2 drive, as in the following:

    FSACCESS B=E

Or use the exclamation point to tell OS/2 not to allow a drive access to the OS/2 file system:

    FSACCESS ! D

Typed without a parameter, FSACCESS lists your current mapping.

Examples

To show how DOS drive letters are currently mapped to OS/2 drives, type the following:

```
FSACCESS
```

Use the following command to stop DOS drives C through E from accessing the OS/2 file system:

```
FSACCESS ! C-E
```

Note

You cannot remap a drive while you are using it.

See Also

FSFILTER
VMDISK

FSFILTER

Purpose

The FSFILTER device driver enables you to access the OS/2 file system from other versions of DOS.

Type

DOS only

Syntax

DEVICE=FSFILTER.SYS

Switches

None

Rules and Considerations

If you run a version of DOS not included in OS/2, you must establish access to the OS/2 file system. The FSFILTER.SYS device driver enables you to do this. Copy FSFILTER.SYS from the C:\OS2\MDOS subdirectory to the disk or partition from which you start your version of DOS. Then include the following statement before any other device drivers in the CONFIG.SYS file that your version of DOS uses:

```
DEVICE=FSFILTER.SYS
```

GOTO

Purpose

In a batch file, GOTO tells DOS or OS/2 to jump to another line that you labeled.

Type

OS/2 and DOS

Syntax

GOTO *LABEL*

Switches

None

Rules and Considerations

GOTO is often used with IF or IF NOT. You can use them to write a batch program that behaves differently, depending on the information it receives or the results of actions it has taken.

GOTO sends the batch program to a label—a string of characters preceded by a colon. A label can consist of any characters except periods. Keep in mind that DOS or OS/2 only considers the first eight characters, so they must be unique within the batch program.

When the batch program arrives at the label, it starts processing again. If you GOTO a label that does not exist, OS/2 halts your batch processing and sends an error message. If you include a label with no accompanying GOTO message, however, OS/2 ignores it and proceeds.

Examples

Issue the following command to instruct the batch program to GOTO a line called COMPLETE:

```
GOTO COMPLETE
```

Next, establish a label at the location you choose:

```
:COMPLETE
```

See Also

IF

GRAFTABL

Purpose

The GRAFTABL command enables a DOS session to display the extended characters of a specified code page in graphics mode.

Type

DOS only

Syntax

GRAFTABL NNN

Switches

/STA   Displays current graphics code page

Rules and Considerations

With the GRAFTABL command, ASCII extended characters can be displayed in graphics mode on most monitors. If you currently display these characters properly, you do not need to change GRAFTABL.

GRAFTABL ? gives you a list of options.

GRAFTABL *NNN* specifies the graphics code page you choose. GRAFTABL can be set to the following:

437   U.S.

850   Multilingual

860   Portuguese

863   French Canadian

865   Nordic

Examples

To see what GRAFTABL options are available, type the following:

    GRAFTABL ?

Type the following to load the U.S. GRAFTABL:

    GRAFTABL 437

Note

If you change GRAFTABL, you do not change your current code page. (See CHCP.)

See Also

CHCP
MODE

HELP

Purpose

The HELP command provides several ways to get system help from the OS/2 and DOS command prompts.

Type

OS/2 and DOS

Syntax

HELP

Rules and Considerations

DOS users quickly find that OS/2 offers a remarkable amount of on-line help. From the Information icon on the desktop, for example, you can access a detailed command reference, tutorial, and glossary. Information on error messages, commands, and many other topics is available from the desktop. Much of this information can be accessed directly from the OS/2 command prompt.

Type **HELP** at the command prompt, and OS/2 provides a list of current options to switch sessions and get help.

HELP=ON adds a help line to the basic OS/2 command display. (HELP=OFF removes it. All other help remains available even with HELP=OFF.)

If you receive a four-digit error message, type **HELP** followed by that number. You get detailed information on the meaning of the error, and what to do about it. (If you get error message 0016, for example, type **HELP 16**.)

To get help on a specific command, type **HELP** and the command's name. OS/2 loads a detailed Command Reference listing that includes syntax and examples of how the command is used.

Sometimes you can use this feature to access information on topics other than specific commands. For example, if you type **HELP PARTITION**, OS/2 locates the relevant command—FDISK—and displays detailed information on that command.

You cannot access the detailed OS/2 Command Reference listings from the DOS prompt, but you can get information on error messages. Some DOS commands also provide help when you add the /? switch.

Examples

Type the following to turn the OS/2 help line on:

```
HELP=ON
```

To get help about error message SYS0112, type the following command:

```
HELP 112
```

Use the next command to get help about the format command:

```
HELP FORMAT
```

The following command gives you information about disks:

```
HELP DISK
```

See Also

VIEW

IF

Purpose

The IF command provides conditional processing of batch file commands.

Type

OS/2 and DOS

Syntax

IF *[NOT] ERRORLEVEL NUMBER COMMAND*
　　　string1==string2 command
　　　exist file name command

Switches

None

Rules and Considerations

The IF command discovers whether the condition you specify is true or false. If true, it performs the following command. If false, it skips that command. (You can use IF NOT to reverse this procedure.)

Sometimes the command that follows IF is GOTO. This indicates that OS/2 must jump to another part of the batch file and begin processing there.

You can use the IF command in the three following ways:

1. To branch, based on the error level returned by a previous action in the batch program. For example, if the batch program did what it was designed to do, and returned an error code of 0, you can instruct it to give the user one message. On the other

hand, if the program returned a different error code, indicating failure, you can make your batch program react differently.

2. To branch, based on whether or not the information in two strings is identical. For example, you can set one string to yes, and then ask the user for yes/no input to be placed in the second string. If yes, the two strings are equal and one action is taken. If no, the two strings are unequal and a different action ensues.

3. To branch, based on whether a file exists. (You may include the wild card characters in your file names.)

Examples

Use the following command to look for an error message. If the message is not 0, display Fail:

```
IF ERRORLEVEL 1 ECHO FAIL
```

Use the next command to see whether the %1 parameter equals yes. If so, display OK:

```
IF %1 == YES ECHO OK
```

To look for the file FILE.DOC, and, if it is absent, to display It's not here, type the following:

```
IF NOT EXIST FILE.DOC ECHO IT'S NOT HERE
```

See Also

GOTO

IFS

Purpose

The IFS CONFIG.SYS statement installs a file system other than FAT, such as HPFS.

Type

OS/2 and DOS

Syntax

IFS=*DRIVE: PATH FILENAME ARGUMENTS*

Switches

/C:*NNN*	Sets amount of memory for file system disk-caching
/AUTOCHECK:*NNN*	Sets the drives to be checked at startup to see whether they were left in an inconsistent state at shutdown
/CRECL:*X*	Sets the maximum record size for caching, from 2K to 64K in multiples of 2K

Rules and Considerations

If you chose FAT when you first installed OS/2, you may later decide to reformat your disk for HPFS. To do so, you must first include the following statement in your CONFIG.SYS file. Include on the same line of this statement the number of kilobytes to be set aside for file system disk-caching—for example, C:64.

```
IFS=C:\OS2\HPFS.IFS\
```

Examples

To install HPFS with a 64K file system disk-cache, include this statement in your CONFIG.SYS file and reboot:

```
IFS=C:\OS2\HPFS.IFS /C:64
```

To also check drive C for inconsistent states at startup, type the following command:

```
IFS=C:\OS2\HPFS.IFS /AUTOCHECK:C
```

Type the next line to also set the maximum cache record size to 16K:

```
IFS=C:\OS2\HPFS.IFS /AUTOCHECK:C /CRECL:4
```

See Also

CACHE
CHKDSK
FORMAT

IOPL

Purpose

The IOPL command determines whether any or all OS/2 processes can issue direct I/O instructions.

Type

OS/2 only

Syntax

IOPL=NO | YES | LIST

Switches

None

Rules and Considerations

To control how programs interact with each other and with I/O devices, OS/2 generally requires them to use OS/2's own I/O services, instead of interacting directly with devices. This default situation is reflected in CONFIG.SYS as IOPL=NO.

If you need to override this and grant all your programs direct access to I/O, insert the statement **IOPL=YES** in your CONFIG.SYS file and reboot.

You may need to provide priority I/O access only to one or two programs. In this case, follow IOPL= with the names of those programs, separated by commas.

Examples

To prohibit programs from accessing I/O directly, include the following statement in CONFIG.SYS and reboot:

```
IOPL=NO
```

To enable all programs to access I/O directly, include this statement instead:

```
IOPL=YES
```

To enable only three programs, EXEC1, EXEC2, and EXEC3, to access I/O directly, include the following statement:

```
IOPL=EXEC1,EXEC2,EXEC3
```

JOIN

Purpose

The JOIN command logically connects a drive to a directory on a different drive. After they are joined, they appear to be located together until you separate them.

Type

DOS only

Syntax

JOIN DRIVE1: DRIVE 2:*PATH*

Switch

/D   Cancels a JOIN command for the drive you specify

Rules and Considerations

In the syntax, DRIVE1 represents the drive you want to connect to a directory on another drive. Notice that you cannot JOIN your current drive. DRIVE2:*PATH* is an empty directory in the root directory of the second drive. If it does not exist, the system creates it for you.

While DRIVE1 is joined to a directory elsewhere, DRIVE1 is no longer recognized on its own by the system. Its contents are shown when you ask for a directory for DRIVE2:*PATH*.

Examples

To join drive B to an empty subdirectory SUBDIR on drive A, issue the following command:

```
JOIN B: A:\SUBDIR
```

Use the next command to see which drives, if any, are currently joined:

```
JOIN
```

The following command separates drive A, which is currently joined:

```
JOIN A: /D
```

Notes

Under DOS, you cannot use the following commands on drives affected by JOIN:

CHKDSK
DISKCOMP
DISKCOPY
FORMAT
LABEL
RECOVER

RESTORE

Do not use JOIN on a network drive, or if the drive being joined is part of a SUBST or ASSIGN.

KEYB

Purpose

The KEYB command chooses a replacement keyboard layout.

Type

OS/2 only

Syntax

KEYB LAYOUT SUBCOUNTRY

Switches

None

Rules and Considerations

The KEYB command gives you a quick way to switch keyboard layouts if you include a DEVINFO statement for your keyboard in CONFIG.SYS. (You get an error message if you call for an alternate keyboard not specified by a DEVINFO statement.)

For LAYOUT, choose a country's initials from the following list. In a few cases, you must include a SUBCOUNTRY value also because the country may have alternate layouts.

Although you can switch to a keyboard layout that does not match your codepage, what you type may not match what you get.

The following keyboard layout tables exist:

Layout	Country	Default	Alternate
AR	Arabic		
BE	Belgium		
CF	Canada (French)		
CS	Czechoslovakia	243	245
DK	Denmark		
SU	Finland		
FR	France	189	120
GR	Germany		
HE	Hebrew		
HU	Hungary		
IS	Iceland		
IT	Italy	141	142
LA	Latin America		
NL	Netherlands		
NO	Norway		
PL	Poland		
SP	Spain		
SV	Sweden		
SF	Switzerland (French)		
SG	Switzerland (German)		
TR	Turkey		
UK	United Kingdom	166	168
US	United States		

Examples

To use the United Kingdom keyboard layout, make sure that you have included it in your DEVINFO keyboard statement. Then, at the full-screen OS/2 command prompt, type the following command:

```
KEYB UK
```

The next command specifies the alternate Italian keyboard layout:

```
KEYB IT 142
```

Note

Run KEYB from a full-screen OS/2 command prompt.

KEYS

Purpose

KEYS gives you an easy way to retrieve earlier commands during an OS/2 session.

Type

OS/2 only

Syntax

KEYS=ON | OFF | LIST

Switches

None

Rules and Considerations

With KEYS on, you can keep up to 64K of old commands in memory, and easily recall them either to use or edit. To list all the commands in memory, type **KEYS LIST**. To find out whether KEYS is on or off, type **KEYS** without a parameter. To include KEYS=ON in your CONFIG.SYS file, use the following statement:

```
SET KEYS=ON
```

When KEYS is enabled, the following editing commands apply:

ESC	Clears command line
Home	Moves cursor to beginning of command line
End	Moves cursor to end of command line
Ins	Inserts characters
Del	Deletes characters
Left arrow	Moves cursor one position to the left
Right arrow	Moves cursor one position to the right
Up arrow	Shows last command
Down arrow	Shows next command
Ctrl-left arrow	Moves cursor to beginning of word
Ctrl-right arrow	Moves cursor to beginning of next word
Ctrl-End	Deletes remainder of line after cursor
Ctrl-Home	Deletes beginning of line up to cursor
Enter	Processes command

Examples

To tell OS/2 to store commands for retrieval, type the following:

```
KEYS=ON
```

Use the next command to tell OS/2 to stop storing commands:

```
KEYS=OFF
```

To list commands entered in this session (up to 64K), type the following:

```
KEYS=LIST
```

Notes

KEYS=ON removes ANSI.SYS extended keyboard support under OS/2.

The closest DOS equivalent to KEYS is DOSKEY.

LABEL

Purpose

The LABEL command enables you to name, view, or change the name of a volume.

Type

OS/2 and DOS

Syntax

LABEL *DRIVE: LABELNAME*

Switches

None

Rules and Considerations

To display your current volume name and be prompted for a new one, type **LABEL** without a parameter.

Volume labels may be up to 11 characters long and cannot use punctuation. You may use more than one word.

Examples

The following command changes the current volume name to NEWVOL:

```
LABEL NEWVOL
```

To change volume on drive A to NEWVOL, type the following:

```
LABEL A:NEWVOL
```

Enter the following command to see the current LABEL on drive C, and be prompted for a new one:

```
LABEL C:
```

To leave the label unchanged, press <ENTER>.

Note

LABEL does not work on drives affected by the ASSIGN, JOIN, or SUBST commands.

See Also

VOL

LASTDRIVE

Purpose

LASTDRIVE tells DOS how many drives it can access.

Type

DOS only

Syntax

LASTDRIVE=X

Switches

None

Rules and Considerations

LASTDRIVE can be any letter from A through Z. It must reflect at least as many drive letters as you have. Because DOS sets aside memory for each drive, do not ask DOS to recognize more drives than necessary. Include enough so that you can use SUBST to replace long paths with new drive letters.

The LASTDRIVE command must be included in your CONFIG.SYS file.

Example

To make DOS set aside memory for eight drives (A through H), include the following statement in your CONFIG.SYS file:

```
LASTDRIVE=H
```

LH or LOADHIGH

Purpose

The LH or LOADHIGH command loads TSR (Terminate-and-Stay Resident) programs into upper memory blocks if they are available.

Type

DOS only

Syntax

LD *DRIVE: PATH FILENAME PARAMETERS*

Switches

None

Rules and Considerations

To load a program "high" (into a UMB), you also must include a DOS=UMB statement in your CONFIG.SYS file. If the statement is not present, or if no UMB is available, DOS attempts to load the program into conventional ("low") memory.

Your LH statement must include the drive, path, and entire file name of the program you are loading, as well as any required parameters. You may want to include LH statements in your AUTOEXEC.BAT file so that they load automatically each time you boot up.

Example

To load the program STAYRES into a UMB, type the following:

```
LOADHIGH=STAYRES
```

See Also

DEVICEHIGH
DOS

LIBPATH

Purpose

The LIBPATH command locates Dynamic Link Libraries (DLLs) for OS/2 programs.

Type

OS/2 only

Syntax

LIBPATH *DRIVE: PATH*

Switches

None

Rules and Considerations

When you install OS/2, your CONFIG.SYS file includes a special
search path for dynamic link libraries, as shown below:

```
C:\OS2\DLL;C:\OS2\MDOS;C:\;C:\OS2\APPS\DLL;SET
```

You can change or add to this search path.

Example

To search only the DLLFILES directory on drive C for dynamic link
libraries, include the following statement in your CONFIG.SYS file:

```
LIBPATH=C:\DLLFILES;
```

MAKEINI

Purpose

Use MAKEINI to create new OS2.INI and OS2SYS.INI startup files
if yours are corrupted.

Type

OS/2 only

Syntax

MAKINI OS2.INI

and

MAKEINI OS2SYS.INI

Rules and Considerations

To re-create your OS2.INI and OS2SYS.INI files, do the following:

1. Insert your OS/2 Installation diskette in drive A; then reboot (<CTRL>-<ALT>-<DELETE>).

2. Remove the Installation diskette and insert OS/2 System Diskette #1 when the OS/2 logo appears. Press <ENTER>.

3. Press <ESC> when `Welcome to OS/2` appears.

4. Change to the drive where you originally installed OS/2—usually drive C—by typing the following:

   ```
   C:
   ```

5. Change to the OS2 subdirectory, as shown below:

   ```
   CD \OS2
   ```

6. Use the following commands to erase current OS2.INI and OS2SYS.INI files:

   ```
   ERASE OS2.INI
   ```

   ```
   ERASE OS2SYS.INI
   ```

7. Enter the following commands to create new OS2.INI and OS2SYS.INI files:

   ```
   MAKEINI OS2.INI INI.RC
   ```

   ```
   MAKEINI OS2SYS.INI INISYS.RC
   ```

8. Remove OS/2 system diskette.

9. Reboot.

MAXWAIT

Purpose

The MAXWAIT command sets the longest time a process can wait to execute before it receives a higher priority.

Type

OS/2 only

Syntax

MAXWAIT=X

Switches

None

Rules and Considerations

As a multitasking operating system, OS/2 sets priorities to execute the various processes that compete for its attention. But some low-priority processes never execute unless OS/2 eventually raises their priority. The MAXWAIT statement in CONFIG.SYS specifies in seconds how long OS/2 waits before it raises the priority of a process.

You can set MAXWAIT from 1 to 255 settings; the default setting is three seconds.

Example

To set MAXWAIT to 30 seconds, include the following statement in your CONFIG.SYS file:

```
MAXWAIT=30
```

See Also

PRIORITY
THREADS
TIMESLICE

MD or MKDIR

Purpose

The MD command creates a directory or subdirectory.

Type

OS/2 and DOS

Syntax

MD *DRIVE: PATH*

Switches

None

Rules and Considerations

OS/2 and DOS support multiple directory levels, with a root directory at the top of each drive. To create a directory within your current directory, type **MD** followed by the name of the new directory. You do not need to use the backslash (\) unless you want to create the directory in the root directory and you are not already there.

To create more than one directory at the same time, specify the drive and path for each new directory, with a space between them.

Examples

To create a directory—DIR1—in the root directory of drive C while you are in another subdirectory, type the following:

```
MD C:\DIR1
```

To create a subdirectory—SUBDIR1—in the directory DIR1 while you are in that directory, issue the following command:

```
MD SUBDIR1
```

The next command creates two subdirectories—SUBDIR1 and SUBDIR2:

```
MD SUBDIR1 SUBDIR2
```

See Also

CD
DIR
RD
TREE

MEM

Purpose

MEM displays used and free memory in your current DOS session.

Type

DOS only

Syntax

MEMD

Switches

/P	Shows memory allocation of programs currently in memory
/D	Shows memory allocation of current programs and drivers, and other programming information
/C	Shows memory allocation of programs in low and upper memory

Rules and Considerations

You can use only one switch at a time.

Example

Enter the following command to show the status of all memory available under DOS:

```
MEM /P
```

See Also

CHKDSK

MEMMAN

Purpose

The MEMMAN command controls OS/2's capability to use virtual memory.

Type

OS/2 only

Syntax

MEMMAN SWAP or NOSWAP
MEMMAN MOVE or NOMOVE
MEMMAN PROTECT

Switches

None

Rules and Considerations

One of OS/2's advantages is its capability to use virtual memory. This means that OS/2 can allocate more RAM than it actually has by swapping some memory segments—"swap files"—to disk. When you run OS/2 from a hard drive, this is the default situation.

The disadvantage of virtual memory is that it takes time and adds system overhead. Some programs require precise timing, and virtual memory swapping creates problems for them. To disable swapping, specify **MEMMAN=NOSWAP** in your CONFIG.SYS file.

MEMMAN provides two other control mechanisms. The MOVE and NOMOVE parameters to control swapping within RAM which are available under OS/2 1.3 also are offered in OS/2 2.0.

You also can add another parameter—PROTECT—to provide some Application Programming Interfaces (APIs) access to protected memory. The PROTECT parameter must follow SWAP or NOSWAP and be separated by a comma.

Example

To provide virtual memory swapping, and give APIs access to protected memory, include the following statement in your CONFIG.SYS file:

```
MEMMAN=SWAP,PROTECT
```

See Also

SWAPPATH

MODE

Purpose

MODE configures devices attached to the system.

Type

OS/2 and DOS

Syntax

MODE *DEVICE ARGUMENTS*

Switches

None

Rules and Considerations

MODE sets communications parameters for serial ports (MODE COM#) and parallel printers (MODE LPT#). It also can control video display characteristics (MODE DISPLAY) and diskette write verification (MODE DSKT).

Serial ports:

Before you use MODE to reconfigure serial ports, make sure that COM.SYS is included in your CONFIG.SYS file. This device driver controls all serial ports except those taken by another driver, such as MOUSE.SYS.

You can use MODE with up to eight serial ports (COM1 through COM8). The syntax is as follows:

MODE *COM#:BAUD,PARITY,DATABITS,STOPBITS,P*

BAUD	Specifies transmission rate. For ports without DMA: 110, 150, 300, 600, 1200, 1800, 2400, 3600, 4800, 7200, 9600, 19200. For ports with DMA: 300, 600, 1200, 2400, 4800, 9600, 19200, 38400, 57600, 76800, 115200, 138240, 172800, 230400, 345600.
PARITY	none, odd, even, mark, space.
DATABITS	5, 6, 7, 8.
STOPBITS	1, 1.5, 2.
P	Tells system (under DOS) to keep trying for 30 seconds if no connection is made immediately. If P is not shown, the system does not keep trying.

These parameters should be separated by a comma, as in the following:

```
MODE COM1:9600,N,8,1,P
```

If you do not want to reset some of these parameters, include commas in their places, as shown below:

```
MODE COM1:9600,,,,P
```

Under OS/2, MODE can set several additional parameters, including xon, data set ready, clear to send, data terminal ready, extended hardware buffering, FIFO, and DMA transfer. See your on-line help for more information.

Parallel printers:

You can use MODE to control output to any of three parallel ports. The syntax is as follows:

```
MODE LPT# CHARACTERS,LINES,P
```

LPT#	Sets parallel port: (LPT1 or PRN, LPT2, and LPT3).
CHARACTERS	Sets characters/line (80 or 132).
LINES	Sets lines/inch (6 or 8).
P	Tells system (under DOS) to keep trying indefinitely if no connection is made immediately. If P is not shown, system does not keep trying.

Again, parameters should be separated by a comma, as in the following:

```
MODE LPT1 80,6,0
```

Video:

You can use MODE to control output to one or two monitors. The syntax is as follows:

```
MODE CON# DISPLAY,ROWS
```

CON#	Sends output to first (CON1) or second (CON2) display.
DISPLAY	Sets display mode: 40, 80, or 132 (characters); BW40, BW80, BW132, CO40, CO80, CO132 (CGA adapters, B&W and color); mono (monochrome monitor).
ROWS	Sets rows that can display (25, 43, 50).

You must include a comma between display and rows, as shown below:

```
MODE CON1 CO80,43
```

Disk write verification:

MODE also determines whether all disk writes are to be verified. The syntax is as follows:

```
MODE DSKT VER=ON¦OFF
```

Examples

To configure your first serial port at 9600 baud, no parity, eight databits, one stopbit, type the following:

```
MODE COM1:9600,N,8,1
```

Enter the next command to configure your second parallel port to print output 80 characters wide, 6 lines to an inch, and to keep trying indefinitely if a connection is not made immediately:

```
MODE LPT2 80,6,P
```

To configure your first monitor for monochrome display, type the command as shown below:

```
MODE CON1 MONO
```

To enable diskette I/O write verification, enter the following command:

```
MODE VER=ON
```

MORE

Purpose

The MORE command displays output, one full-display screen at a time.

Type

OS/2 and DOS

Syntax

COMMAND *FILENAME* | MORE

or

MORE <*DRIVE: PATH FILENAME*

Switches

None

Rules and Considerations

Use MORE to view long directories or files one screen at a time. At the end of each page, the system displays the following:

```
--More--
```

When this message displays, you can press any key to move to the next page or press <CTRL>-<BREAK> to stop.

In the first syntax line shown above, you specify the command and file name you wish to output, followed by the symbol " | " and the MORE command.

In the second line, you begin with MORE, and then take input from your file using the "<" symbol. MORE assumes your current DOS or OS/2 window is maximized vertically, that it extends from the top to the bottom of your screen. Otherwise, text still scrolls off the screen.

Examples

To display the subdirectory C:\OS2 one screen at a time, type the following:

```
DIR C:\OS2 | MORE
```

Use the following command to list the LONGFILE.DOC file on your current directory one screen at a time:

```
MORE <LONGFILE.DOC>
```

See Also

FIND
SORT

MOVE

Purpose

The MOVE command moves files between directories on the same drive.

Type

OS/2 and DOS

Syntax

MOVE *X:\PATH\FILENAME.EXT\PATH*

Switches

None

Rules and Considerations

The MOVE command only works when both source and target directories are on the same disk. If you do not specify a target directory, the files are moved into the current directory. You can use the wild cards * and ?.

While you are moving a file, you also can rename it by adding the new file name and extension after the target directory, as follows:

```
MOVE C:\DIR1\FILENAME.EXT\DIR2\NEWFILE.EXT
```

Examples

To move the file TEXT.DOC from your current directory to DIR1 on the same drive, enter the following command:

```
MOVE TEXT.DOC \DIR1
```

To move the file SPREAD.INKS from DIR1 to DIR2 on the same drive:

```
MOVE\DIR1\SPREAD.WKS\DIR2
```

PATCH

Purpose

The PATCH command enables you to repair software by changing executable code.

Type

OS/2 and DOS

Syntax

PATCH *DRIVE: FILENAME.EXT*

Switch

/A   Automatically implements IBM-provided patches to IBM software and verifies that the patches are correct

Rules and Considerations

Most users rarely need to use PATCH. Use it only if you clearly understand what you are doing or if you are carefully following the directions of a software supplier. Inaccurate changes to a program can easily make it unusable.

First, specify which executable file you need to patch, as in the following:

```
PATCH PROGRAM.EXE
```

(Or, simply type **PATCH**, and OS/2 prompts you for the program name.)

If you are implementing an IBM-supplied patch, add the switch /A, and OS/2 automatically makes and verifies the patch.

If you are implementing a software patch provided on disk by another manufacturer, follow that manufacturer's directions.

If you are manually patching code, PATCH asks you where the patch is to be made. After you provide the correct hexadecimal offset, OS/2 displays the 16 bytes associated with that location.

To change the first byte, type over the existing hexadecimal digits. To move from one byte to another, use the spacebar to go forward and Backspace to go back. If you go past the 16th byte, OS/2 moves to the next set of bytes.

When you are satisfied, press <ENTER>. OS/2 then asks if you want to continue. If so, type **Y**, and provide the next hexadecimal offset location. If not, type **N**. OS/2 shows all your proposed patches, and asks whether you now want to apply them. This is your opportunity to correct any mistakes.

Examples

To patch the file DATABASE.EXE on your current directory, type the command, as follows:

```
PATCH DATABASE.EXE
```

Issue the following command to apply an IBM-supplied patch to the file IBMPROG.EXE:

```
PATCH IBMPROG.EXE /A
```

PATH

Purpose

PATH tells the system where to look for an executable file, if it cannot find the file internally or in the current directory.

Type

OS/2 and DOS

Syntax

PATH *DRIVE: PATH; ...*

Switches

None

Rules and Considerations

You can use PATH at the OS/2 or DOS command prompt, but you also need to include a PATH statement in your OS/2 CONFIG.SYS. This creates a default path for the system to follow each time you use it. For DOS sessions, include your PATH statement in AUTOEXEC.BAT.

The PATH statement must include the drive and path of each directory you want to include. Separate them by semicolons, as shown below:

```
PATH C:\OS2;C:\OS2\DLL;C:\OS2\MDOS;C:\C:\OS2\APPS\DLL
```

Note that PATH looks for the file in the order you have listed the subdirectories. Paths are limited to 127 characters.

To see what paths are currently in effect, type **PATH** without a parameter. To clear all paths, type the following:

```
PATH ;
```

PATH command locates executable files only—files with the extensions COM, EXE, BAT (under DOS), and CND (under OS/2).

Examples

To see the current path from the OS/2 or DOS prompt, type the following:

PATH

To delete the current path and limit OS/2 to searching internal commands and the current directory, enter the following command:

PATH ;

The next command tells the system at startup to search for programs in A:\DATABASE B:\SPREADSH C:\WORDPROC. Include the following statement in your CONFIG.SYS file:

PATH A:\DATABASE;B:\SPREADSH;C:\WORDPROC

See Also

APPEND
DPATH
SET

PAUSE

Purpose

The PAUSE command suspends the processing of a batch file and asks the user to continue when ready.

Type

OS/2 and DOS

Syntax

PAUSE

Switches

None

Rules and Considerations

If you want to add another message in addition to Press any key when ready, you can add a comment to the PAUSE command. This optional message only displays if you also set ECHO to ON.

Examples

To tell a batch file to pause processing and display the message Press any key when ready, type the following:

```
PAUSE
```

Use the next command to add the message Please swap disks now:

```
PAUSE PLEASE SWAP DISKS NOW
```

See Also

ECHO
REM

PAUSEONERROR

Purpose

PAUSEONERROR specifies whether CONFIG.SYS pauses or continues when it encounters an error.

Type

OS/2 and DOS

Syntax

PAUSEONERROR=YES | NO

Switches

None

Rules and Considerations

Unless you specify otherwise, when CONFIG.SYS encounters an error during its processing it stops and shows you an error message. This default situation is equivalent to PAUSEONERROR=YES.

If you know that a CONFIG.SYS error is not a problem, you can instruct the system to ignore it and load your user interface or command prompt as if nothing is wrong. To do so, add the statement **PAUSEONERROR=NO** in your CONFIG.SYS file.

Example

To disable PAUSEONERROR and allow CONFIG.SYS to continue processing even after it encounters an error, type the following:

```
PAUSEONERROR=NO
```

PICVIEW

Purpose

PICVIEW displays a picture file in MET or PIF format.

Type

OS/2 only

Syntax

PICVIEW *DRIVE: PATH FILENAME /MET | PIF*

Switches

/MET	Specifies a metafile
/PIF	Specifies a pic file
/P	Prints the picture
/S	Returns the Picture Viewer window to default

Rules and Considerations

If you type **PICVIEW** at the OS/2 command prompt, the Picture Viewer program loads from the Productivity folder. From Picture Viewer, you can view MET or PIF pictures. If you prefer, you can specify the picture to be viewed from the command prompt. Indicate the complete file name, and then use either the /MET or /PIF switch.

If you also want the picture to be printed, specify the /P parameter at the end of the command line.

If you want the Picture Viewer window to return to its default position, specify /S at the end of the command line.

Examples

To view a PIF file called PHOTO on your current directory, type the following command:

```
PICVIEW PHOTO /PIF
```

Type the next command to view and print the same file:

```
PICVIEW PHOTO /PIF /P
```

PMREXX

Purpose

The PMREXX command provides a windowed environment to display output from REXX procedures and accept input to them.

Type

OS/2 only

Syntax

PMREXX *DRIVE: PATH FILENAME ARGUMENTS*

Switches

None

Rules and Considerations

REXX is a high-level programming language built into OS/2. You can use REXX procedures in place of batch files. The PMREXX command runs your REXX procedures in a flexible, graphical environment instead of at the command prompt. PMREXX also includes a field for entering your input.

To run PMREXX, type **PMREXX** and the name of your procedure. Optionally, you can specify an argument indicated in your REXX program.

Example

To run the REXX procedure FORMDISK from the current directory in the PMREXX window, type:

```
PMREXX FORMDISK
```

PRINT

Purpose

The PRINT command prints one or more files.

Type

OS/2 and DOS

Syntax

PRINT /D:*XXX DRIVE: PATH FILENAME(S)*

Switches

/D:DEVICE	Sets the print device: PRN, LPT1, LPT2, or LPT3. The print command will output to LPT1 if no other device is specified.
/B	Tells system to disregard <CTRL>-<Z> end-of-file markers and print entire file
/C	Cancels file now printing if spooling is on
/T	Cancels all printing if spooling is on

Rules and Considerations

PRINT enables you to specify which files to print, where to print them, and when to cancel printing if necessary.

You can use the wild cards * and ? to print all files in a directory, only files of a certain name, or only files with a certain extension.

Do not use /C and /T together with a file name or with /B.

Examples

To print FILENAME.DOC from your current directory to the default printer LPT1, enter the following command:

```
PRINT FILENAME.DOC
```

To print NEWFILE.DOC from another directory, C:\OTHERFIL, use the command:

```
PRINT C:\OTHERFIL\NEWFILE.DOC
```

The next command sends the same file to LPT2:

```
PRINT /D:LPT2 C:\OTHERFIL\NEWFILE.DOC
```

To cancel printing of the current file, issue the following command:

```
PRINT /C
```

To cancel printing of the current file and all other files waiting to be printed, type the following:

```
PRINT /T
```

Notes

Note that DOS and OS/2 PRINT commands do not use all the same parameters. /U: /M: and /S:, which specify how long a DOS system waits for an available printer, are not available under OS/2. Under DOS, /B: sets the size of the internal print buffer. Under OS/2, this is controlled by PRINTMONBUFSIZE. And /B without the ":" prevents <CTRL>-<Z> from being read as an end-of-file marker. Finally, OS/2 PRINT parameters /C and /T are not available under DOS.

See Also

SPOOL

PRINTMONBUFSIZE

Purpose

The command PRINTMONBUFSIZE sets the size of your parallel port device driver buffers.

Type

OS/2 and DOS

Syntax

PRINTMONBUFSIZE=*X,Y,Z*

Switches

None

Rules and Considerations

Include a PRINTMONBUFSIZE statement in your CONFIG.SYS file to specify print buffer size for up to three parallel ports.

At installation, print buffers for LPT1, LPT2 and LPT3 are each set at the minimum: 134 bytes. Each can be increased up to 2048 bytes. If you increase the size of a print buffer, you can increase the speed of printing but you also may reduce memory available for other tasks.

Example

To keep the LPT1 and LPT2 print buffer settings at 134 bytes, but increase LPT3 to 512 bytes, include the following statement in your CONFIG.SYS file, and reboot:

```
PRINTMONBUFSIZE=134,134,512
```

PRIORITY

Purpose

The PRIORITY command sets priorities for all the independent actions (threads) the processor is asked to handle.

Type

OS/2 only

Syntax

PRIORITY=DYNAMIC | ABSOLUTE

Switches

None

Rules and Considerations

OS/2 assigns priorities to each thread of activity as it begins, and then adjusts these priorities on an ongoing basis to ensure that every thread has adequate processing time. This "dynamic" situation is the default.

If you need to make sure that OS/2's priorities never change—for example, if you have a top-priority program that must always be served first—you can reset PRIORITY to ABSOLUTE.

The PRIORITY command must be included in your CONFIG.SYS file.

Examples

To make sure OS/2 maintains the priority of each thread exactly as it was when it began, include the following statement in CONFIG.SYS:

```
PRIORITY=ABSOLUTE
```

To return to the default situation upon next startup, change the statement to the following:

```
PRIORITY=DYNAMIC
```

See Also

MAXWAIT
TIMESLICE
THREADS

PRIORITY_DISK_IO

Purpose

The PRIORITY_DISK_IO command determines whether applications running in the foreground have priority access to disks.

Type

OS/2 and DOS

Syntax

PRIORITY_DISK_IO=[YES | NO]

Switches

None

Rules and Considerations

If you give your foreground applications priority access to disk, you improve their performance at the expense of background applications. In OS/2, this is the default situation. If you want all applications to have equal access to disk I/O, change the statement in your CONFIG.SYS file to the following:

```
PRIORITY_DISK_IO=NO
```

Example

To give foreground applications priority access to disk, make sure your CONFIG.SYS file contains the following statement:

```
PRIORITY_DISK_IO=YES
```

PROMPT

Purpose

The PROMPT command gives you control over the contents of your command prompt.

Type

OS/2 and DOS

Syntax

PROMPT *TEXT*

Switches

None

Rules and Considerations

OS/2's default system prompt consists of your current directory and drive in brackets, as shown below:

[C:\FILES]

You can change this prompt to include a short message, the current date and time, your OS/2 version number, or a variety of special characters.

You can change your prompt for the current session at the command line. To change your prompt permanently, add a SET PROMPT statement to your CONFIG.SYS file.

To add a message to your system prompt, type **PROMPT** followed by the message.

To add the following special characters to your command prompt, type $ followed by the character.

Command You Type	Special Character or System Response
―	\<Return-Line Feed sequence\>
A	&
B	|
C	(
D	Current date
E	ASCII code 27 (escape)
F	)
G	>
H	Backspace
I	Help line
L	<
N	Default drive
P	Current directory of default drive
Q	=
R	Return code
S	Space
T	Current time
V	Version number

For example, if you want a traditional DOS-style prompt command, type **PROMPT=PG**. You are then prompted with the current directory of the default drive, followed by the ">" character.

If you type PROMPT without a parameter, you return to the OS/2 default prompt.

Examples

To change your OS/2 command prompt to HELLO, type the following at the command prompt:

```
PROMPT HELLO
```

To prompt yourself with the current date and time (instead of directory information), type the next command:

```
PROMPT $D$T
```

To leave a space between the date and time, type the following:

```
PROMPT $D$S$T
```

To get this prompt at startup, include the following statement in your CONFIG.SYS file:

```
SET PROMPT=$D$S$T
```

See Also

DATE
HELP
SET
TIME
VER

PROTECTONLY

Purpose

The PROTECTONLY statement, enables you to choose between a shared OS/2-DOS operating environment and an OS/2-only environment.

Type

OS/2 only

Syntax

PROTECTONLY=NO | YES

Switches

None

Rules and Considerations

Under OS/2, you can run both DOS and OS/2 sessions at the same time. To do this, OS/2 restricts the lowest 640K of memory to DOS programs. This default situation is equivalent to placing the statement **PROTECTONLY=NO** in your CONFIG.SYS file.

If you are sure that you want to run only OS/2 programs, set **PROTECTONLY=YES** in CONFIG.SYS. This gives OS/2 programs access to the lowest 640K, but makes it impossible to run programs in DOS sessions.

Example

To run only OS/2 sessions, include the following statement in your CONFIG.SYS file:

```
PROTECTONLY=YES
```

See Also

PROTSHELL
RMSIZE
SHELL

PROTSHELL

Purpose

The PROTSHELL statement loads OS/2's user interface program and command processor.

Type

OS/2 only

Syntax

PROTSHELL=*DRIVE: PATH FILENAME ARGUMENTS*

Switches

None

Rules and Considerations

Ordinarily, OS/2 automatically loads its user interface program and the CMD.EXE command processor. To do so, OS/2 follows the CONFIG.SYS default instructions listed below:

```
PROTSHELL=C:\OS2\PMSHELL.EXE

SET USER INI=C:\OS2\OS2.INI

SET SYSTEM INI=C:\OS2\OS2SYS.INI

SET OS2 SHELL=C:\OS2\CMD.EXE

SET AUTOSTART=PROGRAMS, TASKLIST, FOLDERS
```

To run a different user interface, first delete the last line (which disables the OS/2 Workplace Shell). Then substitute your user interface's drive, path, and file name for C:0S2\PMSHELL.EXE in the first line.

Examples

To run your user interface program USERINTF.EXE, located in your C:\MAIN directory, include these statements in your CONFIG.SYS file:

```
PROTSHELL=C:\MAIN\USERINTF.EXE

SET USER INI=C:\OS2\OS2.INI

SET SYSTEM INI=C:\OS2\OS2SYS.INI

SET OS2 SHELL=C:\OS2\CMD.EXE
```

See Also

CMD
PROTECTONLY
RMSIZE
SHELL

PSTAT

Purpose

PSTAT gives you detailed information on current processes, threads, system-semaphores, shared memory, and dynamic library links.

Type

OS/2 only

Syntax

PSTAT

Switches

/C	Shows current process and thread-related information
/S	Shows system-semaphore information
/L	Shows dynamic link libraries
/M	Shows shared information for each process
/P:PID	Displays ID-related information of a specific process

Rules and Considerations

You can use PSTAT to determine which threads are currently running, their status, and their priorities. This helps you understand why a thread is blocked or performing poorly. You also get process ID information that can be used by the TRACE utility.

Examples

To show current process and thread-related data, type the following command:

PSTAT /C

The next command shows all dynamic link libraries:

PSTAT /L

To show all system semaphore information, type the command as shown below:

PSTAT /S

Enter the following command to see shared information for each process:

PSTAT /M

To show information related to the process ID 0019, type the next command:

    PSTAT /P:19

See Also

TRACE

RD or RMDIR

Purpose

The RD or RMDIR command removes empty directories.

Type

OS/2 and DOS

Syntax

RD *DRIVE: PATH*

Switches

None

Rules and Considerations

Before you use RD, delete all files and hidden file attributes from the directory you intend to remove. If your directory has sub-directories, you must remove their contents first. Next, remove the subdirectories, and then remove the directory itself.

Under OS/2 only, you can remove multiple empty directories at once.

You cannot remove the following directories:

- Root directory
- Current directory
- Directories affected by JOIN or SUBST

Examples

To remove the subdirectory SUBDIR from your current directory, completely empty it, and then type the following:

```
RD SUBDIR
```

Use the next command to remove the subdirectory files on drive A while you are on drive C:

```
RD C:\FILES
```

Use the following command under OS/2 only to remove the subdirectory DOCFILE from the directory C:\TEXT and to remove the subdirectory ILLOFILE from the directory C:\PUBLISH:

```
RD C:\TEXT\DOCFILE C:\PUBLISH\ILLOFILE
```

See Also

CD
DIR
MD
TREE

RECOVER

Purpose

The RECOVER command recovers files from a disk with bad sectors.

Type

OS/2 and DOS

Syntax

RECOVER *DRIVE: PATH FILENAME*

Switches

None

Rules and Considerations

Occasionally, a disk or diskette develops bad sectors that make a file unreadable, or a directory is damaged so that no files can be read. RECOVER helps to recover those files and file segments that remain on readable sectors.

To use RECOVER, specify the drive, path, and file name of the file you wish to recover.

If the disk directory is damaged, RECOVER assigns new names to the files it recovers, in the following sequence:

```
file0000.rec file0001.rec file0002.rec...
```

You need to view those files, perhaps by using the TYPE command, to determine their contents. RECOVER cannot bring back data lost to bad sectors, therefore, some files may be incomplete.

RECOVER prevents any other process from accessing the disk where you are trying to recover files. This can be a problem if the files are on the same disk as OS/2 or the recover application. To perform the following steps, assume that OS/2 and RECOVER are on drive C:

1. Copy the files C:\OS2\RECOVER.COM and C:\OS2\SYSTEM\OSO001.MSG onto a blank, formatted floppy. Then delete them from drive C.

2. Insert your OS/2 Installation Diskette in drive A, and reboot.

3. To make sure that you are running OS/2 entirely from drive A, type the following at the [A:\] prompt:

```
SETDPATH=A:\
```

```
SETPATH=A:\
```

4. Remove the OS/2 Installation Diskette from drive A, and insert the diskette you copied RECOVER.COM and OSO001.MSG onto.

5. Type the following command:

```
RECOVER C:FILENAME
```

FILENAME is the file and extension you want to save.

Type the following command if the disk directory is damaged and you need to recover all files:

```
RECOVER C:
```

(Remember, you may wind up with hundreds of files named FILE0000.REC, FILE0001.REC, and so on.)

Examples

To recover FILENAME.DOC on drive B, type the following command:

```
RECOVER B:\FILENAME.DOC
```

Use the next command to recover all files on drive B:

```
RECOVER B:
```

Notes

The RECOVER command does not work on the following:

- Network drives
- Drives with ASSIGN, JOIN, or SUBST in effect

See Also

CHKDSK

REM

Purpose

REM enables you to add comments or line tracing on batch files and CONFIG.SYS files.

Type

OS/2 and DOS

Syntax

REM *COMMENT*

Switches

None

Rules and Considerations

Use REM to include comments that make your batch programs and CONFIG.SYS files easier to use or revise. In a batch program, REM statements display to the user if ECHO is ON.

OS/2 does attempt to process a REM statement.

Examples

To include the statement `Currently processing file in your batch file`, type the following:

```
REM CURRENTLY PROCESSING FILE
```

Type the following to add three lines of blank space between one part of your batch file and another:

```
REM

REM

REM
```

See Also

ECHO

REN or RENAME

Purpose

The REN command changes a file name or extension.

Type

OS/2 and DOS

Syntax

REN *DRIVE: PATH FILENAME NEWFILENAME*

Switches

None

Rules and Considerations

To use REN, first specify the location and name of the file you want to rename. Then specify the new file name. The REN command cannot move a file; you must use COPY or MOVE.

You can use the wild cards * and ? to rename all files with the same name, extension, or directory.

In OS/2 sessions, REN also changes directory names.

Examples

To change the name of OLDFILE.DOC to NEWFILE.DOC in the directory C:\ALLFILES, type the following:

```
REN C:\ALLFILES\OLDFILE.DOC NEWFILE.DOC
```

To change the extensions of all file names in your current directory from ABC to XYZ, enter the following command:

```
REN *.ABC *.XYZ
```

See Also

COPY
MOVE

REPLACE

Purpose

The REPLACE command replaces files on one drive with files of the same name on another drive. REPLACE can also copy a list of files to a target drive and ensure that it does not overwrite any files of the same name.

Type

OS/2 and DOS

Syntax

REPLACE *SOURCEDRIVE: PATH FILENAME.EXT*
TARGETDRIVE PATH:

Switches

/A	Copies files from source to target, except file names that already exist on the target
/S	Copies from source to target disk only those files that already exist on the target
/P	Prompts you "Y/N?" for each file

/R	Replaces even read-only files
/W	Waits for you to insert diskette
/U	Copies only source files that are newer than the versions on the target disk (similar to /S)
/F	Halts processing if the source file contains extended attributes and the target disk system cannot support them

Rules and Considerations

The REPLACE command offers an easy way to update or add to files on a disk or directory. If you store new versions of files on a hard drive and older versions on a floppy disk, you can use REPLACE with the /S or /U switch to update all your floppy disk files. Or you can use REPLACE with the /A switch to copy only new files to your floppy backup disk.

You can use the wild cards * and ? to update or copy all files from the same directory or all files with the same file name or extension.

You cannot use /A (which prevents the replacement of existing files) with /S or /U (which require it).

Examples

To REPLACE an old version of NEWSFILE.DOC on the A drive with a new version from the C drive, issue the following command:

```
REPLACE C:NEWSFILE.DOC A:
```

Use the next command to have the system doublecheck that it is actually replacing the older file with a newer one:

```
REPLACE C:NEWSFILE.DOC A: /U
```

To add all the files in directory C:MARCH to the floppy disk in drive A without overwriting any files on drive A, type the following:

```
REPLACE C:\MARCH\*.* A: /A
```

Note

REPLACE does not recognize hidden and system files. You can disable those attributes temporarily, however, by using ATTRIB.

See Also

BACKUP
COPY

RESTORE

Purpose

The RESTORE command restores files that were backed up with the BACKUP command.

Type

OS/2 only

Syntax

RESTORE *SOURCEDRIVE: TARGETDRIVE: PATH FILENAME*

Switches

/P	Asks for permission to restore read-only files or files that have changed since the last backup
/M	Restores files on target disk that have changed since last backup

/B:MM-DD-YY	Restores files on target disk that last changed on or before the date you set
/A:MM-DD-YY	Restores files on target disk that last changed on or after the date you set
/E:HH-MM:SS	Restores files on target disk that last changed before the time you set
/L:HH:MM:SS	Restores files on target disk that last changed at or later than the time you set
/S	Restores subdirectories from backup (source) diskette
/N	Restores files to target disk that do not still exist there in any version
/F	Halts restore if target disk cannot support extended attributes present on backup (source) disk
/D	Lists files on backup disk that also exist on target disk

Rules and Considerations

The RESTORE command only restores files that were backed up with BACKUP, and only to the directory they were originally located in. If you are restoring files from several diskettes, insert them in the same order you used to back them up.

Examples

Type the following to restore OLDFILE.TXT on backup drive A to the root directory on drive C:

```
RESTORE A: C:OLDFILE.TXT
```

To restore all the files on backup drive A to the subdirectory C:\STUFF, issue the following command:

```
RESTORE A: C:\STUFF\*.*
```

The next command restores only those files revised on or before March 15, 1992:

```
RESTORE A: C:\STUFF\*.* /B:03-15-92
```

To restore only files revised at noon or later today, type the command that follows:

```
RESTORE A: C:\STUFF\*.* /1:12:00:00
```

See Also

BACKUP

RMSIZE

Purpose

RMSIZE tells DOS how much memory it can access.

Type

DOS only

Syntax

RMSIZE=*N*

Switches

None

Rules and Considerations

A DOS session can use up to 640K of low memory, but if your DOS sessions require less, you can use RMSIZE to reduce DOS memory, and make more memory available to your OS/2 programs.

You can set RMSIZE from 0 to 640; the default is either 512 or 640, depending on how much low memory you have installed. If you assign DOS more memory than you have available, the system sends you an error message and ignores the command.

Example

To limit DOS to 512K, include the following statement in CONFIG.SYS:

```
RMSIZE=512
```

See Also

PROTECTONLY
PROTSHELL
SHELL

RUN

Purpose

Under OS/2, a RUN statement in CONFIG.SYS loads and starts a system program in the background during system startup. One such program provided by OS/2, LOGDAEM.EXE, records system errors.

Type

OS/2 and DOS

Syntax

RUN=*DRIVE: PATH FILENAME ARGUMENTS*

Switches

If you run LOGDAEM.EXE, the following switches apply:

/E:*FILENAME*	Names your error-log file and places it in C:\OS2\SYSTEM, unless you specify a different path
/W:*N*	Controls the size of your error-log file, from 4K to the default value of 64K

Rules and Considerations

You can load and run some programs directly from your CONFIG.SYS file by using RUN statements that include the program's drive, path, and file name. Programs started by RUN, however, have special requirements. Because CONFIG.SYS starts them before it finishes setting up your system, they must manage their own disk access. They do not have access to OS/2's user interface. (Presentation Manager applications cannot be launched by RUN.)

Your RUN statements execute in the order they appear in CONFIG.SYS.

If a program cannot work with RUN, you may want to start it from a STARTUP.CMD batch file.

One program that works with RUN is LOGDAEM.EXE, which maintains system error logs. (Note the special switches, /E:*FILENAME* and /W:*N*, that apply to LODGAEM.EXE.)

When you include a RUN=LOGDAEM.EXE statement in CONFIG.SYS, also include a DEVICE statement to load the driver LOG.SYS.

Examples

To load and start DOSTUFF from the C:\PROGRAMS directory during system initialization, include this line with your other RUN statements in CONFIG.SYS:

```
RUN=C:\PROGRAMS\DOSTUFF
```

To load and run LOGDAEM.EXE during startup, and to place a 16K log file LOGFILE1.DATD in the C:\OS2\SYSTEM directory, type the following:

```
RUN=C:\OS2\SYSTEM\LOGDAEM.EXE /
E:C:OS2\SYSTEM\LOGFILE1.DAT /W:16
```

Remember to also include DEVICE=*DRIVE: PATH LOG.SYS* in CONFIG.SYS.

See Also

START

SET

Purpose

The SET command establishes, changes, or removes environment variables in your current session.

Type

OS/2 and DOS

Syntax

SET *STRING1=STRING2*

Switches

None

Rules and Considerations

Environment variables affect the way a session looks and acts. SET enables you to control these variables. You can use the SET command at the command prompt or in your CONFIG.SYS file.

If you type **SET** without a parameter, you can see the current environment variables that affect your session. These are commands such as COMSPEC, PATH, DPATH, PROMPT, HELP, APPEND, and KEYS.

From the command prompt, you can change the values of environment variables that already affect your environment, or you can include new ones. In the syntax, *STRING1* is the command you intend to set, and *STRING2* is the new setting.

To eliminate your current path, for example, and replace it with PATH=C:\FILES/C:\PROGRAMS, type the following:

```
SET PATH=C:\FILES;C:\PROGRAMS
```

In a batch file, SET establishes a replaceable parameter. Begin and end the name of your replaceable parameter with a "%" sign, as in *%NEWNAME%*.

Examples

To show current environment variables, type the following:

```
SET
```

The next command clears your current path:

```
SET PATH=
```

Type the following command to create the new path C:\OS2;\C:\MDOS:

```
SET PATH=C:\OS2;C:\MDOS
```

See Also

APPEND
DPATH
KEYS
PATH
PROMPT

SETBOOT

Purpose

SETBOOT enables you to set up the Boot Manager for a hard disk.

Type

OS/2 only

Syntax

SETBOOT

Switches

/T:*X*	Sets length of time Boot Manager menu will appear before default system runs, in seconds
/T:NO	Keeps Boot Manager menu visible until you choose a selection
/M:*M*	Sets menu mode: n (normal) or a (advanced)
/Q	Queries current set startup environment and shows relevant information
/B	Shuts the system down and restarts it
/X:*X*	Sets startup partition, 0-3

Rules and Considerations

The SETBOOT utility program helps set up the Boot Manager.

Examples

To display the startup menu for 30 seconds before moving on, type the following command:

```
SETBOOT /T:30
```

The next command starts Boot Manager in advanced mode:

```
SETBOOT /M:A
```

Enter the following command to determine your current startup environment:

```
SETBOOT /Q
```

See Also

FDISK

SETLOCAL

Purpose

The SETLOCAL command stores current drive, directory, and environment variables and restores them when your batch file finishes processing.

Type

OS/2 only

Syntax

SETLOCAL

Switches

None

Rules and Considerations

See ENDLOCAL.

Example

To store drive, directory, and environment variables before your batch program changes them, include the following statement early in your batch file:

```
SETLOCAL
```

See Also

ENDLOCAL

SHELL

Purpose

SHELL starts COMMAND.COM or another DOS command processor.

Type

DOS only

Syntax

SHELL=*DRIVE: PATH FILENAME ARGUMENTS*

Switch

/P   Keeps command processor in memory until shutdown

Rules and Considerations

Your default CONFIG.SYS SHELL statement is as follows:

```
SHELL=C:\OS2\MDOS\COMMAND.COM C:\OS2\MDOS /P
```

This statement loads the DOS command processor COMMAND.COM with its arguments.

You can substitute, however, another command processor by replacing this statement. You also can move COMMAND.COM to another directory, such as C:\DOS.

Example

To load COMMAND.COM in C:\OS2\MDOS, and to keep it in memory until shutdown, type the following:

```
SHELL=C:\OS2\MDOS\COMMAND.COM C:\OS2\MDOS /P
```

See Also

COMMAND
PROTSHELL
RMSIZE

SHIFT

Purpose

The SHIFT command enables you to use more than 10 replaceable parameters in your batch files.

Type

OS/2 and DOS

Syntax

SHIFT

Switches

None

Rules and Considerations

Normally, batch files can only handle 10 replaceable parameters, %0 through %9. The SHIFT command adds an eleventh parameter as %9, and shifts all the others "down" a notch. This eliminates the first parameter (%0). After you eliminate a parameter, you cannot retrieve it.

Examples

Batch file parameters before you use SHIFT are as follows:

%0='First old parameter'

%1='Second old parameter'

%2='Third old parameter'

After you type **SHIFT**, the results are as follows:

%0='Second old parameter'

%1='Third old parameter'

%2=Empty

SORT

Purpose

The SORT command rearranges the contents of a file, a line at a time, and sends the results to screen, disk, or printer.

Type

OS/2 and DOS

Syntax

SORT <*DRIVE:PATH FILENAME* >*OUTPUT*

Switches

/R	Reverses the sort (Z-A, 9-0)
/+N	Sorts, based on a specific column

Rules and Considerations

SORT is useful when you need to alphabetize the lines in a file or rearrange a simple database. (SORT works with ASCII text.)

The /+N switch makes it easy to arrange, based on any field in a database table, in which each column is separated by a <TAB> or the same number of spaces.

If you use either the /R or /+N switch, place it immediately after the word SORT.

The "<" symbol pulls the file you want to be sorted from its drive, directory, and path. The ">" symbol directs the output to a printer or file name. If you do not specify a destination for the output, it displays on-screen.

SORT is not case-sensitive—in other words, it does not distinguish between uppercase and lowercase letters.

The OS/2 SORT command does not work with files larger than 64K.

Examples

To take input from FILENAME.DOC on the MAINDIR directory on drive A, sort it in reverse order, and print from your first parallel port, type the following:

```
SORT /R <A:\MAINDIR\FILENAME.DOC >LPT1
```

Use the following command to send the same output to a file SORTNAME.DOC on drive C:

```
SORT /R <A:\MAINDIR\FILENAME.DOC >C:\SORTNAME.DOC
```

SPOOL

Purpose

SPOOL redirects printer output.

Type

OS/2 only

Syntax

SPOOL

Switches

/D:*DEVICE*	Sets input device: PRN, LPT1, LPT2, LPT3 (default: LPT1)
/0:*DEVICE*	Sets output device: PRN, LPT1, LPT2, LPT3, COM1, COM2, COM3, COM4 (default: same port you choose for input device)
/Q	Asks system about any current redirections.

Rules and Considerations

Type **SPOOL** at the OS/2 command prompt to activate the spooler. To SPOOL to a serial printer, you must have loaded COM.SYS in your CONFIG.SYS file. Use MODE to make sure your serial port is configured properly for your serial printer.

Some DOS programs do not interact properly with the spooler, therefore, your print file cannot be printed until you close the program. To solve this problem, send your entire file to the spooler: press <CTRL>-<ALT>-<PrintScreen> together.

Examples

To enable the spooler, type the following:

```
SPOOL
```

Issue the following command to redirect input from parallel port #1 to parallel port #3:

```
SPOOL /D:LPT1 D:LPT3
```

See Also

PRINT

START

Purpose

The START command starts OS/2 programs in a different session.

Type

OS/2 only

Syntax

START *"PROGRAM TITLE" /SWITCHES COMMAND COMMANDINPUTS*

Switches

Use no more than one switch from each grouping:

/K	Starts program through cmd.exe and maintains session when program ends (use quotation marks around program title)
/C	Starts program through cmd.exe and closes session when program ends (use quotation marks around program title)
/N	Starts program directly; cannot start internal commands or batch files (do not use quotation marks around program title)
/F	Starts program in foreground
/B	Starts program in background
/PGM	Uses string within quotation marks as name of program

/FS	Runs full-screen DOS or OS/2 application in foreground
/PM	Runs Presentation Manager application in foreground
/WIN	Runs OS/2 application within foreground DOS or OS/2 window
/DOS	Runs program under DOS
/MAX	Opens and maximizes windowed application
/MIN	Opens and minimizes windowed application
/I	Makes new session inherit environment variables in CONFIG.SYS set statements

Rules and Considerations

To open a new OS/2 command processor from the command prompt, type **START** without a parameter.

To load a command in a new OS/2 session, type **START**, the program name you choose in quotation marks, the appropriate switches, and the command you want to execute.

The name you place in quotation marks does not have to be the actual name of the program, as long as you follow with accurate syntax.) For example, the following command opens a session entitled What volume might this be?, and then runs the VOL command:

```
START "WHAT VOLUME MIGHT THIS BE?" VOL
```

You can ask START to load a windowed program in either minimized or maximized state, but it does not always work.

Examples

To start a new OS/2 session from the command prompt, type the following:

START

Enter the following command to run SCRAMBLE in a new OS/2 session:

```
START SCRAMBLE
```

To start a new session that copies all files from the directory A:\FILES to the directory B:\BACKUPS and to show "Copy lotsastuff" as the program name in the new session, type the command, as follows:

```
START "COPY LOTSASTUFF" COPY A:\FILES\*.* B:\BACKUPS
```

See Also

RUN

SUBST

Purpose

The SUBST command substitutes a drive letter for any drive and path. This simplifies access to complicated paths.

Type

DOS only

Syntax

SUBST *NEWDRIVENAME: REALDRIVE:\PATH*

Switch

/d   Deletes a substitution

Rules and Considerations

OS/2 paths can get very long and cumbersome. The SUBST command assigns an unused drive name, such as F, to substitute for a path.

NEWDRIVENAME represents the drive name you wish to use.

REALDRIVE:\PATH represents the drive and path you want to rename.

Make sure that the LASTDRIVE statement in your CONFIG.SYS file supports access to the drive name you are creating.

Examples

To use the drive name K to access files in the subdirectory C:\FILE\SUBFILE\MINIFILE, type the following:

```
SUBST K: C:\FILE\SUBFILE\MINIFILE
```

To end the substitution and restore the original subdirectory access, enter the following command:

```
SUBST K: /D
```

Notes

In DOS sessions, the following commands do not work on drives affected by SUBST:

BACKUP
CHKDSK
DISKCOMP
DISKCOPY
FORMAT
LABEL
RECOVER
RESTORE

See Also

ASSIGN
JOIN

SWAPPATH

Purpose

The SWAPPATH command sets the size and location of the virtual memory swap file.

Type

OS/2 only

Syntax

SWAPPATH=*DRIVE: PATH MINFREE*

Switches

None

Rules and Considerations

OS/2 can allocate more memory than it actually has available in RAM, by swapping some lesser-used data segments to a disk file called SWAPPER.DAT. The SWAPPATH statement in CONFIG.SYS sets a location for SWAPPER.DAT.

Because SWAPPER.DAT can become very large, OS/2 enables you to control how much space it must leave available on disk for other tasks. Set *MINFREE* for any amount from 512K to 32,767K.

Examples

To place the swap file in its default location, C:\OS2\SYSTEM, type the following:

```
SWAPPATH=C:\OS2\SYSTEM
```

Use the next command to make sure that OS/2 leaves 1,024K on disk available for other applications:

```
SWAPPATH=C:\OS2\SYSTEM 1024
```

See Also

MEMMAN

SYSLEVEL

Purpose

The SYSLEVEL command displays your OS/2 corrective service level.

Type

OS/2 only

Syntax

SYSLEVEL

Switches

None

Rules and Considerations

If you type SYSLEVEL at the OS/2 command prompt, the following
information displays:

```
C:\OS2\INSTALL\SYSLEVEL.OS2              (Location of syslevel
                                         data)

IBM OS/2 Base Operating System           (System name)

Version 2.00 Component ID 562107701      (OS/2 version,
                                         component ID)

Current CSD level: XR00000               (Current and prior
Prior CSD level:   XR00000               corrective service
                                         levels)
```

Examples

The following command shows OS/2's corrective service level:

    SYSLEVEL

Type the following to print OS/2's corrective service level:

    SYSLEVEL >PRN

SYSLOG

Purpose

SYSLOG enables you to control OS/2's error log. You can use
SYSLOG to view, print, start, or stop error logging.

Type

OS/2 only

Syntax

SYSLOG

Switches

/S	Suspends error logging
/R	Resumes error logging
/P:*PATH*	Redirects error logging to the path and file you specify
/W:*X*	Sizes your error log (default is 64K)

Rules and Considerations

If you type **SYSLOG** without parameters, an OS/2-compliant mouse-and-windows program loads that tracks system errors. SYSLOG saves error information in a program named LOG0001.DAT, unless you choose another file name.

Examples

To display SYSLOG, type the following:

```
SYSLOG
```

Enter the next command to stop error logging:

```
SYSLOG /S
```

Type the following command to start again:

```
SYSLOG /R
```

The following command redirects log information to a new error file LOGFILE.DAT in C:\OS2\SYSTEM:

```
SYSLOG /P:C:\OS2\SYSTEM\LOGFILE.DAT
```

To set the new file at 48K, type the following command:

```
SYSLOG /P:C:\OS2\SYSTEM\LOGFILE.DAT /W:48
```

Notes

To access SYSLOG, you must include the following two statements
in CONFIG.SYS:

```
DEVICE=C:\OS2\LOG.SYS
```

and

```
RUN=C:\OS2\SYSTEM\LOGDAEM.EXE
```

Use these examples when OS/2 resides on drive C.

See Also

DEVICE
RUN

THREADS

Purpose

The THREADS command sets the maximum number of independent actions an OS/2 session can handle at one time.

Type

OS/2 only

Syntax

THREADS=X

Switches

None

Rules and Considerations

OS/2 applications can have several different processes running at the same time. These processes are called *threads*. OS/2 theoretically can support up to 4,095 threads at once, but the default is 64. You may want to raise the number of threads if you run multiple complex applications or system extensions. To do so, include a THREADS statement in your CONFIG.SYS file.

Example

To raise the number of threads an OS/2 session can support from 64 to 128, include this line in your CONFIG.SYS file:

```
THREADS=128
```

See Also

MAXWAIT
PRIORITY
TIMESLICE

TIME

Purpose

TIME enables you to reset the system clock.

Type

OS/2 and DOS

Syntax

TIME *HH:MM:SS:CC*

Switches

None

Rules and Considerations

Your system displays the time on a 24-hour (military) clock, in hundredth-second increments.

HH   Sets hours, 0-23

MM   Sets minutes, 0-59

SS   Sets seconds, 0-59

CC   Sets hundredths of seconds, 0-99

Hours, minutes, and seconds are separated by a colon or period. Seconds and hundredths of seconds must be separated by a period. You can use the COUNTRY command to change these separators.

Examples

To request the current time and be prompted for a new time, type the following:

```
TIME
```

The following command sets the clock for exactly 3 p.m.:

```
TIME 15:00
```

See Also

COUNTRY
DATE
PROMPT

TIMESLICE

Purpose

The TIMESLICE command establishes the minimum and maximum amount of processor time any thread can receive at once.

Type

OS/2 only

Syntax

TIMESLICE X,Y

Switches

None

Rules and Considerations

To make sure that all processes execute, OS/2 limits the amount of time any thread can monopolize access to the processor. OS/2 controls the length of these time slices and varies them, based on system load and paging activity.

In most circumstances, OS/2 can handle this task better than you can; however, some timing-dependent programs may require specific minimum or maximum "time slices." You can take control over your time slices by adding a TIMESLICE statement to your CONFIG.SYS file.

The *X* parameter sets the minimum length of a time slice in milliseconds (ms), and must be at least 32. *Y* is the maximum length, and it must be less than 65536. Of course, the maximum length must be at least equal to the minimum length.

If you use only one number, it serves as both the minimum and maximum.

Examples

To set the minimum time slice to 64 ms and the maximum to 128 ms, include the following statement in your CONFIG.SYS file:

```
TIMESLICE=64,128
```

To set the minimum and maximum time slices to 64 ms, include this statement instead:

```
TIMESLICE=64
```

See Also

MAXWAIT
THREADS
PRIORITY

TRACE

Purpose

TRACE sets or halts tracing of system events.

Type

OS/2 only

Syntax

TRACE *OFF | OFF TRACEPOINT*

Switches

/P:	Sets a process ID to be traced (/P:ALL traces all processes)
/S:	Suspends tracing but maintains existing trace points
/R:	Resumes tracing current trace points
/C:	Clears trace buffer

Rules and Considerations

The TRACE command is designed to help technical coordinators track system problems. To use it, you must place a TRACE statement in your CONFIG.SYS file. Either TRACE=ON or TRACE=OFF sets a 4K trace buffer in which you can store the tracing data you accumulate. (To enlarge the trace buffer, see TRACEBUF.)

In CONFIG.SYS, you also can specify a major event to be traced, if you know its major event code. The following command is an example of this:

    TRACE=ON,8

After you place a TRACE or TRACEBUF statement in CONFIG.SYS, you also can access TRACE from the OS/2 system prompt. You can trace major events, static trace points, trace definition files, event types, and processes.

Examples

To turn TRACE off at startup, but to make it available from the command prompt, include this statement in your CONFIG.SYS file:

    TRACE=OFF

The following command turns TRACE on at the OS/2 prompt, (after a TRACE statement is placed in CONFIG.SYS):

```
TRACE=ON
```

Note

The commands CREATEDD, TRACE, TRACEBUF, and TRACEFMT are advanced commands normally used with the support of a service technician or technical coordinator.

See Also

TRACEBUF
TRACEFMT

TRACEBUF

Purpose

The TRACEBUF command sets the size of your trace buffer.

Type

OS/2 only

Syntax

TRACEBUF=N

Switches

None

Rules and Considerations

When you include a TRACEBUF statement in CONFIG.SYS, you can establish a trace buffer of any size from 1K to 63K. If you have a TRACE statement in CONFIG.SYS, but no TRACEBUF statement, your trace buffer is set at 4K.

Example

To establish a 24K trace buffer, type the following:

```
TRACEBUF=24
```

Note

The commands CREATEDD, TRACE, TRACEBUF, and TRACEFMT are advanced commands normally used with the support of a service technician or technical coordinator.

See Also

TRACE
TRACEFMT

TRACEFMT

Purpose

The TRACEFMT command displays or prints trace records.

Type

OS/2 only

Syntax

TRACEFMT

Switches

None

Rules and Considerations

TRACEFMT is an OS/2-compliant, mouse- and windows-based program that simplifies how to format, display, and print the information a TRACE generates.

Example

To run TRACEFMT, enter the following command:

```
TRACEFMT
```

Note

The commands CREATEDD, TRACE, TRACEBUF, and TRACEFMT are advanced commands normally used with the support of a service technician or technical coordinator.

See also

CREATEDD
TRACE
TRACEBUF

TREE

Purpose

TREE shows all directory paths on a drive.

Type

OS/2 and DOS

Syntax

TREE *DRIVE:*

Switch

/ F   Lists all file names in each directory.

Rules and Considerations

To show all directories on your current drive, type **TREE** without a parameter. To show directories on another drive or path, specify that drive or path. To show both directories and file names, use the / F switch.

Examples

To list directories on your current drive C, type the following:

    TREE

Use the following command from drive C to list directories on drive A:

    TREE A:

See Also

CD
DIR
MD
RD

TYPE

Purpose

The TYPE command lists file contents on-screen or sends them to a device of your choice.

Type

OS/2 and DOS

Syntax

TYPE *DRIVE: PATH FILENAME*

Switches

None

Rules and Considerations

TYPE displays the contents of any file but is especially suited to ASCII files. For example, you can use TYPE to quickly view a current batch file.

You may want to redirect TYPE output to a printer (>PRN) or view it on-screen one page at a time (| MORE).

The TYPE command displays or prints files without formatting.

Under DOS, you can TYPE one file at a time; under OS/2 you can TYPE multiple files, and even include the wild card characters * and ?.

Examples

To list the file REPORT.DOC on your current directory, use the following command:

```
TYPE REPORT.DOC
```

To send that file to your parallel printer connected to LPT1, type the following:

```
TYPE REPORT.DOC >LPT1
```

Enter the next command to view that file on-screen, one page at a time:

```
TYPE REPORT.DOC ¦ MORE
```

Type the following command under OS/2 to view every file in your current directory, one page at a time:

```
TYPE *.* ¦ MORE
```

See Also

PRINT

UNDELETE

Purpose

UNDELETE recovers deleted files.

Type

OS/2 and DOS

Syntax

UNDELETE *DRIVE: PATH FILENAME*

Switches

/L	Lists files you can recover, but does not try to recover them
/S	Includes all files, including those in subdirectories
/A	Recovers all available deleted files without prompting you at each file
/F	Deletes files permanently

Rules and Considerations

To use UNDELETE, you must first establish directories in which each logical drive can store deleted files. To do this, add the following statement in your CONFIG.SYS file:

```
SET DELDIR=DRIVE:\PATH, MAXIMUMSIZE; NEXTDRIVE:\PATH,
MAXIMUMSIZE
```

From then on, when you ask OS/2 to delete or erase a file, it instead moves the file to this storage area. If OS/2 runs out of room, it permanently deletes the files that have been there the longest.

Examples

To list all files you may be able to recover, type the following:

```
UNDELETE /L
```

Use the following command to recover all files in your current directory, including those in subdirectories:

```
UNDELETE /S
```

To permanently destroy the file SECRET.TXT, issue the following command:

```
UNDELETE SECRET.TXT /F
```

Notes

The UNDELETE command is available in both OS/2 and DOS sessions.

OS/2's CONFIG.SYS file includes a REM statement that you can easily adapt to create a deleted file directory for drive C:

```
REM SET DELDIR=C:\DELETE,512;
```

Delete the word REM and the space following it. Do not forget to create a directory DELETE in your root directory on drive C before rebooting.

See Also

DEL or ERASE

UNPACK

Purpose

The UNPACK command decompresses files and copies files from OS/2 installation diskettes.

Type

OS/2 and DOS

Syntax

UNPACK *SOURCEDRIVE: PATH FILENAME TARGETDRIVE: PATH*

or

UNPACK *SOURCEDRIVE: PATH FILENAME /SHOW*

Switches

/V	Verifies that unpacked files were written correctly
/F	Does not unpack files with extended attributes if the target file system cannot support them
/N:FILENAME	Specifies one file to decompress from multiple files compressed into one packed source file
/SHOW	Lists target paths and file names for all compressed files in a packed file

Rules and Considerations

To UNPACK a packed (compressed) file, specify its drive, path, and file name. Then specify the drive and path where you want to copy the file. (The target file name is already part of the compressed file.)

A compressed file can include the contents of several uncompressed files. Use the /SHOW switch to see the contents of a packed file without unpacking it.

The UNPACK command also copies uncompressed files.

Examples

To UNPACK all the files in a packed file called 1991.CO@ onto the drive A root directory, enter the following command:

```
UNPACK 1991.CO@ A:
```

Use the next command to UNPACK only one file, DECEMBER.TXT, from the packed file 1991.CO@ onto your current directory:

```
UNPACK 1991.CO@ /N:DECEMBER.TXT
```

To see what files exist in the compressed file 1991.CO@, without unpacking them, type the following:

```
UNPACK 1991.CO@ /SHOW
```

VER

Purpose

The VER command displays current version of OS/2 or DOS.

Syntax

VER

Type

OS/2 and DOS

Switches

None

Rules and Considerations

The VER command works under either OS/2 or DOS.

Example

To display a current version of OS/2 or DOS, type the following:

    VER

VERIFY

Purpose

The VERIFY command makes sure that data is written to disk accurately.

Type

OS/2 and DOS

Syntax

VERIFY *ON* | *OFF*

Switches

None

Rules and Considerations

You can set OS/2 to always verify that files are written accurately to disk. If a sector is not written accurately, OS/2 returns an error message. This setting, however, slows down disk writes significantly.

OS/2's default setting for VERIFY is OFF. To enable verification, type **VERIFY ON** at the command prompt.

Example

The following command disables disk write verification:

```
VERIFY OFF
```

See Also

COPY
XCOPY

VIEW

Purpose

VIEW enables you to access the OS/2 on-line Command Reference or REXX Information from the OS/2 command prompt.

Type

OS/2 only

Syntax

VIEW *FILE NAME TOPIC*

Switches

None

Rules and Considerations

You can access REXX Information and the Command Reference from the Information icon on your desktop. With the VIEW command, you also can access these help files from your OS/2 command prompt.

When you install OS/2 with on-line help, two large files—CMDREF.INF and REXX.INF—are placed in an OS/2 subdirectory. To access one or the other, type **VIEW**. Next, type the directory and path in which the file appears—usually C:\OS2\BOOK. Then type the file name. (The extension is not necessary.) Press Enter and the help file loads.

If you know the topic you want—for instance, a command name—type the topic name after the file name, and OS/2 loads that help topic directly.

Example

To access OS/2 Command Reference's detailed on-line help on the format command, type the following:

```
VIEW C:\OS2\BOOK\CMDREF FORMAT
```

See Also

HELP

VMDISK

Purpose

The VMDISK command creates a file with the image of a DOS startup diskette. You can then use that file to create a DOS session.

Type

DOS only

Syntax

VMDISK *SOURCEDRIVE: TARGETDRIVE: PATH FILENAME*

Switches

None

Rules and Considerations

In the preceding syntax, *SOURCEDRIVE:* represents the floppy drive where you place the DOS startup disk. *TARGETDRIVE: PATH FILENAME* are where you place the image file. There must be more space available on the target drive than is used by the source drive.

Example

To create an image file of a DOS 3.3 startup disk in the root directory on drive C, place the disk in drive A, and type the following:

```
VMDISK A: C:\DOS33.IMG
```

Note

Consult Starting a Specific Version of DOS in your on-line help file for details on how to prepare a DOS startup disk.

See Also

FSFILTER
FSACCESS

VOL

Purpose

The VOL command displays the disk volume label and serial number, if the disk has one.

Type

OS/2 and DOS

Syntax

VOL *DRIVE:*

Switches

None

Rules and Considerations

Under DOS, you can only get information on one drive at a time. OS/2, however, can give you information on multiple drives simultaneously.

If you type **VOL** without a parameter, you get volume information on the current drive.

Examples

The following command displays volume information on the current drive:

    VOL

For volume information on drive A, type the following:

    VOL A:

The next command under OS/2, gives volume information on both drive A and drive C:

    VOL A: C:

See Also

FORMAT
LABEL

XCOPY

Purpose

The XCOPY command copies groups of files or subdirectories.

Syntax

XCOPY *SOURCEDRIVE: PATH TARGETDRIVE: PATH*

Switches

/D:*MM-DD-YY*   Copies files revised after the date you specify

/S	Copies subdirectories if they are not empty
/E	Copies subdirectories even if empty (used with /S)
/P	Prompts you before copying each file
/V	Verifies accurate copying of each file
/A	Copies only archive files; does not clear archive attributes
/M	Copies only archive files; clears archive attributes
/F	Halts copying if source file includes extended attributes that target drive cannot support

Rules and Considerations

The XCOPY command makes it convenient to copy large numbers of files, including subdirectories. XCOPY also enables you to control which files are copied, based on date, location, and archive attribute.

You also can use XCOPY instead of DISKCOPY when you copy from one type of disk to another.

Examples

The following command creates a new subdirectory on drive C—YEARFILE—and copies all the files on A:\OLDFILE into it:

```
XCOPY A:\OLDFILE C:\YEARFILE
```

To verify that each of these files is copied accurately, type the following:

```
XCOPY A:\OLDFILE C:\YEARFILE /V
```

Use the next command to copy the contents of A:\OLDFILE onto the root directory of drive C:

```
XCOPY A:\OLDFILE C:\
```

To copy all the files and subdirectories on drive A onto drive C—even the empty subdirectories, type the following:

```
XCOPY A:\ C:\ /S /E
```

See Also

BACKUP
COPY
RESTORE
VERIFY

Index

Symbols

A

B

E

G

J

Q

S

U

X-Z